ATH...
GU...
20...

ATHENS 2004

ALPHA BANK
OFFICIAL BANK

Table of contents

Table of contents

ATHENS GUIDE 2003

Publisher	Anny Eliopoulou
Director	Telis Samantas
Editors in chief	Elli Boubouri
	Panos Deligiannis
Group creative advisor	Stelios Pentarvanis
Journalists	Silia Antoniou, Natalia Bouga, Giorgos Charonitis, Maria Daliani, Evi Fetsi, Nikos Fotakis, Ioanna Gomouza, Charis Kalogeropoulos, Eleni Kouki, Thanasis Koutsis, Maria Kryou, Venia Vergou, Maro Voulgari, Isavella Zabetaki, Despoina Zefkili
Supervision of material	Thanasis Koutsis, Stratis Bournazos
Content coordinator	Sofia Karditsi
Assistant editor	Eleni Komitoudi
Adaptation in english	Anthula Wiedenmayer
Photographs	Zoi Chatzigiannaki, Stavros Kostakis, Pavlos Tsokounoglou, photo library DESMI

Studio

Art director	Constantinos Spaliaras
Assistant art director	Pinelopi Kourmouzoglou
Studio	Paschalis Siozos, Niki Galanopoulou

Advertising department

General advertising director	Spyros Theodoropoulos
Advertising directors	Petros Maidanis, Maria Nounou
Advertising executives	Tzoulia Alysandratou, Marios Dafnomilis, Giorgos Georgiadis, Vasia Kokoutsidi, Grigoris Koutsavlis, Eleni Nitsola, Akrivi Panotopoulou, Loukas Papanikolaou, Ioanna Souchla
Advertising assistants	Christina Boutsika, Anna Miliadi, Mara Tsigka

Production

Production manager	Giorgos Chatzisotiriou
Production coordinator	Betty Karavokyri
Pre-press - films - editing	Ray
Typset and bound by	Iris Printing S.A.

Administration

Administrator and financial manager	Mairi Psarri
IT manager	Thodoris Tsironis
Circulation	Totis Koulis, Vangelis Papoudakis
Public relations	Myrto Apalopoulou
Maps	Odorama - Thanasis Palamiotis Publications

DESMI PUBLICATIONS S.A.
2-4, Mesogeion Ave. (Athens Tower - building B), Athens 115 27
Tel.: 210/7450100, 210/7450200, Fax: Editorial 210/7450227, Advertising 210/7450142, Accounts 210/7450108.
http://www.athinorama.gr, e-mail: aguides@athinorama.gr

The Athens we love

Athens is a puzzle. The body of the city, its structure, even its face, display a fragmentary resemblance, like small pieces of a larger picture, randomly scattered and waiting for someone to put them together, into place, where they will reveal the picture of a vital, vibrant city. The **Athens Guide 2003** wants to take you, its readers, on a wonderful tour of Athens, walking its streets and reconstituting the puzzle of our everyday lives. It searches out the little secrets that can make life in this city easier, friendlier, more fun. Highlighting its best faces, discovering its hidden corners, suggesting clever shopping ideas, decoding the up-and-coming restaurant scene, living the intensity of Athens by night, sketching the diversity of its cultural reality, artistic currents, variety of sounds and spectacles, giving well-researched advice for making the most of your moments of leisure, tracing the emerging new face of the city as it prepares for the 2004 Olympic Games.

Athens is a palimpsest, like one of those ancient parchments whose surfaces were scraped to erase the old writing so that a new text could be inscribed on them. Here, the writer is time: history leaves its indelible traces, but time conceals them beneath or beside the marks of the life that has flowed on uninterruptedly over thousands of years. The **Athens Guide 2003** is designed to be an invaluable tool, an aid to resident and visitor alike in reading the many different layers of this palimpsest, which they will encounter at every step, through an up-to-date, systematic and detailed tour of the monuments, the museums and the modern persona of this amazing city.

Athens is a magic picture: when you look at it from different angles, it changes, constantly, presenting hidden aspects and rapid transformations that, day by day, alter both the overall aesthetic and the services and amenities on offer. The **Athens Guide 2003** explores and records not only the world of entertainment and good living, but also those essential details that help resolve the problems of everyday life. In its pages you will find everything the denizen of a modern metropolis needs to know: from care for body and soul to gourmet shopping and successful parties at home, from how to find expert advice in just about any field to where to have your rare and precious treasures repaired.

So let us help you explore this often confusing, frequently unfriendly but always fascinating city. The **Athens Guide 2003** is the product of real knowledge, based on the accumulated experience of the staff at **Athinorama** magazine, who for 27 years have been recording every aspect of life in Athens. It is also a work of love, written by a team that knows how to discover and enjoy the pleasures concealed under Athens' noisy, often chaotic, outer shell. All you have to do is use it - or better still, enjoy it. Like us, who went through the long, laborious but enjoyable months of preparation required for the creation of the **Athens Guide 2003** with a single slogan: **We Love Athens!**

Telis Samantas

a Bank
with Style

If we were talking about a city with style, it would be a city with history, culture and a contemporary face - it would be Athens. If we were talking about a restaurant with style, it would be a quality place with a trail-blazing cuisine, recipient of a Golden Cook's Hat - it would be our favourite. If we were talking about a film with style, it would be original, entertaining, with Oscar-level performances - we would never get tired of watching it. If we were talking about a production with style, it would sweep the audience polls, be voted the best show of the year - it would be unforgettable. If we were taking about a bank with style, it would be a bank with history and a contemporary profile, with top quality, pioneering services, ready to meet the requirements of this new age - it would be Alpha Bank, the second largest Bank in Greece and the Official Bank of the ATHENS 2004 Olympic Games. It would be our Bank.

Life & Style

Athens Guide 2003

ATHENS 2004

ALPHA BANK
OFFICIAL BANK

a thousand faces
under
one sun

Bathed in the light of Attica, Athens is a crossroads: a place where mountain meets sea, East meets West, a turbulent history meets the contemporary business world. Against this background, it is hardly surprising that the city should have its own vital rhythms, which never fail to astonish other Europeans. Athenians pour the same intense energy into their entertainment as into their work, and they have developed the temperament characteristic of the citizens of any great modern Mediterranean metropolis.

A city like Athens - chaotic, non-conformist, free - is not an easy place to come to grips with. A city where an ancient sense of measure co-exists with the chaos of the modern world, and the relaxed Mediterranean temperament with the inhuman rhythms of international business. Why this should be so, of course, is obvious: Athens is and always has been a busy crossroads. Since its first settlement it has never, despite myriad historical adventures and tremendous population fluctuations over a span of more than five thousand years, ceased to be a city. And a crossroads, particularly a busy one, is not the place to look for order and tranquillity...

Perhaps it all begins with this magical situation: the centre of Attica, a whole cosmos wherein everything exists and everything - mountains and sea, East and West, the soft curves of the landscape and the straight line of the horizon - inter-

Syntagma Square

An unexpected co-existence

sects, to create at their epicentre a basin protected by 'friendly' mountain massifs and punctuated by hills. And the most visible of all is that on which stands the emblem of the city: the Parthenon. The basic ingredient in the city's magic is light. The light of Attica. The characteristic dryness of this part of the country imparts a crystalline clarity to the atmosphere (even if it is now all too frequently clouded by the infamous nephos, or smog) and the sun, reflecting off the marble and limestone of the surrounding mountains, gives the sky a special luminosity. Especially at sunset, these mountains are tinged with a particular purple hue, a colour that made the poets of the 19th century speak of "violet-crowned Athens", the city that Henry Miller gazed upon from the Acropolis - and that gave him the setting for "The Colossus of Marousi" - as he sat there with

George Seferis, the Nobel Prize-winning poet who summed it up in two lines: "There is, I believe, an incarnative function in the light of Greece".
And it is this light that precipitates - how else can one put it? - a release of energy. Light carries a sense of fullness, well-being and zest for life, sentiments widespread among the Athenians when the skies are clear (particularly on certain winter mornings). And by the same token, the absence of light brings on the dismals that we all feel on days when the sky is overcast. In the final analysis, it is the sunshine and the diffuse light that distinguish Athens from other Western capitals.

HISTORICAL CONTINUITY

Modern Athenians are proud of their city; consciously or unconsciously, they are influenced by its history and the civilisation it pro-

Sunshine and a diffuse luminosity set Athens apart from the other great cities of the Western world.

An event at the Herodion Theatre

Fun at a beach bar

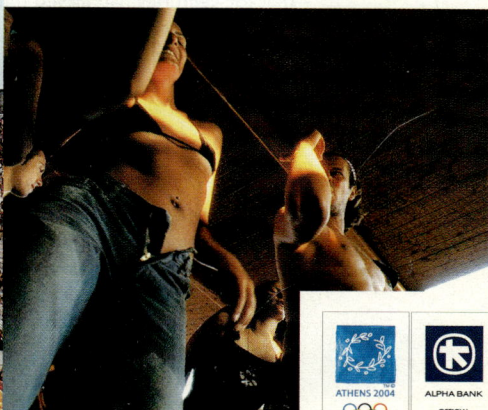

Dining with style, beside the sea

The Womad Festival in Athens

Come nightfall, the enchantment that is Athens reaches new heights: from a vantage point, the view of the illuminated city, vast and pulsating, is totally captivating.

duced. And how could it be otherwise? They live in the same place, and go about their business among the same narrow streets, as the giants of classical antiquity. Merely telling the names of just one small group of people from that brief but glorious Golden Age of 5th century BC Athens is awe-inspiring: there with Pericles, statesman and general, stand the historian Herodotus, Hippodamus the town planner, Anaxagoras the philosopher and Pheidias the sculptor. Meanwhile, a little farther down in the Agora, Socrates is engaged in conversation with students and passers-by, amid the wrestling schools and the stalls of the money-changers, while Aeschylus and Sophocles are busy writing the tragedies that have underlain all representative art to this very day. Their memory has never faded: even those who deliberately debilitated the city that for centuries had played the role of ecumenical university, like the Byzantine Emperor Justinian who in the 6th century ordered the closure of all its schools of philosophy, or Mehmed II, styled the Conqueror, who established Ottoman sovereignty, even they never ceased to respect the legend that was Athens. With such a history, just try persuading the Athenian of today to see himself as an ordinary mortal rather than a companion of the gods...

URBAN ECCENTRICITY

Today, virtually the entire basin is built up. From the coastal areas of Voula and Vouliagmeni in the southeast to Aigaleo, Petroupoli and Liosia in the west; from Ekali and the other posh northern suburbs to the districts of Piraeus and its environs in the southwest; from Ilioupolis and Zografou among the foothills of Hymettus in the east to Thrakomakedones in the northwest: a vast conurbation spreads like a carpet before the observer.

The metropolitan air is a relatively new state of affairs, which developed very rapidly in the aftermath of World War II, when the erstwhile indolent capital of the Eastern Mediterranean was shaken by successive waves of internal migration. The pattern of modernisation was not the usual one of concentric circles typical of other European cities, leaving the historic centre untouched and developing modern uses and aspects around the periphery. The result was an open city, a human and urban continuum with a thousand faces, with neighbourhoods that retain an old-fashioned friendliness next to areas developing at a frenetic pace.

As for the visual result, it is a palimpsest of architectural styles and urban concepts, created largely with no central planning, where the only recognisable style after

The city never sleeps

the neo-classical is the modern Greek apartment block, an austere and strictly functional rectangular construction (not unrelated to the financial conditions which spawned them) with terraced roofs and balconies, in either the predominant white or shades of ochre.

With the exception of Plaka, no section of the city has retained its pre-war character intact. The result is a jumble: in the city centre you can walk past a modern glass building located next to a charmless '70s apartment block rubbing shoulders with a recently restored neo-classical mansion. But even this image of chaos combines with the light and gives forth a charm that harmonises with its surroundings. And by night the enchantment is multiplied a hundredfold in the spectacle of the vast, illuminated, pulsating metropolis...

HUMAN IDIOSYNCRASY

According to the 2001 census, Attica has a population of 3,761,810: the real figure, however, is much higher, since a large proportion of the city's residents prefer to be registered in their places of origin and there is no sure way of counting the number of economic migrants. It is no wonder, then, that those who live in this unique chaos should themselves be unique. On the one hand, since the antiquities are lit-

erally everywhere, the Athenians are peculiarly snobbish with regard to their monuments. They live and move in an open-air museum, accessible at all times, and they are singularly unimpressed by ancient marbles. At the same time, however proud they may be of the past, they adore the present, enthusiastically embracing each new trend - once they have trimmed it to their measure.

The best way to see these different faces is to walk. In the business thoroughfare of Kifisias Ave., with its glass facades and perpetual traffic snarls, the people you meet don't walk: they run. Here in the City of Athens the pace is set by the power executive look, cell phone glued to the ear, step rapid and decisive - business is always pressing and cannot wait. A few kilometres away, in Omonoia, navel of the old city, the scene changes. Here too people move quickly, but the pace is less frenzied. And the look is different: a mixture of all races, classes and ages, who have come downtown for business, pleasure or shopping. Meanwhile, in Kolonaki, the cafes and boutiques are full of elegant people, dressed in the latest fashions, who spend in their everyday lifestyle the wealth generated by the recent economic boom; while in the western suburbs neighbours gossip in the street, as if these were still the days when Athens

Alpha Bank

Alpha Bank is the second largest Bank in Greece. With a network of 470 Branches, the Alpha Bank Group is active in the domestic and international banking markets, with a presence in New York, London and many other cities around the globe.

Since its founding in 1879, it has played an extremely important role in the economic and financial life of the country, providing top quality innovative services. Its experience in the banking sector allows it to be flexible and ensures that it is always in a position to respond to the demands of the times.

It is an acknowledged leader in the introduction of new electronic banking services, such as Alphaphone (via telephone), Alphaline (via computer), Alpha Web Banking (via the Internet) and Alpha Bank m-Banking (via mobile phone).

ALPHA BANK OFFICIAL BANK OF

The Bank of the 21st century

Alpha Bank is at the helm of a group of companies of the financial sector, with a wide range of activities providing comprehensive services to private and corporate clients in the following fields: financing services, investment services, information technology and other services, insurance, real estate, hotels.

The Alpha Bank Group's activities are not limited to the financial sector. For many years, it has demonstrated a practical interest in Greek culture, in all its expressions, by sponsoring -for example- the activities of the Athens Music Hall and the National Gallery.

On February 8, 2001, Alpha Bank was proclaimed Official Bank of the ATHENS 2004 Olympic Games.

Alpha Bank is part of the tremendous national endeavour to prepare this great event, bringing the spirit of collaboration that governs its employees' relationship with customers: "Mazi" *

* "Mazi" in Greek means "together"

THE ATHENS 2004 OLYMPIC GAMES

The Parthenon, eternal symbol of Athens

Musical happening in Dionysiou Areopagitou

was a city where you knew everything about everyone who lived within a radius of a kilometre from your house.

Athens is an open-air city, and its inhabitants love to sit outside, winter or summer. Only two things are required: sunshine and company. This is evident in the plethora of cafes, which are literally countless and come in all shapes, sizes, styles and varieties: they are nooks, breathing spaces, meeting places, necessary refuges from the frantic pace of everyday life. And don't imagine that a cafe has to be confined within four walls: as soon as the sun comes out, with the first breath of milder air, its patrons seem to suffocate indoors. And that is why the best tables, even in the most comme il faut restaurants (which, if they have any self-respect at all, will have an outdoor area), are those in the choicest corner of the terrace, garden, courtyard, next to the water, beside the vine… Company, companions, are an essential feature of the Athenian lifestyle. They are, immediately after the ubiquitous and ever-present family, the nucleus of social life. In all these cafes and restaurants, throughout this great open-air city, you will rarely find people sitting alone. People go out in groups and talk about other groups - people who sit alone do

so either out of dire necessity or from a touch of eccentricity ("can't we ever go out alone?"). An unbroken stream of sociability, contacts and conversations flows through the daily life of the Athenian - and they can't live without it. Here people in the street look strangers in the eye - a habit that has no aggressive overtones, as it would in most European cities, but simply indicates curiosity and a disposition to social intercourse. They also flirt - in the street, in the cafes, in the bars: this everyday undercurrent of eroticism is an essential component of daily life, even if everybody complains that human contact is not as easy as it used to be.

But Athens is not all sunshine. Athenians are also rude, overly familiar and rarely say thank you. They find the city oppressive, fatiguing; it makes them aggressive. They complain about its appearance and are not particularly happy to compare it to the museum cities of Western Europe. But at the same time, the overwhelming majority of Athenians say that they would not change life in Athens for any other city.

The biggest problem here is traffic, in all its forms. Since very few of the city's streets were designed to handle heavy traffic and the road network is based on the narrow back streets and laneways of a

> Nightlife essentially begins after 22:30 - "a quick drink after work and then home" is a foreign concept here.

Out for coffee in Kolonaki

A gala premiere at the Concert Hall

bygone age, the traffic in the centre never seems to stop, day or night. Athenians don't like to walk (and in any case pavements are in many areas virtually non-existent) or to use the proverbially unreliable public transport (although the recent arrival of the Metro has changed that); what they do like is to drive everywhere, in the cars that have become an inseparable part of their being - and which they insist on parking right outside wherever it is they want to go. Add to that an incredibly aggressive road attitude, with more than a touch of exhibitionism and a strong Michael Schumacher streak, and you have an idea of the daily madhouse on the city's streets. This scene is the particular territory of a special category of drivers and yet another of the city's trademarks: its taxi drivers. Perhaps no other social or professional group encapsulates so characteristically the contradictions of everyday life in Athens: everyone speaks of them disparagingly, as if they were a uniform lot who drive capriciously and behave rudely; but at the same time no one could live without them, not only because Athenians use taxis totally indiscriminately, but also because their constant shuttling to and fro through the congested downtown streets has made them an essential cog in the functioning of the city, a blend of psychiatrist, social observer and political/sports commentator, providing their passengers with a flow of opinion, information and personal chitchat as they fray a path through the choked-up roadways. And he who survives...

A CITY OF NIGHT OWLS

The rapid, almost paranoid, pace that has developed over the past few years has so far blended perfectly with the different sense of time that traditionally prevails in this corner of the Mediterranean. The rest of Europe is usually astonished at the resulting cocktail: hard work alternates with long breaks, and the working day ends in a night on the town, which is then succeeded by another hard day's work. The explanation, however, is easy: anything that has to do with having a good time, especially eating, dancing and singing, has pride of place in the life of the Athenian.

Athens has every imaginable kind of nightlife. The number of places of entertainment, their design, their vitality and animation, and the sheer diversity of types of entertainment on offer is truly amazing. Food first: and the spectrum covers everything from the traditional tavernas, mezes bars, grill houses and ouzeris to a nascent gastronomy and rising fine

The Acropolis, from the roof of a nearby gallery

A performance at the Lycabettus Theatre

> Athens breathes an atmosphere of relaxed freedom, heightened by its proximity to the sea.

restaurant scene. And then there are the countless bars, clubs and live music places, which in turn offer a variety of styles from folk to art to classic bouzouki. And all this goes on all the time - without even counting the frequent concerts and festivals billing foreign names, or the lively dance scene and its events.

Nightlife in Athens essentially kicks off after 22:30 - the "one drink after work and then home" philosophy has little currency here. That explains why most restaurants continue to serve well after midnight, while the "big names" on the club programmes do not appear until after 01:00. Since this is as true of weekdays as of weekends, Athens appears to be a city that never sleeps. The night owls returning home at 06:00 or thereabouts will meet others on their way to work - and very often they are the same people. It's all a matter of energy, you see...

There is an obvious atmosphere of relaxed freedom in this city. Which is accented by the fact that it is so close to the sea: the beaches are directly accessible and the traffic, once the weather warms up, shifts to the seafront. For bathing, yes, but also for the nightlife: in the summer, the traffic jams on the shore road in the wee hours are as bad as the peak noon rush-hour congestion downtown.

AND TOMORROW?

Contradictory aspects of a contradictory city. As we noted, the explosion that turned Athens into a modern metropolis was very sudden. As it enters the 21st century, Athens is losing its more or less homogeneous and congeneric character and each neighbourhood is acquiring a style of its own. Many changes have taken place, and many more are on the way. Some of the elements of its easygoing Mediterranean attitude have already vanished, and more will soon follow; on the other hand, it is acquiring metropolitan features unknown until very recently, an aspect that is substantially furthered by a very visible multi-ethnicity.

As for the cost of living, it is already fairly high, especially measured against pay scales that are sensibly lower than the EU average. An espresso costs € 3, a hamburger € 1.50, a ticket to the cinema € 6.50-7 and to the theatre € 20; you can expect to pay about € 80 per person for dinner with wine at a good restaurant, while a bottle of whisky (usually for four) in one of the big clubs will set you back about € 150.

Property prices are also rising, in line with other European cities. The average price for a new apartment varies from approximately € 1200-1400 / m² in western suburbs like Peristeri and Liosia to € 1400-1700 / m² in densely popu-

This time athletes will literally have a shot at making history.

TM©ATHOC 2002, PHOTO COSIDAS

Archery in the shadow of the Acropolis.

In 2004 the Olympic Games return to the place where they were born, where they were revived and where they will be renewed. The ATHENS 2004 Olympic Games are more than an opportunity to participate in the greatest celebration of humanity. They are an opportunity to be part of a story that is as old as history itself. And when it comes to making history, there is really no place like home.

ATHENS 2004. There's no place like home.

Games of the XXVIII Olympiad, Athens 13-29 August 2004
www.athens2004.com

ATHENS 2004

Summer escape in the Greek islands

Summertime, when life moves to the beach

lated central districts like Pagkrati and Ampelokipoi, while in the expensive northern and southern suburbs, like Kifisia and Vouliagmeni, average prices start at € 3000 / m² and may go as high as € 4500 in the choicest areas. Kolonaki, the up-scale quarter in the city centre, is in a class of its own, with property prices - despite the absence of new construction - reaching € 5700 / m², putting it on a level with the most expensive European capitals, like London.

Meanwhile, the fabric of the city is improving, and day by day the changes are becoming visible. The 2004 Olympic Games spurred numerous interventions to the city's urban and social equipment, and more are needed. But beyond the purely Olympic projects, such as the additions to the Olympic Stadium (designed by the famous architect Santiago Calatrava), the fly-overs that will facilitate access to the Stadium and the removal of all billboards, the air that is blowing through the city is fresh and full of renewal: neo-classical buildings are no longer being pulled down, but restored; ring roads are being created to relieve traffic congestion; the new airport, the Metro (with its extensions) and the new tram lines define a transport infrastructure that was long overdue; the waterfront boulevard is being redeveloped and acquiring

Kindled by the prospect of the Olympic Games, a frenzy of activity is bringing Athens into line with the times.

parks and footpaths; Omonoia and the downtown streets are being given a radical face lift; monuments and archaeological sites are being conserved and enhanced (witness the atmospheric pedestrianisation of Dionysiou Areopagitou and Apostolou Pavlou streets); old museums are being renovated and new ones, like the New Museum of the Acropolis, signed by famous architects, prepared; emblematic buildings are springing up everywhere: a riot of activity is bringing Athens to the measure of the times.

ENVOI

Athens, nonetheless, is still a difficult city to discover. Resident and visitor alike have to train their eyes to be selective: to get around in Athens, you have to learn to distinguish, amid the disorder that can be anything from charming to unbearable, what is really worthwhile, where you really should go, how you can have the best time possible. Athens, for her part, will continue to offer in abundance that inimitable feeling of relaxation and freedom, a diversity of options, an intense nightlife and the knowledge that here you can do anything - from best to worst, it's up to you. Because here in Athens you are at an unageing and always unexpected crossroads of mentalities, cultures and behaviours.

Thanks to you, 5 stars* in the sky
belong to Athens International Airport.

ICARUS

★★★★★ *We ranked 2nd in Europe and 3rd in the world.

We are proud to announce that, in the IATA «Airport Global Monitor Survey» for 2001, passengers ranked Athens International Airport impressively high, after only one year of operation. Although this is certainly a good reason to celebrate, we keep on trying for the first place!

ELEFTHERIOS VENIZELOS
ATHENS INTERNATIONAL AIRPORT

together
with
Alpha Bank

This is our city. The whole of Attica, from Oropos to Sounio. Wherever we may go, Alpha Bank will be there too. The second largest Bank in Greece has 178 Branches and 382 ATMs in Attica, assuring immediate service, 24 hours a day, 365 days a year. So let's get to know our city better, together with Alpha Bank.

ATHENS 2004

ALPHA BANK
OFFICIAL
BANK

ALPHA BANK OFFICIAL BANK OF THE ATHENS 2004 OLYMPIC GAMES

Views of the city

Athens Guide 2003

ATHENS 2004

ALPHA BANK

OFFICIAL BANK

snapshots
of Athens

Athens has many different faces, and we have adopted a double-barrelled approach to presenting them. First, we travel the city's main arteries with the eye of the visitor, and then we explore the times and places that the Athenians live and relive. From the high-society of Kolonaki to the multiracial downtown marketplace, from aristocratic Kifisia to neo-classical Plaka, from the waterfront boulevard to Piraeus, a world apart: we recommend ten snapshots that profile the characteristic diversity of this city, the elements that give it its unique vitality.

ATHENS THROUGH THE EYE OF THE VISITOR

Fast forward, to a pan of the city, as seen by a visitor moving through its main thoroughfares.

• The new airport tells the arriving visitor what all Athenians already know, or sense: Athens is changing. Not that the "Eleftherios Venizelos International Airport" has any special architectural character; but it is an ultramodern airport, and the start of the **Attiki Odos**, the Attica Road, probably the city's only truly European-style highway, a road that you can speed along… for a few kilometres, at least, until you catch up with the construction work. The Attiki Odos is literally being built under your wheels, and it brings you down to earth fast as you enter the seedy extension of Mesogeion Ave.

• As you head down **Mesogeion Ave.** towards the centre, you are moving away from exciting places like the new rowing lake and the paradise of the traditional summer

The Parliament Building

In front of the Concert Hall

holiday resorts of Rafina, Loutsa, Zoumperi, Nea Makri. The road is lined with snack bars, family tavernas for impatient Sunday trippers, furniture warehouses, large stores selling household furnishings and garden supplies, agents for pre-fab houses. As you approach the city, however, the streetscape changes: as Agia Paraskevi gives way to Chalandri, past the imposing National Radio & Television Building, you enter the biotope of the recording industry: one after another, from Stavros to the Ministry of Defence and its Metro station, Virgin, Universal, Warner, Sony and Minos-EMI lend a musical/cultural note to an otherwise nondescript stretch of road.

A road that, before the interchange at Katechaki, passes three major hospitals - the General State Hospital, Sotiria and the 401 Military Hospital - before coming to an end in the heart of Ampelokipoi, a densely built up area with extremely heavy traffic. Heading up Pheidippidou, you

come to one of the city's major hubs and the intersection of three of its great downtown thoroughfares: Kifisias, Vasilissis Sofias and Alexandras Ave.

• The western approach to the city **(from the Corinth Highway)** is totally different, for this is where the bulk of postwar industrial development took place. The serpentine coastline (best appreciated from the old national road) is dotted with refineries, chimneys, smokestacks and shipyards. When the high-speed section of the road comes to end and the Athenian drivers are forced to moderate their vertiginous speeds (they seem to be letting go after the traffic snarls in the city), the road narrows at Aspropyrgos. Immediately after Dafni, the city proper begins. Along this ever neglected stretch of road, the gateway into the city for countless domestic migrants, there is an endless succession of car dealerships, used car lots, small industries and supermarkets, inter-

tip
One thing that always confuses visitors is that some of the city's major arteries have two different names: an official one and the one everybody uses. Panepistimiou, for example, is really Eleftheriou Venizelou Street, Patision is officially 28th October Street, while Peiraios is Tsaldari from Omonoia to Gazi and Athinon-Peiraios Ave. from Kifisou to Piraeus!

The modern face of Kifisias Ave.

Views of the city

Athens, a city of "cinemaniacs"

The Stathatos Building on Vasilissis Sofias

The visitor will enter the city either by way of the Attiki Odos and Mesogeion Ave. (coming from the airport) or via Peiraios (from the port) or, if travelling by road, from the national highway.

spersed with the occasional dive or striptease joint. Athinon Ave. takes you to the Metaxourgeio district, where the forlorn facades of older buildings wait for the breeze of urban renewal that is blowing through the neighbourhood to reach them. All journeys come to an end, however; and this road, via Agiou Konstantinou, magnet for immigrants from all over the world and the location of the neo-classical National Theatre, brings you to Omonoia Square.

• If you have arrived by boat and are coming up **Peiraios Ave.**, the cityscape elicits mixed feelings of nostalgia and solitude. This was once the city's industrial heartland, and some of the famous old units are still in operation - e.g. the Elais edible oils plant and, nearer Omonoia, the Pavlidis chocolate plant. Many of these buildings, exceptional examples of industrial architecture, have changed use: along the way you will see the Athens School of Fine Arts and the Foundation of the Hellenic World, occupying former textile and pipe manufactories respectively; while some other similar buildings have been converted into department stores or multiplex entertainment centres. Once past Tavros, with its subsidised tower blocks clustered around the former abattoirs and tanneries, you are in the city proper: here the dominant building is the old gasworks, Gazi, now a Technopolis

hosting exhibitions and happenings. And from here it's a clear run to Omonoia.

• Cut. Back to Ampelokipoi. **Kifisias Ave.**, the road between Ampelokipoi and Kifisia, provides the most representative delineation of how this city grew. From small neighbourhood shops to large shopping centres, from grey apartment blocks to the monsters of "Vovopolis" (most of the huge glass towers around Marousi were built by a contractor named Babis Vovos), from cinema strip (including the summer cinema Ellenis) to multiplex (the Village Center in Marousi), from isolated professional offices in modest buildings to huge banks, advertising agencies, dynamic companies, an explosion of publishers and broadcasters. Kifisias intends to be the city's business hub; and to a certain extent it has succeeded, the only impediment being the eternally snarled traffic, which sometimes leaves the road looking like a crowded showroom for expensive cars.

• **Vasilissis Sofias** is totally different. To drive down this street is to take a journey back in time, to turn back the clock of urbanisation. The signs of the city's first upper middle class neighbourhood remain: the earlier neo-classic villas, succeeded by mansions and luxury apartment blocks - and many examples from each period still stand as they were,

A glass tower, a neo-classical house: the two faces of Athens

Never a boring moment for theatre-goers

which is rare indeed in Athens. The Concert Hall is a contemporary reflection of this current; and it was not chance that located it between the United States Embassy (designed by Walter Gropius, leader of the Bauhaus movement) and Eleftherias Park, whose grassy expanses are a favourite place for casual strollers. Continuing on your way, you pass the Athens Hilton, symbol of the self-confidence generated by rapid post-war development, and head towards the National Garden, still one of the loveliest and most attractive spots in the city. Down one side of the park runs Irodou Attikou Ave., boasting the Presidential Palace, the Prime Minister's official residence and some of the most expensive real estate in the city; it ends at Vasileos Konstantinou and the Kallimarmaro Stadium, which in 1896 hosted the first modern Olympic Games.

• This is the starting point for a new adventure: on the other side of Ardittos hill begins **Vouliagmenis Ave.**, a road that requires considerable patience, as you crawl past endless small shops waiting for the traffic to open up so that you can speed on down to the seaside, either to Glyfada or to Kavouri at the end of this stretch of road.

• And then, of course, there is **Syngrou Ave.**, the broad straight avenue that leads from Faliro and the waterfront boulevard right into the heart of Athens. The role it played in the '70s has been taken over by Kifisias Ave., but the change is celebrated daily - or rather nightly - in the great clubs scattered along its length. Today, it is reclaiming its ancient title, judging by the splendid new buildings that are going up, signed by some of the world's greatest architects.

• Cut. Back once again to Ampelokipoi, this time to go down **Alexandras Ave.** The refugee housing units, which still bear the marks of the Civil War, are being readied for demolition; the Panathinaikos Football Grounds, on the other side of the street, still echo to football games played - as in bygone days - in the heart of the city; farther down is the narrow Argentinis Dimokratias Square, whose name few people know. Pause for coffee, toast or cream cakes at the once again trendy Sonia's, a patisserie with a nostalgic '60s style, before turning into the park of the Pedio tou Areos, an oasis of green in a particularly densely built area.

• **Patision Ave.** waits at the corner. If you've ever come across the a la grecque beat poet Katerina Gogou, you'll find yourself murmuring that your life is "more or less a Patision": this is the most stressed-out street in the city. The Polytechnic School, the School of Economics, Koliatsou, Amerikis Sq., Kypseli, the cafe

tip
On several of the city's main arteries, the numbering is not continuous, but may stop and begin from 1 again two or three times: on Kifisias Ave., for instance, there are two number 12s, one in Ampelokipoi and one in Marousi. To avoid problems, the visitor should make sure he knows the name of the district as well as the street address.

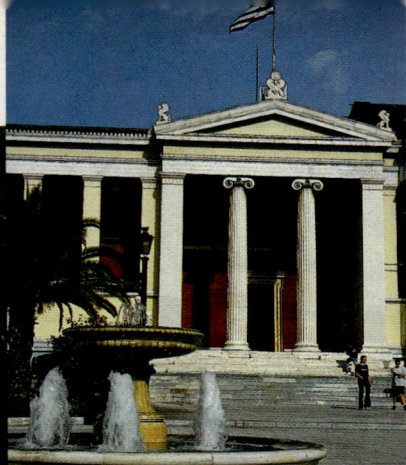
The entrance of the University Building

concourse of Fokionos Negri, Patisia: the neighbourhoods that sheltered the lower-classes dream of post-war residential rehousing became the most densely populated in the Greater Athens Area. And now they are home to people from all over the world, the multiracial dormitory of the capital.

• Change of direction, and return to the centre. **Stadiou Street** has a civilised air about it: as you head up it, you pass Lampro-poulos (one of the city's oldest department stores), the passages through the big old commercial buildings, now proudly renovated (the Stoa Orfeas, for example, with the Theatro Technis, or the Stoa tou Vivliou, abutting the Council of State), the roar of the Stock Exchange wafting up from Sofokleous Street, the big banks, Klafthmonos Square, the mod-ernised Korai Square (with a Starbucks where Floka's used to be), the Old Parliament House, the famous Army Pension Fund block, which once housed Zo-nar's and the Aliki Theatre and is now being converted into the city's biggest shopping centre. Left turn into Voukourestiou. Pause for espresso under the gaze of Moralis, Tsarouchis, Chatzidakis and Pablo Casals at the Brazilian, one of the city's first de rigueur cafes. Some things are truly classic.

• Out onto **Panepistimiou St.**, which for some reason always

looks busier than its neighbour. Perhaps because it's a bit wider, and so has room for more cars - not to mention a bus lane going in the opposite direction. Perhaps because it has even more offices, even more companies, even more passages. Or perhaps because, once you've passed the elegant end, with the Catholic Church, the imposing trio of neo-classical buildings housing the Academy, the University and the National Library, the historic Ideal (cinema and restaurant) and the Rex, where some of the National Theatre's productions are staged, you come back to your starting point. Panepistimiou leads to Omonoia, and the stream of humanity carries you along, trans-forming you from a simple stro-ller to a busy Athenian, always in a hurry to get things done.

• This is the Athens of today; and you sense it if you continue to circulate in the centre, in streets like Akadimias, Solonos, Skoufa, Ippokratous, or the broad flagged pedestrian precinct of Ermou. This is the commercial heart of the city, this is the real down-town core, with few residents but busy night and day: when the shops close in the evening, every-one (and everything) prepares for the next stage, the next wave: those out for an evening's enter-tainment, dinner in a trendy restaurant or a drink in the pleas-ant hubbub of a busy little bar.

ATHENAEUM
INTERCONTINENTAL
ATHENS

The luxury, amenities and quality services that make up the experience of a stay in any of the InterContinental Hotels & Resorts has secured us a place among the world's leading hotel chains.

But we're not resting on our laurels: we are constantly evolving so as to continue to meet the high expectations of our guests, who often include prominent figures, including heads of State, royalty, from the world of politics, business leaders and social celebrities.

We have recently invested in a major renovation programme, which, apart from an extensive renewal of the existing accommodation, public areas and conference facilities, includes among other things the creation of two Club InterContinental floors, as well as of a truly fresh, contemporary all-day dining venue, the cafe**zoe**.

With the completion of this extensive renovation assigned to two of the world's leading designers, Tony Chi and Pierre Yves Rochon, the Athenaeum InterContinental Athens aspires to offer its guests an exceptional choice of services and facilities that are second to none.

89-93, Syngrou Ave., Athens, 210/9206000, fax 210/9206500
e-mail: athens@interconti.com, www.intercontinental.com/athens

A MORNING STROLL IN PLAKA

The most historic part of town, a refuge from the hustle and bustle

Learning to love Athens begins in Plaka. How could it be otherwise? Plaka is essentially the only living witness to the pattern of the city's growth.

Working your way down from the Acropolis to Filellinon is like having a history lesson, noting the traces of antiquity, Byzantium, the years of Ottoman rule, the 20th century: wherever you stop, you realise that at one time this was the heart of the city. The neo-classical buildings are very handsome; but if you look more closely you'll discover humbler (and perhaps more characteristic) examples of Athenian domestic architecture: old two-storey houses with interior courtyards, many of them now simply abandoned. All of these are harmoniously linked to the antiquities on every hand, as well as to the most charming of the "false notes" in this scene: the "Anafiotika", an island town clinging to the foot of the rock of the Acropolis, a masonry memory of the place left behind by the skilled workers who came to build the neo-classical Athens of the 19th century.

But Plaka has been a centre of developments more recently than that. Up until the end of the '70s, this was the heart and soul of the city's nightlife, this was where the younger generation found out what was going on outside their country. Plaka was the natural habitat of the nightclub, which generated what we know as "artistic music" today. It was the rock centre of the city, the home of Mad, the city's first punk club; it was where Giorgos Barakos opened Athens' first jazz bar.

Everything changed in the '80s, when the district was listed for preservation, when governments decided to eliminate noise and leave only the shopkeepers selling their kilted soldiers and miniature Parthenons, their leather sandals and their T-shirts stamped with the opening lines of the Odyssey. You'd think they were doing everything they could to drain the area of its vital sap, to reduce Plaka to a listed monument, a district of museums and Ministry of Culture offices and subservient bodies, a district with a few surviving basement tavernas and "traditional" cafes, bourgeois tavernas serving "Greek moussaka" and old folk songs, coffee shops calling themselves "dairy bars" - a museum piece commemorating an Athens that has long ceased to exist.

A morning stroll down the cobblestone streets is enough to banish this image. You don't need to wait till Carnival time, when the place fills up with rev-

ellers stirring up high jinks. Strolling down Adrianou towards the Tower of the Winds, you see an amazing number of people: families enjoying the sun, parties of friends looking at cheap clothes and toys, couples gazing at a jeweller's display before buying sticky sweets from Kotsolis ("since 1909", says the sign at 112, Adrianou) - a world seemingly uninterested in fads, obsessions and trends, a world that doesn't care that Plaka has been out of fashion for twenty years. In fact, maybe that's what they're looking for: the sweet sense of security you get from being understood when you order a "Chicago" ice-cream in a classic pastry shop on Philomoussou Etairias Square, and not having to endure a scornful glance from a waiter trained to serve pannacotta and pear sorbet.

Between the Scholarcheio with its mezedes and barrels of wine and the Athens University Museum of History, the Goulandris-Horn Foundation and the Amaltheia creperie, the Bakaliarakia and the Museum of Folk Instruments, the Tristrato with its home-style sweets and the Eden vegetarian restaurant, Plaka remains one of the loveliest - and liveliest - parts of Athens. In the afternoon, Dioskouroi and Klepsydra are full of people sitting around tables littered with beer glasses, coffee cups and the last bites of walnut cake, talking about this and that, who's singing at Zygos this year and whether last year's programme wasn't better. Some of them will go on to Esperides and Apanemia, side by side in Tholou Street, where they continue to sing for the assembled company, perpetuating a bygone age.

A SUNDAY ADVENTURE IN MONASTIRAKI

The memory of the city is preserved by its second-hand dealers, street vendors and small shopkeepers.

For the Athenian, Monastiraki is synonymous with a leisurely Sunday morning stroll.

Monastiraki is two streets - well, maybe three: Ermou, Iphaistou and Adrianou. And since Ermou doesn't count - it's too big and busy - Monastiraki is what lies behind it. To be precise, Monastiraki is a promenade: the circuit you make from the electric train station to the edge of Plaka, then down Adrianou to Agion Asomaton and back via Astingos to Iphaistou. Monastiraki is that promenade, absolutely and inextricably interwoven with Sunday morning. Because on no other day of the week can there be the same atmosphere, the same frame of mind. On no other day of the week would you allow yourself to wander aimlessly in and out of bead-sellers' and cheap shoe shops, basement antique dealers and second-hand bookstores; on no other day of the week would you dirty your hands looking through used vinyl LPs, to find Eric Burdon Declares War in amongst the trash. It is no accident that here in Iphaistou you will find 7+7, the legendary Zacharias and Mr Vinyl -or that a little further down you'll find all the old "Illustrated Classics",

old numbers of "Eikones", the first translations of "Asterix" and "Tintin", collections of popular fiction and the epitome of Greek pulp: "Maska", "Maskoula", "Mystirio". These have no connection with ordinary life; there is no place on weekdays for "Maska" and the 45s of the lumpen proletariat. Only on Sunday are you prepared to handle such stuff.

The old flea market of a once tiny Athens is a thing of the distant past, but customs are customs - and they must be piously respected. The rite begins with a rendez-vous at Dioskouroi, behind the station, for coffee and a glance at the morning papers. Which you leave behind on the table - in any case you'll be back later for ouzo, unless you prefer the more European flavour and atmosphere of Kouti. Heading down Adrianou, you check out each and every street vendor. Among his wares - old worn-down shoes, broken telephones, old calendars, odd dishes - you will always find something that takes your fancy: a rusty tin toy, badges for a long-defunct political party, somebody's old postcards. Astingos is full of second-hand bookstores, where you leaf through old magazines, discover the pornography of the '50s - small black-and-white volumes with exotic titles like Strip Tease - and realise that today's hot news will someday enter a whole

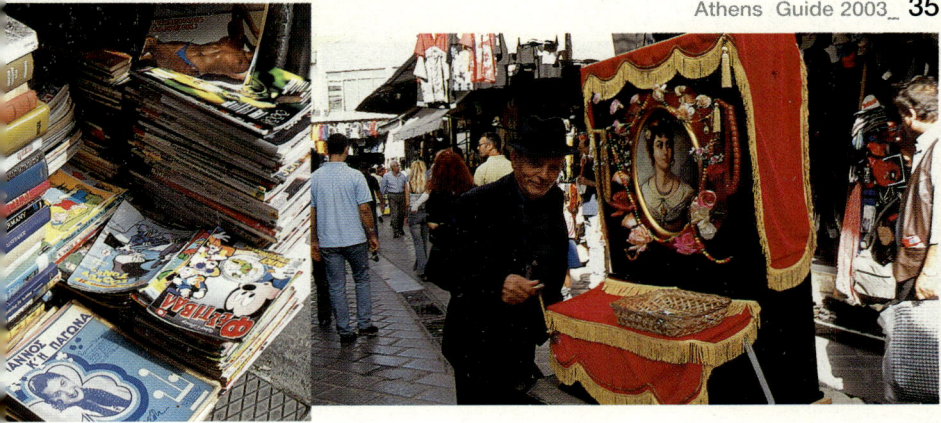

different sphere: the magazines of the '70s are a joke today. But watch out: in Monastiraki nothing is a joke. No one knows this better than the hawkers of Iphaistou Street - felines with roving eyes and a quick tongue, always ready to hook a customer and sell him a pair of boots, a cotton shirt or a pair of trainers at bargain prices. The Underground, on the other hand, with its curious T-shirts, is more selective, and its sign tells you exactly where you stand: "Tourists No. Travellers are welcome".

Monastiraki may look like a lumpen sort of place, but it isn't - or at least it isn't in the sense that you think it is as you walk along between the tumbledown commercial buildings of an earlier age, poor cousins of the neoclassical beauties in Plaka, their wares heaped up anyhow: Monastiraki is selective, even snobbish, in its all-inclusiveness. In the space of a single fifteen-minute walk, we heard in three different places some of the most progressive sounds in contemporary musical output: Badmarsh & Shri, Cinematic Orchestra and DJ Shadow -something that has never happened on Greek radio, for example. With this music in your ears, you go down into Filaretos' basement antique shop, ignoring the photographs of soldiers of the '20s and '30s, and suddenly find yourself

looking at an old player piano, hidden behind a collection of candlesticks. But you haven't the courage to ask how much it costs, so you go back up the steps and, with a sigh, throw yourself back into the fray. Monastiraki is a square.

The oddest square in Athens, since it is formed by two concentric circles. The first, inner, circle is shaped by the concrete booths of the second-hand dealers, while the second is a ring of ordinary shops, some antique shops, a stall with handyman's tools and two of the best cafe-bars in town: the Avissynia Cafe and Inoteka. In the centre of the circle, the junk-dealers spread their wares. Carefully, so as not to tread on anything that might break, you inspect unimaginable collections of venerable china, guns that haven't been fired in decades, photographs, picture frames, kitsch artwork. Small dismantled households, spilling out at your feet. The more you look, the more you wonder how so much past time can be contained within the space of three streets and a square. When you realise that you have spent your Sunday communicating with the accumulated memory of the city, that's when you need a drink, something to set you up, a song. So you follow the sound of the accordion into the Avissynia Cafe.

Monastirakiou Square is the oddest "square" in the city, formed as it is by two concentric circles. Stalls of second-hand goods form an inner ring, within the outer circle of ordinary shops.

SATURDAY NIGHT IN PSYRRI

The most youthful of the city's old neighbourhoods is the ultimate all-inclusive entertainment district.

Psyrri still has its old shops and workshops. But the buildings are really all that is left of the old neighbourhood, and they are now little more than a backdrop.

You are sure to find everyone here: fans of Lazopoulos and the company from the Apothiki, actors, lovers of art music who flock to listen to the current programme at Aeriko, those who jam into the House of Art, smart pop types who drift from One Happy Cloud to Astro and from Spirit to Bee, the young gallery groupies who celebrate new openings with libations at Multi Culti, older folk discovering the joys of luxury mezes bars - a diverse assemblage with a rare oneness of spirit. When about 20 years ago the historic working-class neighbourhood of Psyrri was declared a listed monument, its few remaining residents could never have imagined what would transpire: the restoration of some tumbledown buildings from the interwar period was greeted with sincere relief and pleasure in the aesthetic result, since it also meant that no more ugly four-storey industrial buildings would be springing up amid the old cottages. That was when the change began; and it took place gradually, as first theatres began to open, and then bars, restaurants and mezes bars, creating a chain of development: from the once solitary theatres Apothiki (in the old lumber sheds) and Empros (in the old print works) and the bar Taki 13 to Methystanes with its live street folk, the comfortably trendy Vitrina restaurant (now the Ruby Club), the Multi Culti bar-restaurant, the Ivi theatre, the Kouzina above the summertime Cine Psyrri, the freestyle bar Astro, with its Greek islands atmosphere, the eccentric Padre Padrone restaurant, the gastronomic Agrotikon and the Arabian glamour of Red Marrakesh.

As you move from Iroon Square to Sarri Street, the echoes from the bars create a soundtrack that describes contemporary Greek culture better than anything else: acid jazz and old street folk, rock and world music, Moby and Giannis Kotsiras, Ploutarchos and Chemical Brothers. The climate is relaxed, like being on holiday on an island: you walk along, forgetting that you spent forty-five minutes looking for a parking place before finally leaving your car in Koumoundourou, near the Armenian Church: this is the price exacted by all the formerly deprived areas that become trendy, every "New Athenian Soho", whether it's called Psyrri or Gazi or Rouf or anything else. But that's not the point: what matters is the feeling of relaxed well-being induced by the setting, this old working-class neighbourhood Disneyland that seems to be so far removed from the normal rhythm of the city. This brief escape is what counts, and Psyrri furnishes it most generously.

Values of Life

EURO RSCG

M-Class

ercedes-Benz - a brand of DaimlerChrysler

Freedom...

► Freedom. The ability to spread your ings, to get away, to explore, to evolve. ach values have been ever since the driving rce of Mercedes-Benz, as it was one of the rst companies to develop off-road vehicles. hrough these values, the company has olved and reached perfection in order to offer superior vehicles to people who know how to appreciate them.

As a result, Mercedes-Benz does not just offer cars of unsurpassed quality and technology, with luxury and safety which live up to its name, but it also challenges you to redefine the meaning of life's values.

Mercedes-Benz

mobilo-life
years care-free driving

Mercedes-Benz
FINANCE

Customer hot line: 800-11-76000, www.mercedes-benz.gr

COFFEE TIME IN KOLONAKI

The absolute city-centre meeting-place shares its glamour with all comers.

Kolonaki square is a rite of passage, the place where you stop for a break from shopping, for a drink or a bite to eat, as you watch the endless ebb and flow of people.

It may sound odd, but it's perfectly true: Kolonaki is an "aristocratic neighbourhood" that is open to all. Not that the character of the area has changed: from partway down Skoufa to Vasilissis Sofias, at the level of the American Embassy, in a sweep halfway around the focal point of Lycabettus ("this side" of the hill: for "the other side", Neapoli Exarcheion, once known as "Red Lycabettus", is another kettle of fish entirely), it is still the number one status symbol address. This, of course, is reflected in its real estate prices, not to mention the imperceptible change in tone of voice when someone says "I live in Kolonaki". So to be precise, what has actually opened up to all and sundry is Kolonaki Square. One of the most soothing spots in the city: it is always busy, and always bright, even in the dead of winter. It is full of cheerful people going in and out of shops, chatting, reading magazines or newspapers, buying cigars from one of the two classic newsstands on the square - the ones that are always decked out with foreign publications. It is the absolute meeting place, a ritual passage where you stop for a rest, set down your shopping bags and sip an espresso, eat a brioche or a toasted sandwich, glance at the newspaper. At this precious moment, nothing has any importance except being part of this crowd, all in the same condition as yourself, all talking incessantly, displaying their purchases, planning their evening, discussing (loudly) the economy of the country and the latest gossip from the society pages. At noon in Kolonaki the optimism is all-pervasive: it fills the shops (shoe shops with expensive footwear) and irradiates the streets: Tsakalof, Skoufa, Milioni, Patriarchou Ioakeim - even Leventi, the little back street with the great coffee shop (Misegianni's). There's room for everyone in Kolonaki, as long as they wear their most "I'm here too" face and their most sophisticated clothes: the political and economic bigwigs who lunch with journalists at Prytaneio or Angolo di Milioni, the law students who haunt the Skoufaki alongside the neighbourhood's alternative elements, the intelligentsia who settle back at Filion and talk about the days when it was called Dolce, the students at the British Council and other foreign Institutes sitting next to tables of elegant ladies obviously well-treated by life. Especially at lunchtime on Saturdays, everyone is here, with or without shopping, with or without cigarillos and foreign journals. The old guard, more conservative, take up their quarters at Tops or Lykovrysi; the more modern, or those who pretend to be, go across to Vivliothiki, chat up the good-looking girls and boys at Da Capo or head down to the genial chaos of the Milioni pedestrian passage. They drink a freddo, bask in the sunshine and good humour, and go on to the Central for sushi and salads.

never run out of words.

How are you?

vodafone™

AFTERNOON & EVENING IN KIFISIA

The northern feel of this leafy suburb of villas and cool breezes makes Kifisia a perennial favourite destination for an evening out and a meal.

In Kifisia, designer boutique shopping goes with cosy corners and gourmet refreshment.

Just adding the words "in Kifisia" to a sentence is enough to give it a whole new meaning: saying "I bought a pair of shoes in Kifisia" is totally different from saying "I bought a pair of shoes". However hard they may try to convince us that Kifisia is a misunderstood place, the truth is that it's a whole other world: a habitat where all - ALL - the women wear heels and the older ones don costly jewellery and elegant outfits just to go and buy a packet of cigarettes. Kifisia was built as a place of country houses and villas - you see them on either hand, standing behind their screen of hedges, as you stroll down its tree-lined streets, so different from the rest of Athens. This is why Kifisia, as a residential district, is the number one choice of the British and Americans who come to Greece with their embassies or a multinational company. This is also why it is still a classic destination for a family meal (historic places like the Capricciosa, now gone,

and the eternal Pappa's, which has moved, marked an age when an Italian pizza and a chef's salad were the definition of high gastronomic pleasure). It is perhaps why Kifisia is the place with the rudest sales clerks - in the clothes shops - and the most courteous pastry cooks: this is where you will find the legendary Varsos patisserie (5, Kassaveti St.). And it is the place where, in accordance with some arcane tradition, teenagers stick chewing gum to trees and where their Saturday night entertainment is going out for a burger and bowling.

Despite all this, or perhaps because of it, Kifisia is a fairly civilised place - which makes it a perfect spot for Saturday shopping. However jammed the streets, however crowded the Kifisia Shopping Centre and the countless shops in Kolokotroni, Levidou, Kyriazi, Kassaveti, no one ever loses their cool, nothing ever perturbs the phlegmatic salesgirls, no threats shatter the serenity. It also means that you will rarely - except just before Christmas - see people loaded down with shopping bags. Two at the most: more is considered vulgar.

Shopping in Kifisia always ends with the same rite: a pilgrimage to the temple of chocolate, the Aristokratikon (8, Argyropoulou

St.). After that, there are specific choices: the older residents will go to Berdema (20,Vasilissis Amalias St.) for lunch, but visitors will be unlikely to choose a taverna.

They will probably prefer the Italian cuisine at the Piazza Mela (238, Kifisias Ave.) or at La Soffita (11, Kyriazi St.), while the more "restless" types will opt for Salumaio Di Montenapoleone (3, Panagitsas St.), a more relaxed place, reminiscent of an elegant Italian grocery store.

Hidden in the rambling shopping mall of Levidou Street you will find Sotto Voce, a civilised cafe that serves what has to be the absolute frappuccino in the Northern Suburbs.

As closing time approaches, the focus of interest shifts towards the square, onto which the pleasantly ambling Kolokotroni Street finally debouches. Kefalari Square boasts both the wonderful serenity characteristic of the area and a whole clutch of restaurants and cafes, from the cheerful TGI Friday's to the cool Prytaneio and from Da Lu (for seafood pasta) to Square Sushi (for - what else? - carefully prepared sushi).

Or if you want a fine gourmet meal, you can choose between the French and Greek cuisine of Beau Brummel (which is not really in Kefalari), the trendy Big Deals and the opulent Vardis in the classic Pentelikon Hotel.

But maybe all you want to do is look at the square and the people, enjoy the cool breezes of the northern suburbs (it's always cool here, even in midsummer) and dream of Christmas. Which here is nearly always white.

PIRAEUS: ANOTHER CITY
A nighttime tour of a great port

A sui generis mixture of traditional and contemporary, commercial port and seaside resort, gives Piraeus a character all its own.

The new bridge in Neo Faliro (by the Peace and Friendship Stadium) may be confusing, but don't let it worry you: even if you do get lost and have to go through Piraeus, making a circuit or going through Pasalimani, the heart of the city, you'll find your way out again. And you will have had an opportunity to see something of one of the liveliest sections of the port. At night, Pasalimani (also called Zea) takes on a strange luminosity, as the electrified atmosphere of the great city is reflected in the water and back on to the faces of the people, who never tire of cruising about their town. The cliches are alive and well in Piraeus: the men are men, who stand on their dignity, are cheerful and open-handed and ready to do anything for their girls. Then again, that may be the impression we get as we see them on a pub-crawl, full of nervous energy, crossing Akti Moutsopoulou and through beautiful Alexandras Square to Kastella. There you will see all the contrasts of this town: neo-classical mansions rubbing shoulders with nightclubs, classic restaurants (like Castelo) with fish tavernas and the electric La Rocka, which always has the best live groups in the city. Haughtily scanning the seas, Kastella invites you to explore its back streets, laneways broken by flights of steps, and wander among houses seven and eight decades old and towers new-built to provide office space

for well-turned-out Piraeans. Kastella is splendid at sunset; but the night belongs to Mikrolimano -still called Tourkolimano by the older generation. The yachts and sailboats moored there make you feel as though you've moved from the country's greatest port to some European resort, which would explain the concentration of restaurants, bars and clubs along Akti Koumoundourou. A totally sui generis melange of the traditional and the contemporary juxtaposes old fish tavernas and minimalist restaurants like Plous Podilatou. Fresh fish competes with Jimmy and the Fish's lobster spaghetti, while a little farther down bars like the classic Appalloosa ratchet up the beat, just steps from the summer home of Varoulko, one of the city's very best fish restaurants, in the elegant surroundings of the Yacht Club. Winter and summer, Mikrolimano has the feel of an island, so you ignore the dampness, however overpowering, and follow the crowds of excited youngsters heading in the opposite direction, towards Akti Dilaveri, the Mecca of night-time entertainment: Galla, Iguana, Action Folie try to outdo one another in intensity, revelry, beat and attitude, creating an inimitable to-ing and fro-ing along the waterfront. A little farther down, the traditional Dourabeis watches the goings-on unconcernedly - and for good reason: having spent the past 70 years serving fish to generation upon generation of Piraeans, Athenians and tourists, VIP and non-VIP, it is not easily excited.

NOKIA
7650
Show that you mean

Civilization, History, Greece.
In a move.

NOKIA
CONNECTING PEOPLE

CRUISING ALONG THE WATERFRONT BOULEVARD

The waterfront is not a geographical location: it is a way of life

As winter fades into memory, the Athenians turn to the sea and the urban waterfront becomes the scene of an all-day summer lifestyle.

On the whole, it is fair to say that the inhabitants of the greater Athens area are divided into two basic categories: those who love the waterfront strip... and the rest. And deep down even they, although they turn their noses up at the Southern Suburbs, the holiday homes and the large night clubs, are thankful that their city is so close to the sea, that they can at any time renew their contact with the watery element, which is at most an hour away. This is particularly appreciated by high school students who play truant and end up at Varkiza or Lagonisi, or those who take a winter walk through the marina at Alimos, or who never miss an occasion to visit Alimos so as to drop in at the famous Zefyros (in bygone days) or now at the Skipper, the marina's all-day bar. This is truer still now that the blue flags are flying: in an age when more and more Athenians are cutting their holidays short, it is good to know that you can take a holiday break right in Athens and swim in clean, safe water. Not that it really matters: swimming is the last thing that counts when it comes to water-front entertainment. In the summer months, luxurious hotel complexes and impeccably organised beaches play host to the rising generation: resplendent boys and girls, cool, nervy, full of infectious spirits. This is the target clientele of the waterfront strip, which becomes a vast post-pubescent playground, full of luminous faces radiating optimism. Substitutes for clubbing during the hours when the sun is high, the beaches offer an opportunity for some to indulge in water sports to cool off after a session in the gym, while others dance in their swimsuits, downing beers and isotonic drinks at the indispensable beach bar.

The more refined will head out for lunch - fish, of course - to Kastelorizo, Limanakia in Varkiza, Ithaki, Laimos in Vouliagmeni, or the legendary Lampros on the road to the Lake: just follow the Mercedes, which are almost permanently parked outside. For the waterfront, whatever contemporary lifestylers may believe, is not a thing of the '90s: this is confirmed by the veteran waiters at the legendary Aqua Marina cafe in Laimos, serving ice cream sodas and the best old-fashioned cheese pies on the strip. They have nothing to fear from the parade of fun restaurants that for the past few years have been dominating the area, combining a cool meal out

with the imperative dose of beat that will allow their well-dressed patrons to let it all hang out - starting with their linen shirts. The most recent arrival - Septem, at Asteria Glyfadas - is a worthy competitor to the already classic Island, which has made Limanakia Vouliagmenis feel like somewhere in the Aegean. Not that parallels are necessary. Everyone knows that at night the waterfront comes alive. In the summer the city's migratory nightlife moves to the waterfront clubs and Posei-donos Ave. becomes the busiest street in the whole Athens area, carrying the swarms of clubbers from one place to another, for traditionally everyone moves on somewhere else during the wee hours.

No matter how many unlicensed buildings are torn down, the clubs still find somewhere to go; and no matter where you are on the coast, there will certainly be a big club not far away. If you're in Voula, for example, you're sure

to visit the classic mainstream Tango and Bo. On the Glyfada waterfront you've got the more alternative, smart pop places, like Banana Moon, Buddha, Caprice Del Mar and Club 22.

In Agios Kosmas the intensity of the hot spots of mainstream club-bing, like Privilege and Venue, is balanced by the absolute cool of the newly in vogue Akrotiri Lounge. A little farther along are the summer stamping grounds of the great stars of the nightclub stages: summer 2002 was marked by Giannis Ploutarchos and Giorgos Tsalikis, who packed them into Posidonio and Romeo+ respectively, once again drawing together the big clubs and the popular stages. Which, of course, continue to be represented by the cheerful Frangelico, the classic meeting place on Poseidonos Ave., starting point for the night's post-prandial activities or, more frequently, final refuge of the insa-tiable waterfront night owls, for a last drink before sun-up.

The summertime nightlife that attracts such hordes to the waterfront bou-levard is as leg-endary as the resulting traffic jams.

THE OTHER FACE OF EXARCHEIA

Saturday morning at the street market in Kallidromiou

Exarcheia is not just a rock district, a students' quarter, a magnet for the anti-establishment crowd: it is also a perfectly ordinary, classic downtown neighbourhood.

It's one thing to frequent Exarcheia, and quite another to live there. In other words, it's very doubtful whether those who come down Mavromichali on a Friday night, leaving Alphaville or Technochoros for one of the bars or tavernas in Methonis Street, or its "traditional" population of students, rockers and anti-establishmentarians, have any idea of what goes on in Kallidromiou on a Saturday morning, just below the police station notorious for its clashes with the anarchists. And the tourists staying in the Dryades Hotel are always startled to come down the steps into Benaki Street and find themselves confronting a vociferous tribe calling the freshness and the virtues of their fruits, vegetables, fish and other foodstuffs. The main reason why the Kallidromiou market is so special is its location: this street is one of the handsomest in Athens, lying at the foot of Strefi, its lovely interwar neo-classical buildings bathed in the Saturday sunshine and echoing the lively hubbub of the market - totally different from the somewhat morose greyness of the buildings in the rest of Exarcheia. Small wonder it is a favourite with the local intelligentsia, who mix with the crowd and then follow the example of all the self-respecting locals and withdraw to one of the little places along the street for coffee and the newspaper, shopping bags (bulging proudly with fruit and tomatoes) set neatly on the floor beside them. For the rest, it's like any other street market in Attica: the earlier you go, the greater the choice and the fresher the produce; if you leave it till later, the prices will drop. About one o'clock a restlessness sets in, the vendors begin to think of packing up: "I'm off now, down to Freattyda for a cappuccino and some fish", announces a greengrocer in front of the landmark Enoikos bar, dismantling his stall. The others, who still have stuff to sell, begin lowering their prices. By the time you've covered 150 metres, a euro will buy you five kilos of tomatoes: "Come on, madam, chip in and help bring inflation down", laughs a vendor watching the produce disappear from his stall. The classic wave of humour that ripples through all street markets spreads rapidly through this one - as often as not, for reasons we've never understood, concentrating on the section between Themistokleous and Zosimadon St., where the most dynamic vendors congregate. Yes, apart from a rock centre, the loveliest street in Exarcheia is also something else: a perfectly ordinary Athens neighbourhood.

ATHENS 2004

ΔΕΛΤΑ

GRAND
SPONSOR

Daily exercise is essential for
a strong body. So is the right nutrition.
DELTA Fresh Milk is rich
in proteins of high biological value,
which provide the necessary amino acids
that help build a strong and healthy body.

How much DELTA did you have today?

ΔΕΛΤΑ
φρέσκο
γάλα

We need it

MULTIRACIAL ATHENS

Below Athinas Street, a multinational metropolis is coming into being

Every street has its own ethnic character: Geraniou is Africa, Menandrou is the Indies, while further down in Deligiorgi you suddenly find yourself in the former Eastern Bloc.

Athens today has whole districts where Greek is seldom heard. Where the Greek community seems to be a minority. Where Greeks come to shop when they want a glimpse of an exotic world. However, these areas are some of the liveliest in the city. They are the set of streets below Athinas, the heart of the ancient Agora and its descendant, the modern trading district. In the open markets, stalls and immigrant-run shops, communication is easy, even without a common language.

And all you have to do to get a taste of this world is cross the road: turn your back on the unattractive somnolence of Kotzia Square, cross over to Kratinou Street (next to the City Hall), and step inside the very fancy (for the area's standards) Kleopatra supermarket.

But if you really want to find out what life in a multicultural city is all about, just take a stroll down Sofokleous Street. At numbers 27 and 30 you'll find yourself in a mini Chinatown, among shops sporting signs like Chinese City, Athens-China, etc. Silk robes set the tone, but the real show-stealers are the scads of kitsch wares: toys, lamps, telephones and endless clocks and watches. A few steps farther and you're in the Middle East. At number 47 is the cult kebab joint Raja Jee, next to a shop that proudly bears the inscription Iraq.

Opposite is the Neilos market, one of the most classic in the district, judging by the windowful of newspaper clippings (above a display of sweets that would send a diabetic into a coma just to look at). The farther you go, the deeper you penetrate into what could be the culture of the East today. At number 53 you pause to look at the novelties in the Islamia Store, before you let the stream of young immigrants carry you into the passage.

As you reach the Imtiaz Video, a real underground hangout, your ears are assaulted by a blast of Bollywood soundtracks; so you turn back the way you came - enough of venturing into a Hanif Kureshi story. Leaving, you stumble across another small Chinese clothing shop, next to which, hid-

den deep in a tiny passageway, is the Nargis restaurant: a place for experts and the Indian answer to Telis, who is still serving his classic mini chops on Evripidou Street.

Retrace your route at leisure, straying off into the side streets. In Sapphous you'll find a Pakistani hairdresser's (number 2) and an Indo-Pakistani barber shop (number 11). At number 6, opposite the supermarket, the Suleymana restaurant is neat and quite attractive, ready to welcome families with a taste for the exotic.

In the Chinese supermarket on Theatrou Square (number 24), you'll find dozens of different teas, and be tempted to buy a packet of noodles.

You'll come out onto Menandrou, the city's most multiethnic street, where Chinese clothiers (number 7) rub shoulders with Asian Hairdressers (number 6), while all around them words like Bangla Desh, India and Pakistan re-unite the territories of pre-partition India. The next shop is the Pak Suprem Market, at number 15, where - you can't resist it - you buy a bottle of Djemile henna "for long black shiny hair".

Move on into Geraniou, a small side street off Anaxagora. This is where most of the region's African shops are concentrated. Small grocers' establishments, packed with goods of all sorts: exotic fruit, cosmetics for dark skins, CDs and DVDs. "This is Nigerian music", says the shopkeeper, as you pick up a Fela Anikulapo-Kuti DVD with a suspiciously poorly photocopied cover picture. But for ten euros, who cares if it's pirated; and in any case, you don't find DVDs with an Afro beat even in record stores. To recap: every street has its own ethnic character - Geraniou is the Dark Continent, Menandrou is India, and just beyond, in Deligiorgi, you cross into the erstwhile Eastern Bloc, where emigrants from the former Soviet Union keep a variety of small shops and a plethora of furriers do their best to warm the heart of Athens, as it self-consciously tries to transform itself into a world city, a melting-pot of nations. As unbeknownst to itself it already has, as you will realise the next time you buy a Coke labelled in Arabic from the Kleopatra supermarket, now every bit as good as Carrefour.

Sofokleous is the city's most characteristically multiracial street.

ATHINAIS the new landmark in town

After a long standstill the old silk factory is bursting with new life, converted into a modern "multi-purpose" venue fostering creative human interaction.

GOURMET
RESTAURANT
RED

BRASSERIE
Botavikos

athinais cine

music hall

pierides museum   theatre athinais   cine athinais

BOILER BAR

Including conference halls wich extend over a total area of 1600 sq.m., the Pierides Museum of Ancient Cypriot Art, two restaurants, a bar, a cinema, a theater hall and a music hall, ATHINAIS is a contemporary landmark in the trend-setting part of Athens, offering a novel approach to creative endeavor and reflecting the changing face of Greece on the eve of the 2004 Athens Olympics.

ATHINAIS

34-36 Kastorias str. Votanikos - Gazi 104 47 Athens, Greece,
Tel: 010 34 80 000 (30 γραμμές), Fax: 010 34 80 007
www.athinais.com.gr

music hall   atrium   red   votanikos   boiler

places
with
history

The Battle of Marathon was one of the most important in the Greco-Persian Wars of antiquity. The news of the Greek victory was brought to Athens by Pheidippides, who ran the distance from the battlefield to the city at the cost of his own life: he died proclaiming "nenikekamen - we have carried the day". The Classic Marathon was established in honour of his memory, and in the name of peace and brotherhood of nations. The Classic Marathon is organised every year, following the traditional route from Marathon to the Panathinaikon Stadium in Athens, the site of the first modern Olympic Games. Since 1998, in addition to the Classic Marathon, which every year attracts hundreds of runners from all over the world, the event has also been marked by an open 10 km race starting at Aghia Paraskevi and finishing at the Panathinaikon Stadium. Alpha Bank is the sponsor of this important event from 2001 to 2004, in view of the ATHENS 2004 Olympic Games.

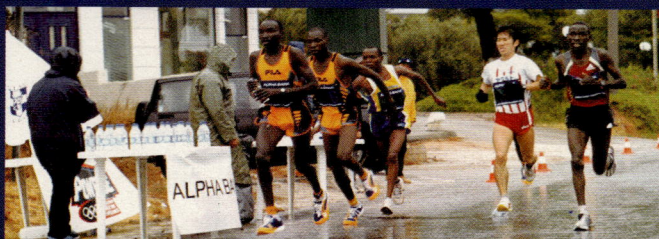

History & monuments

Athens Guide 2003

ATHENS 2004

ALPHA BANK
OFFICIAL
BANK

Athens
5000 years

Every place has its own history, individual and unique. But in the case of Athens we are speaking of a history that, at a certain moment, around the 5th century BC, transcended its narrow geographical boundaries and became a history of global, universal importance. But before Athens could arrive at the golden period of fifty years which it enjoyed in the 5th century BC, it had first to travel a great distance, starting in the Neolithic period, while centuries after its glorious heyday its history continued to be defined by its unique past.

The Acropolis at the beginning of the 20th century

FROM THE NEOLITHIC AGE TO MODERN TIMES

3500 BC - 3200 BC. As the **Neolithic period** was approaching its end, a group of people decided to settle in the heart of the Attic basin. There had, of course, been settlements here dating back three thousand years (on high ground by the coast, in the region of Nea Makri and, later, all down the line of the coast as far as Sounio) but this was the first time a community had decided to stake its survival not on the sea but on the rich plain of the interior. The spot they chose for their new home was a sturdy rock arising from the plain; they could never have imagined, when they sank their shallow wells and dug the pits in which they stored their meagre produce, that they were laying the foundations for the birth of a great civilisation. Not only was the rock they had chosen for their home never to be abandoned, it was gradually to become the heart of an immensely powerful state: it was the Acropolis of Athens.

1300-1230 BC. Time moves slowly onward and the settlements multiply, but without being affected by the earth-shaking changes, which are occurring elsewhere in the Greek world. But towards the end of the **Mycenean period** a leader inspired by the example of the Argolid kings decided to erect a huge palace at the summit of the Acropolis - it is no coincidence that on exactly the same spot, in classical times, the people of Athens would build the Erechtheum, where they worshipped the founders of their city. A generation later and it was decided - probably by the same dynasty - to fortify the rock with an impressive line of walls, known in the historical period as the Pelasgian or Pelargian walls (six centuries later these were the walls behind which the despot Peisistratus was to take shelter - the event which decided the Athenians, after the ousting of the Peisistratid dynasty, to demolish the walls and thereby prevent any future tyrant from finding a fortified position for himself within the city). It must have been at roughly the same time that the first synoecism took place - the administrative unification of the various scattered settlements, an act which tradition attributes to the mythical King Theseus. Theseus is the

supreme example of an Athenian myth: a hero of the Ionian peoples and King of the Athenians, protagonist of feats and adventures in many parts of the Greek world. He was born in Troezen and came as a young man to Athens, while his heroic feats are associated with mainland Greece and the Aegean islands, especially Crete. Scholars believe (whole gallons of ink have been expended on this question) that Theseus does not represent one individual: the mythical figure of Theseus, national hero of the Athenians, combines in one person the acts of many different individuals and ages - with whole centuries between them.

The Athenian kingdom was not destined to last long; at the end of the 12th century new tribes from the north overthrew the civilisation of the Myceneans, while great upheavals in the east impeded the movement of goods and dealt a fatal blow to Achaean trade. The 'dark ages' were beginning, but the Athenians were never to forget this first heyday - most of their myths are historically grounded in precisely this period.

Mid-8th century BC. Along the banks of the River Iridanos (which issued from the slopes of Lycabettus and ran through what is now the centre of Athens, passing through the areas of Syntagma Square and the Kerameikos Cemetery) the aristocratic clans of the

Ermou St. during the days of Othon, with the Acropolis in the background

History

Kerameikos

Stoa Attalus

Athenians buried their dead. Today we can still see a stretch of the Iridanos running through the Kerameikos Cemetery, among reeds and mosses, while another section of the riverbed was uncovered - and preserved - during construction work on the new subway, at Monastiraki. These graves supply us with a wealth of information about the lives of the Athenians at this time - especially the large ceramic vases which they set up to mark the site of the graves. In their severe proportions and geometrical decoration we see the very earliest beginnings of classical art. The artistic flowering which occurred at this time was linked with political developments; it was at this period that the **unification of Attica** was being completed. The foundations of the Athenian state were now in place.

6th century BC. The widespread use of currency now revolutionised the old exchange economy, allowing trade and manufacturing to enjoy their first period of prosperity, but at the same time the changes de-stabilised the old social status quo, creating massive upheavals in society as a whole. At the beginning of the 6th century the fields of Attica were dotted with marker stones known as oroi, stone columns which recorded the mortgage on the property. Borrowing was particularly expensive for the ranks of the small landowners, since the 'security' on their debts was none other than their own person. The members

of the lower social classes risked being reduced en masse into slavery. Moreover, the great aristocratic clans were being shaken by rivalries. In 594 the great **lawgiver Solon** was appointed as a mediator between the various social classes. He introduced a package of radical agricultural reforms, redistributing the land and abolishing in perpetuity and with retroactive effect the right of the creditor to enslave his debtor. This was the celebrated seisachtheia, or shaking off of debts, which released the small landholders from oppression. Solon then went on to introduce a new social order in which the classes would be divided for the first time on the basis of wealth instead of descent. A crucial step towards the emergence of democracy had been taken, since descent, noble or otherwise, ceased to play a role in the Athenian system of government. Yet the road forward would not be easy. After the death of Solon the old rivalries and tensions re-emerged and in 561 Peisistratus, member of a great aristocratic family, made himself tyrant of Athens.
He and his sons retained their hold on power for some fifty years. However, once the tyranny had ended, the Athenians would advance to even more radical reforms of their system of government.

500-479 BC. The vast empire of the Persians now began to turn its attention to the west. In two great campaigns it attempted to conquer

Solon

the city-states of the Greek world. Many of them were prepared to pay tribute to the Persian king, but Athens and Sparta placed themselves at the head of the alliance which fought for independence.
In 493 Themistocles was appointed archon in Athens; he was the politician who would play the decisive role in the impending conflict. He was convinced that the city had to build a powerful fleet, because it was only at sea that the Athenians could hope to prevail - on land the numerical superiority of the Persians was overwhelming. At **Marathon**, in 490 BC, the unexpected victory of the Athenians, fruit of the strategy of Miltiades, one of the Athenian generals, brought the first Persian campaign to an inglorious end. Ten years later, in 480 BC, the Persians launched their second campaign; **the battle of Salamina** proved a veritable catastrophe for the experienced navy of King Xerxes, and an impressive vindication of the newly-constructed Athenian fleet. The war ended one year later with the victory of the Greeks at the Battle of Plataea (479 BC).
The Persian wars had not just been a struggle for independence, but also a journey to self-knowledge. For the first time the Greeks had come to realise their shared traditions, their opposition to Persian absolutism. In the years, which followed, Sparta was compelled to turn back upon itself, owing to severe internal conflicts, but for Athens the moment of glory had come.

477 BC. To protect themselves from the menace of the Persian Empire a number of Ionian cities of Asia Minor, and Aeolian cities of the northern Aegean, had proceeded to form - under Athenian leadership - a naval alliance, to be known henceforth as the **Athenian or Delian Alliance** - Delian, because the dues paid by each member of the alliance were initially kept at the pan-Ionian shrine on the island of Delos. All

too soon however this alliance was transformed from a defensive grouping into an aggressive instrument for furthering the designs of the Athenians, who secured their own total domination of the Aegean, treating their former allies as tributary subjects. At the same time democracy was maturing at home, and reaching its apogee with the reforms of Pericles (the institution of a dole for the poorer citizens introduced for the first time the concept of a welfare state). The intellectual life of the city reflected in its vigour the general prosperity. In 472 Aeschylus presented the tragedy The Persians. The epic majesty of Aeschylus would be complemented by the more human-centred vision of Sophocles, the tragedian who expressed with the greatest lucidity the attitudes of his time, and who made his appearance as a dramatist four years later (468 BC). Philosophers, poets, historians, scientists - a whole host of men of letters and of the arts poured into Athens from every city in Greece, creating a unique cultural environment. It will suffice if we mention only those individuals who made up the immediate circle of Pericles: Herodotus of Halicarnassus, the father of historians, the philosopher Anaxagoras from Clazomenae, the town planner Hippodamus from Miletus, Sophocles and, of course, the sculptor Pheidias. Athens was now enjoying its intellectual golden age; the whole city had been transformed into a vast artistic studio, reaching perfection in the monuments of the Acropolis: these were constructed under the overall supervision of Pheidias, and were to become symbols of classical civilisation that would endure down the ages.

431-404 BC. The rivalry between Athens and Sparta had long been simmering beneath the surface. The expansionist designs of the former brought her into direct conflict with Corinth, a major trad-

ing power at that time and a loyal ally of the Spartans. In 431 BC Pericles pushed the situation to breaking point, and armed hostilities finally broke out. The conflict, known as the **Peloponnesian War**, was to last for some thirty years. Fighting took place not only all across mainland Greece (in one way or another every city in Greece was involved in the conflict) but also in Italy, Sicily, Asia Minor and Thrace, opening up opportunities for the Persian Empire and the Greek colonies of southern Italy to play their part in the hostilities. By the standards of the time, the war assumed the dimensions of a veritable global conflict! Athens was to be defeated; the discontent of her 'allies' and the hazardous campaigns initiated by her demagogues eventually made it possible for Sparta to overcome her old rival. However, the inherently introspective character of the militaristic Spartan state made it impossible for her to capitalise on her victory. The **4th** century proved to be, in general, a ruinous period for the Greek cities, which gradually declined as they battled through one conflict after another. The true victors of the Peloponnesian War were, in the end, … the Persians, who had now acquired the right to intervene in the internal affairs of the Greek cities. The political decline of Athens appears to have liberated the creative potential of its thinkers. It was during the war years that Euripides wrote his dark and melancholy tragedies, while

Aristophanes perfected the Attic comedy in his incisive works which use the robust and unembarrassed humour of the people to express important truths about human folly. The first years of the Peloponnesian War also saw the flourishing of the sophists, the first philosophical movement in the history of human thought to abandon the study of natural phenomena and concentrate instead on human nature. Yet the greatest achievement to rise, almost literally, from the ashes of the war was the chronicle of the war itself, composed by the Athenian historian Thucydides. If, a few decades earlier, Herodotus had fathered the science of history, it was Thucydides who set it firmly on its feet, endowing it with the status of a genuine science: objectivity, understanding not just of the pretexts but the underlying causes of events and, above all, a profoundly rational presentation of human actions, free of magical or divine explanations - these are just some of the innovations introduced to the study of mankind by the Athenian historian.

377 BC. Sparta's domination was short-lived and Athens was quick to seize the opportunity and establish the **Second Athenian Alliance**, one hundred years after the first. A comparison of the two alliances reveals the state to which Athens had been reduced by the 4th century BC. Not one third of the cities who had made up the original alliance were prepared to join the second, while explicit con-

Roman Forum

ditions restricted any aspirations to hegemony that Athens may have entertained. Moreover, new powers were now continually challenging the old Athenian status; Thebes, Thessaly and, finally, Macedonia, a northern state hitherto isolated from general developments, which was - under the rule of its monarch, Philip II - rapidly emerging as the new superpower. There were some, however, notably the Athenian orator Isocrates, who vested their hopes for a union of Greek states in the Macedonian ruler. But Athens was unwilling to surrender the sceptre of power; for the patriotic citizens of Athens the state of Macedonia, with its archaic institutions and absolutist system of government, appeared utterly alien to the traditions of the other Greek cities. In 349 BC the orator **Demosthenes** delivered his first speech against the Macedonian king - the first of his 'Philippics', those fervent and malicious diatribes against the Macedonians, which were to be passed down to posterity as models of rhetorical skill.

338 BC. Although Philip was pursuing a conciliatory policy towards the Greek cities, Athenian persistence succeeded in uniting some of the most important powers in mainland Greece against the Macedonians. Yet the **Battle of Chaironeia** was to demonstrate the absolute superiority of the latter. It was the battle, which decided the fate of Greece, toppling old powers and establishing new ones. The crushing defeat of Athens

meant, in essence, the end of her independence, at least in the realm of foreign policy. The funeral oration for those who had fallen in the battle, delivered by Demosthenes himself in 338, sounded the death toll for the lost grandeur of the city. Of those who fought at Chaironeia we shall do well to remember just one name: the young officer who broke through the ranks of the Boeotian phalanx and settled the Macedonian victory… none other than the son of King Philip, the future Alexander the Great.

307 BC. Alexander the Great died in far-off Babylon, in 323 BC, and his generals immediately proceeded to argue over how his vast empire should be carved up among them. Athens attempted to play a part in this struggle, but it soon became clear that it no longer enjoyed sufficient power to prevail in the new, geo-political game. In 307 BC Demetrius Poliorkitis, son of Antigonus (general and distinguished descendant of Alexander the Great) seized control of Athens from another Macedonian general, Cassandrus. Believing that they had recovered their freedom, the Athenians lavished unprecedented honours on their conquerors; Cassandrus and Demetrius were worshipped as saviour-gods, their gilded statues placed at the most conspicuous point in the Agora. Two new tribes were created in their honour: the Antigonis and the Demetrias. The old commitment to democracy and autonomy appeared to have been aban-

Kerameikos

Stoa Attalus

Columns of Olympian Zeus

doned for ever. Later, when the Romans appeared, Athens submitted relatively painlessly to their rule - in fact the city enjoyed a period of comparative economic prosperity, while also retaining its prestigious status as an intellectual centre. Athens now became a sort of **'international university'**; its schools of philosophy filled with individuals from all over the known world, anxious to share in the benefits of a Greek education.
Although new centres of intellectual activity emerged (Alexandreia, Rhodes, Pergamon, later Rome itself), Athens continued to occupy the first rank among them.
This was why the rulers of the Hellenistic period saw it as a duty to erect opulent buildings in the city - the two most characteristic examples being the Stoa of Attalus in the Ancient Agora, and the Stoa of Eumenes at the foot of the southern slope of the Acropolis.

86 BC. The philosopher Athenion, the leading figure in the political life of Athens at this time, took the fateful decision to side with the King of Pontus, Mithridates, against the Romans. When the Roman general Sulla arrived in the region to suppress the uprising, the city's glorious history did not deter him from permitting extensive looting by his troops - the monuments suffered the most serious damage ever inflicted on them, and the port of Piraeus was set ablaze.
This was the first time the city had been systematically despoiled of its sculptures, which were loaded on to ships to be taken to Rome. Moreover, the indemnities

demanded from the Athenian people by the Roman general - to pay for the continuation of the war - dealt a fatal blow to the already ailing economy of the city.

117 AD. The elevation to the imperial throne of **Hadrian**, an emperor with a profound respect for the classical heritage, created the necessary conditions for a final period of prosperity for Athens. No other city enjoyed such favour from the emperor; no other city was adorned with so many new buildings. These were the years, which saw the completion of the Olympeion, the Library, and the Aqueduct, which solved the old problem of the city's water supply. The city was extended to the south-east - the inscriptions on Hadrian's Gate indicate that the Athenians revered Hadrian as if he were one of the founders of the city, viewing him as a second Theseus. Athens now became the political and cultural nucleus of a new Hellenic world, one which was fully aware of its intellectual independence.

267 AD. Europe was now about to witness the Great Migrations of the People which would change the face of western Europe and mark the end of the ancient world. In 267 AD the Heruli, a Scandinavian tribe, irrupted over the borders of the Greek world and rapidly advanced on Athens. Despite the fortifications it had recently completed, the city was unable to repel the invaders. Athens was never to recover fully from its sacking by the Heruli - the city contracted, confining itself

MISS SIXTY®

Ta Romaiika, a French oil painting from 1843

within narrower boundaries, and was to remain thus confined throughout the whole Byzantine period.

529 AD. More even than the oppressive taxation imposed by the emperors, the collapse of the city's former political independence and the destruction inflicted by the barbarians, one single fact marked the final and permanent decline of Athens: in 529 AD the Byzantine emperor, **Justinian**, ordered the closure of the city's schools of philosophy - their teaching could not be reconciled with the theocratic ideology of the new empire. Athens may have been for a thousand years the most brilliant centre of education and culture in the known world, but the now triumphant Christian faith felt deep suspicion towards the ancient teachings. A few decades earlier the Parthenon, the Erechtheum and other monuments on the Acropolis had been converted into places of Christian worship: Athens was now a Byzantine city.

1182 AD. During the last quarter of the 12th century Athens suffered terrible damage from an incursion by the Saracens, who occupied the city and threatened the Acropolis itself. The wretched picture of the devastated city is painted in his letters by the Metropolitan and eminent scholar Michail Choniatis: the city walls crumbling or totally demolished, houses razed to the ground and turned into fields, people rendered desperate by the terrible famine which afflicted the city. These let-

ters helped to create the mistaken impression that Byzantine Athens was a miserable provincial market town. While the current condition of the city could not be compared with the glory of ancient times, things were not in fact quite as tragic as they have been painted. In the mid-12th century the Arab geographer Al-Idrisi described Athens as 'a populous city surrounded by gardens and well-tended fields'. A few years later, in 1166, the ecumenical patriarch Loukas Chrysovergis, did not hesitate to describe Athens as **'a prosperous and happy place'**. Nevertheless, it was during Choniatis' term as Metropolitan that a series of calamities occurred, the result of the massive turmoil caused by the arrival in the east of the western Crusaders. Finally, in 1204, the Metropolitan himself, seeing that it was useless to offer resistance to the heavily armed crusader knights, surrendered Athens to Boniface of Montferrat, one of the leaders of the 4th crusade.

Over the coming centuries the city would be ruled successively by the Franks, the Catalans, the Florentines, the Venetians and the Florentines again. In 1456 the latter decided to surrender the city without resistance to the Ottoman army of Mohammed II, the Conqueror. Incessant military operations and insecurity had devastated the region.

In the final years of Florentine rule a solution was found to the grave demographic problem of the city:

hardy semi-nomads from the northern parts of Epirus were brought to settle in Attica. These were the Arvanites, who brought their own colourful presence to the whole Attic region and managed to retain their traditions and linguistic idiom well into the 19th century.

First half of 14th century. But Attica did not appeal only to foreign troops. With the revival of interest in classical texts, **travellers** began to arrive in quest of the remains of the city's glorious past. One of the first of these, the important Arab warrior, historian and geographer Abulfeda, referred to Athens with great admiration, describing it as the cradle of Greek philosophy and the place where the knowledge and philosophical teachings of the ancient Greeks had been kept alive. At roughly the same time the German cleric Ludolf, from Sudheim in Westphalia, on a pilgrimage to the Holy Land (1336-1341) travelled through the Peloponnese and, although he never actually visited Athens, recorded the information he managed to gather concerning the city. At the end of the 14th century Athens was visited by the Italian notary from Capua, Niccolo da Martoni, whose account of his impressions is valuable evidence of the state of the mediaeval city. There is no end to the list of travellers - we shall just refer to one case by way of example: Niccolo Machiavelli, ancestor of the great Florentine political theorist, who wrote with unfeigned enthusiasm to his uncle, in 1423 'My dear uncle, you can never have seen a more beautiful place, nor a finer castle!'

1687 AD. One last attempt by the west to recover Attica had fateful consequences for the region's monuments. The Venetian general **Morozini** bombarded Athens with his artillery, inflicting terrible damage mainly on the Parthenon, which had hitherto survived in almost pristine condition.

1754 AD. Chatzali Chaseki was appointed governor of the city. He took advantage of the recent reforms in the administration of the Ottoman Empire, which favoured the delegation of authority to the regions, to levy punitive taxes, while also introducing a series of other arbitrary and highhanded measures. The reaction of the population was one more indication of the discontent seething beneath the surface and which, as the grievances accumulated, would eventually erupt in the War of Independence.

1822 AD. The uprising had already been raging for a year when, in June 1822, the Greek forces laid siege to the Turkish garrison on the Acropolis and, with relative ease, seized control of the city. Five years later the scenario was reversed: this time it was the Turkish troops of General Kioutachi who **besieged the Acropolis**, while the Greeks under Karaiskakis, a brigand chief, attempted to defend the citadel. In August the city itself surrendered, although the garrison on the Acropolis refused to lay down their arms. These hostilities had a decisive impact on the physical fabric of the city, most of its buildings being reduced to piles of rubble.

1833 AD. Following the successful conclusion of the struggle for independence, Athens was proclaimed the **capital of the new kingdom.** Within the territory of the new state there were larger and more important cities (Tripolis, Patra), while Nafplio had repeatedly been proposed as the capital during the course of the War of Independence, but eventually the glorious classical past and international prestige of Athens made the city the undisputed choice for the nation's new capital. Henceforth the fate of the state and the capital city would be inextricably linked. Any account of Athenian history would now necessarily be an account of the modern history of the country itself.

CLASSICAL ATHENS

THE MAKINGS OF THE MYTH

There can be no doubt that classical Athens was the cradle of European civilisation - this is a fact beyond dispute. But sometimes we forget that the achievements of the intellect and spirit were matched by remarkable advances in the standard of living. Here, then, we shall be describing some basic aspects of the life of the Athenians in the 5th century BC, and asking such questions as: What did politics mean for the ancient Athenians? What was the fundamental concern of classical art? Why is philosophy believed to be so integrally related to the life of the city? And some more down-to-earth questions: Which currency was the 'dollar' of antiquity? What was the role of women in the ancient democracy? Can it be possible that even in ancient times Athens had its traffic problems?

PROGRESS TOWARDS DEMOCRACY

Four major reforms in the course of some two hundred years - those of Solon, Cleisthenes, Ephialtes (no relation of the man who betrayed the Greek forces at Thermopylae) and Pericles - led to the appearance of democracy in Athens: a system of direct self-government, where power was in the hands of the people; a system which envisaged that almost every citizen would occupy public office at some point in his life. The system thus combined three radical features: the power of the people (democracy = rule of the Demos), direct involvement in decision-taking (rather than the taking of decisions by representatives) and the alternation of office-holders. The central authority was the Ecclesia of the Demos, the assembly of all citizens, but real power was exercised to a great extent by the Parliament, or Vouli, of five hundred Athenian

citizens (50 from each tribe), whose term of office lasted one year. In 458 BC Pericles introduced a special salary for the members of the Vouli, thereby also allowing the poorer citizens to take part in public life. Naturally, the great aristocratic families never lost their dominant position in political life, but this was still the first time in history that a system of government was established which made provision for the involvement of the lower classes. It has often been emphasised that the Athenian democracy excluded great masses of the population (women, for example), or was based on slave labour; we should not forget, however, the historical context (and let us remember, for example, that women only received the vote in European countries in the early or mid-20th century!). The fact remains that an enormous distance separated the Athenian system from the despotic and theocratic regimes of Mesopotamia or Egypt. What occurred in classical Athens was unprecedented in world history: the will of the despot or the select few was replaced by the opinion of the many, who deliberated and, through a majority vote, governed their own destiny. This is why the Athenian democracy has inspired so many men throughout history - sages, poets, revolutionaries, politicians, all the ardent lovers of freedom in modern times.

The Athenian democracy regarded prominent figures with great suspicion. They were particularly nervous at the prospect of someone wishing to exploit his popularity to endeavour to overturn their delicately balanced political system. The events of the tyranny of the previous century (6th century BC) were still fresh in men's minds. Therefore, in 508 BC, Cleisthenes introduced one of the harshest of Athenian institutions, the ostracism, i.e. the preventive exile of citizens who had acquired dangerously powerful influence in public

Pericles

Horsemen, from the frieze of the Parthenon

affairs. The citizens scratched the name of the man they wished to see exiled on a pottery shard or ostrakon - hence the name of the institution. The ostracism was used at one time or another by the Ecclesia of the Demos to expel almost all the major political figures of Athens, first among them no less a figure than Themistocles, the prime mover in the victory over the Persians.

THE HEYDAY OF PHILOSOPHY

For a thousand years Athens was the ecumenical university of the whole known world. It was here that the most important philosophical systems of antiquity were born: the sophists, the first philosophical movement to devote itself exclusively to human questions; the art of the Socratic dialogue, which encouraged the truth to emerge through a process of question and answer; the idealism of Plato; the empiricism of Aristotle and, in later times, the eudemonism of the Epicureans and the philosophy of the Stoics. Any man who wished to regard himself as cultured had to visit ancient Athens and enrol at one of its schools. This flourishing of the spirit of philosophical inquiry was inseparably linked to the world of classical Athens - the environment of freedom and prosperity, the freedom to question - an environment where men thought and decided for themselves. This was what created the necessary conditions for philosophy to thrive, conditions which did not exist in, for example, a despotic state. Even

The "Pensive Athena"

today the uncovering of those places where the great thinkers once taught is deeply affecting; when it was announced, a few years ago, that the foundations had been uncovered of a palaestra or gymnasium which was once part of the Lyceum of Aristotle, the news travelled to all corners of the earth. After ten centuries of activity the philosophical schools finally closed in 529 AD, by order of the Byzantine Emperor, Justinian - one of the less happy decisions of his reign. Among the last students of the schools, in the 4th century BC, were Gregory Nazianzene and the man later to be known as Basil the Great, two of the most important bishops in the Christian Church: building on the solid foundations established in the course of their studies, they grafted on to the new faith many of the achievements of the classical spirit, creating the hybrid that was to be known as Helleno-Christian civilisation.

THE FLOWERING OF CLASSICAL SCULPURE

If we examine the archaic sculptures in chronological sequence we can clearly see the striving of the Greek artists to achieve a naturalistic art, one which represents faithfully the lines and forms of the natural world. By the early 5th century this endeavour had begun to bear fruit and in Athens, one of the most important artistic centres of the ancient Greek world, the artists had begun to appear who would define the basic principles of the classical perception of beauty: Kalamis, Myron, and, a little later, Pheidias and his pupils, Agoracritus,

Alcamenes, to be followed in the next century by Praxiteles. Most of their creations have been lost in the passage of the centuries, but we have a general idea from the works which have survived, from later copies and from the descriptions of travellers. Classical art was naturalistic without being realistic - we must not expect to find the individualised depictions of the Roman portraits, where the painter renders the less attractive features of his subject or the ravages caused by time. For classical art, the primary concern was to render ideal beauty, supreme harmony. This is why there are no depictions of the aged, and even children are rarely represented. What we might regard as the 'manifesto' of classical art was the treatise by the sculptor Polycleitus, active a little later than Pheidias. In it he expounds the view that beauty is a matter of proportion; he lists the correct dimensions which each part of the statue should have - from the length of the finger to the width of the head - if perfect harmony is to be achieved. This essentially mathematical canon, which was known to later generations as the 'Canon of Polycleitus' was applied by the sculptor himself in his statue of the Spear Bearer (known to us only through copies).

THE ATHENIAN COINAGE: THE 'DOLLAR' OF ANTIQUITY

The silver Athenian four-drachma coin of the 5th century BC, known as the Glauka (owl) because on one side it bore a depiction of the

sacred bird of Athena, was the 'dollar' of its time, the hard currency in which most transactions between states were conducted. In earlier times, of course, other large commercial cities had succeeded in imposing the widespread use of their coinage (e.g. the chelones [turtles] of Aegina) but the wholesale acceptance of the Athenian coinage across the Greek world was without precedent. The 4th century imitations of the Glauka in Egypt and Palestine, even in distant Arabia, speak eloquently of the huge influence of the coinage.

THE ROLE OF WOMEN

The feminists are quite right to remind us that the Athenian democracy was an entirely male affair. In public life women had no more rights than the slaves. While it may be true that in 6th century Lesvos an educational institution was set up for the girls of aristocratic families, or that in 5th century Sparta the women exercised alongside the men, the fact is that in Athens the woman's realm was her home - and even there certain areas were set aside for exclusive male use, and special quarters allotted to the women. Country women, of course, led less confined lives, while in the city the Peloponnesian War, which kept the men far from home for long periods, allowed the women to take on a more public role. Nevertheless, the destiny of woman was clearly articulated in the

THE ANCIENT... TRAFFIC CONGESTION

It may be that the first town planner of antiquity, Hippodamus, lived in Athens, and in the refined atmosphere of that city designed the ideal system of town planning, with its rectangular blocks of buildings and its wide streets. But in fact the city of Athens could not have been farther removed from such an ideal condition. It was an old city, which had grown without any

specific plan, and if we except the monumental area of the Acropolis and the Ancient Agora the rest of the city, with its narrow, winding streets and densely built-up neighbourhoods, suffered from poor conditions of public health and congested streets where movement was slow. Sad but true - Athens has been plagued by traffic congestion since the 5th century BC!

Kilted guards in front of the Temple of Athena Nike, Acropolis, 1853-1854

celebrated saying of an orator of the 4th century BC: 'We have our courtesans for pleasure, our concubines for everyday care and attention, our wives to bear us children and to keep watch faithfully over our houses'. Of these three categories of women, it is the courtesans which have attracted the keenest interest among scholars. The poorest among them were prostitutes in the modern sense, but the most distinguished have acquired immortal renown for their refined intellects and eccentric behaviour. One of these was Aspasia, the companion of Pericles, who was present whenever he entertained friends, to the scandal of Athenian society. Another famous courtesan was Phryne, the companion and model of Praxiteles, whose art earned her great wealth in the 4th century - she commissioned a gold statue of herself to set in the sanctuary at Delphi, among the statues of great generals and kings.

ATHENS: CAPITAL OF MODERN GREECE

'This city is one of the most curious creations of the modern age, and in a certain sense has no parallel except in American experience'; this was the comment, on his first visit to Athens in 1884, of the great German scholar of Byzantium, Karl Krumbacher. The unusual parallel drawn by the learned German philhellenist underlines an important truth which often escapes us: Athens is in fact a very modern city. In 1833, when it was finally declared the capital of the

modern Greek state, the city embarked on a new beginning, erasing to a great extent whole centuries of its history - all the intervening periods, of no significance in the ideology of the time, which separated it from the glories of the classical age. The stereotyped view that Athens was a humble village at the time it was declared capital of Greece has lasted up until our own day, but will not stand up to careful scrutiny. In the mid-18th century Athens numbered some 10,000 inhabitants, and by the standards of the Ottoman Empire was a small but prosperous city, with wide-ranging administrative responsibilities for the surrounding area. But the perception of the foreigners who were now beginning to visit the future capital - and were probably influenced by comparison between the contemporary state of the city and its past glories - was completely different.
The time had come to re-fashion the city. For the visionaries who dreamed of a new Athens, the shabby reality was utterly without value: in the 'gloomy and muddy streets' they saw a tabula rasa, an open field in which they could build the ideal modern city, a neo-classical hymn to ancient glory. The way in which they set about their grand design, and even more so the reasons why they failed, are highly revealing of the desires and the abilities of the new Greek state. The non-implemented blueprint for a new city drawn up by Kleanthis and Schaubert can be seen as an allegory of the whole process of creation of the new

state. In November 1831 the architects Stamatis Kleanthis and Eduard Schaubert, students of perhaps the greatest German neoclassical architect, Karl Friedrich Schinkel, settled in Athens to begin work on their plan for the city. The new Athens would include about half of the old city, while at the same time extending outwards to the west, north and east. The other half of the old city, defined by Ifaistou, Pandrosou and Adrianou Streets, was to be expropriated for archaeological excavations. But even the part of the old city that was spared by the plan was to survive only as a geographical area, since for the most part it was to be divided by new streets and regular blocks of buildings. The main axes would form an isosceles triangle, with its apex at what is now Omonoia Square, Peiraios and Stadiou Streets as its sides and Ermou Street as its base. The whole plan was oriented towards three key points: Piraeus, the Stadium and, above all, the Acropolis - at whose feet the city would lie. The apex of the triangle was marked down as the site where the Palace would be erected - a piece of very obvious symbolism. The planners had identified the precise points for all the public buildings and, more generally, all the main functions of the city: ministries, courthouses, barracks, library, Stock Exchange, parks and so on. The whole scheme was designed to house all the functions of a capital city with a population calculated at 40,000 individuals. The plan reflected the spirit of neo-classical and romantic town planning: quantitative planning, rational use of space and constant historical references -

all the ideals of the 19th century New City. This was a rational City-as-Machine, smooth-functioning, under absolute control, perfectly planned - in a word: the City-Centre, capital of the state and epicentre of power. However, no sooner had the first lines of the plan been drawn on the terrain, and the owners of the old 'malodorous buildings' seen their properties transformed into public buildings, streets, parks and archaeological sites, than a storm of protest was unleashed, accompanied by accusations of profiteering. The outcry led the government of the day, the Bavarian regency, to defer implementation of the plan while it underwent a review. There ensued new attempts to reduce the area of the archaeological sites, introducing new and more 'realistic' modifications to the road network. In fact the process of adjusting the original vision to the demands of reality lasted throughout the 19th century, and eventually laid the foundations for the capital as we see it today. Finally, we should note another radical modification to the original plan: the relocation of the Palace, and consequently of the whole centre of gravity of the city, from Omonoia Square to the foot of Lykavittos pushed the expansion of the city in a north-easterly direction, whereas the original vision had been that Athens should open up towards the sea. Subsequently, therefore, the good neighbourhoods developed towards the north, while the western districts were given over to industrial and manufacturing uses and rapidly degenerated into the disadvantaged quarters of the city.

Panathenian Stadium, Olympic Games 1896

in the
footsteps
of History

Athens is the cradle of Western civilisation. From the end of the 4th millennium BC) up until the present day, the city has never ceased to be inhabited. Periods of glory and prosperity, days of splendour and hours of darkness alternate through the course of the centuries - with the city reaching its apogee in the celebrated golden age of Athenian democracy, the 5th century BC. The modern visitor to the city is privileged indeed: he can read the whole course of Athenian history inscribed, like a palimpsest, on the fabric of the city. There are innumerable fascinating walks to be enjoyed in Athens; But if you want to tread in the splendid footsteps of the history of this city, then come with us on four archaeological and historical circuits that you really should not miss.

FIRST WALK: ACROPOLIS & ENVIRONS

Where: From Dionysiou Areopagitou St. to the Acropolis. From there to Philopappou Hill and the Pnyx, and then via Apostolou Pavlou St. to the Thiseio and Gazi.

What: Without actually walking on the rock of the Acropolis, you can have no real sense of the history of Athens. All roads - the roads of civilisation, thought, the arts, the glory that was ancient Greece - lead to the Acropolis. From Goethe to Flaubert and Le Corbusier, all the great minds have celebrated this place: the sacred rock, the splendid symbol of the classical spirit across the ages. Climbing up to the Acropolis and exploring the surrounding area is something no visitor should miss.

Highlights: Parthenon, Erechtheum, Theatre of Dionysus, Pnyx, Herodeion Theatre.

Duration: 3 hours.

Acropolis: the Propylaia

WALKING ON DIONYSIOU AREOPAGITOU STREET

For decades archaeologists and planners had dreamed of bringing together the archaeological sites of the historic centre into one unified complex of linked sites - and this dream is now becoming reality.

A large open-air museum is being constructed, while the major archaeological sites (columns of Temple of Olympian Zeus, Acropolis, Philopappou Hill, Ancient Agora, Kerameikos) are being linked to form an area that is not bisected by noisy traffic arteries. At the same time the official departments of antiquities are giving the sites a radical facelift, intended to show off the monuments to their best advantage and make them more intelligible to the visitor. This ambitious project should be completed by 2004; already some of the pedestrianised areas - such as Dionysiou Areopagitou St. - are open to the public.

Arrange to meet opposite the columns of the Temple of Olympian Zeus, where Dionysiou Areopagitou St. begins. Make a short detour into the narrow Frynichou St. (about 100m up) where you will find the famous 'Lantern of Diogenes'; this was created by the great Kallikrates in honour of the citizen who had been a choregos, or sponsor. Sponsorship, too, was an invention of the Athenians: the cost of mounting major artistic events (theatrical performances, music and dance competitions) was borne by wealthy Athenians; when the performance or artist they had sponsored was successful in the competition the state awarded the sponsor a prize in the form of a bronze tripod. These were mounted on special choregic monuments, and the one designed by Kallikrates is the only one to have survived of the dozens, which once adorned the 'street of the tripods', the road leading to the Theatre of Dionysus. We now return to D. Areopagitou St. along Vyronos St. At the intersection of these two streets the statue of General Makrygiannis reminds us that it is the general who gave his name to the neighbourhood extending around the southern side of the feet of the Acropolis. Opposite us is the majestic stone Weiler Building (Weiler was the German architect who designed it), one of the first public buildings in the new capital (1834). It now houses the Centre for Acropolis Studies and boasts a rich collection of casts; unfortunately the collection is not open to the public at the moment, since repair work to the damage done by the 1999 earthquake is still not complete. Next to the Weiler Building is the subway station, seeming to emerge from the bowels of the earth; this is the best means of transport to use here, since the district suffers from a

Dionysiou Areopagitou St.: now a pedestrian precinct

Happenings in Dionysiou Areopagitou

shortage of parking places. But even if the subway doesn't appeal to you as a means of transport, it is still worth taking a look inside - all the different levels have been decorated with casts of statues from the Parthenon, while there is also a small exhibition of finds from excavations in the district. This is where we enter the most attractive section of the pedestrian route. To our right the Sacred Rock of the Acropolis looms above us in all its majesty. The precipitous slopes of the south-eastern face are crowned by steep and lofty walls; from immediately behind them there rise the columns of the Parthenon. The walkway continues to the edge of the archaeological site on the southern slope. The ancient ruins stand out from among the pines and arbutus; if you sit on one of the benches there will be the song of the blackbirds to keep you company - dozens of them nest in the vicinity. Take a good look at the fine old 19th and early 20th century houses on your left - particularly numbers 17 and 37, two extremely fine mansions from the inter-war period, now listed buildings. Stop for a rest at the specially designed open-air seating areas and watch the constant movement along the street. If you're lucky you might catch one of the artistic 'happenings', which are occasionally staged here. The characteristic sound of horse's hooves blends with voices and conversations - if

INFO

The Acropolis can be approached either from Dionysiou Areopagitou St. or through the Plaka district (Theorias St. leads to the entrance of the archaeological site), or, finally, from Petralona, ascending Apostolou Pavlou St. The main archaeological site is surrounded by a large copse of trees, open to the public, with beautiful stone-paved paths (designed by the great Greek architect Pikionis). Before you reach the shop there is a canteen with a wide range of food and drink - but at exorbitant prices. In the summer you will definitely need a bottle of water with you, it's a good idea to buy it from the kiosk on Dionysiou Areopagitou St., outside the entrance. There are water fountains within the site, but the water isn't always cold. At the point where they check your tickets you will almost always find guides offering to show you around - at a price. If you prefer not to use their services ask for the leaflet published by the Archaeological Resources Fund. It has a ground plan of the site and valuable information on the various monuments. It is available free of charge, but often the guards forget to give it to visitors. 210/3214172. Open: winter, daily 08.00-sunset, summer, daily 08.00-19.00. General admission: € 12.

you fancy taking a romantic ride in one of the carriages, you'll find them waiting a little farther on, near the Odeion of Herod Atticus.

THE ACROPOLIS AND ITS MONUMENTS

Continuing along Dionysiou Areopagitou St. we come to the point from which our ascent of the Acropolis begins. Prepare yourselves for an intense experience. It doesn't matter what time of year you visit the Acropolis, even in winter it is never quiet. Dozens of tourists from all over the world arrive every minute to pay homage to the cradle of classical civilisation. Life on the rock on which the Acropolis stands began towards the end of the Neolithic period (3500-3200 BC) and has continued since then without interruption. Innumerable myths connect the place with the first kings of the region - Erechtheus, Erichthonius, Pandion… And indeed, up until the 6th century BC this was the home of the city's rulers; after the collapse of the Peisistratid tyranny, however, the Athenians demolished the sturdy Mycenean walls, which surrounded the site in order to prevent any future despot from taking refuge behind them. Since then the hill has been dedicated exclusively to the gods, while its imposing public buildings have made it a symbol of classical civilisation and Athenian democracy. The principal deity of the Acropolis is Athena, the protector of the city. In our imaginations we can re-create that mythical moment, when the two gods, Athena and Poseidon, fought on this very rock for the guardianship of the city. The struggle was hard, but finally Athena - offering the people of the city the valuable gift of the olive tree - prevailed and was proclaimed protector of the city. But leaving the myth aside, the cult of the goddess is attested from as far back as the archaic period (650-480 BC) - her name is inscribed on the many rich gifts (marble korai,

bronze and terra cotta figurines and vases) which the faithful dedicated at her shrine. And what better evidence could there be of the power of the goddess than the three important temples built in the classical period (450-330 BC) on the foundations of earlier temples! All three, the Parthenon, the Erechtheum and the Temple of Nike (Victory), are dedicated to Athena - as Parthena or Virgin, as Poliada or Guardian of the City, and as Apteros (Wingless) Nike respectively.

The Propylaia

Entering the archaeological site we come first to the Propylaia, a central structure flanked by two wings which frame the culmination of the great marble stairway leading up the rock. The Propylaia was built between 437 and 432 BC to designs by the architect Mnesicles. Imagine the northern wing in ancient times, with the paintings, which gave it the name of Pinakotheke - the Picture Gallery. On an area of level ground before the southern wing there stands the small Temple of Apteros Nike or Athena Nike. Don't panic if you can't see it - for the time being it has been dismantled and is being reassembled by restorers - it should be back in its position by 2004. The temple was the work of Kallikrates, who was also one of the architects who built the Parthenon itself, and was built in around 420 BC. The relief frieze (which you can see in the Acropolis Museum) had a representation of an assembly of the gods on the eastern side and various battle scenes on the other sides.

The Parthenon

As we move forward everyone's eye is turned towards the Parthenon. The great temple of the goddess, built entirely of Pentelic marble, dominates the whole site. Today the great level space around the temple is empty, making the monument even more imposing, but in ancient times the picture

Caryatids, the famous korai of the Erechtheum

was very different. Imagine a scene crowded with different monuments: smaller temples and altars (of which the foundations have survived), a host of statues, relief columns and inscriptions with public decrees and regulations. Prominent among them was the great bronze figure of Athena by the sculptor Pheidias, dedicated to the goddess by the grateful Athenians following their victory at Marathon. This was a colossal statue - the great traveller of antiquity, Pausanias, recounts in awe that the visitor could see the head of the goddess' spear and her helmet from the harbour in Piraeus, even before disembarking from his ship. The decision to construct the Parthenon was taken by Pericles, himself the architect of the all-powerful Athenian democracy.

Athena

The man in charge of the whole project was the sculptor Pheidias, assisted by the architects Iktinos and Kallikrates. This supreme monument of ancient Greek civilisation, its symbol around the world, was built in 447-438 BC and decorated between 438 and 432 BC.

The temple, a tangible reflection of the classical spirit itself, impresses the eye with its simple and austere dignity. At first sight the design seems excessively simple. It consists of a large rectangular (in ground plan) structure surrounded by a line of columns (known as the ptero, hence the

term peripteros to describe temples of this kind). However, this apparently simple design was based on extremely subtle calculations, and these are the secret of its sublime harmony. The columns, for example, appear to rise in a straight line, endowing the temple with a heavenly majesty; but the archaeologists have identified a series of deliberate deviations from the rectilinear: at their base the columns are thicker and gradually grow more slender as they rise; they are also not absolutely perpendicular, but lean inwards towards one another (if we extended them indefinitely the columns would eventually converge, forming a pyramid shape). All these details of the construction, planned with geometrical precision, were intended to correct optical illusions, giving the building an imposing sense of geometry combined with a powerful feeling of the natural. The edifice is not built to human scale, the massive steps were not made for human feet to climb. In contrast to the Christian idea of the church as a meeting place for men, the ancient temple was exclusively the home of the gods. The acts of worship were celebrated in the open air; the interior of the sacred edifice was the home of the statue, the image of the deity. In the case of the Parthenon this was the celebrated gold and ivory Athena by Pheidias; the statue has not survived, but there are dozens of descriptions by travellers, which give us an idea of the impression the work aroused. The goddess was ten metres tall and was depicted fully armed, holding a winged figure of Nike. Forty talents of gold were used to cover the statue - more than a thousand kilos! Thucydides describes Pericles as explaining to the citizens of Athens that the gold used to cover the statue could, in case of need, easily be removed from the statue and later replaced. The Athenians have always been known for their practical intelligence …

In the sculptures, which adorned the Parthenon, the creations of Pheidias and his pupils, classical art reached its moment of perfection. The whole frieze - a broad, marble band around the upper part of the temple - depicts the procession known as the Panathenaia, the most splendid of all the ancient Athenian festivals, held every July. The reliefs demonstrate an extraordinary plastic genius in their depiction of horses, riders, young men leading animals to sacrifice, young girls of the aristocratic class - all the figures vivid and lifelike, yet retaining the solemnity appropriate to this sacred occasion. On the exterior, above the peristyle, there were slabs of stone, the metopes, which bore relief scenes of mythical wars involving Titans, Centaurs, Amazons and scenes from the Trojan War. Yet the very finest of all the sculptures were those which adorned the two pediments; at the eastern end was a work depicting the birth of the goddess, leaping fully armed from the head of Zeus, while at the other end the sculpture represented the mythical quarrel between Athena and Poseidon to determine who should be proclaimed guardian of the city. Today barely a single sculpture remains in place on the monument (although a few replicas have been mounted in place of the originals to give the visitor an idea of what the original decoration would have looked like). Some of the originals were destroyed over the course of the

centuries; others are kept for their own protection in the Acropolis Museum, while a large number were stolen by Lord Elgin (among them an important part of the Panathenaia procession and the two famous statues from the pediments which we described in the previous paragraph). The Greek demand that the marbles be returned is not only just but also consistent with contemporary thinking - namely that the individual work of art should be organically integrated into its natural context.

The Erechtheum

To the north, directly opposite the Parthenon, stands the Erechtheum, a temple built to a remarkable design in around 420 BC. Viewing it from the Parthenon we see first the southern side with its famous porch of the Caryatids, an architectural projection from the main structure, its roof supported by six marble korai. The building has two entrances of monumental design, one to the east and one to the north. Its asymmetrical ground plan is a striking contrast to the symmetry of the Parthenon. The site on which it stands is perhaps the most historic point on the Acropolis. It is here that the Mycenaean palace must have stood, the home of the prehistoric rulers of the city. Tradition has it that this was also the site where Cecrops, the first king of Attica, was buried, while on the western side were the two most sacred features of the Acropolis: the spring of salt water offered by Poseidon to earn the favour of the Athenians, and the olive tree which sprung from the ground where it was struck by the javelin of Athena - the olive tree which was known as pankyfos, bowed by the weight of the ages. The Athenians believed that this was the first olive tree the world had ever seen (today, to commemorate the tradition, a young tree has been planted on the spot). In the archaic period a temple of Athena was erected here, housing

The last weekend in September has been designated European Cultural Heritage Days, and the archaeological sites are open free of charge. There are also all sorts of events organised in conjunction with this institution, including guided tours, educational games for children, concerts, etc.

View of the Acropolis from the Areios Pagos (Hill of Mars)

Theatre of Dionysus

a wooden image of the goddess which, according to tradition, was not made by man but fell from heaven. When the question of reconstructing the building (which had been destroyed in the Persian Wars) was raised in 420, the architects had to make allowance for the ancient cults. Thus the main temple is divided into two parts, one dedicated to the worship of Athena and one dedicated to Poseidon Erechtheas (the local deity who incorporated the more ancient cult of some hero of the region, perhaps a king). It is likely that the relief frieze, which surrounded the building on the exterior, represented the birth of Erechtheas. The time has now come for us to visit the small Acropolis Museum, behind the Parthenon. Among the exhibits we will see the famous Moschophoros (a young man carrying a calf to sacrifice), the famous korai with the enigmatic smile of the archaic period, and sections of the frieze depicting the Panathenaia procession (see the more detailed entry in the section on Museums). Finally, the visitor should not fail to take a walk around the perimeter walls, with their panoramic views of the modern city below. The best viewpoint is the eastern end of the enclosure (where the Greek flag flies) with its vast view of Ymittos and (in the distance) the beginning of the Mesogaia plain.

Areios Pagos

As we emerge from the archaeological site we come to a small limestone hill with a long history - the Areios Pagos, the first and oldest of the courts of ancient Athens. It was here that the god Aris was believed to have been tried for the murder of the son of Poseidon - hence the name of the hill (Areios = of Aris, Pagos = rock). One of the many functions of the court, which met here, was to determine whether the new religions introduced to the city by foreigners were consistent with public morality. This is why it was here that the Apostle Paul set forth, in 52 AD, the basic principles of a new faith - Christianity. St. Paul was able to find the appropriate words to appeal to the sophisticated and cosmopolitan citizens of Athens. There was an altar here dedicated 'to the unknown god'. The apostle seized on this concept of the 'unknown god' as the key to winning over his audience in an inspired and philosophical address. An extract from his sermon is carved in a rock suspended at the beginning of the steps leading up to the top of the hill. Climb up to the top and allow the aura of myth and history to enfold you, as you enjoy the superb view across to the Ancient Agora. Be careful on your way down - the steps carved into the rock leading to the top have been worn down and made dangerously slippery by centuries of use.

SOUTHERN SLOPE OF THE ACROPOLIS

It's worth concluding your tour with a short walk to the southern slope of the Acropolis, that area where a large part of the artistic,

Herodion

intellectual and religious life of the ancient city was concentrated. In the archaeological site the trenches, piles of marble slabs and heavy lifting machinery give the place something of the look of a building site, reminding us that the work of unifying the various archaeological sites is proceeding apace. Leaving the ticket office and moving upwards we come to the most important building on the site: the Theatre of Dionysus, one of the oldest theatres in Attica, inextricably linked with the development of the ancient drama itself. Almost nothing has remained of the simple 5th century structure. The theatre whose remains we gaze on now was built under Lycourgos (mid-4th century BC). The orchestra has an opulent paving of coloured marble, and a number of the reliefs, which adorned the stage itself, have survived. The seats are of marble, those of the front rows showing more elaborate workmanship; we can still see the inscriptions, which determined for which of the archons each seat was reserved. It was here that all the great tragedies of Aeschylus, Sophocles and Euripides were staged, as well as the comedies of Aristophanes. The performances, which commenced early in the morning and often went on for up to ten hours, were attended by both men and women. They were a source of entertainment, but also of serious educational value, in that the works performed were not only important artistic creations, still admired today, but also achievements of rational thought, of the

Greek enlightenment - expressing all the great ideas of the classical spirit (from the celebrated notion of measure, or moderation in all things, to the ideas of hubris and nemesis). Farther up, where the rocks begin, we see the choregic monument of Thrasyllos (320/319 BC). This is a natural cave whose entrance has been deliberately modelled and decorated with large columns. In the same area other carvings in the rock indicate the presence of other choregic monuments, which have not survived. After the theatre we come to the Stoa of Eumenes (which owes its name to the King of Pergamon, who is believed to have built it), with its succession of arches constructed of porous stone, and just above it the remains of the sanctuary of Asclepius. Immediately after this (but outside the fence bordering the archaeological site) is the Odeion of Herod Atticus, more simply known as the Herodeion, which was built by the Roman patrician in memory of his wife Regilla, who died in 160 AD. The theatre is semi-circular in design, with an imposing facade of carved porous stone, 28 metres in height. The stage wall was adorned with rich architectural decoration, but this was destroyed - probably - in 267 AD during an incursion by a barbarian tribe, the Heruli, who sacked most of the city's monuments. A small door, just after the Stoa of Eumenes, leads from the Odeion to the rest of the archaeological site, but the visitor cannot be sure of finding it open, so it is best to go out on to Dionysiou

tip
Important: Your admission ticket to the Acropolis is valid for one week and entitles you to visit (more than once) the Acropolis and the southern slope, the Ancient and Roman Agora, Kerameikos and the Columns of Olympian Zeus. You can purchase your ticket at any of the above sites.

Café Dionysos

Pnyka

Areopagitou St. and enter the Herodeion by the main entrance. Every summer the Herodeion is the venue for events in the programme of the Athens Festival. Archaeological site of Southern Slope of Acropolis, 210/3224625. Open: winter, Tues.-Sun. 08.30-15.00, summer, daily 08.00-19.00. General admission € 12, ticket for archaeological site only € 2.

DESCENDING FROM THE ACROPOLIS

Once you have completed your tour of the monuments on the Acropolis, we recommend two possible routes down into the city. The first will take you along to the pine-clad Philopappou Hill, where you can enjoy a cappuccino at one of the nearby cafes and visit the Pnyx, rich in history. The alternative route will lead you to the Thiseio, the temple of Theseus, and the increasingly popular neighbourhood of Gazi.

Philopappou Hill, Loumpardiaris and Pnyx

As you descend from the Acropolis you will find right ahead of you on Dionysiou Areopagitou St. the all time classic Dionysos with its characteristic modern architecture (in the style of the Xenia hotels). From here you will enjoy a panoramic view of the Acropolis. If you're looking for something less high profile, take the pedestrianised road up Philopappou Hill, which begins just at the point where Dionysiou Areopagitou St. joins Apostolou Pavlou St. - also pedestrianised. Look for the little

Byzantine church, the Loumpardiaris, and next to it the tourist kiosk of the same name, which sets out its tables among the pine trees. It was built to designs by the architect Dimitris Pikionis, who also restored the church - note the masterly way in which the design incorporates contemporary building materials to achieve a superb result. When you've finished your coffee it's worth exploring both Philopappou and the adjacent hills, the Hill of the Muses and the Pnyx. An extensive network of stone-paved paths, also the work of Pikionis, leads to the main monuments in the area. Nowadays the area is densely planted with pine trees, but in antiquity it was the site of one of the city's busiest quarters. If you look carefully you will see the foundations of houses and other structures half concealed by the vegetation, such as two chambers carved in the rock and known in the popular imagination as the 'Prison of Socrates' (a sign indicates the path). At the top of Philopappou Hill you will see the funerary monument of Julius Antiochus Philopappus, dating from 114-116 AD, which gave the hill its name. Philopappus was a ruler of Commagene (in Cappadocia) who was exiled, settled in Athens and became an Athenian citizen, occupying both public and religious positions. The northern side of the monument, visible from the Acropolis, is the facade, which retains a number of elements of its originally lavish architectural decoration. Immediately after the

Philopappou Monument

Irakleidon St., Thiseio

Loumpardiaris Church turn right and you will find the path which leads you to a small hill - the Pnyx - of primary historical luster and much admired by visitors. This was the meeting place of the people, the Ecclesia of the demos - the core of the Athenian democracy, the "state of the demos", representing the supreme power of the people.

It was here that the principle of self-determination was realised in practice; it was here that freedom was exalted, that the great decisions were taken - from voting to erect the monuments of the Acropolis to launching the celebrated Sicilian campaign during the Peloponnesian War. You do not have to be a dedicated scholar of antiquity to feel your imagination stirred by the sight of the simple podium carved in the rock. This is where all the great politicians of ancient Athens made their speeches, from Miltiades and Themistocles to Pericles himself, as well as the many famous Attic orators. Apart from its historical interest, the site also offers an amazing view of the Acropolis.

From Apostolou Pavlou St. to the Thiseio and Gazi

A second walk after visiting the Acropolis, for the more … energetic visitor. We continue from Dionysiou Areopagitou St. on to Apostolou Pavlou St., which has also been pedestrianised. We take a gentle stroll down the street, observing the traces of ancient quarrying on our left, at the edge of the Pnyx, and gazing on our right at the Areios Pagos, the Ancient Agora and, of course, the Acropolis. Then we turn on to Irakleidon St., also free of traffic and full of restaurants and bars, with delightful little gift shops in between them. Towards the end of the street the pedestrian-only zone comes to an end and the tall apartment buildings give the neighbourhood a rather less attractive feel. Here you can visit the Melina Mercouri Athens Cultural Centre, housed in the old Poulopoulos hat factory. On the upper floor there is a beautifully arranged permanent exhibition titled Old Athens (a faithful reconstruction, life-size, of a 19th century commercial street in the capital).

You return to Apostolou Pavlou St. by Eptachalkou St., a small pedestrian street (parallel to Irakleidon St.), with picturesque low houses, which follows the train lines - at No. 7 you will find one of the best art galleries in Athens, Bernier/Eliades. If you feel like exploring a little further, carry on to Peiraios St., where you will find the most impressive of the city's old industrial complexes, the Gazi. It was built in 1857 and was the last factory in Europe to carry on working in the traditional way, finally closing in 1984. It has now been re-opened as a cultural venue by the City Council and is known as the Technopolis. If you go farther inside you will discover little houses, small cafes as well as smart restaurants and bars. The Gazi is now one of Athens' fastest developing neighbourhoods. Apart from the select eating places which have been opening over the last few years, plans for the district include the creation of a large 'urban park' with the emphasis on culture - the main feature being the creation of the new Athens Opera.

SECOND WALK: ANCIENT AGORA, ROMAN FORUM, KERAMEIKOS

Where: After visiting the Ancient Agora and its monuments, we move on to Monastiraki. On our way to the Roman Agora, we pause for coffee and a look at the side streets off Adrianou (Kladou, Markou Avriliou, Thrasylou), eventually coming out at Pelopida St. near the entrance to the Roman Agora. From here, we head for Kerameikos via Aiolou and Ermou.

What: The Ancient Agora was the vital heart of Classical Athens. A noisy, bustling crowd daily filled this focal space, the hub of all commercial, political, religious and artistic activity. The Roman Agora, a continuation of the ancient site, expresses the age of the Roman imperium, while Kerameikos, the most famous of ancient graveyards, was the burial place of many of Athens' celebrated orators, philosophers and politicians.

Highlights: Thiseio, Odeion of Agrippa the Roman, Stoa of Attalus, Ancient Agora Museum, Tower of the Winds, Stoas of the Philosophers.

Duration: 3 hours.

ANCIENT AGORA

We enter the Ancient Agora by the central entrance on Adrianou St. Dozens of buildings were erected here during its thousand years of uninterrupted use. A large ground plan strategically placed just beyond the ticket booth explains the lay-out of the site and helps the visitor find his way around the many ruins. Our attention is captured first by a building which has survived intact - the structure known as the Thiseio. Although it takes its name from the representations of Theseus with which it is adorned, it was in fact the Temple of Hephaestus, and is one of the best-preserved of classical temples. Construction of the temple began in 449 BC - two years before work began on the Parthenon. Its architect employed the Doric order and the central structure is surrounded by a peristyle of columns. From the entrance to the temple, which looks down on the Agora from the hill known as the Agoraios Kolonos, you can survey the ruins of the buildings built lower down. To your right you will find it easy to identify the Tholos (460 BC), with its characteristic circular shape. This is where the members of the tribe presiding over the Vouli (those members responsible for preparing proposals to be put to the Ecclesia of the demos) were based, slept and took their meals; it was also where standard weights and measures were kept, necessary for ensuring the integrity of commercial transactions. Next to the

Temple of Hephaestus

Ancient Agora

Cafés beside the Roman Forum

Roman Forum

Tholos are the remains of the Vouleuterion, where the Vouli held its meetings, and of the Metroon, the Temple of the Mother of the Gods, where state archives, the minutes of the Vouli and other documents were kept. In modern Greek the word Metroon is still used to mean a register or official list. To your left you can see the remains of the Basileion Stoa, where the laws of Solon were displayed (most important among them the famous seisachtheia - the decree which cancelled the debts of the oppressed people of Athens) and next to this the Stoa of Eleftherios Zeus, frequented by the philosopher Socrates. Another important building, a little farther on, is the Odeion of Agrippa the Roman - the four colossal statues (tritons and giants) which adorned its facade have survived in excellent condition. On the other side of the archaeological site stands the restored Stoa of Attalus, which now houses the Museum of the Ancient Agora. The humble dirt track which passes in front of it follows the line of the Panathenaia Way, one of the main thoroughfares of the ancient city, rich in religious significance - we must try to imagine the solemn procession which passed along it each July as the people ascended to the Parthenon to dedicate to Athena the new veil which the maidens of the city had woven for the goddess. The procession was led by girls from the prominent families of the city, followed by horsemen and important office-holders (generals, priests and seers); the veil itself was suspended from a pole rolled forward on wheels and the rear of the procession was brought up by an endless line of oxen which would later be sacrificed.

But the site is not only important from an archaeological perspective - it is also of significant ecological interest. There is a fine booklet produced by the WWF-Greece which will provide you with a guide not to the monuments but to the flora of the Agora: arbutus, olive trees, planes and dozens of other species form a unique grove, attracting dozens of birds - the American School of Classical Studies, which is carrying out excavations here, has planted the same types of tree which grew here in ancient times in an attempt to

AN ANCIENT RELIC... FOR YOUR LIVING ROOM?

Close to the Ancient Agora, on Pandrosou St. (one of the busiest tourist streets in the Plaka district) you will find two of the oldest antique shops in the city (Martha Kapsoulaki, at 36, Pandrosou St., and the famous Martinos, at No. 50). They are among the very few dealers in Greece with a licence to trade in antiquities. This means that they can legally sell objects dating from ancient times. Can you think of a finer souvenir than a small vase from the geometrical period, or a Hellenistic oil lamp?

PLAKA HOTEL
ATHENS

HOTEL
HERMES

AH
HOTEL
ACHILLEAS
ATHENS

7, Kapnikareas St. & Mitropoleos
Tel.: 210/3222096-8
Fax: 210/3222412

19, Apollonos St.
Tel.: 210/3235514
Fax: 210/3232073

21, Lekka St., Syntagma
Tel.: 210/3233197
Fax: 210/3222412

Reservations:
Tel.: 210/3222706
Fax: 210/3222412

Kerameikos

recreate the natural setting of antiquity. If you walk past the Agora in the evening you may well hear the voice of the owl, the bird sacred to Athens, which still builds its nest in the dense thickets.
Ancient Agora Archaeological Site, 210/3210185. Open: winter, daily Tues.-Sun., 08.30-15.00, summer, daily, 08.00-19.00. General admission: € 4.

FROM THE ANCIENT AGORA TO ROMAN FORUM

We come out of the Ancient Agora on to Adrianou St., which runs along the whole northern side of the Agora. Along Adrianou St., beside the wire fence surrounding the archaeological site, the cafes put out their tables - conspicuous among them the pop-art plastic chairs of the Kouti restaurant. On the other side of the street you'll find shops selling tourist wares as well as antique shops. You must stop at Pericles (No. 29) to admire the huge collection of beads, while No. 7 (which has no name sign) is one of the largest shops selling old photographs, retro post cards and prints. On weekends, and sometimes during the week, the street fills up with traders selling collector's telephone cards, old coins and notes and a miscellany of second-hand items. Don't be afraid to haggle over prices - it's expected. As we make our way towards the Tower of the Winds and the Roman Forum we make a detour up Kladou St., a narrow passage parallel to Adrianou St., to have a look at the rather seedy second-

hand shops with their endless piles of 1950s magazines. As we approach the entrance to the Roman Forum we admire the simple neoclassical buildings, rather like a theatre set. It's not a bad idea to stop for coffee or a light meal here after our archaeological visit - although the menus are rather tourist-oriented. Along Epameinonda and Panos Streets the waiters are out on the pavement hustling for customers, and a little farther on there is the Mistral cafe, with its tables outside in the shade of the Fetichie Mosque. Finally, on Markou Avriliou St. there is the Aerides taverna, justly boasting that it provides the best view of the Tower of the Winds. But if you're not that interested in getting a close-up view of the monuments and prefer somewhere quieter, then there is the Klepsydra cafe at No. 9 Thrasyvoulou St., with excellent home-made cheesecake.

TOWER OF THE WINDS AND ROMAN FORUM

After that short detour back to the modern world we find ourselves at the entrance of the Roman Forum archaeological site, on Pelopida St. The first sight awaiting us is the famous Tower of the Winds, so named because at the top of each face is a carved relief with a personified representation of one of the winds. It is an octagonal tower built of Pentelic marble with a conical roof, the work of the astronomer Andronicus of Kyrrhos in Macedonia (1st half of 1st century BC), which has survived in excellent condition. There used to be sundials on the exteri-

or, while the interior housed a hydraulic clock. On our right, just beyond the ticket booth, we can see the floor of a much smaller edifice, the only surviving part of what used to be the public conveniences! We enter the Roman Forum itself by the eastern gateway, with its four Ionic columns of grey Ymittos marble. By the 1st century BC the Ancient Agora had become so densely packed with public buildings that there was barely any space left for commercial activities. So, with donations from Julius Caesar and Augustus (the city was now part of the Roman empire) a new forum was built between 19-11 BC, that which we now call the Roman Forum. It was laid out next to the Ancient Agora and was designed exclusively for commercial activity. Before us extends the great marble-paved courtyard, while on the other side - in excellent condition - stands the western gateway, a monumental entrance with four Doric columns and a pediment of Pentelic marble. Finally, on our right we can see the Fetichie Mosque or Mosque of the Conqueror, which was built in 1456 AD over the remains of an early Christian basilica. In its grounds archaeologists have set up dozens of marble architectural fragments uncovered in their excavations - parts of temples, ancient altars, early Christian reliefs, as well as funerary steles from the Ottoman period, incontrovertible evidence that the site has enjoyed a central place in the life of the city for two thousand years.
Roman Agora Archaeological Site, 210/3245220. Open: Tues.-Sun. 08.30-15.00. General admission: € 2.

KERAMEIKOS CEMETERY

We leave the Roman Forum and proceed up Aiolou St. to Ermou St. A short walk straight ahead, past Agion Asomaton Square, and we come to the entrance of the Kerameikos Cemetery. This is not merely one of the largest ancient cemeteries in Athens, but also the most important. The section reserved for public figures, the "Dimosio Sima", contained the tombs of Solon, Cleisthenes and Pericles, as well as famous orators (Lycourgos), philosophers (Zeno), generals (Phormion) and also a large number of common graves containing the remains of men who had fallen in battle. Unfortunately almost no trace remains of this part of the cemetery. A large part of the Kerameikos was occupied by the graves of private individuals, the wealthier among them conspicuous by their lavish funerary monuments, true masterpieces of Attic art. The cemetery began at the Dipylon (one of the most important gateways in the city walls built at the instigation of Themistocles) and extended - at least from classical times onwards - beyond those city walls. We enter the archaeological site from Ermou St., which is significantly higher than the level of the cemetery itself, enabling us to enjoy an excellent view and take in the overall picture before actually making our way in. Right in front of us is one of the most characteristic pathways through the cemetery, with opulent private tombs (the relief stele of Dexileos, the stele of Hegesos, the enclosure of Dionysius of Kollytos with its great marble bull, etc.). The funerary monuments, which emerge so romantically from the undergrowth, are mainly replicas; the originals have been removed to museums. On our right we see three small hills - these are the great tomb mounds of the archaic period. In the distance we can make out the remains of the walls and the Dipylon, as well as the foundations of a large edifice, the Pompeion, where preparations were made for the great Panathenaia procession. The most unexpected 'find' of all, however, is the River Iridanos, which flows through the site cutting it in two; at this location it still flows along the same course as in ancient

Aigli, in the Zappeion Park

Temple of Olympian Zeus

times and has not been covered over - it creates a small wetland in the heart of the modern city. The best time of year to come to the cemetery is definitely the spring, when the gladioli are in flower along the river bed and the dozens of tortoises, almost the official mascots of the site, make their lazy way through the grassy clearings. Kerameikos Archaeological Site, 210/3463552. Open: winter, Tues.-Sun. 08.30-15.00, summer, daily, 08.00-19.00. General admission: € 2.

THIRD WALK:
NATIONAL GARDEN, ZAPPEION, COLUMNS OF OLYMPIAN ZEUS

Where: Starting from the Presidential Palace, we cross the National Garden and Zappeion to reach the Columns of Olympian Zeus and Hadrian's Arch - the boundary between the old and the new city in the days of the Romans.

What: An oasis of green in the heart of the city. Centuries-old trees and unique classical buildings form a bridge between the modern age and ancient Greece (Temple of Olympian Zeus, Hadrian's Arch).

Highlights: The dignified elegance of Irodou Attikou St., the rare and ancient trees in the National Garden, the classical charm of the Zappeion, Hadrian's Gate.

Duration: I hour 30 minutes.

THE MODERN HISTORICAL CENTRE

We begin our walk on Irodou Attikou St., one of the most aristo-cratic streets in Athens. This is the site of the Presidential Palace (which is housed in what was once the palace of the heir to the throne, designed by the architect Ziller), the Maximus Palace (now the official residence of the Prime Minister) and various apartment buildings traditionally the homes of some of the most eminent families in the Attica region (the city's social elite of old-established families) - all looking out directly over the National Gardens.

The gardens - originally known as the Royal Gardens - were designed by Queen Amalia herself, the first queen of Greece, in 1839. The idea was that they would form the gardens of what was then the palace and is now the Parliament building. No fewer than 500 species of plant were ordered, from all the corners of the earth - not the most prudent of schemes, since the dry climate of Athens often proves lethal to plants, which are unaccustomed to it. Nevertheless, the venture was a success and the modern visitor finds himself confronted by a veritable jungle, with lofty, perennial trees rising from dense bushes and climbing plants. You can learn more about the plants at the small Botanical Museum, housed in a neo-classical building constructed in the reign of Otto, within the gardens (210/7215019, open daily,

ALPHA GUIDE 2000
GREECE
THE BEST RESTAURANTS & HOTELS

An annual guide that assesses and evaluates the 1.100 best restaurants, tavernas, large hotel units, small hotels and traditional guesthouses in Athens, the Greek mainland and the islands.

DESMI PUBLICATIONS S.A.
athinorama

ALPHA GUIDE 2001
GREECE
THE BEST RESTAURANTS & HOTELS

700 NEW ENTRIES IN THE 2001 EDITION

It evaluates and ranks the top 1800 restaurants, tavernas and large or small hotels in Greece. The also lively indispensable guide for holidays, weekends and dinner outing.

by the publishers of athinorama

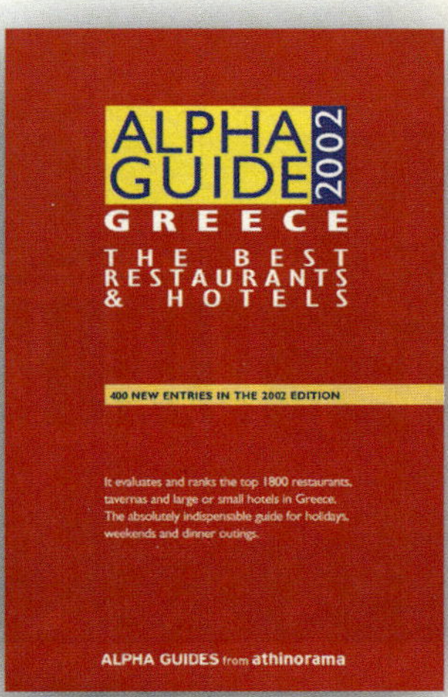

ALPHA GUIDE 2002
GREECE
THE BEST RESTAURANTS & HOTELS

400 NEW ENTRIES IN THE 2002 EDITION

It evaluates and ranks the top 1800 restaurants, tavernas and large or small hotels in Greece. The absolutely indispensable guide for holidays, weekends and dinner outings.

ALPHA GUIDES from athinorama

ALPHA GUIDE 2003
GREECE
THE BEST RESTAURANTS & HOTELS

500 NEW ENTRIES IN THE 2003 EDITION

It evaluates and ranks the top 2500 restaurants, tavernas and large or small hotels in Greece. The absolutely indispensable guide for holidays, weekends and dinner outings.

by athinorama

THE ESSENTIAL GUIDE
FOR YOUR TRIP OR OUTING
FOR THE LAST FOUR YEARS

The Zappeion Palace

The little café in the National Garden

except Monday, 9.00-14.00). Close to the Museum you will find the foundations of a Roman villa, as well as a number of buildings from the reign of Otto, such as the structure, which has now been remodelled to create a charming contemporary Children's Library. Finally you should stop to enjoy a coffee and admire the beauty of the natural setting at the tranquil cafe you will see as soon as you enter the second (coming up from the Zappeion Park) entrance on Irodou Attikou St.

Από τα καταπράσινα ενδότερα
Follow the wooden signs from the lush verdure of the National Gardens and you will come out in the Zappeion Park, on the broad walk which follows the rear side of the Zappeion Palace. If you head downwards you will find yourself in front of the Kallimarmaro, the stadium which hosted the first Olympic Games of the modern era in 1896. It was erected on the remains of an ancient stadium and all its walls are faced with marble. Next to the stadium, on the stone-paved area, you will find an open-air cafe, which does not close till late at night. The Zappeion Park, with its well-tended walks, academic sculptures and imposing flights of steps, is one of the most impressive examples of the neo-classical spirit to be seen in the capital's public open spaces. At the centre stands the Palace of the same name, now a popular venue for exhibitions - it's definitely worth

going through the imposing gateway to admire the superb, circular atrium with its marble colonnades. After that, naturally, you will take a seat at the Aigli Cafe, just next door, which has been a classic meeting place for Athenians for many decades. A light salmon sandwich is just what you need to recharge your batteries.
The natural terminus for your walk will be the archaeological site of the Temple of Olympian Zeus (the entrance, with the ticket booth, is just opposite the Zappeion Palace, on Vasilissis Olgas Ave.). The temple was believed to have been founded originally by the mythical Deucalion. Around 515 BC construction on a temple on this site was begun by Peisistratus the Younger - a monumental edifice which, owing to the overturning of the tyranny, was never completed. Finally the building was completed centuries later by the Roman Emperor Hadrian, in 124/125 AD. The temple, with its lofty columns (a total of 104) in successive colonnades, is just as imposing as when it was new, even though only a small section is still standing. At the north-eastern edge of the site you can see the foundations of Roman houses, as well as those of a Roman baths.
Finally, outside the enclosure, on Amalias Avenue, you will come to Hadrian's Arch, one of the city's most immediately recognisable monuments. This triumphal arch

The National Library

The University

was erected by the Athenians in 131 AD on an ancient road which led from the old city to Hadrian's new Roman city; it was intended to honour the emperor who had brought so many benefits to the city. The architrave bears two inscriptions: the first, on the side facing the Acropolis, 'Here is Athens, the ancient city of Theseus', and the second, facing the other way, 'This is the city of Hadrian, not of Theseus'.

FOURTH WALK: NEO-CLASSICAL ATHENS

Where: Starting from the Parliament Building, we walk down Panepistimiou St., admiring the gems of neo-classical architecture, through the Stoa tou Vivliou to that temple of modern life, the Athens Stock Exchange, and finally to the little Byzantine church of Agioi Theodoroi behind Klafthmonos Square.

What: The history of the city bears the stamp of the classical age. So much so that, centuries later, when Athens became the capital of the newly-established modern state, the architects who built it, Greeks and philhellenes, had recourse to the splendour of the classical period for the monumental public buildings they were designing. Their emblematic neo-classical structures constitute a living link between past and present.

Highlights: Parliament building, Iliou Melathron, Catholic Cathedral, Academy, University, National Library, Arsakeio, Byzantine church of Agioi Theodoroi.

Duration: 1 hour.

FROM SYNTAGMA TO KLAFTHMONOS SQUARE

The starting point for the walk is in front of the Greek Parliament building. This is one of the most central locations in Athens: ministerial Mercedes with tinted glass windows cruise in and out of the building, policemen keep a careful eye on those passing by. But it is possible for visitors to enter the building, or, to be precise, to visit one small part of it: the imposing Eleftherios Venizelos room, which has been laid out as an exhibition venue. If an exhibition is currently being staged you can get in just by producing your ID card and then take the opportunity to sneak a look - into the assembly chamber, for example - as you walk through. Also, if you are looking for rare editions or old issues of the Government Gazette you can visit the library, which is also open to the public. Leaving the Parliament building behind you, make your way up Panepistimiou St. - or rather, Eleftheriou Venizelou St. Most Athenians still know this central thoroughfare by its old name, but officially it now bears the name of the famous politician. This duplication of names always confuses tourists using a map to find their way around the city (and has elicit-

The Old Parliament Building

The Parliament Building

ed caustic comments from many travel guides). Almost every building on this street has its own history, but there are some which are milestones in the architectural development of the city. For example, the Iliou Melathron, the private residence of the great archaeologist Heinrich Schliemann, designed by Ziller. Fortunately the building is now home to the Numismatic Museum, and so it is easy to visit, even if only to admire the wall paintings, inspired by subjects from Pompeii. A little farther on, just past Omirou St. and still on the right hand side we come to the great marble Catholic Cathedral, which was given its final form (a combination of Renaissance and early Christian features) by the Greek architect Lysandros Kaftantzoglou. Note the skill employed in the stained glass windows, all made in workshops in Munich. The most appropriate time for a devout visit is 11am on Sundays, when the second service is celebrated in Latin. On the same block, just beyond the Cathedral, we find a rare example of romantic architecture, the Ophthalmic Clinic, designed by the architect Hans Christian Hansen. With its handsome, stone facade, relieved by ceramic decorative features, and its arched openings, the building represented a unique attempt to create a 'new Byzantine' style - an attempt which failed, however, to find any imitators. On the oppo-site side of the street (17, Panepistimiou) you will be immediately struck by a modern, multi-storey building of marble and glass. This is the home of the city's biggest bookshop, Eleftheroudakis. It has a whole floor dedicated to an excellent collection of travel books, as well as a finely organised foreign language section - but we recommend it as a stop on this walk for its cafe (on the top floor), where you can enjoy an excellent view down Panepistimiou St. - as long as the blinds have not been lowered. Opening up before us now is the impressive vista often referred to as the 'Neo-classical Trilogy' - the Academy, University and Library - the most ambitious 19th century attempt to provide the capital with monumental new buildings. The first of the three is the Academy, which was erected in two phases (between 1859-1863 and 1868-1885) to plans drawn up by the Danish architect Theophil von Hansen. It is regarded as the best of the buildings he designed in Greece. Next comes the University, a severe, symmetrical building, constructed between 1839-1864 to plans by Christian Hansen. Note the wall-paintings on the facade (the work of the Bavarian Rahl and the Pole Lebietski), which depict the revival of the sciences in Greece - typical expressions of 19th century ideology. Finally we come to the Library, with the impressive, ellipsoid, double stair-

Aegli Bistrôt Café

Aegli's Bistro-Café, located in the center of Athens, within the Zappion Gardens, is the ideal choice for your next outing. From early in the morning till late at night, year round, you can enjoy its elegant and friendly surroundings: for your morning coffee, for your mid-day meal or for a dinner under the light of the stars and the illuminated Acropolis.

During summer, restaurant service is out-of-doors. The menu is based on traditional and international dishes, with low calorie and organic ingredients. Dishes of the Day are created depending on the availability of fresh seasonal products, while the extensive wine list offers choices for all tastes from all over the world.

Aegli's Bistro-Café easy access and valet parking are only a few of the factors that will combine to make your visit unforgettable.

ΑΙΓΛΗ

Address: Zappion Gardens
Reservations: 210/3369363, 210/3369364
Valet Parking, Entrance: Vas. Olga's Ave.

way at its entrance, designed by Ernest Ziller (completed in the early 20th century). Despite certain - by no means negligible - shortcomings and excessive rigidity in its operations, it is still the country's most important library, and open to the general public. You should certainly take a quick look inside, even if only to see the reading room with its heavy wood panelling. Directly opposite the imposing 'Trilogy' stands a simple neo-classical building, known as the Yellow House, which reveals a completely different aspect of the architecture of the period. This is the residence of the Soutsos-Rallis family, one of the oldest buildings on Panepistimiou St. (completed in 1842 or 1843) and a characteristic example of bourgeois architecture. Two blocks farther on we come to the Arsakeio complex, the first important project undertaken by Lysandros Kaftantzoglou. From the entrance on Pesmazoglou St. you come straight into one of the finest commercial arcades in the city, devoted to the printed word. All the main publishing houses of Greece have an outlet here, while there is a specially designed underground gallery for exhibitions of books, presentations and other related events. The arcade also has two cafes, one on the ground floor and one on the spacious terrace - the latter also serves food and remains open until late, becoming noisier as the evening wears on.

Leaving Panepistimiou St. for the last time we make our way down Pesmazoglou St., cross Stadiou St. and come to Sofokleous St. Before us stands another imposing neo-classical building, one which has exerted an irresistible fascination for thousands of Greeks in recent years, not because of its architecture - but because it houses the Athens Stock Exchange. On weekdays you will find the entrance crowded with groups of investors excitedly discussing the latest developments. If you take Aristeidou St., which makes an oblique detour around Pesmazoglou St., you come to a small piazza surrounded by fast food outlets (stockbrokers need to eat, just like ordinary mortals). In the centre of the piazza stands a small Byzantine church, set noticeably below the level of the street. This is the Church of Agioi Theodoroi, which dates from the 11th century, as we learn from the plaque set in the wall above the entrance on the western wall. The walls were built using the typical cloisonne system of the Byzantine period - the system which the Ophthalmic Clinic, mentioned earlier, attempted to imitate - on an entirely different scale. This low church, with its elegant dome, is one of the few remains of that time when Athens was no more than a small provincial town, a very long way from the capital city of Constantinople.

The University

The Parliament

The Kaisariani Monastery, an 11th century Byzantine monument on the slopes of Mount Hymettus, is the perfect excuse for an outing "so near and yet so far" from the city.

The building complex has been entirely restored. We can visit the main church (katholikon), which is dedicated to the Presentation in the Temple, and the refectory or bath complex, which during the period of Turkish rule was converted into an oil press. Apart from the inherent archaeological interest of the site, a visit to the monastery allows us to explore one of the loveliest gardens in Attica - and recognised as such by the EU, which in 1993 listed it as one of the "Historic Gardens of Europe".

The laurels here belong to the Athens Society of Friends of the Trees, which has not only seen to the reforestation of an area of 500 hectares but has created around the monastery an enchanting Mediterranean paradise with tidy beds of shrubs and tall shade trees (planes and poplars). Adjacent to the monastery is the historic olive grove, recreated from 17th century engravings. Through it winds a broad path leading (500 metres) to the ruins of the old Frankish Monastery. If you visit the site on a weekday, the Society's nursery garden will be open (revenues go towards the upkeep of the site). Just above the Monastery is the Society's Botanical Garden, with rare Greek species of flora; but this, unfortunately, is not open to the public for now. Leaving the Monastery, our road takes us to the Municipal Tourist Pavilion, a small restaurant that on winter Sundays serves the most fabulous bean soup. If you want to continue your tour, the main road will eventually (after a few kilometres) bring you out to the Asteriou Monastery, a restored post-Byzantine monument.

The monastery itself is unfortunately closed to visitors; but if you follow the footpath from the entrance that leads around behind the building, you will come a marvellous natural balcony with a fabulous view of the entire Attic basin.

info

To get to the monastery, take the Kaisariani Ring Road. The Monastery is open to the public Tues.-Sun. 08.30-15.00; general admission is € 2. Entrance to the gardens and the ruins of the Frankish church is free. For information about the Athens Society of Friends of the Trees nursery and botanical garden, call 210/7231769.

CYPRUS AIRWAYS
Our destination… is you!

Take off with **Cyprus Airways** and discover the shortest way to travelling pleasure, hospitality, lifestyle and gastronomy of Cyprus.

▸ 4 flights from Athens
▸ 1 daily flight from Thessaloniki
▸ 2 weekly flights from Heraklion

operated by **Airbus A 319, A 320, A330** and Holiday packages offered by Cyprair Holidays at very attractive prices.

www.cyprusairways.com

Information
from your travel agent
or at **210/3722740**.

coins
with a past

Even in the age of the Euro, some coins are of priceless value. Historical, cultural, collectible...

Alpha Bank, as part of its contribution to the world of culture, owns one of the finest collections of rare Ancient Greek coins. The Bank's Numismatic collection, which began in 1975 with the purchase of the Andreopoulos and Meletopoulos collections and has been enriched systematically, now numbers approximately 10.000 coins from all over the Ancient Greek world.

Where can you see them? In selected Alpha Bank Branches and in the offices of companies of the Alpha Bank Group, where special touch-screen computers have been installed. Through maps of the ancient world and a list of kingdoms, their history and their coinage, take a journey through time and learn about an important aspect of the influence of Greek civilisation on virtually the entire ancient world.

ALPHA BANK OFFICIAL BANK OF THE ATHENS 2004 OLYMPIC GAMES

Museums

Athens Guide 2003

ATHENS 2004

ALPHA BANK
OFFICIAL BANK

the treasures of the city

2003 will be a year of transition, with Athens' major museums undergoing renovation and modernisation in order to be ready for the 2004 Olympics. When construction of the new Acropolis Museum is complete it will provide a symbol of the 21st century metropolis of Athens, one uniting ancient tradition with contemporary architecture. The Athens of today boasts more than 70 museums, whose powerful appeal lies not only in the wealth of their archaeological exhibits but also in the sheer range of their other collections, covering the whole spectrum of historical periods and subject matter.

There are several museums all around the world which are renowned for their collections of classical treasures, but no student of ancient Greece can claim to have experienced the full range of ancient remains unless he has visited the archaeological museums of Attica, contemplated the enigmatic smile on the faces of the archaic korai of the Acropolis, and the restrained melancholy of the tomb reliefs from the Kerameikos Cemetery. The most important of these museums is the National Archaeological Museum, a veritable treasure house of exhibits from all the most important archaeological sites in Greece. Unfortunately - or fortunately in the long term - the museum is currently closed to the public. But there are also much smaller locations which offer unique experiences to the visitor - at the isolated archaeological site at Ramnous, for example, visitors can marvel at the extraordinary artistry to be seen in the sculptures from the temple of Nemesis, authentic masterpieces from the 5th century BC, the work of Agoracritus, a pupil of Pheidias. But the museums of Athens are not confined solely to the treasures of the ancient world. There are more than 70 museums and collec-

National Historical Museum

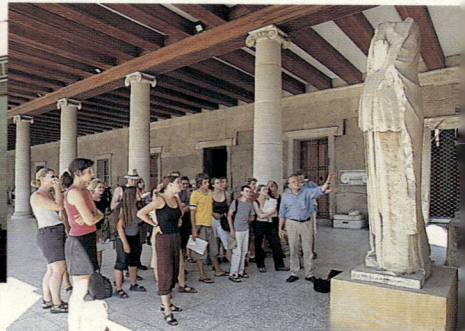
Attalus Stoa

Byzantine Museum

National Historical Museum

tions located all across the region of Attica: public and private, small and large. There are active and enterprising institutions, which are charting the future course of museums here in Greece, as well as sleepy, old-fashioned institutions, where the collections remain for years gathering dust in their display cases. What they share is an extraordinary range of subject matter: there are museums of archaeology, history, technology and natural history, appealing to almost every interest one can imagine, from numismatics to railways, from the Museum of Popular Musical Instruments to the battleship Averof. The museums of Athens are currently experiencing a major period of transition, with the most important among them undergoing renovation. As we mentioned earlier, the National Archaeological Museum is closed for a total renovation of its buildings, to be accompanied by an overhaul of the exhibition lay-out. Extension work is being carried out at the Byzantine Museum, which will involve a ground-breaking network of underground exhibition rooms, allowing the museum to extend its range of exhibits and

introduce more up-to-date display systems. Perhaps the most ambitious innovation of all, however, is the construction of the new Acropolis Museum already in progress. Visitors to the city should not be disappointed however; there are still plenty of other things to see. Some of these are the result of private initiatives: the impressively renovated Benaki Museum, the enterprising Museum of Cycladic Art (with its unique collection of the characteristic prehistoric figurines from the Aegean), the Goulandri Museum of Natural History in Kifisia (recently extended with the new Gaia wing, devoted to environmental education and equipped with state-of-the-art interactive systems) or, finally, the Foundation to the Hellenic World, which introduces the visitor to the ancient world through a range of sophisticated virtual reality systems. All these collections have their own shops selling superb replicas and tastefully designed souvenir and decorative items, as well as elegant cafes or small restaurants - another excellent reason to devote some time to a thoroughly enjoyable museum visit.

tip
The general rule concerning museums that come under the Ministry of Culture is that you can take pictures as long as you don't use a flash or a tripod. In all other museums, you have to have special permission.

tip
In the museums that come under the Ministry of Culture, check out on which days admission is free and who is entitled to a reduced ticket price.

Museum of Cycladic Art

Goulandri Museum of Natural History

ATHENS 2004

ALPHA BANK
OFFICIAL BANK

Museums

ARCHAEOLOGY

Acropolis Museum

Within the Acropolis archaeological site, 210/3214172, 210/3236665. Acropolis subway station. Open: Winter, Mon. 10.30-17.00, Tues.-Sun. 8.00-sunset. Summer, Mon. 12.00-19.00, Tues.-Sun. 8.00-19.00. Admission € 12 (also covers admission to the Ancient Agora, the Dionysus Theatre, the Kerameikos Cemetery, the Olympieion and the Roman Forum).

Just behind the Parthenon the small, old Acropolis Museum, seeming to be carved into the sacred rock, offers an initiation into some of the most important (if not the most sublime) works of classical and archaic Greek art. The narrow galleries are crammed with unique exhibits (undeniable evidence of the urgent need for the new Acropolis Museum). Although the crowded conditions do not make for ideal viewing, this in no way detracts from the value of the works on display.

At the entrance we are welcomed by the marble statue of the cruel Athenian princess, the legendary Procne, who slew her son in order to take revenge on her husband. Just next to her is a marble head of Alexander the Great, an original work by the sculptor Leocharis, dating from 330 BC. The next two galleries are dedicated to the archaic sculptures which adorned the earlier temples on the site of the Parthenon. The large group depicting a lioness devouring a calf, the repellent Gorgon, the demon with three bodies, the small pediment with the apotheosis of Hercules, and many other works besides, all form an excellent introduction to the delights of archaic art. In the centre of the third gallery visitors invariably stop to marvel at the statue of a young man carrying a calf on his shoulders, probably a sacrifice to the goddess. This is the Moschophoros, dating from 570 BC and regarded as one of the most important statues of the period. The next gallery brings alive before our eyes the world of the upper classes of ancient Athens, through their votive offerings to the goddess, all of exquisite artistry. In the first section you will see statues of horsemen and in the second the unique collection of Korai, statues of young women.

Pay special attention to Kore no. 679, known as peplophoros 'the veiled one' (530 BC): the vivid colours of the eyes, lips and wavy hair are remarkably well preserved. Or Kore no. 674 (500 BC), with the oriental almond eyes and delicate robes, so convincingly carved in marble.

USEFUL INFORMATION

• The guide which follows presents the most important museums in Athens and the surrounding region of Attica. Museums are divided into three basic categories: Archaeological, Historical or Special.

• The visitor should bear in mind that although the most important museums we recommend are located within the city limits, it may be necessary to make one or two longer trips outside the city, depending on the individual interests he wishes to pursue. In planning his journey he should also allow from thirty minutes to an hour for looking at the collections in each of the venues we suggest.

• Visitors to Athens will not find it as easy to join a guided tour as it is in other European capitals. Some museums do arrange guided tours to their special exhibitions - the Byzantine Museum is particularly diligent in arranging this kind of tour. The Municipality of Athens does offer free tours every Sunday during the winter season (October to May), visiting museums and archaeological sites - but unfortunately the commentary is only available in Greek. For a full programme, call 210/3231841 and 210/3240762.

• Opening hours, admission prices and holiday openings vary from museum to museum; it's a good idea to check before visiting on an official holiday, the museum may not be open. However, all the museums and sites run by the Ministry of Culture observe the same opening hours. They include the National Archaeological Museum, Acropolis Museum, Archaeological Museum of Piraeus, Byzantine Museum, Inscription Museum, Kanellopoulou Museum, Numismatic Museum, Attalus Stoa, Kerameikos Cemetery, Lavrio Archaeological Museum, Vravrona, Ramnous, Marathonas. The holiday opening hours for these venues are as follows:

6 January, Clean Monday, Easter Saturday,

Acropolis Museum

The rest of the gallery is dominated by the sculptures from the eastern pediment of the archaic Parthenon, whose subject was the Battle of the Giants, while in a specially designed side gallery you can see the frieze from the temple of Apteros Nike (Wingless Victory). Finally, we come to the galleries of Pheidian sculptures (or rather, the meagre remains of these works, since the most important among them are now in the British Museum). Nevertheless, the group with Cecrops, the stone from the frieze of the eastern side of the Parthenon, depicting Poseidon, Apollo, Artemis, Aphrodite and Eros, the metope with the centaur seizing a Lapith woman, as well as a large section of the Parthenon frieze - all combine to give us some idea of the art of the period, which remained a model for artists to emulate for many centuries. Finally we come to the Caryatids, the celebrated statues of young women whose heads supported the upper level of the southern face of the Erechtheum, probably the work of a

Easter Monday, Whitsun, 15 August, 28 October: 08:30-15:00
Good Friday: closed till 12:00
1 January, 25 March, Easter Sunday, 1 May, 25-26 December: closed.
At all these museums there are reduced admission rates for students from non-EU countries, citizens of EU countries aged 65 and over, and members of large families, on presentation of the necessary identification. Admission is free for young people up to the age of 18, on presentation of their ID card; also for students of institutes of further and higher education, on presentation of student cards; students of classical studies or fine arts from non-EU countries, on presentation of student cards; military conscripts, on presentation of service ID; holders of ICOM-ICOMOS cards; guides with Greek Tourist Board accreditation; journalists with official accreditation from the Journalists' Union, and holders of free admission cards.

Finally, at the museums run by the Ministry of Culture there are certain days when admission is free to all: Sundays from 1 November to 31 March; the first Sunday of each month, except July, August and September (when the first Sunday is a public holiday, the second Sunday is the day of free admission); official state holidays; 6 March (Melina Merkouri remembrance day); 18 April (International Monuments Day); 18 May (International Museum Day); 5 June (World Environment Day); the last weekend in September of each year (European Cultural Heritage Days).
The entries below for the above-mentioned museums make no special mention of admission rates or categories of individuals entitled to reduced admission; the general guidelines laid down by the Ministry of Culture are assumed to apply.

ATHENS 2004

ALPHA BANK
OFFICIAL BANK

Museums

Attalus Stoa

pupil of Pheidias, Alcamenes (they date from 420 BC).

Kerameikos Museum
Located within the Kerameikos archaeological site, 148, Ermou St., 210/3463552. Thiseio electric railway station. Open: Winter, Tues.-Sun. 8.30-15.00. Closed on Mondays. Summer, daily, 8.00-19.00. Admission € 2. The beliefs of the ancient Greeks concerning the afterlife, their cults of the dead and funeral practices (so rich in evidence of life in ancient Athens) are all brought to life in the little Kerameikos Museum. The first gallery is dedicated to funerary monuments, providing the visitor with a full introduction to funerary sculpture. Although the most important works from the ancient cemetery are now in the National Archaeological Museum (the stele of Hegesos, for example) it is still possible to see in the remaining works the process of development from the austere relief steles of the archaic period (archaic stele of man with staff and sword, dated 560 BC) to the richly decorated monuments of later times (funerary stele of Dexileus, 394/393 BC).
At the entrance to the museum, on our right, we see the Ampharete relief (430/420 BC), with its moving inscription on the death of Ampharete and her grandchild. Further along on

NEW ACROPOLIS MUSEUM

The ambitious plans drawn up by the Ministry of Culture do not envisage just another museum, but a landmark institution, destined to become an international symbol for the city of Athens. What's more, the new museum is an integral part of the country's endeavours to secure the return of the Elgin Marbles to Greece. In the Parthenon Gallery places have already been designated to receive the works in question, and will remain unfilled until the marbles are returned to their rightful home.
Attaching very great importance to the architectural 'shell', which will house the new museum, the Organisation for the Construction of the New Museum held an international competition to invite tenders. The design finally selected was that of Bernard Tsumi, a celebrated architect who in the 1980s designed and constructed one of the most ambitious of contemporary projects - the La Villette Technological Park in Paris. For the Acropolis Museum he has designed

Attalus Stoa

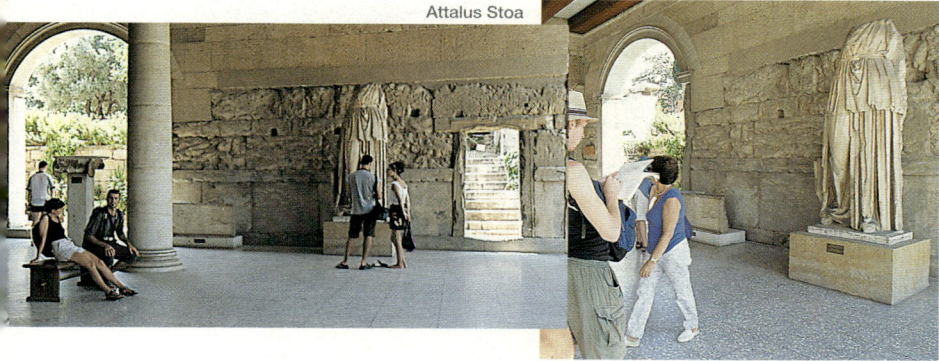

the left there is a simple yet fascinating plinth with a bilingual inscription, in Greek and Carian, a reminder that Athens was home to many foreigners. The following galleries contain vessels and grave goods which represent all the different phases in the life of the cemetery, from the geometrical period (the first period of affluence for the city, attested by the skilfully made vessels, e.g. the large amphora from 860-840 BC,

intended to hold ashes) up until Roman times. Finally, in the showcases containing exhibits from the classical period we see a truly fascinating item: a small doll in a lead case. The bound limbs of the figure leave us in no doubt that that this was intended for some magical use - the casting of an evil spell. On the inside of the case we can still see the names of those whom the maker of the doll wished to curse.

Attalus Stoa (Museum of the Ancient Agora)

Located within the archaeological site of the Ancient Agora, 210/3210185. Monastiraki electric railway station. Open: Winter, Tues.-Sun. 8.30-15.00. Closed on Mondays. Summer, daily, 8.00-19.00. Admission € 2 (covered by the admission ticket for the Ancient Agora archaeological site).
The Museum of the Ancient Agora is housed in the

an austere, geometrical building, whose transparent glass upper level will house the sculptures from the Parthenon. In this way, although the museum will actually be constructed at the foot of the Acropolis, visitors will be able to admire the sculptures and enjoy direct visual contact with the monument itself at the same time.

The intention of the design is that the building should convey a sense of the geology and form of the Acropolis, while also offering an explanation of its evolution down the ages. The first gallery will be dedicated to the shrines located at the feet of the Acropolis, with exhibits hitherto unseen and which highlight the popular character of these shrines, in contrast to the more official forms of worship which took place higher up at the Parthenon itself. This will be followed by galleries containing the impressive sculptures from the archaic temple, the Korai and Kouroi, as well as the works in the 'austere style' (the first phase of the purely classical

style). There will also be hitherto unseen ceramic works and smaller items. Next the visitor will arrive at the Parthenon gallery, the culmination - literally and metaphorically - of the museum display; the walls will be made entirely of glass, bathing the exhibits in the celebrated Attic light and displaying them in as natural an environment as possible. Finally, the last gallery will be dedicated to a display of sculptures from the post Parthenon period. In line with the latest thinking on the role of the museum as a nexus of urban movement, incorporating functions which extend beyond the conventional, purely academic and scientific role of the institution, the new museum will have a restaurant (with, of course, a superb view of the Acropolis), a museum shop and cafe. The New Museum of the Acropolis is scheduled to open its doors to the public just before the
Olympic Games
in 2004.

Museums

National Archaeological Museum

restored Attalus Stoa, which dates from about 150 BC. The exhibits displayed here represent the long history of the area, reminding us that it was continuously inhabited from prehistoric up until Byzantine times. But above all they bring to life some of the most important aspects of the cultural history of classical Athens, as well as the bustling everyday routine of the ancient agora. The earthenware clepsydra for measuring time in the courts of the 5th century evokes the celebrated legal speeches of the ancient orators, while the inscribed bronze shield, a trophy of the Athenian victory over the Spartans at the battle of Sphacteria (425 BC) reminds us of the dramatic events of the Peloponnesian War. The visitor will want to pay special attention to the case with the inscribed pottery shards, the so-called ostraka, which were used for casting votes to ostracise various political figures. We can still make out the names of such celebrated Athenian politicians as Themistocles and Aristides (5th century BC). It is hard to repress a shudder as we pass the case with the innocuous-seeming earthenware phials, when we read that these are vessels found in the prison building and intended to contain the hemlock with which the death sentence was carried out (as every schoolboy knows - it was hemlock with which Socrates was put to death).

Finally, the visitor should pause to examine the exter-

NATIONAL ARCHAEOLOGICAL MUSEUM

This is not only the biggest archaeological museum in the country, but also one of the most important collections of ancient Greek art anywhere in the world. The exhibits come from all over Greece, offering a panorama of the long development of ancient Greek art from the Neolithic period (6th millennium BC) to later Roman times (3rd to 6th century AD). Among the host of items on display the visitor can see the gold finds from excavation at Mycenae, the wall-paintings from prehistoric Santorini, and a unique collection of seven almost perfectly preserved kouroi, an invaluable illustration of the development of archaic art. There are also some of the most important statues from the classical period, including the bronze statue of Poseidon, the funerary stele of Hegesos and the statue of a youth from Antikythira. The austere but imposing neo-classical facade of the National Archaeological Museum with its long portico dominates Patision St., while the little park with its tall palm trees in front of the museum retains something of the splendour of old Athens. Unfortunately the museum is currently closed for renovation and rearrangement of its exhibits. It is scheduled to re-open in April 2004, just in time for the Olympic Games. In the intervening period there will be a total renovation of the buildings, the museum will be equipped with a central air-conditioning system and with special facilities to improve access for the disabled. Auxiliary functions like the canteen, museum shop and educational programmes will be improved, and, most important of all, the collections themselves will be rearranged and reorganised. The most radical changes will be made to the collection of prehistoric (Neolithic, Cycladic, Mycenean) and bronze exhibits.

44, Patision St., 210/8217724. Victoria electric railway station.

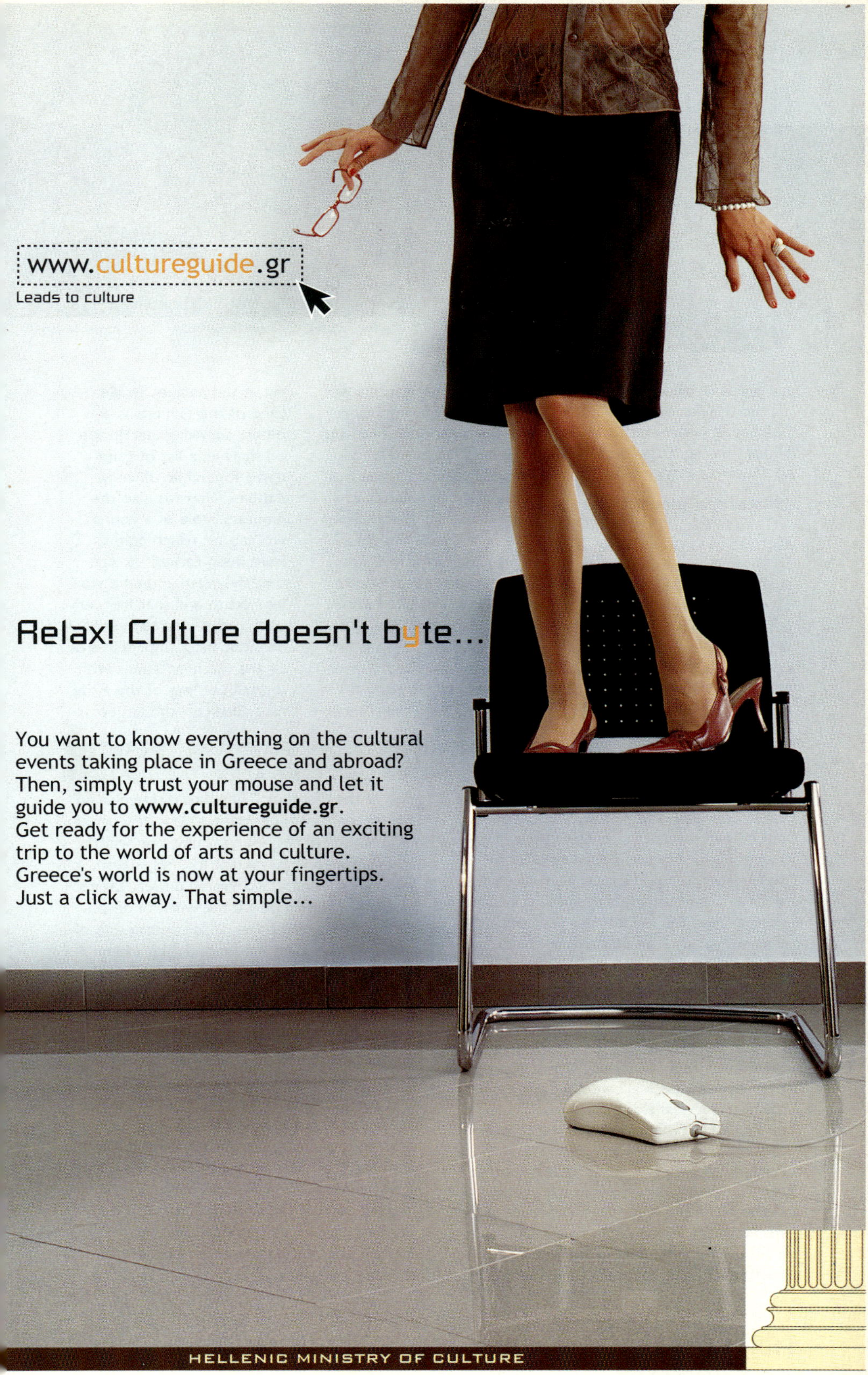

www.cultureguide.gr
Leads to culture
Relax! Culture doesn't byte...
You want to know everything on the cultural events taking place in Greece and abroad? Then, simply trust your mouse and let it guide you to www.cultureguide.gr. Get ready for the experience of an exciting trip to the world of arts and culture. Greece's world is now at your fingertips. Just a click away. That simple...
HELLENIC MINISTRY OF CULTURE

Museums

nal peristyle which runs across the facade of the building: it is decorated with statues dating from the 5th to the 3rd century BC.

Museum of Inscriptions

1, Tositsa St., 210/8217637. Victoria electric railway station. Open: Tues.-Sun. 8.30-15.00. Closed on Mondays. Admission free. Located within the National Archaeological Museum complex, but with its own entrance on the Tositsa pedestrian precinct, the Museum of Inscriptions will remain open during the renovation work on the main museum. This is a remarkable collection, a 'library of stone', whose exhibits are of interest mainly to scholars - in some of the galleries the inscriptions are arranged on special shelves with access designed purely for scholarly research. Two of the galleries have recently been modernised. This is a fascinating collection for those with a specialist interest in the ancient world. One of the exhibits is the oldest surviving inscription on marble, a list of candidates for public office in Athens. There is also the funerary stele of a young woman on which palms have been carved - a sign that the woman died a violent death and that her relatives had sworn to avenge her. But most impressive of all are the huge steles with the tribute lists of the Athenian alliance - the largest is

THE ELGIN MARBLES

Lord Elgin arrived in Athens from England in 1800, intending, like hundreds of travellers before him, to make a study of the monuments of the Acropolis. He had already secured written permission from the Great Vezir of Constantinople to conduct excavations around the foundations (on condition that he would cause no damage to the monuments themselves), to make detailed drawings and take casts of the statues, which would be used to adorn his country house in Scotland. He most certainly had not been granted permission to remove any part of the monuments, something which, moreover, had not been allowed at any time in the past. Nevertheless, during the course of his work Elgin purchased the silence of the Ottoman officials and proceeded to strip the Parthenon of its sculptures, causing untold damage to the monument in the process. His workmen sawed off the rear part of the stones of the frieze, cut in two a capital from the Parthenon and a cornice from the Erechtheum, and in their carelessness broke one of the metopes. They thus dismembered one of the most important groups of works of art in the history of humanity, one which had remained largely intact for more than 2000 years. Within 2-3 years Louzieri, Elgin's assistant, had completed the work of despoliation, even going so far as to remove one of the Caryatids from the Erechtheum. Up until 1811 the cargo of spoils was the subject of protracted and involved diplomatic negotiations, but finally permission was secured to ship the marbles to London. Elgin now entered discussions on their sale to the British government. It is worth noting that there were those in the British parliament itself who branded Elgin a looter and destroyer of antiquities and challenged his ownership of the marbles. However, the government finally agreed to purchase the marbles for £35,000, donating them to the British Museum, where they have since formed one of the main attractions of the museum collection.

about 3.5 metres high, and a small step-ladder is provided for those who wish to scrutinise the whole stele. Those who are interested in reading the texts of the inscriptions will be greatly assisted by the leaflets provided in each gallery and containing transcriptions of all the texts.

Numismatic Museum

12, Panepistimiou St., 210/3643774. Syntagma or Panepistimio subway station. Open: Tues.-Sun. 8.30-15.00. Closed on Mondays. Wed. till 21.00 (winter), or 23.00 (summer). Admission: € 3.
Numismatics - especially the ancient branch of the subject - is an obscure field of study, yet this museum has devised a way of arranging and exhibiting its collections which succeeds in fascinating the ordinary visitor. It is helped, of course, by the extraordinary building which houses the collection - a worthy exhibit in itself!

It is the only museum of its kind in the whole Balkan region, and its collections comprise no fewer than 600,000 coins from the ancient Greek world, Byzantium, the Middle Ages in the West and also from the more modern world. Most of the exhibition space is currently dedicated to ancient coins, but a second area is now planned (on the upper floor, currently closed) to be devoted to Byzantine coins.
The first gallery is dedicated to the museum building itself (the residence built for Heinrich Schliemann). The main exhibition displays the precursors of coinage (talents, etc.) and goes on to describe, with the aid of easily intelligible texts, the art and technique of minting coins. The same gallery also has a display of important treasure troves (hoards of coins found together). This is followed by a section dedicated to the mints of Athens and of the period of

Alexander the Great, as well as a section, which uses coins found at a shrine in Delphi (the Korykeion Andron) to analyse the circulation of coins in ancient times. There is also a fascinating section on numismatic iconography, the various subjects chosen for depiction on coins. The museum has a small shop, selling collector's replicas of ancient coins.

Museum of Cycladic Art

4, Neofytou Douka St., Kolonaki, 210/7228321. Evangelismos subway station. Open: daily 10.00-16.00, Sat. 10.00-15.00. Tues. and Sun. closed. Admission € 3.50.
The third millennium BC saw the flourishing of an extraordinary civilisation on the islands of the Cyclades. The white marble figures created by the Cycladic craftsmen have had a profound influence on contemporary art - Brancusi, Giacometti and Henry Moore

ILIOU MELATHRON

This is the name of the private residence of the renowned German archaeologist Heinrich Schliemann, whose persistence and determination overturned so many of the certainties of the archaeological science of his time. The building was constructed as a home for the archaeologist's dreams and visions: it was here that Schliemann brought the Treasure of Priam, the unique finds he had uncovered in his excavations of Troy.
Work began on the building in 1870. The plans were drawn up by Schliemann's friend and compatriot Ernest Ziller, who opted for a renaissance style, adjusted to suit the neo-classical taste of the period. The house is now regarded as the most representative design by this classically-minded architect. Perhaps the most characteristic feature of the facade are the arched arcades along

Panepistimiou St., which alleviate the austerity of the overall design. The observant visitor will recognise the swastika design in the decorative motifs of the railings around the house. Don't jump to conclusions, however: the swastika is an ancient symbol of the sun, copied from ancient vessels, and with no relation to its subsequent political use. The interior of the house is particularly remarkable, with its mosaic floors and wall-paintings. These are either faithful copies of Pompeian subjects, or depictions of excavation sites and finds uncovered by Schliemann. The building was completed in 1881; on 30 January of that year a glittering reception was held to celebrate its completion. It had cost 439,650 gold drachmas - an astronomical sum at the time.

Museums

are just a few of the modern artists who spring to mind. And as you stroll through the galleries of the museum and contemplate the enigmatic forms of Cycladic art you will immediately understand why.

The museum is an enterprising private institution, with collections of ancient Greek and Byzantine art, but none of the exhibits can compare with the unique Cycladic collection, consisting of 386 exhibits from every period of the 3rd millennium. Ceramic vessels, tools, ritual implements and marble figurines of all types, from the schematic violin-shaped figures to the large human figures. The modern design of the showcases, with their special lighting, explanatory texts and maps, all help to highlight and explain in depth the story behind each exhibit.

The museum also organises important exhibitions on a wide range of subjects, housed in an impressive neo-classical building (the Megaro Stathatou) adjoining the modern main museum building. In the autumn of 2002 there will be an exhibition of 30 paintings and a sculpture by the great surrealist Salvador Dali, under the title Myth and Singularity, while plans are under way for a major archaeological exhibition in spring 2003, as part of the Cultural Olympiad, dedicated to marine communication - 'Navigation: from Sidon to Huelva, 16th-6th century BC'. Don't forget to call in at the museum shop, which has a wide range of superb replicas, dozens of books and many other tastefully designed souvenir items.

In the atrium of the museum there is a very attractive restaurant and cafe, serving a limited but delicious range of dishes.

Archaeological Museum of Piraeus

31, Charilaou Trikoupi St., Pasalimani, 210/4521598.

Open: Tues.-Sun. 8.30-15.00. Closed on Mondays. Admission € 3.

This is a museum which focuses on marine archaeology. The recently renovated building, originally constructed in 1966, houses a display of exhibits from ships, finds associated with the lives of the affluent metics who lived in the vicinity of the harbour, as well as unusual cults which were brought by foreign migrants coming to Attica, and providing a vivid reminder that Piraeus has always been the sea gateway to Attica, open to merchandise, to wealth and to new beliefs.

The showpiece of the collection are the four bronze statues found in Piraeus in 1959. They date from different periods and had probably been collected by a Roman official who planned to have them shipped to Rome. The first probably depicts Apollo; it is the earliest known statue to be cast in metal (520 BC). The other three are female figures, also depicting deities - the two first are probably representations of Artemis and the third (which is an impressive height - 2.35m) of Athena. There is also a bronze tragic mask found in the same excavation.

One of the museum's most impressive features is the specially designed gallery containing the large funerary monument of the metic Niceratos and his son. This is one of the largest ever found in an ancient Greek cemetery, a remarkable edifice seven metres high in the form of a small temple resting on a marble pedestal decorated with scenes from the battle with the Amazons. Three statues

THE WOMAN OF KEROS

Keros is today an uninhabited island, very close to the Koufonisia. During the 1960s it became a paradise for unauthorised excavations: dozens of Cycladic treasures were removed to be sold on the black market for archaeological finds. Authorised and properly conducted excavations carried out subsequently confirmed the wealth of the island's archaeological sites, but the most fascinating discovery was the paradoxical failure to find either settlements or cemeteries. The archaeologists eventually concluded that Keros was used exclusively for religious purposes: in other words, it appears to have been a pan-Cycladic sanctuary, rather as Delos was in classical times. The largest statue in the collection of the Museum of Cycladic Art comes from Keros. It is a beautifully formed female figure, 1.40m high, which can claim to be one of the oldest monumental sculptures in the Greek world. Carved in white marble, the austere but flowing rendering of the woman's features fascinates the museum's visitors. The statue is believed to depict a goddess whose 'home' was the large prehistoric shrine on the island.

Museum of Cycladic Art

rise from within the temple - representing father, son and a slave. Another important gallery is that containing the reconstruction of the shrine of Cybele, which enables the visitor to gain a better understanding of the unusual cult of this goddess.

Lavrio Archaeological Museum
A. Kordella St., Lavrio, 22920/22817. Open: Tues.-Sun. 8.30-15.00. Closed on Mondays. Admission free. The museum contains archaeological finds from the area, with the main emphasis on its mines. Detailed maps are displayed to assist the visitor. The main attraction, of course, are the architectural sculptures from the Temple of Poseidon at Sounio.

Vravrona Archaeological Museum
Vravrona, 22990/27020. Open: Tues.-Sun. 8.30-15.00. Closed on Mondays. Admission € 3 (includes access to whole archaeological site). This is a small museum in the neo-classical style; most of the exhibits are finds from the archaeological site of the sanctuary of Artemis Vravronia. This was a sanctuary where parents dedicated their daughters to the virgin goddess until they

came of age, dressing them as little bears (the bear, of course, was the animal sacred to Artemis). The museum has a remarkable collection of statuary, with sculptures representing young children bearing gifts for the goddess - particularly interesting in view of the fact that representations of young children are so rare in ancient Greek art. The museum is currently planning a programme of renovation, which will probably lead to changes in the present lay-out of the exhibits.

Ramnous Collection of Sculpture
Ramnous, Grammatiko Attica, 22940/63477. Admission € 2 (includes access to whole archaeological site).
A specially designed gallery within the Ramnous archaeological site offers the visitor the opportunity to see the sculptures from the temple of Nemesis. The most striking of the exhibits is the restored entablature of the temple (the part above the capitals, with the triglyphs, metopes and pediment), as well as part of the base of the great marble statue of Nemesis, an original work by the important 5th century sculptor Agoracritus. Unfortunately the gallery can only be visit-

ed by prior arrangement with the 2nd Ephorate of Prehistoric and Classical Antiquities (210/3219792).

Marathonas Archaeological Museum
Marathonas, 22940/55462. Open: Tues.-Sun. 8.30-15.00. Closed on Mondays. Admission € 3 (includes access to the whole archaeological site). A small museum - the main attraction here is the archaeological site itself, with its impressive funerary monuments. However, the museum does have a number of interesting exhibits: in the prehistoric gallery there is a striking collection of Cycladic items found at the site of the only Cycladic colony in Attica. The showpiece of the classical gallery are the finds from the burial mound of the heroes who fell at the Battle of Marathonas (inscriptions, urns, funerary implements).

HISTORY
Byzantine and Christian Museum
22, Vasilissis Sofias Ave., Kolonaki, 210/7211027. Evangelismos subway station. Open: Tues.-Sun. 8.30-15.00. Closed on Mondays. Admission € 4.

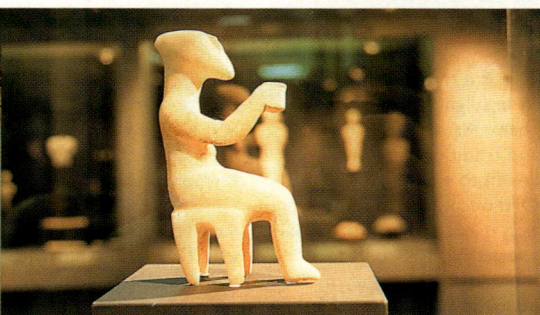

Museums

This is a museum dedicated to highlighting the special character of Byzantine art and tradition, inseparably linked to the history of the Orthodox faith. The collection is housed in the atmospheric Villa Ilissia, built in the mid-19th century by Stamatis Kleanthis, the leading architect of his time, as a 'winter palace' for the celebrated Duchess of Piacenza. The design was based on that of the Italian villa, although certain features - such as the handsome articulation of the facades with their carved blocks of stone - are more reminiscent of mediaeval models.

The first two galleries are dedicated to early Christian sculpture, offering an impressive demonstration of the continuity of the ancient Greek and Byzantine worlds: the work most characteristic of the collection - and probably one of the museum's best-known exhibits - is the Orpheus Group, an allegorical depiction of Christ. Galleries 2 and 4 have been designed as replicas of churches, the former of the early-Christian period and the latter of the mid-Byzantine era. They offer the visitor an excellent opportunity to study the basic features of Byzantine church building. The upper floor houses the icon collection, which includes the fascinating Episkepsis, a rare mosaic icon from the 13th century. There are also collections of miniatures, wall paintings (with works removed from Byzantine churches), ceramics and fabrics.

Work is currently nearing completion on the extension of the museum. The new facilities have been constructed below ground, on multiple levels - forming an 'invisible' ring around the historic building. When complete they will provide an extra 4,500 square metres of exhibition space, allowing a complete re-design of the display of the permanent collections. New gardens are to be laid out around the building, as well as an archaeological park. For the time being some parts of the new galleries are being used to house temporary exhibitions.

National Historical Museum

13, Stadiou St., Kolokotroni Sq., 210/3237617. Syntagma or Panepistimio subway station. Open: Tues.-Sun. 9.00-14.00. Closed on Mondays. Admission € 3, students € 1.50.

The collection is housed in the elegant neo-classical building (designed by the French architect F. Boulanger) which was the home of the Greek parliament until 1934; the assembly chamber is still in its original condition and is one of the most impressive features of the building. The museum has a collection of unique historical items, but unfortunately they are dis-

THE WINTER PALACE OF A DUCHESS

If we could have visited the Villa Ilissia 155 years ago the only sound we would have heard would have been the waters of the river Ilisos, often swollen to a raging torrent by the winter rains. Now the river no longer exists; it was filled in and Vasileos Konstantinou Avenue now runs across the ground where the waters once flowed. In 1848, however, when the Duchess of Piacenza came to live in the villa (only one of the six homes in Attica built for her by Stamatis Kleanthis) this was almost a country district: the house stood just beyond the city boundaries, on the road from Athens to Kifisia. It wasn't long before other prominent Athenians followed her example, building large and opulent mansions along Kifisias St. - the original name of what is now Vasilissis Sofias Avenue) and thereby creating one of the most aristocratic boulevards of old Athens. The Duchess was a strong personality who cannot have failed to exert a powerful influence on the society of the new capital. She was a daughter of the Marquis Francois de Barbe-Marbois. She owed her title to her husband, aide-de-camp to Napoleon himself and Duke of Piacenza or Plaisance. It was not a happy marriage, however, and in 1837 the Duchess came to Athens, where she remained until her death. Previously she had lived in Nafplion, where she was very actively engaged in politics - she sided with the Mavromichalis family against Kapodistrias. She earned immortality in the public imagination through the tales told of her love for the fierce brigand chief Davelis, who was active in Attica in the mid-19th century.

Benaki Museum: the building, and a mural from the café

played with a rather complacent reverence for their value as sacred national heirlooms and with too little concern to explain their historical context to the visitor - there are no explanatory texts. Therefore, in the galleries dedicated to the years before the insurrection the exhibits include the spectacles worn by Korais, a cup belonging to Ypsilantis and a wallet belonging to Tsakalof. In the galleries dedicated to the War of Independence there is a complete collection of compositions painted by the popular artist Panagiotis Zografos at the instigation of Makrygiannis. There is also an impressive collection of the arms borne by important figures in the revolutionary war, such as Kolokotronis and Karaiskakis. There are other galleries dedicated to Mesolongi and Navarino (the carved figureheads of the ships used in the revolutionary war reveal to the visitor a superb aspect of the popular art of the time), to the priesthood (one of the exhibits is the desk, in its original condition, of the Patriarch Grigorios V), the Philhellenic movement and the war at sea. These are followed by a section dedicated to the liberated Greek state (up until 1940).

The tour of the museum comes to an end with a small section dedicated to folk costumes. There is also a superb museum shop with marvellous ideas for gifts or small souvenirs, including silver replicas of tamata (little tokens symbolising a vow or prayer and placed next to an icon), miniature soldiers (collector's copies of old children's toys), puzzles, beautifully produced books and dozens of silver- and gold-plated items.

Benaki Museum

1, Koumpari St., Kolonaki, 210/3671000. Evangelis-mos subway station. Open: Mon.-Wed. & Fri.-Sat. 9.00-17.00, Thur. 9.00-24.00, Sun. 9.00-15.00, Tues. closed. Admission € 6, over 65 € 3, students free. Admission free to all on Thursday.

The impressively renovated Benaki Museum is one of the most popular private museums in the city. Apart from its collections there are also marvellous amenities - the restaurant with its superb veranda opposite the National Gardens and the large museum shop - which compete for the visitors' attention. In general

---

! Don't miss

Museum of the Acropolis: Never before has such a small space contained so many masterpieces of classical art. A unique sculpture gallery, the envy of any major museum anywhere.

Benaki Museum: A prime favourite with the people of Athens. Comprehensive in concept (exhibits from prehistoric times to the 20th century) and offering endless pleasant hours spent in its charming restaurant and art shop.

Museum of Cycladic Art: Follow your initiation into Cycladic Art (one floor of prehistoric finds from the Aegean islands) with a light meal in the "hidden" atrium. The multicultural visiting exhibitions are a perfect complement to the museum's permanent collection.

Byzantine Museum: Well-presented visiting exhibitions and "retro" charm in the permanent collection at the Villa Ilisia. Looking forward to the new rooms to be opened.

Gaia Centre: Spectacular interactive display that will teach you "everything you ever wanted to know" about the environmental problems of the planet.

terms its collections of exhibits cover all the main periods in Greek history, from prehistoric times till the beginning of the 20th century. The first section begins with a display of tools and figures from the Neolithic period. There are unique gold cups from the 'Euboea Treasure', dating from the early bronze age. The classical period is represented by vessels, fragments of statues, Hellenistic figures and many delicate and finely wrought items of jewellery. There are Fayum portraits from the early Christian period, as well as a notable collection of Coptic fabrics. The early centuries of Byzantium are represented by a variety of exhibits from Syria, Egypt and the Greek world. Without doubt the most bountiful feature of the Museum is its folklore collection, with the costumes, embroidery and, finest of all, the two rooms preserved intact from splendid old mansions in Kozani and Siatista, with their wealth of wood-carved decoration. Also of great interest are the small showcases on the third floor, dedicated to pre-revolutionary Greece and highlighting such areas as shipping, the world of letters, etc. The last floor is dedicated to the liberated Greek state, from Otto to Venizelos, and the collection is dominated by the massive showcase of costumes from the royal Greek court. The museum has a small gallery for temporary exhibitions - of which it makes the fullest possible use, organising significant events here all year round. Up until 10 December 2002 the gallery will be home to an exhibition of Armenian treasures from Cilicia. During the Christmas and New Year holidays the gallery will be used for a presentation of the multi-faceted work Nekuia by the artist Chronis Botsoglou, and this will be followed in February by an exhibition of work by the great Greek photographer Kostas Balafas. Finally, in mid-March an important archaeological exhibition - The bull in the Mediterranean - will be opening here as part of the programme for the Cultural Olympiad.

Kanellopoulou Museum
12, Theorias St. & Panos St., Plaka, 210/3212313. Monastiraki electric railway station. Open: Tues.-Sun. 8.30-15.00. Closed on Mondays. Admission € 2. The museum houses a I varied private collection, which was donated years ago to the state. The neo-classical building of the museum stands at the foot of the Acropolis (above the Ancient Agora). The first section is dedicated to Byzantine art, with important portable icons (such as the Dormition of the Virgin, School of Constantinople, from the late 14th century, and the Martyrdom of Agia Paraskevi, signed by Michail Damaskinos, dating from the 16th century). The mezzanine and first floors have a large number of small objects, vessels and figures, dating from prehistoric to Roman times. There is a particularly rich display in the showcase containing dozens of elegant Tanagra figurines (female figures in terra cotta), as well as caricatured figures of characters in the New Comedy of the Hellenistic period.

Museum of the City of Athens
7, I. Paparrigopoulou St., 210/3246164. Panepistimio subway station. Open: Mon., Wed., Fri. 9.30-15.00, Sun. 10.00-15.00, Tues. and Thur. closed. Admission € 5, students, schoolchildren and over-65s € 3.
One of the oldest neo-classical complexes in Athens (once used as a temporary home for the first royal couple of Greece) now houses a collection of paintings, miniatures, sacred relics and architectural models - a collection which tells the story of the city's history from the rule of the Franks to the 20th century, but with the main focus on the 19th century.
Particularly striking are the galleries with the drawing room of Otto and Amalia, while the most unexpected reconstruction is that of the kitchen (!) of the palace of the royal couple (all the utensils are authentic).

Centre for the Study of Modern Ceramics
4-6, Melidoni St., Kerameikos, 210/3318491. Thiseio electric railway station. Open: Mon., Tues., Thur., Fri. 9.00-15.00, Wed. 12.00-20.00, Sat. closed, Sun. 10.00-14.00. Admission € 2, students € 1.
Dedicated to research into and promotion of the functional ceramics of the last three centuries, this little museum next to the Kerameikos Cemetery throws light on the often ignored daily life of the modern Greek world. The

Museums

The battleship Averof

first gallery introduces the visitor to the subject through maps, drawings, photographs, texts and audio-visual media, while in the following galleries the visitor can study presentations of the basic types of ceramic workshop. The final gallery is dedicated to the traditional potter, his life and work. In the courtyard there is a fascinating reconstruction of an open-air workshop. There are frequent temporary exhibitions to supplement the permanent collection, while in the shop the visitor will find a variety of interesting ceramic wares.

War Museum

2, Rizari St., Kolonaki, 210/7244464. Evangelismos subway station. Open: Tues.-Sun. 9.00-14.00. Closed on Mondays. Admission free. Weapons, weapons and more weapons - from the stone age to the 2nd World War. The purpose of the museum's founders - and of the Ministry of Defence, which is now responsible for the museum - was to display important military objects and to commemorate the sacred military struggles of the Greek nation. The first galleries of this massive, contemporary-style building are dedicated

to ancient times, to Byzantium and to the period of Frankish rule, but there are also extremely interesting sections on modern Greece (Balkan Wars and 1940), containing important historical items. Young children are usually delighted by the rear courtyard with its military planes - in some of which you can actually climb into the cockpit.

Naval Museum

Zeas Marina, 210/4516264. Open: Tues.-Fri. 9.00-14.00. Sat. 9.00-13.30, Sun. and Mon. closed. Admission € 1.50, over-65s and students € 1. The history and evolution of ships and shipping in Greece, illustrated by 2500 exhibits - uniforms, models of ships, paintings, etc. For those fascinated by the sea the museum (housed in a long and narrow contemporary-style building) has a number of surprises in store, such as the collection of model ships made of bone from the early 19th century, formerly displayed on the yacht Christina, owned by Aristotle Onasis. In the courtyard visitors can see the tower of the legendary submarine Papanikolis, as well as naval arms and equipment from various periods. There is a

museum shop selling books, posters, CD-ROMs, etc.

The Battleship Averof

Trocadero Marina, Palaio Faliro, 210/9836539. Winter opening hours (after clocks change): Mon., Wed., Fri. 11.00-13.00 & 16.00-18.00, Sat. and Sun. 11.00-15.00. Summer opening hours: Mon., Wed., Fri. 11.00-13.00 & 17.00-19.00, Sat. and Sun. 11.00-15.00. Tues. and Thur. closed. Admission € 0.80, children free. The battleship was the pride of the Greek fleet during the Balkan Wars (1912-1913), playing a decisive role in the critical naval encounter involving Elli and the one at Limnos. It is now moored at the Trocadero Marina in Faliro. Largely renovated it offers an opportunity to young and old to feel at first hand the aura of glory that hangs over a historic battleship, walking its corridors, inspecting its facilities and - of course - ascending to its bridge. Some parts of the ship have been laid out to house temporary and permanent exhibitions, such as the personal possessions of Admiral Kountouriotis, arms of the period and the ship's own weapon systems.

SPECIALIST MUSEUMS

Goulandri Museum of Natural History

13, Levidou St., Kifisia, 210/8015870. Kifisia electric railway station. Open: daily 9.00-14.30, Fri. closed. Admission € 3, children and students € 1.20.

The museum's galleries use highly detailed signs, special diagrams and visual reconstructions to introduce the visitor to the natural kingdom. The collection is housed in a little palace built in northern European style concealed behind the high perennial trees of Levidou St. in Kifisia. The first galleries are dedicated to flora, and followed by others focusing on fauna, starting with the simplest life forms and moving up to the mammals. There is a very impressive section on minerals, with dozens of colourful exhibits, and children will be enchanted by the palaeontology section, staring fascinated at the huge skeleton of the triceratops dinosaur. Make sure you visit the excellent museum shop and leaf through the superb books published by the museum. You must also visit the Gaia Centre, just opposite, which is run by the museum but charges a separate admission fee.

Gaia Centre

100, Othonos St., Kifisia, 210/8015870. Kifisia electric railway station. Open: daily 9.00-14.30, Fri. closed. Admission € 4.50, children and students € 1.50.

The Gaia Centre - the new autonomous wing of the Goulandri Museum of Natural History - is devoted to environmental research and education. The research is conducted in the state-of-the-art laboratories of the underground levels, while the purposes of education are served by a remarkable spectacle which is designed not just to enchant the visitor but also to make him stop and think. The exhibition was designed in association with the Museum of Natural History in London. Superb use has been made of audio-visual systems, video, atmospheric lighting and music. The tour of the museum begins with a presentation of the planet Earth and continues by introducing us to the ecosystems and the way they interact

The ultra-modern Gaia Centre

with human activities. The final section is dedicated to the major environmental issues of our time: energy policy, transport systems and their impact, the over-exploitation of natural resources, the adequacy of supplies of food and water. The Centre also has a large shop (selling the same things as the main Museum of Natural History shop, but more attractively displayed) and an elegant restaurant - Ammonitis - where you can sit and enjoy a coffee.

Foundation of the Hellenic World

254, Peiraios St., Tavros, 210/4835300. Open: Winter (15/9-14/6): Mon., Tues., Thur. 9.00-14.00, Wed. & Fri. 9.00-21.00, Sun. 10.00-15.00, closed on Saturdays. Summer (15/6-14/9): Mon., Tues., Thur., Fri. 9.00-16.00, Wed.

9.00-20.00, Sun. 11.00-15.00, closed on Saturdays. Admission free.

A museum without museum exhibits! It sounds illogical but this is the new principle of museum science implemented at the Foundation to the Hellenic World. Not that there are no exhibits, of course, it's just that they are not the original items we are used to seeing in other museums.

The purpose of the Foundation is to familiarise us with the world of ancient Greece (as well as other periods in Greek history) through state-of-the-art electronic interactive systems and educational displays. The most impressive feature are the virtual reality 'theatres' on the ground floor. The most sophisticated of these is the Ark, in which you can take a tour of ancient Miletus, the Temple of Zeus at Olympia, and

the magical world of Greek costume. The Magic Screen is the second, and simpler, virtual reality programme, which introduces the visitor to 'The traditional olive press' and 'Ancient vessels with depictions of Olympic sports'. The upper floor currently houses a temporary exhibition on 4000 years of Greek costume, which will last until November 2002, or possibly until the end of the year. Next year a major exhibition dedicated to mathematics is planned. Finally there is the permanent exhibition with the title 'On this day each year…', which is dedicated to important national anniversaries.

The Foundation organises a large number of educational programmes, has an Internet room and large shop selling books, souvenirs and educational CD-ROMs.

THE LAST OF THE ATHENIAN BATHHOUSES

During the period of Turkish rule there were a number of public baths in Athens, places of high symbolic importance used not just for personal hygiene but as social meeting places, especially for women. By the beginning of the 20th century all the baths had been closed and their buildings demolished, with one exception - the bathhouse known as the Aeridon Baths, on Kyrristou Street. The bathhouse was

recently fully renovated and can be visited on Wednesday and Sunday (10.00-14.00). The interior, with its domes and marble baths, is a delightful sight. On the mezzanine floor there is an exhibition with information on the water supply to the city of Athens in modern times.

8, Kyrristou St., Plaka, 210/3244340. Monastiraki electric railway station. Open: Wed. & Fri. 10.00-14.00. Admission free.

Foundation of the Hellenic World

Museum of Greek Folk Art

17, Kydathinaion St., Plaka, 210/3229031. Acropolis or Syntagma subway station. Open: daily 10.00-14.00, closed Monday. Admission € 2, over-65s € 1, students free.

The building on Kydathinaion Street reminds us of the period when the collection was first assembled as we know it today - 1973. Since then there has been no major renovation - although various sections have undergone remodelling, with the result that the quality and character of the displays vary strikingly from floor to floor. The entrance hall, dedicated to works of embroidery, is remarkably gloomy; the lighting is so poor that you can hardly see the exhibits - a pity, since they are all of exceptional quality. There is a small shop here, with interesting replicas (including tamata -little tokens symbolising a vow or prayer and placed next to an icon). The galleries used for temporary exhibitions and silver-work, however, are both modern in style, painted in appealing earth colours and with proper display cases to show the exhibits at their best. Despite its defects, the fact

is that the museum boasts a comprehensive collection, which helps the visitor to understand the folk culture of Greece. Of particular interest are the shadow theatre figures, one of which is reversed to display a dedication written by the maker of the puppet to the puppeteer. Just next to these is a display of costumes used at carnival events. Also impressive are the wedding crowns with their special crests (in the silver-work collection) and the whole top floor with its display of costumes.

The museum also runs two independent annexes, the Mosque on Monastiraki Square, which houses the V. Kyriazopoulou Collection of Popular Ceramics, and the bathhouse at 8, Kyrristou St., known as the Aeridon Baths, because of its proximity to the monument of that name.

Museum of Greek Popular Musical Instruments - Foivos Anogeianakis Collection

1-3, Diogenous St., Aeridon Square, Plaka, 210/3250198. Monastiraki electric railway station. Open: Tues. & Thur.-Sun. 10.00-14.00, Wed. 12.00-18.00, closed Monday. Admission free.

This fine old house in the

Plaka district, next to the Aerides (the Tower of the Winds, which was built to house a hydraulic clock in the Roman Forum) is home to an extremely comprehensive collection representing the history and evolution of Greek popular music. The collection is the result of fifty years of research by the musicologist Foivos Anogeianakis. It is the largest collection of such instruments in Greece, and one of the most important in Europe. It was donated to the Greek state in 1978. The museum was established under the supervision of the collector himself and opened in June 1991. The exhibits are displayed on three levels and arranged in categories of musical instrument (wind, strings, percussion, etc.). Next to each showcase are earphones which the visitor can use to enjoy the sound of the instrument in the case. The music has been selected with great care and if you are a devotee of folk music you will find yourself spending a long time listening to the long drawn-out sounds of the clarinet, the Dionysian rhythms of the zournades,

the more western melodies of the mandolin. Of particular anthropological interest are the idiophone instruments and sounding objects (animal bells, clapping boards, children's whistles, etc.), which remind us of the importance of sound in every aspect of daily life.

The shop stocks a superb collection of folk CDs. There is also a very fine catalogue of the museum's collection. The Centre for Ethno-Musicology, which is housed in the same building, organises annual courses in playing popular instruments - the oud, the touberleki, clarinet, Cretan lute (taught by Psarogiannis) and many others - as well as singing lessons.

Jewish Museum

39, Nikis St., 210/3225582. Syntagma subway station. Open: daily 9.00-14.30, Sun. 10.00-14.00. Sat. closed. Admission € 3, schoolchildren and students € 1.50.

The museum is housed in an austere, neo-classical building in the Plaka district and the designers have shown considerable ingenuity in adapting the premises - not ideally suited for a museum. The collection is arranged in five sections. To the left of the entrance we can admire the authentic interior of the Romaniote Synagogue in Patra. We move on to a display of liturgical implements and instruments associated with the Jewish calendar. The next section contains documents referring to Jewish involvement in the Greek struggles for liberation and in the Resistance. This is followed by a particularly

moving display, dedicated to the Holocaust. The final level offers a picture of the daily life of the Jews in Greece from the 18th to the 20th century - particularly moving is the showcase with a display of children's clothes.

Ilias Lalaounis Museum of Jewellery

Kallisperi St. & 4a, Karyatidon St. (Dionysiou Areopagitou passage), 210/9221044. Akropoli subway station. Open: Mon., Thur., Fri., Sat. 9.00-16.00, Wed. 9.00-21.00, Sun. 11.00-16.00, Tues. closed. Admission € 3, over-65s € 2.30.
Admission free for children under 10 and each Wednesday 15.00-21.00 & Saturday 9.00-11.00.

This early 20th century building designed in the eclectic style houses a collection of three thousand items of jewellery, created during his fifty-year career by the celebrated Greek jeweller Ilias Lalaounis. Of particular interest is the original goldsmith's workshop, where visitors can watch the application of ancient and modern techniques. From time to time the museum organises temporary exhibitions, lectures and seminars. The museum shop has a collection of 2000 designs, while it is also possible to commission special items. There is a delightful cafe, which also functions as a restaurant.

Railway Museum

4, Siokou St. (vertical to 301, Liosion Avenue), 210/5126295. Tues. and Thur. 9.00-13.00, Wed. 17.00-20.00, Fri.-Sun. 10.00-13.00. Admission free. If you're a train fanatic this

collection, with its historic Hellenic Railways rolling stock, will bring back all the charm and splendour of the glory days of the Greek rail network.

There are steam locomotives dating back to 1884 (including steam engines from the mine railways), hand- and foot-operated draisines, old-world trams, instruments, tickets and other documentary exhibits. Among the most striking items are the royal coaches and the smoking car of the sultan's train of Abdul Hamit.

Postal Museum

5, Panathinaikou Stadiou Sq., Pagkrati, 210/7519066. Open: daily 8.00-14.00, Sat. and Sun. closed. Admission free.

A small but comprehensive collection of special interest to philatelists, with Greek stamps from 1861 to the present day as well as a range of other documents and exhibits on the history of the Greek postal service.

Spathareio Shadow Theatre Museum

Kastalias Sq. (V. Sofias Ave. & D. Ralli St.), Marousi, 210/6127245. Marousi electric railway station. Open: daily 10.00-13.30, Sat. & Sun. closed. Admission free.

A small collection of items associated with the popular shadow theatre. The original core of the collection was assembled by Evgenios Spatharis, one of the most famous of all shadow puppeteers. There are black-and-white and coloured Karagkiozis figures, as well as other types of traditional shadow puppet.

H|P
HOTELS

Athens at its most relaxed

- **Peaceful Location:** at the foot of the Acropolis, in the museum neighborhood, within an easy stroll from Plaka, providing easy access to the main shopping, business areas and metro station.
- **Unique View of the Acropolis**
- **Comfort:** at the elegant and well equipped 90 guest rooms of Herodion hotel and 50 rooms of Philippos hotel, some ideally spacious for big families.
- **Taste:** Mediterranean cuisine at the atrium coffee shop viewing the green back garden and at the restaurant.
- **Cocktail Bar:** after an impressive performance at the Herodion Ancient theater you may continue your evening with a drink in a pleasant and friendly environment.
- **Roof Garden:** an impressive space, an enticing suggestion for private occasions, celebrations, dinners.
- **Conference and Banquet Facilities**

Shopping

Athens Guide 2003

ATHENS 2004

ALPHA BANK
OFFICIAL
BANK

the art
of shopping

Do you like shopping? Are you one of those who jump at any occasion to visit the shops? Are you an unredeemed bargain hunter who forages through the markets armed with your trusty credit card? Does the joy of discovering a secret source give you as much pleasure as the purchase itself? Or do you prefer to kit yourself out fully at the beginning of the season? Whatever your shopping style, these pages of the Athens Guide have been designed as an irreplaceable tool to help you get the most out of your shopping experience.

We will share our shopping philosophy and practice with you, and give you a guide to shopping in the five Athens districts where the heart of the city's marketplace beats most strongly. Five districts where you will not only find the most interesting stores, but feel the rhythm of the marketplace and have a good time as you go. Shopping can be the best way to begin or end a difficult day. And by this we don't mean just hitting the stores (expensive or otherwise), emptying your wallet, pushing your credit limit. We also mean browsing through a good bookshop for something that will take you to new destinations, buying a gadget spotted in a window that is just the thing to brighten up your desk, choosing a small treat for yourself or a gift for a friend, splurging on

Shopping in Levidou St., Kifisia

Pumps by Casadei, at Kalogirou

something from Gucci or Armani. Shopping can be lots of things, a combination of all those moments that give you a lift: visiting the shops, having coffee with a friend, opening the bag at home, experiencing the pleasure of that special purchase that makes you feel good or look even better. Shopping, in other words, can be a marvellous... form of alternative therapy.

A look at the shops in Athens is enough to persuade even the most difficult shopper that Greece's capital is perfectly at ease among the world's fashion metropolises. And this is not only because all the great designer names and global brands are there in its shops, and at prices that can compete with any city in Europe: Greece, and Athens in particular,

creates fashion, international fashion. From Giannis Galatis in the '60s to Sofia Kokosalaki, the pet of today's international catwalks, Greek designers are at the heart of things.

Let's be on our way, then, for a relaxed and relaxing tour of the city, for shopping and coffee: we'll go to Kolonaki, to the "Historic Centre" of Athens, to Neo Psychiko and neighbouring districts along Mesogeion Ave., to Kifisia and Glyfada.

In each district we selected the shops that mark its particular life style and define its particular character. Among them you will discover small gems, the places we call 'secret shopping', as well as easy solutions to ordinary or more difficult shopping problems. So, let's go shopping!...

In Athens, there is no single "shopping district". While this means that you'll have the fun of constantly discovering new spots, you should be aware of a few focal areas.

Patriarchou Ioakeim St., Kolonaki

Ora Kessaris, in Kifisia

Prada

Antonios Markos

Patriarchou Ioakeim: one of the city's finest shopping streets

Mageia

KOLONAKI

From the heart of the Athenian aristocracy and the meeting place of a closed elite, Kolonaki Square has slowly but surely transformed itself into a broad-based Babel of contemporary urban trend. Noisy, colourful, full of people at any hour of the day or night, it still retains intact its splendid and somewhat aloof character.

If you always want to be at the hub of things, if you like to shop and sightsee at the same time, if you're a child of the city and your adrenalin keeps pumping even when you're shopping, then Kolonaki is your kind of place. This is where the heart of Greek fashion beats, this is where it all happens, this is where life has a touch of Sex and the City. Choose a little table at Da Capo and sit down for a quick coffee in the company of some of the city's Very - or not so Very - Important People. Around the square, you'll see all the great Greek fashion houses. We always adore the very individual style of Charis & Angelos, the delicately feminine dresses chez Loukia, and the minimal Deux Hommes. Angelos Frentzos and Sofia Kokosalaki are still tops at Bettina's, while at Luisa's you'll be able to look

The key to enjoying shopping in Kolonaki is not to be rushed: here, a leisurely stroll, coffee and perhaps lunch are every bit as important as your actual purchases.

through the new lines from Cavali, Etro and Plein Sud.

Outside Everest, kids in wide designer jeans hang out, languidly flirting in their own idiom; at Vivliothiki, stylish ladies gossip over coffee. At Sotris you'll pick up something from Alexander McQueen, Comme des Garcons or Marni, while the new Rere Papa has clothes by Joseph Font and jewellery from Xenia Vitou. At Mahjong you'll find hand-tailored men's suits from Kiton, at Le Streghe son Tornate you'll select vintage accessories and at Mageia you'll discover the handbags by Kimonos & Kaos.

As you stroll along, you'll pass hurried businessmen talking animatedly into their hands-free and accompanied by super trendy girlfriends carrying designer shopping bags - they may well be models on their way to the next casting session, their books under their arms.

Moving on, you'll come to Marianna Petridi (progressive jewellery from Greek designers) and Gavello (his black diamonds are to die for). At the Feng Shui House you'll learn the secrets of Zen spatial design: Designers Guild has the most beautiful upholstery fabrics in the city. You'll eat at Maritsa's, along with some of the city's elite, or at the Sea Satin in

Angela Rapti

Lakis Gavalas

the winter (Saturday lunchtime, you may even find yourself dancing on the bar), or possibly at Kiku's for world-class sushi. Don't neglect the stores that you won't find elsewhere in the city. Choosing between the handbags at Louis Vuitton and those at Tod's is admittedly always difficult, while this year Lakis Gavalas presents his own line of clothes and accessories and has for you a waiting-list for a bag from Fendi. This section of the Guide will tell you all the little secrets of shopping in Kolonaki: where to order hand-made stilettos, for example, or where to find street wear from England, Turkey, Spain. So go for it - and have fun.

CIGARS

Casa del Habano
The temple of the cigar in Athens. The Balli company, Greece's exclusive importers of Cuban cigars, have the largest collection of Cuban cigars in the country plus, since this was the first Dunhill boutique in Athens, a wide selection of Dunhill accessories.
25, Voukourestiou St., 210/3608425. 258, Kifisias Ave., Neo Psychiko, 210/6773438-9.

Curivari
The paradise of non-Cuban cigars. Resident expert Andreas Throuvalas selects and imports some of the top brands from the Dominican Republic, Nicaragua and Honduras.
24, Kolokotroni St., Kifisia, 210/8088257.

Mefisto
Cigars and a variety of accessories, many of them imported by the owner, Mr Lampris, himself.
6, Xanthou St., Kolonaki, 210/7218084.

Rentzis
One of the oldest tobacconist's in Athens, where apart from shopping you can probably find the answers to any questions about the world of tobacco. Good selection of cigars (kept in a humidor) at accessible prices.
13, Ippokratous St., Stoa Operas, 210/3637122.

The Cigar
The busiest cigar store in Athens. Their humidor contains a very good selection of famous Cuban and Dominican cigars, plus some of the top brands from Nicaragua and Honduras.
21, Kanari St., Kolonaki, 210/3603725.

KOLONAKI
CLOTHES

Antonios Markos
21, Skoufa St.,
210/3623036.
Clothes and accessories for "cartoon" types, in a colourful, playful setting. The Paul Frank lines of (men's and women's) clothing and accessories with his trademark, the monkey. Jewellery from Antonios made with marbles and bottle caps and other assorted objects in extraordinary and striking combinations. The hat collection is fascinating.

Aslanis
16, Anagnostopoulou St. & Irakleitou, 210/3600049.
The blue-eyed boy of Greek fashion designs very feminine clothes for both evening and day wear. And if wedding bells should be in the offing, remember that Michalis has dressed many a VIP bride.

Bettina
4, Voukourestiou St.,
210/3238759.
Wonderful clothes selected with flair, and a faithful clientele who are now bringing their daughters. Here among other things you will find creations from Angelos Frentzos and Sofia Kokosalaki - chez Bettina they believe in Greek designers.

Boudoir
22, Anagnostopoulou St.,
210/3390966.
A breath of Mykonos in the heart of the city - the original shop was on the island of the winds. Playful and intensely feminine clothes and accessories plus, in the summer, swimsuits, pareo and fabulous beach sandals.

Caprice
21, Voukourestiou St.,
210/3630984.
Unpretentious shop known for years as a reliable source of women's wear, predominantly simple in line but always chosen with taste. Also elegant accessories, like the Nicky Sommers sandals that were the hit of summer 2002.

Carla G.
29, Anagnostopoulou St.,
210/3615032.
Understated and particularly elegant decor. Modern, stylish and very feminine clothes, for the up-to-the-minute, sexy woman who thrives on change. Prices more than reasonable.

Carouzos
12, Kanari St.,
210/3627123.
Synonymous with big name shopping. Men's and women's lines from Prada, Jil Sander, Fendi etc., plus distinctive accessories, shoes and bags. Impeccable service from the extremely polite staff. The hand-made shoes by John Lobb are a must.

Central Prince Oliver
3, Anagnostopoulou St.,
210/3645401.
The all-in-one shopper's delight. Clothes and accessories that perfectly reflect the fashion of today, and perhaps of tomorrow as well. For men and women, from Patrick Cox, Etro, Fake of London, Paul Smith, Kenzo, Alessandro del Aqua, Yohji Yamamoto, Issey Miyake to name just a few… Don't overlook the ties and cufflinks, or the accessories for women.

Christos Kostarelos
44, Charitos St.,
210/7228261.
Visit the atelier of one of Greece's most talented young designers for garments that do honour to Greek fashion at home and abroad. Clothes that flatter, without requiring a catwalk figure. The fluffy shawls are a very hot item.

Colori
3, Patriarchou Ioakeim St.,
210/7218158.
Casual chic in a sleek attractive environment that sets them off beautifully. All day clothes notable for their intelligent details and youthful style. We loved the vine leaf beach sandals from the summer accessories collection.

Costas Faliakos
53, Patriarchou Ioakeim St., 210/7229259.
Greek haute couture. Heavy evening wear, cut from costly materials, hand sewn and embroidered with beadwork and rhinestones, for very special occasions.

Deux Hommes
18, Kanari St.,
210/3614155.
Modern clothes, interesting lines, chosen with flair and attention.

Diesel
14 Tsakalof St.
The well-known jeans and T-shirts, sweatshirts, bouffant jackets, shoes and many other sportswear items. Youthful atmosphere, with a "made in USA" flavour.

DKNY
8, Solonos St.,
210/3603775.
A name that needs no introduction. A New York

dame who is passionate about clean lines and simple fabrics, with ideas for men and women who want easy-to-wear designer clothes.

Emporio Armani
4, Solonos & 5, Milioni St., 210/3389101.
Three floors dedicated to the luxury of absolute Italian style. Well-known clothes for men and women, simple in line and perfectly finished. On the ground floor, one of the best cafe-restaurants in Athens, with authentic Italian cuisine.

Enny di Monaco
18, Irodotou St., 210/7217215.
The Mecca of the trendy shopper. The kind of clothes and the accessories that you drool over in the fashion magazines and until recently could only find in London or New York. Designers like Luella, Luella, Adam Jones, Diane von Furstenberg, Cesare Fabbri, superb quality and taste, and a touch of eccentricity. Prices to match. And the accessories are worth a visit in themselves: designer faux, fabulous bags and shoes - the Christian Louboutin and Rodolphe Menudier are an absolute must.

Eponymo Via Solonos
33, Solonos St., 210/3629906.
An atmosphere of simple elegance, setting off collections from designers like Montana, Vivienne Westwood, Ferré, Genny, Gaultier, Michel Perry and the like. Winter highlight: cheap and chic Moschinos.

Ermenegildo Zegna
18, Skoufa St.
The famous Italian suits, synonymous with high quality and business chic. Superb pure wool and pure cashmere fabrics, always with the fine finishing touches that befit a truly great name.

Free Shop
75, Charitos St., 210/7290151.
Alternative modern ambience, for men's and women's clothes with real character - something between avant-garde and decontracte. Lines from (among others) Marcella, Day, Claude Pierlot, wonderful bags from Orla Kiely and accessories from Maria Calderara.

Harris & Agelos
19, Voukourestiou St., 210/3621060.
The Damon and Pheidias of Greek haute couture, in a harmonious partnership with the persistence of an expensive cologne. Charis Chourmouzis designs, Angelos Tasis looks after the … more technical aspects, and the ladies bless them both. Original clothes, costly fabrics, impeccable finishing and collections that would not be out of place on the most fashionable international catwalk.

Hugo Boss
19, Amerikis St., 210/3389080.
Blue chip men's wear, plus accessories, ties and watches. Hugo Boss caters for a wide range of tastes and fancies.

Kanari 5
5, Kanari St., 210/3392597.
Stylish new multishop, with clothes, shoes, accessories, jewellery, ornaments, cosmetics, CDs and occasional small pieces of furniture, all by top designers (Blumarine, Pinco Pallino, Byblos, Replay, Simonetta, Cavalli, Moschino, Primal, Calderara) and all sharing the same progressive aesthetic. Come in and indulge in the ultimate shopping therapy. And bring your daughters - there's plenty here for "little women" as well.

Katerina Stylianou
18, Anagnostopoulou St., 210/3626631.
Well-made modern clothes for all occasions for the bigger-than-life woman. Clothes with style and personality in sizes up to a European 56 (Greek 70), at prices that will come as a pleasant surprise.

Kathy Heyndels
21, Alopekis St., 210/7239780.
One of Greece's oldest fashion houses, still very popular, and now in the hands of the next generation. Classic clothes, and very interesting leather creations.

Kenzo Boutique
30, Tsakalof St., 210/3626044.
Trendy and full of character, like the eye-catching clothes in the window. Modern lines, but not overstated - clothes that whisper rather than shout.

Lakis Gavalas
50, Voukourestiou St. & Tsakalof, 210/3629785.
Lakis Gavalas is more than

Get to know ATHENS with

Would you like to know more about Athens? Explore its history? Enjoy its restaurants and nightlife? Or perhaps you simply want to shop? Just choose the way you want to spend your free time in the city and ... go right ahead.

Because whatever your choice, Alpha Bank is there. The Official Bank of the ATHENS 2004 Olympic Games has created for you the ATHENS 2004 VISA cards, credit and banking cards, so that you easily fulfil your wishes and enjoy unique "Olympic Privileges". Live a carefree life with the ATHENS 2004 VISA GOLD or the ATHENS 2004 VISA SILVER, and become a contributor of the ATHENS 2004 Olympic Games.

Choose the GOLD ATHENS 2004 VISA and enjoy «golden» privileges

- 9% Interest Rate. The lowest interest rate on the market today, applicable all through the card's validity (plus Law 128/75 contributions) and transfer of balances from other non-Alpha Bank cards.
- One-time subscription fee. The membership fee of € 350 covers not only the card's entire period of validity up until 31.12.2004, but also the fee on your next Alpha Bank card, of equal prestige, until 2008.
- Acquisition of an additional card at half the fee.
- A collector's Limited Edition Card. Only a limited number of Gold ATHENS 2004 VISA personal or corporate cards will be issued.
- Actual participation in the ATHENS 2004 Olympic Games. When you acquire a Gold ATHENS 2004 VISA, € 70 of your membership fee will be contributed to the Games. In addition, every time you use your card for purchases or services, the Bank will give approximately 25% of its income from the use of the card for this cause.
- "EPATHLON" Rewards Scheme. Through this programme, you can win authentic ATHENS 2004 products, "Olympic collectors items", tickets to the Games, unique goods and services.

ALPHA BANK OFFICIAL BANK

ΕΠΤΑΘΛΟΝ

Your ATHENS 2004 VISA card not only gives you freedom but also allows you to participate in the "EPATHLON" Rewards scheme, which has been designed exclusively for ATHENS 2004 VISA cardholders.

How does the programme work?

The programme works on the basis of "ATHLA"*, which you collect each time you use your ATHENS 2004 VISA Gold or Silver card to purchase goods or services. The more often you use your card, the more prizes you will win. "ATHLA" are also awarded for:

- delivery of your card
- transfer of balances from cards issued by other banks
- payment of card balances by standing order on your bank account
- recommendation of family members or friends for an ATHENS 2004 VISA Gold or Silver card, once the card is approved
- participation in special programmes and draws on landmark dates.

What can you win?

You can use your accumulated "ATHLA" to win:

- Authentic ATHENS 2004 products, such as men's, women's and children's wear, articles for home, kitchen, bathroom and office, accessories, jewellery and gift items.
- Collector's Olympic items that will be designed exclusively for you.
- Tickets for the ATHENS 2004 Olympic Games.
  This programme will be announced by the ATHENS 2004 Olympic Games Organising Committee, on the basis of declaration of interest and pre-purchase.
- Products and services with particularly favourable terms - just for you - in collaboration with other sponsors or firms.

For more information about the "EPATHLON" Rewards Scheme, call the "EPATHLON" Rewards Scheme Customer Service Bureau at 801 111 2004.

* Athlon, plural athla, noun, neuter [contracted from the Homeric aethlon: prize of contest]: prize awarded to the victor in an athletic competition.

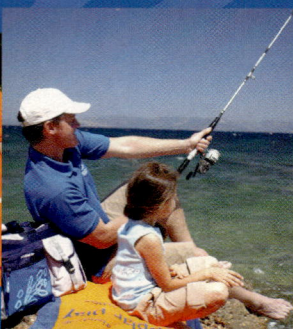

ALPHA BANK OFFICIAL BANK OF THE ATHENS 2004 OLYMPIC GAMES

a cult fashion figure: he is also a trend setter. Progressive clothes, chosen with taste, imagination and a touch of sauciness, from famous designers like Cavalli, Yves Saint Laurent, Missoni, Fendi, Burberry's, Miu Miu. He will also put your name on a waiting list for sold-out must-haves like Fendi's "baguette" and "croissant" bags.

Liana Camba
26-28, Anagnostopoulou St., 210/3641027.
Feminine clothes, airy fabrics, flattering lines and original designs. Clothes chosen by a woman who likes women and knows how to cleverly hide the little imperfections and highlight the hot spots.

Loukia
24, Kanari St. (1st floor), 210/3627334.
Famous for her totally feminine clothes and fabulous wedding gowns. Airy lines with a good dose of romanticism, soft fabrics that hug the body lovingly, hand sewn creations that are a hymn to womanhood.

Louis Feraud
4, Xanthou St., 210/7215789.
Classic shop, one of the oldest in the area, presenting year in year out the newest collections of clothes and accessories from the famous French fashion house.

Luisa
17, Skoufa St., 210/3635600.
A shop that doesn't merely offer fashion, but makes a statement about absolute style. Expensive clothes,

specifically selected for her chosen clientele. Collections of Cavalli, Pucci, Missoni, Etro and Plein Sud. True worth. The Kolonaki shop is the largest and most stylish, and carries complete collections from all the fashion houses.

Mahjong
14, Kanari St., 210/3622860.
Its highlight are the outstanding Kiton suits: unique fabrics, impeccable Italian tailoring, costly linings, astounding finishing and waiting lists all over the world. And if the suit you choose needs any alterations, you can pick it up just a few hours later - there is always a tailor on standby in the shop. Also Joop shirts, Windsor overcoats and car shoes.

Max Mara
19, Kanari St., 210/3602142.
Classic clothes in subdued colours, with the emphasis on quality fabrics and impeccable finishing. Also a few more modern pieces, but the absolute investment here is an all time classic coat.

Mohnblumchen
7, Dexamenis Sq. & Spefsippou, 210/7236960.
The heart and soul of this place is Katerina (a familiar figure in Kolonaki's better-known day & night spots), who chooses progressive sports clothes (New York Industry, Costume National), fabulous jeans (men's and women's) and accessories for both that give just the right touch of distinctive difference to any outfit.

Paul & Shark
6, Anagnostopoulou St., 210/3392334.
Elegantly designed and maintained, classic decor in shades of blue and dark wood. Full designer line for men who like classic sports clothes. Exceptional quality, wide variety, sizes up to 4XL.

Rere Papa
62, Skoufa St., 0977693410.
Renata Papazoglou and Rebecca Papastavrou channelled all their flair and enthusiasm into this exceptionally elegant shop, which has really taken off with its collection of creations from young English, Finnish and Spanish designers (Joseph Font, Ivana Helsinki and Patrick Sweeney among others). Complement them with jewellery from Xenia Vitou and gorgeous Italian shoes.

Sofos
5, Anagnostopoulou St., 210/3618713.
A shop that veered away from its classic tradition a few years ago to follow a more modern line. Clothes that tread a nice balance between the trendy and the comme il faut, giving even those whose sartorial preferences tend to the conventional a decided air of fashion.

Sotris
30, Anagnostopoulou St., 210/3639281.
Thanos Sotiropoulos was one of the first to bring the trend concept to Athens,

Shopping

many years ago. All the hottest fashion names parade through his windows: Voyage, Prada, Miu Miu, McQueen, Marni, Joseph, Comme des Garçons, Diego Dolcini, Ghost, Dolce e Gabanna and AngelosFrentzos. If you're wise you'll pay him a visit at the beginning of the season to see what's in the wind.

Spicy Cookie
0938973995.
Fabulous hand-painted shirts, trousers and bouffant jackets, with designs inspired from films, music, books and great love stories. Kelly Stamouli, a lawyer by trade, has raised her hobby to a fine art; and her unique creations have taken London by storm, selling in the Golden Kiosk boutique at the Sanderson Hotel for prices in the £800-1000 range!

Stenia
9, Kanari St., 210/3627697.
Uncluttered modern space, friendly ambience, impeccable service, reasonable prices, Matoula's unerring instinct and lots of people, in one of the hottest shops in the area.
Clothes from Juicy Culture, Paper Denim, Age, Dice Kayak and Cyuso, accessories from Dior Jewellery, Streets Ahead and Phorms. Two particularly interesting lines from "ex's": Venera Arapou, who designed the Chloe collection before Stella McCartney, and Gaowei+Xin Zhan, formerly of Gaultier.

T-Store
15, Tsakalof St., 210/3619743.

The Trussardi store with clothes from the designer's collection and the trendy accessories that we all love. Sporting the famous whippet trademark and in defiance of the times, a little leather bag or a metal cigar case with a wooden lid is a gift that is always appreciated.

The Martin's
7, Dexamenis St., 210/3614690.
Casual items from designers like Blumarine and D&G, fabulous jeans and T-shirts from Goldings, cheerful feminine clothes from Homeles and other interesting stuff.

This n' That
7, Leventi St., 210/7293790.
In this veritable bazaar of a shop, redolent of faraway places, you will find handmade garments and accessories from India, Peru, Thailand and Africa. Bags, pareos, scarves, sandals and caftans in wonderful colours, for ethnic fashion fans.

Tokyo Life
6, Xanthou St., 210/7299366.
Colourful shop, walls plastered with comics and graffiti - there's an air of London about the place. Young casuals from Miss Sixty, Energie and Custo, original T-shirts with Buddhist Punk prints.

Trade Shop
29, Skoufa St., 210/3603264. 52, Patision St., 210/8826054. e-mail: info@trade.com.gr
Provocative window display, and collections of new gen-

eration extreme that you simply won't find - under one roof - anywhere else. Check out the Miss Sixty (full collection), Energie, fantastic Michico Koshino jeans, must-have Royal Elastics, Mambo, Ra.Re, Religion and saucy Meltin' Pot, amid a treasure house of accessories with a London air about them. There is a second Trade Shop at

Yiorgos Elefteriades
38, Pindarou St., 210/3615278.
Another of the young Greek designers that are doing us proud. Beautifully designed clothes, easy and very feminine, with a progressive stylishness.

Zara
13, Tsakalof St., 210/3638677.
Clothes inspired by the great designers at very affordable prices, popularising styles that were once addressed to a select few. Like all the other stores in the chain, this one too carries lines for men, women and children.

STOCK
After Season
42, Pindarou St., 210/3640445.
"After Season" Genny, Donna Karan and Moschino, at enticing prices.

Enny di Monaco
8, Alopekis St., 210/7229075.
Off-season remainders from the Psychiko and Kolonaki stores, at up to 50% discounts.

Escada Stock
33, Tsakalof St.,

210/3613918.
In-store stock, in the basement. Unique bargains and discounts up to 70%.

Luisa Stock
17, Skoufa St.,
210/3646079.
60% discount on remainders from last year's lines. Some real bargains, especially in shoes and handbags.

Nine Below
9, Karneadou St.,
210/7233949.
Second hand store where you'll find authentic Levi 501s, leather jackets, suede shirts and fantastic '60s and '70s coats.

Sotris Stock
30, Leventi St.,
210/7223686.
Clothing and accessories for men and women from past

lines and odd sizes at half price. The discount is rather less than at some other similar stores, but it's still worth taking a look.

LINGERIE

Aerakis Exclusive
18, Anagnostopoulou St.,
210/3635957.
Athens' best known and most elegant lingerie shop. Cobwebby laces, silk negligees, matching feathered mules, leggings in all colours and designs, swimsuits and ski socks (the ones with the multi-coloured toes).

La Perla Boutique
14, Spefsippou St.,
210/7299720.
Lingerie for all occasions - romantic, sensual, sporty or sexy. In this super-luxurious shop (the opening was

attended by famous "Druna" designer Milo Manara), you will find the company's complete line of innerwear, including nighties and swimsuits.

Nota
17, Akadimias St.,
210/3606163.
Nighties, dressing gowns and underwear in classic lines and exceptionally fine quality. Gorgeous sets, flowered pyjamas, comfortable undies and lovely slippers.

Secret Elements
Xanthou & 2, Spefsippou St., 210/3625558.
Elegant new boutique with a fine selection of cheerful innerwear and swimwear from Okay Brazil and Cores do Sol.

Sine Qua Non
25, Patr.Ioakeim St.,
210/7292537.
The most expensive kinky and sexy underwear in Athens, in a tasteful doll's house of a shop. Don't look for anything ordinary - the laces and microscopic strings and outrageous colours point directly to absolute style for intimate moments.

CHILDREN'S
Frattina
21, Kanari St.,
210/3610262.
Ultra chic children's clothes for designer tots. DKNY jackets, shoes with attitude, swimsuits and accessories for junior socialites.

Jack in the box
13, Charitos St. &
Loukianou, 210/7258735.
Fairytale name and fairytale merchandise, enough to enchant any small person. A very good place to shop for gifts.

Mothercare
23, Voukourestiou St.,
210/8087325.
Clothes for children of 0 to 10, and for mothers-to-be. Also baby needs, small toys, shoes for tots, even baptismal gifts.

SHOES - BAGS
Aigner
25, Voukourestiou St.,
210/3647983.
Leather goods with the trademark horseshoe, silk scarves, and clothes for those who insist on classic style.

Angela Rapti
36, Voukourestiou St.
(mezzanine), 210/3535445.
Paradise for shoe maniacs. Choose your style and colour, and Angela will assure a perfect fit, in anything from a dressy pump to a beach sandal. Also bags and distinctive accessories.

Gucci
5, Tsakalof St., shopping centre Melathron,
210/3602280.
Italian style, dreamy clothes and accessories, in one of the hottest shopping spots in town - men and women yield to temptation here without the slightest struggle.
The famous shoes crafted out of velvety soft leather are synonymous with absolute desire.

Kalogirou
4, Patriarchou Ioakeim St.,
210/7297960.
There can't be anyone who has never shopped once, or at least window-shopped, at Kalogirou. Men's and women's shoes from Prada, Tod's, Ungaro, Miu Miu and other equally sensational names. Just remember that if you see something you like, buy it, because it probably won't be there tomorrow.

Left
1, Leventi St.,
210/7238937.
Shoes with attitude, for the young crowd and those who want something different. Summer sandal shoppers will have a terrible time choosing among all the fabulous styles by Ioannis Alexopoulos.

Longchamp
7, Tsakalof St.,
210/3637552.
An historic name in leather goods. In recent years there have been some delightful surprises, like the design-it-yourself bag, where the customer puts together her own colours and styles.

Louis Vuitton
19, Voukourestiou St.,
210/3613938.
From handbags and luggage to accessories, his leather goods have long been an international status symbol. The pleasure of buying the bag of your dreams and carrying it home in its soft cotton case is beyond price. And the elegant brown gift box with the discreet LV logo is sure to elicit an enthusiastic response from your favourite people.

MCM
12, Milioni St.,
210/3646460.
German leather goods, monogrammed handbags and luggage. Cosmopolitan luxury and quality.

Nine West
Filikis Etaireias Sq. &
Tsakalof, 210/3387650.
The answer to the excruciatingly expensive Italian and French designers. Stylish youthful shoes from the famous firm, at very reasonable prices. This is how to always be in fashion without mortgaging your future.

Petridis
6, Kolonakiou Sq.,
210/7238434.
Men's and women's shoes from Parallele, Camper, Charles Jourdan and many other names, in one of the city's perennial favourites. The house lines are also very interesting, crafted in classic styles out of beautiful leathers.

Preview
19, Patriarchou Ioakeim
St., 210/7224731.

SIZES
14
UP TO
32

KATERINA STYLIANOU

NEO PSYCHIKO: 20, EL. VENIZELOU Str. Tel. 010 6748921-2 Fax: 010 6712876
KOLONAKI: 15-17 ANAGNOSTOPOULOU Str. Tel./Fax: 010 3626631
GLYFADA: 7, I. METAXA Str. - "CORNER" SHOPPING CENTER (2nd Floor) Tel./Fax: 010 8940129
Monday, Wednesday, Saturday 10:00 - 15:00 Tuesday, Thursday, Friday 10:00 - 20:30 (Continuous)

For alternative footwear. Creations from Kallisté, Clergerie, Menudier and other eccentric designers. Season to season, this is where the drummer for the lower extremities beats most forcefully. So fall in step!

Tod's Boutique
13, Voukourestiou St., 210/3392200.
The familiar soft leather shoes with studded soles, in their original version. Entirely hand sewn, from leathers so soft you'll hardly realise you're wearing them. Classic timeless value.

ACCESSORIES

Ananda
17, Pindarou St., 210/3616376.
Large variety of faux bijoux and accessories in semi-precious stones and silver as well as humbler materials - a mosaic of colours you won't be able to resist.

Bianca Verti
34, Voukourestiou St., 210/3638812.
Superbly designed Italian faux, always in the swing of international fashion. Creations from Armani and other famous fashion houses that you've admired in foreign Vogue magazines.

Cravatterie Nazionali
5, Valaoritou St., 210/3620996.
The temple of the silk tie, hallmark of the well-dressed man. This tiny shop is a veritable treasure house of select items signed Armani, Trussardi, Valentino, Ferré, Versace, Calvin Klein and the like. Our information is that its patrons include such well-known newscasters as Nikos Chatzinikolaou and Terence Quick.

Eccentrics
59, Skoufa St. & Matzarou, 210/3646055.
Colourful shop, full of scent and music, reflecting the flair and enthusiasm of owner Stella Pournatzi. Jewellery and accessories with personality, from France, Spain, Belgium and Greece.

Furla
8, Patriarchou Ioakeim St., 210/7216154.
Superb Italian bags, accessories with character, silver jewellery with hearts, stars and moons, and beautiful key chains. The little coin purses for euros with the lion or mouse faces on them are a must.

Galia
14, Tsakalof St., 210/3637475.
The Mecca of alternative accessory shopping. The main theme, for years now, has been the hair slides and clips in an unimaginable variety of colours and designs. Also small bags, scarves, faux bijoux.

Le Streghe Son Tornate
9, Charitos St., 210/3233555.
A very special shop, where you will find not only distinctive jewellery and accessories but also clothes. And all of them vintage. Browse to your heart's content and discover treasures seemingly made just for you.

Lito
25, Irodotou St., 210/7295177.
An open studio where you can find some of the season's most beautiful pieces of jewellery. Semi-precious stones in fabulous designs and combinations, for truly unique outfits.

Mad Hat
23, Skoufa St., 210/3387343.
Hats, woollen caps, bags, scarves, gloves, beach sandals, accessories for all seasons in fabulous designs and colours. And at very reasonable prices.

Mageia
18, Charitos St., 210/7240697.
Ileana Makri's impressive and recently redecorated boutique is a treasure house of lovely pieces of jewellery, gorgeous bags, accessories (for men and women) and supremely decorative objets d'art. Whatever you do, don't miss the fabulous bags from Kimonos & Kaos and the gorgeous Michael Stars tops. And the Elena Syraka creations are always favourites with us.

Penny Papadopoulou
1, Irakleitou St., 210/3629952.
Her hats are famous, her accessories selected with imagination and flair. In this lovely little shop you are bound to find just what you need to give that final touch to your outfit and make you feel like a star.

JEWELLERY - WATCHES

Arsenis
13, Voukourestiou St., 210/3633057.
Unique pieces of jewellery, distinctive for their austerity of line and for the purity of the gemstones that ornament them.

Bvlgari
8A, Voukourestiou St., 210/3247118.

MISS SIXTY®

'EN⊖RGIE®

Exclusive Store / 29, Skoufa str. Kolonaki / tel.: 210 3603264

Jewellery of gold and semi-precious stones, the trademark look of the international fashion house. Also watches and leather accessories, including bags, briefcases and diaries with ornate silver fasteners.

Cartier
3, Stadiou St.,
210/3235727.
The epitome of French chic in watches, jewellery and accessories. Here you will find all Cartier's new lines (and some older ones as well), or you may just bring your watch in for cleaning. In any case, just looking in the windows is pure temptation.

Dafnomilis Megas
14, Valaoritou St. (1st floor), 210/3639578.
Atelier with a luxurious showcase salon and a 50-year tradition in jewellery. Modern designs. The adjacent area is devoted exclusively to cufflinks in gold and platinum for day and evening wear.

Elena Votsi
7, Xanthou St.,
210/3600936.
Large, striking and unique pieces of jewellery, in shapes inspired by the curves of the human body and the materials used by the designer. Gold and semi-precious stones (for the most part) blend harmoniously in stunning creations.

Fanourakis
23, Patriarchou Ioakeim St., 210/7211762.
Jewellery with real character - most unlikely to go unremarked. Designs in gold and platinum with dia-

ANTIQUES & SECOND-HAND DEALERS

Alexandra Sapountzi
Atmospheric shop full of rare china and glass, old doors and shutters, hand-painted wooden panels. Check out the authentic signs from old shops and cafes.
50, Solonos St., Kolonaki, 210/3631949.

Ellie Konortou
Large shop full of furniture and antiques that will take you back to the early 20th century. One-of-a-kind pieces from England and from old Greek houses (nothing later than 1950), old silver plate flatware, lamps and small ornaments, in a very veritable treasure house of an antique shop.
218, Mesogeion Ave., Cholargos, 210/6544252.

Gallery Zoumboulaki
Old furniture and objets and contemporary works of art. A combination that for years has made the Zoumboulaki Gallery one of the top places for antiques and collector's art. New merchandise arrives constantly and inexhaustibly from all over the world: candlesticks, china, amber beads, silver, antique furniture, refectory tables, embroideries, authentic pieces that have stood the test of time, all unique and constantly changing.
26, Charitos St., Kolonaki, 210/7252488.

Giannoukos
2-4, Amalias St., Syntagma Sq., 210/3232220.
French, Italian, Greek, Austrian (mostly) and the occasional English piece of furniture, in a shop that is considered one of the best and most knowledgeable in Athens. You will doubtless find lamps and dinner ware and some jewellery here, but the bulk of the merchandise is antiques from Central Europe, genuine pieces and very well preserved.

Goutis
No antique furniture here but instead you will find old Greek jewellery and other articles of exceptional quality and rarity. Goutis has been mining Greek history since 1934, his prices are eminently fair, and most pieces are 19th century. The attractive gift boxes and the weight of the Goutis name in the world of antique objects guarantee a gift that is certain to be appreciated.
10, Dimokritou St., Kolonaki, 210/3613557.

Mimis Tzilalis
One of the city's best known antiquaries, with a long family tradition in the business. After thirty years at "Monastiraki tis Kifisias" and the Society of Greek Auctioneers, Mimis Tzilalis has created a new and very atmospheric space in the old "Anatolia" carpet factory, where he sells (and auctions) antiques and works of art: furniture, vases, porcelain, objets, paintings. It was Mimis Tzilalis who auctioned the items that belonged to Dora Stratou and Eleftherios Venizelos.
2, Vyzantiou St. & Arganon, Kalogreza, 210/6777947.

monds and semi-precious stones that look like ribbons, in bows or gracefully suspended. All unique and all so beautiful it's almost impossible to choose among them.

Folli Follie
25, Solonos St., 210/3632487.
The shop that made gold and silver combos a fashion item. Now the windows display costlier pieces in gold, ethnic lines in silver and semi-precious stones, and superlative accessories

including bags, watches and silk shawls.

Ilias Lalaounis
6, Panepistimiou St. & Voukourestiou, 210/3610645.
The ambassador-at-large of Greek jewellery. The displays in the windows always include, among many other things, some of the gorgeous pieces based on designs from ancient Greek jewellery. The new generation is now making its own mark with similar success.

Jaloux
6, Tsakalof St. & Anagnostopoulou, 210/3638518.
Zircon-studded silver and silver-gold combos, watches and accessories. Alternative fashions in excellent taste and at prices for every pocket.

Kassis
Stadiou & Voukourestiou, 210/3229382.
The harmonious pairing of two great international names. Choose a piece by De Grisogono, set with black diamonds, or from

To Palio Sentouki tou Manthou
An unusual kind of a place, but with a special charm of its own. Small, and absolutely crammed with chests and desks and lamps, as well as china dinner services, old glass and ink wells. An enticing jumble of one-of-a-kind pieces that attracts the collector like a bee to nectar.
14, Ymittou St., Cholargos, 210/6548499.

Peggy Loutou
Peggy Loutou, the store's heart and soul, is a licensed antique dealer. Old engravings, authentic paintings, decorative and useful articles all personally selected, in a shop of equal interest to the collector and the art lover alike.
56, Perikleous St., Cholargos, 210/6544117.

Quelchemanca
"Quelchemanca" means "what are you missing?". An absolutely fascinating shop in Kolonaki, with many genuine antiques from the 19th century (Murano, Muller, Limoges, etc.), mostly art deco and art nouveau: occasional furniture, ornaments, china pieces, old tiles, etc. Most of the furniture comes from Venice.
26, Kleomenous St., Kolonaki, 210/7251876.

Stavros Michalarias Art
The building in Alopekis Street is a real magnet for lovers of antique objets d'art. Art

appraiser Stavros Michalarias assembles Byzantine collections, genuine articles and pieces of furniture whose creators, age and origin are documented - many of them in fact are signed. This is where VIPS from the world of politics and the arts come when they want a very special gift with a history of its own.
1, Alopekis St., Kolonaki, 210/7237838, 210/7213079.

Tania Dimitriadi
Make an appointment with Tania and let her introduce you to the world of batik. Silks dyed in wonderful patterns and colours using this difficult technique create unique art-to-wear garments.
4, Daskalogianni St., 210/6460987.

To Palaiopoleion
One of Kolonaki's most centrally located, oldest and most authoritative antique shops. If you're looking for antique French or Greek furniture, you will probably come to Kostas Katsianos in Irodotou Street; but what he is best known for is old porcelain ware: plates, whole or partial dinner sets, old fashioned Limoges breakfast sets, canisters, wash basins and jugs complement the furniture and occasional pieces. He also has an interesting collection of valuable small perfume bottles.
18, Irodotou St., Kolonaki, 210/7243922.

one of Chopard's beautiful lines with their suspended diamond creations - but it won't be easy to make up your mind between them.

Katerina Lolou
10, Lykavittou St.,
210/3630337.
More an atelier than a shop, in atmosphere. Unique pieces, hand-crafted from gold and semi-precious stones, with the stamp of creative artistry, and beautiful wreaths of tiny silver flowers.

Kessaris
7, Panepistimiou St.,
210/3310600.
Athenian high society's favourite bijoutier. The best diamonds in the city, set in white gold in unique designs, and wonderful lines in pearls and precious stones.

Liana Vourakis
32, Anagnostopoulou St.,
210/3617705.
The loveliest silver baptismal gifts in Athens, tied up with colourful silk ribbons.
Rattles, rocking horses, hearts, boxes and many other ideas for the bonbonniere mementoes of your little angel's christening day.

Loggetta
6, Leventi St.,
210/7226679.
An unusual little shop, kept by Anna Skiadaresi and Nikos Dilaverakis, who create lovely designs in dull gold and decorate them with sapphires, tourmalines and aquamarines.

Marianna Petridi
34, Charitos St.,
210/7217789.

More a gallery than a jewellery shop. In addition to the owner's own designs, you will also find pieces by other jewellers (Katerina Anesti, Christina Dara, Maria Mastori, Vasilis Vasileiou, Paola Lakah, La Luna και Par). Different styles, same good taste. We loved the amusing play-with pins by Abbot & Ellwood.

Ora Kessaris
5A, Panepistimiou St.,
210/3310600.
Heaven for watch maniacs. From costly articles by Frank Muller and Harry Winston to trendy pieces from Ikepod and Locman, you're bound to find a watch to suit your fancy - and your pocket.

Pentheroudakis
19, Voukourestiou St.,
210/3613187.
Solid classic jewellery, set with precious stones for impressive outings. One of the oldest jewellers in Athens, and it has lost none of its image or prestige.

Rinaldo Gavello
5, Neofytou Douka St.,
210/7258101.
The famous Italian designer has created a jewel of a shop in which to display his new lines, set with brown diamonds. Or for a more summery style, choose something with turquoise or rose quartz.

Rolex
1, Kolokotroni St.,
210/3227053.
Swiss mechanisms, heavy gold bracelets (preferably) and diamond-studded faces - still a status symbol in the world of watches.

Swatch Center
8, Kapsali St.,
210/7248307.
The most hippy and trendy watches in the world renew the date with their fans with every changing season. Select your watch and then pair it with distinctive matching accessories.

OPTICAL
Laskaris
3, Kolonakiou Sq.,
210/3645929.
Large variety of eyeglasses and sunglasses, in classic lines. Armani, Versace, RayBan and other top names. Do try the coloured contact lenses - who knows, green eyes might be just your style.

Mark Aalen
5-7, Skoufa St.,
210/3617987.
Young style, and thousands of frames on display - pick up and try on whatever appeals to you. There's bound to be something to suit, for they carry all the big names: Calvin Klein, DKNY, D&G, Oakley, Chloe, Escada, Gucci, Valentino, Ray Ban, Dior, Prada, Celine, etc.

Stavrou
20, Kanari St.,
210/3616417.
One of the largest opticians in Athens. Frames from Chanel, Gucci, Prada, Max Mara, Byblos, Armani, Celine, Moschino, D&G. You can also find featherlight titanium reading glasses here, from Air.

THIS & THAT
Elements
53, Deinokratous St. &

Marasli, 210/7228688. Modern art house, with all kinds of options. You can look at the exhibitions in the new artists gallery, take in a plastic arts event, relax over coffee while leafing through the art books and magazines, or visit the all-about-art gift shop on the mezzanine level, with original gift ideas created by the exhibiting artists.

Omnia Armandos Moustakis
7, Xanthou St., 210/3608242.
The ultimate in gadgetry, in a shop where everything has a touch of humour about it. From the collector's radios and coffee mugs to the key chains and bookmarks, everything is designed to relieve a little

of the tedium of everyday routine.

Paper Shop
14, Al. Soutsou St., 210/3632654.
Occasional furniture, ornaments and useful articles, all made of paper - and recycled paper at that - for people with taste and an ecological conscience. Also super desk items, diaries, writing paper, greeting cards, etc.

HOUSEWARES

Carousel
21B, Loukianou St., 210/7293513.
Ornaments and occasional pieces, chosen with flair in a shop with character for shoppers of discernment. The Venetian masks are a must.

Designers Guild
29, Tsakalof St., 210/3619226.
Discover the colourful world of Tricia Guild. The famous designer, who draws her inspiration from the colours and the scents of Tuscany, has upholstery fabrics, wallpapers and household linens in strong designs and bright colours - to fill your rooms with light and cheerful optimism.

Gata pou ti lene Uccello
19, Al.Soutsou St., 210/3642246.
Ornaments and occasional pieces, chosen with imagination and exceptionally fine taste, to give your home a very special atmosphere. Wonderful wooden furniture, amazing lamps, pieces reminiscent of Wales,

Cornwall, Tuscany as well as ethnic items.

Giannis Deloudis Objet
3-5, Spefsippou St., 210/7235684.
Unique collection of useful and decorative articles for the home from the great international houses and designers. Don't miss the art de la table lines, with superb china and crystal and sensational flatware.

Ikia
5, Loukianou St. & Ypsilantou, 210/7245749.
Bath and kitchen shop, with a good collection of ornamental items. We particularly liked the dishes and glasses, the design fans, the coconut straw mats, the wonderful bathroom scales and the pretty aluminium lamps.

Kyros Interiors
23, Irodotou St., 210/7251136.
Wide variety of upholstery fabrics, curtains and carpets. The in-store experts are there to help you choose.

Lalique
11, Voukourestiou St., 210/3610645.
Famous French glassware to grace your home and … your evening out! Yes, that's right, crystal jewellery for an out-of-this-world style.

Meli Interiors
41, Voukourestiou St., 210/3609324.
Integrated solutions for interiors with character. From garden furniture and cushions to ornaments and wallpapers with matching borders - and it all comes with expert advice from experienced decorators.

Oikos
26, Irodotou St., 210/7231350.
Occasional furniture, CD cases, small hippy console tables, useful and ornamental articles with an air of gadgetry for the house and design gifts for friends with a sense of humour.

Olas
42, Sina St., 210/3627829.
Colourful shop with a strong ethnic element and carefully selected objets for the home. Ideas from every corner of the world just waiting for you to choose the one that best suits your own particular style.

Pavillon Christofle
5, Koumpari St., 210/3620483.
A famous house with a long history. Splendid silver flatware patterns, themselves an ornament to any table, silver serving pieces, fabulous porcelain dinnerware from Christian Dior and Lacroix.

Room Service
33, Irodotou St., 210/7230629.
Design ornaments and occasional pieces for the home. Spare geometric shapes and clear strong colours for the wallpaper style so beloved of late of the Greek stylists.

Rouga
3, Dexamenis Sq., 210/3605954.
Unique hand crafted lamps, as beautiful as they are functional, created with flair and imagination by owners Giorgos and Roula.

Studio E Creations
4, Irodotou St., 210/7225886.
A shop that looks like it was beamed straight in from London. Useful articles, many of them in rattan that would be right at home in the cupboards of a little cottage in Wales.

Virginia Ventouraki
5, Tsakalof St., shopping centre Melathron, 210/6450773.
No introduction needed. All Philippe Starck's an Alessi gadgets, for a house full of colour, humour and alternative attitude. For the gourmet, a super line of pots and pans, but at these prices you'd almost expect them to do the cooking for you. Note the dwarf tables and the iron wheel CD stand.

BOOKSHOPS - STATIONERY

Elpinor
5, Irakleitou St., 210/3606781.
A different sort of bookshop, quite unlike the impersonal department store type place. After years in Milioni Street, now in new quarters in Irakleitou. As you go down the three steps into the shop, you are greeted by the smell of paper and the wonderful feel of a traditional bookshop. Browse, leaf through books at leisure, chat with the owner, and experience the real joy of reading.

Libro
8, Patriarchou Ioakeim St., 210/7247116.
This small but elegant bookshop/publisher has Greek and foreign titles in all fields, selected with real flair. Their strongest point is the very interesting collection of art books and periodicals upstairs, making this a gathering place for art lovers.

Ermou St.

HISTORIC CENTRE

This is the warm and vital heart of the city, and an area where past and present mingle sweetly: every street, every laneway has its own history. Charged with memories and redolent of ages long past, a stroll through the historic centre of Athens is in itself a real event.

Forget the fumes, the horns and the stress for a moment, and let yourself be won over by the human mosaic of people from every race on earth, the dynamic new stores and the little old shops carrying their decades of history. In this kind of district, of course, shopping has many faces. We have opted to emphasize the alternative dimension, since you can do your designer shopping in Kolonaki, while Monastiraki and Plaka are degenerating into mere tourist attractions. Here, then, you'll find spices of every kind, curious accessories from the four corners of the world, "treasures" in hidden nooks and crannies. And you'll relax over coffee while leafing through an interesting book. At Out of Africa you'll choose accessories and clothes with an ethnic flavour, at Apriati you'll drool over unique pieces of gold or silver jewellery and then cross the road to the little cafe with the umbrellas for a quick espresso. At Mitropoleos 31 you'll discover a genuine book-lover's dream, while at Tilt you'll find contemporary and collectible comics. At Neon you'll sample oriental ice creams, at

Aiolis you'll enjoy a light lunch, and a chance to watch would-be TV stars in pre-casting for the upcoming season's shows. At Mac you'll buy cosmetics, knowing that the proceeds will go to help combat AIDS, while at Petratos you'll order made-to-measure men's shirts at exceptional prices. As you cross Stadiou St., take a look at the old Army Pension Fund Building that, as we write, is being converted into a new shopping centre - the buzz is that it's going to have some seriously up-scale stores, such as Chanel and Bvlgari, as well as a Galeries Lafayette. Stadiou is rapidly becoming one of the city's most vital shopping streets, as its old buildings are being restored and leased to several very interesting tenants.

By this time you'll probably have worked up an appetite, so you'd better head for Savvas' for one of the best souvlakis in town, or perhaps to Bairaktaris, just next door, for super traditional cooked dishes. Ready to continue? On to Spiliopoulos, then, where you'll practically join battle for a pair of stilettos (but when they tell you the price you'll agree it was worth it), or to Closet, for street wear from Mambo, Buddhist Punk and Gusto. In this section of the Guide we will also try to answer some of your questions: Where can I buy genuine vintage clothes? Have a pair of shoes made for me? Find collectible tin soldiers? Just look in the Guide, and you're on your way.

The stylish pedestrian precinct of Ermou Street is traditionally the place where the commercial pulse of the city beats most strongly.

Strolling along Ermou St.

Closet

HISTORIC CENTRE

CLOTHES

Artisti Italiani
22, Ermou St.,
210/3313857.
Greek fashion with an Italian air. Beautifully finished, uncluttered clothes for a trendy made-in-Greece style.

La Stampa
44, Perikleous St.,
210/3316775.
Now with the entire collection, which used to be broken up among different stores. Feminine clothes, with flattering lines that artfully conceal any little imperfections. Very reasonable prices.

Lucifair
53, Ermou St.,
210/3217052.
Stylish women's clothes that manage to be both trendy and easy to wear, day or evening.

Lussile
37, Ermou St.,
210/3215615.
Clothes for women who love fashion but want to adapt it to their own personal style. Fine quality and finishing, sizes for real-life women, interesting accessories.

Petratos
12, Nikiou St.,
210/3233230.
Tailor-made shirts for men who pay attention to every detail of their appearance. Variety of fabrics in different qualities, patterns and colours, fabulous finishing, extra collars and cuffs, mother-of-pearl buttons, monogrammed pockets for real elegance.

Replay Stores
53, Ermou St.,
210/3245217.
American style store with the entire Replay range of clothes and footwear. For men, women and children who go for casual sportswear.

Strongylos
25, Stadiou St.,
210/3229493.
One of the oldest stores in Athens. Tradition, classic style and quality in men's and women's wear that includes Burberry lines of clothing and sumptuous cashmere sweaters.

Tsantilis
23-25, Ermou St.,
210/3239401
Part of the history of Athens. Dressmaker fabrics of superb quality and patterns for clothes that you usually admire in shop windows. And upstairs, ladies' wear for clients who insist on classic style and values.

Zara
9, Ermou St.,
210/3252579.
Designer-inspired clothes at very affordable prices, opening a once-select market to the general population. All stores in the chain carry men's, women's and children's lines.

VINTAGE CLOTHING

American Market
19, Sofokleous St.
The first and best second-hand clothing store in Athens. With a little rummaging, you'll unearth authentic Levi 501s, leather and suede jackets and all sorts of other treasures.

Vintage Clothing Sale
29A, Agiou Markou St. (2nd floor), 210/3216337.
Genuine vintage clothes, exactly the same as those pictured in the fashion magazines, just waiting for you to come and discover them. The prices are a pleasant surprise.

STOCK

Berlin
59B, Kolokotroni St.,
210/3245602.
Recently moved from Miltiadou Street into these bigger and brighter premises. Clothes and accessories from Prada, Moschino, Exte, Chanel, Calvin Klein and

top foreign boutiques, at prices that are more than affordable.

Kalogirou
12, Pandrosou St., 210/3356410.
Shoes from famous houses that are sold in designer boutiques. Ends of lines and odd sizes, at extraordinarily low prices. There can't help but be something for you!

SPORTING GOODS
Nike Exclusive Stores
54, Ermou St., 210/3317017.
Paradise for the athletic shopper, in a super-stylish store that stocks sizes from 0 to XXXL. They have everything here, from microscopic infant trainers to gym gear in all possible styles and colours, for outfits that make a statement in the chic gyms.

CHILDREN'S
Mothercare
44, Ermou St., 210/3238695.
Clothes for children from 0 to 10, plus maternity clothes and baby needs (cots, prams, push-chairs etc.). Also small toys, shoes and baptismal gifts.

Prenatal
29, Ermou St., 210/3221384.
For babies and mothers-to-be. Layettes and baby clothes, furniture for baby's room, loose comfortable clothes for Mum, soft toys for babies with no teeth to chew on.

Th. Troupakis
15, Aiolou St., 210/3213087.
Looney Tune toys and clothes featuring Tweety, Silvester and other favourite cartoon characters.

SHOES - BAGS
K. I. Kontou
6, Ag. Theklas St. (mezzanine), 210/3215381.
Any sort of footwear you might want, from classic pumps and sandals to boots and flip flops, made to measure. Excellent prices, courteous service, rapid delivery.

Lemisios
6, Lykavittou St., 210/3611161.
At the same address since 1912, and still making fine shoes from exceptional quality leathers at very reasonable prices. His flat slippers are the best in town - a real must-have item.

Spiliopoulos
63, Ermou St., 210/3227590.
50, Adrianou St., 210/3219096.
Wonderful Italian shoes at exceptionally good prices, but they don't carry many sizes. The shop is on the small side for the number of people who come in here every day, but your acquisitions will more than compensate you for any inconvenience. Also men's and children's shoes, and the fabulous Coccinelle handbags at prices that will astonish you.

ACCESSORIES
Achilleas Accessories
38-40, Kolokotroni St., 210/3239970.
Large collection of accessories at very good prices. Shawls, bags, pareos belts, beach sandals, hats and much more, to complement any outfit.

Anastasia
5-7, Leocharous St., 210/3231172.
Stylish accessories, always in

tune with the latest seasonal trends. Carefully chosen to add the right note of style and brio to your outfit.

Closet
28, Sarri St., Psyrri.
Very modern shop, with loud music and a young style atmosphere. Clothes from Swear, Mambo, Energy, Gusto and Buddist Punk. Truly eccentric shoes and accessories for bold young girls who truly want to stand out.

Franca
11, Miaouli St., Psyrri, 210/3214112.
Trendy little place, with a constant turnover of new bags, belts, hats and pareos, always following the latest fashion dictates.

Out of Africa
13, Perikleous St., 210/3233682.
Unusual accessories and faux bijoux with an ethnic air, to turn even the simplest outfit into something truly special.

JEWELLERY - WATCHES
Apriati
9, Pentelis St. & Mitropoleos, 210/3229020.
Unique creations in silver and gold, designed by Athena with imagination, style and humour. Ask for the cat earrings and you'll see what we mean.

Folli Follie
37, Ermou St., 210/3230601.
The shop that made gold and silver combos a fashion item. Now the windows display costlier pieces in gold, ethnic lines in silver

Shopping

and semi-precious stones, and superlative accessories including bags, watches and silk shawls.

Gofas
3, Stadiou St.,
210/3244981.
The absolute magnet in his window display is always the collection of cheery colourful pieces by Pasquale Bruni. Hearts with "Love" picked out in diamonds, many-hued flower bracelets and rings gorgeous enough to take your breath away.

Swatch
5, Ermou St., 210/3313833.
The most hippy and trendy watches in the world arrange for a new date with their fans with every changing season. Select your watch and then pair it with distinctive matching accessories.

Time Center
14, Voulis St.,
210/3235933.
Large collection of Timberland, Nautica, Ellesse, Saint Honoré and other watches, perfect for casual wear.

COSMETICS
Chilia Aromata
58-60, Ermou St.
Old-fashioned shop, full of little bottles and flasks of every description, just waiting for you to have them filled with the scent of your choice.
Here you will find all the familiar perfumes in bulk - excellent imitations and even better prices.

MAC
44, Ermou St.,
210/3258260.
Minimal, stylish interior, expert make up artists and new-style, new-technology cosmetics. Check out the

special lipstick: proceeds from all sales go to help AIDS victims.

THIS & THAT
Octopus
18, Solonos St.,
210/3636677.
Original gifts and gadgets for the house. We loved the fish and cow shaped "mice" with their matching mouse pads, the portable fish radio, the plush picture frames and the super wow mobile phone cases.

Selini
22, Char. Trikoupi St.,
210/3645694.
Particularly elegant and stylish 2-in-1 jewellery and gift shop. Watches and clocks in amazing designs, beautiful bathroom accessories, small pictures for walls… with an attitude.

DEPARTMENT STORES
Fokas
11, Ermou St.,
210/3257770.
Everything from cosmetics and accessories to toys, clothes and household linens. When you're tired of shopping, stop for coffee at the in-store coffee & cake shop upstairs.

Hondos Center
4, Omonoia Sq.,
210/5221335.
Giant superstore that is strikingly modern and uncluttered in design. And it really does have everything: from classic clothes, shoes and accessories for the entire family, through house wares, cosmetics, cigars and electrical appliances to Vefa Alexiadou kitchen goodies. And since it is all too easy to spend the entire day

here, remember that there is a roof garden with a coffee shop-cum-restaurant.

Lampropoulos
99, Aiolou St. & Lykourgou, 210/3245811.
The city's most historic department store now operates on the "shops in a shop" principle, with some 400 different "boutiques" occupying a total of 14,500 m² on 7 floors. You'll find everything here, from clothing and accessories to cosmetics and small appliances. Free parking and home delivery.

Marks & Spencer
33-35, Ermou St.,
210/3240804.
Four floors of clothes (men's women's and children's), underwear, shoes, house wares, foodstuffs, etc. The styles may tend to classic neutral, but the quality is always excellent. The food department includes, among other things, some very interesting wines and ready-to-use sauces.

HOUSE WARES & INTERIORS
Elmaloglou Bros
22, Aiolou St.,
210/3234993.
Those who "know" about interior decorating swear by this place. Exceptionally fine quality fabrics at unbelievable prices. Arm yourself with patience, for you'll have to search for what you want - but the results are guaranteed to be satisfactory.

Happyland Cuisine
21, Stadiou St.,
210/3247808.
Cheerful unfussy place that invites you to explore its secrets. Fabulous design cookware, tastefully simple

Παριά Βουλή
Piano Ristorante

The Art...of Mediterranean Taste

AVANTGARDE ADV.

With respect to the name
of the "Old Parliament"
and creative spirit,
we transformed a place
into an ultimate restaurant.
Open at noon
with greek classic home made dishes
and mediterranean cuisine.
...at night we offer you
a gastronomic journey
with favorite melodies
from live piano and vocals....
...in summertime we have created
in the middle of Athens,
an oasis of gastronomy.
...everyday from 8 a.m. till sunrise,
you can enjoy drinks and coffees
at the "Old Parliament, Café - Bar".

7, Karitsi Str., Athens
Tel.: 210.32.11.311, 210.32.34.803

tableware, kitchen implements, dinner mats and kitchen accessories.

Madura
9, Stadiou St.,
210/3239953.
Upholstery fabrics and made-up curtains in an incredible range of patterns, colours and sizes. Also wonderful matching throws for your sofas, skirts for any kind of chair, cushions and even little footrests ... for your feet only.

Palladium
24, Ermou St.,
210/3221487.
Ornaments, household articles and linens, tablecloths and much more, to give character and personality to your home.

Sarlas
61, Ermou St.,
210/3233300.
Wide selection of upholstery fabrics and curtains at exceptionally good prices. There are often excellent bargains to be had in remnants, with discounts of up to 50%.

BOOKSHOPS - STATIONERY

Eleftheroudakis
17, Panepistimiou St.,
210/3258440.
European-style multi-level bookstore, where the emphasis has traditionally always been on foreign books. Among their strong points are their specialised sections on practically anything you care to name, from wines and cigars to collector's art books, books on Formula I and, of course, travel and tour guides. Happenings are organised in the children's section for young booklovers. On the top floor

there is a pleasant little coffee shop and a music department with all the latest CDs.

Estia bookstore
60, Solonos St.,
210/3615077.
The oldest publishing house and bookstore in Athens. Much has changed since the days when George Souris was writing poems about it, but with its vast collection it is still the benchmark for any booklover.

Mitropoleos 31
31, Mitropoleos St.,
210/3221281.
A wonderful place, full of wood and the scent of paper - you'd swear it was an old traditional bookshop. But no, it's a brand new modern store that stays open every day (except Sunday) till 9 at night. If you're a booklover, be sure to drop in and browse.

Naftilos' Library
28, Charilaou Trikoupi St.,
210/3616204.
An oasis for the booklover, in the heart of the city. In this miraculous little shop you will find not only contemporary titles but rare and out of print books as well. A favourite haunt of writers and intellectuals, especially on Saturday mornings. George, the pillar of the establishment, is an absolute mine of information.

Pallis
8, Ermou St., 210/3242115.
A shop with a long history - our parents and possibly even our grandparents all shopped here. Now fully renovated, it has one of the largest collections of stationery supplies and writing materials in Athens. There

is also a special print shop where you can order cards and invitations.

Tilt
37, Asklipiou St.,
210/3636028.
Simple, friendly, bright and cheery - as befits a shop of this kind. Tilt has become one of the best places in town for comics fans. Dragonball, Blade, Spawn, Kabuki and Lenore are just some of the names you'll see on its shelves. And if you look, you'll find some interesting re-issues of older series.

MISCELLANEOUS

Kalyviotis
8, Ermou St.
Braid, ribbons, and buttons - it's like Ali Baba's cave in here. A cult supplier, beloved of generations of Athenians. However unusual, impossible or recherche the item you're looking for as a finishing touch, you're bound to find it here.

O Molyvenios Stratiotis
185-187, Ippokratous St.,
210/6447602.
Little tin soldiers? Yes, but these are collector's items. Lead sailors, musketeers, cavalry officers, policemen, guardsmen and captains, each with its own history. And George Emmanouilidis will be more than happy to tell you their tales, and explain how he puts a price to them.

Tsiapara Bros
21, Pallados St.
Buckles, buckles and more buckles. Enormous variety of designs and materials. Choose one and the next thing you know it will have been fastened to a leather belt for you - your own unique creation.

Shopping

DESTE

NEO PSYCHIKO MESOGEION

With its more relaxed mode and shops that will satisfy even the most demanding consumers in the city, Neo Psychiko is the alternative trendy market for the northern suburbs. Of course, the on-going road works on Kifisias Ave., at the Faros junction, will make access difficult for at least another year. But no amount of bother can deter the designer shopping fanatics who relish the area's combination of uptown and downtown qualities. So welcome to Neo Psychiko, another of the city's hot shopping spots.

At Enny di Monaco you'll buy Colette Diningan and Jimmy Choo, at Free Shop you'll choose clothes by Marcela and handbags by Orla Kiely, while at Gem & Gem you'll adore the collections from Plein Sud and Garage. At Carouzos you'll select hand-sewn men's shoes from John Lobb, while at Lacoste you'll find sizes up to 9 for the larger than life. At Body & Soul the ladies will choose oils from Kiehl's for their hair and powder from T. Leclerc for a truly professional maquillage. Tired? Stop for coffee with the newscasters and celebrities at Deals, or savour a cup of jasmine tea at Lotus, or if it's lunchtime drop into Dioskouroi to sample

their light-style Greek cooking. If you've shopped all day, maybe it's time for an early dinner at Cosmos combined with a visit to DESTE for progressive gifts with attitude. Choose some goodies from Spuntino's delicatessen or order hand-stitched linen sheets from Essential for the ultimate in sweet dreams. In this section of the Guide you'll also find a few little secrets: where to find exceptional bargains in designer stock, where to order an opulent evening dress, where to buy modern clothes in extra large sizes. In recent years, Athenian shoppers have been discovering the attractions of another nearby area, along Mesogeion Ave. into Agia Paraskevi and Cholargos, while heading towards Kifisias, Chalandri displays a wonderful blend of tradition and contemporary dynamism. More low profile than their neighbours in Psychiko, the shops in these areas add their own note to shopping in the city. We found fine clothes and accessories (Saks Tsiantaridis, Casa di Hermes), "colonial" style dresses in linen and silk (Caravan Gallery), shoes that would grace any shop window in Rome (Mostre), and some lovely and interesting gift ideas (Tabacchi, Ble Fonto, The Gift Shop).

The up-and-coming shopping spot of the northern suburbs is gradually expanding towards Mesogeion Ave.

Oilily

Eqvus

NEO PSYCHIKO
CLOTHES

Anel
292, Kifisias Ave., Psychiko Shopping Centre, 210/6773226.
Women's clothes, made to measure, just like the good old days. Choose your fabric, and a pattern from Kyria Eleni's stylebook, come in for a fitting or two, and let her experienced hands do the rest, while you simply enjoy the process.

Aquila
292, Kifisias Ave., Psychiko Shopping Centre (lower level), 210/6745749.
Armani jeans and collections for men and women, casual and trendy. Also some very unusual clothes and accessories, like the painted military belts that were all the rage last winter.

Camomilla
300, Kifisias Ave., 210/6774000.
Everyday clothes and accessories at reasonable prices, focusing on all day fashion - the quintessence of colour combos. Summer hits include delightful beach sandals and pretty shawls for cool evenings.

Carouzos
240, Kifisias Ave. & Solomou, 210/6778884.
One of the star stores of this great chain, with a broad front on Kifisias Ave. Synonymous with big name shopping. Men's and women's lines from Prada, Jil Sander, Fendi etc., plus distinctive accessories, shoes and bags. Impeccable service from the extremely polite staff. The hand-made shoes by John Lobb are a must.

Colori
240, Kifisias Ave. & 2, Solomou St., 210/6755990.
Casual chic in a sleek attractive environment that sets them off beautifully. All day clothes notable for their intelligent details and youthful style. We loved the vine leaf beach sandals from the summer accessories collection.

Enny di Monaco
9, Stratigi St., 210/6725691.
It may not look the part, but this is the Mecca of the trendy shopper, with the kind of clothes and accessories that you drool over in the fashion magazines and until recently could only find in London or New York. Designers like Luella, Diane von Furstenberg, Adam Jones, Cesare Fabbri, superb quality and taste, and a touch of eccentricity. Prices to match. And the accessories are worth a visit in themselves.

Eponymo
7, Omirou St., 210/6744744.
The famous Kolonaki store recently acquired a baby brother in Psychiko. And the family resemblance is obvious: same atmosphere of simple elegance, setting off collections from designers like Montana, Vivienne Westwood, Ferré, Genny, Gaultier, Michel Perry and the like. Winter highlight: cheap and chic Moschinos.

Free Shop
10, Lykourgou St., 210/6741914.
Alternative modern ambience, for men's and women's clothes with real character - something between avant-garde and décontracté. Lines from (among others) Marcella, Day, Claude Pierlot, wonderful bags from Orla Kiely and accessories from Maria Calderara.

Gem & Gemm
12, Omirou St. & Stratigi, 210/6748508.
Avant-garde creations from labels like Plein Sud, Garage etc. These clothes are expensive, but you won't meet yourself coming and going: they only bring in one or two of each item - clientele oblige.

Jade Avenue
258, Kifisias Ave., 210/6711584.
The Versace lines in the windows tell you what to expect. Glamorous day and evening wear, clothes that

the essential home collection

THE ESSENTIALS

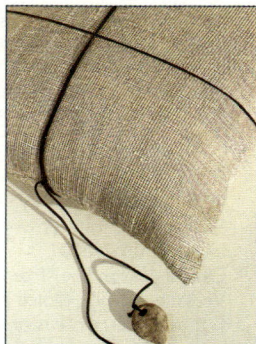

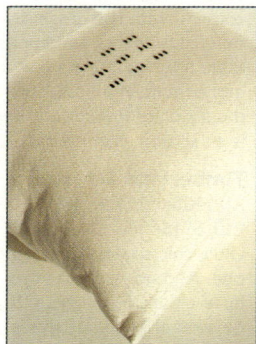

Hand made creations for your home

Curtains throws cushions rugs bedspreads pillows
tablecloths linensheets towels and monogrammes

RETAIL/WHOLESALE

54 EL. VENIZELOY STR. • GR-15451 • N. PSYCHIKO • GREECE • THΛ. & FAX: +30210-6715701

make their wearers look as though they'd just stepped out of "Dynasty".

Katerina Stylianou
20, El. Venizelou St., 210/6748921
Well-made modern clothes for all occasions for the bigger-than-life woman. Clothes with style and personality in sizes up to a European 56 (Greek 70), at prices that will come as a pleasant surprise.

Lacoste Corner
1, Psychari St., 210/6721270.
The famous crocodile that once stood for trendy luxury in cotton shirts. They also stock large sizes, but these tend to disappear quickly.

Max Mara
1, Psychari St., 210/6714839.
Classic clothes in subdued colours, with the emphasis on quality fabrics and impeccable finishing. Also a few more modern pieces, but the absolute investment here is an all time classic coat.

Timberland & Nautica
212, Kifisias Ave., 210/6718408.
Ultra chic sportswear, two in one. And no need to introduce either. Highlights include Timberland boat shoes and Nautica windbreakers - for all-weather fashion.

Trinia
4-6, Solomou St., Stoa Shopping Centre, 210/6744746.
Alternative modern dressing, with clothes that may not have designer labels but are in the spirit of the times. Wide range of clothes at very good prices, nicely balanced between the trendy and the easy-to-wear. And you can always dress them up with appropriate accessories - just take a look, for example, at the denim bags.

Yoschi
1, Psychari St., 210/6749250.
Clothes by Calvin Klein and a few less famous names on the ground floor. But the big secret is on the mezzanine: in-store stock from the same label at very good prices, plus ends of lines from the previous season.

STOCK
Apothiki
1, Psychari St. (1st floor), 210/6756488.
Stock from Danny Shop. Timberland, New Balance, Two, Car Shoes, Passenger's and many other labels, at less than half price.

Gem & Gemm
12, Omirou St. (lower level), 210/6748508.
Out-of-season clothes from Gem & Gem at amazing prices. Ask before you come, for the shop is not always open. Also, there are no mirrors, and space is very limited, but the low prices cancel out any inconvenience.

Griff
292, Kifisias Ave., Psychiko Shopping Centre (lower level), 210/6718641.
Out-of-season lines from Versace, DKNY, Dolce e Gabbana, Ferre, Trussardi jeans, Valentino, etc., at very low prices.

SPORTING GOODS
Harley Davidson
268, Kifisias Ave., 210/6712463, 210/6728015.
Indisputably number one in the biker hierarchy. Helmets, back packs, T-shirts, belts, boots, and the most trendy accessories for biker boys and girls. The leather jackets with the raised pattern on the back are practically a cult item.

Nike Exclusive Stores
268, Kifisias Ave., 210/6776687.

Paradise for the athletic shopper, in a super-stylish store that stocks sizes from 0 to XXXL. They have everything here, from microscopic infant trainers to gym gear in all possible styles and colours, for outfits that make a statement in the chic gyms of this upscale neighbourhood.

LINGERIE
Nota
10, Omirou St., 210/6741912.
Nighties, dressing gowns and underwear in classic lines and exceptionally fine quality. Gorgeous sets, flowered pyjamas, comfortable undies and super slippers.

CHILDREN'S
Eqvus
10, Perikleous St., 210/6779777.
Beautiful shop full of fabulous ideas for all ages. Wooden toys by Sevi, unique origami constructions, plush animals and much much more. Wonderful ornaments, too, like the plump metal ladies from Diva that serve as bookends. As the kite-flying season approaches, stop in for a designer model that will last a couple of seasons. And come Easter they have a wonderful selection of candles.

Frattina Exclusive
246, Kifisias Ave., 210/6777528.
Ultra chic children's clothes for designer tots. DKNY jackets, shoes with attitude, swimsuits and accessories for junior socialites.

Oilily
4-6, Solomou St., Stoa Shopping Centre, 210/6755632.
"Elegant" fashions from Oilily for kids up to 10. Original styles, progressive colour combinations and imaginative

NOTA
LINGERIE

Dunhill lighter, at Casa del Habano

accessories. The little girls' clothes, in particular, are fabulous.

To Trenaki
3, Omirou St., 210/6712931.
Toys for children of all ages, defying the department store, as-seen-on-TV, mentality. Wide variety of board games and wooden toys for tiny tots.

Trotinette
292, Kifisias Ave., Psychiko Shopping Centre (ground floor), 210/6749895.
Trendy casual for fashion-conscious kids and parents. Children's lines from Replay Jeans, Gant and other ... progressive labels.

SHOES - BAGS
Keds
4-6, Solomou St., Stoa Shopping Centre, 210/6779523.
Canvas shoes that have set a trend, classic and easy-to-wear. Always in fashion for your morning or Sunday casuals. Lovely children's styles, especially those for little girls, with lots of pink and a real Barbie look about them.

Petridis
250, Kifisias Ave., 210/6725230.
Men's and women's shoes from Parallele, Camper, Jourdan and many other names. The house lines are also interesting, crafted in

classic styles out of beautiful leathers.

ACCESSORIES
Sacs Etc.
11, Omirou St., 210/6728344.
Bags by Furla and Coccinelle, some faux bijoux, pretty shawls, original shoes, and a few lines of "little" clothes, in a shop that has far more varied merchandise than you'd think at first glance.

Sfendoni
292, Kifisias Ave., Psychiko Shopping Centre (ground floor), 210/6719738.
A shop with character, with a store of real treasures in its drawers. Not that the windows lag behind, mind you... Elegant faux bijoux, embroidered bags, mules and shawls to set off even the simplest look. This year's highlight: the corded and tasselled jewellery from Anesti.

COSMETICS
Body & Soul
11, Omirou St., 210/6774554.
A minor paradise for those who fancy alternative cosmetics. Powder from T. LeClerc, hair oils from Kiehl's, face creams from Aesop and many other interesting products. Also aromatic candles, vanilla-scented pot pourri, and the fabulous tweezers by Twezerman.

Shocking Pink
2, Solomou St., 210/6772072.
The Shocking Pink line of make-up products for young faces. Exclusive distributors of these English products that glitter and sparkle: gold dust powder, glitter mascara, luminous eye shadow and nail colour, and innocent semi- transparent pink make-up products for young debs.

OPTICAL
Laskaris
258, Kifisias Ave., 210/6724625.
Large variety of eyeglasses and sunglasses, in classic lines. Armani, Versace, Ray Ban and other top names. Do try the coloured contact lenses - who knows, green eyes might be just your style.

Ofthalmos
11, Omirou St., 210/6728040.
This is a more trendy sort of place. Multi-coloured frames, brands like Cutler and Cross and an air of modernity even in the decor.

THIS & THAT
DESTE
8, Omirou St., 210/6729463.
Art store in the heart of Neo Psychiko. Browse along the shelves and display cases, and you'll find wonderful ideas for gifts: bags and jewellery by Katerina Pleioni, small numbered paintings by

Ioannidou, design office supplies, curious T-shirts… The cow computer cover is a real must-have item.

Ypografi
292, Kifisias Ave., Psychiko Shopping Centre (lower level), 210/6756977.
Unusual lamps, Looney Tune mugs, faux bijoux, original clocks, greeting cards, clever board games. We loved the original shower curtains - but they're not always in stock.

HOUSEWARES - INTERIORS

E & M
Psychari & Stratigi St., 210/6746481.
Coloured crystal glasses, velvet rosebuds, sumptuous linen and lace tablecloths, superb decorations for a very special table setting.

Laura Ashley Home
10, Omirou St., 210/6727052.
Romantic flower print upholstery fabrics, decorative cushions, place settings for two, pot pourri, scented lining paper for your drawers and much more. For those who like the Little House on the Prairie look.

Omnishop
292, Kifisias Ave., Psychiko Shopping Centre (ground floor), 210/6771120.
Table and kitchen ware for houses with humour, taste and character. Original mugs, beautifully painted cookie jars, and wonderful ideas for Christmas and Easter gifts.

Sandra
292, Kifisias Ave., Psychiko Shopping Centre (1st floor), 210/6726329.
Occasional furniture, beautiful picture frames, candles

and the loveliest holiday items in town. The Christmas tree decorations are out of this world, and the Easter candles the prettiest we've ever seen.

www.home.com
10, Omirou St. & 7 Stratigi, 210/6721710.
Benroubi company's answer in expensive table settings. Table ware and tablecloths, candles, bath boutique and pet supplies, all in beautiful designs at exceptionally reasonable prices. A highlight for the housekeeper with attitude: scented water for the steam iron.

HOUSEHOLD LINENS

Descamps
10, Omirou St., 210/6777678.
Superb quality household linens from a famous French house. Fluffy bathrobes and

towels, sheets with matching quilts, and an excellent children's line, for a quality lifestyle, every day.

The Essential Home Collection
54, El. Venizelou St., 210/6715701.
The finest household linens on the market. Monogrammed sheets and pillowcases, superb tablecloths and curtains. Also, fluffy towels and bathrobes (mostly to order). Very interesting line of summer clothes - we particularly liked the loose linen trousers and the wide shirts, made to measure.

BOOKSHOPS - STATIONERY

Chartopolis
1, D. Vasileiou & Kifisias Ave., B.C. Shopping Centre.
Up-to-date Greek and foreign literature section and interesting children's series. If you can't find what you're looking for, they'll have it for you the next day. Stationery department with filofax and knock-on-the-door with beautiful pop-up cartoons.

Ex Libris
4-6, Solomou St., Stoa Shopping Centre (1st floor), 210/6779482.
Very interesting bookshop specialising in foreign titles. Wide range of subjects: books on feng shui and cookery, art and architecture, and of course literature.

MESOGEION (AMPELOKIPOI, CHALANDRI, CHOLARGOS, AGIA PARASKEVI)

CLOTHES

Caravan Gallery
15-17, Aristofanous St., Chalandri, 210/6840164.

146, Charilaou Trikoupi St., Nea Erythraia, 210/6254139.
Natural fibres only - linen and real silk. Colonial style and desert colours, in loose garments that all women love. Hand sewn Spanish shoes and sandals from Minorca, made from exceptionally fine leathers. The handbags are by London designer Jas Sehmbi - Bohemian, distressed-look, truly fabulous.

Christoforos Detsikas
13, Kolokotroni St., Chalandri, 210/6891912.
A mixed bag: some of the clothes we really loved, others not. But it's always worth having a look. Good variety, and very good prices. We particularly liked his embroidered cotton shirts and loose woven tunics, with a real '70s look to them.

Elle Style
34-36, Pentelis Ave., Vrilissia, 210/6852037.
Athanasia Evangelinou abandoned her university career without thinking twice about it, to devote herself full time to her real passion: the world of clothing! Not only does she import clothes and accessories (chosen on her buying trips to Italy), but she creatively improves them as well, hand-painting them with a special technique. Bring her any solid colour article of clothing you're tired of, and see what she can do with it!

Flash
Ymittou & 72, Aspasias St., Trilithon Shopping Centre, Cholargos, 210/6545348.
Cholargos is not a small market, but even here it's unusual to find so many big names under one roof: Roberto Cavalli, Exte, Fendi, Plein Sud, Blumarine, etc. They pride themselves on

their personal service, so do make full use of the sales staff - you'll really appreciate their patience, their excellent advice and their good taste.

L' Angolo
18, Pentelis Ave. & 2, 28th October St., Vrilissia, 210/6824019.
Very elegant shop stocked with imports, tasteful window displays, and an exceptionally polite staff. French and Italian clothes that simply radiate quality in the very latest fashions: well-sewn costumes, elegant trousers, feminine skirts cut to flatter the figure... Probably the most stylish boutique on Pentelis Avenue.

Mala
56, Perikleous St., Cholargos Centre, Cholargos, 210/6546050. 18, Agiou Ioannou St., Agia Paraskevi, 210/6012105.
Young styles, but without the cheap look that sometimes characterises boutiques that target this market. Club gear for girls: stretch dresses, Capri pants, bustiers, all cleverly designed with a distinctive touch of elegance.

Margo
Grigoriou E, Chalandri, 210/6853395, 210/6846170.
All well-loved imported lines (Sweet Soffio, Bump's, Carmen Martinez and Arabesque) plus her own creations in leotards, tights and costumes. Pointe, jazz and character shoes, as well as fabulous leotards for everyday wear. Ask for Mr Antonis Koletsis.

Sakis Tsiantaridis
76, Agiou Ioannou St., Agia Paraskevi, 210/6016092. 17, Chaimanta St., Chalandri, 210/6834198.

HOME BOY

MISS SIXTY.

ENERGIE

KILAH

gsus

NO.L.ITA N.Y.C.

MELTIN' POT

ecko unltd.

custo
BARCELONA

mambo

ROYAL
ELASTICS

Ra.Re

Buddhist Punk

JEANS
MICHIKO KOSHINO

stock
SHOP

STOCKSHOP >> 10, Messogion str., Athens
> tel.: 210 7473435 (close to the Tower of Athens)

DESTE

The best boutique, by far, in Agia Paraskevi: this is the only place where you'll find clothes by Valentino, Fendi, Versace, P.A. Gaspari (the real thing, not seconds), plus shoes from the same designers. Sakis, a prime favourite with the ladies of Agia Paraskevi, makes frequent buying trips to New York and brings back designer accessories (bags, scarves, even luggage) and sometimes very original pieces of jewellery.

Do make a point of going up Agiou Ioannou street and visiting this boutique - unless you prefer the outlet in Chalandri.

Zino
33, Pentelis Ave., Chalandri, 210/6892657.
The most up-to-date shop in the Zino chain. If you like Versace, D&G and Artisti Italiani, you'll find clothes and accessories (the belts are fabulous) at very good prices - they import their own, and you'll find special offers on most things all year round. The men's department is every bit as good as the women's.

STOCK
Stock Shop
10, Mesogeion Ave., Ampelokipoi, 210/7473435.
Miss Sixty, Energie, Killah Babe, Formarina, Home Boy, Mambo, Royal Elastics: these

are the clothes we found in the Stock Shop - and it's equally strong on accessories. The London touches in hats, belts and handbags attract people of all ages who want to lighten up a somewhat classic wardrobe.

LINGERIE
Eso Orama
56, Perikleous St., Cholargos Centre, Cholargos, 210/6512415.
Full of cheerful colour, pyjamas with cartoon characters, snug homewear, socks, and other things to make your indoor life more comfortable. Welcome to the most playful underwear store in town!

Linea Donna
2-4, K.Varnali St., Chalandri, 210/6836101.
Nina Ricci, Millesia and other designer lingerie in a very elegant shop in Chalandri. Also a selection of homewear, and some Ferré and Valentino articles.

ACCESSORIES
Eleni Pylarinou
56, Perikleous St., Cholargos Centre (1st floor), Cholargos, 210/6545912.
Eleni travels all over the world, and this year has brought back a surprise line of wonderful leather jewellery. Apart from what she imports from Paris and Spain, she also designs her

own articles, often using Swarovski crystals.

Gilda
56, Perikleous St., Cholargos Centre (1st floor), Cholargos, 210/6537064.
Gilda's is a totally crazy place, and one of the most progressive shops around. Bags, shawls, headscarves, fur pieces and many more accessories, chosen with exceptional taste. Which explains her faithful clientele: the neighbourhood girls come in regularly to check out the new arrivals.

THIS & THAT
Ble Fondo
4, Dimokratias Sq., Cholargos, 210/6543496.
Despite its name, the Ble Fondo (= blue background) is actually a very colourful place. Original items, featuring mainly pop style and eccentric designs. Carefully selected young-at-heart articles for one-of-a-kind gifts.

The Gift Shop
56, Perikleous St., Cholargos Centre (1st floor), Cholargos, 210/6541715.
For alternative gifts, particularly featuring natural and intelligently used materials. Diaries, books, picture frames in wood, stone and paper, small boxes, pencil holders, photo albums, and a wonderful collection of hand-made greeting cards.

Kessaris

Gallé

KIFISIA

Under the centuries-old, shady plane trees of the place that was once a favourite holiday resort for Athenian high society there is now a high-flying marketplace that is the northern suburbs' answer to Kolonaki. A marketplace with a high income (and very demanding) customer base, that offers a combination of a leisurely excursion atmosphere with by far the best service in the city.

If you want luxury with a sense of exclusiveness, if you don't like breezing through your shopping in a spare half hour, if you're tired of searching for a parking place, if you like a lordly atmosphere, then Kifisia is the perfect shopping place for you. Here the ambiance changes and the rhythm turns cool. In the streets there are expensive cars and bikes with baby seats or shopping baskets, and on the pavements dozens of dogs bask undisturbed in the sun. As for the shops, the opportunities are endless. At Nicole Farhi you can browse through minimal "made in London" styles, at the corner of Kassaveti and Levidou you'll find yourself surrounded by the best-dressed kids in Athens, at Galle you'll love the Anya Hindmarch accessories, and at E-Play you'll see how casual dressing can become a real fashion statement. At Rossi, when the weather's nice, you'll sip your freddo in the shade of the plane trees. At Central Prince Oliver you'll select cufflinks by

Tateossian, while at Gianneto you can order a custom-made suit or shirt with a monogrammed pocket. At Varsos, when you stop in for some of the best whipped cream ever, you'll encounter elegant figures from another age, while a little farther along, at the corner of Levidou and Kolokotroni, a horse-drawn caleche will take you on a journey back through time. At Preview and Kalogirou you'll wish you were a … centipede, while at Longchamp you'll find superb leather change purses. You can have a light lunch at Piazza Mela in company with women you'll recognise from the society pages, stock up on succulent delicatessen items from Salumaio di Montenapoleone or enjoy the tastiest sandwiches at the Artisti Italiani Cafe. The wonderful - and wonderfully youthful - jewellery in Venetia Vildiridi's window will surely tempt you, while at Etiquette you'll find everything you need for the trendiest table settings imaginable. Finally, at the La Prairie Spa you can spend the whole day basking in absolute relaxation and opulence.

One trip to Kifisia is enough to show you why the people who live in these suburbs no longer bother going downtown for their shopping, except perhaps at Christmas. We, in this section of the Guide, will not only tell you about the familiar standard shops but will also share our own secret alternatives with you. Shopping Kifisia-style awaits you, with its splendours and its enchantments.

Always a place apart, Kifisia is the absolute centre for designer shopping combined with a feel of easy-going luxury.

Virginia Ventouraki

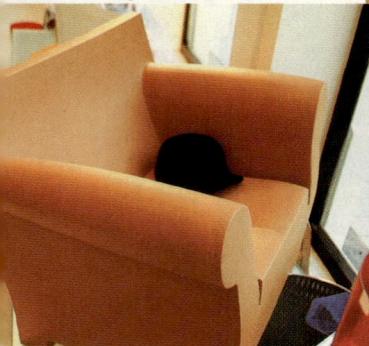

Gallé

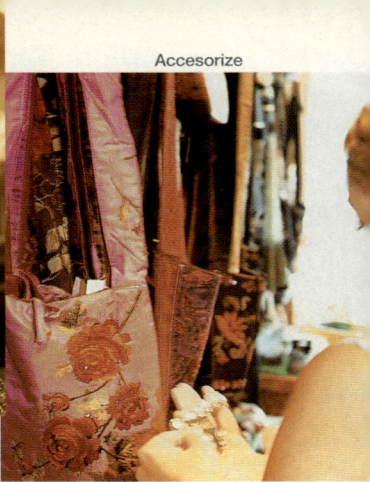

Accesorize

KIFISIA
CLOTHES

Carla G.
16, Levidou St.,
210/8085770.
Understated and particularly elegant decor. Modern, stylish and very feminine clothes, for the up-to-the-minute, sexy woman who thrives on change. Prices more than reasonable.

Central Prince Oliver
Kifisias Ane. & Panagitsas,
210/6231873.
The all-in-one shopper's delight. Clothes and accessories that perfectly reflect the fashion of today, and perhaps of tomorrow as well. Clothes from Patrick Cox, Etro, Fake of London, Paul Smith, Tateosian, to name just a few... Don't overlook the ties and cufflinks, or the accessories for women.

Chevron
30, Kyriazi St.,
210/8017278.
Jeans, jeans, jeans!!! The heart of casual trendy is here, and so are crowds of kids in their habitual blare of music. Leather biker's jackets are a strong winter season feature.

E. Play
8, Kolokotroni St.,
210/8080565.

Striking interior, full of music and colour. And clothes to match - they couldn't go unremarked if they tried. Vivid colours and unusual fabrics in strange combinations that make teasing statements about life and routine.

Escada
19, Kassaveti St.,
210/8013761.
Classic chic, fine quality, understated luxury and carefully tailored simple elegance, in a shop to match.

Esprit
26, Kyriazi St.,
210/8017482.
In a warm but unfussy setting, casual sportswear for any time of day. For those who adopt a carefully un-put-together look, in a deliberately youthful style.

Gallé
10, Kolokotroni St.,
210/6230859.
An unassuming shop that you might easily not even notice, but the clothes, from the selected Camper shoe lines and Mira Mikati T-shirts to the Anya Hindmarch collections of clothes and accessories, are very elegant. Chosen with flair and imagination, for those who insist on style and character.

Giannetos
40, Kyriazi St.,
210/8014864.
Suits and shirts tailored sur mesure, from one of the oldest outfitters in Athens. Choose your fabric from a wide range of samples, decide on collar, cuffs and - if you wish - monogram, and your personalised, tailor-made shirt will be ready for you in just a couple of days.

Ginestra
5, Levidou St.,
210/8085423-4.
Clothing and accessories with an Italian air, understated fashion for everyday wear. Excellent value.

Gucci
8, Kolokotroni St.,
210/8089034.
Italian style, dreamy clothes and accessories, in one of the hottest shopping spots in town - men and women yield to temptation here without the slightest struggle.
The famous shoes crafted out of velvety soft leather are synonymous with absolute desire.

Henry Cottons
8, Kolokotroni St.,
210/8089350.
Shirts and sweatshirts in

MammaRò

a rainbow of colours, perfect for casual dress.

Hugo Boss
15, Kyriazi St.,
210/8011503.
Blue chip men's wear, for a wide range of tastes and preferences. Customers have been known to "forget" to remove the Hugo Boss label from their sleeve...

Joseph
3, Panagitsas St.,
210/8088368.
London style in a minimalist decor that that serves as a perfect foil for these distinctive clothes. Simple lines, neutral colours, fabulous fabrics, extreme style. Very trendy shoes.

Kenzo
8, Kolokotroni St.,
210/8089055.
Trendy and full of character, like the eye-catching clothes in the window. Modern lines, but not overstated - clothes that whisper rather than shout.

L' Altra Moda
5, Levidou St.,
210/6231666.
"Little" clothes to beautifully complete your outfits, stylish accessories and clever ideas for final touch shopping. Look out for the Lollipops line in the summer.

Levi's
1, Papadiamanti St. & Levidou, 210/6233249.
American atmosphere and all time classic jeans. Between the music and the youthful customers, Saturdays are a bit of a bazaar.

Litta
11, Kassaveti St.,
210/8083711.
One of the first boutiques to enjoy the custom of the fashion-conscious ladies of the northern suburbs. Big on Blumarine strass casuals and embroidered evening wear. Also pashminas, a must for winter and even summer evenings.

Luisa
12, Kolokotroni St.,
210/8012991.
A shop that doesn't merely offer fashion, but makes a statement about absolute style. Expensive clothes, specifically selected for her chosen clientele. Here, if you don't belong to the right set you may get a disapproving glance. But the clothes are worth every penny.

Nicole Farhi
3, Panagitsas St.,
210/8010624.
Pure London. Totally unfussy clothes, with clean lines in trendy and absolutely neutral colours - this is what distinguishes London fashion from Paris or New York. Superb finishing, expensive fabrics, and quiet understated elegance.

Polo Sport
19, Kassaveti St.,
210/8085550.
Classic collection for elegant casual dressing. Leisure outfits sporting the famous pony, as at home at the club in Ekali on Sunday morning as on the younger representatives of the northern suburbs in some fashionable night spot after dark.

Rossi
14, Kolokotroni St.,
210/8085182.
Classic quality, with Italian elegance and style. For men who know what they want and are willing to pay for real excellence.

Sofos
14, Levidou St.,
210/8012677.
A shop that veered away

from its classic tradition a few years ago to follow a more modern line. Clothes that tread a nice balance between the trendy and the comme il faut, giving even those whose sartorial preferences tend to the conventional a decided air of fashion.

Sotris
11, Levidou St., 210/6233547.
Thanos Sotiropoulos was one of the first to bring the trend concept to Athens, many years ago. All the hottest fashion names parade through his windows: Voyage, Prada, Miu Miu, plus Christopher Kontentos. If you're wise you'll pay him a visit at the beginning of the season to see what's in the wind. The Kifisia store may be the smallest Sotris, but it's got everything.

T-Shirt Factory
16, Agiou Dimitriou St., 210/8019140.
Choose, print and wear! All kinds of stamps ready to apply to your T-shirt or sweatshirt. The more daring opt for a magazine page, a postage stamp or snapshots of themselves.

T' Store
8, Kolokotroni St., 210/8089056.
Handsome, minimalist Trussardi shop with clothes from the designer's sportswear collection and the trendy accessories we all love. Sporting the famous whippet trademark and in defiance of the times, a little leather bag or a metal cigar case with a wooden lid is a gift that is always appreciated.

Yves Saint Laurent
8, Kolokotroni St., 210/8089030.
Princess or top model, if only for a night! Selected lines from the famous fashion house with that unmistakable Parisian air - the absolute expression of haute couture. And of course, accessories that are a status statement in themselves.

STOCK
Fifty - Fifty
6, Kassaveti St. & Miltiadou, 210/6230081.
Discount and more, as the shop's cards say. Clothes and accessories from Cacharel, Calvin Klein, Cerruti, Furla, Lolita Lempicka, La Perla etc., all below cost.

Rollini
6-8, Kyriazi St., 210/8088710.
Off-season shoes and handbags, odd sizes and ends of lines, and very low prices.

LINGERIE
La Femme
11, Panagitsas St., 210/8012370.
Undies, nighties and swimsuits, tempting, tasteful and teasing. Laces and satins for ... progressive seduction.

CHILDREN'S
Bonbons
16, Levidou St., 210/8082993.
One of the best children's wear stores in Athens, with beautiful clothes from Quincy and Marie Chantal. And so trendy that you'd probably buy the accessories for yourself if the size was right. These, you see, are the clothes that

Madonna buys for her little Lourdes. This winter's must are the animal-face galoshes.

Kollitiri
4B, Kassaveti St., 210/8080551.
Unusual toys for creative kids. Emphasis on wooden constructions and board games. For those who want something other than Pokemon for their offspring.

SHOES - BAGS
Il Gatto
8, Argyropoulou St., 210/8081610.
Good quality wallets, handbags, umbrellas, scarves, in a wide range of colours and designs and at very reasonable prices. The charming little euro-coin purses are a must.

Kalogirou
5, Panagitsas St., 210/6236800.
There can't be anyone who has never shopped once, or at least window-shopped, at Kalogirou ... Shoes from Prada, Tod's, Ungaro, Miu Miu and other sensational names. In Kifisia, the men's and women's departments are separate (essentially in two separate stores), and the service is better. Just remember that if you see something you like, buy it, because it probably won't be there tomorrow.

Longchamp
6, Panagitsas St., 210/6231635.
An historic name in leather goods. In recent years there have been some delightful surprises, like the design-it-yourself bag, where the customer puts together her own colours and styles.

The shop is small, however, and can be over-crowded.

Preview
6, Panagitsas St.,
210/8011120.
For alternative footwear. Creations from Kallisté, Clergerie, Menudier and other eccentric designers. Season to season, this is where the different drummer for the lower extremities beats most forcefully. So fall in step!

ACCESSORIES

Accessorize
5, Levidou St.,
210/6236540.
The newest spot for accessories. Wonderful selection, constantly renewed, at very affordable prices. The hats are a must: winter or summer they're all fabulous, and so cheap you can buy them all! As you might expect, the place is usually jammed.

Armandos Moustakis
1, Levidou St.,
210/8011964.
The place for faux bijoux for more than a decade. Top quality and pieces with real character.

Bianca Verti
8, Kolokotroni St.,
210/8089040.
Superbly designed Italian faux, always in the swing of international fashion. Creations from Armani and other famous fashion houses that you've admired in foreign Vogue magazines.

Erietta P.
4, Alonion St.,
210/8085265.
Hand-crafted jewellery, small bags and accessories: the shop may be small, but the variety is astonishing. The wire-and-bead bracelets are a must for summer island-holiday wear.

Fragonard
9, Kyriazi St.,
210/8080584.
Bags, accessories and firo-lite jewellery (an artificial diamond indistinguishable from the real thing except by special apparatus). Knock 'em all dead with your fabulous rocks, at breathtakingly low prices.

Rave Xilone
10, Papadiamanti St.,
210/8085803.
Traditionally a shop for threads and knitting yarns (the name means 'sew and unpick'), but this summer

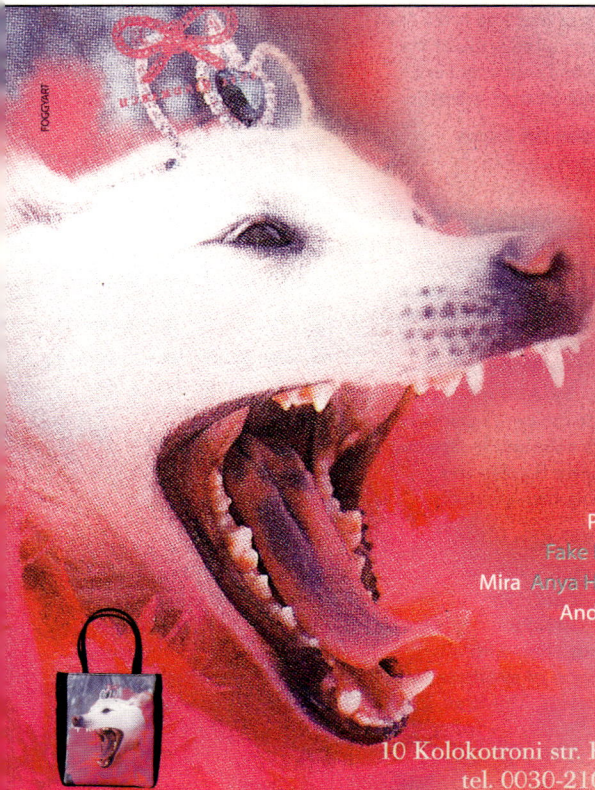

we saw fabulous beach sandals, mules and a very interesting collection of hats.

Sock Shop
14, Kolokotroni St.,
210/8011794.
Socks, socks, socks!!! In every colour, design and size you could possibly imagine. For kids and their young-at-heart parents. Don't forget to buy a pair of soft woolly-lined sleep socks - come the winter, you'll bless us.

JEWELLERY-WATCHES
Bvlgari
238-240, Kifisias Ave.,
210/8089508.
A name that needs no introduction. Italian design in jewellery and watches that are absolute status symbols. This gem of a shop also carries the designer's famous accessories.

Fanourakis
6, Panagitsas St.,
210/6232334.
Jewellery with real character - most unlikely to go unremarked. Designs in gold and platinum with diamonds and semi-precious stones that look like ribbons, in bows or gracefully suspended. All unique and all so beautiful it's almost impossible to choose among them.

Kessaris
238-240, Kifisias Ave.,
Mela Shopping Centre,
210/8089500.
Athenian high society's favourite bijoutier. The best diamonds in the city, in a veritable gem of a store. You will also find watches from Frank Muller and Ikepod, as well as unusual

gift items in silver for the special people on your list.

Venetia Vildiridis
19, Kassaveti St.,
210/6236617.
The younger generation of the famous bijoutier family in a shop targeting a young modern clientele. Superb pieces set with diamonds and semi-precious stones, and those Technomarine watches with the fabulous straps (exclusive dealer).

COSMETICS
Beauty Works
8, Kolokotroni St., Aigli Shopping Centre,
210/6231688.
Rare cosmetics for those who pamper their skin and prefer exclusive products. You'll find excellent products from Acqua di Parma, Kiehl's, Neal's Yard and of course the super line from Japanese make-up artist Sue Uemura - the pride of the store and sold only here. Striking abstract metal decor.

Heaven on Earth
16, Levidou St.,
210/8081151.
A veritable paradise of boutique cosmetics. Here you'll find the very fashionable Annick Goutal perfumes (sold also in crystal collector's bottles), and Jao, the antiseptic world travellers swear by. Also the Fresh line of cosmetics made from cow's milk, and Hollywood's favourite Bumble and Bumble bath products.

OPTICAL
Eye Q.
36B, Kyriazi St.,
210/6233326.
Trendy shop with a large selection of eyeglasses and sunglasses. The large selec-

tion of children's sunglasses is super - and the mums love them as much as their kids do.

HOUSE WARES - INTERIORS
Baccarat
238-240, Kifisias Ave.,
Mela Shopping Centre,
210/6236698.
The luxurious brilliance of crystal in glassware, ornaments and original pieces of jewellery. The coloured hearts that you wear on a velvet ribbon around your neck are a real must-have item.

D.L. Interiors
8, Argyropoulou St.,
210/8012747.
Ornaments and occasional pieces selected with flair and taste. We particularly liked the bright swags of flowers, for that special touch in your home.

Etiquette
9-11, Kolokotroni St.,
210/6232842.
From the very first glance you know that this is a shop for people with excellent taste and pockets deep enough to indulge it. One-of-a-kind dinner services displayed in cases like fine jewellery - some of the most beautiful pieces we've seen on the market. The household linens are also well worth looking at.

Facade
9, Kolokotroni St.,
210/8017920.
Upholstery fabrics, occasional furniture and ornaments made of natural materials with an ethnic air. Carefully chosen and very interesting ideas for comfortably relaxed interiors with char-

COME FOR THE FOOD.

STAY FOR THE FUN.

Every time you come in a TGI FRIDAY'S® restaurant you'll find a relaxed atmosphere, friendly servers and original FRIDAY'S® recipes that satisfy every taste.

Start off with the very best cocktails made by the best bartenders in the world. Then choose from our menu full of incredible appetizers, pastas, salads, chicken, steaks and of course our great tasting burgers, all freshly cooked especially for you, from FRIDAY'S® chefs.

Add to that our signature Jack Daniel's Grill and it's easy to see how FRIDAY'S® casual brand of dining makes everything just that much better.

So, visit TGI FRIDAY'S® where the high quality food, the refreshing cocktails, the pleasant atmosphere, the friendly environment and your fun is our top priority. Let us show you what good food and good times is all about!

T.G.I. FRIDAY'S

35 Kolokotroni St. • 14562 Kifisia • Tel.: 010 6233947-8

17 Akti Dymaion St. • Shopping Center "Veso Mare" 26222 Patra • Tel.: 0610 362020

In here, it's always Friday.™

FRIDAY'S BAR & CAFE

110 Imittou St. • Pagrati Shopping Center Athens Millennium Tel.: 010 7560544-5

acter and taste. The organdie mosquito nets and the old Blanc d' Ivoire console tables are absolute musts.

Ikia
20, Kyriazi St., 210/8018878.
House wares and ornaments selected with taste for modern homes with attitude and character. We particularly liked the doormats in various designs, the coconut straw mats, the colourful mugs and the bathroom accessories.

La Taste
7, Kolokotroni St., 210/8080603.
Possibly the oldest of the house wares stores. Their merchandise is strong on character, in a predominantly country style. Lovely mini-checked dishes in wicker picnic baskets, fabulous cookie jars, flatware, straw doormats and all sorts of other things for your country home.

MammaRò
238-240, Kifisias Ave., 210/8083833.
The internationally famous company, now in Greece in a lovely shop full of colour and wood, with a decided air of Tuscany about it. House and kitchen wares in a light rustic style - everything from dishes, flatware and tablecloths to home style jams.

Natura
21, Kyriazi St., 210/8012811.
Useful and ornamental objects for the house, chosen with flair and enthusiasm and a note of romanticism. Lace, pot pourri and the prettiest shower curtains on the market.

Past & Present
1, Kolokotroni St. (1st floor), 210/6231299.
Sets of dishes, picture frames, small gifts and other articles for the house, including the fabulous line of wicker products from Tohu Bohu, so perfect for the stylish country house.

Virginia Ventouraki
11, Levidou St., 210/8081210.
No introduction needed. All Philippe Starck's and Alessi gadgets, for a house full of colour, humour and alternative attitude. For the gourmet, a super line of pots and pans, but at these prices you'd almost expect them to do the cooking for you.

Wax & Craft
14-16, Kyriazi St., 210/8081733.
Candles in fabulous shapes and colours, with symbols of the seasons hidden in their hearts.
Dried flowers, leaves, shells, rope - they make wonderful gifts (why not treat yourself, too?).

MISCELLANEOUS
Anemos
36, Kyriazi St., 210/8082027.
A client-friendly gallery that generally exhibits Greek artists. Don't hesitate to come in, browse, ask questions - there'll be no pressure to buy. Exhibitions change frequently, so it's worth stopping in from time to time.

Kamarinos Engravings
20, Panagitsas St., 210/8017079.
Atmospheric shop, and something of a time

machine to boot. Lovely engravings, tastefully framed, old books, and other ideas for gifts or for the home.

Hallmark
7, Kolokotroni St., 210/8011827.
Colour and cheerful humour reign supreme. Original greeting cards, clever party invitations, paper plates with matching cups and napkins, paper chains and swags, plush animals and wonderful bags and boxes to put them in. The special photo albums for weddings, baptisms and other festive occasions are a real must.

Papasotiriou
10, Kolokotroni St., 210/6231854.
Everything you might need for your computer, from books to CDs.
Huge selection of titles and games, sensibly arranged so that you can easily find what you're looking for. Well-informed staff that give the impression of knowing each and every game inside out... Every job has its up side!

Type Center
9, Kyriazi St., 210/8083671.
Distinctive invitations, cards and writing paper. A wealth of designs and papers, at hefty prices. If you like pens, this is your place. Do ask for the sampler - the shop has an impressive collection. And since everybody who is anybody comes in here, be sure to look at the display case - there are bound to be invitations for weddings and parties that made a tremendous splash...

Octopus

Stenia

Shopping

GLYFADA

Although the NATO base has gone, the American influence is still there: many (for the size of the market, at least) malls, pubs springing up in the back streets, gangs of kids on their skateboards. If you like shopping combined with a lively beat, if you enjoy exploring shopping centres or if you simply happen to live in one of the southern suburbs, then Glyfada is the hot shopping spot for you.

Strolling about, you'll find youngsters chilling out, kids on roller blades, ladies with that total jean look, and of course tourists - the big stores are full of groups of Italians animatedly bargaining over everything.

You'll sip your freddo at Egomio, watching the world go by, and at Panino's delicatessen, a favourite artists hang-out, you'll buy something delectable to take home. At First you'll browse at the amazing window displays with clothes by Holly, Vent Couvert and of course Christopher Kontentos. Baskets of merchandise frequently stand on the pavements. At Soho Soho Private (by appointment only), you'll fall in love with the leather caftans by Angali, the painted shirts from Spicy Cookie and the fabulous Lost Toys. Enjoy a tasty salad or a light meal at The Cafe, the most it place in the district, or pick up a freduccino and a marvellous sandwich on an unusual bun at the Style Cafe. At Ensayar you'll shop for Cavali, Voyage and Yazoo, and at Pinko you'll rave over the sweaters. At Stenia you'll adore Matoula and her fabulous alternative street wear, from Juicy Culture, Dice Kayak and Vera Arapon. Aioli has wonderful spaghetti, and Antonio has real Italian pizza with a thin crispy crust. At the Art & Deco House you'll find the nicest invitations, and at Crabtree & Evelyn you'll select beautifully fragrant bath products and pot pourri, and some fine English delicacies.

We have selected for you some of the most interesting shops in this area, and have shared some secret tips. So if you want to know where to find ethnic clothing from Java and India, where to look for the most provocative undies, where to buy jasmine pearls for your tea or antistress quartz crystals, just consult this Guide and... have fun!

The southern suburbs are a shopping paradise with a recognisably American flavour.

ATHENS 2004

ALPHA BANK
OFFICIAL BANK

GLYFADA
CLOTHES

A La Mode
27, Ang. Metaxa St., 210/8982024.
Attractive, uncluttered place and a clientele with attitude and taste. Clothes and accessories (men's and women's) from Dolce & Gabbana, Miu-Miu, Prada, Dries Van Noten, Marni, Collection Privée, Garage and Ric Owens.

Attitudes
17, Al. Panagouli St., 210/8942113.
Men's and women's casual chic clothing. Paul Smith, Armani jeans, etc., for sporty but very elegant dressing.

Carouzos
23, Ang. Metaxa St., 210/8941474.
Synonymous with big name shopping. Men's and women's lines from Prada, Jil Sander, Fendi etc., plus distinctive accessories, shoes and bags. Impeccable service from the extremely polite staff. The hand-made shoes by John Lobb are a must.

Colori
16, Gr. Lampraki St., 210/8982146.
Casual chic in a sleek attractive environment that sets them off beautifully. All day clothes notable for their intelligent details and youthful style. We loved the vine leaf beach sandals.

Ensayar
24-26, Ang. Metaxa St., 210/8943694.
Another of the neighbourhood's progressive stores. Distinctive and elegant women's clothes, selected from the collections of D&G, Cavalli, Moschino, Gaultier, Voyage, Exte, Simultaneous, Burberry's, Yazoo and Cacharel. Next door, at number 22, is the men's shop, with clothes and accessories from the same fashion houses.

First
16, Gr. Lampraki St.
One of the best stores in the neighbourhood, and the window displays are absolutely stunning. Gold background, red and white roses, design lighting with little prisms, wonderful clothes and accessories from Holly, Vent Couvert, Blumarine and D&G. Don't miss - here's a plug for Greek design - the eccentric styles from Christopher Kontentos, who this year has created some fabulous boots, fit for a fairy tale prince!

Free Shop
1, Botsari St., 210/9680123.
Alternative modern ambience, for men's and women's clothes with real character - something between avant-garde and decontracte. Lines from (among others) Marcella, Day, Claude Pierlot, wonderful bags from Orla Kiely and accessories from Maria Calderara.

Gloria Caram
29, Ang. Metaxa St., 210/8946947.
Young contemporary clothes that faithfully reflect foreign fashion trends while adapting them to the style of the modern Greek woman. Excellent prices.

Kathy Heyndels
13, Gr. Lampraki St., 210/8982224.
One of Greece's oldest fashion houses, still on the top list, and now in the hands of the next generation. Classic clothes, and very interesting leather creations.

La Strega
2, Giannitsopoulou St., Esperidon Sq., 210/8981480.
Italian clothes and accessories that follow the prescriptions of the most it trends of the season. Lace, neo-hippy, and new stock all the time - owner Antigoni pops over every two weeks to renew her collection.

Luisa
21, Ang. Metaxa St., 210/8940358.
A shop that doesn't merely offer fashion, but makes a statement about absolute style. Expensive clothes, selected from the collections of Cavalli, Pucci, Etro, Missoni and Plein Sud. In the Glyfada shop, we saw the heaviest and most heavily embroidered pieces, starting with the leathers and caftans from Cavalli.

Max Mara
25, Ang. Metaxa St., 210/8949855.
Classic clothes in subdued colours, with the emphasis on quality fabrics and impeccable finishing. Also a few more modern pieces, like the embroidered jeans from Max Sport, but the absolute investment here is always an all time classic coat.

New Cult
9, Ang. Metaxa St., 210/8940362.
Clothes and accessories for men and women. Young trendy style, for youthful and very with-it dressing. Check out their website (www.new-cult.gr) for a preview.

Oberon
10, Foivis St. & Ang. Metaxa, 210/8949639.
A small shop, full of magic, to wing you away to another world. Colourful clothes and accessories from India and Java, with the ethnic flavour that was so popular last summer. You will find them simply enchanting.

Paul & Shark
18, Dousmani St.,
210/8947969.
Elegant classic decor in
shades of blue and dark
wood. Full designer line for
men who like classic sports
clothes. Exceptional quality,
wide variety, sizes up to 4XL.

Pinko
16, Gr. Lampraki St.,
210/8980196.
Minimal interior and Italian
design for very modern clothes with character and personality. Delectable leather
trousers, wool skirts with
applique flowers, bulky
pullovers with extra long
sleeves. Intriguing detail: chif-
fon blouses with sleeves
made from real woollen
socks!

Precetto
6, Ang. Metaxa St.,
210/8948522.
Embroidered dresses and
trousers for a very dressy
evening. Also the accessories
you need to complete your
outfit. Extremely helpful sales
staff and reasonable prices.

Central Prince Oliver
23, Ang. Metaxa St.,
210/8982927.
The trendiest and most
youthful shops in the Tou-
manidis Group. Eccentric
creations in clothes and
accessories from Paul & Joe,
Issey Miyake, Patrick Cox,
Kenzo, Malloni, Hugo, Paco
Rabanne, Alessandro del
Aqua, Sonia Rykel, Etro, Paul
Smith and Yohji Yamamoto.
Shopping paradise for men
and women who go for bold
and beautiful.

Replay Stores
11, Ang. Metaxa St.,
210/9680180.
American style store with
pale wood, old advertising
signs and the maker's entire
collection of clothes and

shoes. American sportswear
for men, women and chil-
dren.

Sofos
21, Ang. Metaxa St.,
210/8946660.
A shop that veered away
from its classic tradition
a few years ago to follow
a more modern line. Clothes
that tread a nice balance
between the trendy and the
comme il faut, giving even
those whose sartorial preferences tend to the conven-
tional a decided air of fashion.

Soho Soho Private
122, Gounari St.,
210/9622159, 0944660499.
By appointment only. But
don't let that put you off - in
this wholly renovated shop
you will find (exclusive and
one-of-a-kind) treasures:
accessories from Vasileia,
hand-painted shirts from
Spicy Cookie and trousers
from Katerina Vagia, fabulous
trainers from Roberto
Cavali. And more: dresses
from Colyn B. (new designs
every week), clothes and
accessories from Lost Toys,
super trendy leather caftans
from Angali and, of course,
Katerina Pleioni's wonderful
unique accessories.

Stefanel
22, Ang. Metaxa St.
Simple everyday clothes for
soigne casual dressing. For
men and women who like
the clean cut look. Neutral
colours, excellent quality and
a few more progressive
items, saucy touches on a
rather classical background.

Stenia
70, Kyprou St, Esperidon
Sq., 210/8941321.
Uncluttered modern space,
friendly ambience, impeccable service, reasonable
prices, Matoula's unerring

instinct and lots of people, in
one of the hottest shops in
the area. Clothes from Juicy
Culture, Paper Denim, Age,
Dice Kayak and Cyuso, acce-
ssories from Dior Jewellery,
Streets Ahead and Phorms.
Two particularly interesting
lines from "ex's": Venera
Arapou, who designed the
Chloe collection before Stella
McCartney, and Gaowei+Xin
Zhan, formerly of Gaultier.

Tsantilis
35, Ang. Metaxa St.,
210/8983028.
Dressmaker fabrics of
superb quality and pattern
for clothes that you usually
admire in shop windows.
Also, ladies' wear with the
attention to detail that gives
them an air of luxury. For
clients who insist on classic
style and value.

Zara
2, Ang. Metaxa St. 2 & 21,
Lazaraki St., 210/8945600.
Designer-inspired clothes at
very affordable prices, opening a once-select market to
the general population. All
the stores in the chain carry
lines for men, women and
children.

STOCK
Carouzos Stock
41, Ang. Metaxa St.,
210/8946202.
All last year's clothes and
accessories (men's and women's), in ends of lines and
odd sizes, at discounts of
70%. This store is in itself
reason enough to come to
Glyfada!

CHILDREN'S
Bambineria
19, Ang. Metaxa St.,
210/8943031.

Shopping

The good shopper... starts young. Designer clothes and accessories for the junior set: Armani, Henry Cottons, Christian Dior, Byblos, Simonetta, Cacharel, Fiorucci, Miss Blumarine, La Perla, Tartine & Chocolat and Agatha Ruiz Della Prada etc.

Frattina
37, Ang. Metaxa St., 210/8983376.
Ultra chic children's clothes for designer tots. DKNY jackets, shoes with attitude, swimsuits and accessories for junior socialites.

Mothercare
33, Ang. Metaxa St., 210/8982739.
Clothes for children aged 0 to 10, plus maternity clothes and baby needs. Also small toys, shoes and baptismal gifts.

To Paichnidi
11, Botsari St., 210/9680825.
Lots of interesting toys and games for pre-schoolers and their older siblings. Huge collection of plush animals, plus those wooden toys by Sevi that the kids love and their parents collect.

SHOES - BAGS

Borsa & Arte
31, Lazaraki St., 210/8948384.
Superb leather and other - handbags. All you have to do is choose the one that looks best with your favourite outfit.

Kalogirou
72, Kyprou St., Esperidon Sq., 210/8900830.
There can't be anyone who has never shopped once, or at least window-shopped, at Kalogirou. Men's and women's shoes from Prada, Tod's, Ungaro, Miu Miu and other equally sensational

names. Just remember that if you see something you like, buy it, because it probably won't be there tomorrow.

Longchamp
9, Dousmani St., 210/8982814.
An historic name in leather goods. In recent years there have been some delightful surprises, like the design-it-yourself bag, where the customer puts together her own colours and styles. The Glyfada shop puts on a more modern face than the others, but holds to the same traditional classic style of the parent house.

MCM
15, Dousmani St. & Botsari, 210/8942658.
The full collection of leather goods with the familiar monogram logo. Also Versace-type clothes and accessories with lots of gold trimmings.

Petridis
18, Ang. Metaxa St., 210/8944638.
Men's and women's shoes from Parallele, Camper, Jourdan and many other names, in one of the city's perennial favourites. The house lines are also interesting, crafted in classic styles out of beautiful leathers.

ACCESSORIES

Accessorize
24-26, Ang. Metaxa St., 210/8985301.
The newest spot for accessories. Wonderful selection, constantly renewed, at very affordable prices, which makes it hard usually to get through the door! The hats are a must: winter or summer they're all fabulous, and so cheap you can buy them all!

Calzedonia
4, Esperidon Sq., 210/8944646.
Socks and tights in the winter, swimwear in the summer, all in such fabulous variety as to satisfy the most demanding shopper.

Starstrass
6, Ang. Metaxa St., 210/8948522.
Huge variety of men's and women's accessories, at good prices. Ring the changes on your favourite outfit, adapting it to your every mood.

JEWELLERY - WATCHES

Folli Follie
8, Ang. Metaxa St., 210/8947850.
The shop that made gold and silver combos a fashion item. Now the windows display costlier pieces in gold, ethnic lines in silver and semi-precious stones, and superlative accessories including bags, watches and silk shawls.

Jaloux
6, Ang. Metaxa St., 210/8941484.
Zircon-studded silver and silver combo jewellery, watches and accessories. A different look for elegant dressing, at very accessible prices.

Li-La-Lo
16, Gr. Lampraki St. & Ang. Metaxa, 210/8982554.
Silver and silver combo jewellery, in a large bright sleek-looking store that immediately attracts the attention. Also an interesting collection of silver baptismal gifts.

Michalis
166, Ang. Metaxa St., 210/8982607.
Heavy jewellery in gold and platinum, flashing diamonds and Vacheron et Constantin watches, for big spenders.

san marzano

pizza pasta vino e birra

ΥΔΡΑΓΩΓΕΙΟ

Close to you every day

Creative Cuisine

Shopping

COSMETICS

Body 'n Soul
17, Foivis St., 210/8945737.
A bit of paradise for those who fancy alternative cosmetics. Powder from T. LeClerc, hair oils from Kiehl's, face creams from Aesop and many other interesting products. Highlights include aromatic candles, vanilla-scented pot pourri, and the fabulous tweezers by Twezerman.

Crabtree & Evelyn
16, A. Papandreou St., 210/8981032.
Elegant and very green, with an air of London about it. Scented candles, pot pourri, scented hangers, shelf paper and drawer bags, bath oils and other bathroom items, fragrances, and an interesting men's line (the classic wooden shaving soap bowl is a real must-have). And there is a fine food section, with jams and marmalades, biscuits and aromatic oils, for your own kitchen or for a gourmet gift made in England.

Heaven on Earth
11, Botsari St., 210/9680564.
Alternative cosmetics, obeying the recent dynamic trends in this sector. Cosmetics by Philosophy and Talika, Milk Fresh bath products smelling deliciously of chocolate, coffee or mocha. And don't forget the original "Oh my dog, oh my cat" products, for pampered pets.

THIS & THAT

Natura
46B, Ang. Metaxa St., 210/8944692.
Useful and ornamental objects for the house, chosen with flair and enthusiasm and a note of romanticism. Lace, pot pourri and the prettiest shower curtains on the market. Gifts for friends or for yourself, for an added touch of quality in everyday living.

Octopus
33, Ang. Metaxa St., 210/8980428.
Original gifts and gadgets for the house. We loved the fish and cow shaped "mice" with their matching mouse pads, the portable fish radio, the plush picture frames and the super wow mobile phone cases.

HOUSEWARES - INTERIORS

Art & Deco House
27-29, Ang. Metaxa St., 210/8982618.
Small shop with lots of hand-crafted ornamental items, like wooden picture frames, small pictures, bright pretty swags. Lovely and very original line of comfit boxes, invitations and photo albums for weddings and baptisms - you'll fall in love with them for sure.

Carousel
61, Kyprou St., 210/8946961.
Ornaments and occasional furnishings, chosen with flair, for shoppers of discernment. The Venetian masks are a must.

Gata pou ti lene Uccello
1-3, Botsari St. & A. Papandreou, 210/8981931.
Ornaments and occasional pieces, chosen with imagination and exceptionally fine taste, to give your home a very special atmosphere. Wonderful wooden furniture, amazing lamps, pieces reminiscent of Wales, Cornwall, Tuscany and ethnic items.

Gallis Lighting
27, Lazaraki St., 210/8942301.
Light, more light! Choose one of the hundreds of lamps in this wonderful collection to light up your evenings.

Ikia
2A, Esperidon Sq., 210/9680264.
Bath and kitchen shop, with a good collection of ornamental items. We particularly liked the dishes and glasses, the design fans, the coconut straw mats, the wonderful bathroom scales and the pretty aluminium lamps.

Kosta Boda
16, Lazaraki St., 210/8940347.
One of the oldest names on the Greek scene. Crystal ornaments for the home from famous Danish and Norwegian designers, dinner services, rattan and fabric furniture, and a particularly interesting line of kitchen wares from Swedish wood.

Laura Ashley
59, Kyprou St., 210/8943611.
Romantic flower print upholstery fabrics, decorative cushions, place settings for two, pot pourri, scented lining paper for your drawers and much more. For those who like the Little House on the Prairie look.

Room Service
16, Foivis St., 210/8946700.
Design ornaments and occasional pieces for the home. Spare geometric shapes and clear, strong colours for the wallpaper style so beloved of late by Greek stylists.

MISS SIXTY.

ENERGIE

Killah

gsus

NO.L.ITA N.Y.C.

MELTIN POT

ecko unltd.

custo

mambo

ROYAL

Ra.Re

Buddhist Punk

SHOP

SHOP >> 52, Patission str., Athens
> tel.: 210 8826054 > info@trade.com.gr

the Golden
Athens of
taste

ALPHA 2004
Limited Edition
4532 0123 4568 2004
VISA

You are demanding. Satisfied with nothing but the best. When you go out, everything has to be perfect. What you want is... the city on your plate.
And you know that gold is a universal guarantee of excellence.
Like the Golden Cook's Hat, the gustatory Oscars that the "Athinorama" awards every year to indicate you the best restaurants in the city. The Athens of taste is coloured in gold. And you can enjoy its most gourmet side, with the ATHENS 2004 Gold VISA, the collectable card created by Alpha Bank for the demanding, for you!

ALPHA BANK OFFICIAL BANK OF THE ATHENS 2004 OLYMPIC GAMES

Eating out

Athens Guide 2003

ATHENS 2004

ALPHA BANK

OFFICIAL BANK

a gastronomic
metropolis
is born

The year 2003 will put the final touches to a process that has been under way in Athens for several years now: namely, its rapid and steady conversion into a gastronomic metropolis, in tune with the times but with its own distinct personality. On the city's constantly evolving restaurant scene, taste trends mesh with traditional Greek and Mediterranean nexus, while ethnic cuisines give polished Gallic flair a run for its money. The result is a colourful and wonderfully flavourful fusion that has won the enthusiastic approval of a public that truly relishes the good things of life.

Today's Athens can justifiably claim to be a gastronomic metropolis. Its restaurant scene may not be as well developed as those of New York or London, but it does share some of their vital characteristics: it is lively, it is to a significant degree determined by trends and fashions, and it displays a diversity that includes a very satisfactory representation of ethnic cuisines from different parts of the world.

This, of course, has not always been the case. But for the past several years the restaurant market has progressed amazingly: dozens of restaurants open every year; there is substantial investment in the sector, with many business figures branching out in this direction; and famous chefs from around the world come to work in Athens, while the menus in some of the city's best known restaurants are overseen by some of the most celebrated French chefs (at present). At the same time, a new and very promis-

Beau Brummel

Plous Podilatou

Spondi

The Spondi wins a Golden Hat

ing generation of Greek chefs is emerging. This progress is reflected in the "Golden Hat" awards published every year by "Athinorama" magazine, an institution that in 2003 will be celebrating its 10th birthday. The number of "best restaurants" (those awarded a certain number of points or more and which are eligible for one of the prize awards) is continually growing, while with every passing year it becomes harder and harder to choose the top ten. Even the very conservative Michelin Guide has acknowledged this change, giving two of the city's restaurants (Vardis and Varoulko) a star apiece - and we are persuaded that in its next edition Athens will feature with at least three and possibly four stars. For never have the city's top restaurants been better. Spondi, ruled over by chef Jerome Serres under the watchful eye of (Michelin 2 star) chef

Jacques Chibois, continues to evolve and to impress with its achievements. Vardis, under the guidance of (Michelin 2 star) chef Manuel Martinez, continues zealously to produce fine results; plans, however, call for it to close for a few months during 2003 for a complete overhaul, to turn it into the "restaurant for all seasons" promised by owner Charis Vardis. Meanwhile, the Beau Brummel pursues its scintillating course, with the fabulous Jean de Grillot at the helm. Nor must we forget to mention Red, in the Athinais complex, or Aigli, in Zappeion Park - two more restaurants that are becoming ever more interesting. An exciting new restaurant that will soon be opening its doors - and from which we expect great things - is the "48" in the Ileana Tounta Gallery, which is to be in the talented and capable hands of chef Christoforos Peskias, who has

tip
Athinorama's "Golden Hats" are awarded to Athens' top restaurants in an annual competition that is now in its tenth year. The "Golden Hats" have become an institution, and have played a significant role in the upgrading of the city's restaurant scene.

Chrysopsaro

Alekos Metropolitan

Eating out

Central

Fogg's

Aegli Bistrot Café

been training with such top chefs as Ferran Andria, Marc Meneau and Joël Robuchon.

At the same time, ethnic cuisines are becoming steadily better represented, with arabesque (Red Marrakesh, Habiba), Indian (Yoga Bala, Jaipur Palace, Shalimar) and sushi (now served in many restaurants, regardless of any Japanese affiliation) at the top of last year's charts, while fusion and Mediterranean cuisine dominate the trendier restaurants, as is the fashion everywhere.

But while Athens certainly follows international trends, she also creates her own. Last year witnessed a remarkable rise in the fortunes of Greek cuisine, a trend that is expressed in two different ways. First of all, many of the city's finest chefs have been experimenting with Greek recipes and ingredients, proposing in their "modified Greek" restaurants dishes that could well stand as the paradigm of modern Greek cuisine. Lefteris Lazarou at Varoulko, Chrysanthos Karamolegkos at Aristera-Dexia, Giannis Geldis at Orizontes Lykavittou and Giannis Baxevanis at Mezzo-Mezzo, and to a lesser degree Michalis Lytrivis (Edodi), Herve Pronzato (Ruby Club) and Jean-Yves Caratoni (Atelier Agrotikon) are some of the celebrated

chefs who propose some of the most creative Greek cuisine in the city, raising it to a whole other plane with the aid of French (for the most part) techniques. We have also tasted interesting dishes at such modern Greek restaurants as Kitrino Podilato, Plous Podilatou, Gefseis me Onomasia Proelefsis, Kallisti and Ydragogeio.

But it is not only in the fine and creative restaurants that we see Greek cuisine making a dynamic comeback: the ever-popular taverna is also changing its style. Traditional small tavernas where the grill is hot, the fish fresh and the cooked dishes well-prepared still exist and always will; but they are being joined by "modern tavernas" that, while preserving the simplicity and relaxed atmosphere of the genuine article, have embraced a more modern, aesthetically more progressive style, moving away from the classic or the impersonal and appealing to a younger and trendier public. In an age when the mannered and the complicated seem to predominate, the taverna "sells" simplicity of cuisine and service, virtues that everyone seems to appreciate. Some of these "new style" tavernas add to the mix a party atmosphere featuring powerful Greek music: e.g. Sea Satin, Taverna and

ΣΠΟΝΔΗ
(Restaurant)

5, PYRRONOS ST., VARNAVA SQ., PAGKRATI (behind the Kallimarmaro Stadium)
tel.: 210/7564021, 210/7520658, fax: 210/7567021
www.spondi.gr

Eating out

Balthazar

Red

Dirty Str-eat. But the most durable fashion is the one that combines food and a bar ambience, for it rests on the cheerfully extroverted character of the Athenian public and on their tendency to combine food and entertainment. Thus, for many years now some of the most interesting and most talked-about places fall into this category. The list is endless, but includes places like Interni, Big Deals, Balthazar, Central, Island, Cosmos, Alekos Metropolitan and many more. The restaurants in the city's great hotels are also evolving and steadily improving, carried along by the dynamic of the market and the general orgy of renovation and up-grading that is sweeping the hotel landscape in view of the 2004 Olympic Games. The exceptionally interesting Karavi in the Airport Sofitel, in the hands of the very capable Marc Morel, the Grand Balcon in the St. George Lycabettus, with its fine young Swedish chef Mark Enderborg, the gorgeous Polynesian Kochylia in the Grand Resort Lagonissi, the gourmet Cafe Tabac in The Margi, the Mediterranean Olive Garden in the Titania, the now classic Kona Kai in the Ledra Marriott, the idyllic Mythos in the Divani Apollon Palace & Spa, the classic Captain's House at the Asteras: these are just some of the fine hotel restaurants that are distinguished for both their gastronomic standards and their atmosphere. We also expect great things of the brand new Café Zoe in the Intercontinental, Brown's in the Divani Caravel, and of course the new restaurants in the Grande Bretagne and the Hilton, which are scheduled to open in February.

Meanwhile - and largely because of these developments - wine continues to strengthen its position in the city's restaurants. Wine lists have never been longer or more sophisticated, and in virtually all the city's best restaurants include - among their 100-150 or so labels - wines from all over the world. And it's more than just diversity of choice. More and more cellars are opening, and more and more restaurants are endeavouring to acquire an expert wine-service.

In this Guide you will find the most important restaurants and tavernas in Athens, classed in a way that we think will help you make your choice, so that you can navigate as confidently as possible through the multiform landscape of gastronomic Athens.

Eating out

RESTAURANTS
GOURMET

Aigli Bistrot Café
Aigli Zappeiou,
210/3369363-4.
Open: Year round,
daily, noon-evening.
Price: € 36-42.
One of the most delightful
spots in Athens, surrounded by pines and overlooking
Zappeio Park and the
Acropolis. Chef Jean-Louis
Capsala is attuned to modern Mediterranean frequen-
cies, and his cuisine, while
acknowledging certain classics, bears the definite
imprint of France and Italy.

Beau Brummel
9, Agiou Dimitriou St. &
Agion Theodoron, Kifisia,
210/6236780. **Open:** Year
round, daily (except
Sunday), noon-evening.
Price: € 70-90 (Downstairs,
fixed price menu € 65).
Epic restaurant by the standards of Athens (3rd place
in the 2002 Golden Hat
awards), with a luxurious
formal gourmet dining
room and a thoroughly
modern lounge-bar. Chef
Jean De Grylleau bases his
cuisine on the finest ingredients, superlative technique

and the charm of simplicity.
Don't miss the fabulous
crayfish with lasagne. The
service is superb and the
wine list, drawn mainly
from the vineyards of
Greece and France, impressive. The lunch menu fea-
tures classic French and
Greek cuisine at reasonable
prices.

Edodi
80, Veikou St., Koukaki,
210/9213013. **Open:** Year
round, daily (except
Sunday), evenings.
Price: € 35-40.
Theatrical gourmet restaurant (that received a 2002
Golden Hat award) with
matinee prices and many
echoes of the creative cuisine of the late lamented
master chef of the old
Bajazzo, Klaus Feuerbach.
Owners Michalis Lytrivis as
sous-chef and his brother
Giorgos, who orchestrates
and directs the presentation
of the dishes in their raw
state, before they are
cooked, follow in the creative footsteps of their
mentor. Ample and well-
chosen wine list, with selections from all over the
world.

Karavi
Athens International Airport
(Hotel Sofitel), Spata,
210/3544000. **Open:** Year
round, daily, evenings.
Price: € 60-95.
Contemporary design,
warmly modern dining
room and an interesting
creative cuisine based on
Mediterranean ingredients.
This gastronomic vessel
(moored on the 9th floor of
the Sofitel hotel) is com-
manded by talented young
chef Marc Morel.

Le Grand Balcon
2, Kleomenous St. (Hotel
St. George Lycabettus),
Kolonaki, 210/7290712.
Open: Year round, daily
(except Sunday-Monday),
evenings. **Price:** € 33-39.
Newly arrived and very
promising Swedish chef
Marc Enderborg creates a
light modern Mediterranean
cuisine for the gourmet
restaurant in the St. George
Lycabettus hotel. Come
April, the panoramic view
of the city will be set off by
an airy decor signed by
Angelos Angelopoulos.

Orizontes Lykavittou
Lycabettus Hill,
Kolonaki, 210/7227065.

Enastron

Interni

Open: Year round, daily, evenings. **Price:** € 40-60.
The summit of Lycabettus has finally (summer 2002) acquired the quality cuisine befitting this marvellous situation. Chef Giannis Geldis weaves deftly between simple excellence and baroque creativity. This winter he will be experimenting with a creative Greek cuisine. Elegant, luxurious dining room with retro touches and a breath-taking view of the city.

Red
Athinais: 34-36, Kastorias St., Votanikos, 210/3480000.
Open: Year round, daily (except Sunday), evenings.
Price: € 38-50.
Chef Giannis Tzelepis of the gourmet restaurant in the Athinais Cultural Centre proposes an opulent Mediterranean cuisine, enriched with exotic elements. The dining room is the most atmospheric in the city, with its deep red sofas and stone walls, and the service is superb.

Spondi
5, Pyrronos St., Pagkrati, 210/7520658, 210/7564021.

Open: Year round, daily, evenings. **Price:** € 42-53.
The best restaurant in Athens (Golden Hats 2002) - and de facto in Greece -, with a cuisine of an audacious simplicity that is never anything less than first-class. Superlative (2 Michelin stars) French chef Jacques Chibois is in charge of the menu, in collaboration with his excellent restaurant chef Jerome Serres. In this marvellously elegant dining room you will be treated to such fabulous dishes as perfectly grilled sea bass with a feather-light sauce of rose petals and vanilla-scented oil, or scallops with a cauliflower puree. The signature dessert is a tantalising symphony of flavours: lotus with mandarin sorbet on a bed of pineapple/banana puree, candied olives and a drizzle of vanilla-scented olive oil, with a sauce composed of basil, saffron and curry! Impeccable service, and cellars that this year will feature more than a thousand labels.

Vardis
66, Diligianni St. (Hotel Pentelikon), Kifisia,

210/6230650-6. **Open:** Year round, daily (except Sunday), evenings.
Price: € 65-85.
One of the country's top restaurants (2nd place in the 2002 Golden Hat awards, I Michelin star), with dishes that are outstanding in their artistry and aromatic expressiveness. Elegant room, combining classical luxury and modern decorative allusions. Since the autumn of 2001 Manuel Martinez (two Michelin stars) has been responsible for the kitchen, represented on the spot by his sous-chef Bertrand Valegeas. To complete the picture: an extensive but classic list of French and Greek wines, a cheese trolley, and superlative service.

Varoulko
14, Deligiorgi St., Piraeus, 210/4112043, 210/4221283.
Open: Year round, daily (except Sunday), evenings.
Price: € 42-50.
Always a prime favourite, regularly awarded a Golden Hat, and the first Greek restaurant to win a Michelin star (in 2002). In its elegant, uncluttered dining room,

Kona Kai

Royal Thai

Eating out

Prytaneio

the Varoulko realises an imaginative and contemporary Greek cuisine, introducing new ideas, concentrating the essence, refining its specialities.

Characteristic dishes include the wonderful marinated parrot-fish with creamed broccoli, truffle oil and balsamico and the cult steamed monkfish with vegetables. Owner-chef Lefteris Lazarou - the heart and soul of the place - orchestrates the service and the composition of very special menus at each table. Excellent new wine list.

TRENDY

Alekos Metropolitan

74, Mitropoleos St., Syntagma Sq., 210/3319650. **Open:** Year round, daily (except Sunday), evenings. **Price:** € 20-25.

Stylish simplicity and an abstract elegance, animated by a crowd of executives and beautiful people. Expressive Italian flavours, imaginative combinations, sophisticated experiments from chef Fabbrizio Bouliani. Excellent sweets, including the best chocolate dessert in Athens (perfetta).

Aristera - Dexia

3, Andronikou St., Rouf, 210/3422380. **Open:** Year round, daily (except Sunday), evenings. **Price:** € 27-33.

A cuisine at once time-honoured and incredibly creative, the best cellars in Athens and a striking, truly modern decor combine to make this one of the most successful restaurants in the city. Nor does its summertime offshoot lag behind: Apla Aristera Dexia is a progressive and creative taverna that plays intelligent variations on traditional Greek mezedes.

Azul

43, Charitos St., Kolonaki, 210/7253817. **Open:** Year round, daily (except Sunday), evenings. **Price:** € 24-30.

Light, creative, Mediterranean-inspired dishes and casual-trendy finger food. Explosive colours (orange, fuchsia, blue), and Plexiglas shelves at the bar that change colour with the changing light.

Balthazar

27, Tsocha St. & D. Soutsou, Ampelokipoi, 210/6412300-9. **Open:** Year round, daily, evenings. **Price:** € 39-47.

Neo-classic stateliness combines with modern design in one of the loveliest bar-restaurants in the city. Talented chef Christoforos Peskias plays creatively with tradition, proposing a very interesting and personal cuisine.

Big Deals

50, Charilaou Trikoupi St., Kifisia, 210/6230860. **Open:** Year round, daily, evening. **Price:** € 35-45.

Huge, atmospheric, with modern design and a bar that is always packed. Creative modern food, attractively presented. Fast, courteous service, varied and extensive wine list. Good selection of cocktails, cigars and spirits.

Central

14, Filikis Etaireias Sq., Kolonaki, 210/7245938, 210/7241059. **Open:** Winter only, daily, noon-evening. **Price:** € 35-45.

Elegant room with Japanese effects, warm colours and a great sushi bar. The main lounge is a real hot spot, and always full whatever the hour, not least because of

Καράβι
(Karavi)

SOFITEL ATHENS AIRPORT

Sofitel Athens Airport welcomes you "on board" of the most gourmet experience you have ever tasted. The gastronomic restaurant "Karavi" conveys you the ultimate gourmet experience with refined dishes created by the French chef, Marc Morel right behind a wall of frosted glass in the restaurant's show kitchen. From the 9th floor of Sofitel Athens Airport where "Karavi" is situated, the only "disruption" you might have from your gastronomic ritual is its panoramic view over the airport and the vineyards of Mesogeia plain.

SOFITEL
ACCOR HOTELS & RESORTS

Sofitel Athens Airport, Athens International Airport "Eleftherios Venizelos", tel.: 210/3544000, fax: 210/3544444.

ACCOR ▶ European leader and worldwide group in the universe of Hotels and Services.

Eating out

the excellent music (ethnic, dance, trip-hop). Good food, blending Mediterranean and exotic elements, and a fine selection of post-prandial cigars and spirits.

Cosmos
8, Omirou St., Neo Psychiko, 210/6729150-3. **Open:** Year round, daily (except Sunday), noon-evening. **Price:** € 30-39.
Modern unfussy interior, shared by a quiet room for formal dining and a cheerful bar-restaurant. Chef Christos Tzieras combines classic favourites and exotic creations. Adequate wine list.

Fogg's
10-12, Kifisias Ave. (Agora Center), Marousi, 210/6846690. **Open:** Winter only, daily, evenings. **Price:** € 36-45.
The most impressive bar-restaurant in the city. Atmosphere and opulence, in a decor marrying Eastern exoticism and Western elegance. Chef Vangelis Driskas offers perfectly executed fare with a markedly exotic flavour.

Frame
2, Kleomenous St. (Hotel St. George Lycabettus), Kolonaki, 210/7290712. **Open:** Year round, daily, noon-evening. **Price:** € 29-32.
Lounge restaurant decorated in a progressive , striking 60s-70s style by Angelos Angelopoulos. Attractive, simple modern cuisine from TV chef Alexandros Papandreou. Good bar.

Interni
152, Ermou St., Gazi, 210/3468900, 210/3468352. **Open:** Winter only, daily (except Sunday), evenings. **Price:** € 40-50.
Famous architect and designer Paola Navone has created one of the loveliest restaurants in Athens, beautifully integrating Japanese minimalist style into a Western formal concept. Excellent fusion cuisine with a pronounced Asian colour, and real flair in the combination of ingredients. Extensive, varied wine list, satisfactory service.

Island
Km 27, Athens-Sounio road, Varkiza, 210/9653563-4. **Open:** Summer only, daily, evenings. **Price:** € 39-50.
Long a favourite, classic choice for summer dining. Magical location, Greek islands decor with modern designer touches. Light Mediterranean cuisine in more or less inventive combinations, plus interesting sushi. Excellent and well-balanced wine list.

Mezzo - Mezzo
58, Syngrou Ave., 210/9242444. **Open:** Winter only, daily (except Sunday), evenings. **Price:** € 50-60.
Chef Giannis Geldis offers a pared-down version of his sumptuous modern cuisine in this impressive navy-style place, designed around its aquariums. Impressive cellars, one of the best wine lists in Athens and an attractive smoking lounge for your post-prandial cigar.

Mommy
4, Delfon St., Kolonaki, 210/3619682. **Open:** Winter only, daily, evenings. **Price:** € 24-27.
The freestyle '60s atmosphere and second-hand furniture scattered about the various rooms in this villa make you feel as though you've walked into a friend's house. Pleasant menu of finger food and fusion dishes.

Sea Satin
1, Fokylidou St., Kolonaki, 210/3619646. **Open:** Winter only, daily, noon-evening. **Price:** € 25-38.
Fun restaurant that provided the sensation of the year last season, importing the lively original formula from Mykonos to Kolonaki. The warmth and luxury of a good bar-restaurant ideally complement the simple well-prepared fish-taverna food. The cheerful chaos of Saturday and Sunday lunchtime is due to the successful musical cocktail of Greek songs.

Septem
58, Vas. Georgiou II St. (Asteria Seaside), Glyfada, 210/8941620. **Open:** Summer only, daily, evenings. **Price:** € 45-55.
The most attractive place on the waterfront, with a theatrical minimalist decor on a beautiful deck by the sea. The illuminated pool, the palm trees and the sofa beds of the Balux Club (with which it shares this space) create a dreamy setting. Chef Jean-Yves Caratoni creates a light cuisine that is a blend of refined simplicity and flavour intensity.

TBWA\ATHENS

Reservée

Nicole

Penelope

[They shared the same man.
Will they share dessert?]

Uptown and Downtown,
Ethnic and Nouvelle,
Bar and Restaurant...
Come together.
businesslunch@Cosmos

Cosmos — COSMOS BAR RESTAURANT — 8, Omirou str., Psychiko - Tel. (210) 67 29 150

KITRINO
Ποδήλατο
KITRINO PODILAT

ΠΛΟΥΣ ΠΟΔΗΛΑΤΟΥ

RESTAURANT
PLOUS PODILATOU

ΑΚΤΙ Α. ΚΟΥΜΟΥΝΔΟΥΡΟΥ 42 ΜΙΚΡΟΛΙΜΑΝΟ
TEL.: 210 4137910, 210 4137790

SERVICE 12:00 PM. - 12:00 AM.

Eating out

CHIC

Boschetto
Evangelismos Grove, Kolonaki, 210/7210893. Open: Year round, daily (except Sunday), evenings. Price: € 43-56.
Ultra chic restaurant (a favourite in bohemian and business circles) in the pleasant grove at Evangelismos. The classy Italian specialties are good, but don't justify the reputation the place enjoys. Excellent wine list, with some hard-to-find Greek vintage reds and many fine New World reds also.

Café Tabac
11, Litous St. (Hotel Margi), Vouliagmeni, 210/9670924. Open: Year round, daily, noon-evening. Price: € 24-33.
Particularly well-designed interior, with warm earth tones, stone walls, ethnic details and wonderful lighting. A cuisine that just keeps on getting better, and more modern, as it acquires a more pronounced Mediterranean and exotic colouring. Excellent service, and a wine list that girdles the globe.

Chrysa
81, Dimofontos St., Ano Petralona, 210/3412515. Open: Winter only, daily (except Sunday), evenings. Price: € 30-34.
Attractive, uncluttered, recently renovated place, and sophisticated cooking from a wonderful hostess. The menu changes frequently, and the results are highly satisfactory.

Chrysopsaro
61, Papanastasiou St.,

Kastella, 210/4120333. Open: Year round, daily, evenings. Sat.-Sun. also at noon. Price: € 30-40. Gorgeous realisation of a tasteful bright pop modernism with a view of the port of Kastella. Its modern seafood-based cuisine successfully transfers classic elements to the framework of the modern bistro.

O Kyrios Pil Poul
51, Apostolou Pavlou St. & Poulopoulou, Thiseio, 210/3423665. Open: Year round, daily (except Sunday), evenings. Price: € 50-62.
Ambitious restaurant in a neo-classical building that once housed the Poulopoulos hat factory. Classically luxurious, elegant winter dining room and, for the summer months, the most beautiful terrace in Athens: a magnificent luxurious setting overlooking the Acropolis, Lycabettus and the Observatory, with black and white marble and atmospheric music. The cuisine is creative but disciplined, with French and Mediterranean influences.

Olive Garden
52, Panepistimiou St. (Hotel Titania), Omonoia Sq., 210/3838511. Open: Year round, daily, noon-evening. Price: € 27-30. Well-tended roof garden, with olive trees beautifully framing the view of the Acropolis. Imaginative menu, firmly rooted in the Mediterranean tradition, well-chosen ingredients, technical mastery, but overly timid with regard to flavour intensity.

Piazza Mela
238, Kifisias Ave. (Mela Shopping Centre), Kifisia, 210/6236596. Open: Year round, daily (except Sunday), noon-evening. Price: € 33-45.
Extremely elegant all-day cafe-restaurant, with classic Italian dishes executed with unusual flair. Reined-in inspiration and excellence of technique are its basic characteristics. The best gorgonzola in Athens, fabulous panna cotta and creme brule, wonderful espresso.

Plous Podilatou
42, Akti Koumoundourou St., Mikrolimano, Piraeus, 210/4137910, 210/4137790. Open: Year round, daily, noon-evening. Price: € 30-40.
The Piraeus version of the Kitrino Podilato: modern Greek cuisine, careful execution and a wealth of flavours (mainly maritime) and aromas that solo and team up equally well. Decor of an exemplary abstractive elegance that flirts with the summery, holiday mood of the seaside.

Ratka
30, Charitos St., Kolonaki, 210/7290746. Open: Winter only, daily (except Sunday), evenings. Saturday only at noon. Price: € 25-35.
A place that has a page of its own in the history of the city's social life, with a faithful clientele and an unshakeable adherence to its established image and philosophy. Multi-ethnic cuisine, now also featuring excellent sushi. Amazing collection of eaux de vie.

Robin's Hood
34, Vas. Georgiou, Chalandri, 210/6834907,

Taverna

THE CLASSIC

GREEK "TAVERNA"...

...AND NOT ONLY!

236, Kifisias Ave., Filothei

📞 +30210-6728053-4

Eating out

210/6812840. **Open:** Year round, daily (except Sunday), noon-evening. **Price:** € 28-35.

Austere but warm design, and an intensely red bar that links the dining room to the attractive small lounge. The menu maintains a good balance between the classic and the trendy.

Sugar Grill
30, Spefsippou St., Kolonaki, 210/7210655, 210/7233348. **Open:** Winter only, daily (except Sunday), noon-evening. **Price:** € 25-35.

Warm, modern restaurant, wood and stone decor, open kitchen. Interesting food, with a variety of shellfish for starters and delectable steaks to follow. Try the oysters Rockefeller with spinach, the excellent rib-eye steak and the tasty hamburgers.

Symposio
46, Erechtheiou St., Herodion, 210/9225321. **Open:** Year round, daily (except Sunday), evenings. **Price:** € 36-43.

Nicely designed place, with a glassed-in atrium for the winter and a summer terrace overlooking the sacred rock of the Acropolis. The Epirote owner proposes a variety of good things from his native province, with a preponderance of simple dishes. He also has the best bread in Athens!

BAR - RESTAURANTS
Avalon
20, Leokoriou St. & Sarri, Psyrri, 210/3310572. **Open:** Year round, daily, evenings. Sun. also at noon. **Price:** € 21-24.

Famous for its fantastic mussels: fleshy, cooked with Thessalonian flair and mastery in classic or unusual taste combinations, and extremely appetising. The wide selection of beers adds to the feeling of a French brasserie.

Bara
23, Ploutarchou St. & P. Ioakeim, Kolonaki, 210/7217178. **Open:** Winter only, daily, evenings. **Price:** € 24-27.

Warm ambiance, lots of wood and leather, loud, well-chosen music. Good food, both international and modified Greek. Fast, friendly service. Wine list unexpectedly complete and extensive.

DeLuxe
15, Falirou St., Makrygianni, 210/9243184. **Open:** Winter only, daily (except Sunday), evenings. **Price:** € 21-27.

Attractive place, featuring a highly modern combination of '60s and '70s decorative elements with sounds that range from (chiefly) funk through electronica to acid jazz. Moderately original food, and an interesting wine list including a fair number offered by the glass.

Dirty Ginger
46, Triptolemou St., Gazi, 210/3423809. **Open:** Summer only, daily, evenings. **Price:** € 12-18.

One of the most pleasant downtown summer eating places: a cheerful taverna whose beautiful courtyard has a holiday air. Well-prepared appetisers, perfect

fried potatoes, an assortment of meats from the grill and the spit, all flavourful and perfectly cooked. The loud cheerful music heightens the bar atmosphere.

Dirty Str-eat
12, Triptolemou St., Gazi, 210/3474763. **Open:** Year round, daily (except Sunday), evenings. **Price:** € 21-27.

The former Dirty Fish has metamorphosed into the Dirty Str-eat as its menu has expanded to include meat dishes. The simple but intelligent cuisine continues to address traditional recipes and humble ingredients with imagination and flair. The whole place has the feel of a modern mezedopoleio, and you may well round off your evening with a shot or two at the bar.

Malvazia
3, Agathimerou St., Rouf, 210/3417010. **Open:** Year round, daily, evenings. **Price:** € 35-42.

A place redolent of the mediaeval fortress of Monemvasia, its stone walls, wooden tables and countless candles creating a striking atmosphere. The menu proposes Mediterranean flavours, with modern touches enhancing traditional Greek recipes. The candlelight (after 01:00 there is no other lighting) and carefully chosen music invite you to prolong your evening at the bar.

PJ's
322, Kifisias Ave., Neo Psychiko, 210/6714054, 210/6716790. **Open:** Year round, daily, evenings.

The Three Little Pigs have now settled into their new home at Skoufa 73, Kolonaki... an ultra-modern and very stylish setting in the center of town.

Their friends are invited from the morning for coffee, snacks, meals and drinks till very late at night...
Ground level for dining and drinks, upper level for chilling out on sofas and lower level for clubbing and partying.

Their old houses of straw, wood and brick have been transformed into very trendy toilets, each with its own DVD show...

Τα Τρία Γουρουνάκια

Ta Tria Gourounakia (The Three Little Pigs)
CAFE BAR - RESTAURANT
SKOUFA 73, KOLONAKI, TEL.: 210-36.04.400

... the talk of the town!

Price: € 27-30.
Combination club-restaurant and grill-house, in a very English-style setting. Wood, warm bright colours, comfortable sofas, very good very loud music and... fun. The menu features mainly steaks and burgers, with a few more exotic items.

Stoa
101, Patision Ave. & Kodrigktonos St., Patisia, 210/8253932. **Open:** Winter only, daily, evenings. **Price:** € 21-24.
A cafe-bar, a club and a restaurant, all under one roof. The new multispace on Patision Ave. has an air at once modern and classic, with a preponderance of wood in the decor and a glass dome that creates a sense of open space.

Ta Tria Gourounakia
73, Skoufa St., Kolonaki, 210/3604400. **Open:** Year round, daily, evenings. **Price:** € 24-30.
Modern, youthful, trendy, stylish, hip, with a decor inspired by the familiar story of the Three Little Pigs. Light menu, well-prepared food.

Taverna
236, Kifisias Ave., Filothei, 210/6728053-4. **Open:** Winter only, daily, noon-evening. **Price:** € 22-30.
Modern taverna with good, older Greek music and a swinging, up-beat mood. The food is simple, classic and tasty. Do sample the pitas (we liked the cockerel pie) and mezedes, but the real focus is on the grill and spit. The cooked dishes are also excellent: don't miss

the leg of kid baked in a lemon sauce.

The Man Ray by Ginger
10-12, Dorylaiou St., Mavili Sq., 210/6451169. **Open:** Winter only, daily, evenings. **Price:** € 21-27.
With a name acknowledging the surrealist American photographer, the former fun restaurant Ginger has become a trendy club-restaurant with famous DJs on the decks. The restaurant has moved upstairs, where it offers ethnic dishes (with the emphasis on India) and a selection of light finger foods.

The Place
7, Vasileos Georgiou, Chalandri Sq., 210/6856282. **Open:** Year round, daily, noon-evening. **Price:** € 21-25.
All-day cafe-bar-restaurant combining warmth and an elegant, accessible luxury. The cuisine is characterised by finesse of flavour and solid technical skill. Very diverse menu, plus tapas and multi-ethnic appetisers.

MODERN GREEK CUISINE

Gefseis me Onomasia Proelefsis
317, Kifisias Ave., Kifisia, 210/8001402. **Open:** Year round, daily (except Sunday), evenings. **Price:** € 27-33.
Atmospheric place with a period flavour: an old mansion in a beautiful garden. The cuisine, under the direction of Ilias Mamalakis, is evolving classic Greek recipes. Trump cards: the exquisite attention to detail on every level (even in the

soft drinks!), the unique cheeses that Ilias gathers from all over Greece, and the intelligent service.

Kallisti
137, Asklipiou St., Neapoli Exarcheion, 210/6453179, 210/6445476. **Open:** Winter only, daily, evenings. **Price:** € 21-30.
Bright attractive restaurant with a modern air. A cuisine that is constantly exploring and a menu that soaks up new ideas. Certain weaknesses in technique keep some of her dishes at a level more mundane than arresting.

Kitrino Podilato
116-118, Kerameikou St. & Iera Odos, Gazi, 210/3465830. **Open:** Winter only, daily (except Sunday), evenings. **Price:** € 30-40.
One of the most creative cuisines in Athens. Chef Dimitra Valla seeks out ingredients of exceptional quality and creates works of art as pleasing to the eye as to the palate, with inventive Mediterranean combinations. Charming modern room with over-sized photos of collector's items. Well-composed wine list, emphasising Greek labels.

Ydragogeio
12, Agiou Konstantinou, Glyfada, 210/8947139. **Open:** Winter only, daily (except Sunday), evenings. Sunday, noon only, buffet. **Price:** € 30-36.
Lovely, warm friendly place, that creates the impression of an old aqueduct.
The menu draws on all of Greece and beyond for its inspiration, proposing delectable and very special dishes.

Eating out

TRADITIONAL GREEK CUISINE

Apangio
4, Megistis St., Alimos, 210/9839093, 210/9881329. **Open:** Year round, daily (except Monday), evenings. Sunday also at noon. **Price:** € 12-18.
Angeliki Maniaki has collected recipes from all over Greece, and prepares them in the traditional manner. The result? Absolutely delicious food, but usually very heavy.

Asklipiou Gonia
130, Asklipiou St. & 2, Valsamonos St., Neapoli Exarcheion, 210/6452318. **Open:** Winter only, daily, evenings. **Price:** € 20-24.
Lovely restored neo-classical building, tasteful dining room. Good food, and relatively simple, based on traditional flavours, although not lacking in ideas or technique.

Kallimarmaron
13, Eforionos St. & Eratosthenous, Pagkrati, 210/7019727, 210/7017234. **Open:** Year round, daily (except Monday and May-Oct. Sunday), noon-evening. **Price:** € 15-21.
Homey, bourgeois, hospitable ambiance. Tasty food that respects tradition and follows the seasons.

Kioupia
End of Politeia Sq., 210/6200005, 210/6206433. **Open:** Year round, daily, evenings. Sunday only at noon. **Price:** € 35-40.
A Homeric epic of a restaurant. An impressive display of well-prepared traditional dishes will appear on your table, unless you select and order just those you particularly want. Large room decorated in neo-traditional style, and a beautiful courtyard with a panoramic view of the whole of Athens.

Sodeia
41, Dionysou St., Kifisia, 210/8012697. **Open:** Year round, daily (except Monday), evenings. Sat.-Sun. also at noon. **Price:** € 18-22.
Cuisine that selects recipes from all over the country, prepares them in the lightest possible way and transforms them into dishes of quality. Wonderfully tranquil place, with a super garden.

Spyros
17, Ethnikou Stratou St., Ano Kifisia, 210/8017869. **Open:** Year round, daily (except Sunday), evenings. **Price:** € 15-20.
The attractively simple room and professional service placed this famous taverna among the restaurants. Classic home-style Greek cooking, featuring delicious dishes like lamb in grease-proof paper and perfectly fried hake.

ETHNIC RESTAURANTS

Alexandreia (Egyptian)
13, Metsovou St. & Rethymnou, Mouseio, 210/8210004. **Open:** Year round, daily (except Sunday), evenings. **Price:** € 15-21.
Simple modern decor that still manages to suggest the exotic roots of the place. The menu proposes two basic types of cuisine: Egyptian, and a quasi-Mediterranean style featuring dishes like kebab hala and aubergines, black-eyed beans and yoghurt baked in an earthenware casserole.

Altamira (multi-ethnic)
28, Perikleous St., Marousi, 210/6128841, 210/6142767. **Open:** Year round, daily (except Sunday), evenings. **Price:** € 18-24.
A passion for food and an insatiable curiosity are what make this restaurant a Mecca for lovers of exotic flavours and audacious combinations. Four exotic cuisines (China, Mexico, India and the Middle East) meet in two beautiful villas, in Marousi and Kolonaki, with colourful rooms and ethnic decorative features. (The Kolonaki version is more opulent.)

Bee Garden (Chinese)
30, Kydonion St., Nea Smyrni, 210/9319711-2. **Open:** Year round, daily, evenings. Sunday also at noon. **Price:** € 15-21.
Chinese cuisine in an austere and occidental setting. Strong colours. The spacious modern dining room is a truly delightful surprise. So is the music: Eastern pop! The food is good, the prices pocket-friendly and the service cheerful.

Far East (Chinese)
54, Diligianni St., Kifisia, 210/6233140-4. Lazaraki and Pandoras St., Glyfada, 210/8940500. 7, Stadiou St., Syntagma Sq., 210/3234996. **Open:** Year round, daily, evenings. Sunday also at noon. **Price:** € 30-40.
Luxury chain of three fine restaurants, featuring an

Eating out

excellent poly-Asian cuisine characterised by technical skill and unwavering quality. All three restaurants - in Kifisia, Glyfada and Syntagma - are extremely attractive, a pleasant blend of western lines and an understated Chinese luxury. They prepare the best version of Peking duck, and the service is professional and irreproachable.

Freud Oriental (Japanese)
21, Xenokratous St., Kolonaki, 210/7299595, 210/7299597. **Open:** Year round, daily (except Sunday), evenings. Sat. also at noon. **Price:** € 30-38.
The dining room, in a neoclassical villa in Kolonaki, is a Freudian analysis of the oriental aura of sushi in a modern western setting. Trendy Athens relaxes in its soft seats to enjoy such dishes as inside-out maki-sushi (the rice enrobes the seaweed, instead of the more usual reverse) with exceptionally good shrimp tempura and aji tataki: lemony-hued raw cubes of marinated horse mackerel.

Golden Phoenix (Chinese)
131, Tatoiou St., Nea Kifisia, 210/8078640. 120, Vouliagmenis Ave., Elliniko, 210/9644889. 85, Pentelis Ave., Chalandri, 210/6825017. Ch. Trikoupi & Gortynias St., Kifisia, 210/8013588. **Open:** Year round, daily, evenings. Sunday from the morning. **Price:** € 24-30.
Chinese aesthetic and opulence in all their grandeur, but attractive nonetheless. As for the food, the Chalandri Golden Phoenix

is better than the Nea Kifisia one, while both Chalandri and Kefalari have sushi bars.

Habiba (Arabian)
224, Patision Ave. & 2, Astypalaias St., Kypseli, 210/8673722. **Open:** Year round, daily (except Monday), evenings. **Price:** € 21-28.
Manages to combine Arabian decorative elements with the stripped-down contemporary face of a trendy restaurant. The music - live on the weekend - is on the same wave length. The food is excellent, with the weight on traditional cooked dishes from a variety of Arabian countries.

Jaipur Palace (Indian)
73, Themidos St. & Agiou Konstantinou, Marousi, 210/8052762-3. **Open:** Year round, daily, noon-evening. **Price:** € 25-40.
Epic-style Indian restaurant! Stunning dining room, with strong colours, authentic furniture and ornaments, large atmospheric garden and a ground floor shop selling Indian furniture and other articles. The vast menu proposes genuine Indian cuisine, with many dishes prepared in a traditional tandoor (clay oven in which food is cooked over charcoal).

Kiku (Japanese)
12, Dimokritou St., Kolonaki, 210/3647033. **Open:** Year round, daily (except Sunday), evenings. **Price:** € 30-42.
Japanese restaurant that would be remarkable in any gastronomic capital in the

world. Fabulous sushi and sashimi and fresh raw fish, and a special menu for Japanese patrons, featuring dishes that are extraordinarily delicious and supremely elegant. Fragile fried dumplings, deeply flavourful yakisoba (noodles with prawns), and udon (plump pasta in broth) that will win you away from their Italian counterparts!

Kochylia (Polynesian)
Km 40, Athens-Sounio road (Grand Resort Lagonissi), Lagonisi, 22910/76000. **Open:** Year round, daily, evenings. **Price:** € 70-90.
The Grand Resort Lagonissi's Polynesian restaurant is one of the most attractive in Attica. A gigantic aquarium full of tropical fish, amazing lighting and a view of the sea compose a striking minimal setting designed in accordance with the principles of feng shui. And the food is up to the same standard, with sushi and Polynesian dishes of superlative quality.

Kona Kai (Polynesian)
115, Syngrou Ave. (Hotel Ledra Marriott), 210/9300000. **Open:** Year round, daily (except Sunday), evenings. **Price:** € 42-50.
Timeless Polynesian restaurant, responsible for educating Athenian palates to a taste for gastronomic paradise. Although from time to time it has known minor qualitative hiccups, these past two years it has been in absolutely top form. The kitchen staff are master technicians, especially when it comes to frying. Superlative service.

seafood therapy

(piperia)

Πιπεριά
Πιπεριά
Πιπεριά
Πιπεριά
Πιπεριά
Πιπεριά

Πιπεριά

seafood

210 6729 114 + 210 6728 438
mob.: 0944 921 128
www.piperia-seafood.gr
chiltoman@hotmail.com
8, Ag. Sikelianou & Adrianiou str., N. Psichiko

Eating out

Lviv (Oukrainian)
27A, Mithymnis St.,
Amerikis Sq., Kypseli,
210/8659429. **Open:** Year
round, daily, evenings.
Price: € 12-15.
Fine Ukrainian bar-restaurant in a lovely neo-classic building in Kypseli (?). Neat interior, well-prepared Ukrainian specialties, and Russian pop music that brings patrons to their feet even in the middle of their dinner, creating a spirited, festive ambience.

O Kitrinos Skiouros
(Brazilian)
21, Dimitressa St., Ilisia,
210/7211586. **Open:** Year
round, daily, evenings.
Price: € 15-21.
Bar-restaurant, artsy and very cosy, where the "Girl from Ipanema" caresses your ears and the imaginative food your taste buds. Every dish has an exotic note: e.g. the wholly representative fesoàda, in which the rice is combined with delicious black beans, wonderful sausages and meats, spinach and orange.

Red Marrakesh
(Moroccan)
3, Agatharchou St., Psyrri,
210/3317646-8. **Open:** Year
round, daily, evenings.
Price: € 40-45.
Fabulous authentic decor, reminiscent of the interior of a Moroccan palace, and music (alternating between live and DJ) that gradually ratchets up - carrying the ambiance with it. The excellent Moroccan cuisine is exemplified by dishes like pastiya (a classic Moroccan pie with thin crispy pastry dusted with sugar and cinnamon) and a filling of

chicken, almond and eggs. In the summer they move down to the seaside (On the Rocks).

Royal Thai (Thai)
12, Zirini St., Kifisia,
210/6232323. **Open:** Year
round, daily, evenings.
Price: € 30-35.
The best Thai cuisine in town, and one of the best exotic/ethnic in general. Skill and audacity bring out the flavours in these delicious and impeccably executed dishes. Oriental ambiance, with no excesses or intrusive modernity.

Shalimar (Indian)
5, Maiandrou St.,
Ilisia, 210/7220824.
Open: Year round, daily
(except Monday), evenings.
Price: € 25-33.
Lovely Indian restaurant, with a colourful pop ambience and very good food. Its signature dishes are fried dory with green spices and curry, and a very hot kali mirch ka murg (chicken with spicy curry, black pepper and nutmeg).

Square Sushi (Japanese)
56, Diligianni St., Kifisia,
210/8081512, 210/8081881.
Open: Year round, daily,
evenings. Sat.-Sun. also at
noon. **Price:** € 22-27.
Relatively small place, warm and friendly despite the minimal ambience befitting a Japanese restaurant. Well-organised menu, with a large variety of well-prepared classic and original maki and nigiri sushi and sashimi, as well as a few soups and salads.

Sveik (Czech)
6, Roumpesi St., Neos
Kosmos, 210/9018389.

Open: Year round, daily
(except Monday), evenings.
Price: € 21-24.
Warm and atmospheric, with dark colours. Two levels and a courtyard (reminiscent of an old train station). Fine Czech cuisine, focusing on cooked dishes, plus delectable schnitzels.

The Sushi Bar (Japanese)
38, Georgiou Vlachou St.,
Neo Psychiko,
210/6729333. Varnava Sq.,
Pagkrati, 210/7524354.
15, Konstantinoupoleos St.,
Glyfada, 210/8942200.
Open: Year round, daily,
noon-evening.
Price: € 15-21.
Pop Japanese minimalism in Pagkrati, Neo Psychiko and Glyfada. Expert Oriental chefs prepare satisfactory nigiri (without seaweed) and maki (rolls with seaweed, rice, fish) sushi, using a wide variety of raw fish (tuna, sea bass, salmon, bonita, squid). Very good ambient and ethnic background music.

Tora Tora Tora (Asian)
4, Andronikou St. & Tzaferi,
Rouf, 210/3424994.
Open: Year round, daily,
evenings. **Price:** € 27-33.
Modern oriental style, warm colours and a beautiful bar separating the lounge from the other tables. The cuisine (generic Asian) features good sushi and main dishes served in the western manner.

Ya Hala (Lebanese)
37, Kolokotroni St., Kifisia,
210/8015324-5. **Open:** Year
round, daily, evenings.
Fri.-Sun. also at noon.
Price: € 18-21.
Modern Lebanese restaurant, with decent food in a

KIR·YIANNI

The red *Paranga*, the white *Samaropetra* and the rose *Akakies*
are Yiannis Boutaris' new wine selections.

Unique blends of indigenous and foreign varieties produce
modern New-Old world wines of distinctive character.

www.kiryianni.gr
Tel.: 210 6716050

ating out

very pleasant setting. The meats are properly marinated, but the short order dishes are not always successful.

Yoga Bala (Indian)
5-7, Riga Palamidou St., Psyrri, 210/3311335. **Open:** Winter only, daily, evenings. **Price:** € 26-35.
Indian bar-restaurant with a style of its own, combining ethnic and kitsch. Bright fuchsia colours, heavy pure white tables and an old Venetian suite set the stage for a refined and restrained (that is, not excessively hot) cuisine. Sorbets, lassa and excellent cocktails at the ground floor bar.

Won Ton (Chinese)
89, Poseidonos Ave. & 1, Zisimopoulou St., Glyfada, 210/8943373. 15, Poseidonos Ave., Vouliagmeni, 210/9673152. 57, El. Venizelou St., Nea Smyrni, 210/9316997. 47, Poseidonos Ave., Moschato, 210/9483141. 62, I. Drosopoulou St., Kypseli, 210/8847475. **Open:** Year round, daily, noon-evening. **Price:** € 18-21.
Popular chain that is constantly expanding, winning new converts to Chinese cuisine. They all share the same basic features: simple modern premises, extensive menus and excellent prices.

CASUAL
Atelier Agrotikon
48, Sarri & 6, Tournavitou St., 210/3240121, 210/3240231. **Open:** Winter only, daily (except Sunday-Monday), evenings. **Price:** € 30-36.
Light and airy. The long bar and sofas extending down one side set the tone. The

menu bears the seal of chef and co-owner Jean-Yves Caratoni, but is simpler and more direct than what he has accustomed us to in recent years. The dishes are less complicated, less fussy and more elegant in their presentation, and the flavours are sharper. The meats are excellent, and we particularly enjoyed the fricassee of wild mushrooms. Exceptionally good sweets, satisfactory wine list.

Chic
32, Kallirois St. & Petmeza (Hotel Athenian Callirhoe), Fix (210/9215353. **Open:** Year round, daily, evening-noon. **Price:** € 30-35.
The restaurant of the recently renovated boutique business hotel. Mediterranean cuisine, with some interesting ideas developed from creative Greek cooking. The elegant - predominantly orange - dining room suggests an updated '70s mood, and the stylish roof garden has a view of the Acropolis and Lycabettus.

Enastron
4, Mikonos St. & Karaiskaki, Psyrri, 210/3212755, 210/3216796. **Open:** Winter only, daily (except Monday), evenings. **Price:** € 18-21.
Bottero's well-fed ladies sway gently through this warm, friendly place, exculpating the customers. Unpretentious delicious Mediterranean cuisine, delectably priced. The style of the (live) music and the overall atmosphere of the place are quite untypical of the district.

Ex-Party
17, Eforionos St. & Agiou Spyridonos, Pagkrati, 210/7019291. **Open:** Year round, daily (except Sunday), evenings. **Price:** € 24-30.
Continuing the tradition of the '90s Party, the Ex-Party is a playfully decorated place, with an intensely cheerful friendly atmosphere. The agreeable Mediterranean cuisine is most successful in the simpler dishes.

La Pasteria
18, Tsakalof St., Kolonaki, 210/3632032. 6, V. Katraki St., Bizaniou Sq., Glyfada, 210/8945085. 15, Konstantinou Palaiologou St., Nea Smyrni, 210/9319146-7. Village Park, 228, Thivon St., Agios Ioannis Rentis, 210/4922960. 58, Patision Ave., 210/8250315. Konstantinoupoleos & Charilaou Trikoupi, Peristeri, 210/5775133. 213, Alexandras Ave. & Pouliou, Ampelokipoi, 210/6455220. Athens International Airport, building 42 (Olympus Plaza complex), 210/3538282. **Open:** Year round, daily, noon-evening. **Price:** € 15-18.
Eight cheerfully modern restaurants in different parts of the city, plus the airport at Spata. Very popular Mediterranean cuisine, with the accent on (surprise, surprise) pasta.

Oineas
9, Aisopou St., Psyrri Sq., 210/3215642. **Open:** Year round, daily, noon-evening. **Price:** € 18-20.
One of the classiest places in Psyrri. Good, and reason-

seafood
το βαρούλκο

1st PRIZE FOR BEST GREEK CUISINE
ONE OF THE 10 BEST RESTAURANTS IN GREECE
Golden Hat award in the "Athinorama" 2001-2002
for the 9th year running

1 STAR IN THE GUIDE MICHELIN

Imaginative seafood dishes from chef Lefteris Lazarou

14, DELIGIORGI ST., PIRAEUS
TEL.: 210/4112043 - 210/4221283 - 0944/320193
e-mail: varoulko@internet.gr

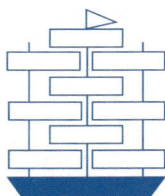

ARISTERA DEXIA.
LEFT AND RIGHT.
THE NEW DIRECTION
IN MEDITERRANEAN CUISINE.

ΑΡΙΣΤΕΡΑ ΔΕΞΙΑ

3 ANDRONIKOU STREET
ROUF
ATHENS
210 3422380
210 3422606

ably creative, food in stylish premises decorated with old advertisements in pale shades.

Palmie Bistrot

29-31, Iofontos St., Pagkrati, 210/7258826. 72, Solonos St. & Massalias, 210/3641794. Closed Sundays. 5, Viktorias Sq., 210/8836592. 1st EOT Beach, Voula, 210/8954054, 210/8952403. 35, Kolokotroni St., Kefalari Sq., 210/8012411, 210/8085590. **Open:** Year round, daily, noon-evening. **Price:** € 10-12.

These light, young-style places are cropping up all over the city. A wide range of choices for a light meal at any hour of the day.

San Marzano

13, Konstantinoupoleos St., Glyfada, 210/9681124. **Open:** Year round, daily, noon-evening. **Price:** € 18-21.

The Greek "branch" of the international Pizza Express, in an elegant modern setting in Glyfada. Light and delicious Mediterranean cuisine, classic and original pizzas.

Sousouro

2, Konitsis St., Eleftherias Sq., Goudi, 210/7770038. **Open:** Year round, daily, noon-evening. **Price:** € 20-22.

Carefully studied cuisine featuring Mediterranean (mainly Greek and Cypriot) dishes, based on the strength and flavour of appropriate seasonal ingredients. Each month spotlights a different ethnic cuisine. Attentive, personal service.

Tartare

52, Panagouli St., Glyfada, 210/9680320. **Open:** Year round, daily (except Sunday), evenings. **Price:** € 30-40.

Casual modern bistro, nicely decorated, with a pleasant courtyard. Classic, well-executed French cuisine. Unbeatable for flavourful meats with a variety of sauces, excellent thin-cut fried potatoes and a perfect chocolate souffle.

TGI Friday's

35, Kolokotroni St., Kefalari Sq., Kifisia, 210/6233947. **Open:** Year round, daily, noon-evening. **Price:** € 20-25.

American atmosphere in Kefalari and Pagkrati. Both have the same cheerful American-style service, but the food is much better in Kefalari.

Votanikos

Athinais: 34-36, Kastorias St., Votanikos, 210/3480000. **Open:** Year round, daily, noon-evening. **Price:** € 15-21.

The all-day restaurant in the Athinais multi-centre (cinemas, galleries, museum, events halls, shops) occupies a spacious industrial-style room. Simple well-prepared food, Mediterranean with a predominantly Greek colouring. Good service.

LUNCHTIME FAVOURITES

47 Maritsa's

47, Voukourestiou St. & Fokylidou, Kolonaki, 210/3630132. **Open:** Year round, daily, noon-evening. **Price:** € 27-32.

Timeless Kolonaki restaurant, classic Greek cuisine, wide variety of appetisers and entrees centred on the grill. Attractive classic dining room. Courteous service, but can be very slow at peak hours.

Alexandra's

10, Alexandras Ave. (Park Hotel), Pedion Areos, 210/8832711. **Open:** Year round, daily, noon-evening. **Price:** € 15-18.

Classic cuisine on the ground floor of the Park hotel, ideal for business lunches in the Champ de Mars area.

Cellier Le Bistrot

10, Panepistimiou St. (in the passage), Syntagma Sq., 210/3638525. **Open:** Year round, daily, noon-evening. **Price:** € 30-33.

The high-ceilinged dining room of the legendary Apotsos has been transformed into a modern bistro, maintaining a perfect equilibrium between the ordinary and the luxurious. Simple, classic, timeless (international and Greek) cuisine, generally well-executed without being original. Wine list extensive, diverse and well-organised.

Deals

10, Vasileiou St., Neo Psychiko, 210/6773183. **Open:** Year round, daily, noon-evening. **Price:** € 20-30.

One of the busiest and trendiest places in the northern suburbs, with a highly successful modern everyday cuisine. Delicious salads and sandwiches, spaghetti and steaks, as well as more ethnic flavours. Satisfactory wine list, famous ice cream topped brownie.

Eating out

Emporio Armani Caffè
5, Milioni & 4, Solonos St., Kolonaki, 210/3389107. Open: Year round, daily (except Sunday), noon-evening. Price: € 33-39.
Super elegant designer cafe-restaurant offering quality Italian cuisine and classic simplicity in the socialite ambience of Milioni St. Most of the ingredients come from Italy, and the relatively short menu changes frequently. Excellent classic sweets.

Kouti
23, Adrianou St., Monastiraki, 210/3213229. Open: Year round, daily, noon-evening. Price: € 27-33.
A favourite downtown restaurant returns after a two-year absence. Elegant setting, arty ambience. The food is tasty, and generally fairly simple, with filling salads and the signature honeyed pork strips.

L' Angolo di Milioni
Milioni & Irakleitou, Kolonaki, 210/3390756. Open: Year round, daily, noon-evening. Price: € 30-36.
Classic elegance on Kolonaki's fashion catwalk. Mediterranean cuisine, creative, soigné. A variety of interesting salads, and the signature coq aux fines herbes. Excellent espresso.

La Terrasse
66, Diligianni St. (Hotel Pentelikon), Kefalari, 210/6230650. Open: Year round, daily, noon-evening. Price: € 30-35.
Post-modern art nouveau atmosphere on the ground floor of the Pentelikon hotel. Good fusion-style cuisine with modern touches.

Palia Agora
26, Kechagia St. & M. Renieri, Filothei, 210/6837037. Open: Year round, daily, noon-evening. Price: € 27-32.
Austerely modern, with colourful Philip Stark chairs and a striking vase ornamenting the central pillar. Well-prepared modern cuisine, offering both inventive dishes (e.g. the delectable chilli prawns with yellow rice) and classic favourites. Substandard service.

Palia Vouli
9, Anthimou Gazi & 7, Karytsi St., Syntagma Sq., 210/3234803. Open: Year round, daily, noon-evening. Monday only at noon. Price: € 18-24.
Pale pastels and classic lines create an elegant air of discreet formality. Relaxingly beautiful exterior area, opposite the old parliament building. Well-prepared classic cuisine, plus some Greek dishes.

Prytaneio
37, Kolokotroni St., Kefalari, 210/8089160-2. 7, Milioni St., Kolonaki, 210/3643353. Open: Year round, daily, noon-evening. Price: € 30-36.
Two lovely stylish places with art touches, in Kolonaki and Kefalari. Both have tables outside, on the pavement or square respectively - observation posts on two society promenades. Cuisine simple, generous, with an Italian accent.

San Paolo
10, Lykourgou St., Neo Psychiko, 210/6740052-3. Open: Year round, daily, noon-evening Price: € 21-27.
Modern cafe-restaurant, simple lines and shades of grey, and the unusual feature of... closing early in the evening. An abundance of salads, a few pasta dishes and plenty of grilled meats. Good service.

Silentio
3, Mantzarou St., Kolonaki, 210/3633144. Open: Winter only, daily (except Sunday), noon-evening. Price: € 15-21.
Warm, multi-level space with an atrium for sunny mornings and a fireplace for cold winter nights. Comprehensive international menu based largely on products from their own farm. Good value for money.

Valaoritou Brasserie
15, Valaoritou St, Kolonaki, 210/3641529. Open: Year round, daily (except Sunday), noon-evening. Price: € 30-38.
Minimal ambience, dark colours, and the feeling of a modern brasserie. The large noisy room is a popular lunch spot with business people and shoppers. We found the Mediterranean cuisine a little simpler this year, and the lunch menu has been expanded to include some of Greece's classic cooked dishes.

Verde
Korytsas & Pentelis Ave., Alsos Papagou, Agia Paraskevi, 210/6533086. Open: Year round,

ασκληπιού γωνία
ΕΣΤΙΑΤΟΡΙΟ

Every night we wait for you
in our marvellous neoclassical building
at Asklipiou street.
Try the tastes we have loved
from Greece and the world
in a warm and friendly atmosphere.

ASKLIPIOU GONIA - restaurant
130 ASKLIPIOU str. and 2 VALSAMONOS str , ATHENS, TEL.: 210 6452318

Malvazia

210 34 17 010

Agathimerou
3.Rouf

daily, noon-evening.
Price: € 20-25.

Stylish and relaxed chalet atmosphere, amid the greenery of the park. Even the interior gives you the feeling of being outside under the pines. Mediterranean cuisine of an acceptable standard.

SEAFOOD

Ammos

10, Markou Botsari St., Glyfada, 210/8986020. **Open:** Year round, daily (except Sunday), evenings. **Price:** € 35-38.

Lovely oyster bar/restaurant, where sand and water feature as impressive, abstract decorative elements. In addition to oysters, cockles and hard clams, the menu also includes a number of carefully-devised creative fish dishes.

Bouillabaisse

28, Zisimopoulou St., Amfithea, 210/9419082, 210/9425203. **Open:** Year round, daily, noon-evening. July-Aug. evenings only. **Price:** € 24-27.

A place with a long tradition, that is turning the urban fish taverna into a comme il faut seafood restaurant. Choose your fish from the tantalising marble slab, and they will grill it to perfection or fry it extremely lightly. And their bouillabaisse is spicy, aromatic and deliciously thick.

Club House

Astir Palace Hotel, Vouliagmeni, 210/8902000. **Open:** Summer only, daily, evenings only. **Price:** € 70-90.

A breathtaking view of Saronikos Gulf and a sense of classical luxury. The chefs at the Club House maintain the tradition of fine quality seafood cuisine.

Ithaki

28, Apollonos Ave., Laimos Vouliagmenis, 210/8963747, 210/8963739. **Open:** Year round, daily, noon-evening. **Price:** € 43-56.

Modern designer luxury, magical view of Asteras bay. Cuisine that is not out to win any prizes, but uses the freshest of ingredients and treats them with respect. Impeccable service, satisfactory wine list, stiff prices.

Jimmy and the Fish

46, Akti Koumoundourou, Mikrolimano, Piraeus, 210/4124417. **Open:** Year round, daily, noon-evening. **Price:** € 24-30.

Wooden deck, striped director's chairs and a fabulous tourist-poster view (the marina is dead ahead). They specialise in perfectly cooked fresh fish - if you fancy anything more complicated, you're in the wrong place.

Kastelorizo

2, Platanon St., Nea Kifisia Sq., 210/8075408. Poseidonos Ave., Limanakia Varkizas, 210/9655022. 334, Thiseos Ave., Tzitzifies, 210/9429027. 28, Vas. Georgiou St., Glyfada, 210/8948246. **Open:** Year round, daily, noon-evening. **Price:** € 27-30.

Professional service, carefully selected ingredients, absolute mastery of grill and frying pan. The food is not earthshaking, but the fish are perfectly fresh. Of the four restaurants in the group, the one in Varkiza, with its seaside location, is the most attractive.

O Mythos tis Thalassas

10, Agiou Nikolaou St. & Ilia Iliou (Hotel Divani Apollon Palace & Spa), Vouliagmeni, 210/8911100, 210/8911256. **Open:** Year round, daily (except Sunday), evenings. **Price:** € 33-39.

Lovely restaurant in the recently renovated Divani Apollon. Particularly attractive in the summer, when the tables are set outside on the pier. Fresh fish, conservative cuisine, adequate wine list.

Ou gar oidasi

15, Konstantinou Palaiologou, Chalandri, 210/6821730. **Open:** Year round, daily (except Sunday), evenings. **Price:** € 24-30.

Two people armed with flair and enthusiasm have created an elegant ethereal restaurant that is a paean to the prawn. Fried, spicy, braised, al pesto... twelve different versions, classic and original, but all delicious. Friendly service.

Sonar

8, Spefsippou St., Kolonaki, 210/7257756. **Open:** Year round, daily, evenings. Sat. also at noon. **Price:** € 30-36.

Oyster bar, perfect for an early evening aperitif or an atmospheric seafood dinner. Futuristic design, large aquariums full of colourful fish, ambient music. Service slow and uncoordinated.

Eating out

Thalatta
5, Vitonos St., Gazi, 210/3464204. **Open:** Year round, daily, evenings. Sunday only at noon. **Price:** € 21-24.
Pleasant modern room, combining industrial features with "old neighbourhood" warmth. The cuisine relies heavily on perfectly fresh ingredients and, while not lacking in imagination, is perfectly at home with classic recipes.

Vythos tis Gefsis
9, Asomaton Sq. & 1, Adrianou St., Monastiraki, 210/3211966. **Open:** Year round, daily, evenings. Sunday also at noon. **Price:** € 27-30.
Lovely room, all wood and stone, in the historic centre of Athens. Tables outside, with a view of the Acropolis. Classic dishes displaying a moderately creative approach, but not always perfectly executed.

PASTA PROWESS

Casa di Pasta
11, Gortynias St. & Charilaou Trikoupi, Kifisia, 210/6233361-3. Apollonos & 2, Litous St., Vouliagmeni, 210/8964122. **Open:** Year round, daily, evenings. Sunday also at noon. **Price:** € 33-45.
These two spaghetti houses introduced the fashion for authentic Italian pasta a decade ago. Perfectly cooked pasta, and well-balanced non-bastardised sauces (no cream), warm luxurious interiors, superlative service.

Classico
36, Evangelistrias St., Nea Erythraia, 210/6201572.

Open: Year round (except August), daily, evenings. Sunday also at noon. **Price:** € 27-36.
Simple, elegant room, polished art de la table. One plus feature is the ample space and uncrowded table arrangement. Tasty food, dishes generally well executed, fresh pasta made on the premises.

Clavdios
38, Veikou St., Koukaki, 210/9235140. **Open:** Year round, daily, noon-evening. **Price:** € 20-25.
A simple, modern Italian taverna where you can eat a quality casual meal. Classic dishes, unpretentious and perfectly prepared. Extra emphasis on hospitality from Italian proprietor Claudio.

Da Lu
77-79, Pentelis Ave. ("Ermeion 1" Shopping Centre), Chalandri, 210/6892430. **Open:** Year round, daily (except Monday), evenings. Sunday also at noon. **Price:** € 36-39.
Lovely modern room, but overcrowded. Famous for its lobster spaghetti (which does not 100% deserve its reputation), also serves several other good seafood pasta dishes. Quite good service, wine list barely mediocre.

Il Parmigiano
254, Kifisias Ave., Filothei, 210/6778765. 3, Grivaion St., Kolonaki, 210/3641414. 40, Ekalis St., Nea Erythraia, 210/6254151-2. **Open:** Year round, daily, noon-evening. **Price:** € 15-21.

Good value for money and stylish design have made these Italian eateries extremely popular. Delicious pasta, fabulous pizzas (with thin crispy crusts), friendly service.

Il Tinello
54, Knosou St., Alimos, 210/9828462. **Open:** Winter only, daily (except Sunday-Monday), evenings. **Price:** € 21-27.
Simple well-kept place with an air of a traditional Italian trattoria, but too often suffocatingly overcrowded. Special service from owner Stefano, who doubles as a waiter, creating an atmosphere of intimacy. Properly cooked pasta and superb sauces.

La Soffita
11, Kyriazi St., Kifisia, 210/8014800. **Open:** Year round, daily, evenings. **Price:** € 18-24.
Pleasant attractive room, next to the open kitchen where you can watch the preparation of the various dishes. Tasty, rustic, well-made genuine Italian trattoria food. Attentive friendly service.

Padre e Padrone
24, Lepeniotou & 16, Ogygou St., Psyrri, 210/3318184. **Open:** Year round, daily, evenings. **Price:** € 20-25.
Modern room, designer aesthetic, dark colours, and a roof that opens and closes to give a summertime feeling. Refined rustic version of the cuisine of Sicily.

Sale e Pepe
34, Aristippou St., Kolonaki, 210/7234102. **Open:** Winter

only, daily (except Sunday), evenings. Sat. also at noon. **Price:** € 48-60.
One of the warmest and most welcoming restaurants in town, and one of the city's two best cellars. Owner-sommelier Ivan Otaviani will guide you through a wine list full of good deals, and nearly a thousand labels long! Italian cuisine, tasty and relatively simple, based on the excellence of the ingredients.

Santa Pasta
73, Pentelis Ave., Chalandri, 210/6854755. 46, El. Venizelou St., Nea Smyrni, 210/9370064. 66, Voutsina St., Cholargos, 210/6561300. **Open:** Year round, daily, noon-evening. **Price:** € 15-18.
Wide selection of pasta dishes in any of three simple, popular restaurants with open kitchens and friendly prices. Impressive variety of pastas, of a satisfactory quality for the type of restaurant.

Trattoria
19, Anaxagora St., Nea Erythraia, 210/6253633. **Open:** Year round, Tues.-Sat., evenings. Sunday also at noon. **Price:** € 21.
Parade of ten to twelve different dishes that change daily depending on the season and what the Italian chef finds in the market. Authentic flavours, well-prepared, in an attractive if somewhat crowded setting. Good value.

STEAK HOUSES

Epicure
12, Aiolias St., Nea Kifisia, 210/8078095. 16, Metaxa

St., Voula, 210/8953544. 17, Poseidonos Ave., Vouliagmeni, 210/8961237. **Open:** Year round, daily, evenings. Sat.-Sun. also at noon. **Price:** € 15-18.
American aesthetic in Voula, Nea Kifisia and Vouliagmeni, where the hamburgers rival the steaks and the Roquefort dressing is the unbeatable trump card.

Silver Star
37, Ionias St. & Troias, Kifisia, 210/8000108. Apollonos & 4, Litous St., Kavouri, 210/9671164-5. **Open:** Year round, daily, evenings. Sun. also at noon. **Price:** € 30-39.
Two airy restaurants, in Vouliagmeni and Kifisia, that tread a successful balance between the modern and the rusticity of an authentic steak house. Classic menu, with the accent on a variety of Mexican-style fried appetisers, salads and of course meat (steaks, T-bones, rib eye, etc.), all tasty and well-prepared. Rich classic sweets.

Tilemachos
19, Fragkopoulou St., Kato Kifisia, 210/8077460. **Open:** Year round, daily, evenings. **Price:** € 20-25.
The traditional taverna-grill house has become a warm, modern bistro. Grill and spit retain their primacy, in the face of a deluge of not always successful appetisers.

VEGETARIAN

Eden
12, Lysiou St. & Mnisikleous, Plaka, 210/3248858. **Open:** Year round, daily

(except Tuesday), noon-evening. **Price:** € 15-18.
Vegetarians and (vegetarian) tourists flock to the attractive dining room in this pleasant villa. The emphasis is on vegetables, and while the dishes are agreeable they are not always sufficiently well-flavoured.

AFTER-HOURS

Gyalino
143, Syngrou Ave., 210/9315855, 210/9315306. **Open:** Year round, daily, noon-evening. Till 03:30, Fri.-Sat. till 06:00. **Price:** € 18-27.
The modern and stylishly austere bistro-restaurant in the "Gyalino Music Theatre" stays open very late - or more correctly, until very early... in the morning. Interesting and well-set-up cuisine, that combines traditional Greek dishes, progressive international specialties, pasta, pizza and sushi.

BEER RESTAURANTS

1920
110, Agias Paraskevis St., Chalandri, 210/6813029. **Open:** Year round, daily, evenings. **Price:** € 16-18.
Tasteful brasserie in an attractive and relatively quiet environment. Menu with something for every taste, with cured meats, cooked dishes and some ethnic fare. Lovely garden.

Alexandra
14, Argentinis Dimokratias St., Panathinaia, 210/6450345. **Open:** Year round, daily, evenings. Sunday also at noon. **Price:** € 12-21.

eX party
restaurant|bar

17 Evforionos str. and Agiou Spiridona str., Pagrati – Tel.: 210 70 19 291

Εναστρον
BAR - RESTAURANT

A century-old mansion restored with full respect
for its architecture, a friendly environment, simple
chic that is warmed by Bottero's plump figures.
A cuisine that is honest and sincere, proposing tasty
Mediterranean dishes, and quality music to animate
the elegance of Enastron.

4, Mikonos St. & Karaiskaki, Psyrri Sq., 210/3212755.

Eating out

Lovely room in stone and wood, friendly ambience. Satisfactory list of (properly classified) beers, and excellent snack platters.

Beer Academy
100, Agiou Ioannou St., Agia Paraskevi, 210/6007913. 336, Kifisias Ave. & 45, N. Karela St., 210/6817170 (closed on Sun.). 29, Stournari St., Exarcheia, 210/3816962. 115, Karaiskou St., Terpsithea Sq., Piraeus, 210/4297278. 79, El. Venizelou St., Nea Smyrni, 210/9334142. 14, N. Zerva St., Glyfada, 210/8980121. 42, Paraskevopoulou St. & Zalokosta, Bournazi, 210/5785116. 38, Pousoulidou St., Ilioupoli. 60, Agias Lavras St., Ano Patisia, 210/2281339. **Open:** Year round, daily, noon-evening. **Price:** € 15-21.
In each of the 9 branches you will find a variety of sausages and cured meats and a selection of tasty dishes. Rustic decor, informative journal-menu, wide variety of beers, knowledgeable waiters.

Craft Brewery & Restaurant
Main Square, Chalandri, 210/6832670.
205, Alexandras Ave., Ampelokipoi, 210/6462350. **Open:** Year round, daily, noon-evening. **Price:** € 15-21.
The first craft brewery restaurants in the country. Modern premises, industrial design, dominated by the stainless steel tanks in which the various beers are brewed. The menu is more ambitious than that of the traditional brasserie, even

including some Polynesian dishes. Our advice would be to stick with the simpler stuff.

Octoberfest
82, Agiou Ioannou St., Agia Paraskevi, 210/6082999. **Open:** Year round, daily, noon-evening. **Price:** € 18-21.
Brasserie with a classic rustic air - the expertise and enthusiasm of the owners make all the difference. Dozens of well-chosen beers, lots of draft beers (and glasses that hold up to 5 litres!) and a menu that includes both classic and creative dishes.

Tar
34, Irakleiou Ave., Patisia, 210/2237717. **Open:** Year round, daily, evenings. **Price:** € 12-21.
One of the first brasseries in the city. Atmospheric premises, arty disposition, musical evenings. Simple, tasty food with a pronounced Mexican accent, frequent "featured flavours".

Zythos
45, Eleftherias Ave. (continuation of Amfitheas Ave. towards the sea), Palaio Faliro, 210/9850478.
13, Kifisias Ave., Marousi, 210/6890220. 28, Karaiskaki St., Psyrri Sq., 210/3314601-2. **Open:** Year round, daily, evenings. Sunday also at noon. **Price:** € 15-21.
In its three Athens locations, Zythos lists 130 different beers. The draft beer is kept in a special cold room, so that it's just the right temperature when it's pulled. Good food, including mussels and seafood pasta.

TAVERNAS
FISH TAVERNAS
Avra
Nea Makri (waterfront, end of Poseidonos Ave.), 22940/91518. **Open:** Year round, daily, noon-evening. **Price:** € 15-24.
Little tables set out next to the tranquil shore road - an almost idyllic setting. Satisfactory variety of fresh fish, incomparable skill with the frying pan (dry and crispy).

Dourabeis
29, Akti Protopsalti, Piraeus, 210/4122092. **Open:** Year round, daily, noon-evening. **Price:** € 24-33.
One of the most celebrated fish tavernas in Attica. Classic appearance and flavour, perhaps a little tired after sixty-odd years in the business.

Kanaria
119, Kanari St., Moschato, 210/9422119. **Open:** Winter only, daily (except Sunday), evenings. **Price:** € 12-21.
A surprise fish taverna. Very simple place, packed inside with celebrity and socialite diners. (The luxury cars parked outside give the game away). The freshest of fish and prawns. Masters of the grill, magicians with the frying pan.

Kollias
3, Stratigou Plastira St. (Kalokairinou & Dramas), Piraeus, 210/4629620. **Open:** Year round, daily (except Sunday), evenings. Sundays and holidays also at noon. **Price:** € 21-24.
Tasos Kollias is a legend in the city's marine gastronomy world, having turned his

«kouti»
All time classic café-restaurant in the old area of Athens.
Closed to the ancient Agora with a privillege view of Acropolis.
Open all week. All credits cards are accepted.
Adrianou 23 str, Monastiraki
Res.: 210 3213229 - 210 3213029, FAX: 210 3314136

To sousouro

Talk of the Town

Restaurant

When you have customers
you are happy,
when you have FANS
you are proud.
Here we have the second!

2, Konitsis & Ifestionos str.,
(Eleftherias sq.), Goudi
Tel.: 210-77.70.038, 210-77.70.068

back on the banal and systematically cultivated the authentic, the unfamiliar, the sophisticated. Choose a special treat from his assortment of rare iodine-rich deep-water oysters, blowfish from Kalymnos, gobies and hagfish. Well-chosen wine list.
Directly opposite his fish taverna, Tassos Kollias is opening "Ta Epta Piata", a clever young-style meze-dopoleio serving seven sets of seven dishes of seafood and other mezedes for a fixed price of € 7.70.

Margaro
126, Chatzikyriakou Ave., Piraeus, 210/4514226. **Open:** Year round, daily, noon-evening. Sunday only at noon. **Price:** € 15-18.
Margaro's frying pan next to the Naval Academy in Piraeus is a miraculous utensil that produces a steady stream of prawns and red mullet. Cult fish taverna, always jammed.

O Giannos
70, Aristotelous St., Drapetsona, 210/4614355. **Open:** Year round, daily (except Sunday), evenings. Winter Sundays also at noon. **Price:** € 15-21.
Well-tended, spotlessly clean fish taverna, with marble tables. Fresh fish, perfectly grilled or fried, plus some more "progressive" dishes.

O Psaras
54, Elaion St., Nea Kifisia, 210/6205925. **Open:** Year round, daily, evenings. Sundays and holidays, only at noon. **Price:** € 21-24.
Take a guided tour of the refrigerators, which contain

a treasure trove of seafood preserved at the right temperature: fresh fish, cockles, hard clams and razor-shells. Small but select cellar, and good non-bottled wine. The fish is expensive here, but worth every penny.

Psarras
16, Erectheos & 12, Erotokritou St., Plaka, 210/3218733. **Open:** Year round, daily, noon-evening. **Price:** € 12-21.
Inside: bare stone and atmospheric lighting. Outside: a cool veranda or the shade of the plane tree. Fresh fish, grilled or fried to perfection.

Thalassinos
32, Lysikratous St. & Irakleous, Tzitzifies, 210/9404518. **Open:** Year round, daily (except Sunday and Monday), evenings. Sat.-Sun. also at noon. **Price:** € 18-24.
Attractive fish taverna with a repertory that goes beyond the classic, without neglecting simple well-prepared fresh fish. Carefully chosen ingredients, and expertise with grill and frying pan.

Trata o Stelios
7-9, Anagenniseos Sq., Kaisariani, 210/7291533. **Open:** Year round, daily, noon-evening. **Price:** € 21-24.
The best fish taverna (by far) in Kaisariani. Exclusive arrangements with fishermen ensure perfectly fresh fish that are fried or grilled with real expertise. Well-prepared appetisers, and friendly, family-style service.

Trechantiria
52, Akti Koumoundourou St., Mikrolimano, Piraeus, 210/4127900. **Open:** Year round, daily, evenings. **Price:** € 15-20.
A small pearl in the sea of fish tavernas in Mikrolimano. Apart from the picturesque view of Kastela and the proximity of the fishing boats, you will enjoy fresh fish and specialties from the island of Mytilini.

Xypolitos
1, Georgiou Papandreou & 25th March St., Agios Nikolaos, Loutsa waterfront, 22940/28342. **Open:** Year round, daily, evenings. Sat.-Sun. also at noon. **Price:** € 18-21.
Fish taverna with a tradition of more than half a century in incomparable fresh fish, on the waterfront at Agios Nikolaos, between Rafina and Loutsa.

Zoumperis
Zoumperi waterfront, Nea Makri, 22940/96866. **Open:** Year round, daily, noon-evening. **Price:** € 25-27.
Attractive fish taverna with a lovely terrace right by the sea. Their fresh fish and well-prepared appetisers draw a clientele including many politicians and artists.

GRILL - COOKED DISHES

Agios Merkourios
Agios Merkourios (open-air pavilion), 22950/98383. **Open:** Year round, daily, noon-evening. **Price:** € 9-12.
In this former hunting lodge on the green slopes of Mount Parnitha the menu is short, but the grilled food

THALATTA seafood restaurant

...where Aegean Seas meet the center of... Athens

onos str. gazi, athens-greece, тег. +3210 3464204, fax +3210 3416657, www.thalatta.gr

L'angolo di Milioni
Restaurant

Downtown Athens, in one of the most well-known pedestrian walks, is "L'angolo di Millioni", a classy restaurant, where you can enjoy a meal with flavours of high quality mediterranean cuisine.

Tel.: +30210 339.0756
Fax: +30210 363.0778

L'angolo di Milioni
Alta gastronomia e cafee

Milioni&Iraklitou str., Kolonaki

in particular is delectable. Drink in a view that stretches all the way to Evoia, and savour pan-fried liver-and-lights, grilled baby beef steaks, huge and well-aged, and fresh coarse-cut potatoes.

Agroktima tou Regkoukou
Amygdaleza, 210/6217898, 210/8143351. **Open:** Year round, daily (except Monday), evenings. Sunday only at noon. **Price:** € 12-18.
Farm on the eastern slopes of Mount Penteli, with vegetables, poultry and rabbits. Home-style food prepared from their own produce. Some dishes are decidedly better than others. The place is small, but the excursion to Amygdaleza is well worthwhile.

Bakaliarakia (tou Damigou)
41, Kydathinaion St., Plaka, 210/3225084. **Open:** Winter only, daily, evenings. Sunday also at noon. **Price:** € 9-12.
Traditional basement eatery, brimming over with atmosphere and history. Famous for its truly excellent, light and crispy fried hake, and the potatoes that are cut on the spot and fried in a deep cast-iron pan! All this in a room that is genuinely old and sparklingly clean.

Berdema
20, Vasilissis Amalias St., Kifisia, 210/8013853. **Open:** Year round, daily, evenings. Sunday also at noon. **Price:** € 15-27.
Modern taverna, with lamps made out of graters and

sieves serving (successfully) as ornaments. The cuisine honours both Greek and Constantinopolitan recipes. We loved the sardines baked in the oven with vegetables and herbs, as well as the gyros and the tasty kebabs.

Chani
24, Zisimopoulou St. & Syngrou, Amfithea, 210/9403660. **Open:** Year round, daily, noon-evening. **Price:** € 15-18.
A music taverna with an unusual feature: the dual entertainment provided by the Katsamba brothers on stage and the old Greek films projected onto the walls. Extensive menu of traditional Greek dishes.

Katsarina (Stamoulis kai Anna)
311, Kifisias Ave., Kifisia, 210/6254072. **Open:** Year round, daily (except Wednesday), noon-evening. **Price:** € 12-18.
Comfortable winter dining room and spacious garden. Good meats (like the monstrous, succulent stable-raised baby beef), well-cooked, and perfect appetisers. The fastest service in the city.

Lefkes
100, Galatsiou Ave., Galatsi, 210/2924458, 210/2927233. **Open:** Year round, daily (except Sunday), evenings. **Price:** € 12-15.
Attractive rustic ambiance, lovely courtyard reminiscent of Mexico (!) and flocks of young people. Good, simple food. Fast friendly service, cheerful atmosphere.

Manginas
1, Ethnikis Antistasis Sq., Melissia, 210/8046143. **Open:** Winter, Tues.-Sat. and summer, daily, evenings. Winter Sundays, also at noon. **Price:** € 9-12.
Simple, traditional taverna, famous for its spit-roasted suckling pig: succulent flesh, crispy skin. Excellent kokoretsi and splinantero. In the summer, the cool shade of the plane trees is heavenly.

Metsovo
Stamata, in the square, 210/6218138. **Open:** Year round, daily, noon-evening. **Price:** € 12-16.
Warm, well-cared for place with a fire burning in the grate all day in winter. The origins of the proprietor are as obvious in his pitas as in the name of his restaurant. Don't miss the pita with wild greens and cornmeal pastry. Tasty cooked dishes, fantastic lamb chops and fabulous Metsovo-style kebabs.

Papas
2, Strymonos St. & Dramas, Thrakomakedones, 210/2431573. **Open:** Year round, daily, evenings. Sat.-Sun. and holidays, also at noon. **Price:** € 12-15.
Beautifully kept dining room, all stone and wood, and a lovely terrace with Athens spread out below it like a carpet. Fabulous home-made pitas (don't miss the hortopita), perfectly fried courgettes, aubergines and potatoes, delicious chops and patties. In the winter, you may be lucky and find game.

Papoutsis
1, Markou Botsari St., Vrilissia, 210/8043244.

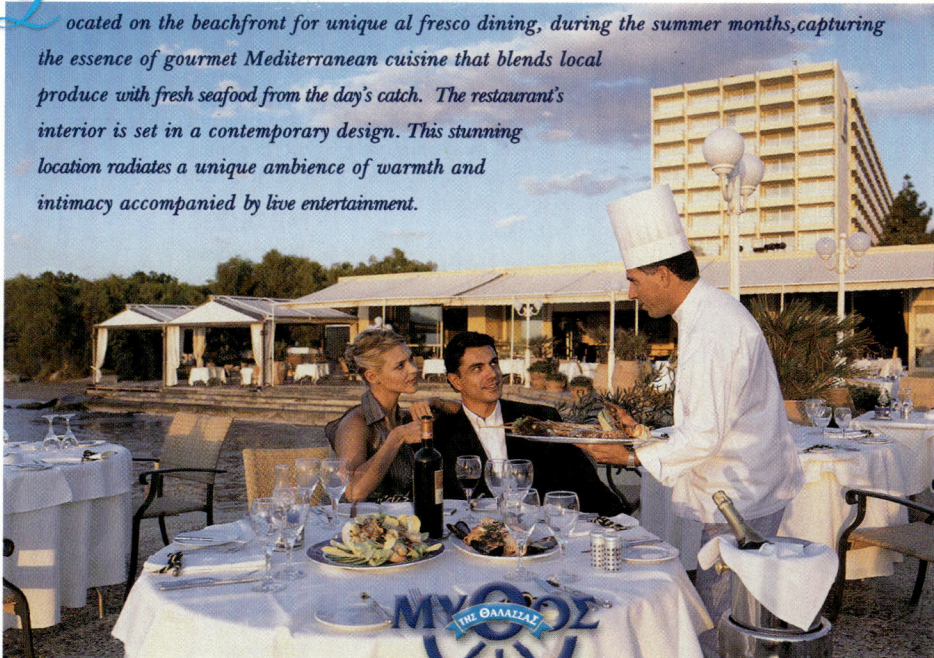

Eating out

Open: Year round, daily, evenings. Sundays and holidays also at noon. **Price:** € 12-15.

For nearly half a century, here in Ano Vrilissia, Thanasis Papoutsis has been teaching Athenians what a T-bone steak is. Choice meats from Karystos, served with thick and feather-light hand-cut fried potatoes.

Platanos
4, Diogenous St., Plaka, 210/3220666. **Open:** Year round, daily (except Sunday), noon-evening. March-May & Sept.-Oct., Sundays also at noon. **Price:** € 9-12.

Ancient taste temple with 60 years of service beneath the sacred rock of the Acropolis. Succeeds in serving unadulterated traditional Greek cuisine and in pleasing even the noblest of palates.

Skoufias
63, Troon St., Ano Petralona, 210/3412210, 210/3412252. **Open:** Winter only, daily (except Sunday), evenings. **Price:** € 12-15.

Charming, tasteful contemporary version of the traditional Greek taverna, with an intellectual clientele. The top hits from the kitchen are the fabulous honeyed pig's trotters and the tantalising hounkiar beyendi. The cook's special spaghetti (cream, vegetables, nuts) is a dish worthy of any great chef.

Stou Xynou
4, Angelou Geronta St., Plaka, 210/3221065. **Open:** Year round, daily (except Saturday/Sunday), evenings. **Price:** € 9-12.

Traditional rustic decor and classic tasty food. With its truly magical saucepans, the Xynos is one of the better places for a meal in tourist-ridden Plaka.

Tavernaki tis Despoinas
16, Evangelistrias St., near the square in Nea Erythraia, 210/8072262, 210/6205008. **Open:** Year round, daily (except Sunday), evenings. **Price:** € 12-15.

Despina Merkel may call it a "tavernaki", but the cheerful proprietor of this attractive place has brought back from America a trunkful of expertise in public banqueting. Warm ambiance, super-home-style cooking.

Vasilis
Km 27, Marathonos Ave., 22940/79075, 22940/75666. **Open:** Winter, Fri-Sun., noon-evening. Summer, daily, evenings. Sat.-Sun. also at noon. **Price:** € 12-15.

The traditional taverna at its best! Varied fare of unrivalled quality. Superb suckling pig, superlative small-size kokoretsi, sublime courgette patties. All this in a large and comfortable restaurant in Mati.

Vlasis
8, Pasteur St., Mavili St., 210/6463060. **Open:** Year round, daily, noon-evening. Sunday only at noon. **Price:** € 11-15.

Simple place, but tasteful and well-tended. Classic Greek cuisine at its very best, from the excellent cheese pie to the aromatic soutzoukakia. The cook is blessed with a lightness of touch that assures delicious

flavour without heaviness. In the summer they move to Zoumperi (22940/50290).

MEZEDES

Chochlidaki
41, Pentelis Ave., Chalandri, 210/6848043, 210/6820943. **Open:** Year round. Winter, daily (except Sunday), evenings. Sat.-Sun. also at noon. Summer, daily, evenings. **Price:** € 12-18.

One of the most famous mezes places in Athens. Well-designed room, with green marble and lots of private corners. Impressive platter with sixty or so different mezedes.

Ellinikon
124, Agias Paraskevis St., Chalandri, 210/6823394. Km 20, Parnithas Ave., 210/2469586. **Open:** Year round, daily, noon-evening. **Price:** € 15-20.

Pleasant, friendly, tastefully decorated rooms that attract a mix of people. The extensive menu is a tribute to the authentic flavours of Greece: from the charcoal-grilled aubergine seasoned with a tangy cheese spread and garlic vinegar to a delicious vegetable stir-fry from Pontus. Extremely courteous service.

Esy oti peis...
31, Perikleous St., Chalandri, 210/6851227, 210/6847640. **Open:** Year round, daily (except Monday), evenings. Sunday also at noon. **Price:** € 15-18.

Pleasant wood-and-stone dining room, and a large cool summer courtyard. Constantinople-style appetisers, a creative approach

Eating out

to traditional flavours, and particular attention to healthy cooking techniques.

Mania
67, Aigaiou & 13, Kyzikou St., Nea Smyrni, 210/9315016. **Open:** Year round, daily, evenings. Sunday also at noon. **Price:** € 12-18.
Authentic Greek and very flavourful repertory, including taste treats like honeyed chick peas baked in an earthenware dish, or the pork with a fabulous date-and-prune sauce. Casual cosy atmosphere, with hostess Kyria Mania very much to the fore.

Monippo
12, Drosini St., Kifisia, 210/6231440. **Open:** Year round, daily, noon-evening. **Price:** € 12-15.
Casual, smart, modern place. The mezedes include a broader range than is usual, with a number of creative dishes plus some traditional recipes from the owners' home province of Thessaly.

Ouzadiko
25-29, Karneadou St. (Lemou shopping centre), Kolonaki, 210/7295484. **Open:** Year round, Tues.-Sat., noon-evening. **Price:** € 12-15.
Microscopic wood-trimmed room, outside tables, in the atrium of Kolonaki's quietest shopping centre. Tasty food and abundant enthusiasm and flair. The largest collection of ouzos and tsipouros in Athens: 380 kinds!

Paei Kairos
16, Taki St, Psyrri Sq.,

210/3212858. **Open:** Year round, daily, evenings. Sat.-Sun. also at noon. **Price:** € 18-20.
One of the most popular eateries in Psyrri, always full and a bit too crowded. Greek mezedes and live music.

Piperia
Angelou Sikelianou & Adrianeiou, Neo Psychiko, 210/6728438. **Open:** Year round, daily, evenings. Sunday only at noon. **Price:** € 20-22.
Cheerful modern mezes place, nice people, and a decor that changes with the seasons. Sophisticated creative versions of traditional Greek mezedes, plus some Asian-inspired offerings (e.g. the squid sauteed with ginger, balsamic vinegar, sesame and finely chopped nori) and fresh mussels prepared in various intelligent ways.

Stou Korre
20-22, Agion Anargyron St., Psyrri, 210/3215291. **Open:** Year round, daily, evenings. Sat.-Sun. also at noon. **Price:** € 18-20.
Perhaps the most studied musical mezedopoleio in Athens! Musician Nikos Korres has created an impressively elegant and very modern place. Honest and refreshingly light Greek cuisine. Barrel wine from Thebes, served in tasteful earthenware goblets.

Tzitzikas kai mermigkas
4, Papadiamanti Sq., Ano Patisia, 210/2232376. 26, Aeschylou St. & Agiou Georgiou, Chalandri, 210/6810529. **Open:** Year round, daily (except Sun-

day), evenings. **Price:** € 15-20.
Modern establishments in Chalandri and Patisia, with a light and tasty menu. Both classic and creatively modified Greek mezedes. Fast friendly service.

Zeidoron
10, Taki St. & Agion Anargyron, Psyrri Sq., 210/3215368. **Open:** Year round, daily (except Monday), noon-evening. **Price:** € 12-18.
Probably the best mezedes place in Psyrri, overlooking some of the busiest streets in the district. Warm, friendly, but also crowded. Good food, not always entirely reliable.

ETHNIC TAVERNAS
Al Mawal
18, Maragkou St., Glyfada, 210/8944227. **Open:** Year round, daily, noon-evening. Monday, evenings only. **Price:** € 18-21.
Large well-kept dining room, with discreet reminders of the restaurant's Arabian origins. Authentic and successful Lebanese cuisine, plus water pipes with aromatic tobacco and belly dancers on Saturday night.

Anachita
3, Chrysostomou Smyrnis, Chalandri, 210/6891222. **Open:** Year round, daily, evenings. **Price:** € 12-15.
Authentic taste of Persia and points east, in an attractive small place patronised equally by native and oriental Athenians.

Axum
183, Drosopoulou St.,

Kypseli, 210/2011774.
Open: Year round, daily
(except Monday), evenings.
In summer, closed also on
Tuesday. **Price:** € 11-15.
Ethiopian cuisine in a rural
setting. Sample the large
assortment of cooked
meats and salads, accompanying each bite with injeras
pita, but be sure to consult
the friendly staff first about
the degree of fieriness you
want!

Buffalo Bill
13, Kyprou St., Glyfada,
210/8943128, 210/8947033.
Open: Year round, daily
(July-Aug. closed Sunday),
evenings. Sunday also at
noon. **Price:** € 18-24.
Probably the best Tex-Mex
restaurant in town, in a
small villa with a warm
atmosphere and plenty of
ethnic features. Excellent
chilli, perfect (and huge)
T-bone steaks and a fabu-
lous frozen Margarita that
you can order by the
pitcherful.

Furin Kazan
2, Apollonos St., Syntagma
Sq., 210/3229170. **Open:**
Year round, daily (except
Sunday), noon-evening.
Price: € 18-21.
Quality Japanese fast food -
perfect for a quick sushi
meal. Their sushi are some
of the best in the city.

Maracana Grill
55, Kolokotroni St. (from
296, Thiseos St.), Kallithea,
210/9400801. **Open:** Year
round, daily (except
Monday), evenings.
Price: € 15-21.
A whole parade of meats
comes to your table, in
accordance with the pre-
scriptions of the Brazilian
tsouraskeria. Interesting

side dishes on the buffet,
cheerful modern decor in
Brazil's national colours.

O Serkos kai
ta tessera asteria
28, Xenofontos St. & Zep-
pou, Glyfada, 210/9649553,
210/9634920. **Open:** Year
round, daily, evenings.
Winter Sundays, only at
noon. **Price:** € 12-15.
Probably the best kebab
place in town: simple and
spacious, and the food is
fabulous. Super lahmatzoun,
doner and Adana kebabs
and yiaourtlou, and an
unimaginably delectable
earthenware dish of veal,
pureed aubergine and melt-
ed cheese. And for afters,
the best kiounefe you have
ever tasted.

Pak Indian
13, Menandrou St., Psyrri,
210/3219412, 210/3242225.
Open: Year round, daily,
noon-evening. **Price:** € 9-12.
Like a well-set-up Indian
taverna, in the heart of
Athens' Indo-Pakistani district. Sometimes sparklingly
clean, sometimes, unfortunately, not.

Pera
20, Dekeleias St., Nea
Chalkidona, 210/2533896.
Open: Year round, daily
(except Monday), evenings.
Sunday also at noon.
Price: € 9-12.
Large room, with the
atmosphere of an Istanbul
eating-place. Among the
dozens of good things,
you'll find all sorts of kebabs, familiar and unfamiliar.
The beiti kebab is excep-
tionally good, and the lamb
gyros very tasty.

Poly-polis
7, Sinopis St., Athens

Tower, Ampelokipoi,
210/7484788. **Open:** Year
round, daily (except
Monday), noon-evenings.
Sunday only at noon.
Price: € 15-18.
A multiethnic team, with
members from Ghana, the
Middle East and Eastern
Europe, prepares ethnic
home cooking in a small
warm eatery.

Santa Fe
30B, Agiou Georgiou St.,
Chalandri, 210/6859690.
Open: Year round, daily
(except Sunday), evenings.
Price: € 15-18.
Simple place, with Mexican
touches in the decor and a
wonderful "Mexican" courtyard behind. We would suggest Mex starters and Tex
entrees (including perfectly
grilled steaks). Tasty hamburgers.

Suzanna
5, Chariton St. & Orfeos,
Amfithea, 210/9428129,
210/9404004. **Open:** Year
round, daily, evenings.
Sunday also at noon.
Price: € 12-15.
Irresistible temptations to
gluttony from various eastern countries, in this very
attractive "Hellenised"
eatery.

Valentina
253, Lykourgou St.,
Kallithea, 210/9431871.
Open: Year round, daily,
noon-evening.
Price: € 12-15.
Delicious Russo-Pontian
cuisine and sweet prices are
an unbeatable combination.
Don't miss the light-as-air
Ukrainian pelmeni, the
impeccable piroshki, the
tantalising marinated meats
and the fragrant hand-made
lipotska bread.

Night life

Athens Guide 2003

ATHENS 2004

ALPHA BANK

OFFICIAL
BANK

all-night beat

The Athens clubbing scene has something for everyone, all night long: potent house music alternates with Greek popular hits, and top dance floor DJs make way for sophisticated underground listening. So it should come as no surprise that its chiefcharacteristic is multiplicity of form. And this year, clubbing in Athens is linked with artistic events, theme parties and good food, whilethe fanatical clubbers impatientlyawait the explosion of energythat comes with the dance festivals.

Lots of top name DJs (Sasha, John Digweed, Dave Seaman et al.), plenty of big open air dance festivals (Just Dance, Energy, Athens' Dance), guest appearances by members of pop/rock groups who DJ their own sets, all kinds of bar-clubs with arts features (theatrical performances, art exhibitions, film screenings): these are the components of the Athens clubbing scene in 2003, a year that promises to be exceptionally interesting. The big winners again this year are the dance clubs (Plus Soda, Venue, U-Matic), which have secured their places on the map of the world's best venues, with incredible DJ line-ups, and of course the big fashion mainstream clubs (Privilege, Envy, Kalua), that will once again play host to the cream of the country's celebrities.
It's obvious: Athens clubbing is evolving, and the growing tendency (this year stronger than ever) to do away with the compartmentalisa-

U-Matic

Club 22

tion that restricts it to musical entertainment lets it display a multiplicity of form that, umbrella-like, covers a variety of artistic elements and activities (theatre, cinema, exhibitions, live, drag shows, audio-visual projects). Clubbing is also tending to break away from identification with specific locales, i.e. the clubs themselves. It is no accident that lately the best dance evenings have been at dance festivals, nor that more and more party teams (Jungle, Floorfiller, Dazzle, Magna) prefer not to be associated with a specific club but organise events in a variety of venues, from concert stages to cinemas.

Clubbing is also conducting a flirtation with dining, making bars and club-restaurants the top - 2 in 1 - choice for an evening out, while every self-respecting trendy new bar or club (De Stijl, Mommy, De Luxe) also places great emphasis on its cuisine.

This is all happening because Athens is a city that never sleeps. Forget the Friday-and-Saturday-night-out routine: in Athens the clubbing is fast and furious seven days a week.

From the big fashionable mainstream clubs, where you can easily find yourself at five o'clock on a Wednesday morning in the middle of a wild and glamorous party, to the daily "fiesta" in Mavili

square, where the bars and the square merge into one party that goes straight on till morning, this city offers its night owls all kinds of choices. Having embraced contemporary musical trends, while at the same time creating new ones or insisting in certain locales on projecting a distinctive, particular and wholly Greek character, Athens can justifiably claim to have it all. With dance clubs, big fashion mainstream clubs, small prive clubs, classic bars, rock clubs, Latin clubs, freestyle bars, live music bars and even ellinadika, Athens clubbing has little or nothing to envy from any other late night capital in the world - and in many cases quite the reverse.

Only in Athens (and in Greece in general, for in this domain the rest of the country tends to imitate the capital) will you find big clubs where the programmes move smoothly from house dance hits to Greek popular hits and the patrons dance on bar and tabletop, tossing carnations and paper napkins as if they were at a bouzouki place!

Of course, the fashion for ellinadika (which was launched by Vasilis Tsilichristos at the Mercedes in the '80s, when he played Greek music in a club for the first time and nearly caused a riot, and was taken up by the Vareladiko,

tip
To get past the severe face control you will need: a date, proper evening or trendy dress (depending on the place) and possibly a reservation.

tip
Expect to pay substantially more than usual when there is a guest DJ.

Kalua

Clubbing

which instituted the term elli-nadiko) is tending to fade in recent years. But even today many mainstream clubs (Prime, Liberty, Privilege) continue to devote a large part of their programme to Greek music. The city's fashion mainstream clubs all seem to have adopted a golden recipe for success: huge premises (downtown in the winter, on the beach in the summer, and not always the same - like the names of the clubs), a decor that changes with the season but always follows the latest fashion (last year minimal, this year oriental), stringent face control, many reserved tables and a programme of nothing but hits (Greek and foreign).

In these places the atmosphere is less one of good cheer and high spirits (which doesn't mean that you can't have a good time) than of posturing and power dressing, which creates the impression that you belong to the "chosen few", members of a select society.

But it's dance clubbing that has changed the most in recent years. Some club and party teams embraced the rave movement of the early '90s, slowly creating a hard-core dance music scene, with parties and events featuring all the big names of the world dance scene. In time, house music became mainstream, and inevitably the fashion mainstream clubs began inviting famous foreign DJs as featured guests (always based on the box office value of the name), dangerously eroding the boundaries between them and the dance clubs. The result was that some dance clubs went even further underground (in order to differentiate themselves), winning themselves a place on the list of the best dance clubs in the world and being cited as hot spots on the DJs' CVs.

But with the electronic music

generation of the '80s moving into its thirties, a demand has arisen for smaller, cosier places. This explains the genesis of the freestyle bars, which have recently become the strongest trend on the clubbing scene. Tiny, with colourful decors and DJs who know how to marry every variety of electronic and other music on their consoles, the freestyle bars have provided opportunities for less commercially-oriented listening and dance scenes throughout the week, while some them slipped easily into the lounge mode that was all the rage last year. Many of them, in fact, turned into miniature nightclubs, with very loud music and foreign guest DJs.

This preoccupation with famous foreign guest DJs is still very obvious on the club scene in Athens, with big names appearing every week in dance clubs, freestyle bars, fashion mainstream clubs, even rock clubs; and it has created a tendency for evenings to be considered "compelling" only when there is a guest name. This has been further reinforced by the dance festivals, which are getting bigger every year, and will of course peak in 2004, when we can expect to see some truly great events.

Greek summers are perfect for open air dance festivals (Energy, Just Dance), and places like the Foundation of the Hellenic World also permit the organisation of such events in the winter as well: the huge success of these events justifies calling them an alternative form of Athenian dance clubbing, outside the clubs, reminiscent of the English warehouse parties of the early '90s.

Fluid, progressive and dynamic, the Athens clubbing scene is again this year ready to offer us evenings and venues that will be the talk of the town.

tip
Look for the "theme parties". They have become very popular in recent years and are usually great fun.

tip
Many clubs will only hold reservations until 01:00. Don't be late!

tip
Parking valets accept only tips. They can't quote you a rate (usually € 5) unless it's a private parking lot.

FASHION MAINSTREAM

Alekos
Agioi Apostoloi,
22950/82338, 22950/85104.
One of the loveliest and
most historic summer clubs
in Attica. The air of a mediaeval manor house created
by the stone walls surrounding its lush garden is enhanced by the gauzy lamps and
myriad candles. It attracts
large crowds of young, mainly Athenian enthusiasts that
dance all night to a pro-
gramme of house hits.
Recently the management
has also been stressing the
restaurant side of the place.

Atlantis
Chalkoutsiou Ave., Oropos,
22950/31832.
One of the biggest summer
clubs in the environs of the
city, with a huge garden full
of enormous trees and
countless candles and plants.
The decor of the large
wood-panelled interior,
including details like the bell-
tower, suggests the grandeur
and solemnity of a
monastery. The soundtrack
plays only hit music, Greek
and foreign. A couple of
years ago the Atlantis Prive
opened next door: equally
verdant, with a small pool,
plenty of salons and a console that plays music from
across the decades as well as
artistic Greek, it is designed
to please a thirtysomething
crowd.

Balux
58, V. Georgiou II, Asteria
Glyfadas, 210/8941062,
210/8941620, 210/8941109.
The name means "golden
sands" in Latin, which is
totally appropriate for a club
located next to the sandy
Asteria beach. This is one of
the city's newer summer

clubs: discreetly lit by scores
of candles and torches, with
wooden floors, lounge
atmosphere in the salons
next to the console and
king-size lounge chairs
around the pool. The soundtrack frequently diverges
from the strictly mainstream,
since it hosts famous DJ parties. There are tentative
plans for a winter Balux
beginning in the 2003-4 season.

Banana Moon
5, Stadiou Sq. & Agras,
Pagkrati, 210/7521768.
Diadochou Pavlou, Glyfada
waterfront, 210/8946018.
A winner since it first
opened in the Zappeion gardens, it became the absolute
must summer fashion main-
stream club downtown.
Recently, however, it abandoned its garden site for
permanent (winter-summer)
premises - all bright colours
and minimal decor - directly
across the road, on the piazza in front of the Kallimarmaro Stadium, doubling up in
the summer with a twin spot
on the waterfront, in the
left-hand section of the
Palmeras Group in Glyfada.
The music is mainstream
plus Greek.

Budha
Peiraios & Andronikou St.,
Rouf. Diadochou Pavlou,
Glyfada waterfront,
210/8945992.
Its winter home on Syngrou
Ave. is huge, with an oriental
decor and a gigantic Buddha
presiding from behind the
console. The music leans
heavily towards commercial
house and dance hits, but
they also play a bit of Greek
on Fridays and Saturdays and
often invite guest DJs from
abroad. In the summer, the
whole scene moves to Glyfada, to quintessentially sum-

mer premises - featuring a
vast illuminated pool - on
the waterfront.

Camel
74, Irakleidon St. (formerly
at 115, Peiraios St.),
Thiseio, 210/3476847.
The only club in the city that
features glam rock. Impressive industrial decor and a
crowd that, outwardly very
comme il faut, are inwardly
committed rockers! The
console covers the whole
spectrum of rock music,
from indie and '80s elec-
tropop to contemporary
alternative British and American pop/rock. The resident
DJs include familiar radio figures, like Dimitris Papaspy-
ropoulos and Takis Chris-
tidis.

Club 22
22, Vouliagmenis Ave.,
N. Kosmos, 210/9249814.
Diadochou Pavlou, Glyfada
waterfront, 210/8944422.
The most off-beat club in
town. It organises crazy car-
nival-style theme parties (e.g.
Kitscherella, with a strictly
kitsch dress code!), wel-
comes famous foreign guest
DJs, screens short films,
organises art exhibitions,
presents shows (everything
from illusionists to stand-up
comedy, drag queen shows
and folk singers!), stages theatrical performances and in
general brings together birds
of very different feathers.
Musically it covers a wide
range of sounds, from alternative rock to house and
pop (all decades), with a
regiment of resident DJs.
Attracts a young crowd,
knowledgeable and no com-
plexes. Its winter premises
are at the beginning of Vou-

Clubbing

liagmenis Ave., and in the summer it moves to the waterfront, to the Palmeras Group in Glyfada.

De Stijl
11, Vouliagmenis Ave., Glyfada, 210/9602611-2. "Eirinikos": 4, Poseidonos Ave., Voula, 210/8952403. Taking up where the legendary Mercedes left off, this club - under the management of Niko Bure - is part of the Vasilis Tsilichristos group. Glamourous VIP crowd, very strict face control, dynamic and enthusiastic atmosphere driven by a lively programme of hits - including the Greek hits that really get people going. In the winter you'll find it in Glyfada (in premises that are strikingly like the old Mercedes), while in the summer it moves to the waterfront.

Envy
123, Syngrou Ave., Neos Kosmos, 210/9355665. 2, Gr. Lampraki St., Asteria Glyfadas, 210/8944558. In essence a chain of clubs, cafes and bar-restaurants: the summer Envy Club on the beach (huge, awesome decor, in the old Asteria Glyfadas); the winter Envy Club (on Syngrou Ave., where the old Tunnel was, minimal decor); the winter Envy-Voyage (bar-restaurant with ethnic decor in the old Mercedes on Kifisias Ave.); the summer Envy-Glam (bar-restaurant with pool, on the site of the old Mustang in Politeia) and Envy Cafe (Kefalari Sq.). All of them attract a trendy (and in general quite young) crowd with a good sprinkling of local celebrities. Resident DJ and part owner Takis Chatzakis plays only foreign hits (plus the odd Greek song); the Envy Club often features foreign guest DJs, always from the mainstream/pop house scene.

Fogg's
10-12, Kifisias Ave. (Agora Shopping Centre), Marousi, 210/6846690. Stunning winter club, with a decor that breathes opulence and around-the-world glamour, with separate corners inspired by different parts of the globe (Japan, Morocco, India...). The same world-mix concept also governs the soundtrack that, while remaining solidly in the mainstream, weaves in music from all over the world, introducing clever suggestions of ethnic, arabesque, Asian... Other drawing cards include the sensual dance show by a group of dancers and the theatrical costume-uniforms sported by the staff.

Island
Limanakia Vouliagmenis, 210/9653563-4. Summer club rightly numbered among the classics, in premises that are still among the most beautiful on the waterfront strip. Marvellous sea view, atmospheric decor with a Mediterranean aura, candles, gauzy curtains, cascades of bougainvillaea. One of the city's most "preppy" club-restaurants, with good food and good dance music.

Kalua
6, Amerikis St., Syntagma, 210/3608304. Porto Rafti (Avlaki), 22990/75415. One of the older downtown clubs, and for twenty years never off the top 5 favourites list. Its winter home is the now legendary basement on Amerikis St., in the heart of the city. Always packed - even midweek - with a very preppy gossip column crowd. Extremely strict face control, and a console that will play a bit of Greek. Come summer it moves to a huge garden by the sea at Porto Rafti, and functions as a club/beach bar.

Karina
Akti Alimou, Alimos, 210/9858654. Open-air summer club-restaurant giving directly onto the sandy beach, with a fabulous sea view. Simple, unfussy decor, dominated by two large main bars with masts holding aloft the characteristic blue navigation lights of a sea-going vessel, creating the illusion that you're aboard a yacht. Soundtrack features mainly hits.

Liberty - Comeback
10-12, Kifisias Ave. (Agora Shopping Centre), Marousi, 210/6840392. Liberty is a mainstream club-restaurant that opened successfully in Kolonaki but moved to Marousi about a year ago. The style is generally retro, harking back to the Athens of the '80s, with a console that plays the hits of that period plus lots of current (as well as older) Greek hits. Very strict face control. Enthusiastic celebrity crowds that generate a party atmosphere every day of the week. In the summer it changes its name to Comeback and moves to the waterfront.

On the Road
1, Ardittou St. & 1, Ilissou, Mets, 210/3478716. Summer club that occupies a narrow island-garden between two main roads, next to the Kallimarmaro Stadium. Last year's move to abandon mainstream for worldbeat music with a fair

injection of electronic proved highly successful. Trump cards: the attractive flower beds and the lively parties deejayed by top-flight foreign guests.

Privilege

Ag. Eleousis & Kakour-godikeiou, Monastiraki, 210/3317801. Agios Kosmas Beach, Elliniko, 210/9852993.
The most famous mainstream club in Athens is owned by Vasilis Tsilichristos, one of the best-known figures on the city's nightlife scene. Local celebrity crowd, very strict face control, nothing but hits (Greek and foreign) from the console. It has a restaurant, and its premises are always large and richly decorated. For the 2002-3 winter season it is adopting a multiplex style, with the club and restaurant on the ground and first floors of its new habitat, while the second floor will be given over to the Bedroom, featuring mainly electronic music and a decor redolent of the opulence of the '30s. In the summer it moves to the beach at Agios Kosmas.

FREESTYLE

I-22

122, Doukissis Plakentias St. & Panormou, Ampelokipoi.
In contrast to the walls, which are a riot of colour, the console shows a decided penchant for black: sounds from hip-hop to reggae and drum 'n' bass, with a fair dose of electronica. Solid weekly programmes, many special guests from abroad, but what really counts is the tiptop console and the relaxed style of proprietors and patrons.

7 Heaven

22, Pheidippidou St. & Mesogeion, Ampelokipoi, 210/7709146.
Located on the third floor of a shopping centre, with one side covered in stained glass and the other overlooking the street. Often cranks up the beats, even playing techno, making it more like an underground club than a freestyle bar.

Almodobar

60, Konstantinoupoleos St., Gazi, 0932145757.
New freestyle bar with a deliberately kitsch decor, and a strong contender for a top spot in its category. Owner and resident DJ Panos D has gathered a team of well-known Greek DJs, several of whom have made recordings abroad.

Astron

3, Taki St., Psyrri, 0977469356.
Bar in Psyrri that for two seasons was hugely successful, particularly in the summer, since Taki St. at this point looked more like an Aegean island than downtown Athens and sitting, drink in hand, outside Astron became a must for those in the know. Today, however, although it still has good freestyle residents, some of the glamour has worn off.

Bee

Miaouli & Themidos, Psyrri, 210/3212624.
Describes itself as a bar-restaurant, but feels intensely like a club. In this trendy place with its pop decor you'll meet mainly stylists, fashion designers, models, media men, and the mood is always gay-friendly. The console plays mainly electronica and often jacks up the bpm. Always packed, this is the

perfect place for a close-up of those who support or belong to the local star system.

Briki

6, Dorylaiou St., Mavili Sq., 210/6452380. 18, Frynis St., Pagkrati, 210/7518637.
The Lilliputian bar on Mavili Sq. is the "big" brother of the even more microscopic brasserie in Pagkrati. Funky colourful decor that stops just short of kitsch and changes about every three months, and a very eclectic soundtrack, with a base ground of electronica interwoven with rock, pop, ethnic, and even disco. Popular with artists and media types in recent years, it is packed every day of the week.

DeLuxe

15, Falirou St., Makrygianni, 210/9243184.
In essence, this is a stylish bar-restaurant that in recent years has adopted a lounge mode. The owners were the creators of one of the first freestyle places in town (the legendary Zoo), and in DeLuxe they put the emphasis on the console, which marries electronica with '60s music and touches of ethnic. All this in a pop art setting to which the country's entire media-lifestyle set repairs en masse.

Inoteka

3, Avissynias Sq., Monastiraki, 210/3246446.
Small, friendly place, with a smart, uncomplicated (and unaffected), and very mixed crowd. Prime time is the summer, when they set the tables out on the square. The penchant is for freestyle and electronic (all sorts), but

Clubbing

they're happy to play ethnic and even rock music as well. Cult details: kitsch elements in the decor (float mattress, singing fish…), Louisa shots, aquarium at the bar.

Loop
3, Agion Asomaton Sq., Thiseio, 210/3247666.
Long, colourful, mini-size bar, where on weekend nights they crank up the beats and morph it into a club. Kids who like good freestyle adore it, because the resident DJs play just about everything from the electronic music scene. The decor, which keeps changing, was simpler this past year, the basic element being the pom-pom type lamps hanging over the bar.

Micraasia
90, Konstantinoupoleos St., Gazi, 210/3464851.
Beneath the banner of worldbeat music and with a very active arts stage (live performances, visual arts exhibitions), Micraasia endeavours to marry western (mainly electronic) music and Anatolian culture. Owners Dimitris and his Turkish wife Charla have converted the ground floor of his family home into a very attractive bar, with lots of oriental touches (painted ceilings with arabesque motifs, souvenirs of Constantinople, Arabian tiles) in the decora-

tion. You'll hear good freestyle, NY house, and live performances of the music of Asia Minor and Arabia. By summer 2003 they hope to have completed their projected chill-out roof bar, with a view of the Acropolis.

Mommy
4, Delfon St., Kolonaki, 210/3619682.
Popular with artists, media folk and the trendy crowd. Lounge-style atmosphere, although the Greek DJs at the console play mainly freestyle. The decor, which changes regularly, is colourful, pop, artistico. It has a restaurant, and there is talk of opening a club in the basement. Each month there is a different visual arts exhibition.

Nipiagogeio
8, Kleanthous St. & Elasidon, Gazi, 210/3458534.
This very attractive little place owes its name ("kindergarten") to the fact that its summertime garden once belonged to a nursery school. Colourful decor, colourful cocktails and colourful music, covering the entire contemporary electronic scene, interspersed with plenty of more classic listening, like jazz, soul, funk…

One Happy Cloud
12, Aristofanous St.,

Psyrri, 210/3222264.
Small bar, unimaginative decor (except when there is an art exhibition), but the music is fabulous, leaning heavily towards good electronica and black sounds. Attracts some of Greece's most popular DJs as residents, and foreign guests who are not necessarily the most commercial names. Generally popular with alternative freestyle fans.

Soul
65, Evripidou St., 210/3310907.
New in place from the team that created De Luxe and before that Zoo. Artistic decor, electronically-oriented console (but not exclusively so) that welcomes all the top Greek DJs and an enthusiastic crowd any day of the week. In the summer the scene moves outside, to the small courtyard.

Stavlos
10, Irakleidon St., Thiseio, 210/3467206.
Multiplex (gallery, restaurant, cafe, club) named for the old royal stables it used to occupy. The cobblestone courtyard has become Thiseio's summer meeting spot, and even in the winter you can sit outside and watch the sky from under a clear plastic awning, This year the club was taken over by the Modular Expansion group, who converted it into a very attractive freestyle place that covers the entire spectrum of electronic music, from hip-hop and drum 'n' bass to techno.

Vibe
1, Aristofanous St., Iroon Sq., Psyrri, 210/3244794.
Stylish minimal look bar, with a console handled by the cream of Greece's freestyle

---

DISCO

Vinylio
The only discotheque in the city, and one of the liveliest places in town. The console plays only hits from the '70s on, while the decor is original disco, with mirror balls, polished dance floor, mirrors and lots of strobe lights. It is not retro, or cult, just an ideal place for pure unadulterated fun for all ages - the ages on the dance floor go from teens to forty plus.
33, Poseidonos Ave. (hotel Emmantina), Glyfada, 210/9681056.

FOGG'S

TASTE OF THE WORLD

DEEP INTO LOUNGE... DEEPER INTO PLEASURE...
Some times the trip around the world takes one night!

LOUNGE FUN RESTAURANT
AGORA CENTER, 10-12 KIFISIAS str., MAROUSI, TEL. 210 6846690, 210 6858056

Clubbing

artists, with frequent guest appearances by top foreign DJs. Private club atmosphere, popular with arts types and lifestyle media editors. Its collaboration with the restaurant Interni and its continual endeavours to organise events set it apart from the other bars in its category, and give it a foreign bar-club style. Ask for a glass of red wine and settle back to enjoy your drink in a goblet the size of the Holy Grail!

DANCE CLUBS

Bossa Nostra Noir

3, Zoodochou Pigis & Akadimias, 210/3840205.
One of Athens' best-known dance clubs, it first caught our attention with its deep red decor and lounge atmosphere, since the music, although mainly house, had a tendency to drift towards freestyle. This season, however, the Bossa Nostra has opted for black: it has moved from Psyrri into the centre, renamed itself Bossa Nostra Noir and gone farther underground, deeper into the club style. The black background to the decor is broken by splashes of colour in a '50s/'60s style, and there is a dark room with a film screen. Resident famous Greek DJs like Akylla and Costas Marousopoulos man the console, with frequent foreign guests.

Free Your Base

110, Ermou & 6-8, Avliton St., 0932076122.
Although it opened just two years ago, it is already one of the most important and most alternative of the winter dance clubs. Beautiful deep red space with Moroccan decor, celebrated Greek and foreign DJs, frequent

happenings with live percussionists and sax-players, visual arts exhibitions.

Plus Soda

161, Ermou St., Thiseio, 210/3456187.
The city's most famous dance club has acquired an international reputation, with its weekly guest stints by the cream of the world's house-progressive DJs; meanwhile, the careers of its resident artists are rocketing skywards. Here you'll see extreme outfits, casual clubbers, stylish celebrities and media people.

U-Matic

268, Vouliagmenis Ave., Agios Dimitrios, 0945363700.
In its three years of existence the city's most underground club has wholeheartedly embraced the techno and progressive house scene, creating an ideal habitat for fans of the genre. It has two stages, and a crowd that seems to have stepped straight out of the pages of "Face". If you can't take the cranked-up bpm, then better give it a miss; but if you like quality techno and want to listen to some of its top exponents, then you'll love the place.

Venue

7, Sina St. & Kifisias Ave. (next to OTE), Marousi, 210/6106869. Agios Kosmas Beach, Elliniko, 210/9852995-6.
Dance culture with the glamour and attitude of the mainstream clubs. The result is an impressive mass-style house club, with very strict face control and a young but far from lumpen crowd. Owner and resident DJ is the famous Vasilis Tsilichristos,

and there are often guest appearances by big names from the international house scene. In the winter you'll find it at Gazi, while in the summer it usually moves to the beach.

CLASSIC ROCK ALTERNATIVE POP/ROCK

45°

18, Iakchou & Voutadon, Gazi, 210/3479625.
Its two great loves are classic rock music and Harley Davidsons - and it makes no attempt to hide either of its weaknesses. Far from it! Even the name is a tribute, being the angle formed by a Harley's cylinders... Occupies a two-storey industrial-style building in Gazi, and the decor has the feel of an American rock club/bar, with its 12-metre bar, countless bits and pieces and Harley posters on the walls. The soundtrack covers the whole rock spectrum, and the music is often live. In the summer they move up to the roof, which has a fabulous view of the Acropolis and the entire surrounding area, and show films and video and concert clips on the big screen.

Argo

35, Ploutarchou St., Kolonaki, 210/7254093.
The Athens version of the Mykonos rock club (that wrote its own page in the history of the nightlife on the legendary island) spends the winter in Kolonaki. Residential-type locale with many rooms and gracious arty touches (candles in niches in the walls, vases of flowers on the bar, fresh fruit in bowls on the tables) that enhance the lovely and very comme il

'EN⟨RGIE®

Clubbing

faut atmosphere of the place. The music covers the full rock spectrum. Order one of the fancy cocktails - you won't be disappointed.

Blue
8, Mesolongiou St., Chalandri Sq., 210/6815505.
Rock place with a long history in Chalandri, and a console that is handled by some of the best known radio DJs, who play everything from classic rock to the latest from the American and European pop/rock scene. There is a bar on the ground floor and a mini club upstairs, while in the summer the roof terrace, dripping with jasmine and climbing plants, becomes a small chill-out bar where the freestyle music ranges from low beat electronica to ethnic.

Chorostasio
2, Skouleniou St., Klafthmonos Sq., 210/3314330-1.
Occupying both storeys of a beautiful neo-classical building in the centre of Athens, the Chorostasio is one of the most atmospheric winter rock spots in town. Resident DJ and soul of the place is Giorgos Fakinos, who manages to create a programme embracing whatever is new and fresh on the rock scene, lots of '80s stuff, a fair bit of electronica and many musical tributes, new recordings and of course his celebrated gothic parties, a must for fans of the genre. The ground floor is occupied by Chorostasio Downstairs, open year round and occasionally imitating a freestyle bar, lacing the rock music with electronic.

Decadence
69, Voulgaroktonou & 2, Poulcherias St., Strefi Hill, 210/8823544.
Small rock club with a long history (more than twenty years!), and a hard sell drive that definitely does not mean it's musically inferior to the other clubs in its category. On the contrary, it's one of the most active places in town, with a full weekly programme (musical tributes, record presentations, guests), many DJs and party teams and a console that plays anything that rocks (in the widest sense). It also organises hip theme parties, like indoor beach volleyball and blonde bashes! Located in a neo-classic building - the small bar (Down) on the ground floor acts as a second stage.

Komis
15, Laskaratou St., Ano Patisia, 210/2013176.
The soul of this place is Defkalionas (who calls himself Komis - "the Count"), a typical rock figure. This is evident both here, where the walls are plastered with posters in true old-fashioned rock style, and in the neighbouring brasserie of the same name in its beautiful neo-classic building. In the summer, especially, the brasserie's delightful garden, with its quality rock sound (Greek and foreign), is a very pleasant place to be.

Mad
110, Ermou & 6-8, Avliton St., 210/3227663.
One of the city's oldest rock clubs, which continues to present the new status of the international alternative rock scene. In fact, it goes further than that, experimenting with other alternative sounds and including hip-hop parties, reggae nights, gothic parties and experimental electronica evenings in its weekly programmes. Musically sophisticated crowd, extreme dressers and generally very young.

GAY BARS

Alekos Island
Historic bar, always with the same unique bartending and exceptional lounge music.
42, Tsakalof St., Kolonaki.

Alexander's
Fun atmosphere, with Greek music on the ground floor and foreign dance hits downstairs.
44, Anagnostopoulou St., Kolonaki, 210/3646660.

City
Drag queen show Fridays and Saturdays.
4, Koryzi St. & Vourvachi, Makrygianni, 210/9240740.

Granazi
Mainly Greek music. Very friendly ambience, no posturing.
20, Lempesi St., Makrygianni, 210/9244185.

Lamda
The "clubbiest" of the gay joints. House and Greek. In the basement also a dark room.
15, Lempesi St., & 9, Syngrou Ave., Makrygianni, 210/9224202.

Lizard
Every Friday, Cyberdykes party with euro-gay disco & house music.
31, Apostolou Pavlou St., Thiseio.

Memphis

5, Ventiri St., Hilton,
210/7224104.
The DJ is obviously partial to
'80s rock, devoting a large
part of his programme to it.
But there are also musical
tributes to electronic
sounds, and he covers the
full range of contemporary
rock. For years now Tues-
days have been gothic nights,
featuring industrial, gothic
and electro pop music. In the
summer they move out into
the little courtyard with its
designer furniture and screen
of plants, while the dance
floor in the air-conditioned
interior is a jungle.

Mo Better

32, Koletti St. &
Themistokleous,
Exarcheia, 210/3812981.
The most popular rock bar
in the city is in Exarcheia, is

packed every day of the
week and is called Mo Better. It occupies the first floor
of a neo-classic building,
changing its colour scheme
every year but always retaining its attractive cosy
ambiance. The console
moves easily from hip-hop
on Tuesdays to hardcore
rock on Thursdays, with
British or American pop and
rock in between.

Mojo

36, Papadiamantopoulou
St., Ilisia, 210/7757033.
One of the cosiest and most
attractive rock bars in the
city is located in an old stone
building with discreet atmospheric lighting and a console
that plays everything, from
classic rock, soul, funk and
'70s psychedelic to the latest
British and American rock
hits. Excellent bar, with a

good selection of pure malts.
In the summer they also use
the interior garden courtyard - a small oasis among
the apartment blocks of Ilisia.

Pop

10B, Kleitiou St.,
210/3220650.
Lilliputian corridor-bar (!),
extremely popular with
those who take an interest
in the alternative music
scene. The decor is bright
and cheerful, the service
very friendly, the ambience
cosy and the console truly
stylish, playing mainly British
pop/rock.

JAZZ - BLUES - FUNK

Empleon

20A, Laskaratou St., Ano
Patisia, 210/2280402.
Located in a beautiful neo-
classic building with an equal-

Clubbing

ly beautiful garden. The console plays mainly funky and jazzy grooves, but is happy to deliver some rock, and even mainstream! Especially in the summer, when the action moves into the garden, this is one of the most atmospheric places in town.

Half Note Jazz Club

17, Trivonianou St., Metz, 210/9213310.
Synonymous with some of the biggest names in jazz and ethnic music. Cosy place, a favourite with thirtysomething live music fans. Weekly programmes feature groups from all over the world, plus top-flight local bands.

Jazz

15, Tatoiou St., Kifisia, 210/8014036.
One of the most popular places in the northern suburbs, with a soundtrack that explores 'all that jazz' - everything from acid jazz to jazzy freestyle beats. Its great assets are its wonderful garden - in the summer a hidden cool oasis in the city - and the superb bartending.

Parafono

130A, Asklipiou St., Exarcheia, 210/6446512.
Historic bar, that regularly presents all kinds of groups, but mainly jazz.

Thirio

1, Lepeniotou St., Psyrri. Miniature place, with a dreamy colourful decor and a contrastingly lively atmosphere, since the console, which is handled by connoisseurs of jazz and funk, sometimes verges on freestyle.

ETHNIC - LATIN

Cubanita

28, Karaiskaki St., Psyrri Sq., 210/3314605-8.
Exotic cocktails plus live music from Cuban groups make this one of the liveliest stages in the city.
The ground floor (the restaurant is on the mezzanine level) literally goes wild, with a crowd of thirtysomethings dancing within kissing distance of the musicians.

Folie

2, Esselin St., Ampelokipoi, 210/6469852.
Small cosy club, with a

colourful decor (changes regularly) and a bar with a strong tradition in cocktails, Folie is particularly fond of ethnic and Latin listening, but has nothing against the black sounds of funk, acid jazz and hip-hop. Cult feature: the Brazilian dancers among the patrons, who really get the place jumping on Brazil nights!

Palenque

41, Farantaton St., Goudi, 210/7752360.
The oldest and best-known Latin/ethnic place in town is always packed, and its weekly programme is always full of DJ parties, lots of live music, plus evenings devoted to the tango (tangeria) and Latin dance lessons.

Red Marrakesh

3, Agatharchou St., Psyrri, 210/3317646-8.
The impressive and ethnic decor takes you to Morocco (you guessed?), as does the music (DJ sets and live). But it's the belly dancing that really stirs things up.

GREEK FOLK

Enigma

130, Dimitrakopoulou St., Koukaki, 210/9245983.
Small club, predominantly wood decor, walls decorated with small nautical items (life vests, anchors, cables), windows imitating portholes. The ambiance is friendly, especially on weekend nights when the place fills up with students.
The console plays all the latest Greek hits.

Kolones

66, Agias Paraskevis Ave., Bournazi.
Although they also play foreign beat hits, the real forte of the place is Greek folk and pop hits, with a dose of

---

PUBS/BARS

Au Revoir

Classic barroom, with something of the flavour of an English pub.
136, Patision St., Mouseio, 210/8223966.

Flower

Cheap drinks, and a favourite haunt of the twenty/thirtysomething crowd.2, Dorylaiou St., Mavili Sq., 210/6432111.

Galaxy

Cushioned bar, for drinkers with attitude.
10, Stadiou St. (in the

stoa), Syntagma, 210/3227733.

Loras

An "old-timers" joint, with the classic Nikos at the bar.
7, Soutsou St., Mavili Sq., 210/6428473.

Low Profile

Jazzy soundtrack and serious boozing.
6, Lykavittou St., Kolonaki, 210/3620200.

Toy

A favourite with journalists and students.
10, Karytsi St., Karytsi Sq., 210/3311555.

tsifteteli. In the western suburbs it is considered the
hottest spot around, and the
ambiance is always lively and
cheerful. Decor somewhat
exaggerated and slightly
kitsch.

STRIP SHOWS

A Million Dollars
166, 3rd Septemvriou St.,
210/8643557.
Admission with drink € 10,
bottle of whisky € 90.

Aphrodite Club
177, Syngrou Ave.,
210/9319750, 210/9311494.
Admission with drink € 10,
bottle of whisky € 88.

Aphrodite Palace
137, Syngrou Ave.,
210/9319750, 210/9311494.
Admission with drink € 10,
bottle of whisky € 88.

Athens Queen's
Glyfada Sq. (Deliolani complex), 210/8981732. Drink at
the bar € 7.34, bottle of
whisky € 73.37.

Athens Queen's
250, Athinon Ave., Chaidari,
210/5816288. Drink at the
bar € 7, bottle of whisky
€ 80.

Baby
201, Syngrou Ave., Nea
Smyrni, 210/9349444. Drink
€ 10, bottle of whisky € 85.

Millionaire
3, Athanasias St.
& Eftychidou, Plastira Sq.,
Pagkrati, 210/7524143,
210/7560418.
Drink € 6, bottle of
whisky € 73. Closed Mon-
days.

Princess
3, Chrysafi St. & Posei-
donos Ave., Kalamaki,
210/9886930. Drink € 10,
bottle of whisky € 90.

Sirocco
255, Syngrou Ave.,
Nea Smyrni, 210/9424986.
Admission with a drink at
the bar € 10, bottle of
whisky € 85. Fridays and
Saturdays, male strippers,
admission € 15. Closed
Sundays.

String
195, Athinon Ave.,
Chaidari, 210/5811012.
Drink € 7.34, bottle of
whisky € 73.37.

Tessera
117, Peiraios Ave.,
Gazi, 210/3423198,
210/3423228. Admission
with drink € 9, bottle of
whisky € 76 (with trim-
mings). Closed Sundays.

Tutti Frutti
417, Irakleiou Ave., Irakleio,
210/2810200. Admission
with drink € 10, bottle of
whisky € 75.

intensity
and eroticism

Dance clubs and night clubs, musical theatre and rebetika, bouzouki and electric guitar, tsifteteli on the table and audiences rapt and reverent: Athens loves to be out and doing after dark, which is why it has probably the most distinctive night life in Europe. This year, the climate on stage favours pairing names and schools, cross-matching sounds and attitudes.

Athens is a city that manifests itself intensely and extroversively - and this of course includes a dynamic nightlife. Despite its gradual Europeanization, it sticks to its role as the wayward diva, retaining an immediacy, a naturalness, a light-hearted animation. "Athens is so vital, so full of energy", we often hear foreigners say, usually enthusing about the daily programmes: "Here, the singers give concerts every day of the year!" The heavy artillery of the mainstream nightclubs and musical theatres is concentrated in Gazi, downtown Athens and Syngrou. The shore road, meanwhile, is passing into history, as one by one the night clubs that in the '70s and '80s used to keep a large portion of the city's population awake till dawn with their programmes headlined by the great names of Greek folk song close down. The reason for this decline lies in a shift in customs and habits, but the coup de grace was given by the construction associated with athe Olympic Games. This year, the interest focuses on combinations, encounters, cross-matchings of names and schools, past and present, making classifications more and more relative. Alkisti Protopsalti with Antonis Remos, Giannis Parios with

Romeo

Anna Vissi, Despoina Vandi with Tolis Voskopoulos - and that's just for starters. Art songs and pop music, attentive listening and sumptuous spectacle, everything is subservient to the integrity of a global programme with a strong aesthetic point of view and designed to satisfy all the requirements of an evening out in the spirit of the times. Compared to the past, when all that mattered was having a good time, fuelled by the presence of the singer and his hit songs, this situation seems very artificial; but within the European space, the warmth and individuality of the Greek temperament still stand out. Besides, the big changes in the nocturnal landscape of Athenian life took place in the '90s. The Greek popular music scene moved away from what we used to mean by "bouzoukia" - heavy consumption and display, with cases of champagne being sent to the singer, flowers falling like snow, plates being smashed by the dozen and big spenders, well-heeled and well-lubricated, plonking down wads of cash to pay for a pair of scissors to shorten the singer's evening gown to a mini dress! Now live performances are more likely to resemble open concerts or clubbing, with the requisite adjuncts of tables and dancing. The modern sound, where the electric guitar competes with the bouzouki, the rhythms, which have a touch of rock and funk, and the show, which often accompanies the programme with effects like those in a video clip, plus the casual dress and younger age of the patrons, are banishing the traditional - and until recently, given - image of the classic bouzouki place. The old-time big spenders at the front tables have been replaced by groups of twentysomethings who go out once in a while for a Friday or Saturday night fever.
As for the music itself, the "civil war" between commercial and quality music is beginning to simmer down. Now, there is no longer a clear distinction between

"quality" and "commercial" artists, since many of the latter have improved their quality of sound, production and repertory, while the former are paying more attention to the fact that people want to be entertained and are moving away from introspection and melancholy. Today, then, the number of night spots offering pure entertainment and relaxation has been whittled down to a dynamic core of big names, with a proportionate increase in the number of places putting on short-stay "content programmes". More specifically, on the basis of the different venues and the style that each one represents, we note that the modern, cosmopolitan, post-industrial, classical/historical clubs that are synonymous with Greek good-time entertainment continue to anchor their programmes to the big name club singers, while the music stages present programmes by contemporary songwriters and the repertory of older composers (artistic Greek, rock, ethnic, etc.) and focus on listening, on enjoyment of the music. The basic (identifiable) trends are a fusion of folk and rock or traditional music, and mixes within the framework of world music. The folk music stages and rebetadika that carry on the tradition are of course in a category of their own. The former continue to present the classic repertory of the great songwriters, plus the neo-folk music of the past twenty years. As for the rebetadika, the musicians will be either groups of young performers or real old-timers. Recently there has been a tendency to include older folk songs in their programmes, which are very closely related to authentic rebetiko. Completing the picture are the "hot" bouzouki joints, the dressy dance halls that draw today's action crowd, the ones out for a spanking good time. And as the big halls close, the hot spots multiply to meet the demand for all-night fun.

tip
The usual tariff is a bottle of whisky per four people or a bottle of wine per two.

tip
Where programmes are aimed at a younger audience, the price of admission is usually just a drink at the bar. Admission automatically implies a minimum expenditure, which is covered by your order.

VENUES
SHOWS

Apollon
259, Syngrou Ave., Nea Smyrni, 210/9427580-3. Lounge atmosphere without the usual crowding - and there's a balcony. And usually plenty of company in the bar. The programme usually features the young, rising stars of contemporary folk pop, like Antonis Remos, Nikos Kourkoulis, etc. This season: Kaiti Garmpi, Giorgos Tsalikis.

Fever
Syngrou Ave. & 25, Lagoumitzi St., Neos Kosmos, 210/9217333, 210/9217622. Huge hall with ultramodern stage mechanisms, set up last year in record time. Opened with the great "Vissi-Garmpi in concert" programme, then changed its name to Kosmos to present Sfakianakis in a show that went largely unappreciated. This season: Anna Vissi, Giannis Parios, One.

Fos
7-9, Iera Odos, Gazi, 210/3428053-5. Most recent incarnation of the Chaos club, not unlike Gazi, but with a somewhat more pronounced club or live rock stage atmosphere. Became famous as the setting for Anna Vissi and her shows. For the past couple of years it has switched to a more alternative style, first with Kotsiras - Tsaligopoulou and then with contemporary Greek pop from Michalis Chatzigiannis, Iro and Eleni Peta. This season: musical show with Natasa Theodoridou.

Gazi
9, Ierofanton & 96, Peiraios St., Gazi, 210/3474477, 210/3450038.

The first club to adopt the "new concept" trend, with its stark industrial, metallic style. Initially presenting artistic programmes (Protopsalti-Kraounakis-Nikolakopoulou), it later turned to classic popular entertainment shows featuring names like Pantazis, Dimitriou, Theodoridou. This season: Notis Sfakianakis, Giorgos Mazonakis.

Gefyra
26-28, Poseidonos Ave., Tzitzifies, 210/9409221-3. Makis Christodoulopoulos' home stage is a large, unfussy place. At the end of the season (late spring/early summer) the club may feature other singers, usually of the more or less classic light folk persuasion. This season: Makis Christodoulopoulos, Angela Dimitriou.

Iera Odos
18-20, Iera Odos, Gazi, 210/3428272-276. A modern place with an inherent grandeur - perhaps because of its size. From Giorgos Dalaras, who was also its first artistic director, it moved to Sfakianakis and other big recording stars - Terzis, Garmpi, etc. Sometimes, particularly in off-peak periods, it hosts less artistic programmes (Arvanitaki) or jazz festivals for a few days. This season: Paschalis Terzis, Dimitris Mitropanos.

Maskes
22, Vouliagmenis Ave., Neos Kosmos, 210/9248705. Occupying the former Prime club (all lounge seats and bars). This season's headliner is Peggy Zina - who stood out as a runner-up for Eurovision with "Love is a wonderful thing" - in a cheerful young-style programme.

Neraida
3, Poseidonos Ave.,

Kalamaki, 210/9812004, 210/9813950. Entertainment duplex: the large room has for years now been turned over to clubbing, while the smaller one opens in the summer with a classic entertainment programme featuring folk and pop music with the likes of Giorgos Alkaios, or Adamantidis and Pantazis, etc. Enclosed but not oppressive, somewhat amphitheatrical, with a prominent bar.

Posidonio
18, Poseidonos Ave., Elliniko, 210/8941033-35. Somewhere between lounge and club style, with a long bar and lounge seats. Still a top fun spot, as it was in the glory days of Antypas, then under the sign of "Gorgones kai Magkes", and more recently with a series of young stars who were born right on this stage - Kourkoulis, for example, and now Giannis Ploutarchos, who is your host from May till January 7th.

Rex
48, Panepistimiou St., 210/3814591, 210/3825842. The historic theatre (and cinema) with its handsome classical facade has for the past ten years or so been operating as a nightclub or occasionally as a dance hall. In recent seasons, newly renovated and fitted out with all the new technology, it has been presenting spectacular shows featuring big name recording stars like Sfakianakis, Terzis, Vandi. The old boxes are still there. This season: Despoina Vandi, Tolis Voskopoulos.

Studio Peiraios 130
130, Peiraios St. & Alkyoneos, Gazi, 210/3411330. The club premises that once

housed Privilege, the city's "absolute absolute" mainstream club, have now acquired a modern stage for Alkistis Protopsalti and Antonis Remos, one of the season's most unexpected duos.

LIVE MUSIC STAGES

Athinais

34-36, Kastorias St., Votanikos, 210/3480000.
The musical stage Athinais (in the well-known multispace) is under the direction of Stamatis Kraounakis, who last winter presented both the musico-theatrical production "Sold Out" and a solo show with Dimitra Papiou. Stone and wood, small readily convertible stage. Combine a visit with some of the other attractions in the multispace - restaurant, exhibitions, bar, cinema.

Grammes

111, Konstantinoupoleos St., Gazi, 210/3414350, 210/3462283.
They stripped the old factory building down to its stone, added metal balconies, dressed it in atmospheric lights. The stage created by Kostas Kaldaras focuses on artistic, artistic folk and experimental fusion, and has welcomed a host of distinguished musicians, from Savvopoulos to Nikolopoulos, from Savina Giannatou to Glykeria. This season begins under new management.

Exodos Kindynou

255, Syngrou Ave., Amfithea, 210/9400345, 210/9401990, 210/9401980.
Last year the renovated premises of the former bouzoukerie were transformed into a kind of music

hall, with showman Takis Zacharatos. This season: Lakis Lazopoulos will be directing Iro in a programme with many guests.

Kerameikos

58, Kerameikou St. & Marathonos, Kerameikos, 210/5222222.
Large building, newly built in a classical architectural style along the lines of a music theatre, beautifully designed and thought out, with state-of-the-art equipment. Inaugurated by Alexiou and Machairitsas. The marked "dinner atmosphere" on the main floor and in the boxes created by the tablecloths and table settings clashed with the musical stage concept. The inaugural show was followed by the phantasmagoric spectacular Calor Cubano from Havana.
The kitchen serves hot snacks. This season: Dionysis Savvopoulos and Nikos Papazoglou.

Medousa

2, Makri St., Makrygianni, 210/9218120, 210/9218272.
The underground club that became famous under Giorgos Marinos, who for years presented a series of music hall/cabaret/theatrical programmes. It continued as a musical stage, operated for a short period as a club, and recently, again as a musical stage, it has welcomed Lidakis, Galani, Makedonas, Nikolopoulos-Glykeria, etc. This season: Panos Katsimichas, Babis Stokas, and later Nikos Portokaloglou.

Metro

83, Kalvou St. & Gyzi, Gyzi, 210/6461980, 210/6439089.
Historic hall, former cinema, with gallery. The old seats have been replaced by simple

tables. The bar at the back usually fills up with young fans. Features big names from the contemporary artistic scene. Casual, intellectual, student atmosphere, but the programmes are addressed to music-lovers of all ages. This season: Stavros Logaridis, Miltiadis Paschalidis, Elli Paspala, Melina Kana, Orfeas Peridis, Eleni Peta, Sokratis Malamas, Dionysis Tsaknis.

Sfentona

22, Alexandras Ave., Pedio Areos, 210/8253991-2.
The musical stage directed by Vasilis Papakonstantinou (who appears once or twice a year himself) has also welcomed the entire vanguard of the alternative scene, particularly its rock and artistic exponents. The theatre - arranged like a cinema, with a balcony - has a student concert atmosphere and is easily imagined without its seats, which doesn't happen, however, since the programmes often also attract a 40+ audience. At the back, lots of hatches and bars for the young crowd. This season: opens with Eleni Tsaligopoulou, Manolis Lidakis and later Giannis Kotsiras.

Stavros tou Notou

37, Tharypou St. & Frantzi, Neos Kosmos, 2109226975, 2109239031
The most dynamic live rock stage in town. The emphasis is on Greek rock, but its programmes also include international rock, old and new. Always two core groups, frequent guests, sometimes special programmes. Lively atmosphere, with kids crowded around

the tables, often midweek as well as weekends. This season, the stage will be moving downstairs to the ground floor, so that the classic upstairs room can be turned over to big name programmes, while the Apenanti opposite will be reserved for artistic and folk.

Vox
16, Iera Odos St., Gazi. New spot, inaugurated by the duo Eleftheria Arvanitaki and Lavrentis Machairitsas.

Zygos
22, Kydathinaion St., Plaka, 2103241610 Historic boite that has recently made a dynamic comeback with quality programmes from Galani-Tsanaklidou, Dalaras and the like. Former cinema, semi-basement, soigne but simple. This season: opens with Giorgos Dalaras followed by Dimitra Galani and Michalis Chatzigiannis.

FOLK CLUBS, LIVE

La Notte
10-12, Kifisias Ave., Agora Center, Marousi, 210/6846139-40. Lively good-time repertory, plus resplendent love songs of the kind cultivated by Poulopoulos, Voskopoulos, Parios, etc. Another curios feature: the headliners always include musical leader Nikos Giatroudakis and Antonis Zafeiropoulos - Christos Kalogranis made his debut here last year (son of the popular singer Menidiatis). Fanatical audiences, enthusiastic revellers.

Papagayo
1, Asomaton Sq. & Ermou St., Thiseio, 210/3252889, 0932600052. Ensconced for a few years

now in the old Loft (later Charis Alexiou's Nefeli). Club-style room for plenty of action. This season headlining Christos Antoniadis (former feature star at Romeo) with Prodromos (from Big Brother).

Plaisir
Dimitros & Kastritsis, Ekali, 210/8132892, 210/8135490. Well off the beaten track, lost in the wilds of Ekali. Here too you'll find faithful patrons and good low profile voices. The programmes always include a substantial dose of foreign rep, sometimes Latin, sometimes soul rock, bringing back memories of old-fashioned nightclubs. Let the good times roll...

Romeo
4, Kallirrois St., Columns of Olympian Zeus, 210/9224885, 210/9232648. Last year it moved into the "big programme" class, as the rise of Giorgos Tsalikis changed all the parameters. But it is still philosophically one of the hot places, as it has been for many years now. In the summer it moves to premises on the shore road. This season: Andreas Stamou, Elli Kokkinou.

FOLK REBETIKA

Charama
Kaisariani Rifle Range, 210/7664869, 210/7669742. The historic home of the legendary Tsitsanis came to life again in the '90s (thanks to the stage designer Manolis Pantelidakis) and resumed its place on the Athens night scene with names like Dimitra Galani, Viki Moscholiou, Polykandriotis, Kouka etc. The low-ceilinged, stable-

type room is a very atmospheric place that takes you back to the turn of the century. Food usually available. This season: Glykeria with famous guests.

Magiopoula
9, Odemisiou St. (by the Near East football grounds), Kaisariani, 210/7214934, 210/7226616. The refugee cottage in Kaisariani has been a perfect setting for neo-rebetis, neopopular songwriter Vangelis Korakakis. Very natural sound, authentic interpretations from his associates - the friendly, intimate atmosphere is sustained right to the mezedes. This season: once again Vangelis Korakakis.

Mnisikleous
22, Mnisikleous St. & Lysiou, Plaka, 210/3225558, 210/3225337. An old place in Plaka, set up for tourists, it is true, but with a solid history of top flight names and programmes - notably Mostrou. In recent seasons the host has been the mellow-voiced neo-rebetis Babis Tsertos, who has a particular penchant for artistic rebetiko. The custom of the house includes dinner. In the summer, it opens as a taverna on the terrace. This season: Babis Tsertos, Sotiria Leonardou, Giouli Tsirou.

Perivoli t'Ouranou
19, Lysikratous St., Plaka, 210/3235517, 210/3222048. Typical Plaka-style place, long a political meeting-place, universally respected, popular with celebrities. Blond rustic, classic food. Former animator Tsertos has in recent seasons been replaced as musical director by the great high priestess of rebetiko,

Mario. This season: Mario again, with Giorgos Tzortzis.

Stoa Athanaton

19, Sofokleous St. & Stoa Athanaton, Central Market, 210/3214362, 210/3210342. Made a splash in the '90s. Single upstairs room, hidden in one of the galleries in the main meat market, which of course is the perfect atmosphere for rebetiko. All the old rebetes - Koulis Skarpelis, Takis Binis, etc. - have sung here.

SINGERS
SHOW BIZ

Angela Dimitriou

It's impossible to separate Angela the performer from Angela the persona. Authentic popular diva in the sense that she reflects the popular culture of the age with no second level, she has been absorbed by her market image. Fodder for the yellow press, arabesque figure in the Middle East, significant sales in Turkey - but when she sings her original street folk songs you know she feels it with every cell in her body.

Stelios Dionysiou

Very close in colour and style to his father Stratos, and outstanding in his interpretations of his great hits, he adheres to that tradition but within the framework of the modern club. He is rightly appreciated and has a faithful following in what are difficult circumstances for the type of folk he performs.

Kaiti Garmpi

Commanding presence, star quality, the classic sparkling-eyed beauty who is also a first rate interpreter of everything from street folk to the most demanding pop

repertory. And not only that, but as a performer at the peak of her career whose private life gives rise to very little gossip, she is all the more appreciated for being less talked about.

Giorgos Mazonakis

Street pop with a tendency to a slow, melancholy beat, plus classic, verging on the heavy, repertory folk. Firmly in the mainstream, but he creates an atmosphere all his own that has won him a solid following.

Giannis Ploutarchos

More romantic than Remos or Kourkoulis, for the past two years he has been top of the pops on the Athens nightlife scene, largely because of his amazing success in up-dating the erotic, atmospheric '70s Poulopoulos climate. Blond and very noble in appearance, a suave jeune premier for the ladies and one of the lads for their escorts, he enchants his audiences and, like Remos and Kourkoulis, is happy to entertain them for hours. A fixture at the Posidonio.

Antonis Remos

Typical star of the new generation, more modern than either Kourkoulis or Ploutarchos. He strikes a nice balance between folk musical expression, the new sound, international influences and top-of-the-charts hits, but his songs always have a solid content and he steers well clear of kitsch. In addition, Remos has a lovely chromatic voice, and on stage gives his all to the audience. Intimate, and a first class entertainer with or without a show, this year he excelled with his new album signed by Giorgos Theofanous.

Sakis Rouvas

Now trying his wings in France, with the help of his own company and his friend Nana Mouschouri. Considered the greatest pop star ever to come out of Greece, with his slim, elegant body and handsome, smiling young European face he has attracted the whole pop marketing machine. Stunning shows, teenage hits, and above all an image that the girls adore.

Notis Sfakianakis

His occasionally daring pronouncements in social matters, which offend his grassroots supporters, coupled with the heavily inflated prices at the Fever made this a less than successful year. Nonetheless, he is still the people's prince, the pop star who has succeeded in surrounding his image with an aura of sagacity, intellectual curiosity and melodrama - a new and up-dated Voskopoulos. Excellent well-coloured voice, careful orchestration, original touches, broad repertory (classic folk, arabesque, rock, Latin) and impressive shows with a very ceremonial atmosphere.

Natassa Theodoridou

The girl with the smile from Thessaloniki, whose authentic voice-of-the-people style quickly set her apart. She is one of those good young singers whose solid training enables them create modern hits that preserve a popular flavour. Successful and widely appreciated, even by the difficult fans of older styles.

Giorgos Tsalikis

The prince of the Romeo. Who knows how long he

Venues

will last, but for now, at the beginning of his career, he is already at the top, and rightly so. His enthusiasm on stage is wholly infectious, touching even the most morose. Such brio, such sweetness, such charm of presence are rare, and in the entertainment world are sufficient attributes. But added to them is a very pleasant voice that is steadily improving, and the hits are coming thick and fast.

Despoina Vandi
The newest show-woman. Young, beautiful, with a ` dynamic stage presence, a voice that sounds good and a steady supply of hit songs by Foivos, she has rocketed to the top. The inevitable comparisons with Anna Vissi and image of an imitator are beginning to fade, as it becomes more and more obvious that the attributes that got her where she is are not borrowed. And she's churning out the discs as fast as she can.

Anna Vissi
Last winter she starred in the musical "Mala" (author Nikos Karvelas is her permanent associate, former husband, lifelong friend and a great hit-maker), an impressive production worthy of any London stage. She started out singing artistic and art folk music, gradually moved into straight pop (everything from lounge to quasi-tsifteteli), tried her performance wings in the rock opera "Demons", and was the first (in the '90s) to bring world class shows to the Greek nightclub stage. First-rate singer, excellent show-woman, with a dazzling presence and a forceful personality, she is the greatest star in

the Greek pop culture firmament and shows no signs of burning out.

Tolis Voskopoulos
Still quite successful in his appearances, he hit the headlines once again in a duo with young singer Giorgos Lempesis. The last of the great performers of a bygone era, lord of the music stage, he continues to draw on the legend that was born from his film days. He has sung every kind of folk music, but his great strength has always been in the love songs that magnetise his audiences. Romantic, melodramatic, courtly, placing woman on the loftiest of pedestals, with a stage presence that is equally ceremonious: always impeccably and formally dressed, and with a certain stateliness of movement. His songs are the ones that are inevitably chosen as the closing number on a club's programme.

NEO-FOLK & ART POP

Charis Alexiou
One of the greatest voices of the past thirty years, she sang songs of Smyrna, folk and art pop traditions in a manner that never failed to magnetise: she could in fact almost have been set up as a national songstress and a benchmark for future generations. It is to her great credit that, in spite of this success, like a true artist she pursued other, more modern, forms of expression (although lately she has tended to forsake them).

Eleftheria Arvanitaki
Recently (at Diogenes) she has given a new vocal-orchestral dimension to her material. She began (with the

then famous "Opisthodromiki Compania") as the perfect interpreter of the songs of Smyrna, and gradually found her voice in unusual artistic forms by contemporary composers. She has developed into a fully-fledged artist with a musical mind of her own, rising in the esteem of the public and earning herself a place in the European modern music scene with her participation in important ethnic festivals.

Michalis Chatzigiannis
Burst onto the scene three years ago with "Mono sta oneira", and then proceeded to demonstrate that he has more than one string to his bow. His programme at Fos with Iro and Eleni Peta caused a sensation. Artistic pop-rock ballads, with the sensitivity of a bygone age plus a contemporary freshness.

Giorgos Dalaras
In 2002 he chose to present a review of his own history on stage at Zygos. For the overwhelming majority of the public, he is the number one singer of Greek songs - folk, classic art folk from the great composers, contemporary, even Latin. A lead player in Athens' musical life for the past thirty years, with considerable success outside Greece as well, he shares his stage with promising young singers and groups as, always alive to new trends and currents, he continuously explores the dimensions of his art.

Dimitra Galani
For the past two years she and Tania Tsanaklidou have been successfully reviving a boite atmosphere at Zygos. The younger crowd know

252 _Athens Guide 2003

her best as a folk singer, and some perhaps from her electronica work with Konstantinos Vitas; but she is a true artist, a performer of rare sensitivity, and has been one of the most important interpreters of the artistic song from the days of Chatzidakis to the present.

Alkinoos Ioannidis
In last winter's programme - he sings alone, accompanying himself on the guitar - he impressed us with the richness and force of his performance. He started out (he came from Cyprus to study acting) as a young and sensitive art song voice, and has developed into a true artist with a profound feeling for things.

Iro
2002 was her year. A highly skilled musician and composer, with roots in light jazz and pop rock, she has achieved a mature personal form of expression that today's audiences understand and appreciate. Songs like "Etsi eimai ego", "Tipota" and "Etsi ein' oi scheseis" are an oasis amid the predominantly eastern sound of this country.

Melina Kana
Last year she performed her songs with a more highly coloured, ethnic approach. The Muse who inspired Sokratis Malamas and Thanasis Papakonstantinou, she has a rich, mature voice free of folk characteristics and effects. Her name is associated with a branch of the modern Greek scene characterised by a fusion of tradition, rock ballad and folk elements, plus a healthy dose of elitism that stands out against the mass consumer ethos.

Vangelis Korakakis
A maker of neo-rebetiko, neo-folk songs, who chooses to work and find expression as if he were living in the '70s. In performance he renders, in the most authentic way, with the most natural sound, the urban folk tradition of which he is an extremely promising exponent.

Giannis Kotsiras
Formed a very successful duo with Basis at Sfentona in a dynamic, aggressive programme. A dyed-in-the-wool folk voice with rock potential, he was selected by Mikis Theodorakis for Axion Esti, is a born star, presents a seductive Renaissance figure, and seems to be made to measure for contemporary art folk music.

Manolis Lidakis
A great folk artist, whose rich colour and Cretan musical background have made him one of the top performers of the past two decades. Once a more regular performer, now rarely seen on stage, he continues to record and occasionally makes brief appearances.

Lavrentis Machairitsas
Last winter he joined forces with Charis Alexiou at Kerameikos. From "Didymoteicho Blues" and "Gattos" to "Thalassa", he had a whole string of hits in the '90s. A singer-songwriter of genius who started out with the successful rock group Termites, he has acquired a very personal style as a balladeer and canzonettist. Often works with his "soul brother" Dionysis Tsaknis.

Kostas Makedonas
Last winter he sang with Katerina Kouka in a musical

show organised by Stamatis Kraounakis, before going on tour with the composer's "musical company". At his best he recalls Bithikotsis, off peak he is more like Dalaras, but he is always a strong figure in the folk and art song field, and a great crowd-pleaser who will never go out of fashion.

Sokratis Malamas
Independent singer-songwriter from Thessaloniki, whose ballads are a distillation of Greek rock and folk elements. Very individual body of work, hermetic, seductive - with very keen fans. His strong point is not centred on his albums, but rather on his live performances, achieving a profound, but not mass, resonance.

Dimitris Mitropanos
From "Agios Fevrouarios" to "Tis psychis to parakato", his most recent and extremely meaty stage programme was a great crowd pleaser. A very distinctive voice, masculine and intensely poetic, he started out working with composers like Dimos Moutsis, sang the craving, nostalgic ballads of Takis Mousafiris and, after a short period on the wane, has come back (with composers like Mikroutsikos and Papadimitriou) as a classic.

Vasilis Papakonstantinou
"Vasili, hooray, we live to hear you play", roars the gallery at the Sfentona. The Kazantzidis of Greek rock, who moved from more artistic paths to become the great voice of the powerful all-time classic songs, and a

Venues

composer on the scale of Nikolas Asimos. This year with new songs from Manos Xydos.

Nikos Papazoglou
The singer from Thessaloniki who, along with Dionsysis Savvopoulos, was the first to inject a rock dynamic into Greek folk song. Ever since "Ekdikisi tis yiftias", Nikos Papazoglou has been one of the leading lights in the sphere of Greek ethnic sound.

Giannis Parios
For several years now he has preferred to perform straight listening programmes in good venues, in a recital atmosphere. He has recently worked with Theodorakis in a review of the composer's love songs.
A great interpreter - also a good composer and sensitive lyricist - of love songs, he is a top-flight artist who never loses his appeal. It is no accident that his "Nisiotikia" albums are all-time top sellers.

Nikos Portokaloglou
A notable presence again this year with his "Thalassa mou skoteini", not to mention his collaboration with Eleni Tsaligopoulou and Giorgos Andreou at Metro - a programme that also included Kazantzidis' songs. Leading figure in the world of Greek rock, creator and guiding spirit of "Fatme", he continues his creative career.

Alkisti Protopsalti
Of late, more and more artistic, elitist. A voice at once subtle and powerful, one of those voices that are not charged with strong characteristics but, like an actor, assume a colouring through interpretation.

She started out with the heroically artistic music of a heavily politicised age, and since the '80s has been the muse of the Kraounakis /Nikolakopoulou compo-ser/lyricist duo- the team that brought to song a new mythology, a new musical age.

Dionysis Savvopoulos
A singer who can capture an audience the way Chatzidakis did. Actor and thinker, unceasing confessor and examiner of our social reali-ty, wholly idiosyncratic. With an initial debt to Bob Dylan and an obvious affec-tion for Lucio Dalla, he is the songwriter who created and defined Greek rock: the style, the sound, the delivery, everything. Thirty years later, it is still hard for his succes-sors to get past him.

Eleni Tsaligopoulou
Her most recent collabora-tion was with Nikos Por-tokaloglou. From folk music with a pronounced Smyrna flavour she moved on to contemporary art sound, demonstrating extraordinary flexibility.
A marvellous vocalist who comes close to ethnic jazz, adhering firmly to the quali-

ties of pure folk. A voice that has improved immensely since he collaboration with her partner and composer Giorgos Andreou.

Tania Tsanaklidou
Made history with Dimitra Galani, electrified rock at the Stavros tou Notou, and with Michalis Delta haunts the consoles of emotional elec-tronica.
Greece's answer to Edith Piaf, waif-like, vibrant, artistic, dramatic, cheerful - the most magical on stage singer/actor we have known in the past thirty years.

REBETES
Agathonas
The rebetis from Thessaloni-ki with the look of a '70s rocker, known and recog-nised as a type across the country from his commer-cials. Old-fashioned style, atmospheric performer.

Babis Goles
One of the last of the his-toric rebetes, he came to Athens for a short stint from Charama in Patra and never left. Considered one of the great interpreters of the genre, with a voice like an old gramophone disc that takes you back to the now mythical life of the pre-war period.

Mario
Historic partner (after Lili) of the legendary Chontron-akos in Thessaloniki, she is the Bouboulina of rebetiko, respected by music-lovers everywhere. Distinguished for her genuine sentiment and her vital stage presence. In her company (recently she has been appearing at Periv-oli tou Ouranou) the last half-century might never have happened.

Ktima Papaioannou

NEMEA 1998

* Gold medal - Thessaloniki 2001
* Gold medal - London 2001 (Wine & Spirit Competition)
* Award GMF & OPE Best Greek Wine 2001

Odeon
Alpha Odeon

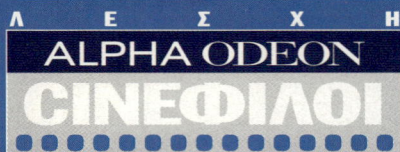

No matter how many years have passed by, since the first frames found their way into darkened rooms, no form of entertainment has ever been able to replace the magic of the big screen.

Of course, many things have changed since then - and especially our expectations of quality, both in films and in services provided.

Since September 1999, Alpha Bank, in cooperation with the Odeon cinemas, has shaped the new cinematic reality that goes by the name of ALPHA ODEON: high quality aesthetic, latest technology projection systems, innovative privileges and specialised services (like advance booking with a phone call to 801 11 60000 or 210 678 6000).

Other privileges available to members of the Alpha Odeon Cinephile Club include premiere screenings, parties, competitions with great prizes, information about the cinema and, of course, reduced ticket prices at the 30 cinemas of the chain.

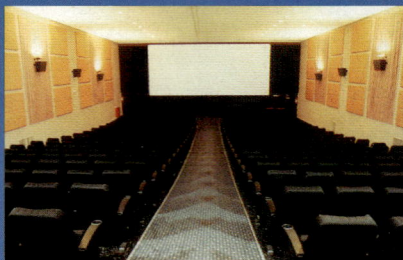

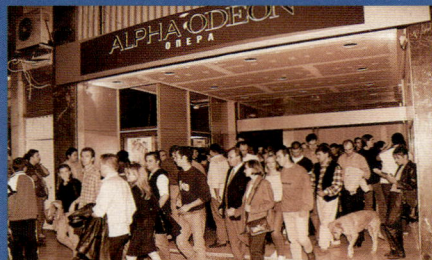

ΛΕΣΧΗ
ALPHA ODEON
CINΕΦΙΛΟΙ

ALPHA ODEON

Shows
& music

Athens Guide 2003

ATHENS 2004

ALPHA BANK

OFFICIAL
BANK

theatre:
a never-ending feast

A classic version of Chekhov or dramatisations of comics. Angry young writers from the in-your-face generation or deconstruction of Shakespearian texts. Hallmark theatre evening dressed in red velvet or wooden seats for avant-garde experimental in an old factory. Ancient Greek drama or bar theatre. No, Athens is not a theatrically divided city: it has simply raised the bar very high, and it rivals the best-known theatre capitals. New theatres, new theatre districts, young companies, fresh ideas, powerful interpretations, avant-garde productions - this is a city where theatre-lovers need never be bored...

In the land where tragedy was born, it would be impossible for there not to be a living and vital theatrical reality. This is not sterile ancestor worship, but a simple statement of fact: Athens is a vibrant theatrical capital, with a number of particularities that make it exceptionally theatre-fan-friendly.

The key factor is diversity. Whatever you want to see, you can. From classical and semi-classical productions to ultra-experimental performances, from ancient tragedy laced with contemporary barbs to the latest Broadway and West End hits.

The situation is further helped by the many and different theatrical districts, each with its own physiognomy and its own air.

The most highly developed are those in the historic centre (Psyrri, Gazi, Metaxourgeio, Piraeus), which are attracting more and more theatre companies, especially from the new generation. The city's old classic theatres are still powerful mag-

Amore Theatre

The "Lyriki Skini"

Modern dance

Herodion

nets, usually with a more mainstream - but always fresh - orientation: they are concentrated in the Syntagma-Ippokratous-Panepistimiou-Omonoia area. The Kypseli district has its own history, with theatres that opened about twenty years ago as stages for companies following with their own particular star (these were the ones that prepared the way for the subsequent theatrical explosion) and theatres occupying the erstwhile "fringes" of the downtown theatre core (Polygono, Kallithea, Zografou, Ilisia). And the theatres themselves are just as varied. From Italian-style stages like that of the National Theatre to classic parquet circles with red velvet seats, and from renovated former cinemas to converted factory buildings which, in their transformation, have acquired a whole new stylised aesthetic that is perfectly adapted to modern theatrical discourse: here, too, the key word is diversi-

ty. Which, not surprisingly, is supplemented by a series of happenings and experimental performances staged in theatre foyers, in after-hours performances and (the latest fashion) in bar theatres - a self-contained evening out where the theatre experience is combined with a drink and/or music. As for the people who make up this living community, they are as diverse as all the rest. Alongside the impresarios, old and new, we find companies that create their own space right from the word go; alongside the actors who head their own companies, we find the lone "snipers" with their portfolio of great roles. And as far as the directors are concerned, they come in all flavours, from the head-hunters looking for a dream team to the professionals who regularly mount solid, well-set-up productions. A lot of water has gone under the bridge since the days when the modern Greek theatre was defining the terms of

Psyrri, Gazi, Metaxourgeio: these are just some of the districts in the historic city centre where theatre companies, especially from the new generation of creative artists, have found a home.

Herodion

Ancient tragedy

Ancient comedy

Omada Edafous

Neos Kosmos Theatre

its specific entity, with classic directors like Dimitris Rontiris and Alexis Minotis, or indeed Karolos Koun, the "heretic" of the postwar period, who created the preconditions for the emergence of the director-auteur; but it is still a real achievement that there should continue to be such lively and intensely productive theatrical fermentation given the (often disputed) government subsidy policy and with general budgets that are not in the same league as those in the world's other great theatre capitals.

The Athenian public does full justice to this sumptuous celebration. And it does so in two theatre arts seasons: the winter season, from October to May, is marked by the opening of the shows that will be talked about (and that this year are distinguished, after years of exploration in modern "raw realism", by a return to a more classic repertory and to contemporary Greek theatre) and the summer season, from June to September, during which the prevailing breezes are lighter and more international. Lighter, because summer is the season for revues, a particular modern Greek form of satire on current events, in open theatres, with lots of music, songs and recognisable stars. International, because it is the season of festivals, which bring to theatre audiences some of the greatest per-

formers from other countries in unique heritage settings like the Herodion and Epidaurus theatres. Then, of course, there is dance, which plays an often underrated role on the theatrical scene. Although the objective conditions for its evolution are exceptionally difficult, young companies with modern perceptions have in recent years been creating dance theatre in performances that have produced powerful resonances. It is no accident that Dimitris Papaioannou, one of the protagonists in Greece's dance renaissance, has been charged with organising the opening and closing ceremonies for the 2004 Olympic Games…

In sum, theatre suits the Athenian temperament. Multifarious, hip, profound and exhilarating, the theatrical reality in Athens excites the public, which in turn has adapted it to its customary habits: a visit to the theatre isn't complete without the "apres-theatre" part, which means that as soon as the curtain falls people are making their plans for the rest of the evening - perhaps heading for a nearby spot to relax and chat over a meal or a drink, or quite possibly hitting the clubs. Not bad at all for the descendants of the theatre-goers of Sophocles' days, who experienced the dramatic tetralogies as an opportunity for socialising as well as refreshment for body and soul.

tip
From October to May, "Athinorama" organises weekly avant-premieres for its readers, issuing free passes to that week's featured production.

THEATRES

Amore

10, Prigkiponison St.,
Polygono, 210/6468009.
The permanent stage of the
Theatro tou Notou (Theatre
of the South), an artistic
mini-state which offers a
series of numerous productions over the course of the
season, always oriented
towards quality contempo-
rary and alternative work.
It gives pride of place to
European trends, young
actors and innovative directors, approaches and plays.
It was created by Giannis
Chouvardas, who is its director, now seconded by his talented young assistant

INFO

• Evening performances
usually begin at 21:00.
There are generally mati-
nees on Wednesday and
Saturday at 18:00. Many
theatres have adopted the
practice of a single Sunday
performance at 19:00.
• For the 2002 -2003 sea-
son, ticket prices with be
around € 20.00. Matinees
(Wednesdays and
Saturdays) are half-price.
Students and soldiers get a
50% discount. Some the-
atres offer reduced rates
for a set of productions.
• Seats can be booked by
telephone, but the tickets
must be picked up at least
an hour before curtain
time.
• A theatrical performance
in one of the ancient theatres (e.g. Herodion or
Epidaurus) is a unique
experience. Spectators
should, however, be aware
that they will be seated on
the stone tiers, and not in
comfortable seats. Ladies
are advised not to wear
high-heeled shoes.

Thomas Moschopoulos.
They introduced the institution of the pre-performance
interval, when the audience
gets to meet and talk to the
cast and back-stage princi-
pals, and "Try-outs", a double (pre- and post-season)
festival of experimental productions by theatrical new-
comers at low ticket prices.
This year, the Central Stage
will be offering: David Graig's
"Mainstream" (till 2/2), Noel
Coward's "Private Lives"
(21/2-20/4), and "Tapper",
by Ioanna Portolou and her
Griffon Dance Theatre (7/5-
1/6). The Exostis will have:
Karl Shechner's "Devil
Woman" (till 26/1) and
Ronald Schimmelpfennig's
"Push-up" (5/2-20/4).

Amphi-theatro

111, Adrianou St.,
Plaka, 210/3233644.
Permanent home of director
Spyros Evangelatos, one of
the most classic and well-
established directors in
Athens. The plays he stages
are mainly drawn from the
classic repertory, while in
recent years he has introduced the Athenian public
to a number of unfamiliar
works by great dramatists.
The leading lady on his stage
is his wife, Lida Tasopoulou.

Aplo

4, Charilaou Trikoupi St.
(behind the Panteio),
Kallithea, 210/9229605.
Home of director Antonis
Antypas, a low profile theatre type who manages
every year to make an event
out of his productions. This
is owing to a very faithful following that is always interested in his ideas, and also
his choice of programme.
He has a penchant for Pinter,
and his trump cards are his
uncanny knack for casting
and the music written for

him by internationally famous
composer Eleni Karaindrou.
The 2003 programme starts
with "Translations", by Irish
playwright Brian Friel, with
Dimitris Kataleifos, Mania
Papadimitriou and Stelios Ka-
logeropoulos, followed by
Joe Penhall's "Blue/Orange",
directed by Roula Pateraki,
with Ilias Logothetis, Alexandros Stavrou and Stavros
Kalligas.

Attis

7, Leonidou St., Metax-
ourgeio, 210/5226260.
Guild theatre, performing
plays classic and modern,
Greek and foreign, with
small casts, simple sets and
emphasis on lighting. Director Theodoros Terzopou-
los has brought a number of
top foreign artists to his stage, and is himself one of the
prime movers of the International Festival of Ancient
Drama held every summer
(usually in July) in Delphi.
The Attis company is the
strongest Greek presence
on the international theatre
scene, always with performances of ancient drama. The
2003 programme will carry
over Dimitris Dimitriadis'
"Lethe" and Samuel Beckett's
"Rockaby" into their second
season, while a production
featuring fragments of lost
tragedies by Aeschylus is
scheduled to open early in
April.

Exarcheion

69, Themistokleous St.,
Exarcheia, 210/3300879.
Located in a classic rock
neighbourhood, director
Takis Vouteris' theatre has
acquired a devoted public.
His programmes are drawn
mainly from the classical
repertory, and his produc-

Theatre

tions are always very solid pieces of work. In 2003 he will be repeating the very popular "Mrs Klein" (Nicholas Wright), starring the grande dame of Greek theatre, Eleni Chatziargyri.

Ilisia - Denisi

4, Papadiamantopoulou St., Ilisia, 210/7216317. Owned by actor Mimi Denisi, the glamour star of the Greek theatre. She generally stages expensive productions from Greek and foreign repertory. This year will see a continuation of "The King and I", one of last season's smash hits.

Ivi

21, Sarri St., Psyrri, 210/3215127.
Greek satire from one of the top exponents of the genre, Lakis Lazopoulos, who this year will be repeating his very successful revue "Ta Leme", with some changes in cast.

National Theatre

Central Stage, New Stage, Experimental Stage, Empty Space: 22-24, Agiou Konstantinou St., Omonoia Sq., 210/5223242.
Kotopouli-Rex: 48, Panepistimiou St., 210/3305074.
The country's premier theatre is housed in one of the most beautiful neo-classical buildings in the city (designed by Ziller). Since the beginning of 1930 it has supported the Greek dramatic arts and the cultural education of the Greek public with first class actors and directors and with plays from the Greek and international repertory. In the early '90s its repertory was expanded to include contemporary drama, two new stages were added and an actors' and directors' workshop instituted. The Central Stage (the most

beautiful of them all) is being renovated for 2004, and so the production of Eugene O'Neill's "A Long Day's Journey into Night" has been moved to the Theatro Kappa (2, Kypselis St., 210/8831068). The Kotopouli will be staging Ibsen's "Peer Gynt" and Jean Giraudoux' "La Folle de Chaillot". The New Stage will have Pantelis Horn's "Sentzas" and Pirandello's "Six Characters in Search of an Author". The Experimental Stage will be continuing its successful production of Shakespeare's "Love's Labours Lost" as well as presenting the "Twentieth Century", a work based on contemporary Greek poetry, Brecht's "Baal" and Gogol's "The Overcoat". Performances at the Empty Space (non-house productions by young companies) begin in May and last for one month.

Neos Kosmos Theatre

7, Antisthenous St. & Tharypou, Neos Kosmos, 210/9212900.
Home of actor/director Vangelis Theodoropoulos, who stages solid productions of works by authors from Ravenhill and Strindberg to Chekhov and contemporary Greek playwrights. This year's programme will include "The Seagull" (Anton Chekhov), "Loop" (Makis Papadimitriou) and Ludmilla Petrushevskaya's "Immortal Love".

Odou Kykladon

11, Kykladon St. & Kefallinias, Kypseli, 210/8217877.
Every production in which actor/director Lefteris Vogiatzis is involved is a challenge to the public. He is primarily dedicated to quality theatre, producing contemporary Greek and foreign works with a young team of actors

and technical artists. This year he will be staging Loula Anagnostaki's latest work "S'esas pou me akoute".

Peiraios 131

131, Peiraios St., Gazi, 210/3450922.
The light comedies and other works produced by the successful author/director duo of Michalis Reppas and Thanasis Papathanasiou on this stage are always extremely popular with audiences. This year's show is their brand new comedy "Ta mora ta fernei o pelargos".

Porta

59, Mesogeion Ave., Ampelokipoi, 210/7711333.
At Xenia Kalogeropoulou's theatre, you can be sure of getting a good show, no matter what your age, social condition or style, and many of her excellent productions have also been box office successes. This winter she will be producing the stage version of the hit film "Full Monty", directed by Stamatis Fasoulis, with Thodoris Atheridis, Antonis Loudaros and Sofia Philippidou.

Stoa

55, Biskini St. (3rd stop in Zografou), Zografou, 210/7770145, 210/7702830.
Theatrical home of actor/director Thanasis Papageorgiou and his leading lady Lida Protopsalti, who are passionately devoted to the Greek theatre and have for thirty years been introducing audiences to the works of the best Greek playwrights. This year, however, they will be producing one of Lorca's most significant plays, "The House of Bernarda Alba".

Theatro Technis - Ypogeio

5, Pezmazoglou St., City Centre, 210/3228706.

Theatre

Karolos Koun, founder of the Theatro Technis, began to make his mark on contemporary Greek theatre in the late 1950s. A progressive and inspired director, he was the first to give ancient drama a new and realistic dimension, to stage young and (then) unknown Greek playwrights (Kechaidis, Anagnostakis, Skourtis) and to introduce modern European and American repertory theatre into Greece. In his productions he worked with the cream of the Greek intelligentsia (Chatzidakis, Tsarouchis), and he created a theatre school that has produced a number of important interpreters. Since his death, his theatre has followed a more conventional path, but continues to be a meeting point for important theatre people. The 2003 programme will include a reprise of Vasilis Papavasileiou's production of "Eleni"

(by Giannis Ritsos), and Botto Strauss' "Large and Small" directed by Thodoros Grapsas.

Thiseion

7, Tournavitou St., Psyrri, 210/3255444.
The name of director Michail Marmarinos and his "Diplous Eros" company is synonymous with some of the best avant-garde theatre Athens has ever seen. His daring interpretation of classic and contemporary texts is always focused on the spectacular and the astonishing. After a reprise of "National Anthem", a performance combining narrative, interview and memory, the 2003 programme will feature Shakespeare's "Romeo and Juliet".

BAR THEATRES

In recent years, the city's freestyle and alternative bars have proven to be fertile ground for exploratory theatre. And their more aware patrons are happy, along with the music, to feel with the actors and participate in the show.
Such places are: the **Bar Kelsos** (63, Vouliagmenis Ave. & 4, Kelsou St., Neos Kosmos, 210/9217951), the **Enallax** (139, Mavromichali St. & Vatatzi, Exarcheia, 210/6437416) and the **Mikro Mousiko Theatro** (35, Veikou St., Koukaki, 210/9245644).

FESTIVALS

In the long Greek summer, the Arts take to the countryside. Ancient and Roman theatres, theatres carved out of the rock, theatres in gardens and groves all welcome colourful crowds come to enjoy music, theatre, opera and concerts. June to September is festival time in Attica, with many of the municipalities in the greater Athens region organising

ETHNIKI LYRIKI SKINI (NATIONAL OPERA COMPANY)

The country's only opera theatre. On the central stage, fans of opera and classical ballet can see famous operas and premiere performances of new works with the theatre's permanent company and foreign guests, while the second stage (in the Akropol Theatre) is reserved for operetta and children's opera performances. For the past three years it has been making its mark on the international scene with selected works from the international repertory. From November to May, this year's interesting programme brings to the Central Stage a number of hopeful operatic and dance productions, including three world premieres:

Pavlos Karrer's "Marathon-Salamis", directed by Isidoros Sideris (9, 12, 14, 16/2); Vivaldi's "Orlando Furioso", directed by Maria Gyparaki (10, 12, 15, 17, 19/1); William Walton's "The Bear", directed by Spyros Evangelatos, together with Giancarlo Menotti's "The Medium" (23, 26, 28/2, 2/3); Verdi's "Macbeth", a joint production with the Municipal Theatre of Berne, directed by Aike Grams (15-28/3). The rest of the programme includes performances of "Carmen", "Sleeping Beauty", "La Boheme", "Romeo and Juliet" etc.
In the summer, the company will be performing Saint-Saens' opera "Samson et Dalida" (June) and the ballet

"Don Quixote" (July) at the Herodion Theatre.
The Akropol (9-11 Ippokratous St., 210/3643700) is the only theatre in Greece to stage operettas, a form of light musical theatre that first appeared in Greece in the early decades of the 20th century. It was brought back into style a few years ago by the Lyriki Skini, which staged works by two of the most important exponents of the genre, Theophrastus Sakellaridis and Nikos Chatziapostolou. Giorgos Remoundos will be directing a production of the latter's "To koritsi tis geitonias" this season.
59-61, Akadimias St., 210/3612461.

Theatre

their own cultural events, the lion's share being represented by ancient Greek comedies and tragedies, with a fair quantity of Greek artistic music. The biggest and most historic festival in the country is the multi-faceted Athens Festival, whose events are held at the Herodion Theatre (Odeio Irodou Attikou), the unique ancient theatre in Epidaurus and the theatre on Lycabettus (the loveliest of the city's hills). The local municipal festivals also generally embrace a variety of art forms.

Athens Festival
210/9282900,
www.greekfestival.gr

• Herodion
Dionysiou Areopagitou St., Acropolis, 210/3232771.
Every summer the art-loving public, residents and visitors alike, flocks to the foot of the Acropolis. The Herodion Theatre, a magnificent Roman Odeum built in 161 AD, seats an audience of 4500 and hosts some of the most important theatrical, operatic, dance and musical events of the summer season. Countless international stars have acknowledged the applause of enthusiastic audi-

ences, their eyes turned to the illuminated rock of the Acropolis... For the 2003 season, the Festival programme will include seven sections: Symphonic Music & Great Performers, Lyric Theatre, Dance, Theatre, Greek Creative Artists & Interpreters, Modern Spectacle, and Special Events.

• Epidaurus
At Ancient Epidaurus, near the village of Lygourio in the Prefecture of Argolida, 27530/22026.
An evening at the theatre in the magical setting of Epidaurus is an experience you will remember for the rest of your life. Thousands of Greek and foreign visitors flock to the performances of ancient drama that are given here in the months of July and August by the National Theatres of Greece and Cyprus and many other companies. In recent years internationally renowned directors of the likes of Peter Stein, Peter Hall and Lina Wertmuller have created productions specifically for Epidaurus. Audiences thrill to the words of the ancient dramatists (Sophocles, Aeschylus, Euripides, Aristophanes), eternal in their truth and beauty.

• Lycabettus
Lycabettus Hill, 210/9282900.
Located in the heart of the city, the Lycabettus Theatre was the first open-air stage to thrill the people of Athens with concerts starring big names from the world rock, ethnic and Greek music scene. From June through August the theatre mainly hosts concerts and dance events by foreign artists, while in September the programme also features theatrical performances.

Summer in Marousi
210/8760120-27-28, www.amaroussi.gr
Situated near the Olympic village, from June till early September, the Municipality of Amarousion brings some of the best Greek productions to the stage of the Anavryton Theatre (Syngrou Park), and top names from the Greek artistic and rock music scene to Iroon Square. Admission free.

THEATRE ON THE RAILS

Seven cars and an old diesel locomotive on the tracks at Rouf make up one of the most atmospheric places in the city. The stage, the musical stage and the dining car in the "Rouf Train" offer an exceptionally original combination for an evening out. On stage, with live music, is Lena Divani's musical "The Angry Beauty", directed by Tatiana Lygari, while the musical stage is the scene of the music-and-poetry show "Thelete dendra anthisete, thelete maratheite", in which minor key music from piano, flute, mandolin and double bass sets off selected verses from the works of Greek poets, brought to life through the art of the singer or actor. At the station on Konstantinoupoleos St., between Iera Odos and the Chamosterna bridge in Rouf, 210/5298922, 0937604988.

Greek sounds,
multi-ethnic
situations

Greece is a country with a strong musical tradition - and Athens a city with its own sound. And although in practice you can probably go out and listen to just about anything you want (from classical music to house and from heavy metal to authentic rebetiko), the musical genius loci is pre-eminent. Greek music today is a polymorphous beast. Aphorisms of the type "art song" or "modern folk pop" may be general currency, and are perhaps helpful for purposes of classification, but they miss the essence. Things are far simpler; for the sound of the city is as much synthesiser as bouzouki, as much saxophone as clarinet, as much sampling as santouri.

Perhaps we would all like to see and hear more, and more varied, things from outside Greece; but already the means at our disposal are far from paltry: we can hear great classical composers and performers at the Athens Concert Hall and, in the summer, at the Athens Festival, we can enjoy the world in miniature if we keep up with what's going on at the Half Note Jazz Club, Rodon or Lycabettus, we can find authentic rebetika and clarinettists right in our neighbourhood, and we can always, in any well-designed nightclub pro-gramme, get the full flavour of live Greek vocal music.

Because Athens has places that play classical music, rock, jazz, blues, Latin, ethnic sound rhythms, on a permanent or at least a regular basis. And there are times (particularly in the summer) when the city finds itself in full festival mode. Athens is no different (qualitatively) from any other European metropolis - and things are getting better all the time. But what predominates is Greek sound, and this is not characteristic

Lycabettus Theatre

Megaron Mousikis

of the past ten years. A little historical investigation makes things clearer. If we go back a bit, to the time when (internationally) music was turning into pop (popular, that is, and it happened in the first decades of the 20th century with the advent of the phonograph and the radio), we will see that the sound of this city of ours was roughly characterised by two main types of urban song that, apart from their social references, form an aesthetic East-West polarity: these are the rebetiko and the so-called light music. These two types, each with its own distinctive style and texture, formed the main body of Greek popular song until shortly after World War II.

After that, the existence of great, ingenious musicians and songwriters of the ilk of Vasilis Tsitsanis gave meaning and substance to the concept of "Greek folk song" and provided musical models that served as the foundation for an astonishing artistic structure. Great musicians of extraordinary sensitivity, like Mikis Theodorakis and Manos Chatzidakis, provided the next stage in the sequence; while in the '60s the popular (Greek) cinema, which was one of the few musical media of the period, creating more hit songs than good films, brought new musical worlds into the limelight with Mimis Plessas, Stavros Xarchakos, Giorgos Zampetas…
In this politico-social context, and

with the high aesthetic quality of the popular song tradition (whether "pure" or "artistic"), foreign musical idioms like rock and jazz (which were mainstream for the rest of the western world) had little chance - but they did have a fanatical young audience. Only Dionysis Savvopoulos (in a class by himself) paved the way for real fusion - and a new kind of song writing. Meanwhile, two or three rebetiko revivals, a "return to the roots" by the proto-ethnic Giannis Markopoulos (who established a new contact with the demotic song), a powerful post-post-dictatorship rock and jazz boom and the concomitant opening to the rest of the world brings us to the early '80s, when Greek folk was also redefined (Rasoulis, Xydakis, Papazoglou, "Cheimerinoi Kolymvites"), Greek rock became a solid entity (Fatme and Porto-kaloglou) and the dives… well, they had a charm of their own. Meanwhile, an eager and informed public, with knowledge gleaned from specialised radio stations and publications, was taking an interest in new rock, new jazz, the ethnic music of the world, the magic of the poetry of a global village…
A magic which, although never rebuffed by the acoustic sensor of the Athenian, was always filtered through the components of Greek sound, thus creating the particular musical landscape that surrounds us in Athens today…

tip
The Stoa Opera (59, Akadimias St.), with its many excellent shops, is the place to go for classical music.

Womad Festival

Half Note Jazz Club

CONCERT VENUES

AN
13-15, Solomou St., Exarcheia, 210/3305056. The oldest live club in Athens, for 20 years the springboard for each new wave from the Greek rock scene, has been renovated and entirely revamped. Black and white photographs from the '50s on the walls, a second bar and more room (now accommodates 150 seated and 250 standing), vegetarian food and a sales point inside for cigars, CDs, videos and DVDs. As for the programme, there are DJ sets and daily live appearances by Greek and foreign artists.

Gagarin 205
205, Liosion Ave., Thymarakia, 210/8547600-2. Music and cinema are the prime players in this brand new multi-arts venue, which hosts rock and jazz concerts, film screenings and from time to time converts itself into a club or disco. Regular features include the rock 'n' roll-oriented Gimme Shelter Film Festival, weekly concerts featuring American and European groups, the Thursday cinema club (eg. cult Greek cinema week), and DJ sets.

Half Note Jazz Club
17, Trivonianou St., Metz, 210/9213310. Bar with a great history, and still the sole "temple" of live jazz, it has also embraced world music. Every week there are live performances by groups from all over the world.

Rodon Club
24, Marni St., 210/5247427. The stage that has welcomed all the most important names on the Greek and international rock scene, from the Ramones, John Lurie, Iggy Pop and Dr. John to our own Stereo Nova and Trypes: artists and groups that have been influential, but not necessarily fashionable. For years it was the only concert stage in Athens, and is still important, and beloved of Athenian rockers of all generations.

FESTIVALS

Womad Festival
Incomparably greater than any ordinary music festival, with its years of travelling around the globe and its comprehensive inclusion of all forms of musical expression, Womad is the focal reference point of world music. Towards the end of June 2003, Womad will be at the Kentro Ippasias in Goudi. For the three days of the festival everyone and everything will exist on equal terms: the great stars of international pop and rock together with the finest folk artists from a variety of countries.

European Jazz Festival in Athens
The European Jazz Festival is usually held at the end of May in the city's Technopolis in Gazi. This institution focuses on the promotion of the European jazz scene with purely artistic criteria, lots of good music and outstanding musicians.

MEGARON MOUSIKIS (ATHENS CONCERT HALL)

The cultural outline of any great city begins with its classical monuments, but continues with the buildings that are created along the way and that give it a distinctive character. The Athens Concert Hall adds to the value and the specific gravity of the image and the essence of our modern civilisation. Designed on contemporary functional principles to serve to the fullest the requirements of world class productions, not to mention those of a demanding, knowledgeable and aesthetically aware public, the result bears comparison with any of the world's great concert halls. With its admirable architecture, concert rooms designed to ideally accommodate any size of musical or theatrical company (from great symphony orchestras to small chamber ensembles and from large opera companies to solo performers), acoustics and sound specifications that can be modified to meet the requirements of the specific concert or spectacle, functional spaces and foyers that are used for a variety of artistic events, conference and seminar rooms, music library, record shops, bar and restaurant, the Athens Concert Hall is an outstanding arts complex that enhances the modern cityscape. The Concert Hall's annual season is from October to June. The events on its calendar are in the main related to what is generally understood by classical music, but also include jazz concerts, world music and Greek music. Vas. Sofias & Kokkali, 210/7282333.

ATHENS 2004

ALPHA BANK
OFFICIAL BANK

a city
of cinemaniacs

"Citizen Kane", "Lord of the Rings", or a Fellini festival? Love seats in a multiplex, jasmine and popcorn in a summer garden cinema, or style and luxury in Athens' most aristocratic cinema?

Whatever the components of a film buff's dream evening, Athens is today more than ever in a position to provide it. The 7th art is not only alive and well in Athens today - it is stronger and more vigorous than ever. On average, five or six new films appear on the city's screens every week, opening virtually at the same time as in the US and Europe.

Today's Athenian is one of the most demanding film-goers in Europe. He was brought up on the masterpieces of the world's cinema (reprints come out within the year), and follows all its great new international and Hollywood productions with an eager and critical eye - some of them in world premiere screenings ("Star Wars II"). September and October are film festival months. The "Opening Nights" Festival, organised by the monthly periodical "Cinema", and the "Panorama of European Cinema" Festival, organised by "Eleftherotypia" newspaper, mark the beginning of each new season.

Season? What season? Winter has traditionally been the time for new films; but more and more the distributors are bringing new releases - including blockbusters - out in the summer months; and in Athens, as in America, the new season now essentially begins in the summer. For many Athenians, May through

"Dexameni" summer cinema

Village Centre

Attikon

September is in fact the best time for going to the show, when the summer cinemas are open. These open-air cinemas have for decades made their own contribution to the aesthetic and the culture of the capital (and indeed the whole country).

The most traditional have retained their old-fashioned colour, their gravel-strewn gardens like cool oases in the summer city. Some have broadened the scope of their entertainment, and now set out small tables where food may be served during the show (anything from souvlaki and cheese pies to… sushi!). At the other end of the spectrum are the Village Cool cinemas, which have given summer cinema in Athens a whole new image. Opened in the summer of 2002, these cinemas feature "love seats" (double seats) for couples, sound and picture quality every bit as good as in the winter Village multiplex, and lounge seats for even more comfortable viewing.

Of the winter cinemas in the centre, the historic and wholly renovated "Attikon" and "Apollon" cinemas stand out for their glamour and elegance: these are the cinemas that host the biggest film festivals, and welcome avant-premieres of European productions along with their directors. The art cinemas (Trianon) focus on programmes for cinema buffs, and organise mini festivals year round, paying homage to great film-makers. Finally, there are the stylish American-type cinemas (Etoile), with plasma screens in the entrance showing previews of upcoming programmes, brilliantly lit popcorn-scented foyers and irreproachable air conditioning.

And if the cinema-goer has a fair selection of type of cinema to choose from, his options with regard to type of film are even more varied. There are films for every taste - and indeed the

Athenian cinema audience is one of the largest target groups in the city. Today "Citizen Kane" (in reprint), tomorrow a Hollywood adventure, the next day a new Indian film, and after that the sequel to "The Lord of the Rings", "Harry Potter" or "Matrix".

The distributors - there are four majors (ODEON, PROOPTIKI, U.I.P., WARNER) and six independents (Ama Films, Art Free, P.C.V., Play Time, Rosebud, Spentzos) - bring to Greece's screens films from the big Hollywood studios and from around the world, as well as Greek productions. Greece's film industry is year by year producing more titles and more new filmmakers. Unfortunately, Greece has no university-level Cinema or Film Studies Academy (nor even a National Film Library), but only a single private School of Film Direction (the Stavrakou School). But it has nonetheless produced great films that have won important international awards, films like Jules Dassin's "Never on Sunday" (1960) starring the great Greek actress Melina Mercouri (best actress award at the Cannes Film Festival). Cannes looked Greece's way again in 1998, awarding Theo Angelopoulos, Greece's only internationally recognised auteur, the Palme d'Or for his Mia Aioniotita kai mia mera (Eternity and a Day). There is no unified cinematographic current in contemporary Greek film, as there is in certain other European countries (e.g. the Danish School). But the industry's fairly large output (assisted by subsidies from the Greek Film Centre, www.gfc.gr) every year yields good films by talented new filmmakers. Their participation in major international festivals and the awards they win there are for the moment sufficient to compensate for the lack of a national film academy.

One feature of the city's cinematographic landscape is its open-air summer cinemas, which are constantly renovated to catch the pulse of the times.

Athenians can - and do - watch a wide variety of films from around the world, not just Hollywood productions.

Cinema

CLASSIC CINEMAS

Alpha Odeon Avana
234, Kifisias Ave. &
3, Lykourgou St., Chalandri, 210/6715905. Pre-bookings: 210/6786000,
801-60000. Dolby DTS.
Classic cinema with an old-fashioned atmosphere.
Excellent sound, and a large bar with little tables. Mainly American feature films.

Alpha Odeon Opera 1 & 2
57, Akadimias St.,
210/3622683. Pre-bookings: 210/6786000,
801-60000. Dolby Digital.
Metro: Panepistimio.
Classic downtown cinema, with 2 theatres (one fairly small). Little tables in the spacious foyer. Shows mainly Odeon features, including avant-premieres.

Alpha Odeon Tropical 1 & 2
223, Eleftheriou Venizelou St., Kallithea, 210/9594422.
Pre-bookings: 210/6786000,
801-60000. Dolby Digital.
Two screens that include mainly commercial hits in their weekly programme, but occasionally feature interesting social issue films. One of the district's classic cinemas -

MULTICENTRE

Athinais
Elegant multicentre that has changed the landscape in Votanikos. It features a stylish cinema hall with comfortable seats, an elegant foyer, a restaurant ("Votanikos") serving Mediterranean cuisine at the entrance, and a very tasteful art shop with a variety of small articles.
34-36, Kastorias St.,
Votanikos-Gazi,
210/3480000. A/C.

with a summer venue on the terraced roof.

Apollon Renault
19, Stadiou St.,
210/3236811. Dolby Digital.
A/C. Metro: Syntagma or Panepistimio.
One of the most popular downtown cinemas, it opened in 1960. Now renovated in modern style, with comfortable (blue) seats and its trademark giant posters (by Vakirtzis and Touliatos: two motifs, each in four successive phases). It screens "Opening Nights" and "Panorama" Festival films, "Athinorama" avant-premieres, and its regular programme features mainly European films.

Attikon Renault
19, Stadiou St.,
210/3228821. Dolby Digital.
A/C. Metro: Syntagma or Panepistimio.
Plaster arches round the balcony and gallery and an amazing chandelier that bathes the fantastically comfortable deep red seats in glorious light. The city's flagship cinema - designed by architect Alexander Nikoloudis - opened in 1914 as a theatre, and was converted four years later to a cinema (the first to show talkies). It attracts large audiences of film buffs to its Festival screenings and its annual programme, which features quality American and European films. Elegant foyer.

Danaos Ericsson 1 & 2
109, Kifisias Ave.,
Ampelokipoi, 210/6922655.
Dolby Digital Sr. A/C.
Metro: Panormou.
Far more stylish than the other cinemas on Kifisias Ave., this duplex has a faithful audience that keeps it full year round, not just during the "Opening Nights" festival.

Film books in showcases in the foyer. Room 1 is large (there is a balcony), with simple wood surface decor and high quality sound.
Room 2 is small. Films for demanding audiences.

MULTIPLEX

Aello Cinemax
140, Patision St.,
210/8259975, 210/8215327.
Dolby Digital. A/C.
Six screens in a modern area decorated in purple, blue and orange-salmon. Films of all kinds. Mainly young audiences.

Alpha Odeon Marousi 1, 2, 3
215, Kifisias Ave., Marousi,
210/6128993. Pre-bookings:
210/6786000, 801-60000.
Dolby Surround, A/C. ESAP (electric train): Marousi.
The haunt of Marousi's younger set. Two or three shows daily in each theatre, with films aimed mainly at this target group.

Athinaion Cinepolis 1, 2, 3, 4
7, Zisimopoulou St. &
Ang. Metaxa, Glyfada,
210/8983238. DTS, Dolby Digital. A/C.
The youth of the whole district flocks to Glyfada's multiplex cinema. Three or four shows daily on each screen, with films for all tastes - from American comedies and science fiction to European art films.

Kifisia Cinemax Ericsson
1 & 2: 245, Kifisias Ave.,
Zirineio, Kifisia, 210/6233567,
210/6232808. 3: 16, Drosini St. (opposite Varsos), Kifisia,
210/6231601, 210/6231933.
Dolby Digital. A/C. ESAP (electric train): Kifisia.
Spacious rooms with comfortable seats and good sound quality. Bar on two levels, large car park.
American films.

Village Centre
Fragokklisias & Granikou, Marousi, 210/6156300. Dolby Sr. (in some rooms also THX, DTS). A/C. Greece's first multiplex. Ten screens, modern rooms seating a total of 2431, and two to four shows a day each. Large central foyer, internet cafe, shops. Parking for 600 cars.

Village Cinemas
110, Ymittou St. & Chremonidou, Athens Millennium Shopping Centre, Pagkrati, 210/7572440. Dolby Digital, DTS. A/C. Youthful, modern place, with five screens (total seating capacity 777), each with three or four shows a day. Parking for 800 cars.

Village Entertainment Park
Petrou Ralli & Thivon, Agios Ioannis Rentis, 210/4278600. Dolby Srd. DTS. A/C. The biggest multiplex in the Village chain (total seating capacity 4491), in Greece's biggest shopping centre, with restaurants, cafes, playground, designer boutiques. Twenty spacious rooms, ultramodern sound systems, lounge seats and American-style love seats. Films from Warner and other American studios. Parking for 1000 cars.

ART CINEMAS
Attika Cinema 1 & 2
5, Amerikis Sq., 210/8674078, 210/8674252. Dolby Digital. A/C. Wholly renovated duplex cinema with new Italian armchairs and a new look in the bar. Its new profile also extends to its programme, since it now mainly screens art films.

Trianon
21, Kodrigtonos St. (off Patision, at number 101), 210/8215469. Dolby Sr. ESAP (electric train): Victoria station. Beloved of the really arty Athens audiences. In the winter, they showcase great film-makers, organise screenings of classic films with live orchestral music, and house film festivals (such as the films from the annual Drama Short Film Festival). They also organise preview screenings with "Athinorama". In the summer they switch chairs, add some small tables and open the roof. Classic foyer.

OPEN AIR CINEMAS
Aigli Village Cool
Zappeio Park, 210/3369369-70. Dolby St. Metro: Syntagma. One of the oldest summer cinemas in the city, set in the grounds of the Zappeio park - the palm trees next to the screen set a very special tone. On the balcony you can enjoy a meal on properly-laid tables. Since it was acquired by the Village chain, it shows mainly American commercial films.

Aphrodite
7-9, Andronikou St., Rouf, 210/3425890, 210/3425316. DTS. Totally modern summer cinema. Chaises longues in the front row, comfortable seats and extremely stylish pop-trendy foyer-buffet.

Cine Psyrri Lipton Ice
40-44, Sarri St., Psyrri, 210/3247234. Dolby Sr. ESAP (electric train): Thiseio. Almost a cult cinema for many Athenians, who queue patiently (the films are

always smash hits) for a place in the garden beneath the big screen. And afterwards, they head to the restaurant next door for a drink or a meal with a Mediterranean flavour.

Dexameni
Dexamenis Sq., Kolonaki, 210/3623942, 210/3602363. Dolby Sr. Synonymous with late night Saturday screenings of art films and box office hits. The foyer is a cool courtyard.

Paris Refresh Cinemas
22, Kydathinaion St., Plaka, 210/3222071, 210/3248057. Stereo Sound. Metro: Acropolis. Summer on a terrace, but not just anywhere. In Plaka, in a cinema for film buffs against the backdrop of the best preserved part of the old city.

Thiseion
7, Ap. Pavlou St., Thiseio, 210/3420864, 210/3470980. Dolby Sr. ESAP (electric train): Thiseio. It's no small thing to sit outside on hot summer evening in a cinema overlooking the Acropolis and watch a good film. Here an evening at the pictures is an experience; and since the area is closed to traffic you can enjoy a very pleasant stroll before or after the show. Covered section in case of rain. Quality films.

Village Cool
228, Thivon St. & Parnassou, Agios Ioannis Rentis (in the Village Park garden), 210/4278600. Dolby Digital. Love seats and lounge seats for cocooning in the biggest and most comfortable summer cinema in the Park.

play
and learn

Let's play a game together. Can you draw a picture of the house you dream of? Great! Now, let's put your family in that house, shall we?

No, no, you don't have to draw that! Alpha Bank will make it happen. Through Alpha Family Housing Loan, with a favourable interest rate of just 3.9%* (fixed for the first year), insurance coverage of the loan's reimbursement, in case of unexpected events - at no charge - and, finally, a loan of up to € 3,000 for the "initial installation costs", at the same favourable interest rate.

So, visit one of the Alpha Bank's Branches today, and give your family the home they deserve. Alpha Bank can help you make your dream come true!

* Plus the contribution of Law 128/75

ALPHA BANK OFFICIAL BANK OF THE ATHENS 2004 OLYMPIC GAMES

Children

Athens Guide 2003

ATHENS 2004

ALPHA BANK
OFFICIAL
BANK

recreation
and
creative play

Large cities are never a children's paradise, and Athens is no more child-friendly than any other metropolis. However, even in a city like this, where the air is polluted, the pavements are narrow and the recreation facilities sometimes outmoded, children will always find a way to escape. And the past few years have seen a vast increase in the number of available activities, party facilities and places to play and be creative, giving the city's children many more opportunities to observe, to listen, to play, and to run and shout to their hearts' content.

Athenian children love going to the National Garden (a traditional Saturday outing), playing in the lush green Pikioni Park (Filothei), riding their bikes in the "Pedion tou Areos" or on Mt Ymittos. On winter Sundays they go to the theatre, laughing at the antics of Karaghiozis and his friends in the traditional shadow theatre, or delighting in the enchantment of a puppet or marionette show.

In the summer, their days are filled with games and activities at the many organised day camps, while year round the playgrounds are a favourite place for burning off surplus energy and making new friends.

Art lovers or simply those who feel that play and creative activity go together know how much fun a visit to a museum in Athens can be: many of the city's museums have special areas where children can play and sing and learn to express themselves in craft work while learning about the museum's collection.

As for the red-letter days on every child's calendar, from Christmas and May Day to birthdays, there is plenty of scope for arranging a very special party, just the way your child wants it, whether at home or in some other place that they prefer.

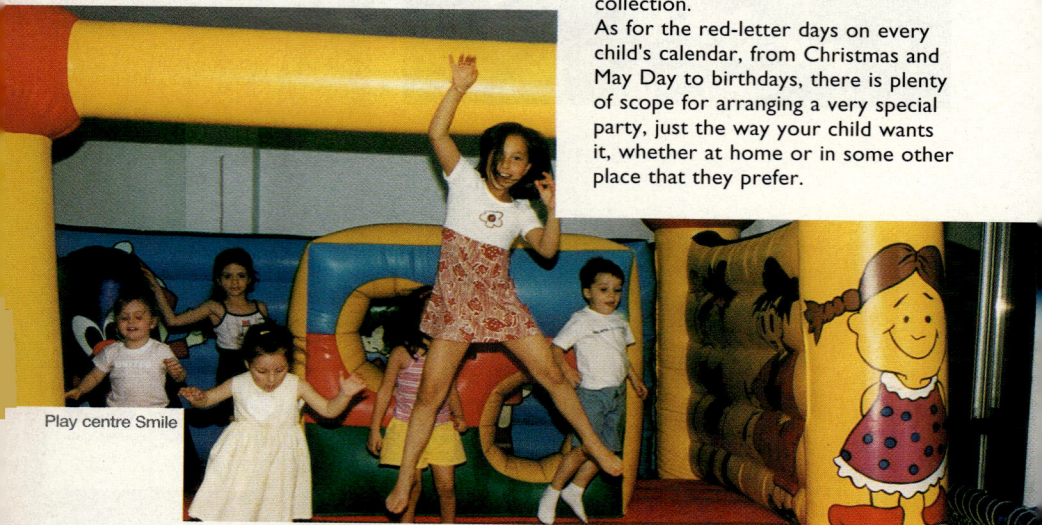

Play centre Smile

THEATRES

Chora
20, Amorgou St.,
Kypseli, 210/8673945.
Theatro "Chora" makes a dynamic entry into the world of children's theatre this year with Kakia Igerinou's tale "…Just Like Pinocchio". The show was based on a collection of songs by Mikis Theodorakis, from the record "Songs for little children and kids".
The live participation of the Mikis Theodorakis Popular Orchestra.

Ethniki Lyriki Skini
59-61, Akadimias St.,
210/3612461.
Despite the initial hesitations of Carmen Roungeri's targeted audience, her opera productions for young people have been triumphantly successful. She, as the director, and her long-standing associates Christina Kouloumpi (sets and costumes) and Petros Gallias (choreography) have that special gift that adds a touch of magic to the telling of a story. This year's production is an unfamiliar tale by Weber, which will transport the audience into a romantic era. In the early summer, the previous year's winter production is revived at the Herodion Theatre. During the summer of 2003, it will be the turn of Mozart's "The Magic Flute", adapted and directed by Carmen Roungeri. Be sure to book early - these productions always sell out very fast.

Kivotos
115, Peiraios St., next to the Poulopoulos Millinery and the Technopolis, Gazi, 210/3417000.
Carmen Roungeri's new stage has just completed its first year. This new season will open with a continuation of last year's record-breaking "Snow White and the Seven Tall Dwarfs", while a new show is in the works for performance in mid-season.

National Theatre Children's Stage
24-26, Agiou Konstantinou St., Omonoia, 210/5223242.
With stylish productions of classic tales, enhanced by lavish sets and costumes, the city's premier theatre opened its doors to junior audiences, creating an additional permanent stage for the National Theatre Company: the Children's Stage, on Panepistimiou Street. For this year only, the Children's Stage has moved to the National Theatre's main building, with its production of Jules Verne's "Around the World in 80 Days". In the summer, the company takes to the road, bringing the winter's production to children all over Greece.

Peiraios 131
131, Peiraios St., Gazi, 210/3450922.
Carmen Roungeri's "Mythologies" troupe will be making its debut with "Hercules", the first of a series of productions intended for High school-age audiences and based on tales from Greek mythology. A second production, "Coming with me", will be opening in mid-season; this show is based on a book written by the director in 1993.

Porta
59, Mesogeion Ave., 210/7711333.
For thirty years Xenia Kalogeropoulou's "Mikri Porta" has been entertaining generations of young the-

atre-goers while also promoting emerging young actors and directors. Her productions, all written, adapted and directed by herself, have always been enthusiastically received by her young audiences. A few years ago Xenia Kalogeropoulou joined forces with co-director Thomas Moschopoulos, who shares her love of, and ideas about, children's theatre. Together they wrote and produced "Beauty and the Beast", which was first performed to rave reviews in 1994 and has been revived, in an all-new production, for this winter's season.

SHADOW THEATRE

Figoures kai Koukles
30, Tripodon St., Plaka, 210/3227507. Sun. 11.00 & 17.00. Admission: € 3.05.

Thanasis Spyropoulos
Lamprinis & 9, Ersis St., Galatsi, 210/2629046, 210/2613501. Sun. 11.00 & 17.30. 37, Dodekanisou St., Ag. Anargyroi, 210/2629046. Sat. 18.00 & 20.00, Sun. 12.00 & 19.00. Admission: € 3.00.

Theatro Desylla
4, Isaia Salonon St., Gyzi Sq., 210/6430739, 0944691819. Sun. 11.00, Wed. 22.00. Admission: € 3.00 (Sun.), € 4.05 (Wed.).

CREATIVE MUSEUM ACTIVITIES

Benaki Museum
1, Koumpari St., Kolonaki, 210/3671000.
The educational programmes

Children

are related to the museum exhibits, which present the history of Greece. Children of 10-13 flock to the Museum for these programmes at Carnival time, on "Clean Monday" (the first day of Lent), at Easter and in the spring.

Byzantine and Christian Museum
22, Vas. Sofias St., Kolonaki, 210/7211027, 210/7232178.
Two Saturdays a year, one in the autumn and one in the spring, the museum organises an educational programme entitled "A Day at the Byzantine Museum".

Children's Museum
14, Kydathinaion St., Plaka, 210/3312995-7. Open: Tues.-Sat. 10.00-14.00, Sun. 10.00-18.00 (September-June). Admission free.
Multiple-interest museum where children can exercise all five senses in experimental and creative play using the museum exhibits (subway train, attic, computers and much more).

Foundation of the Hellenic World
254, Peiraios St., Tavros, 210/4835300.
The constant theme of this cultural centre is the Greek cultural heritage, which is presented both through the (unique in Greece) virtual reality theatres "Kivotos"

and "Magic Screen" and the exhibition on "The Olympic Hero", and through its periodical exhibitions and educational programmes. These are thematic in nature, and are organised all year round, especially at national holidays and celebrations (25th March, Easter, etc.).

Greek Folk Art Museum
17, Kydathinaion St., Plaka, 210/3239813.
One weekend a month from November through to April creative workshops are held for children aged 6-12, on themes inspired by seasonal customs

Greek Folk Instrument Museum
1-3, Diogenous St., Aeridon Sq., Plaka, 210/3250198.
Children can see and listen to modern and traditional string, wind and percussion instruments during a simple museum visit. But the museum also organises educational programmes, mainly on themes relating to folk tradition and local customs.

Modern Pottery Study Centre
4-6, Melidoni St., Kerameikos, 210/3318491-6.
Children are taken on a journey across the centuries, where they learn about the uses of clay at different periods of Greece's history and about the customs associated with its use.

Museum of Cycladic Art
4, Neofytou Douka St., Kolonaki, 210/7228321-3.
The periodical exhibitions organised by the museum serve as a framework for exploring one of the best collections of Cycladic Art in the world. The educational programmes, which are held at weekends under the general title "Play and learn", have a specific theme and are accompanied by special educational material. The museum shop has a collection of games and toys relating to the exhibits.

Museum of Greek Children's Art
9, Kodrou St., Plaka, 210/3312621.
Open: Tues.-Sat. 10.00-14.00, Sun. 11.00-14.00 (September-June).
The walls are covered with artwork by children who took part in the museum's drawing competitions and artistic workshops. On Saturdays children from 5-8 can experiment with painting materials and techniques.

CHILDREN'S PARTIES
ORGANISERS
Anakatosoures
210/2580806.
Clowns, Harlequins, Mickey and Minnie Mouse, Charlie Chaplin, Aladdin and other favourite characters turn children's parties into veritable fairy tales.

Art 'n' Party
210/9967583, 210/9946142.
Maria and Spyridoula create scenarios, make puppets and present puppet shows that take children to "witch land", to the "circus", to the "amusement park", to "outer space", to a world of fun and games.

INFORMATIONS

• Tickets for children's performances cost about € 11.00 per person. Most theatres offer special group rates, but do check first.
• The weekly magazine Athinorama has discount coupons for children's shows on its children's pages throughout the winter.
• Most cinemas in the city show children's films at the weekends mostly in the winter. Show times start at 16.00 on Saturday and 11.00 on Sunday.

Bourboulithres

210/6424306.

Clowns, magicians and animators organise games using puppets, magic tricks and balloon constructions.

Mad Science

21, Nerantziotissis St., Marousi, 210/6146581-2, 0977411659.

When the Mad Scientist decides to entertain his young friends (5-12), bottles and tubes will smoke and foam and produce fountains of bright coloured liquids, as one mad experiment in Physics or Chemistry succeeds another. And when it's all over, the children will make fantastic scientific constructions to take home, and will be solemnly sworn in as Assistant Mad Scientists and take the oath of Mad Science.

Magikes Svoures

210/9853609.

The magic top spins and opens the door to fairy tales,

theatre games and workshops in drawing, modelling, scene painting, craftwork, music and rhythmics.

Seven Stars

210/5151155.

Your house will turn into a fairyland with brightly coloured balloon creations, and the fireworks will really get things going. For entertainment, you can choose between a clown, a magician, a shadow theatre (Karaghiozis), a juggler or an illusionist.

Trekking Hellas

210/3310323.

"Alternative parties" with lots of action games: centipede, spider web, archery, etc.

Vynios Sotiris

210/9928174, 0977142766.

For Shadow Theatre parties. Performances of traditional and modern Karaghiozis stories in halls, schools, theatres or your home.

PLACES

Ho Ho Camp

160, Varis-Koropiou Ave., 210/9654500.

In this green setting children's parties become Indian festivals, with guests sporting war paint on their faces and going for pony rides in the park. There are also two playgrounds for running and team games. Older children can play soccer in a separate part of the park at the back, while parents can relax in the cafeteria/bar.

Playmobil Funpark

9, Matsa St., Kato Kifisia, 210/8075404.

Pirates, doll's houses, Indians - the whole Playmobil world has been set up as a playplace for children during their leisure time (daily 10.00-20.00, except Monday). Special facilities for Playmobil parties. The site includes a coffee shop and a Playmobil market.

KARAGHIOZIS

Shadow theatre has a long tradition in Greece. Since the 19th century and to this day, the irrepressible figure of the sagacious buffoon known as Karaghiozis has been entertaining successive generations of Greeks. The wandering hunch-backed hero of the popular Greek Shadow Theatre is at once an uncompromising barefoot revolutionary and a sly lazy-bones, a figure who satirises historical, political and everyday events with an audacious peasant wit. From the beginning this theatre has been performed by self-taught popular artists, each of whom is a whole theatre company in himself: moving the figures, preparing the music and the sets and creating all the voices. The figures are cut out of cardboard or painted on leather or plastic, and are operated from behind a translucent (cloth) screen. One of the oldest performers in Greece, with a long family tradition in the genre, and whose voice now is that of Karaghiozis, is Evgenios Spatharis. Since 1942 he has given countless performances in Greece and abroad, and has also written plays and illustrated stories about Karaghiozis (1960-1970). In 1995 he donated a collection of shadow-theatre gear (figures, sets, tools, etc.) that had been used by his family to the municipality of Marousi, enabling it to create the "Spathareio Shadow Theatre Museum of the Municipality of Marousi" (Vas. Sofias & D. Ralli, Kastalias Sq., Marousi, 210/6127245), a magical place that reveals the wealth of an entire art form.

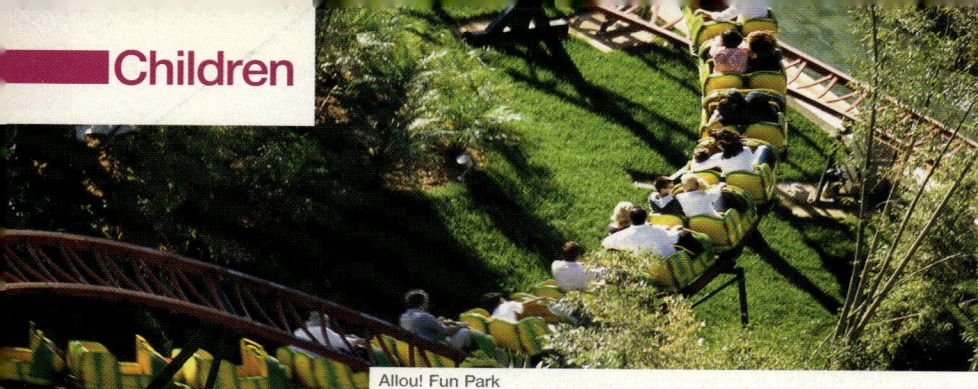
Allou! Fun Park

PLAY CENTRES

Balloons

210/9949234, 210/9957620 (main office).

At "Balloons", the rainbow-coloured inflated toys become a veritable magic kingdom "on air" for children aged 1-7. There are 16 "Balloons" centres in Athens each with its own decor but all operating in the same way. Baby-sitting available. Catered children's parties organised.

Paramythi

25B, Ifigeneias St., Nea Ionia, 210/2711811, 210/2716716. Open: Daily 10.00-14.00 and 17.00-22.00, Sat. 10.00-23.00 and Sun. 10.00-22.00.

Apart from the classic slide, bouncing frame, etc., the 3-storey castle with its ropes and tunnels is a real challenge for young explorers, who will finally make a fantastic exit via a chute into a tub of balls. Parties are held on the first floor and resemble a theatrical show. Parties also organised for children with special needs. Parents sit at little wooden tables at the bar in front of the entrance.

Renti Family Park

Petrou Ralli & Thivon, Agios Ioannis Rentis, 210/2381975. Open: 19.00-01.00.

In the Renti Village Park, children can play (under supervision) with the inflated climbing toys and constructions while their parents watch a film in one of the centre's 20 theatres. After 23.00, parents are allowed to join in!

Zouzounoparea

98, Pentelis Ave. & Grammou, Vrilissia, 210/8049524. Open: Tues.-Sun. 10.30-21.00, Mon. 17.00-21.00. Supervised play for children aged 2-9, on the labyrinthine slides that end in tubs of coloured balls and on the climbing frame with its tunnels and chutes.

TRIPS AND OUTDOOR FUN AND GAMES

Allou! Fun Park

Kifisou Ave. & Petrou Ralli, Agios Ioannis Rentis, 210/4256999.

The Allou Fun Park, the only one of its kind in Greece, is located near the Village Park (multiplex cinema) in Agios Ioannis Rentis. It occupies an area of 2 hectares, full of amazing amusements for young and old - everything from the traditional bumper cars to most impressive things. There are also a number of meeting points: for the youngsters, popcorn stands, sweet and lollipop booths, the Events Plaza and Kiddie Show (under construction) where happenings are hosted; for their seniors, a number of coffee shops and eating places. Admission to the park is free, and the various attractions cost between € 2 and € 4.

Attica Zoo

Yalou St., Spata, 210/6634724. Open: Daily 09.00-17.00, Weekends 09.00-18.30. Admission: € 8 (adult), € 6.50 (children 3-12). Home to 2,000 birds (30 species) and mammals (deer, lynx, wallabies, etc.). Playground and coffee shop.

The "Archelon" Society's Centre for the Protection of the Sea Turtle

Glyfada waterfront, 3rd Marina, 210/8982600. Open: Daily 10.00-14.00, Weekends 10.00-17.00. Learn about the sea turtle and its protection programmes in the permanent photo exhibit, and visit the large pools where injured turtles can live safely.

Ymittos (Mt Hymettus)

With multiple access points and many roads and trails, the mountain that looks down on Athens is not only ideal for walking but also the best place around for mountain biking. Starting from Moni Kaisarianis, if you follow the paved road up towards Papagou, you will come 4 km later to a dirt road that goes off to the right, towards Karea. There are also lots of other smaller dirt trails in this area.

MUNICIPALITY OF AMAROUSSION
PEACE AND CULTURE PROGRAMME 2004

Painting

Publications

Ceramics

Visual Communication

Sculpture

International Olympic Sculpture Park

Theatre

Dancing

Documentary

MUNICIPALITY OF AMAROUSSION

Tel.: 0108760123-127-128

Allou! Fun Park

... of the ordinary experience in Athens! ... 0,000 m2 surrounded by approximately 10,000 tropical plants and a ... of 31 extreme and family rides has been created with one and only purpose: ...o provide unprecedented fun for all types of people and of all ages. Happenings and events are organized for your entertainment in an attempt to amuse you, give you the opportunity to relax and loosen up, or even pump up your adrenaline levels. We are here to provide you the variety and you are entitled to make the final choice.

- **Shock tower.** Try it if you are the extreme type; avoid it if you are not. The drop from a height of 40 meters with tremendous speed will leave you speechless.
- **Panorama.** Maybe it is not the wheel of fortune but it certainly is the largest wheel you have come across in the whole of Greece. Take a ride and give yourself the opportunity to get a panoramic view of Athens. It is magical!
- **Top Spin.** For the most topsy-turvy time of your life
- **Big Apple.** Have you ever taken a ride on a caterpillar? Now is your chance to do so together with your friends or your family.
- **Carousel.** A charming, maybe even romantic ride. Ride the most elegant horses and fairytale carriages.
- **La Isla.** Rafting for everyone on the waterfall lake which will take you around the lounge bar.
- **Pirat.** The most adrenaline charged ship. All aboard! (Friendly tip if you want to see your parrot again just leave him behind)
- **Crazy Mouse.** How crazy can a mouse be? Take a wicked ride on the most crazy spinning coaster of the park. Make sure, however, that you avoid this ride right before lunch or dinner!

Test your shooting skills at the Saloon and the Corsaro, drive like a maniac the bumper cars of New York and Boom-Boom. Allow the toddlers to enjoy a ride on Bongo's little elephants or the canoes in the Indian village of tatanka. Say yes to a sweet temptation from Caramellou or a savory snack from Fritas, Gorilla, Grillizo, Everest...

As for the hot spots of the park; toddlers like to gather at the kiddy show, teenagers at the area if Mahallou while all ages meet at the Events Plaza.

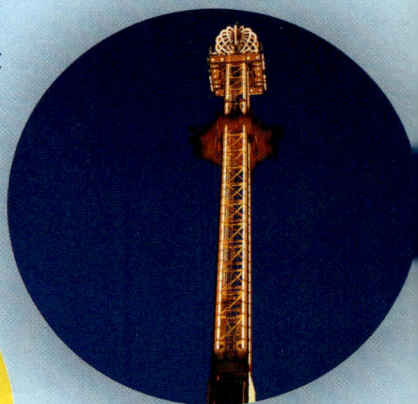

Allou!
Fun Park ®

Info: Allou! Fun Park, Kifisou Ave. & Petrou Ralli, Agios Ioannis Rentis, 210/4256999. Open: Monday-Thursday 17.00-01.00, Friday 17.00-02.00, Saturday 10.00-02.00, Sunday 10.00-01.00.

Park admission free. For the rides, pick up a rechargeable Fun Card, charge it (at the cashier's booths) with as many units as you want, and they are automatically deducted when you check in at a ride. Use it every time you come to the Allou! Fun Park. Free parking for 3500 cars

works
of art

Alpha Bank, the second largest Bank in Greece, plays a major role in the economic and financial life of the country. The Alpha Bank Group's activities are not limited to that. For many years now, it has demonstrated a vital and practical interest in important events that promote culture in this land. By sponsoring such significant cultural events as the "Great Orchestras - Great Conductors" series at the Athens Music Hall, the Alpha Bank Group makes its own contribution to the continuing evolution of the cultural and educational level of the country, by facilitating the contact of a wider public with sights and sounds that promote awareness of, and interest in, cultural movement and creation. Alpha Bank also owns a significant collection of works of art, consisting of rare paintings, sculptures and engravings. The Bank regularly organises exhibitions of works from its collection all over Greece, or lends them for thematic or artist-oriented exhibitions organised by other institutions.

ALPHA BANK OFFICIAL BANK OF THE ATHENS 2004 OLYMPIC GAMES

Art

Athens Guide 2003

ATHENS 2004

ALPHA BANK
OFFICIAL
BANK

tableau vivant

The world of the arts in Athens today is more vibrant, more active, more exciting than ever. Dynamic and brilliant, it is conquering the international visual arts market, keeping up with currents and developments on all fronts, starring in major cultural events, organising world class exhibitions and festivals, converting industrial sites into centres of cultural creation and expression, making statements with alternative fashion shows, popping in and out of art boutiques carrying eccentric handbags and collector jewellery.

The long-awaited Museum of Contemporary Art is now a fact, new galleries are springing up like mushrooms, the big names on the international art scene appear promptly in the city's exhibition spaces, while more and more people are visiting art spaces, not only to see exhibitions but also to watch alternative fashion shows or purchase art jewellery and handbags. Year by year the Athens of the arts is emerging from its regional shell, taking a more dynamic place in the round of international visual arts movements and cultural exchanges, reaching a wider public and reducing the gap that separates it from the great art metropolises of the world. The euphoria of the past five years has been both quantitative and qualitative. The first sign was an increase in the number of galleries exhibiting young Greek and foreign artists, with no corresponding decrease in the number of older

National Museum of Contemporary Art

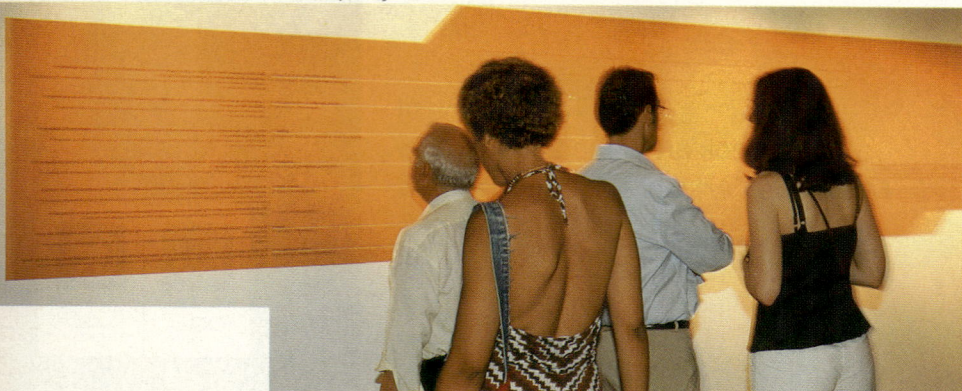

A.D. Gallery

National Museum of Contemporary Art

Rebecca M. Kamchi Gallery

Art

galleries working with established figures from the Greek visual arts world. In a parallel development, foreign currents are reaching the Greek galleries much faster and more systematically than ever before, while the presence of Greek artists at international exhibitions is becoming more marked. The establishment of the Museum of Contemporary Art in the converted Fix brewery at the end of the year 2000 filled a significant gap, paving the way for a more serious engagement with contemporary art - in the end a less "difficult" subject than many imagine - and helping make it more accessible to a broader public. And the Fix factory is only one of many disused industrial premises that are enjoying a new lease of life, most of them as multiple use art and culture centres. Typical examples are the factory in Renti now housing the School

of Fine Arts, the City of Athens Technopolis in Gazi, the Foundation of the Hellenic World in Renti, DESTE in Neo Psychiko and the Athinais art space in Votanikos. Nor is the National Art Gallery - the city's oldest and most important art museum - being left behind: it is renovating its rooms and displaying its permanent collections accompanied by the use of audio guides, which may be taken for granted in all major museums abroad, but are new to Athens.

Before Psyrri developed into a major entertainment district, and at a time when the city's Central Market still belonged to the cheese vendors, Rebecca Kamchi opened (in 1995) a contemporary art gallery on the 5th floor of a pre-war hotel in Sofokleous St., and a new plastics arts forum came into being. By the end of the decade, the district had

tip
The National Art Gallery is famed for its collections of 19th century Greek art.

Fine Arts Factory

become a key centre for contemporary art, attracting not only new galleries but also older ones like AlphaDelta and Artio, which left Kolonaki to settle among the industrial blocks and immigrant social clubs. Pakistani video clubs, squares with tiny Byzantine churches, flower markets, brightly painted benches, abandoned lofts, trendy new restaurants and bars: this is an ideal backdrop for art expeditions.

The galleries are more organised and effective with every passing season, instituting various festive "days" (when, for example, they stay open till midnight with exhibitions, drinks, a buffet, and the gallery owners there to talk to their visitors) that encourage a younger public to visit them. In addition, a map-card with the locations of all the galleries in the historic centre of Athens is available at any of them. And while the Psyrri galleries are inviting DJs to their openings and distributing flyers in lieu of invitations, the traditional artistic community in Kolonaki continues to talk of vernissages, bump into Panagiotis Tetsis at the Friday street market in Xenokratous St. en route to the galleries in Dexameni, and wait impatiently for the next Moralis exhibition at the

Zoumpoulakis Gallery.

Day by day, the city is witness to the determination of the contemporary art scene to escape from the narrow confines of the typical "white box" modern gallery and move into the streets: happenings on pavements, squares and terraces, festivals that bring together many different types of art (Medi@terra, e-phos, Trash Art etc.), "use by" exhibitions in empty houses scheduled for renovation (What if?), cheap art bazaar-exhibitions (Cheap Art) and exhibitions of art objects intended for practical use (Art 2 Use, Art 2 Wear).

The pioneer, and most integrated exponent, of this trend is of course the DESTE Contemporary Art Centre in Neo Psychiko, whose exhibition programme is not restricted to simple visual arts presentations but also includes events examining the relations between the plastic arts and music, cinema, architecture, design, fashion and modern culture in general. Every self-respecting new restaurant or bar buys works of art to decorate its walls and entrusts its decor to professionals from the art world; and, in the interim until the art hotel project collector and DESTE founder Dakis Ioannou is working

tip

The map-card listing all the galleries in the city centre is available at each one.

A work by Vassiliki

The Cosmos restaurant in the DESTE Contemporary Art Centre

Art Athina

Bernier/EliadesGallery

A work by Chryssa in the Metro

a.antonopoulou.art Gallery

A work by G. Zongolopoulos in the Metro

on takes shape, more and more of the city's hotels are adding art notes to their dynamic. Athens may fairly be described as a living open air museum of antiquities, but with regard to modern public art, the city still has a long way to go: Varotsos' famous Runner is still a lonely figure among the busts of generals and heroes of the 1821 Revolution. Opposite the Runner, Giannis Moralis' engravings on the Hilton are a point of reference, as are Giorgos Zongolopoulos' umbrella sculptures a littler higher up, on Kifisias Ave. (at Neo Psychiko). The Metro, of course, endowed Athens with a few more umbrellas (cf the Syntagma station), and in general a few more public works of art, and these are expected to multiply as the Olympic Games draw nearer and the city's open spaces are refurbished. Already Marousi has announced the creation of an International Olympic Sculpture Park in which every Olympic city will be represented by a piece of sculpture; and we hope that initiatives like that of the Single Archaeological Sites Organisation, which organised exhibitions by students from the School of Fine Arts on the pedestrian precinct of Dionysiou Areopagitou Street, will encourage more contemporary art out on to the streets and squares of this city.

tip
Most Athenian galleries are closed on Monday.

tip
At Trash Art's open workshops you can watch artists on the job.

ATHENS AS INSIPIRATION

From Konstantinos Parthenis' expressionistic "Around the Acropolis" landscapes and Spyros Vasileiou's naif "Kathara Deftera" tables set against the backdrop of the great rock, to Dimitris Tsoumplekas' photomontages of a black granite Parthenon a la northern suburbs office building, the landscape of Athens has inspired countless artists, in ways congruous with the artistic concerns and style of each period. An "imaginary gallery" of the city could also include Giannis Tsarouchis' coffee shops on Omonoia Square, which record the ordinariness of everyday life against the backdrop of neo-classical Athens, the monumental "Street Market" paintings by Panagiotis Tetsis, who endeavoured to capture the light of Greece in colour, the cubist neighbourhoods by Nikos Chatzikyriakos-Ghikas, Vlasis Kaniaris' "Homage to the walls of Athens" series, Alekos Fasianos' be-hatted cyclists, as models of interwar bourgeois photography, Nikos Tranos' photographic compositions of doorbells and building entrances, not to mention TAMA, Maria Papadimitriou's temporary autonomous museum in Menidi.

GREEK ART IN THE 20th CENTURY

The omnipotence of the academic style of painting as expressed by the Munich School, which had defined the 19th century, came to an end in the first decade of the 20th. The first symbolist works by Gyzis, Konstantinos Maleas, Dimitrios Biskinis and others blazed the trail for the modernist movements. Impressionism came knocking at the door in Konstantinos Parthenis' landscapes, which brought a new optic into formal and spatial expression with their characteristic flatness and virtually monochromatic composition.

By the second decade of that century, a lone spirit in the person of Giorgos Bouzianis was beginning to unveil a new aspect of expressionist painting, based on the expression of a dark personal psychism. One of the most important art movements of all, which was born in interwar Athens and continues to dominate Greek art and thinking to this day, was the so-called "generation of the '30s". These artists - Giannis Tsarouchis, Nikos Chatzikyriakos-Ghikas, Nikos Engonopoulos, Spyros Vasileiou - share a common aim, which was to define what it was to be Greek. Of course, the plastic media selected by each artist as his means of expression differ, and incorporate elements both from the western currents of modern art and from new readings of Byzantine iconography and folk tradition. After 1940, and despite the turbulent social and political conditions, Greek art entered another new phase, with the work of Giannis Gaitis, Alekos Kontopoulos, Giannis Spyropoulos etc and their ilk reflecting abstract trends. The so-called '60s generation (Vlasis Kaniaris, Pavlos, Daniil, Nikos Kessanlis) sought - for the first time - to dynamically embrace the reality of international art, aligned itself with current trends and made its presence felt at major events. The socio-political upheavals of the mid-'60s provided food for a politicised and critical art, while the 1972 exhibition of the "New Greek Realists" (K. Digka, G. Valavanidis, K. Katzourakis, C. Botsoglou, G. Psychopaidis) at the Goethe Institute was to stand as a landmark and rallying point for the artists and intellectuals of the resistance.

The profusion of morphoplastic currents that sprang up on the Greek visual arts scene, as in the rest of the world, in the mid-'70s continued unabated for two decades. By the mid-'90s a new generation was beginning to make its presence felt (Nikos Navridis, Alexandros Psychoulis, Dimitris Kozaris, Danae Stratou and many others), which, international in outlook and extremely dynamic, turned its back on the question of Greekness that had tormented the entire century and opened itself to universal concerns and new means of expression.

tip
Wide selection of foreign art magazines, special publications, newspaper inserts, etc., at the two newsstands on Kolonaki Square.

tip
Defining Greekness was what preoccupied the artists of the '30 generation, like Giannis Tsarouchis, Nikos Chatzikyriakos-Ghikas, Nikos Engonopoulos.

A work by N. Kessanlis in the Metro

National Art Gallery

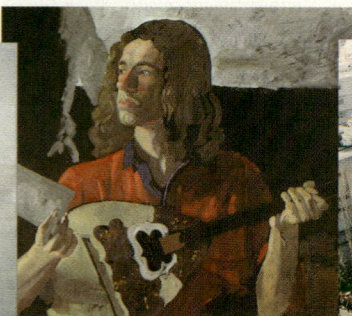

A work by G. Tsarouchis

MUSEUMS
ART GALLERIES
COLLECTIONS

National Museum of Contemporary Art

Kallirois & Amv. Frantzi (former FIX brewery), 210/9242111-2. Tues.-Sun. 11.00-19.00. Thurs. 12.00-22.00. Admission € 3.00, students € 1.50. Thursday evening (17.00-22.00) admission is free for children under 12, seniors over 65 and persons with special needs (and their companion).

Until October 2000, when the National Museum of Contemporary Art opened in temporary premises on the ground floor of the former Fix brewery, Athens had no museum of this nature.

Its occasional acquisitions are exhibited in the form of periodical exhibitions; purchasing policy emphasises the classic video artists (Nam June Paik, Bruce Nauman, Bill Viola, Gary Hill etc.), video performance, video installations, new media young artists, and works by Greek artists of the '60s generation (Kaniaris, Pavlos, Kessanlis etc.) and later. The Museum also organises exhibitions of the work of up-and-coming Greek experimental artists in video and multimedia installations.

Particular importance is attached to educational programmes, guided tours and artists lecturing about their work. The Museum's current accommodation is temporary, and the development programme is expected to be completed in time for the 2004 Olympics.

National Art Gallery

1, Michalakopoulou St., 210/7235857, 210/7235937-8. Mon.-Fri. 9.00-15.00. Sun. 10.00-14.00. Admission € 6.46, students € 2.93.

The city's most important modern art museum. Its strong point is its collection of 19th century Greek art, now hung in the Gallery's newly renovated wing. The last half of the 20th century has only a limited amount of space devoted to it, and is presented in the form of a periodical exhibition.

Apart from the permanent collections, the museum also organises periodical exhibitions of major figures in modern Greek art (e.g. Gyzis) or of collections of great masters from foreign museums. There are a number of educational programmes, audio guides to the permanent collections, and a small shop selling exhibition catalogues and posters. Future plans include the creation of a sculpture gallery in a pair of 19th century stables in Goudi. The "Century of Picasso" exhibition will be presented here until 27/1/2003.

Fine Arts Factory

256, Peiraios St., Agios Ioannis Rentis, 210/4801315.

The old factory at 256 Peiraios Street, which now houses the Athens School of Fine Arts, is one of the most ideal venues for exhibitions of contemporary art. In 2001-2 it hosted two of the most important shows of the season (British artists Gilbert and George, and the Dutch Van Abbe Museum), but its programmes vary.

The graduating class exhibition organised every summer is a classic event. Plus points include the library and the general bohemian atmosphere. Opening hours and ticket prices vary with the exhibition.

DESTE

8, Omirou St., Neo Psychiko, 210/6729460. Mon.-Fri. 12.00-20.00, Sat. 12.00-16.00.

Its name ("International Greek Contemporary Art") and its exhibitions remind us that we too are members of the global village of contemporary art, and its bar-restaurant ("Cosmos") and art shop are the most complete art-outing package in the city. Child of collector Dakis Ioannou, it is housed in a disused paper warehouse in Neo Psychiko and its exhibitions constitute an on-going record of current trends in international - including Greek - contemporary art and open new horizons for dialogue between the plastic arts and other forms of artistic creation (fashion, design, etc.). Guided tours can be arranged, and it offers an annual prize for artists exhibiting for the first time.

Athens Municipal Art Gallery

51, Peiraios Ave., 210/3231841. Daily 9.00-13.00 & 17.00-21.00, closed Sunday afternoon and all day Saturday.

A lovely neo-classic building (1875), housing changing exhibitions of modern Greek art from the collection of the Municipality of Athens (mainly 20th century

painting and engraving, from academic to abstract), and a variety of thematic exhibitions in collaboration with foreign cultural institutions.

Piraeus Municipal Art Gallery

91, Iroon Polytechneiou St. & Kantharou, 210/4194585. Tues.-Fri. 10.00-13.00 & 17.00-21.00. Sun. 10.00-14.00.

Permanent collection of 19th and 20th century Greek painters, focusing mainly on landscapes, seascapes and port life. Housed in a renovated neo-classic mansion. There are also two small rooms devoted to the work of self-taught Piraeus painter Kyriakos Tsakiris and folk artist Stamatis Lazarou.

Giannis Tsarouchis Foundation

28, Ploutarchou St., Marousi, 210/8062636. Wed.-Sun. 9.00-14.00. Admission € 1.47, students € 0.73. Sundays free.

Paintings and stage scenery - including watercolours painted as a child and his last sets, which were never used - by one of the most famous of the '30s generation of artists, exhibited in a lovely villa designed by Tsarouchis himself. The art shop has books, silk screens on Plexiglas, dishes, magic cubes that turn to reveal well-known works by the artist, etc.

Phrysira Museum

3-7, Monis Asteriou St., Plaka, 210/3234678. Wed.-Fri. 11.00-19.00. Sat., Sun. 10.00-15.00. Admission € 6.00, under 25 and seniors € 3.00.

Relatively new private museum, housed in two neo-classic buildings. The main, three-storey building (1860) houses the permanent collection, cafe and art shop. The other building, a listed monument from the early years of the 20th century with a vaguely Ionic facade and a lovely interior courtyard, is used for periodical exhibitions. Both the permanent collection and the periodical exhibitions focus on 20th century European paintings of the human form. The museum also organises History of Art seminars, guided tours and educational programmes.

Portalakis Collection

8, Pesmazoglou St., Athens, 210/3318933-4. Wed. 14.00-20.00, Sat. 11.00-15.00.

Collector primarily of abstract expressionist Theodoros Stamos, Zacharias Portalakis inaugurated his new gallery in the centre of Athens with an exhibition of the artist's early period. There will be more Stamos later, as well as exhibitions of famous 20th century European and American painters from the same collection.

CULTURAL CENTRES

Parko Eleftherias Arts Centre

Eleftherias Park, Vasilissis Sofias Ave., 210/7232603. Daily 9.00-13.00 & 17.00-21.00, closed Sunday afternoon and all day Monday.

The City of Athens Cultural Centre uses the space behind the statue of Venizelos for various interesting exhibitions organised by divers bodies and institutions.

City of Athens Cultural Centre

50, Akadimias St., 210/3621601. Daily 9.00-13.00 & 17.00-21.00, closed Sunday afternoon and all day Monday.

Located in a neo-classical building (formerly the "Elpis" municipal hospital) in the centre of the city. Occasional exhibitions of (mainly) Greek artists. Also lectures, book presentations and tributes. The coffee shop is a classic student haunt.

Melina Cultural Centre

Irakleidon & Thessalonikis St., 210/3452150. Daily 9.00-13.00 & 17.00-21.00, closed Sunday afternoon and all day Monday.

An old factory in Thiseio has been converted by the city into a cultural centre to accommodate a variety of exhibitions with a different profile. There is also a permanent exhibition space, the "Journey through Athens", which takes us on a tour through the life of different parts of the city.

Technopolis

100, Peiraios St., Gazi, 210/3467322. Daily 10.00-22.00.

One of the loveliest industrial multispaces in the city and the trademark of Athens' trendiest district; its exhibitions, however, are generally fairly low profile. As is generally the case with public spaces used for a variety of events with no guiding exhibition policy of their own, here too you may happen upon just about anything, from a tribute to mark x years since the death of Engonopoulos to the Trash Art Recycling Marathon.

BERNIER / ELIADES

Haluk Akakçe

Giovanni Anselmo

Dirk Braeckman

Herbert Brandl

James Casebere

Tony Cragg

Gilbert & George

George Hadjimichalis

Cristina Iglesias

Donald Judd

Takis & Stella Kavallieratos

George Lappas

Richard Long

Mario Merz

Yan Pei Ming

George Navridis

Albert Oehlen

Tony Oursler

Eric Poitevin

Thomas Schütte

Jim Shaw

Marc Trivier

Boyd Webb

Franz West

Sue Williams

Jane & Louise Wilson

Katerina Zacharopoulou

ΩΡΕΣ ΛΕΙΤΟΥΡΓΙΑΣ ΓΚΑΛΕΡΙ / GALLERY OPENING HOURS
ΤΡΙΤΗ - ΠΑΡΑΣΚ. / TUESDAY-FRIDAY: 10.00 - 20.00
ΣΑΒΒΑΤΟ / SATURDAY: 12.00 - 16.00

ΕΠΤΑΧΑΛΚΟΥ 11, 118 51 ΑΘΗΝΑ • ΤΗΛ.: 010 3413935 -7, FAX: 010 3413938
11, EPTACHALKOU, GR-118 51 ATHENS • TEL: +30 10 3413935 -7, FAX: +30 10 3413938
E-mail: bernier_eliades@attglobal.net

Art

GALLERIES

PSYRRI HISTORIC CENTRE

a.antonopoulou.art
20, Aristofanous St., Psyrri, 210/3214994. Tues.-Fri. 12.00-21.00, Sat. 12.00-16.00, and the first Sunday in each month 11.00-15.00. 200 m² of space in a 4th floor loft in a '70s industrial building, devoted to exhibiting the work of talented young Greek artists like Alexandros Psychoulis, Andreas Savva, Lina Theodorou, etc. An added bonus is one of the finest "Psyrri view" sunsets.

Alpha Delta
3, Pallados St., Psyrri, 210/3228785. Tues.-Fri. 12.00-21.00, Sat. 12.00-16.00.
Classic example of a former Kolonaki gallery that moved to Psyrri at the end of the '90s, following the spirit of the times. Usually mounts one-man shows of new and established Greek and foreign artists who work in a variety of media: you might chance upon anything from the classic mec-art work of Nikos Kessanlis to the minimalist installations of Angus Fairhurst (cf Young British Artists) or Dimitra Vamiali's post-modern picnics.
The gallery shares the same address with Artio, in an apartment block in Pallados St.

a-station
8, Protogenous St., Psyrri, 210/3317431.
Alternative contemporary art centre in a loft in Psyrri. It organises intercultural exhibitions and projects on themes like "Mass culture in fringe countries" or "Suburbia - the vast expanses of the Athenian suburbs".

The apartment
21, Voulis St., 210/3215469. Wed.-Fri. 12.00-20.00.
The most domestic of the city's galleries (hence the name) is a model of how to utilise an ordinary apartment in an old apartment block below Syntagma. In its barely two years of existence it has mounted some very interesting exhibitions (mainly painting and photography), with participations from important figures on the international plastic arts scene with works created specifically for the occasion. Details that make all the difference: the old lift, and the hallway with its periodicals and catalogues.

Artio
3, Pallados St., Psyrri, 210/3211602. Tues.-Fri. 12.00-16.00 &18.00-21.00, Sat. 12.00-16.00.
Another gallery that left Kolonaki for Psyrri. In this terrazzo-floored flat in the same building as the AlphaDelta gallery in Pallados St., you will see installations and constructions by such well-known contemporary Greek artists as Angie Karatza and Paris Chaviaras. The view of the colourful merchandise spread out beneath the picture windows of the gallery by the small shopkeepers on Agiou Dimitriou Square is an added attraction.

Art Tower
10, Armodiou St., 210/3249626. Wed.-Fri. 15.00-20.00, Sat. 12.00-16.00.

Diana Gallery Down Town
10, Armodiou St., 210/3249606. Tues. & Fri. 12.00-20.00, Wed., Thurs. 17.00-20.00, Sat. 11.00-16.00.

Five art rooms, an auction hall and plans for a rooftop cafe: that is the Art Tower in the city's Central Market. The Diana Gallery Down Town on the 2nd floor focuses on paintings, although we prefer its holiday "Art to Use and Art to Wear" bazaars. The other rooms (Cleio, Erato, Urania and Muses) are under common management and are used mainly for commercially oriented exhibitions with the emphasis on decorative articles. The Auctions Hall is on the 8th floor. The higher you go, of course, the more spectacular the view of the Acropolis and the more attenuated the smell of cheese from the market!

Bernier/Eliades
11, Eptachalkou St., Thiseio, 210/3413935. Tues.-Fri. 10.00-20.00, Sat. 12.00-16.00.
Historic gallery, founded in 1977 by Jean Bernier in Alexander Iolas' first house on the Marasli steps in Kolonaki. Since its very first Giannis Kounellis exhibition, the mission of the Jean Bernier (later Bernier/Eliades) Gallery has been to bring the work of avant-garde European and American artists to the modern-art-starved public of the day. The boom in the contemporary art market at the end of the '90s found the Bernier/Eliades in a neo-classical building in Thiseio, four-square in the spirit of the times, with more and more Greek and foreign artists in its portfolio. From its owners' initial attempts (in the late '70s) to convert the Fix Ice Factory into an art space to its recent organisation of two major

exhibitions at the Fine Arts Factory (Gilbert and George, and the Dutch Van Abbe Museum), the activities of the Bernier/Eliades Gallery go far beyond the narrow boundaries of a private gallery.

Els Hanappe Underground
2, Melanthiou St., Psyrri, 210/3250364. Thurs.-Sat. 14.00-20.00.
A basement opposite the little Byzantine church of St Dimitrios is the home of one of the most active contemporary art galleries in the city. Art historian and curator, Els Hanappe has repeatedly presented some exceedingly interesting examples of the work of up-and-coming and established Greek and foreign - mainly British and American - visual artists (Eva Rothschild, Adam Chodzko, Vangelis Vlachos, Dimitra and Kaiti Barba, etc.), making optimum use of the very limited space.

Rebecca M. Kamchi
23, Sofokleous St., 210/3210448. Wed.-Fri. 12.00-20.00, Sat. 12.00-15.00.
Opened in 1995, on the 5th floor of a pre-war hotel in Sofokleous St., opposite the Central Market, launching a whole new visual arts district, and still an institution in the field today. The gallery mounts exhibitions of artists like Rita Akerman, Ross Bleckner, Nan Goldin, Tracey Moffat, Julian Opie. Well worth a visit, if only for the feeling of the place, from the industrial lift to the terrace overlooking the Acropolis.

Kappatos
6, Agias Eirinis St., 210/3217931. Wed.-Fri.

12.00-20.00, Sat. 11.00-15.00.
Classic gallery in the historic city centre, in an old building just below the flower markets on Agias Irinis Street. At the top of the serpentine wooden staircase you're likely to find exhibitions of artists of the calibre of Louise Bourgeois and Marina Abramovic, as well as less well established young Greek artists.

Nisos Art
14, Sarri St., Psyrri, 210/3250058. Tues.-Fri. 11.00-14.00 & 15.00-20.00, Sat. 11.00-14.00.
New low profile place on the 4th floor of an apartment block in Sarri St. Offshoot of the Nisos publishing house, it organises book presentations and discussions in addition to its exhibitions of young Greek and foreign artists (mainly in applied and plastic arts). There is also a mini library/bookshop with books on subjects of social and philosophical interest.

Stigma
20-22, Agion Anargyron St., Psyrri, 210/3221675. Tues.-Fri. 16.00-21.00, Sat. 12.00-15.00.
Relatively new gallery in the centre of Psyrri, with exhibits of the work of young Greek artists, mainly in the fields of painting, photography and constructions (V. Geros, D. Tzamouranis, A. Tsekoura).

Unlimited
1, Kriezi St., Psyrri, 210/3314375. Tues.-Fri. 15.00-20.00, Sat. 12.00-16.00.
Solid institution in Psyrri since the day it opened in

1996. Representing mainly coming Greek and foreign artists, with a preference for video, photography and new media (Uri Tzaig, Theodoros Raftopoulos, Myrto Vounatsou etc), although there have also been some interesting installations, such as Erwin Wurm's famous one minute sculptures.

Zygos
48, Nikis St., Syntagma, 210/3317902. Tues.-Fri. 11.00-21.00, Sat., Sun. 11.00-16.00.
For decades Frantzis and Nitsa Frantziskakis' Zygos gallery (opened in 1956) was, together with the art periodical of the same name, the reference point for the city's art-loving public. It was re-opened in 2001 by their son Ion, in new premises on the ground floor of a listed building on Nikis St., with an exhibition of old associates. Future plans include exhibitions of unknown Greek and American artists.

KOLONAKI
Athens Art Gallery
4, Glykonos St., Dexameni, 210/7213938. Tues.-Fri. 10.00-14.00 & 18.00-21.00.
Historic gallery that first opened in 1963 in the Athens Hilton with a Giannis Moralis exhibition that attracted the cream of the society of the period. The 1967 dictatorship found it packing up an exhibition by Vaso Katraki, and a few years later it closed, to re-open in its present location in a semi-basement opposite the reservoir in Dexa-

meni Square. Exhibits established Greek artists.

Astrolavos

• **Astrolavos Dexameni**
11, Xanthippou St.,
210/7294342-3. Tues.-Fri.
10.00-14.00 & 18.00-21.00,
Sat. 10.30-14.30.

• **Astrolavos artlife**
11, Irodotou St.,
210/7221200. Mon., Wed,
Sat. 11.00-15.00, Tues.,
Thurs., Fri. 11.00-20.30.
One of the newest and
trendiest Kolonaki galleries,
in a modern multi-level
space in Dexameni Square,
with an art shop, a place for
periodical exhibitions and a
repository with works by
known and new Greek
artists. In 2002 they opened
Astrolavos - artlife, which is
basically an art shop (miscellaneous stationery items,
art books, jewellery, silk-
screened table mats, etc.)
but also has a small exhibition space for periodical
exhibitions of well-known
artists, such as Giorgos
Zongolopoulos.

Zoumpoulaki

• **Contemporary Art**
20, Kolonaki Sq.,
210/3608278, Tues.-Fri.
10.00-14.00 & 18.00-21.00.,
Sat. 10.00-14.00.

• **Graphics and Editions**
7, Kriezotou St.,
210/3631951, Mon., Wed. &
Sat. 10.00.-15.00, Tues.,
Thurs. & Fri. 10.00-20.00.

• **Art and Antiques**
26, Charitos St.,
210/7252488, Tues.,
Thurs. & Fri. 10.00-14.00 &
17.00-20.00. Wed. & Sat.
10.00-15.00.

• **Multiple Event Art Loft**
37, Agathodaimonos & 199,
Peiraios Ave., 210/3414214.
Tues.-Fri. 8.30-16.30,
Sat. 8.30-15.00.
Tasos Zoumpoulakis and his
wife Peggy took the family

tradition one step further
(his father had been the
proprietor of a well-known
antique store since 1912),
when in 1961 they opened
a modern art space in
Kriezotou St., presenting
the then rising generation
of Chatzikyriakos-Ghikas,
Tsarouchis and Moralis.
Forty-plus years later, the
family has 4 galleries, the
Zoumpoulakis name
inspires awe in the hearts of
art lovers and the Moralis
exhibition held every five
years is still a major visual
arts event. The gallery on
Kriezotou St. has now been
turned over to the publishing side and is also used for
multiple happenings. The
main exhibition space is in a
large basement area on
Kolonaki Square; there is
also an antique shop, as
well as a multiple event
area in a factory on
Peiraios St.

Nees Morfes
9, Valaoritou St.,
210/3616165. Tues.-Thurs.
10.00-14.00. & 18.00-21.00,
Fri. 10.00-21.00 & Sat. 10.00-
15.00.
A leader on the city's visual
arts scene since it opened in
1959, exhibiting the artists
that represented the avant-
garde of that time (Giannis
Spyropoulos, Achilleas
Apergis, Giannis Gaitis,
Marthas, etc.) and bringing
the Athens public into contact with the German
expressionists, Picasso and
Kandinski. It has also supported studies and critical
appraisals (Eleni Vakalo), in
the absence of any public
art museum. Still at its old
location in pedestrianised
Valaoritou St., it presents a
varied exhibition pro-
gramme (paintings, video,
installations) featuring established Greek artists.

Stavros Michalarias Art
1-3, Alopekis St.,
210/7213079. 24, Kanari St.,
210/3606552. Mon., Wed.
10.00-18.00, Tues., Thurs.,
Fri. 10.00-21.00, Sat. 10.00-
15.00.
Whether you go to the
neo-classical building on
Alopekis or the basement
gallery on Kanari you will
be able to stroll about in
the company of works by
Pavlos, Takis and Chryssa
and buy lithographs, icons
and objets d'art. Watch for
the opening of their pro-
jected Art City in Malakasa,
with space for exhibitions,
restaurant, library, etc.

Photography
Circle - Photospace
44, Tsakalof St., Kolonaki,
210/3645577, 210/3615508.
Mon.-Fri. 12.00-22.00,
Sat. 12.00-20.00.
Champion of black and
white art photography,
Platon Rivellis' Photography
Circle is the city's number
one photo club. With about
300 members, it organises
seminars and meetings, has
a 3500-volume library, dark
room, exhibition hall and
coffee shop.

ACROPOLIS
EXARCHEIA
AMPELOKIPOI
Eleni Koronaiou
5-7, Mitsaion St., Makry-
gianni, 210/9244271.
Tues.-Fri. 11.00-13.00 &
17.00-20.00, Sat. 11.00-
14.00.
Whoever said there's no
room for contemporary art
in the shadow of the Acropolis? Apart from the pic-
ture-lined passages, from its
headquarters in a small
basement room Eleni Koro-
naiou's art gallery presents
artists representing the
entire spectrum of contem-

porary creativity, with the emphasis on painting and photography - both by established artists (Axel Hutte, Paul McCarthy) and new-comers (Michel Majerus, John Bock).

Ileana Tounta

20, Armatolon kai Klefton St. & 16, Argyroupoleos, 210/6439466. Tues.-Fri. 13.00-15.00, Sat. 11.00-15.00.

Ensconced since 1988 in an old factory on Armatolon kai Klefton Street, Ileana Tounta's Contemporary Art Centre is a solid player on the city's visual arts scene, and has become, for its size, a remarkably multi-faceted art space. Its facilities include exhibition rooms, a special Art & Technology Department for video art exhibitions, an outdoor area for performance art, a cafe

and an art shop; and it pursues an exhibitions policy that is broad-based and moderately progressive - from Alexis Akrithakis and Kostas Varotsos to Rosemarie Trockel and Dimitris Tsoumplekas.

Statement

15, Bouboulinas St., Exarcheia, 210/8820066. Tues.-Fri. 12.00-20.00, Sat. 12.00-17.00.

Relatively new gallery, in a ground floor apartment - just like home - in Exarcheia. Presents the work of young Greek artists (Nikos Kryonidis, Fiona Mouzakiti, Niki Kapokaki, Giorgos Tserionis), many of whom have previously exhibited at Cheap Art. If you're looking for art for your loft, make straight for the pop depot at the back.

EVENTS

Art Athina

Helexpo Exhibitions Centre, 39, Kifisias Ave., Marousi, 210/6168888. For information, contact Artproductions, 210/6913943.

This annual art fair is held towards the end of March in the Helexpo Exhibitions Centre, with dozens of participating galleries from Athens, the rest of Greece and abroad. It lasts for four days, and attracts all the city's art lovers to a preview of the season's visual arts movements, a look at the new art books and all the associated buzz. In the context of this event, the Association of Greek Art Galleries every year organises a contemporary art exhibition focusing on a specific country.

Art

Cheap Art
25, A. Metaxa St. & Themistokleous, Exarcheia, 210/3817517. Mon.-Sun. 14.00-21.00.
Visual arts group that organises happenings and inexpensive art shows. Their performances satirise the commercialisation of art, and their classic pre-Christmas arts bazaar in their premises in Exarcheia and at a.antonopoulou.art are the perfect place to browse for art gifts at astonishingly low prices.

Vavel Comics Festival
Information at Vavel, 1, Lontou St. & Zoodochou Pigis, Exarcheia, 210/3825430.
Faithful to its annual rendezvous with fans of the genre, the Vavel Comics Festival inaugurates the new visual arts season each year with its international event. Exhibitions, happenings, installations, concerts, projections, graffiti, street performances and video dance attract the city's most alternative crowd, and you have to wonder where they hide themselves the rest of the year!

Month of Photography
Information at the Greek Photography Centre, 210/9210545, http://month of.photography.gr
Somewhere between September and October a new month begins for art lovers: the Month of Photography. It is organised by the Greek Photography Centre in conjunction with the Association of Greek Art Galleries, and participants include not only galleries but also institutions with a broader scope, like DESTE and the Hellenic-American Union, presenting solo and group exhibitions. Sometimes exhibited works are auctioned off towards the end of the month.

e-phos
Information from the ALAS Digital Culture Organisation, 210/7520064-5.
Annual international cinema and new art media festival, organised by the ALAS Digital Culture Organisation in venues that change every year. Special emphasis is on film projections, but you may happen upon multimedia interactive theatre performances, parties, workshops, exhibitions, digital media presentations, lectures, electronic music festivals, etc.

Medi@terra
Information at Fournos, 168, Mavromichali St., Exarcheia, 210/6460748.
Annual international art and technology festival organised by Fournos, embracing multimedia, interactive art and video art exhibitions, net workshops, events, parties, concerts, video theatre performances, etc. The venue(s) change every year.

Trash Art
Information from Ozon, 210/3387133-4.
Open workshops where you can watch the artists create works of art out of cheap materials, and buy whatever takes your fancy. Interactive installations, recycled electronic music, performance and fashion shows with recycled materials: these are just some of the highlights of the annual Recycling Marathon organised by the Ozon Group in the city's Technopolis.

ART SHOPS

Athinais
34-36, Kastorias St., Votanikos, 210/3480000.
Ceramics and jewellery from well-known Greek artists, books, T-shirts with work-of-art stamps and much more, in the art shop of the Athinais multispace.

Anemos
36, Kyriazi St., Kifisia, 210/8082027.
Kifisia gallery art shop, where you can find works of art and art objects (from jewellery to raku and blown glass) by well-known artists (e.g. Zouni, Karras, Papagiannis). Also occasional exhibitions.

Astrolavos artlife
11, Irodotou St., 210/7221200. Mon., Wed., Sat. 11.00-15.00, Tues., Thurs., Fri. 11.00-20.30.
New art shop with the seal of the Astrolavos Gallery. Numbered works from celebrated names, pieces by younger artists, silk-screens, dishes and housewares with motifs by famous painters, art gifts for all ages, jewellery and more.

Artstore DESTE
8, Omirou St., Neo Psychiko, 210/6729460. Mon.-Fri. 12.00-20.00, Sat. 12.00-16.00.
The temple of progressive art shopping, with a great - and constantly changing - variety of articles of all kinds, both originals from young designers and mass produced items; clothes (the baby-gro sleepers from Toby Pimplico are a must), handbags, hair clips, jewellery, lamps, plastic-flowered dustpans from Sugar Line productions, Keith Haring sheets, Marilyn hot water bottles, alternative

Alpha Bank.
Your
Bank

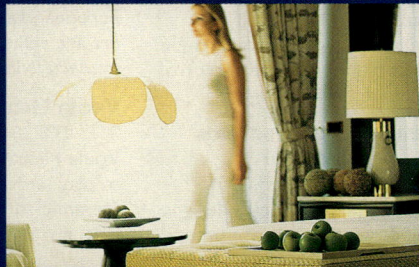

handmade holiday orna-
ments. Also books and international art magazines. And
they're open till midnight,
which is a life saver when
you suddenly remember, on
your way to a party, that it's
your host's name day and
you've forgotten to bring a
gift.

Zoumpoulakis Graphics & Editions

7, Kriezotou St.,
210/3634454. Mon.-Wed. &
Sat. 10.00-15.00. Tues.,
Thurs., Fri. 10.00-20.00.
One of the best art shops
in town, with silk-screens
and small sculptures by
famous artists (from Aidinis'
painted constructions to
Moralis' bronze doorknobs),
posters, and a wide variety
of art objects for the whole
family: Niki de Saint Phalle
pop blow-up animals,
Magritte playing cards,
Picasso mugs, etc.

DESIGNERS

Fragiskos Bitros

39, Marasli St., Kolonaki,
210/7257580.
Chandeliers of gold leaf and
tiny Swarovski crystals, flo-
ral bouquets, lamps of wire
mesh, a flower pot sporting
a lamp in the shape of a
rose, the famous shoe-tree
lampshade(!), a luminous
ball with butterflies and, of
course, the famous Japanese
lamps that throw pencils of
golden light through pleats
of white fabric: this is
Fragiskos Bitros. From his
studio "F+M FOS", he
makes his own neo-baroque
intervention in the sector of
unique designer lighting.

Panagiotis Drantakis

5, Ag. Fanouriou St.,
Pagkrati, 210/7514217.
Panagiotis Drantakis designs
and creates articles in metal

(iron or steel). Well worth
taking a look at are his
modern, geometric votive
lamps, the centre secured
by a screw, bringing mod-
ern industrial design to
these Byzantine artefacts.

Anastazia Fotiadou

10, 28th October St., Palio
Psychiko, 210/6711420,
0932273323.
Her background is in fashion,
textile and accessory design
(Milan), but her real passion
has always been construc-
tions. Believing that things
always have another side to
them, she also adores trans-
mutations. She creates
pieces of furniture out of
wood and wire, amazing
lamps out of fabric, paper
and "curious" materials. She
will also undertake to decorate an entire interior (e.g.
the restaurant ZAZA),
where she reveals her penchant for heart-shaped
objects and the colour red.

Mariona Katrani

210/9619233, 0945450767.
A graduate of the Glasgow
College of Commerce,
Katrani is at home with all
styles and techniques. She
gives old articles of furniture new life, lightening
their antique heaviness
without stripping them of
the distinctive characteristics of their age and maker.
Old Venetian mirrors share
space with "converted"
Baroque stools and tables,
while chandeliers from
European second-hand dealers are refinished to adorn
modern living rooms.

Voula Michalitsianou

210/4532280.
Voula Michalitsianou loves
to play with light. Her lamps
(ceramic torches on metal
feet) are tall, slender, aus-

tere, functional, and dream-
like. She is very hard to
pigeon-hole: modern
ceramist or pureblood
designer?

Dimitris Naoumis

30, Nikopoleos St.,
Patisia, 210/8645898.
Famous for his fabulous
designer doorknobs, candlesticks and letter-openers,
Naoumis is the pet of the
deco glossies. His designs,
filled with hollows and
curves, give the impression
of molten shiny metal that
has escaped from its mould.
The liquid lines and intelligent design often make you
want to query the identity
of his witty and inspired
creations.

Kostis Thomaidis

39, Polydefkous St.,
Piraeus, 210/4122839.
In his English-loft-style atelier Kostis Thomaidis dis-
plays unique (and signed)
candlesticks and sculptures,
crafted chiefly in iron. His
metal tables, mirrors and
uniquely designed chairs
hover between articles of
sculpture and articles of furniture. Come on Saturdays
(open house) to select
unique art gifts (weekdays
by appointment only).

Stamatis Zannos

210/7513707.
Interior decorator, stage
designer, jewellery designer.
His creations are erotic,
fabulous, composing living
narratives and moving in an
atmosphere of dreams and
ideals. His work, both jewellery and other articles, has
been displayed in designer
shops and major museums
in Greece.

Accommodation

Athens Guide 2003

ATHENS 2004

ALPHA BANK
OFFICIAL
BANK

rooms
with a view
of 2004

Many fine five-star city hotels, a handful of boutique hotels and resorts, small guesthouses, standard hotels in every category: this is the accommodation map of the city, but it is changing day by day. These changes are geared in view of 2004 and the Athens Olympic Games, and in the hotel sector sights have been set very high indeed. Most hotels have been fully renovated or are in the process of upgrading their facilities, while at the same time new "hotel construction sites" are springing up in various parts of the city, to fill in the single gap in the spectrum: providing specialty hotels (art hotels, spa hotels, small hotels, all suite hotels) reflecting the current accommodation trends of the times.

Never before has there been such activity in the city's hotel sector: you'd think they were all making a bid for an Olympic gold in hospitality. Already, the historic duo of the Grande Bretagne - ornamenting Syntagma Square - and the Hilton - the architectural paradigm of 20th century modernism on Vasilissis Sofias - are ready to re-open, after radical overhauls that have left nothing but their history to recall the past.

The luxury Athens hotels operated by the international chains Intercontinental and Marriott on Syngrou Ave. are following the same path of renewal. Their gradual renovations are day by day raising the level of their already high standard of services. The arrival of the five-star Sofitel at the Eleftherios Venizelos International Airport has filled another gap in this sector.

As for the traditional Greek hotel

Grande Bretagne

Asteras Vouliagmenis

Novotel Athènes

Athenaeum InterContinental

chains, they are mounting a counter-attack: the Divani hotels (Divani Caravel, Divani Palace Acropolis, Apollon Divani Palace) have completed their renovations, and the Apollon's Thalassotherapy Centre is expected to open in the 1st half of 2003. Grecotel, with three hotels in the historic centre, has set April 2003 as the opening date for its grand new resort near Cape Sounio. A little farther north, at Lagonisi, another major Greek chain - Ilios - has already inaugurated what is currently Attica's top resort: the Grand Resort Lagonissi, which provides a holiday feeling just a few kilometres outside Athens. Lovers of the Athenian Riviera remain faithful to the three Asteras Hotels, which occupy one of the finest situations on the shore road from Athens to Sounio, and offer a classic atmos-

phere. And in general all of Attica's seaside hotels are changing aspect, with global or partial renovations.

The same is true of the historic centre. Large conventional units are freshening up, while small guesthouses are exploiting the advantages of their location (for the most part, these are in the historic centre, no more than a stone's throw from the main sights and the Acropolis), in an attempt to attract a younger clientele and to face up to the coming competition. Many small boutique hotels are already being planned for the city centre, in lovely neo-classic or modern buildings, to supply a very obvious deficiency. The choice of a hotel always depends on the type of visit. Individual travellers generally prefer the central hotels

Adrian

NJV Athens Plaza

Metropolitan

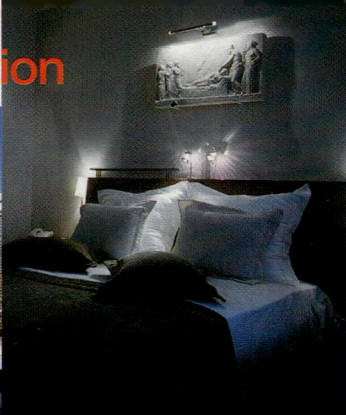
Sofitel Athens Airport

Divani Apollon Palace & Spa

(Syntagma, Plaka, Pillars of Olympian Zeus, Makrygianni St.) and those on the periphery of the core (Syngrou Ave., Alexandras Ave., Michalakopoulou St.), so as to be near the main sights. In this zone there are hotels for every purse: from de luxe to standard to small guesthouses (especially in Plaka). Tour groups stay in the large hotels on Syngrou Ave. and the outskirts of the city. These are also preferred by business travellers, since the large luxury hotels have many facilities for professionals (most now have executive floors with special services) and many have invested in conference tourism, creating perfectly set-up rooms fitted with all the latest technology and equipment. Some of those whose business requires them to remain for more than just a few days in Athens prefer to stay in a luxury apartment, like those in the Andromeda Athens and the Holiday Suites (fully equipped and with a homey feel). This category also includes the Kefalari Suites (for those who need to be in the northern suburbs) and the Blazer Suites (in the southern suburbs). Finally, those who choose a hotel on the waterfront do so in order to combine a short seaside break with easy access to the city and the airport. To recap, the city currently offers high standards of accommodation, but has some way to make up in the specialty hotel sector prescribed by contemporary trends in hospitality. We can affirm with full confidence, however, that the picture is changing with every passing day.

Omonia Grand Hotel

Herodion

NORTHERN ATHENS

Over € 400

Pentelikon

66, Diligianni St., Kifisia
☎ 210/6281600,
210/6230650
Fax 210/8010314.
e-mail: pentelik@otenet.gr
Internet: www.hotelpentelikon.gr Open: Year round.
Rooms: Standard 37, suites 7.

❄ 📺 ▼ 🍴 ▼ 📶 🔆 🌊 P cc VISA

Famous luxury hotel, occupying a neo-classical building set in lush gardens with a simple pool, just off the main square in Kefalari. Public areas small but perfectly adequate, with leather sofas, deep carpets, marble facings, fine paintings. Classic decor in the bedrooms, which are gradually being renovated.

From € 300 to € 400

Grand Chalet

38, Kokkinara St., Politeia
☎ 210/6233120-6
Fax 210/8085426.
Open: Year round.
Rooms: Standard 45.

❄ 📺 ▼ 🍴 ▼ 📶 🔆 🌊 P cc VISA

A hotel reflecting the period when Ekali was far from the city and the foothills of Penteli the perfect place for a mountain holiday. Small public areas, bedrooms comfortable but conventional, old-fashioned furniture (currently under renovation). Ask for a back room, overlooking the beautiful quiet gardens.

Kefalari Suites

1, Pentelis St. & Kolokotroni, Kifisia
☎ 210/6233333 Fax 210/6233330. e-mail: info@kefalarisuites.gr
Internet: www.kefalarisuites.gr Open: Year round. Rooms: Suites 12.

❄ 📺 ▼ 📶 🔆 P cc VISA

Boutique hotel, with small public areas and spacious, comfortable suites. The decor is sophisticated, and each suite is different: the "Daphne and Chloe", for example, has a neo-classical elegance, the "Hydra" is like an island mansion, the "Deck House" is the epitome of casual luxury. Somewhat cramped bathrooms detract from certain of the suites.

Theoxenia Palace

2, Filadelfeos St., Kifisia
☎ 210/6233622-6
Fax 210/6231675. e-mail: info@theoxeniapalace.com
Internet: www.theoxeniapalace.com Open: Year round. Rooms: Standard 67, suites 4.

❄ 📺 ▼ ▼ 🔆 🌊 ♻ ≋ 🏃 🏃 P cc VISA

Occupies a lovely neo-classical building, with smallish public areas but exceptionally elegant and comfortable bedrooms - spacious, beautifully decorated, with a sense of easy luxury in the fabrics and soft furnishings. The bathrooms are small but adequate, and the fine 3-room suites all have CD player and Jacuzzi.

From € 100 to € 200

Katerina

3, Mykonou St. & Kolokotroni, Kifisia
☎ 210/8018495
Fax 210/8015218. e-mail: admin@hotelcaterina.com
Open: Year round. Rooms: Standard 36, suites 10.

❄ 📺 ▼ ▼ 📶 🏃 cc VISA

Ideal for business travellers. Frequently renovated, with all modern conveniences. Public areas small but attractive; bedrooms simple, with small but fully renovated bathrooms. Wide range of business services. Relatively inexpensive for the area.

USEFUL INFORMATION

• The hotels recommended in this Guide have been inspected and selected to provide a wide range of profiles covering every style and budget. The accompanying texts describe the main features and particular characteristics of each.
• Listings have been arranged first by area, then by category on the basis of price range, and finally in alphabetical order. The areas are: Northern Athens, Centre, Southern Athens, Piraeus and Resorts. The price ranges are: over € 400, from € 300 to € 400, from € 200 to € 300, from € 100 to € 200 and under € 100.
• Rate classification is based on the lowest posted rate for a standard double room with breakfast. Usually these rates remain fixed throughout the year, but some hotels do apply low, middle and high season rates. The high season is October through January, the middle season runs from February to Easter, and summer is the low season. Depending on the season and on the tourist traffic, hotels may offer preferential rates. Ask the hotel directly or, for more general information, enquire from the Union of Hotel-Keepers of Attica (210/3235485).

Accommodation

CENTRAL ATHENS

Over € 400

Andromeda Athens
22, Timoleontos Vassou
St., Mavili Sq. ☎
210/6415000 **Fax**
210/6466361. **Open:** Year
round. **Rooms:** Standard
17, suites 9, studios 4,
apartments 12.

❄ 📺 🍸 🍴 🍷 ⛹ ♻ 🐾
P CC VISA

Atmosphere and luxury.
Objets d'art and designer
furniture in the small lobby.
The rooms, each one unique,
are romantic in style, with
classical touches. The twelve
apartments (opposite the
main hotel building) are
exceptionally fine: large, with
a minimalist classic decor,
they combine the atmos-

EXPLANATION OF SYMBOLS

👁	Wonderful view
❄	Rooms ai-conditioned
📺	TV in all rooms
🍸	Mini bar available
RF	Fridge in your room
🍴	Restaurant
🍷	Bar
⛹	Business facilities
♻	Conference rooms
🏊	Outdoor pool
🏊	Indoor pool
🏃	Courts
🏄	Sea sports
🏋	Gym
🚶	Sauna
💆	Massage - relaxation
SPA	Spa
♿	Rooms for persons with special needs
🐾	Pets allowed
P	Parking
CC	Credit cards accepted
VISA	Will accept Visa

phere of a private apartment
with the luxury and service
of a fine hotel. The excellent
Etrusco restaurant in the
hotel serves Italian and
Mediterranean cuisine.

Grande Bretagne

Syntagma Square
☎ 210/3330000
Fax 210/3228034.
Internet: www.HotelGran-
deBretagne_ath.gr
Open: Year round. **Rooms:**
Standard 290, suites 37.

👁 ❄ 📺 🍸 🍴 🍷 ⛹ ♻
🏊 🏊 🏄 🚶 💆 SPA ♿
P CC VISA

The historic Athens hotel,
one of the most famous in
the world, is in the final
stages of renovation. One
section should be ready to
open in February 2003, and
the official re-opening is
scheduled for the autumn of
the same year. Kings have
slept in its rooms, and legendary personalities of the
19th and 20th centuries; and
in this new phase of its existence it expects once again
to be the emblematic hotel
of the city. Large rooms,
with modern fittings, large
marble bathrooms and a
classical decor that bridges
its past and its present. A
modern city spa and pool
are being created on the
lower level, and the roof garden will have an open pool,
restaurant and club (open
May-October).

Hilton

46, Vasilissis Sofias Ave.
☎ 210/7281000
Fax 210/7281111.
Open: Year round. **Rooms:**
Standard 498, suites 19.

👁 ❄ 📺 🍸 🍴 🍷 ⛹ ♻
🏊 🚶 ♿ 🐾 P CC VISA

Landmark hotel, with its
impressive architecture (classic modernist) and excep-
tional location (a stone's
throw from the centre, the
museums, the many local
points of interest).
Unrecognisable after the
recent radical renovations
and the addition of a new
wing, the hotel has taken on
a new lease of life (it is
expected to re-open in the
first half of 2003). Its standard rooms, decorated in
contemporary minimalist
style (marble and wooden
floors) are now larger, with
bigger bathrooms (tub and
shower). The best are those
on the top floors (10th,
11th, 12th), now set up as
executive wings. With its
new restaurants and bars, it
is aiming to regain its status
as one of the city's classic
meeting places.

Holiday Suites

4, Arnis St., Ilisia ☎
210/7278000 **Fax**
210/7278600.
e-mail: holinn@ath.
forthnet.gr **Open:** Year
round. **Rooms:** Suites 34.

❄ 📺 🍸 🍴 🍷 ⛹ ♻ ♿
CC VISA

Apartment-suites, 40-55 m².
All are studio design, with a
discreet partition separating
bedroom, workspace (fully
equipped office) and kitchenette. Bathrooms spacious
and aristocratic. Your fully
equipped kitchenette enables
you not only to prepare
breakfast the way you like it,
but also to invite someone
to dinner. The public areas
are tiny, but guests may use
those in the sister hotel
Holiday Inn on
Michalakopoulou St..

NJV Athens Plaza

Vasileos Georgiou & Sta-
diou, Syntagma Sq.
☎ 210/3352400
Fax 210/3235856. e-mail:
sales-njv@grecotel.gr **Open:**
Year round. **Rooms:** Standard 156, suites 26.

In the heart of Athens, right
on Syntagma Square, next to
the Metro station. Favoured
by businessmen. Warm
modern design, with character. Politicians and business
people often take time out
for coffee in the lobby. The
best rooms are those on the
outside on the 8th and 9th
floors, with a view of Plaka
and the Acropolis.
Magnificent presidential suite.

From € 300 to € 400

Alexandros

8, Timoleontos Vassou St.,
Mavili Sq. ☎ 210/6430464
Fax 210/6441084.
e-mail: airotel@otenet.gr.
Internet: www.airotel-
hotels.com **Open:** Year
round. **Rooms:** Standard
74, suites 19.

Ideal for business travellers,
and for tourists who want
good value for money.
Contemporary modern aes-
thetic, with designer furniture in the lounges and
reception area. Spacious
rooms, all alike, except that
those with no balconies are
slightly bigger. Fully equipped
with all modern conven-
iences.

Athenaeum Inter-Continental

89-93, Syngrou Ave.
☎ 210/9206000 **Fax**
210/9206500.

e-mail: athens@intercont.
com **Internet:** www.inter-
conti.com **Open:** Year
round. **Rooms:** Standard
220, standard superior 248,
studios 15, suites 59, presidential 1.

Large modern palace in the
well-known chain, in one of
the most central locations in
the city. The radical renovations to the lobby and
restaurants (Premiere and
Zoe Cafe) should be com-
plete by the first part of
2003. All the VIPS (artists
and politicians) who have visited Athens in recent years
have stayed in its suites.
Exceptionally spacious reception areas. The rooms and
public areas are decorated
with works by Greek artists
from the owner's private
collection. Rooms are large,
and fully equipped. Those on
the 8th and 9th floors (61
rooms, 17 suites) provide
enhanced services for
patrons who want a superior
level of personal service and
comfort: separate check-in /
check-out, club floor lounge
with a view of the Acropolis,
special breakfast room.
Impressive conference centre.

Divani Caravel

2, Vasileos Alexandrou St.,
Pagkrati ☎ 210/7207000.
Fax 210/7253770. **Internet:**
www.divanicaravel.gr
Open: Year round. **Rooms:**
Standard 423, suites 48.

Just a stone's throw from
the centre of Athens, this is
a meeting place for business
travellers. Large rooms, the

best being those on the two
executive floors (2nd and
5th), with their own check-in
/ check-out and a series of
other non-standard services.
Large and exceptionally elegant public areas. In the summer, the outdoor pool
(enclosed during the winter
season) and pool bar are a
tranquil oasis with a unique
view encompassing the
Acropolis, Lycabettus and
the entire Attic basin. Ask
for one of the 35 rooms
overlooking the Acropolis.

Golden Age

25, Michalakopoulou St.,
Ilisia ☎ 210/7240861-9
Fax 210/7213965.
e-mail: goldenage@ath.
forthnet.gr **Open:** Year
round. **Rooms:** 122.

Impeccably renovated hotel,
addressed mainly to business
travellers and those who
want the luxury and comfort
of a large hotel. Spacious
rooms decorated in a somewhat official style. Large
warm public areas, four conference rooms.

Holiday Inn

50, Michalakopoulou St.,
Ilisia ☎ 210/7278000
Fax 210/7278600.
e-mail: holinn@ath.forthnet.
gr **Internet:** www.hiathens
greece.com **Open:** Year
round. **Rooms:** Standard
188, suites 4.

Just a stone's throw from
the heart of the commercial,
historic and financial centre.
The rooms are large and,
apart from the standard

services, feature closed circuit video, automatic check-
out, computer hook-up and
voice mail. There are executive rooms with extra services, and wheelchair-accessible
rooms for those with special
needs. Outdoor pool and
restaurant (summer months)
on the top floor.

Ledra Marriott

115, Syngrou Ave.
☎ 210/9300000
Fax 210/9359153.
e-mail: marriott@otenet.gr
Internet: www.marriott.com
Open: Year round.
Rooms: Standard 259,
suites 15, presidential 1.

The Athens Ledra Mariott
has just completed its renovations and is in the process
of expansion (50 more
rooms). The large standard
doubles are fully equipped
and elegantly decorated,
while the 39 rooms on the
executive floor have their
own service, separate check-
in / check-out and private
breakfast room. The suites
vary in style and size (from
50 to 120 m²), the most
impressive being the presidential suite. Added attraction: the Kona Kai restaurant, with its fine Polynesian
cuisine.

Park

10, Alexandras Ave.,
Pedion Areos
☎ 210/8832711-19
Fax 210/8238420.
e-mail: park_hotel@
otenet.gr **Internet:**
www.park_hotel.gr **Open:**
Year round. **Rooms:** Standard 127, suites 19.

Opposite the "Pedion tou
Areos" (Champ de Mars),
the Park is one of the city's
classic businessman's hotels.
Recently renovated, with
comfortable functional
rooms, the best being those
facing the park. Small
rooftop pool.

Royal Olympic

28-34, Athanasiou Diakou
St., Makrygianni
☎ 210/9288400
Fax 210/9233317.
e-mail: royaloly@hol.gr
Internet: www.royal
olympic.com **Open:** Year
round. **Rooms:** Standard
288, suites 10.

Opposite the pillars of
Olympian Zeus and
Hadrian's Gate, within
whistling distance of Plaka
and the Acropolis. The front
rooms have an unrestricted
view of the archaeological
sites and Lycabettus; the
back rooms are quieter.
Most rooms have recently
been renovated, although
work is still going on. The
hotel has a fully equipped
meeting room (seats 15) on
the top floor, with a fabulous
view of the archaeological
sites and the city.

From € 200 to € 300

Athenian Callirhoe Exclusive Hotel

32, Kallirois Ave. &
Petmeza St., Fix
☎ 210/9215353
Fax 210/9215342.
e-mail: hotel@tac.gr
Internet: www.tac.gr
Open: Year round. **Rooms:**
Standard 66, executive 15,
suites 3.

New ultra chic hotel (of the
unit that preceded it on this
site, only the shell was
retained) distinguished for its
aura of privacy, trendy decor
and superior services. Stylish
public areas with a minimalist
elegance (lounge bar,
Mediterranean restaurant
and bar restaurant with full
view of the Acropolis and
Lycabettus). The rooms
combine luxury, comfort and
a homey feeling. Special facilities for businessmen.

Athens Acropol

1, Peiraios Ave., Omonoia
☎ 210/5282100
Fax 210/5231361.
e-mail: fom-acr@grecotel.gr
Internet: www.grecotel
city.gr **Open:** Year round.
Rooms: Standard 160,
suites 7.

Businessman's hotel in the
heart of the city. Recently
renovated public areas, comfortable bedrooms decorated with executive elegance
(metal details and leather,
black-and-white framed photographs). Good service.

Divani Palace Acropolis

19-25, Parthenonos St.,
Makrygianni
☎ 210/9280100
Fax 210/9214993.
e-mail: acropol@otenet.gr
Open: Year round. **Rooms:**
Standard 234, suites 7.

A favourite with foreign visitors - its location right
beneath the Acropolis is its
greatest advantage. Large
rooms, with spacious bathrooms, fully equipped. The
best are those between the
4th and 7th floors overlook-

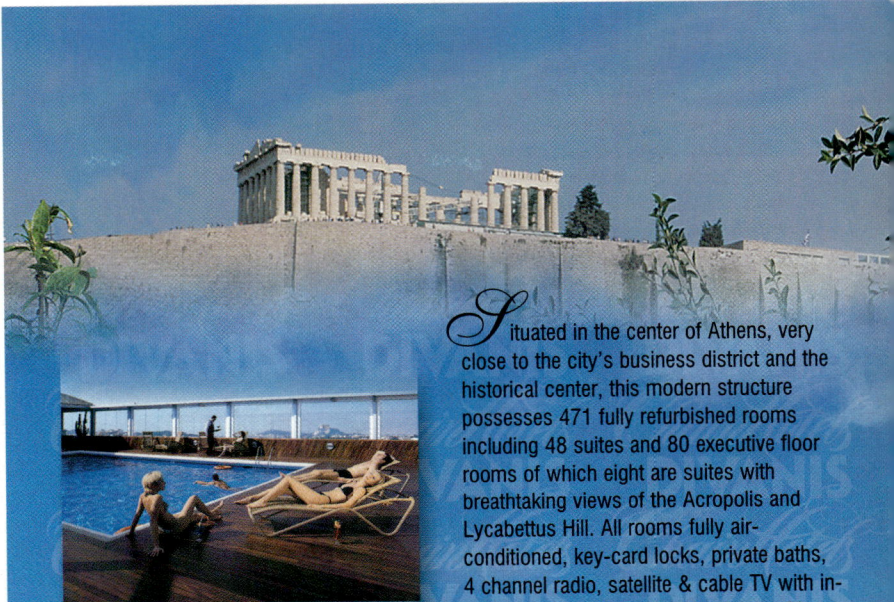

ing the Acropolis. In the summer months, BBQ buffet with live music in the roof garden overlooking the illuminated Acropolis. A surprise feature is a section of the Long Walls of classical Athens, which has been incorporated into the centre of the hotel.

Esperia Palace

22, Stadiou St., Syntagma Sq. ☎ 210/3238001-9 **Fax** 210/3238100. **e-mail:** esper@otenet.gr **Internet:** www.esperia.gr **Open:** Year round. **Rooms:** Standard 183, suites 1, studios 1.

In the centre of Athens, and on one of its busiest streets. The rooms are simple, functional, furnished with restored pieces by Saridis and equipped with everything you need for a short stay in the city. The best are those on the facade, especially those on the upper floors (7th and up, with a view of the Acropolis), and the studios on the 9th floor, with a panoramic view of the city.

Katerina

Karolou & Psarron, Metaxourgeio ☎ 210/5226115 **Fax** 210/5228529. **Open:** Year round. **Rooms:** Standard 51.

Small friendly hotel - immaculately clean - in a still underdeveloped part of the city. The rooms are small, but beautifully kept. Courteous staff. Small cafe at the entrance and on the mezzanine.

Omonia Grand Hotel

2, Peiraios Ave., Omonia ☎ 210/5235230 **Fax** 210/5234955. **e-mail:** fom-gcr@grecotel.gr **Internet:** www.grecotelcity.gr **Open:** Year round. **Rooms:** Standard 112, suites 3.

Modern, comfortable, youthful, contemporary, and right on Omonoia Square. Minimal public areas, the most attractive being the "Omonia Times" restaurant on the mezzanine level, a place for business meetings and casual encounters. Comfortable rooms, modern decor: the best are those facing the square on the top floor, which have a view of Lycabettus.

Parthenon

6, Makri St., Makrygianni ☎ 210/9234594-8 **Fax** 210/9235797. **e-mail:** airotel@netplan.gr **Internet:** www.airotel-hotels.com **Open:** Year round. **Rooms:** Standard 79.

On a quiet street behind Syngrou Ave., near the Acropolis and the pillars of Olympian Zeus. Large public areas, contemporary hotel design, friendly ambiance. Good base for exploring the archaeological sites and for shopping expeditions, also for quiet business meetings. The rooms have all the essentials for a comfortable stay. One of them has a view of the Acropolis, and some have large balconies.

Saint George Lycabettus

2, Kleomenous St., Kolonaki ☎ 210/7290711-9 **Fax** 210/7290439. **e-mail:** info@sglycabettus.gr **Internet:** www.sglycabettus.gr **Open:** Year round. **Rooms:** Standard 142, suites 15.

On the lower slopes of Lycabettus, in the Kolonaki district, with a panoramic view of the city. Spacious rooms, some decorated in colonial and some in modern style. The best are the 73 south-facing rooms overlooking the city and the Acropolis. The finest of all is the presidential suite with its 100 m² balcony and breathtaking view of the Acropolis. Pool with a view on the top floor. Two fine restaurants: the gastronomic "Grand Balcon" with its magnificent view and the trendy fan restaurant "Frame" on the ground floor.

From € 100 to € 200

Amalia

10, Amalias Ave., Syntagma Sq. ☎ 210/3237301 **Fax** 210/3238792. **e-mail:** hotamal@hellasnet.gr **Internet:** www.amalia.gr **Open:** Year round. **Rooms:** Standard 98, suite 1.

In the heart of Athens, opposite Syntagma and the National Garden, very near Plaka and the commercial heart of the city. Contemporary hotel design, attractive lobby with cafe. Comfortable rooms, fully equipped with all the necessities for a short stay in the city and, despite the central location, very quiet. The best

Accommodation

are those on the front, with their wonderful view of the National Garden, Panathenian Stadium, Parliament Building and Lycabettus.

Athens Atrium

21, Okeanidon St., Agios Sostis ☎ 210/9319300-2. **Fax** 210/9319305. **e-mail:** athensatrium@hotmail.com **Open:** Year round. **Rooms:** Standard 40.

Small hotel behind Syngrou Ave., currently undergoing radical renovation, which is scheduled for completion by the middle of 2003 and will wholly transform the place. The new business rooms are very large, as are their bathrooms, most of which have hydromassage. The rooms on the 5th floor also have large balconies.

Electra

5, Ermou St., Syntagma Sq. ☎ 210/3223223 **Fax** 210/3220310. **e-mail:** electrahotels@ath. forthnet.gr **Open:** Year round. **Rooms:** Standard 106, suites 3.

In the heart of Athens. Ideal for tourists who want to be near the archaeological sites, and for business travellers. Small public areas. Comfortably sized rooms, with small bathrooms. 46 of them overlook Syntagma and Ermou St.

Herodion

4, Rovertou Galli St., Makrygianni ☎ 210/9236832-6 **Fax** 210/9211650. **e-mail:** herodion@otenet.gr **Internet:** www.herodion.gr

Open: Year round. **Rooms:** Standard 86, suites 4.

At the foot of the Acropolis, in a very quiet location. Near the archaeological sites and opposite Plaka, with easy access to downtown Athens. Stylish reception areas, particularly the cool Atrium with its cafe-bar, a few steps up from ground level. Of the 90 rooms, the best are those at the back, overlooking the Acropolis.

Novotel Athènes

4-6, Michail Voda St., Vathi Sq. ☎ 210/8200700 **Fax** 210/8200777. **e-mail:** H0866@accor-hotels. com **Internet:** www.novotel. com **Open:** Year round. **Rooms:** Standard 190, suites 5.

Fully renovated, and a pleasant surprise in this relatively under-developed district. Spacious and stylish, the lobby and atrium restaurant bear the unmistakeable stamp of the parent chain. The rooms are comfortable, those giving on to the inner courtyard being substantially quieter. Attractive roof garden with pool. Its proximity to the railway station (Stathmos Larisis) makes it ideal for those planning to continue their journey by train.

Olympic Palace

16, Filellinon St., Syntagma Sq. ☎ 210/3237611 **Fax** 210/3225583. **e-mail:** hoteloly@hol.gr **Internet:** www.ellada. comhoteloly.html **Open:** March-15 Nov. **Rooms:** Standard 90.

Its location near the main archaeological sites and the city's business centre make it ideal for tourists and business travellers looking for a modern downtown hotel. Most of the rooms overlook the city, the best being those on the top floors that have a view of the Acropolis.

Philippos

3, Mitsaion St., Herodion ☎ 210/9223611-3 **Fax** 210/9211650. **e-mail:** Philippos@herodion. gr **Internet:** www.herodion.gr/philippos **Open:** Year round. **Rooms:** Standard 46, suites 4.

Small and comfortable, with modern decor and small public areas. Attractive airy atrium, where you can have a cup of tea or simply read your paper. Perfect for families or couples who want to visit the archaeological sites and museums, and for business travellers who want quiet surroundings and a friendly ambiance.

Titania Hotel

52, Panepistimiou St., Omonoia Sq. ☎ 210/3300111, 210/3809611. **Fax** 210/3830497. **e-mail:** titania@titania.gr **Internet:** www.titania.gr **Open:** Year round. **Rooms:** Standard 386, executive 10, suites 4.

Downtown hotel, currently undergoing gradual renovation, which has been completed in the spacious comfortable rooms, decorated in a contemporary classic style.

NOVOTEL

ACCOR
hotels

BUSINESS TRIP or CITY BREAK?

Whatever is the reason for your visit to Athens, Novotel guarantees the comfort of a great hotel chain at a central location in the heart of the city. Functional elegance and understated luxury in 195 spacious rooms.

Panoramic view of the Acropolis and Lycabettus Hill from the roof garden with the pool, bar and the romantic Clair de Lune restaurant. Special services for professional or social activities in the hotel's fully equipped conference facilities.

NOVOTEL ATHENES

4-6, Mich. Voda St., Athens, tel.: 210/8200700, fax: 210/8200777, www.novotel.com

Large bathrooms. The best (and biggest) rooms are those on the 8th and 9th floors. Fabulous view of the Acropolis from the Olive Garden restaurant on the roof.

Zafolia
87-89, Alexandras Ave.
☎ 210/6449002
Fax 210/6442042.
e-mail: zafoliahotel@compulink.gr Open: Year round. Rooms: Standard 184, suites 8.

Hotel for business travellers, recently renovated. Public areas comfortably spacious, and decorated with modern furniture in austere lines. Minimal aesthetic in the rooms, which are entirely furnished by Silvestridis. The rooms on the upper storeys have large balconies. Attractive roof garden with pool.

Under € 100
Achilleas
21, Lekka St., Syntagma Sq. ☎ 210/3233197, 210/3222706
Fax 210/3222412.
e-mail: achilleas@tourhotel.gr Internet: www.achilleashotel.gr Open: Year round. Rooms: Standard 24, suites 10.

Radically renovated downtown hotel, combining a central location, a style of its own and a cosy feel. Minimal decor in the public areas, which are limited to the absolutely essential, and classically styled rooms.

Acropolis Select
37-39, Falirou St., Koukaki
☎ 210/9211611 Fax

210/9216938.
e-mail: select@otenet.gr
Internet: www.acropoliselect.gr Open: Year round.
Rooms: Standard 72.

Near Syngrou Ave., and just steps from Plaka and the Acropolis. Striking and stylish reception area, atmospheric restaurant. Comfortable rooms, far better equipped than required by its category. Warm earth tones in the soft furnishings. Thirteen rooms have a view of the Acropolis, the best of these being numbers 401-405.

Adrian
74, Adrianou St., Plaka
☎ 210/3221553 Fax 210/3250454. Internet: www.douros-hotels.com Open: Year round.
Rooms: Standard 22.

Small friendly guesthouse on Plaka's busiest street. Conventional rooms, furnished in classic hotel style. The little balconies on the third floor at the back, and the lovely roof garden, awash with flowers, where breakfast is served in the summer, almost touch the rock of the Acropolis.

Astor
16, Karageorgi Servias St., Syntagma Sq.
☎ 210/3351000
Fax 210/3255115.
e-mail: astor@astorhotel.gr
Internet: www.astorhotel.gr Open: Year round.
Rooms: Standard 133.

Classic hotel, fully renovated, in a single 1960s building. Comfortable rooms, the best being those with a view

of the Acropolis. The public areas have a standard mass tourism air. View of the Acropolis from the (conventional) 10th floor restaurant, which is also the breakfast room.

Athens Center
26, Sofokleous St. & Kleisthenous, Kotzia Sq.
☎ 210/5248511-6
Fax 210/5248517.
e-mail: athcen@hol.gr
Internet: www.athenscenter.gr Open: Year round.
Rooms: Standard 136.

Recently renovated '70s hotel, behind the City Hall on Kotzia Square, near Omonoia, Psyrri and Monastiraki. The rooms are fully up to contemporary standards, as are those of the public areas that have been renovated - work on the rest, namely the restaurants and the pool area (which has a panoramic view of the Acropolis and Lycabettus) should be completed within 2003.

Athens Cypria
5, Diomeias St., Syntagma Sq. ☎ 210/3238034
Fax 210/3248792.
e-mail: diomeia@hol.gr
Open: Year round.
Rooms: Standard 71.

Recently fully renovated hotel in a multi-storey building, just steps away from the pedestrian precinct of Ermou St. Comfortable rooms in mass production style. Rudimentary public areas.

Cecil
39, Athinas St., Psyrri
☎ 210/3217079
Fax 210/3218005.
e-mail: cecil@netsmart.gr

Accommodation

Internet: www.netsmart.gr/cecil **Open:** Year round. **Rooms:** Standard 39.

❄ 📺 🧗 CC 💳

Older (inter-war) hotel, fully renovated but retaining much of the charm of the past. Small public areas, spacious high-ceilinged rooms decorated in a style that, while impersonal, respects the history of the building. Ideal for people who want to be near the great sites/sights of central Athens (Acropolis, Plaka, Kerameikos).

Diethnes
52, Paioniou St., Stathmos Larisis ☎ 210/8836855 **Fax** 210/8230582. **Internet:** www.interland.gr/diethnes **Open:** Year round. **Rooms:** Standard 20.

❄ 📺 🍽 🍴 🍽 🧗 CC 💳

Reasonably priced hotel, ideal for those travelling by train from Stathmos Larisis, although the area is not one of the best. The rooms have high ceilings and lovely architectural details, but the decor does not do them justice.

Dorian Inn
15-17, Peiraios Ave., Omonoia Sq.
☎ 210/5239782
Fax 210/5226196.
e-mail: dorianho@otenet.gr
Internet: www.greek hotel.com/athens/dorian-inn **Open:** Year round. **Rooms:** Standard 146.

❄ 📺 🍴 🍽 〰 CC 💳

Freshly renovated hotel in a multi-storey building on Peiraios, offering a central location and a stab at the amenities of a big hotel. Comfortable rooms furnished in classic hotel style, panoramic view from the

modest 12th floor roof garden, with its cafe and small pool overlooking the Acropolis and Lycabettus.

Ermis
19, Apollonos Ave., Plaka
☎ 210/3235514-6
Fax 210/3232073.
e-mail: hermessa@ath.forthnet.gr **Open:** Year round. **Rooms:** Standard 45.

❄ 📺 🍽 CC 💳

A modest but comfortable hotel in the heart of Athens, between Syntagma and Plaka. The rooms (all alike) are spacious, and equipped with all the essentials. Small balconies, with no particular view. But you can see the Acropolis from the small roof terrace, where in the summer drinks are served and a few sunbeds set out.

Jason Inn
12, Asomaton St., Asomaton Sq. ☎ 210/3251106
Fax 210/3243132. **Internet:** www.douros-hotels.com **Open:** Year round. **Rooms:** Standard 57.

❄ 📺 RF 🍴 🍽 CC 💳

Modest and dignified downtown hotel, ideal for visitors who want to be near the restaurants, bars, theatres etc. of Psyrri as well as Thiseio, Monastiraki and the Acropolis. Conventional rooms, furnished in conventional hotel style. Panoramic view from the simple modern roof garden, whose bar-restaurant is open to the public.

King Jason
26, Kolonou St., Metaxourgeio ☎ 210/5234721, 210/5234906 **Fax** 210/5234786. **Internet:** www.douros-hotels.com

Open: Year round. **Rooms:** Standard 114.

❄ 📺 RF 🍴 🍽 🍽 CC 💳

Renovated downtown hotel in a part of the city that, although depressed, is beginning to improve with the arrival of the Metro and a clutch of theatres and music stages. Official-chic rooms, cheerful airy public areas.

Museum Best Western
16, Bouboulinas St., Mouseio ☎ 210/3805611-3 **Fax** 210/3800507. **Internet:** www.bestwestern.com **Open:** Year round. **Rooms:** Standard 57, suite 1.

❄ 📺 🍽 🛎 🍽 CC 💳

Small, official-style city hotel behind the Polytechnic School and the Archaeological Museum. The rooms, although somewhat cramped, are fully renovated. Perfect for business travellers. Good value.

Oscar
25, Filadelfeias St. & Samou, Stathmos Larisis
☎ 210/8834215
Fax 210/8216368.
e-mail: oscar@oscar.gr
Internet: www.oscar.gr
Open: Year round. **Rooms:** Standard 162, suites 2.

❄ 📺 🍴 🍽 🍽 〰 CC 💳

Rudimentary standard-type hotel in two multi-storey buildings (one with just rooms). Plus point: its proximity to the Metro and railway station. Panoramic view from the roof garden and pool. The marks of time are visible, but renovations are scheduled for the winter 2002-3. Spacious conference rooms, also available for events.

Accommodation

Pan

11, Mitropoleos St., Syntagma Sq. ☎ 210/3237816-8
Fax 210/3237819.
e-mail: panhotel@hol.gr
Open: Year round.
Rooms: Standard 33.

❄ 📺 ▼ cc 💳

Simple classic hotel, largely renovated, within whistling distance of Plaka and Syntagma. Comfortable rooms, rudimentary public areas.

Plaka

7, Kapnikareas St., Plaka
☎ 210/3222096
Fax 210/3222412.
e-mail: plaka@tourhotel.gr
Internet: www.plakahotel.gr
Open: Year round. **Rooms:** Standard 67.

👁 ❄ 📺 RF ▼ cc 💳

Ideal for those who want a small, warm, comfortable hotel just steps away from Plaka, the shops of Ermou St. (pedestrian precinct) and Monastiraki. Fully renovated (you'd think it was brand new), with a wonderful view of the Acropolis from the modern roof garden.

Pythagorion Best Western

28, Agiou Konstantinou St., Omonoia Sq.
☎ 210/5242811-4
Fax 210/5245581. **Internet:** www.bestwestern.com
Open: Year round. **Rooms:** Standard 56.

❄ 📺 ▼ ▼ 🎲 cc 💳

Decent accommodation with the guarantee of the international hotel chain, for those who prefer to be in the centre of the city. Comfortable, recently renovated rooms in classic hotel style, public areas satisfactory if impersonal.

Zinon Best Western

3, Keramikou St. & Zinonos, Omonoia Sq.
☎ 210/5245711-4
Fax 210/5245581. **Internet:** www.bestwestern.com
Open: Year round.
Rooms: Standard 55.

❄ 📺 ▼ cc 💳

Renovated classic hotel unit, offering decent and affordable accommodation in the centre of the city, with the international standards guaranteed by the name.

SOUTHERN ATHENS

From € 300 to € 400

Divani Apollon Palace & Spa

10, Agiou Nikolaou & Il. Iliou, Vouliagmeni
☎ 210/8911100
Fax 210/9658010. **Internet:** www.divaniapollon.gr
Open: Year round. **Rooms:** Standard 279, suites 7.

👁 ❄ 📺 ▼ 🍴 ▼ 🏊 🎲 🌊 ⚒ ♿ P cc 💳

Its great advantage is its proximity to both the centre of Athens and the airport, making it ideal for weekend and conference tourism, but also for holidays. The intelligent architectural design gives every room a view of the Saronikos Gulf, the best being those on the front (executive wing), where the balconies have a panoramic view. These rooms are also larger, with designer furniture in warm earth tones and every modern convenience. The suites are amazing, the public areas spacious and the conference centre impressive. The "Pelagos" bar in the lobby is particularly atmospheric, as is the seafront "Mythos" restau-

rant. The Thalassotherapy Centre should be open by mid-2003. Member of the Leading Hotels of the World.

The Margi

11, Litous St., Laimos Vouliagmenis ☎ 210/8962061
Fax 210/8960229.
e-mail: margihouse@hol.gr
Internet: www.themargi.gr
Open: Year round. **Rooms:** Standard 99, suites 11.

❄ 📺 ▼ 🍴 ▼ 🏊 🎲 🌊 ♿ P cc 💳

Luxury hotel on a small back street in Vouliagmeni, not beside the sea. Studied sophistication in the decor of the public areas, and cleverly designed small pool court. Standard rooms reasonably sized, and with their marble baths, large beds, animal prints and ethnic touches create a very satisfying whole. The suites are lovely (especially the VIP suite, with its minimal zen aura), with a combination of antiques and modern furniture.

From € 200 to € 300

Asteras Vouliagmenis

40, Apollonos Ave., Vouliagmeni ☎ 210/8902000
Fax 210/8962583.
Internet: www.astir.gr
One of Greek hotellery's most impressive complexes, and one of the first resorts in Attica. Renovations in progress. Located on the headland at Laimos Vouliagmenis, in about 30 hectares of pine-clad grounds with a panoramic view of the Saronikos Gulf. Comprises three autonomous hotel complexes, the "Aphrodite", the "Nafsica" and the "Arion", plus independent bungalows.

Accommodation

• Arion
Open: Year round. **Rooms:** Standard 150, suites 18, bungalows 73.

The "Arion" has more of the air of a city hotel (and it remains open over the winter). Large public areas decorated with neo-classic simplicity. Very comfortable rooms, with marble baths and classic decor, the best being those on the upper floors, which have large verandas and a panoramic view of the sea.

• Aphrodite
Open: May-Oct. **Rooms:** Standard 165, suites 4.

The least sophisticated unit in the group, ideal for family holidays. Radically renovated just a year ago. Comfortable rooms, with large beds and balconies that are perfect for drinking in the view of the sea (recalling your island holidays). Those with large wardrobes will appreciate the ample closet space.

• Nafsika
Open: Apr.-Nov. **Rooms:** Standard 161, suites 9, presidential 1.

The largest rooms in the complex, but renovations are still in progress. The '70s character of the rooms is unchanged. Large public areas, lovely pool, same services as the rest of the complex.

Blazer Suites
1-3, Karamanli Ave. (former-ly Alkyonidon), Voula ☎ 210/9658801-7 **Fax** 210/9658808. **Open:** Year round. **Rooms:** Suites 28.

Small apartment-suites, fully equipped. Though the furnishings are neither expensive nor luxurious, the warmth of the decor creates a friendly atmosphere. The kitchens are small but functional, and fitted with all the necessary appliances (including microwave). The bathrooms are narrow, inferior to the rest of the apartment. The grounds have been designed to accommodate a pleasant pool area with a very attractive cafe.

Metropolitan
385, Syngrou Ave., Delta Falirou ☎ 210/9471000 **Fax** 210/9471010. **e-mail:** metropolitan@ chandris.gr **Internet:** www.chandris.gr **Open:** Year round. **Rooms:** Standard 362, suites 10, presidential 1.

Luxury hotel on one of the city's busiest streets. Ideal for business travellers. The public areas, at once classic and modern, are reasonably large. There are rooms for events and conferences, and a super luxurious ballroom. Rooms spacious, with beautifully chosen furnishings. The executive rooms on the 7th floor - the only ones with balconies - overlook the Acropolis and Kastella. The rooftop restaurant, beside a small pool, is open in the summer.

From € 100 to € 200
Coral
35, Poseidonos Ave., Paliao Faliro ☎ 210/9816441 **Fax** 210/9831207. **e-mail:** info@coralhotel.gr **Open:** Year round. **Rooms:** Standard 82, suites 2.

Perfect for businessmen who need to be in the southern suburbs and the centre of Piraeus. The rooms are comfortable, and fitted out with adequate, brand new modern furnishings. 23 of the rooms have a view of the sea, and those on the 6th floor have large verandas. On the top floor there are a small gym, events room and a tiny pool that is more of a hydromassage unit.

Glyfada
40, Poseidonos Ave., Glyfada ☎ 210/8944081, 210/8944106 **Fax** 210/8985068. **e-mail:** info@glyfadahotel.gr **Internet:** www.glyfadahotel. gr **Open:** Year round. **Rooms:** Standard 40, junior suites 8.

Right on Poseidonos Ave. and just steps from the centre of Glyfada, this recently renovated hotel is ideal for businessmen. The rooms, although small, are equipped with all the essentials for a comfortable short stay. The best are the junior suites. Ask for a room with a sea view.

London
38, Poseidonos Ave., Glyfada ☎ 210/8942106.

Located right on the waterfront of Paleo Faliro, a seaside suburb of the city of Athens, **Best Western Coral Hotel** offers panoramic views of the Saronic Gulf and genuine Greek hospitality. Recently awarded Best Western Premier certification and a Four Star property since 2001, **Best Western Coral Hotel** confidently provides guests with fine accommodations and services.

Best Western Coral Hotel offers newly renovated guest rooms, with all modern conveniences for the comfort of our guests. Many rooms have a panoramic sea view. Three function rooms with spectacular sea view, a dedicated staff, stylish surroundings and an inventory of equipment combine to make **Best Western Coral Hotel** a desired location for successful social events, meetings and conferences. The indoor counter current swimming whirlpool and exercise facility completed in 2002 offer our guests a refreshing experience.

The **Best Western Coral Hotel** Restaurant features traditional Greek and Continental cuisine and is open for Buffet Breakfast, Lunch and Dinner. The hotel's Bar offers all day light menu service, coffees and pastries, sandwiches and salads. In the evening, drinks and cocktails are served in a cosy
atmosphere with background music and friendly service.

Built in 1963 and transformed into an elegant hotel in 2002, we, at **Best Western Coral Hotel**, make it our business to make your stay enjoyable whether you travel for business or pleasure.

Best Western

BEST WESTERN
Coral Hotel

Paleo Faliro
Athens 175 61, GREECE

Best Western Coral Hotel
35 Possidonos Avenue, Paleo Faliro 175 61, Athens, Greece
Telephone: +30 (210) 98 16 441
Fax: +30 (210) 98 31 207
www.coralhotel.gr www.coralhotel.com
Email: info@coralhotel.gr

SAVOY HOTEL

The recently renovated Savoy Hotel in the centre of Piraeus is ready to host your next event, with spacious multi-purpose rooms suitable for receptions, seminars, exhibitions, etc. And for your business meetings the luxurious restaurant proposes a lavish breakfast buffet, cold lunch plates or salad bar and international cuisine à la carte.

Iroon Polytechneiou Ave.
Tel.: 210/4284580
Fax: 210/4284588
e-mail: savoy@otenet.gr
www.savoyhotel.gr

OY HOTEL • SAVOY HOTE

e-mail: htllondon@hellasnet.gr **Internet:** www.greekhotel.com/athens/london/home.htm **Open:** Year round. **Rooms:** Standard 75.

Businessman's hotel, although its location near the sea on Poseidonos Ave. suggests holiday accommodation. Comfortable rooms, simply decorated.

Oasis Hotel Apartments
27, Poseidonos Ave., Glyfada ☎ 210/8941662 **Fax** 210/8941724. **e-mail:** oasis@ath.forthnet.gr **Internet:** www.oasishotel.gr **Open:** Year round. **Rooms:** Apartments 70.

Two-room apartments in a classic-style hotel, with a pleasant view of the shore or overlooking the very attractive interior courtyard. This is the hotel's best feature and includes a large pool, children's pool and Jacuzzi, all surrounded by carefully tended flowerbeds.

Plaza Vouliagmeni Strand Hotel
14, Litous St., Vouliagmeni ☎ 210/9670196-8 **Fax** 210/9670139. **e-mail:** capital@otenet.gr **Internet:** agn.hol.gr/hotels/plaza/plaza.htm **Open:** Year round. **Rooms:** Standard 76.

Occupying a modern apartment building in Vouliagmeni, and thus without grounds. Ask for a corner room - they have a wonderful view of the sea. This is a simple but perfectly decent hotel in an expensive part of Athens.

Under € 100
Emmantina
33, Poseidonos Ave., Glyfada ☎ 210/8980683 **Fax** 210/8948110. **e-mail:** emmantina@emmantina.gr **Internet:** ww.emmantina.gr **Open:** Year round. **Rooms:** Standard 80.

Entirely respectable city hotel (though not more than 150 metres from the sea), patronised mainly by businessmen and others who simply want to be in the southern suburbs. Pleasant public areas; rooms functional, and double-glazed for soundproofing. Small rooftop pool.

Poseidon
72, Poseidonos Ave., Palaio Faliro ☎ 210/9822041, 210/9822161 **Fax** 210/9829217. **e-mail:** sales@poseidonhotel.com.gr **Internet:** poseidonhotel.com.gr **Open:** Year round. **Rooms:** Standard 90.

Fine choice for those who want to be in the neighbourhood of the organised beaches and marinas of Floisvos and Alimos but prefer the comfort and services of a city hotel. Ask for a room with a sea view on one of the upper floors.

PIRAEUS
From € 100 to € 200
Cavo d' Oro
19, Vasileos Pavlou St., Kastella ☎ 210/4113744-5 **Fax** 210/4122210. **Open:** Year round. **Rooms:** Standard 75.

Dark public areas, rooms in need of renovation - but the best view in Kastella. The best accommodation is on the upper floors, where the rooms have large verandas.

Savoy
93, Iroon Polytechneiou St., Piraeus ☎ 210/4284580 **Fax** 210/4284588. **e-mail:** savoy@otenet.gr **Internet:** www.savoyhotel.gr **Open:** Year round. **Rooms:** Standard 68, suites 3.

Well-maintained classic hotel, for good accommodation within walking distance of the Port of Piraeus and the marina at Zea. Comfortable rooms decorated in classic style, functional public areas.

Under € 100
Mistral
105, Vasileos Pavlou St., Kstella ☎ 210/4117150 **Fax** 210/4122096. **Internet:** www.mistral.gr **Open:** Year round. **Rooms:** Standard 77, suites 3.

Well-maintained hotel, and it is this careful attention that enables it to keep up its standards. Bright, comfortable public areas; rooms simple, well-kept, with double-glazing and small bathrooms. The front rooms overlook Mikrolimano.

RESORTS
Over € 400
Mare Nostrum Club Méditerranée
Akti Vravronas ☎ 22940/47700 **Fax** 22940/47790. **e-mail:** cmcomm@clubmed.gr **Internet:** www.clubmed.

com **Open:** Year round.
Rooms: Standard 313 in main building, bungalows.

What makes this place different from the run-of-the-mill Club Med holiday complex is the thalassotherapy centre (extra charge). The public areas are large, the rooms comfortable and fully equipped - the best being the bungalows and the "superior" rooms on the 3rd floor of the main building. Well-tended garden. The quoted rate is for one week's stay with full board, per person.

From € 300 to € 400
Grand Resort Lagonissi
Km 40, Athens-Sounion road, Lagonisi
☎ 22910/76000
Fax 22910/24514.
e-mail: lagonissi@lagonissi resort.gr **Internet:** www.lago nissiresort.gr
Open: Apr.-Nov. **Rooms:** Standard 114, suites 4, bungalows 95, villas 38.

Fabulous resort on the shore road between Athens and Sounio, and a member of the Leading Hotels of the World. Main building, bungalows and villas set amid lush gardens on an idyllic promontory with 16 white sandy beaches and a panoramic view of the Argosaronikos. Stunning accommodation in the main building, with a sophisticated elegance in the decor.
The bungalows, in restored or new buildings, with all modern conveniences and a touch of luxury, come in var-

ious types: with garden, with private pool, executive waterfront suites, family cabins, etc. The "Grand Resort Lagonissi" has also invested heavily in its gastronomic amenities.
The food and service in all its restaurants (classic in the Aphrodite, Polynesian in Kochylia, Italian in Captain's, Greek in Poseidon and the Ouzeri) bring the Athenians all the way down to the coast.

From € 200 to € 300
Sofitel Athens Airport
Eleftherios Venizelos International Airport, Spata ☎ 210/3544000
Fax 210/3544444. **e-mail:** H3167@accor-hotels.com
Internet: www.sofitel.com
Open: Year round.
Rooms: Standard 345, suites 13, presidential 1.

Impressive modern architecture, directly opposite the terminal building at Athens' new airport. The public areas are simple and very handsome. Comfortably spacious standard rooms, with sophisticated decor, large beds, and a full range of equipment and services especially designed for travellers: for example, they are fully soundproofed, and can be totally darkened.
The Karavi gastronomic restaurant on the roof garden, with a view over the airport, has a shipboard-style decor. One of the hotel's best features is the enclosed roof garden pool, with a thrilling view spanning both runways. Impeccably equipped conference rooms.

Under € 100
Eden Beach
Km 47, Athens-Sounio road, Anavyssos
☎ 22910/60031
Fax 22910/60043.
e-mail: info@eden.gr
Internet: www.eden.gr
Open: Apr.-Oct.
Rooms: Standard 250.

Holiday complex, not far from Athens, and very good value for money. The gradual renovations have been steadily improving its image. Two buildings, set in gardens with flowers and tall trees. Simple, austere, clean, with spacious balconies (most rooms have a sea view) and large bathrooms. Another plus is the underground passage leading to the clean sandy beach, with its European Union "blue flag" of quality.

Marathon Beach Hotel
12, Marathonos Ave., Nea Makri waterfront
☎ 22940/91292, 22940/91255
Fax 22940/95307.
e-mail: hotelmb@otenet.gr
Internet: www.marathon beachhotel.gr **Open:** Apr.-Oct. **Rooms:** Standard 166.

Right on the waterfront in Nea Makri, this is an ideal place for a holiday near Athens, or a relaxing weekend break. The rooms are comfortably sized, all with veranda and view. Seawater pool, garden for receptions. Good base for excursions to Delphi, the islands in the Argosaronikos and Mykonos.

distance
servicing

ATHENS 2004

ALPHA BANK
OFFICIAL
BANK

We are children of our age. By a click on the computer we avoid queuing and bureau-cracy. By a telephone call we perform all our transactions. At any hour of the day or night. Wherever we may be. Thanks to Alpha Bank, the Bank that respects our time and responds to the needs of the times - before anyone else is even aware of them. Its electronic services Alpha Web Banking (transactions via the Internet), Alpha Bank m-Banking (transactions via your mobile phone) and Alphaphone (transactions over the phone), all available at no extra charge, accompany us even on excursions and holi-days, allowing us absolute freedom. Subscribe to Alpha Bank's electronic services today, and let the others run home to pay a forgotten bill.

ALPHA BANK OFFICIAL BANK OF THE ATHENS 2004 OLYMPIC GAMES

Beaches

Athens Guide 2003

ATHENS 2004

ALPHA BANK

OFFICIAL
BANK

endless
shades
of blue

Sand or pebble, rugged or placid, organised to offer all imaginable facilities or beautifully unspoiled, Attica's beaches are a microcosm of the entire Greek coastline: reminiscent of the Cyclades in the south, green like Chalkidiki or the Ionian in the east and west, socialising with neighbouring Evoia in the north. Their heyday was the period from the '50s to the '70s, when they were graced by the socialites of Athens and the starlets of the Greek cinema, who introduced the bikini and the wild beach party. Later they fell into decline; but in recent years the tide seems to have turned, and as they win more and more blue flags they are once again dynamically claiming their place in the sun.

Athens is one of the few European capitals that can boast of a coastline of such length, extent and variety. Beaches for maritime relaxation against a vast backdrop of blue, beach clubs that get the adrenaline going with water sports, pumped-up decibels and... "beer battles", empty shores combining an idyllic charm with a prospect of archaeological monuments, tame sands that are an irresistible attraction to family groups. In Attica, the choice is virtually inexhaustible.

In the Alpha Guide Athens 2003, we have divided the beaches of Attica into two categories: organised beaches, where you pay an entrance charge and enjoy a host of facilities - even massage parlours -, and free beaches. Those in the first category have the distinct advantage of being near the city, and the recent impressive innova-

Eden Beach

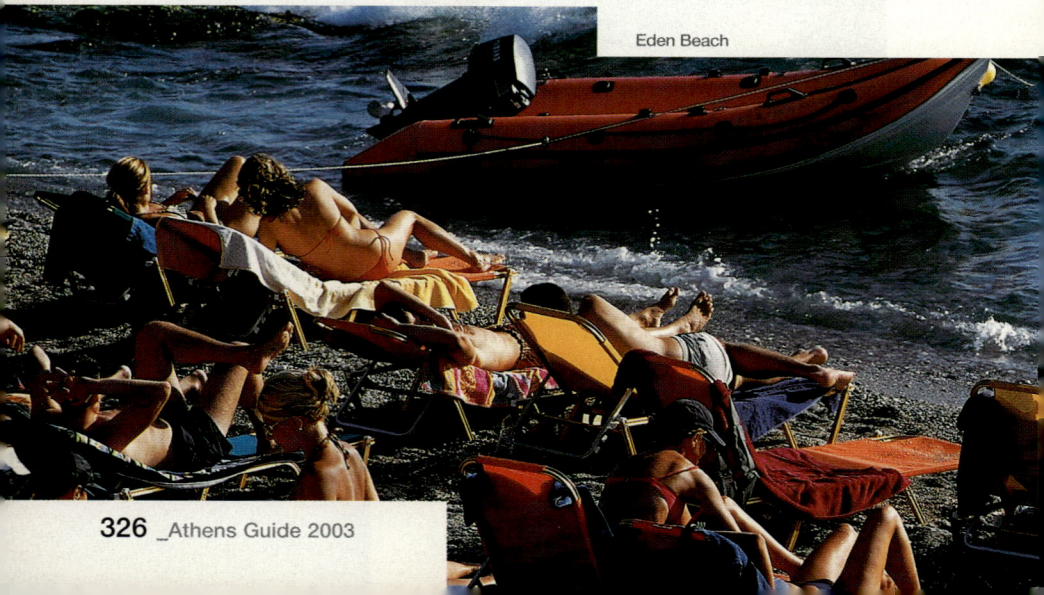

Beach bods and... surprises

tions guarantee high quality services - at a price, of course. Most of these beaches are in the southern part of the county, and include the former EOT (Greek National Tourist Board) beaches, now privately run, and the private beaches of Attica's great seaside resort hotels.

The changes began in 2002, and will be completed by the Olympic year of 2004. The competition for the favour of the public is fierce, but fortunately the ultimate winners are always the residents of Athens, who can now swim in clean clear water, from beaches with every imaginable facility, within easy reach of the city.

At the free beaches (and that means most of the coastline) there is no entrance charge, but you do pay a price in the greater distance from the city and the

weekend traffic jams - but this is the only way to experience a different type of scene, in settings with incomparably more character. Here, you either bring your own umbrella or grab the tree with the best shade. Sun-bed? The choice is up to you: a flat rock in some deserted cove or a comfortable chaise longue at a beach bar with a booming beat. Wherever you go along the coastline of Attica you will find free beaches.

Where to go? That's entirely up to you. But remember that, although most beaches are in popular resort areas, the atmosphere midweek is very different to the weekend scene - especially in July and August, when even the remotest stretches of shore are packed with people escaping for a short break from the heat of the city.

tip

The arrival of winter does not mean empty beaches. The members of the various "Polar Bear" clubs continue to enjoy their dips all year round, at beaches like Vouliagmeni, Voula and Palaio Faliro.

Balux, Asteria Seaside

Grand Beach Lagonissi

Grand Resort Lagonissi

Beaches

ORGANISED BEACHES

THE BEGINNINGS OF AN ATHENIAN RIBIERA

Massage by the sea, finger food delivery to your sun-bed, water parks with floating trampolines, tracks for extreme games and seaside facilities for special events: these are just some of the amenities offered by Attica's organised beaches. With the privatisation of the Tourist Board (EOT) beaches, and things hotting up in view of the 2004 Olympics, the beaches are just getting better and better, almost rivalling those of Barcelona! Canvas umbrellas and straw sun-beds add colour to the wholly renovated installations, which now also feature squads of security guards as well as lifeguards, first aid centres and cleaning crews. These services, coupled with the clean waters of Saronikos Gulf (the result of recent improvement works in the region), are attracting more and more bathers. Before you head south, however, bear in mind that construction work for the Olympic Games may be temporarily affecting some of the coastal areas in this direction, and that admission rates may change.

Grand Beach Lagonissi

Last year the Grand Beach swept the board on Attica's new map of beach fun. The recently renovated and very impressive Grand Resort Lagonissi now offers some of the most luxurious accommodation in

Attica, and its waterfront is of the same high standard. The gently shelving turquoise waters, wooden footbridge and floating bar call to mind some exotic lagoon. The special body parlours for massage (shiatsu, Thai, relaxation and reflexology), body painting and henna tattoo - overlooking the sea - add a spa note, while tranquil relaxation is implicit in the cane sun-beds, casually disposed and considerably spaced. The Poseidon restaurant serves light, beach-friendly food, and spoils us by delivering snacks right to our sun-bed. Naturally, the prices of even basic necessities like water are as elevated as the general aesthetic of the beach.

Active types - including the members of the Greek national beach volley team - work out on shore on the volley, beach volley and mundialito 5X5 pitches (likely to be used for tournaments), while the left-hand end of the bay is given over to water sports: parasailing, water-skiing, banana and tubes. And the extreme games track (climbing wall, rappel, fly fox) on the right is the envy of even Cretan resorts. The fun gets fast and furious with events like the aerobic marathon, racquets tournament (umpire imported from abroad!) and marine treasure hunt, while Radio DeeJay broadcasts live at weekends from the beach, sparking impromptu beach parties. And for an atmospheric long drink in the evening, there's nothing like the floating wooden bar enhanced with underwater lighting - reached

tip
Some of the resorts in Attica have a very advantageous visitor pass system for regular visitors even if they are not hotel guests.

Asteria Seaside

by a torch-lit bridge. You can, of course, also enjoy the luxury of the Grand Beach by staying in one of its bungalows or suites. And for an exceptional gastronomic experience, the complex has two outstanding restaurants to choose from - the Italian Captain's House, with a deck sweeping out around the sea, transforming it into a pool, and the extremely stylish Polynesian Kochylia, decorated in accordance with the dictates of feng shui.

Open: 8.00-21.00.
Admission: Mon.-Fri. 8.00-15.00 € 7, 15.00 till sunset € 4.50. Weekends € 10.50. Children, half price Info: 22910/76000.

Asteria Seaside

The Asteria Seaside in Glyfada is a dynamic contender on the organised beach scene, going for gold with features like well-kept gardens, all day beach bars with attractive wooden pergolas, a self-service restaurant with elegant

marble tables and recreation areas that are quite out of the ordinary. Enjoy the fine golden sand brought in from Chalkidiki, and savour the finger food delivered to your cane sun-bed. The water is kept clean by an ultra-modern filter net and a team of divers who comb the seafloor daily.

As for the activities, these come as a very pleasant surprise. Apart from the all-wooden playground, the Asteria offers an amazing aqua park with inflatable constructions: an "iceberg" for scaling, three water trampolines, see-saws, catapults and an aqua volley area. There are also one official and two unofficial beach volley pitches and a mini football field where tournaments are played. This is the summer broadcasting base of the "Rhythmos" radio station, music events are organised on an almost weekly basis, and the TV channel "Mad" schedules live summer broadcasts from the Asteria Seaside.

Waterfront bar

Aqua Park, Asteria Seaside

Asteras Vouliagmenis

If you want more privacy, head for the small section of beach in front of the Balux all day club. Unwind at this glamorous summer hot spot with a massage in their parlour, stretch out on one of the "colonial" daybeds around the pool, and savour light meals from the Septem restaurant (after 13:00). By summer 2003, the redevelopment plans will have been completed, transforming the whole Asteria Seaside waterfront into a multifaceted summer complex: the cabins at the left-hand end of the beach will have become private summer units (each with its own pool), the former Amphitheatre will re-open as a night club, and there will also be a conference centre.
Open: 8.00-21.00. Admission: Mon.-Fri. € 7, Children € 3.50. Weekends and holidays € 10, Children € 5.
Admission to Balux beach: Weekdays € 10, Weekends € 13. Info: 210/8945676.

Apollonies Aktes (Beaches A and B at Voula)

These were traditionally the "people's beaches", popular with young and old on account of their sandy shore, shallow water and relatively short distance from the city centre. The management company that has taken them over ("Apollonies Aktes") began revamping them in the summer of 2002, with a view to making them even more attractive.

Phase one focused on Beach A, where (apart from the familiar waterslides and water sports centre) we now find white canvas umbrellas, blue cane sun-beds and a beach bar with wooden pavilions. The beach has become extroverted and event-friendly, mixing Hawaiian cocktails at the Hula Moon bar and hosting special events (e.g. Latin concerts under the full moon) in its open-air venues Blue Water and Verde. The next phase will include a Hawaiian restaurant (Aloha), new sports facilities, a playground and a pool. Beach B (one kilometre away on Poseidonos Ave.), greener, but with a similar sandy shore and shallow water, is being made over along the same lines.
Open: 7.00-21.00. Admission: € 3, Children € 1.50 (1 month, 6 month and 12 month passes available). Info: 210/8951646.

Asteras Vouliagmenis

Wholly distinctive with its tree-covered private promontory and attractive '70s-style architectural features, the Asteras is a legendary part of summer in Athens. The resort's familiar cabins have welcomed many a Greek politician and artist, and the beach is one of the "hottest" in Attica. The fine white sand is graced by the current stars of the catwalk, and you may well see a clutch of famous footballers on the beach volley pitch, presenting their own version of the game complete with kicks and

ATTICA

ANO SOULI
AG. MARINA
LIMNI MARATHONOS
MARATHONAS
KATO SOULI
KRYONERI
AG. STEFANOS
SCHINIAS
THRAKOMAKEDONES
ANOIXI
BARYBOBI
STAMATA
ORMOS MARATHONA
FYLI
DIONYSOS
ATTIKI ODOS
N. MAKRI
ANO LIOSIA
ACHARNAI
MEG. ALEXANROU AVE.
ASPROPYRGOS
ZEFYRI
KOMVOS KYMIS
PENTELI
AG. MARINA
PATISION
PENTELIS AVE.
ELEFSINA
KOMVOS METAMORFOSIS
KOMVOS GERAKA
RAFINA
ATHINON AVNUE
CHALANDRI
KIFISOU AVE.
KOMVOS STAVROU
KOMVOS PALLINIS
MARATHONOS AVE.
THIVON
KIFISOU AVE.
GLYKA NERA
KOMVOS GL. NERON
PIKERMI
ATHINA
KANTZA PALLINIS
LABRAKI
KOMVOS SPATON
SPATON AVE.
ARTEMIDA (LOUTSA)
PERAMA
PEIRAIOS AVE.
KOMVOS KATECHAKI
PAIANIA
KOMVOS SPATON
SPATA
PEIRAIAS
ATTIKI ODOS
ELEFTHERIOS VENIZELOS AIRPORT
ELLINIKO
KOMVOS KOROPIOU
POSEIDONOS AVE.
LAVRIOU AVE.
MARKOPOULOU AVE.
KOROPI
MARKOPOULO
PORTO RAFTI
VARIS-KOROPIOU AVE.
AVLAKI
VARI
KALYVIA
VOULIAGMENI
VARKIZA
AG. DIMITRIOS
KOUVARAS
KAKIA THALASSA
FLEVOPOULA
LAGONISI
KERATEA
DASKALEIO
FLEVES
NEW LAVRIOU AVE.
PLAKA
SARONIDA
ANAVYSSOS
LAVRIO
SARONIKOS KOLPOS
PALAIA FOKAIA
ARSIDA
THYMARI
LEGRAINA
SOUNIO
PATROKLOS GAIDOURONISI
ARCHI

ATHENS 2004

ALPHA BANK
OFFICIAL BANK

CENTRAL ATHENS

NEAPOLI

LYKAVITTO HILL

KOLONAKI

LYKAVITTOS CABLE-CAR

LYRIKI SKINI

PANEPISTIMIO

PATR. GRIGORIOU

PALAMA SQ.

LYKAVITTOU SQ.

FILIKIS ETAIREIAS SQ.
(KOLONAKIOU)

BENAKI MUSEUM

ANCIENT ART MUSEUM

BAS. SOFIAS AVE.

BYZANTINE MUSEUM

MARTIAL MUSEUM

SYNTAGMA SQ.

AGNOSTOU STRATIOTI

HOUSE OF PARLIAMENT

NATIONAL GARDEN

ZAPPEIO MEGARO

PYLI ADRIANOU

STYLOI OLYMPIOU DIOS

PANATHINAIKO STADIO

ARDITTOU HILL

Street names

SOLOMOU, KOLETTI, TZAVELLA, A. METAXSIOU, ALTETSIOU, ZOODOCHOU, TILEMACHOU, P. SERGIOU, NIKIF. OURANOU, DAFNOMILI, DOXAPATRI, SARANTAPICHOU, ROMANOU MELODOU, ASKL, DAMASKINOU, ARKA

SOULIOU, MESOLONGIOU, CHAR. TRIKOUPI, DERVENION, KORONIS, AG. ISIDOROU, CHRYS. SERRON

KIAFAS, GENNADIOU, NAVARINOU, MAVROMICHALI, IPPOKRATOUS, ASKLIPIOU, PATR. FOTIOU, LEONTOS SGOUROU

KAPLANON, DELFON, PRASSA, MERLIE, STATHA G., DIMAKI, CHERSONOS, OITIS, RONGAKOU, XANTHIPPOU, ARISTIPPOU

SINA, DIDOTOU, SKOUFA, MANTZAROU, OMIROU, LYKAVITTOU, DIMOKRITOU, ANAGNOSTOPOULOU, FOKYLIDOU, STR. SYNDESMOU, LOUKIANOU, GLYKONOS, SPEFSIPPOU, KLEOMENOUS, DEINOKRATOUS, ACHAIOU, XENOKRATOUS, PLOUTARCHOU, MARASLI

AKADIMIAS, RIGA FERAIOU, SINA, VISSARIONOS, AMERIKIS, VALAORITOU, AL. SOUTSOU, AKADIMIAS, PINDAROU, IRAKLEITOU, MILIONI, TSAKALOF, IRODOTOU, CHARITOS, PATR. IOAKEIM, ALOPEKIS

EDOUARDOU LO, STADIOU, VOUKOURESTIOU, KRIEZOTOU, ZALOKOSTA, KANARI, MERLIN, SEKERI, KAPSALI, KARAOLI DIMITRIOU, KARNEADOU, VAMVA, DOUKA N., PLOUTARCHOU

CHR., VOULIS, SERVIAS, VAS. GEORGIOU I, ERMOU, MITROPOLEOS, FILELLINON, XENOFONTOS, VAS. AMALIAS AVE., KOUMPARI, MOUROUZI, LIKIOU, STISICHOROU, RIGILIS, VAS.

NIKIS, SKOUROU, SOURI, IRODOU ATTIKOU, ISIODOU, VAS. GEORGIOU II, MELEAGROU, VAS. KONSTANTINOU AVE., KTISIOU, AMYNTA

DIMOU, KORROU, SIMONIDOU, TSATSOU K., DAIDALOU, ARAVANTINOU, AGRAS, EFORIONOS, FOKIANOU, AG. SPYRIDONOS, ARKTINOU, IRONDA, STASINOU, PAPSANIOU, ARRIANOU, TELESSILLIS, POLEMONOS, ELLANIKOU, FAIDROU

MON. ASTERIOU, PITTAROU, VAS. OLGAS AVE., ERATOSTHENOUS, THEOFRASTOU, IRONOS, IPPODAMOU, ARISTOXENOUS, NIKOSTHENOUS, EFRANORI

ARDITTOU, THEOTOU, TSIKLITIRA, ATHANASIAS

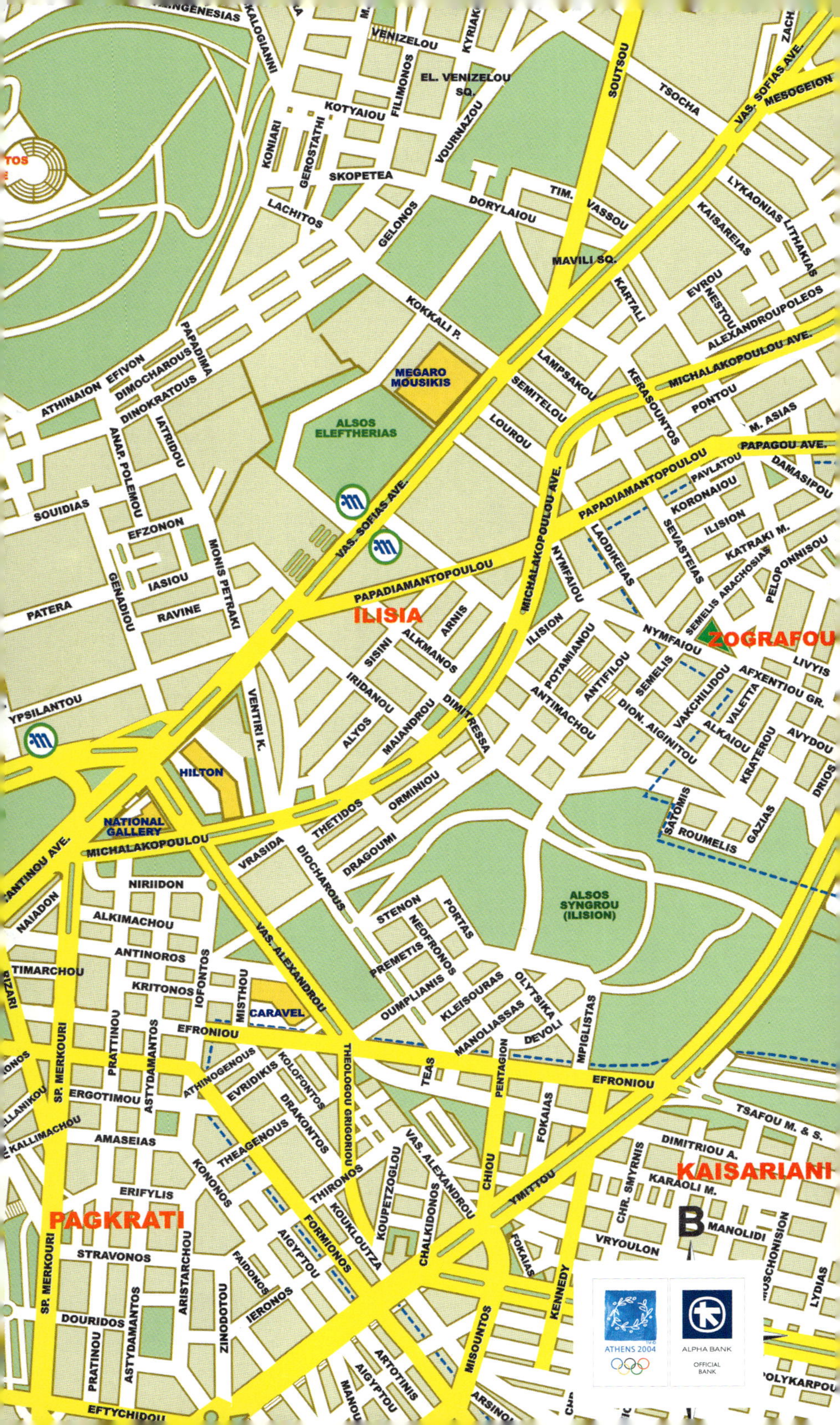
ILISIA
ZOGRAFOU
KAISARIANI
PAGKRATI
B
ALSOS ELEFTHERIAS
ALSOS SYNGROU (ILISION)
MEGARO MOUSIKIS
HILTON
NATIONAL GALLERY
CARAVEL
VAS. SOFIAS AVE.
MICHALAKOPOULOU AVE.
PAPADIAMANTOPOULOU
PAPAGOU AVE.
MESOGEION
VAS. ALEXANDROU
EFRONIOU
YMITTOU
SP. MERKOURI
EFTYCHIDOU
KENNEDY
SOUTSOU
TSOCHA
MAVILI SQ.
EL. VENIZELOU SQ.
TIM. VASSOU
DORYLAIOU
KOKKALI P.
LAMPSAKOU
SEMITELOU
LOUROU
KERASOUNTOS
PONTOU
M. ASIAS
DAMASIPOU
PAVLATOU
KORONAIOU
ILISION
KATRAKI M.
SEVASTEIAS
SEMELIS ARACHOSIAS
PELOPONNISOU
NYMFAIOU
LAODIKEIAS
LIVYIS
AFXENTIOU GR.
VALETTA
ALKAIOU
KRATEROU
AVYDOU
DRIOS
GAZIAS
ROUMELIS
SATOMIS
DION. AIGINITOU
VAKCHILIDOU
SEMELIS
ANTIFILOU
POTAMIANOU
ANTIMACHOU
DIMITRESSA
MAIANDROU
IRIDANOU
ALYOS
SISINI
ALKMANOS
ARNIS
ORMINIOU
THETIDOS
DRAGOUMI
DIOCHAROUS
VRASIDA
VENTIRI K.
MONIS PETRAKI
GENADIOU
PATERA
RAVINE
IASIOU
EFZONON
SOUIDIAS
ANAP. POLEMOU
IATRIDOU
DINOKRATOUS
DIMOCHAROUS
PAPADIMA
ATHINAION EFIVON
YPSILANTOU
ANTINOU AVE.
NAIADON
NIRIIDON
ALKIMACHOU
ANTINOROS
TIMARCHOU
RIZARI
KRITONOS
IOFONTOS
MISTHOU
STENON
NEOFRONOS
PORTAS
PREMETIS
OUMPLIANIS
KLEISOURAS
OLYTSIKA
MANOLIASSAS
DEVOLI
MPIGLISTAS
TEAS
PENTAGION
THEOLOGOU GRIGORIOU
FOKAIAS
CHIOU
TSAFOU M. & S.
DIMITRIOU A.
KARAOLI M.
CHR. SMYRNIS
VRYOULON
MANOLIDI
MOUSCHONISION
LYDIAS
POLYKARPOU
PRATTINOU
ASTYDAMANTOS
ERGOTIMOU
KALLIMACHOU
AMASEIAS
ERIFYLIS
STRAVONOS
DOURIDOS
PRATINOU
ARISTARCHOU
ZINODOTOU
IERONOS
FAIDONOS
AIGYPTOU
FORMIONOS
KOUKLOUTZA
THIRONOS
KOUPETZOGLOU
CHALKIDONOS
MISOUNTOS
ARTOTINIS
MANOU
ARSINOIS
ATHINOGENOUS
EVRIDIKIS
KOLOFONTOS
DRAKONTOS
THEAGENOUS
KONONOS
LACHITOS
GELONOS
SKOPETEA
GEROSTATHI
KONIARI
KOTYAIOU
FILIMONOS
VOURNAZOU
VENIZELOU
KYRIAKOU
KALOGIANNI
KAISAREIAS
LYKAONIAS
LITHAKIAS
EVROU
NESTOU
ALEXANDROUPOLEOS
KARTALI
ATHENS 2004
ALPHA BANK
OFFICIAL BANK

"One visit is not enough"
thought **Francois Mitterrand** after
re-election for the second time.

For the first time
Anthony Quinn felt like a real King.

Watch out!
His name is Moore. **Roger Moore**.

When **Jane Fonda met Ted Turner**.
After a while, they decided to buy CNN.

et into the star system!

ot of famous people have visited Astir Palace at Vouliagmeni, the
endary five star hotel near Athens, Greece. Now it is your turn. Get
e treatment you deserve: luxury, outstanding service, fun, action!
oose one of the three hotels, Arion, Nafsika or Aphrodite, and live
e dream! The magnificent view of the sea and the surrounding
ands are waiting for you. As well as everything else: three private
aches, one indoor and three outdoor swimming pools, seven bars,
nnis courts, a health club, all water sport facilities, and the
lyfada Golf Course". Whether for business or for pleasure, visit
tir Palace and get into the star system!

ASTIR PALACE VOULIAGMENI S.A. Affiliate of the National Bank of Greece
phone: ++3210 8902000, Fax: ++3210 8963194, E-mail: aspa-res@astir.gr, Website: www.astir.gr

ASTIR PALACE

Akti Vouliagmenis

headshots. On the broad beach, the fine sand and gently shelving bottom attract bathers of all ages. The very friendly staff at the water sports centre (mostly twentysomethings who did their military service in underwater commando units) will initiate you into the world of water skiing and wind surfing, or you can hire the motorboat for a trip from Voula to the little island of Fleves. Two of the highlights of this beach are the ruins of the Temple of Apollo (5th c. BC) and the modern wooden playground. A higher-priced ticket (€ 30 on weekdays and € 45 at weekends) gives you admittance to all the beaches and pools on the promontory, from the pool-like Aphrodite Beach to the "Zolotas", the secluded green cove named after the Greek politician and "Polar Bear" whose favourite spot it was. You might want to prolong your day at the beach by staying over at one of the resort's three complexes, or dining at one of its restaurants. Taverna 37 (Greek cuisine on the waterfront) is always reliable, while the Club House offers an unbeatable combo of gastronomic seafood cuisine and a fabulous view of the Saronikos Gulf.
Open: 8.30-18.00.
Admission: Mon.-Fri. € 8, Children € 4. Weekends and holidays € 11, Children € 5.
Info: 210/8902000.

Attiki Akti Vouliagmenis
The deep clean water, urban holiday atmosphere and proximity to the city make this a very popular beach. Taken over last year by the "Attikes Aktes" management company, the revamped Vouliagmeni Beach enjoys the warranty of an EU blue flag. The elegant wooden sun-beds, canvas umbrellas, brand new cabins, bars and wholly renovated washrooms, together with the modernisation of the entire infrastructure, have raised the standard significantly. There is also a First Aid Centre, operated by the Attica Medical Centre. Future plans include a variety of sports facilities, including 5X5 mini football pitches.
Open: 8.00-20.00.
Admission: € 3.
Info: 210/8960906.

Agios Kosmas Beach
As soon as you enter, the elegant aesthetics of the whole area with the attractively designed brick buildings immediately create a good impression. The beach is small (accommodating no more than 700 bathers), but is the only one with a signboard at the entrance to tell you when all the sun-beds are occupied! There is a snack bar (sandwiches and drinks) and areas for beach volley and racquets. Don't leave without having a look at the neighbouring Venue by day. Since the Olympic sailing events are to be held nearby, it

Divani Apollon Palace & Spa: the beach and the pool

is likely that construction work will be affecting the general image of the beach.
Open: 8.00 till sunset.
Admission: € 5, Children € 2.
Info: 210/9852993-4.

Limni Vouliagmenis

The scenery has a flavour of Central or Northern Europe, with abrupt rock faces encircling a small dark lake, isolating it from the surrounding area. A silent serenity pervades the place, while the "forbidden" caves at the far end create a sense of mystery.

Stay in the shallows unless you're a good swimmer: the heavier water doesn't have the buoyancy of the sea. The water temperature varies between 20? and 27?, and its therapeutic properties (for neuralgia and skin diseases) explain the relatively high average age of the bathers - in fact, the whole thing may remind you of a scene from "Cocoon".

! Don't miss

Grand Beach Lagonissi: Shiatsu massage with a view of the sea.
Asteria Seaside: Water trampoline and climbing "iceberg" for children ... of all ages; sunset parties and finger food at the poolside couches at the Balux Club.
Apollonia Akti Voulas: Hawaiian cocktails at the Hula Moon.
Limni Vouliagmenis: Absolute sense of mystery.

Around the lake there are umbrellas, sun-beds, showers and changing cabins, and plans for the renovation of the old hydrotherapy unit are in the pipeline. The cafe serves (until 14.00) mezedes, snacks and a daily special. The fish taverna Akti and the cafe Agnanti across the road are reliable places for a meal or an ice cream.
Open: 7.30-19.30.
Admission: € 4.50. Info: 210/8962237.

Akti Varkizas

The most recently privatised of the former Tourist Board beaches. Plans call for the creation of a seaside recreation area with mini football pitches, open-air cinemas, a separate playground and seasonal shops. Its very real advantages include clean broad sands and shallow water. The First Aid centre on the beach is operated by the Metropolitan Hospital. Another advantage is the proximity of the neighbouring swimming/sailing club (NAOBB), where you can take wind surfing, Optimist, Laser, kayak or swimming lessons (210/8974305). And don't be surprised if the faces of some of the sailboarders look familiar: that might well be Nikos Kaklamanakis zipping past you, since Greece's Olympic wind surfing champions put Varkiza high on their list of favourite spots.
Open: 8.00-20.00.
Admission: € 3, children under 5 free. Info: 210/8972438.

Now you can carry out your

You finally managed to get away for the weekend. You're already in a relaxed mode when you realize that... you forgot to pay your electricity bill. For some people, this would put a definite damper on their spirits, but for you, it means spending just a few minutes to take care of this minor inconvenience.

Because Alpha Bank is by your side, wherever you go. With a series of electronic services that include Alpha Web Banking, Alpha Bank m-Banking and Alphaphone, you can carry out your transactions 24 hours a day, easily, quickly and with complete security.

ALPHA WEB BANKING

Banking transactions via Internet

The service that offers you the opportunity to carry out, completely free of charge, a large range of banking transactions from hotels, airports, beaches, your home or your office, using your personal computer. Via Internet you have the opportunity to:

- Pay your utility bills (electricity - telephone - water), credit cards, mobile phone bills, subscription channels.

- Give instructions for money transfers from one account to another, either yours or a third person's.

- Access information on your account balance, the interest and transactions of your account and card.

banking transactions on the spot, no matter where you are

ALPHA BANK M-BANKING
Banking transactions via mobile telephone

If your mobile telephone has WAP technology, then this service offers you the opportunity to carry out all of the above transactions using your mobile telephone. You simply give instructions from your phone's keypad and read the results on your screen. So that when you're on vacation, you have complete freedom, wherever you are and whatever time or day it may be.

ALPHAPHONE
Banking transactions via telephone

The service that offers you the opportunity to carry out your banking transactions, completely free of charge and with just one call, even from abroad, and within seconds!
The electronic tele-service system Alphaphone connects you to Alpha Bank's Computer Center via a tone telephone. All you have to do is dial +210 326 6666, listen to the instructions and dial the corresponding keys on your telephone. Alphaphone does the rest.

Save time! Become a subscriber to Alpha Web Banking, Alpha Bank m-Banking or Alphaphone. Fill out the corresponding subscription application form and drop it off, together with the necessary supporting documents, at your nearest Alpha Bank Branch, today!

OF THE ATHENS 2004 OLYMPIC GAMES

Limanaki Vouliagmenis (the second cove)

Thymari: Kyra-Antigoni's taverna

FREE BEACHES

FAMILIAR AND YET UNKNOWN

Along the hundreds of kilometres of coastline around the Prefecture of Attica, there are bays and beaches for every taste. The wilder South, with both rocky and sandy shores, emanates a sense of freedom and serenity. In this hottest and most expensive stretch of coastline, the luxurious summer properties extend from Lagonissi to Sounio, impressive new resorts are springing up and property prices exceed 3,000 € / m². In the east, the various beaches are inextricably linked to resort centres. Diving at Erotospilia, wind surfing off Loutsa, clubbing till dawn at Porto Rafti. Farther north, from Oropos and Kalamos all the way to the Prefecture of Voiotia, you will find family beaches and beaches for all-day fun at the beach bar.

SOUTH

Rocky shores and sandy bays, expensive summer houses and cult cafes, swimming in the shadow of the Temple of Poseidon at Sounio, diving to the shipwreck off Patroclos Island, midnight bathing under the full moon in the second cove (Deftero Limanaki) at Vouliagmeni. Southern Attica, with its wealth and varied scenery, will enchant you.

VOULIAGMENI

Deftero Limanaki Vouliagmenis (second cove)

Held within the rocky embrace of the Attic coastline, this cove is mainly popular with the young. To get there, you have to walk (unless you have a jeep) down a short track with a panoramic view of the deep dark water. On the rocks around the long, narrow cove there is room for everyone: groups of teenagers mark off their territory with music blaring from portable radios, nudists seek out the quieter corners, bright bikinis bake on the multi-level wooden decks, diving schools explore the natural well in the area or take off for the open sea in their Zodiacs. The loungers settle in at the wooden bars by the water, sipping their coffee or beer in the shade of the overhang. The cafe-bar stays open till the wee hours, part and parcel of an idyllic summer moonlight scene. After your (morning or evening) swim, the cult place to go

CHOOSE YOUR BEACH

We have grouped the free beaches in the prefecture by area (north, south and east), and present them here in order, moving counter clockwise from the south. Each beach is described in detail (sea, morphology, facilities), and at the end of each section you will find information on where to eat, what to buy and where to stay, should you decide to hang around the area a little longer.

Sounio

Eden Beach

Beaches

for coffee is the canteen bar and biker stop just above Deftero Limanaki.

ANAVYSSOS
Eden - Thymari

All along the coast from Anavyssos to Legraina you will find many beaches populated by a mixture of day-trippers (Greek families out for a Saturday or Sunday at the beach) and summer residents. Broad sands, dotted here and there with tamarisk, and a gently shelving, moderately stony, sea floor. One of the best is the beach in front of the Eden hotel, which sports one of the EU's blue flags. Fine sand and relatively stone-free (for the area) turquoise water. Amenities include a water sports centre, snack bar, changing rooms,

sun-beds, umbrellas, toilets and showers, designed to meet the requirements of the (mostly foreign) hotel guests but open to "non-hotel guests" as well.

A little farther along the road, on Souniou Ave., you come to Thymari, with a similar sea but no facilities other than a small but pleasant playground. The two benches, deep in the shade of the pine trees alongside, invite you to choose your favourite ice cream from the little shop across the way and savour it as you gaze languidly at the little island of Argenta. "Where to eat" in Thymari means Kyra-Antigoni's taverna (on the Sounio road), where everything is prepared from fresh local ingredients: milk and cheese from her sheep, eggs from her hens, meat from the flocks that pasture on the slopes

INFO - SOUTH

Where to stay
Divani Apollon Palace & Spa
(10, Agiou Nikolaou St. & Il.Iliou, Kavouri Vouliagmenis, 210/8911100) The renovated Apollon at Kavouri can now fairly be called a resort.
Asteras Vouliagmenis
(40, Apollonos St., Vouliagmeni, 210/8902000) One of the finest hotel complexes in Greece.
Eden Beach
(km 47 Athens-Sounio road, Anavyssos, 22910/60031) Large holiday complex, with attractive gardens and an underground passage to the beach.
Grand Resort Lagonissi
(km 40 Athens-Sounio road,

Lagonissi, 22910/76000) Attica's finest resort (at the moment). Standard double rooms in the main building, luxury bungalows in the gardens.
Neptune Villas
(Pounta Zeza, at the turn for the Olympic Marine of Lavrio, 22920/22171/5) 2-storey villas (sleeping up to 5) on the shore.
The Margi
(11, Litous St., Laimos Vouliagmenis, 210/8962061) Small hotel offering a holiday atmosphere in an urban setting.

Where to eat
Akrogiali
(Sounio, 22920/39107) The defini-

nearby and fish brought in by the local fishing fleet! Better book ahead, though, because the place fills up quickly.

SOUNIO

Legraina

The distance from Athens discourages most beach-goers, allowing those who persist (mainly families and couples) to enjoy relative peace and quiet. Once you've passed the only stoplight on Souniou Ave., you'll come to a dry area that looks like the Wild West. Turn right, and look for the bay in front of the abandoned Hotel Amphitriti. The turquoise water and sandy beach framed by low trees and bushes with red flowers make a charming setting for a picnic. Better avoid the classic beach to the left of the fishing port at Legraina. Although the broad sands are very enticing (note the miniature sand dunes), there are large stony slabs in the shallows that make bathing awkward. On the other side of the bay you will see a whole string of little beaches. The nearest ones, which are just as attractive and relatively more isolated, are easy to get to, by the bush-ridden path leading up the hill. In the village of Legraina, on

the other side of the highway, you will find a mini market and Stamoulis' taverna - his earthenware pot-roasted meats are delicious. And there are always the fish tavernas a little farther down the road, beside the highway.

Temple of Poseidon

Sounio calls up an idyllic image of swimming in blue water at the foot of the Temple of Poseidon. Unfortunately, the morphology of the terrain means that only the most daring (or commando-trained) will actually be able to put themselves in the picture. From the top of the cliff you can peer down at two deserted cave-like "beaches" at the foot of the temple. Fishing addicts and thrill-seekers may attempt the descent, but most people will prefer the tamer and more accessible beach, with a view of the Temple, in front of the adjacent Hotel Aigaio. On the sands there are trees and umbrellas with sun-beds for hotel guests (mainly foreign), while an accumulation of details make up a picturesque and wholly typical Greek summer scene: two tiny tavernas overlooking the sea, the waterfront one awash with flowers, its tables covered with blue and white check tablecloths, and

tion of the picturesque fish taverna: awash with flowers and right on the water, with a view of the Temple of Poseidon.

Asimakis
(km 60 Lavrio-Sounio road, Sounio, 22920/39442) Fish, by the sea.

Kyra-Antigoni
(km 55 Sounio Ave., Thymari, 22910/39367) Everything from her own... barn, from meat to milk.

Stamoulis
(Legraina, 22920/51147) Lamb and chicken cooked in an earthenware pot.

Syrtaki
(km 69 Athens-Sounio road,

Sounio, 22920/39125) Good Greek cooking with a view of the sea.

Trigono
(36, Athinon St., Kalyvia, 22990/48540) Exceptional meats from Mytilini.

What to buy

Ideal Fresh Gelateria
(2, Saronidas Ave., Saronida) Many of the unusual flavours (e.g. Blue Curacao and bubble gum) from the Kayak dairy.

Fruit stalls
(on the Sounio shore road) Fresh fruit (figs-grapes) and vegetables from around the area of Markopoulo.

a wooden jetty pointing to colourful fishing boats bobbing at their moorings... A few luxury yachts farther out provide a discreet reminder that we are on one of the higher-class stretches of the Attic coastline. For the rest, you can always combine a good swim with acknowledgement of the exceptional archaeological interest of the site - with an afternoon visit to the Temple, for example. This will assure a magical finale, with the postcard perfection of a sunset witnessed from the temple.

EAST

Cosmopolitan Porto Rafti swims and clubs at Erotospilia and Kalua, Nea Makri sunbathes in front of La Costa, organises dives, swims at the picturesque Kokkino Limanaki (= red cove) and has "beer battles" at Prova, the more popular Loutsa raises kitsch to cult status at Agios Nikolaos beach, while the sea breezes up and down the coast fill the sails of the sailboards. Past Marathon, the summer villas thin out and the day-trippers take over. From the family-oriented pine forest of Schinias and the crazy young crowd at the Karavi beach club to the deserted rocks of Dikastika, the Ancient Greek air of Ramnous or the paradise of the free camping site at Sesi, there is a place on the shoreline for everyone.

PORTO RAFTI
Kakia Thalassa

Open to the currents of the Evoiko Channel, with deep and often turbulent water -the swimming is wonderful. Kakia Thalassa is the port that serves Keratea (a small and not particularly pretty village), and it dominates this superb coast surrounded by huge rocks - wholly unlike the nearby but more conventional Daskaleio. It is, of course, an open secret. At weekends a fair number of people flock to it, mainly families from the neighbouring countryside, but it is large enough not to appear crowded. Avoid days with an onshore wind: the waves will pile heaps of seaweed on the beach. Amenities: coffee shop, playground, small shallow pool, shower-heads and an open-air cinema for the evening. There is another coffee shop a little farther back. The choice of what to eat is simple: fish or fish. The best-known taverna is Giorgaki's, the first one you come to as the road turns toward the sea. The menu is rather limited, but the service is impeccable - even on busy Sundays. If you don't want fish, go back to Keratea and head for Kalyvia (about 10 km), where you will find Trigono, one of the most famous chasapotavernas ("butcher's" taverna, where they cut their own meat) in the region.

PATROCLOS ISLAND

Lost in the vastness of the sea, off the coast between Thymari and Sounio, is a speck of land: the rocky islet of Patroclos. Its lovely sandy beaches are all the more attractive for being easy to get to: About 300 metres past km 60 on Leoforos Souniou, turn right at the Kasidiara area and ask for Kyrios Kostas (22910/37326), who will take you across in his boat. This shuttle service starts at 10.00 and continues - every 10 minutes - till 20.00 (fare € 5).

Porto Rafti Beach

One of the stalwarts of the Greek family holiday! Most summer visitors converge on the main beach, each planting a beach umbrella to stake out their few square metres of sand. Water wings, buckets and spades, rackets and balls run riot under the sun, Zodiacs skim over the waves in the distance, and the older generation retire to the shade of the tamarisk trees. Picturesque notes are supplied by the little church of St Spyridon and the fishing boats off to the left. To the right, a pavilion serves as a beach bar, while on the basketball court the nets are waiting for the day when their broken backboards will be replaced. The holiday resort atmosphere is heightened by the fresh fruit and vegetable stalls set up in the parking lot behind the beach. If you get hungry, Avlaki is the best place for fresh fish and Bibikos for tasty fish mezedes.

Erotospilia

Despite the romantic name (= lovers' cave), the beach at Erotospilia is no longer an idyllic secret. This small sandy bay bordered by rocks and small caves attracts many people from Porto Rafti and Athens, who arrive in two "shifts": families with young children in the morning, and their seniors after lunch around 2 pm, when the sand toys and water wings are replaced by racquets and beach fun. A pavilion overlooking the sea in the shade of the pines provides the necessary: soft drinks, beer, sandwiches and cheese pies. In addition to his other duties, the amiable Thanasis also keeps the beach clean, removing every morning the traces of the previous day's occupation. The water gets deep quite suddenly and the bottom, a mosaic of stone, sand and rocks, offers undersea explorers the surprise of a "shipwrecked" sunken automobile. If you swim out into

Erotospilia

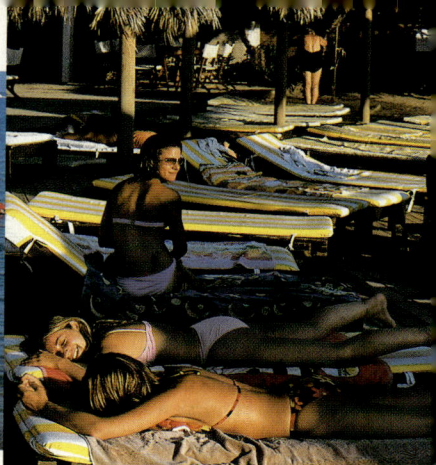

open water, the enclosed bay of Porto Rafti (which appears almost in its entirety) looks like a large lake, and the pyramid-shaped island opposite Erotospilia is a curious sight. A little farther along, handsome houses dot the green hill behind the beach, next to the glamorous Apollo resort complex. The Erotospilia beach is itself the access to a number of private houses - with their own private beaches - farther down the shore. That is why there is a "no entry" sign on the road to the beach, and a picturesque old gentleman who serves as a parking attendant, assuring a clear passage for the local VIPs. Your own access will be harder, especially at the weekend, for space is limited.

But if you want something more for your trouble, go to the miniature Erotospilia, which is far more worthy of the name. Head up the dirt road to the left of the bar (on foot or by motorcycle), sneak a quick look at the gardens of the luxury villas and, after about five minutes walk, turn right down a leafy path towards the sea. The narrow rocky cove on the right is a favourite haunt of young lovers who come up from Athens and of the dressy local teenagers, who appear on the beaches decked out in the latest word in fashion beach wear. At weekends, of course, even this bit of coast fills up with gangs of kids who scramble up the rocks and dive off "Acapulco-fashion". For the full flavour of the

most cosmopolitan resort in Attica, head for the main drag of Porto Rafti after your swim and relax over a freddo or a cappuccino in one of the many waterfront cafes. If the green slopes on the other side of the bay weren't so built up with blocks of flats, you could mistake the place for one of the Greek islands.

As for the local night life, the clubs in Avlaki can match just about anything in Athens. Some of them, in fact, are Athenian: the Kalua, for example, is spending its third summer here, on a huge pier that is now also used for daytime beach parties. By day, stretch out on your sun-bed and dig into a giant fruit salad - half a watermelon filled with bits of just about any seasonal fruit you can think of. In the evening - and especially Friday and Saturday nights - the place goes wild, with the beats mounting dangerously. Along the same strip, the Bossa Tres (mainstream music), the Congas' Lounge (lounge and freestyle), the Del Mar (freestyle and "black sound") and the Dance Floor (good electronic music) complete the entertainment landscape, making Porto Rafti the king of summertime clubbing.

VRAVRONA - ARTEMIS
Chamolia
This little strip of sand is the easy answer for those spending the summer at Vravrona. The shallow water is a magnet for families with

young children, their seniors prefer the nearby basketball courts, and the large kiosk-shop sells just about everything you might require. About 200 metres farther on, the smooth rocks offer an alternative base for quiet bathing. Enjoy the deep cool water and, while you're sunbathing, watch the little crabs scuttling in and out of the cracks in the rocks. If you walk along to the headland of this rocky cove, you'll find yourself in a little crescent of sand - an easier way into the water. On the road from Vravrona to Chamolia, do stop to have a look at the little temple of Artemis.

Agios Nikolaos
Artemidos Beach

This is such a popular beach it's almost a cult. The broad sands and the - annoyingly - shallow water are packed with noisy humanity - families, gangs of teenagers, pensioners. You'll retain some very picturesque images out of this colourful human mosaic: the grandfather enjoying a stately swim in his captain's cap with his pipe alight, the kids with their wallets and cell phones tucked into their bathing suits, the Africans flogging CDs with the latest hot hits to the

beach backgammon enthusiasts. Crowning the whole scene, which is worthy of Almodovar, is the amazing beach bar reigning at the left end of the beach: '70s style lounge furniture set out on the beach and a straw roof fringed with bird cages complete with canaries.
A little farther to the left, sailboard-mania has created an entirely different scene: two clubs serve as bases for those who prefer the winds on this side of the mainland. Summer and winter alike, dozens of sails can be seen darting across the bay. And when they return to shore, the Austrian sailboard coach Paul (22940/24823) and the all day windsurfing club Aiolos (22940/26326) are there to talk over the day's sailing. Both places offer lessons, as well as sailboard storage. Finally, serious fish eaters will wind up their day at the beach with a meal at the Xypolitos fish taverna in Agios Nikolaos.

RAFINA
Marikes Beach

One of the most popular destinations for day trips from Athens in the 1960s (perhaps this is why songwriter Vasilis Tsitsanis, cites it

INFO - PORTO RAFTI, VRAVRONA, ARTEMIS

Where to stay
Mare Nostrum Club Med
(Akti Vravronas, 22940/48412) Club Med specifications and thalassotherapy centre.
Kyani Akti (km 40 Agias Marinas St., Porto Rafti, 22990/86401) Small hotel, recently renovated, right on the seafront.

Where to eat
Avlaki (108, Avlakiou Ave., Avlaki - Porto Rafti, 22990/87663) Fresh fish by the water.
Ippokampos (2, Thessalonikis St., next to the town hall, Gerakas, 210/6047456) Fish from Evoia, in a taverna that has fed just about

every politician in the country.
Psaropoula-Bibikos (118, Avlakiou Ave., Avlaki - Porto Rafti, 22990/71292) Number one for fish mezedes.
Xypolitos (1, G. Papandreou & 25 Martiou St., Agios Nikolaos, Loutsa Beach, 22940/28342) Fresh fish backed by fifty years of tradition - an unbeatable combination.

What to buy
Kayak Ice Cream (Alonistra Industrial Zone, Koropi, 210/6628466) Your road back from Koropi takes you very near the home of Kayak gourmet ice creams - why not stock up while you're here?

Kokkino Limanaki

Artemis

as the place of assignation of his immortal pair of lovers ... the bream and the crab!) As the area developed into a major port and important urban centre, its character as a focal point for excursions petered out. As a comfortable seaside town, of course, Rafina has beaches that are mainly frequented by the locals. Marikes is a fairly large beach, with a place for everyone: the local old-timers sit in the shade of the trees on the left side of the beach, the teenagers wait for the sun to go down at the little bar (Akri) to the right or come back there at sunset, and there is plenty of room in the middle for playing racquets and football and beach volley. The great slabs in the shallows that catch the water in little pools are a relic of history and the German Occupation.

Kokkino Limanaki

Although the name ("little red cove") suggests something tiny, Kokkino Limanaki is actually rather extensive. The red in the affair is justified by the colour of the long hill forming the backbone of the coastline (and providing welcome shade in the afternoon), while the green of the bushes and the stone of the serpentine benches add cheerful notes to the scene. The shore has both fine pebbles and sand, and the seaweed that washes ashore when the waves build up never seems to bother the families and couples that visit this beach. The signposting on the roads in this area is not all it should be, and to find Kokkino Limanaki you will have to be on the watch on the last kilometre of the Rafina-Mati

In the area of Markopoulo there are a number of Byzantine churches dating from the 12th century. Those particularly worth visiting are: Panagia Mesoporitissa in Merrenta, Gennisi tis Theotokou and Panagia Varampa in Vravrona, and the twin churches of Ag. Paraskevi and Ag. Thekla in Markopoulo.

road, so as not to miss the steps that lead down to the shore. You can of course always go down through the Kokkino Limanaki campgrounds, but there are more steps that way. After your swim, make your way up to the cafe-restaurant Balkoni, which serves tasty Greek dishes on a terrace overlooking the shore from on high.

NEA MAKRI
Zoumperi

Popular with summer people from Mati, Zoumperi and Nea Makri, and usually crowded. Here the sands are divided into two distinct zones: the area belonging to the vast beach bar La Costa, and that belonging to the "thematic" Divers Club. At La Costa everything is oversize, from the numberless tables to the gigantic umbrellas and the huge parking lot. The sandy beach is the domain of a youthful crowd that gathers from all around to enjoy hours in the sun, watch the sunset and dance the night (and day) away to powerful beats. Down the beach, the scuba divers have set up their own waterfront club, serving coffee and fresh juices. The agenda here includes games of beach volley and beach football, diving from the club boat to interesting underwater sites up and down the coast, and meticulous keeping of the log book. If you're not intending to dive the next day, the mainstream club Prova monopolises night life in Nea Makri, with happenings including everything from beauty contests and guest DJs to water fights

that are the stuff of legend. Its day-time brother, the beach bar Prova (a few kilometres farther along, towards Marathonas), attracts the fashionable youth of the region and the northern suburbs of Athens. Day clubbing usually ends with spectacular "beer battles", with empty beer cans used as missiles by the enthusiastic crowd.

Those who holiday at Mati either stay on the small coves and "mili-tary" beach of Agios Andreas (a wire fence separates the free part of the beach from the end belong-ing to the Greek Army's holiday complex), or go to neighbouring beaches like Kokkino Limanaki and Zoumperi.

Nea Makri Beach
Extends from the Nireas Hotel to the taverna Avra and is divided into smaller stretches of sand punctuated by rocks. The clean water and gently shelving bottom and the

(well-spaced) umbrellas provided by the Municipality of Nea Makri attract all sorts and conditions. The biggest and most open stretch of sand, which is obviously the most popular, is the section to the right of the little harbour of Nea Makri (looking from the shore).

MARATHON
Schinias - Karavi
The word 'Schinias' means three different things to the pre-2004 Athenian: a green pine forest by the sea, cool beats in the kingdom of beach-clubbing Karavi, and the (awaited) Olympic rowing site. Although construction work at various points on Marathonos Ave-nue makes access difficult, Schinias and Karavi are still two of the most popular beaches in Attica. Schinias is a combination of endless sands, pine trees and little tavernas in the shade. Marathonos Avenue runs for several kilometres along-

Karavi - Schinias

side the pine forest on the right and is intersected at numerous points by short tracks leading down to the endless shore. The sandy beach and shallow water have the feel of an immense playground, with hordes of small children turned loose to enjoy themselves with their buckets and spades (unfortunately, all too often the family's rubbish is turned loose as well). This is also where the summer camps in the neighbourhood bring their campers to swim (the areas near the end of the beach are generally the quietest). Be patient as you walk out in search of deeper water: you will eventually get to a depth of 2-2.5 metres of clean, clear turquoise water, where you can swim in (relative) peace. When you come out again, don't resist the temptation to sit down at one of the tables set out on the sand by the sea in the

shade of the pines for an ouzo. If you head for the other end of the beach, leaving the picturesque element behind, you will enter another dimension of this seaside world, as defined by the beach club Karavi: noisy groups of students, voluptuous bikinis, well-built lifeguards, sun-tanned wind surfers, bananas and tubes, enough balls and racquets to carpet the whole beach, all to the rhythm of a cool powerful beat. It was the Karavi that first brought the concept of beach fun to Attica, organising whole series of events and tournaments in a modern place with lots of sports grounds, greenery and cool beat bars with wooden decks. Annual wind surfing, beach football and beach volley tournaments are held here, interspersed with events like the aerobic marathon and the string (!) contest. Another hot feature of Karavi is sail boarding

Stop at the Tomb of Marathon to pay tribute to the brave warriors of the Battle of Marathon, and visit the Archaeological Museum with its collection of important finds from the region.

If you're in the area of Vravrona, do visit the ruins of the ancient Temple of Artemis and the neighbouring archaeological museum.

INFO - MARATHON

Where to stay
Athenia Club Med
(Marathon, 210/9301191) A small village with all Club Med services.
Leon Anti Village Inn
(Schinia shore, Marathon, 22940/56910) Attractive complex with bungalows.
Marathon (25, Agiou Panteleimonos St., Marathon, 22940/55122) Recently renovated, right on the waterfront.
Ramnous Camping (Rizari - Schinias, 22940/55855) 115 sites, with several services.

Where to eat
Kavouri (Marathon shore,

22940/55243) Fresh fish, modern environment, by the sea.
Kali Kardia (221, Schinias Ave., 22940/63353) Good meat and freshly cut potatoes.
Ta Tria Adelfia (Marathon shore, 22940/56461) Delectable fish mezedes, by the sea.

What to buy
Perivoli tou Kyr Diamanti (shortly before the Tomb at Marathon) Organic products and fresh produce.
Steki tou Bakoula (Marathonos Ave., past Nea Makri) Ewe's milk ice cream and yoghurt.

Prova Club, Nea Makri

Dikastika

champion Toni Fran, on hand to initiate newcomers into the secrets of her sport. On the negative side: the shallow water that wears you (and your patience) out before you get more than knee-deep, and the probability that your search for a free sun-bed will prove to be a long-term activity. Other beach clubs are beginning to spring up in the vicinity of the Karavi (Cafe del Mar, Schinias Bay '04), multiplying the fun potential of the area.

Dikastika

If the idea of a rocky shore with deep turquoise water tickles your fancy, then come and have a look at Dikastika (near Marathonas). Leave the shallow water and crowded beach of Schinias behind, and follow the road up to the development called "Dikastika". The environment here is totally different, with the flat bay of Marathonas ending in a rocky headland. Sheer cliffs with touches of green create a sense of wildness, which is softened by the scattered small villas. The well-tended properties, in conjunction with the serpentine slopping road and the American-style rectangular green road signs, have something of the flavour of the resort hills of the west coast of America. Take the second turn into the development and, just before the road ends, leave your car and continue along a short green path. At weekends, the cool shade attracts hordes of families with their straw mats and beach chairs, who jostle for a place under the pine trees - and leave behind them a full complement of rubbish.

Keep on going, and you will come to the large slab of rock that serves as the main beach, forming smaller semi-separate coves on either side. The rock that separates them is so high in places that it looks like the wall of a tumble-down house, creating a physical barrier from any "neighbours". In the deep, clear greeny-blue water you may well spot columns of strange rising bubbles, or bits of diving gear or even frogmen - this area is often used by the diving schools of the city's northern suburbs. Follow their traces (as far as you comfortably can, of course), and explore the interesting rocky depths with mask and flippers. Note that access to the water is not easy here, since there are no steps, decks or docks to help you over the rocks. As for supplies, on the way to Dikastika you will see a sign for the "Magazaki tou Schinia", the little shop at Schinia, which sells - among other things - ice water that is literally ice. And you can buy fresh fruit and vegetables from the roadside stands. The nearest tavernas, with a view of the sea from the shade of the pines, are just a few kilometres away, on the beach at Schinias. For fish and mezedes, go to Kavouri or Tria Adelfia, and for meat (roasts or on the spit) to Kali Kardia.

NORTH

The ancient Athenians used to go to Kalamos and the sanctuary of Amphiaraos to be cured of their mental and bodily ills. Today's Athenians go for a different sort

CYPRUS

CYPRUS AIRWAYS

Cyprus
Tourism Organisation
One Island, A World of Options

‹ History: The Island's tumultuous past is evident from the large number of ancient sites and monuments which go back to 10000 years.

‹ Nature: Situated at the crossroad of three continents, Cyprus enjoys a mild climate, offers a wide variety of landscape and favors a rich and inique flora and fauna.

‹ Accomodation: There are many fine hotels from large and luxurious to small and simple - from the grandeur of the international chain to the convenience of hotel apartments with self catering facilities as well as traditional houses in remote villages.

‹ Gastronomy: Cyprus cuisine is particularly varied and delicious, Mediterranean in character. "Koupepia", "Sheftalia", "Afelia" and "Haloumi" are some of the most traditional dishes you can expect to be served.

‹ Alternative Tourism: Impressive thalassotherapy spas, maritime tourism, agrotourism, conference centres, multiple adventures! Whatever you are looking for - you will find it here! In the year - round light and warmth of the Cyprus Mediterranean sun.

Cyprus Tourism Organisation: 38 Voukourestiou St. Athens, 210/3610178, 210/3610057.
A panorama of information for Cyprus in our website: www.visitcyprus.org.cy

of release: swimming, clubbing and dining by the sea. The coast of Oropos - the king of the 70's - is very similar, with beach clubs stretching right to the borders of the Prefecture of Attica.

OROPOS

Agioi Apostoloi / Kalamos Shore (Rera, Agona)

The first thing that comes into the mind of the lifestyle-conscious Athenian who hears the word "Kalamos" is the club-restaurant Alekos: the popular club and excellent restaurant with the designer French Provincial interior are always a favourite with the Athenian crowds. And of course a night out at Aleko's can easily be combined with a swim at a nearby beach, either as an afternoon prelude or as an early morning finale. Day clubbing is synonymous with Agona beach, being the basic activity of both the local beat generation and of the day-trippers who come out from Athens. The young crowd gathers at the beach club Agona for frappes in the garden, volleyball or racquetball on the courts, sunbathing on the beach and wind surfing off shore.

At Rera beach, a little farther along (towards Agioi Apostoloi), things are quieter. There are fewer people on the pebble beach or in the clear turquoise water, and Agamemnon and Kochyli are both good places for a tranquil meal. Near here are both the

---

INFO - NORTH

Where to stay

Agamemnon (Rera - Kalamos shore, 22950/83806) Small family hotel.

Alkyonis Hotel (Markopoulo shore, Oropos, 22950/32490) Excellent sea view. Renovations nearly complete.

Calamos Beach (Rera - Kalamos shore, 22950/81465) Large '60s-style hotel with a manmade sand beach.

Paradise Hotel (Athinon Ave. - Skala Oropos, from Malakasa, 22950/35965) Particularly well-kept small hotel.

Where to eat

Agamemnon (Rera, Kalamos shore, 22950/84708) The red courtyard by the sea has an Aegean island air about it. Grilled fish and meats, cooked dishes.

Amphiaraeia (Agioi Apostoloi shore, 22950/81249) The freshest fish in the area, within a "homely" courtyard.

Batis (Agioi Apostoloi shore, 22950/81276) Tradition in fresh fish, in nicely kept surroundings.

Giannis Tsadaris (Afidnes, 22950/22745) Country-style bread, home-made pies and delicious lamb chops, on a lovely terrace.

Koutsoukos (Afidnes, 22950/22213) Traditional pan-bread and lamb chops in the shade of the plane trees next to the picturesque railway station in Afidnes.

Paralia (Chalkoutsi Oropos, 22950/71288) Fresh fish in a simple setting.

Entertainment

Alekos club restaurant (Agioi Apostoloi, 22950/82338) Designer French Provincial: mediaeval monastery meets modern design. People come out from Athens both for the soigne Mediterranean cuisine and the cool beats at the club.

Atlantis Club (on the road between Skala Oropos and Chalkoutsi, 22950/31832) Gothic decor, dance delirium and large garden. Lounge atmosphere around the pool at the Atlantis Prive.

Watersplash (on the road between Skala Oropos and Chalkoutsi, 22950/37570, 10.30-19.30, admission € 8, under 12 € 6.50) Attractive small water park.

Karvounoskala

Alekos club-restaurant, Kalamos

Agamemnon Hotel and the Calamos Beach, which has covered its
stretch of beach with sand and set
out umbrellas and sun-beds. At
Agioi Apostoloi, family groups and
summer residents gravitate to the
long narrow central beach: parents, small children, grannies and
string-clad nymphs rub elbows
under the tamarisks on the pebble
beach, while the broad pavement
is transformed into a pitch for racquets and football. Strung out on
the other side of the narrow road
are a whole row of fish tavernas,
and the small sailboats bobbing
about in the bay complete the picture of summertime. For fresh fish,
go to Batis taverna, Amphiaraeia
with its homely courtyard or
Agamemnon (the garden and Aegean island atmosphere are very
refreshing). For your frappe or
freddo, there are many places
along the waterfront, but we particularly like the light and stylish
Alekos Cafe (Haagen Dazs ice
cream and sweets) and the cafe-
bar Agnanti with its no-limits view
of Evoia. Or combine swimming at
Kalamos with an excursion to the
verdant slopes of Mount Parnitha
and a meal in one of the appetising
tavernas in Afidnes or Agios
Merkourios.

Oropos - Nea Palatia

Ask any Athenian where to go for
a swim and a coffee by the sea, and
the answer will probably be
Oropos. The water is deep, and
the pebble beach dotted with

straw umbrellas extends literally
for kilometres, attracting bathers
of all ages and situations: families,
pensioners, parties of teenagers,
romantic couples. Doughnut-sell-
ers wander up and down the
beach with large trays on their
heads, hot dog vendors do a roar-
ing trade, and an orange pavilion
(in both colour and shape) sells
soft drinks and fruit juice. The
teenage end of the beach is clearly
demarcated by the beach bar
Karvounoskala, featuring a DJ as its
highlight who operates from the
lifeguard's tower. From time to
time the municipal authorities ban
the bar's wooden installations from
the beach, and then the Karvounoskala remains limited to the far
side of the road. Whatever the situation, this part of the beach has
a steady clientele that happily alternates between bathing and clubbing all day and all night.
A little farther along, you can hire
a pedal-boat or play beach volley
on the public pitch. Other leisure
attractions include the cute Watersplash (water slides and lazy
river), a go-kart track and a campi-
onato mundialito 5x5 pitch, all on
the road leading out of Skala Oropos towards Chalkoutsi. Coffee
with a view of the sea from one of
the cafes in the harbour (Aithrio,
Aqua, Mango Beach) is a must,
while the fashion mainstream
Atlantis Club with its huge garden
and the easy listening Atlantis Prive
are reason enough to prolong your
stay into the evening.

time
and
money

ATHENS 2004

ALPHA BANK
OFFICIAL
BANK

They say that when you have the time you don't have the money, and vice versa.
Alpha Bank knows that our time is as valuable as our money, and offers us a way to
enjoy it, with a comprehensive series of Alpha Consumer Loans.
Alpha Consumer Loans have been designed to cover the needs of contemporary living,
by offering significant advantages, such as immediate approval of the amount of the
loan, favourable interest rates and flexible repayment systems. All with no hassle or
time wasted.
With the Alpha Consumer Loans time is on our side!

ALPHA BANK OFFICIAL BANK OF THE ATHENS 2004 OLYMPIC GAMES

Leisure

Athens Guide 2003

ATHENS 2004™

ALPHA BANK
OFFICIAL BANK

under
the sign
of well-being

From gyms, spas and beauty centres to swimming pools, riding clubs and tennis courts, quality facilities for leisure activities that help cultivate fitness and well-being have been multiplying like mushrooms in Athens in recent years. The only sure guide to maximum enjoyment of the luxuries of leisure is proper information about the services available in this city. In the pages that follow you will find a list of carefully selected places that, in one way or another, offer beauty, fitness and relaxing activities for your leisure hours.

All listings have the wherewithal to provide genuine services in a responsible manner - neither poor imitations of other facilities or promising more than they can perform. The city spas that lead off this section are real urban spas exploiting the beneficial effects of water. These, of course, do not include those institutes that, in their agonised efforts to bring their facilities up to date, squeezed some tubs into their already over-crowded premises and purchased the odd thalassotherapy product.

Nor do they include the large and well-advertised slimming centres, on the one hand because these are so easy to find if anyone should want one, and on the other because our readers are used to seeking more personal service, especially when it comes to health and beauty.

The gyms we list include both classic and alternative facilities. The

Relaxing massage

Universal

Cocoon Urban Spa

Yoga exercises

classic gyms we chose as "impressive productions", well-equipped places that offer variety, flexibility and a bit of socializing. The alternative gyms are more "monastic" in style, for initiates of contemporary holistic pursuits, where the object is not luxury but cleanliness and dedication. What is important, however, is less your individual preference - many people dabble in both equally successfully - but taking regular care of your body.

When it comes to beauty care, there have been great changes in the city in recent years. Beauty centres are both numerous and good; beauty counsellors have introduced trends from London and New York that have won an immediate response from Greek women, who are both coquettish and always willing to try something new; hair salons have been transformed into luxury studios with much higher standards and improved services; and the beauty institutes (some of them, at least) are gradually morphing into spas or centres offering laser treatments and minor plastic surgery. As for the laser treatment and plastic surgery centres, we believe that they will gradually

replace the classic beauty institutes, since they are staffed by both aestheticians and doctors and can thus provide both lighter and more drastic treatments.
In the world of cosmetics, too, things are changing. The great empires appear to be struggling against a rising tide of products - mainly herbals - from small manufacturers who are revolutionising the personal care sector and dominating the full-page tributes in the fashion magazines.
The same criteria governed our choice of studios offering nail care or the delights of a good massage: places with a positive aesthetic that keep up with the latest trends and that more than meet all quality and health specifications.
Finally, to help you manage your leisure time, we add a comprehensive list of swimming pools, tennis clubs and other sports facilities for lovers of open spaces, team sports and model cars (and planes, trains, etc.). Because we mustn't forget that for today's city-dweller health, beauty and fitness are all connected and depend directly on their sense of personal consummation and well-being.

tip
It's interesting to discover what sort of massage suits you best. It's even more interesting to discover your own therapist, for massage is an extremely personal thing.

tip
Don't yield to pressures to pre-register or get a card from an institute. These are just ploys to secure custom, and they show how uncertain they are that you'll go back. Pay for no more than what you do. If you're pleased, you can always go again.

CITY SPA

Anne Semonin
36, Anagnostopoulou St., Kolonaki, 210/3634014.
Anne Semonin opened her first ateliers de beaute in Paris and Geneva, before going on to create day spas in all the major metropolises of the world. Most people come for the massage, and you'll certainly want a nail treatment while you're here. This is also the only place where you can get the famous Semonin beauty products - simple packaging, and sold at extremely reasonable prices. The masks and the eye serum are the top hits.

Caroli Health Club
65, Kyprou St., Glyfada, 210/8980746.
Site of the Empire Spa, a latter-day Roman bathhouse. The succession of different temperatures, judiciously calculated, in the different rooms is extremely beneficial, and creates a marvellous sense of relaxation and well-being.

Clarins
80, Gargittou St., Agia Paraskevi, 210/6081945.
A name that has been in the service of female beauty since 1954 is now attached to a beauty centre in Athens, providing care based on the unsurpassed massage and physiotherapy expertise of the chain's founder, Jacques Courtin Clarins. The method is based entirely on manual skill, and the results are visible immediately: rejuvenated face, glowing skin, smooth, well-toned firmer body, total well-being.

Cocoon Urban Spa
9, Souliou St. & Erifylis, Chalandri, 210/6561975,
e-mail: cocoonurbanspa@hotmail.com
Three floors decorated in bamboo tones, with a simple and understated aesthetic that is totally unlike anywhere else. Special rooms for floor bar, tai chi, yoga, ballet, Pilates, body control etc. The Cocoon Urban Spa has a pool, a genuine marble hamam, a sauna and, of course, a Jacuzzi.

Day Treatment
8, Kolokotroni St., Kifisia (enter from Beauty Works), 210/8089070.
Exotic environment and exotic massage, in a setting where the atmosphere plays the leading role and the natural beauty products - literally straight out of the kitchen: the fruit juice that is to be applied to your face is squeezed right in front of you - follow close behind. The colonial atmosphere and water cures are out of this world.

Elisabeth Spa
96, Vas. Sofias St., Mavili Sq., 210/7772082, 210/7780268.
Total therapeutic massage with 144 jets to energise all body zones, for a sense of well-being and a more active metabolism. The Spa Bouvier Hydro machines (ISO 9001 certified) offer thalassotherapy programmes as good as any in the world.

La Prairie Daily Spa
24, Kanari St., Kolonaki, 210/3601350, 210/3601450. 238-240, Kifisias Ave., Mela Shopping Centre, 210/6230101-2.
All kinds of massage - firming, toning, moisturising, revitalising - with all kinds of techniques - shiatsu, aromatherapy, lymphatic, muscle relaxation - singly or in combination. Only La Prairie products are used: not only the current lines of face products, as used by the La Prairie clinics in Switzerland, but also the creams and body oils that are used with every massage.

PERSONAL TRAINING

The latest trend is to have your own personal fitness trainer. The programmes vary, from stretching and tae bo (this combination of martial arts and aerobic exercise is the latest thing in fitness training) to yoga and dietary advice.

Dimos Diplaris
0942127304.

Exercise Personal Training Experts
210/9949018, www.exercise.gr

Sofia Gerani
0946798285.
For women (singly or in small groups) and couples in the southern suburbs.

Charis Karalis
0942323562.

Antigoni Lougani
0977405350.

Efi Petropoulou
0946011600, 210/9767522.
Women only.

Niki Petroulaki
0944763276.
Women only.

Ioannis Tziolas
210/9249067, 0977957984.

GYMS

Hercules Fitness Club
35, Ethnikis Antistaseos St., Nea Erythraia, 210/8073834, 210/6204462.
4000 m² of space, three gyms, heated indoor pool (9x12 m), plus special facilities for massage, hydromassage, solarium, sauna and hamam. Baby park. The fitness room (more than 1000 m²) has a special free weights area and 200 conventional resistance machines for all muscle groups. Plenty of parking.

Holmes Place
40, Agiou Konstantinou St., Aithrio Shopping Centre, Marousi, 210/6179316.
This is a huge place, with absolutely everything: squash, aqua aerobics in an Olympic-sized pool, studio aerobics, Pilates, floor bar, huge spinning room where you can watch the enormous cardio-theater screens as you cycle, sauna, hamam… and Salumaio's, an elegant light bar where you can meet your friends for a healthy snack. The brand new Holmes in Marousi is at once an exercise gym, a luxurious club and a relaxing spa.

Palestra
Central gym: 2-4, Mesogeion Ave., Athens Tower, 210/7770606, 210/7483333.
Luxury gym with alternative touches: Sauna, steam baths, comfortable changing rooms, nice people, carefully selected trainers. This is a members-only club; if you work for a large company, ask about the company packages.

Universal
Central: 1, Ypsilantou & 54 Skylitsi St., Piraeus, 210/4220895. 376, Patision St., Patisia, 210/2110147.
Big outfit, with gyms all over Greece. Members can use any of the gyms, some of which, like the one in Piraeus, have large pools (12x17 m) and swimming machines. You will also find hydromassage and all kinds of studio classes (aerobic, Swedish, step etc.).

ALTERNATIVE GYMS

Anima Soma
7, Aiolou St., Agia Paraskevi, 210/6015688, e-mail: anima-so@otenet.gr (Information: Marina Katsika & Alexandra Antoniou)
Alternative gym, yoga and shiatsu centre in Agia Paraskevi. This is the only place in Athens that teaches NLP (Neuro-Linguistic Programming, which is fairly similar to the Silva method). You can also take Callanetics classes (slow gymnastics based on exercise repetition) or have a lymphatic massage, reflexology, aromatherapy, rejuvance, the new Bowen technique or shiatsu.

Isadora and Raymond Duncan Dance Study Centre
34, Chrysafis St. & Dikaiarchou, Vyronas, 210/6920317, 210/7621234. (Information: Penelope Iliaskou)
Initiation into the magic of dance and movement, in a historic building that Isadora Duncan designed, built and lived in. The Duncan Dance Centre has classes for professionals and for total beginners, in children's and adults groups. They also hold tai chi chuan and dance therapy classes, and Body Mind Centering seminars.

Seresta Dance Studio
7A, Ierotheou St. (off Ag. Konstantinou St.), Omonoia, 210/5226359.
In creating this centre, well-known dancer Christina Beskou was seeking to overcome the old mentality that saw schools of dance as closed, severe, institutional, and to give anyone who wanted it a chance to become acquainted with their body through the freedom of dance. And so, with the classical ballet that she teaches herself, the Callanetics, the African dance, the flamenco lessons and, of course, the Argentinean tango, the Seresta has become an open art centre for both professional dancers and people who just love to dance.

Sinequanon
10, Plataion St., Kerameikos, 210/3457393, www.sinequanon.gr, e-mail: info@sinequanon.gr
The members of the Sinequanon group display their fluid movements and love of dance in their bright spacious studio in Kerameikos - and it's very infectious! Classes in floor bar, partnering, axis and techniques that are a combination of all of these, to get you moving lightly, with none of the coercion of gymnastics.

PILATES

Bodycentric
23, Ilidos St., Ampelokipoi, 210/7473754.
Pilates studio, with a team of experts to teach you to stand, move and use your body correctly and special modern equipment to work out on.

Corpus Ray

100, Kifisias Ave. & Panormou, Ampelokipoi, 210/6984779, 210/6926209.
One of the best Pilates studios in the city. Evgenia Papadopoulou trained with Romana Kryzanowska, a devoted student of and continuator of Pilates. This is the address of her new, large studio, which has just opened.

PERSONAL MASSAGE

Julie Hardenberg

18, Stratigou Ioannou St., Metz, 210/7521450.
Rejuvance is a gentle rejuvenating technique applied to the face and neck. It was developed in America by Stanley Rosenberg, and has been practised in Greece for four years now. Julie's hands loosen and relax the tension zones that draw and distort the face, releasing the connective tissue beneath the skin. The face will "lift", giving you in effect a temporary facelift.

Alexandra Iatridou

210/8031372, 0932875589.
Natural essential oils, new age energy therapies, shiatsu and four seasons massage, craniosacral balancing, crystallotherapy, Dasira Narada, meditation, tai chi, dietary techniques. Will come to your house (this applies to women and children only).

Gioula Karakosta

13, Evgeniou Voulgareos St., Metz, 210/9215218.
Therapist and tai massage instructor, graduate of the European Shiatsu School and of the Old Medical Hospital of Chang Mai, Thailand. Tai massage, a mixture of yoga, reflexology and shiatsu, is

not only the most popular and refreshing but also the most effective form of massage, since the therapist performs passive stretching upon you.

Angeliki Papageorgiou

0945471438.
Reflexologist with experience in both large spas and small alternative centres with the most stringent specifications.

Elena Zerva

0942461212.
Reflex zone autotherapy, reflexology, aromatherapy, practised by one of the best masseuses in the city. Will also come to your house.

SLIMMING & BEAUTY INSTITUTES

City Spa

10, Skoufa St., Kolonaki, 210/3643444.
Pleasant environment, courteous staff, good value for money. It is not the most luxurious centre in town, but for the same amount you would spend in an ordinary institute you get high tech machines and professional medical care for face, body, nails, slimming and depilation. The manicure/pedicure spa is a real asset.

DNA

801-11-11900.
Three centres in Attica (Mavili Square, Syntagma and Piraeus), offering individualised local fat and cellulite loss, anti-ageing and photo depilation programmes, with a supporting staff of experienced doctors, psychologists, dieticians and physiotherapists. Also diet/nutrition programmes specially designed for men.

Envie

5, Tsakalof St., Kolonaki

Sq., 210/3390888.
Micro crystal method for eliminating wrinkles, freckles, scars and stretch marks. The institute also applies the MT Peel (micro peel) method, which can be used to reveal your new skin even in the summer since it doesn't irritate the skin or cause photosensitivity.

BEAUTY CONSULTANTS

Ekfrasis

22, Papadiamantopoulou St., 210/7249961.
A studio with professional maquillage products (for photo shoots, TV appearances and very special evenings), and the exclusive distributors of the German Kryolan line.
They also carry such props for your talent and imagination as false beards, moustaches, wigs, eye lashes, noses, etc.

House of Colour

63, Ag. Ioannou St., Foinikas Shopping Centre, Agia Paraskevi, 210/6016116, 210/6394598, 0932850248. 1A, Mykinon St., Glyfada, 210/9637637.
Determine your colour type and find out how to avoid style and colour mistakes. The excellent stylist Aleka Retzepoglou may suggest a few strategic wardrobe moves, and perhaps some changes to hair and make-up, for a striking and classy appearance.

Kaiti Tomazinou

210/5710682.
Katie Tomazinou is a professional maquilleuse who specialises in theatre make-up and special effects. If you're getting ready for a very special event or photo shoot, she will make you up at home.

Become Slim in a City Spa

Leisure

Maria Micha

210/6217224, 0946682080.
Maria Micha studies your appearance and suggests purchases to renew your wardrobe, your style and your make-up. Ideal for women who have neither the knowledge nor the time to shop. She will also work closely with you before an important event or a major change in your life (e.g. a career change).

The Styling Club

24, Dimokritou St. (2nd floor), Kolonaki, 210/3615723, 210/3630884. A club for busy women who have no time to shop. Experienced stylists discuss your needs with you, then do your shopping for you. Any alterations are made by the club's own seamstress, and the clothes are delivered to your home. The fees are not prohibitive, and the club already has 6500 members.

Yanna's Fashion Studio

12, Spefsippou St., Kolonaki, 210/7212252. Yanna Papazisi teaches colour analysis, maquillage and styling to groups or individuals. She will prepare you a personal colour chart, make you up and teach you to choose according to your colour range. You can also renew your hairstyle, since the studio has a permanent hairdresser - who is also a trained colour system specialist.

EXCLUSIVE COSMETICS

Honey-based cosmetics

3, Veikou St., Makrygianni, 210/9234133.
Pure honey-based products for baby's tender skin, for women's facial care and for men who want something simple, pure and economical for their skin. They also carry honey masks, and a very effective propolis line for the treatment of acme, all made up by chemist Maria Vasilakopoulou.

Kavalieratos

18, Irodotou St., Kolonaki, 210/7213860.
Takis and Pampitsa Kavalieratou use materials from their property in Anavyssos to produce cosmetics (Cavalier) for a select clientele in their institute on Irodotou St. They are both aestheticians, and their quite interesting, exclusively herbal cosmetics can be purchased only here.

Korres Natural Products

Central supplier: 20-26, K. Manou St., Athens, 210/7565800, www.korres.com
Their small pharmacy has blossomed and flourished like the fragrant rose petals they use in their original hypoallergenic lotions. Active aloe bubble bath with a creamy foam, body milk that feels like powder for a matt effect and, their best seller this year, a line of aromatic body waters that perfume and moisturise without leaving a trace of greasiness. Available in many pharmacies across Athens, and very successful abroad.

Santa Maria Novella

11, Levidou St. & 7, Papadiamanti, Kifisia, 210/6232360.
In her marvellous traditional pharmacy, Irini Prifti carries exclusive lines of fragrances, powder, medicines, pomades, marvellous liqueurs (like the liqueur of the Medici), an ethereal rose water called "the queen's water", and one of the finest soaps in Europe, the Vellutina Crema di Sapone, still packaged in the same old romantic wrappings.

HAIR STYLISTS

Angelos

17, Omirou St., 210/3626011. 258, Kifisias Ave., 210/6742228.
Angelos can fairly be considered the founder of haute coiffure in Greece, since he taught not only advanced techniques but also the service to be expected of a European hair salon today. He will always be remembered for ancient Greek pseudonyms he gave his stylists (not to mention the rain bonnets they still hand out as required).

Athina-Janet Korosi

2, Tsakalof St., Kolonaki, 210/3624730.
Stylist - colourist Athina Janet Korosi is famous for her skill with extensions, which can either be permanent or removable, if you want to take them out at night. Her clientele includes a long list of models and celebrities.

Central Hair

3, Riga Palamidou St. (opposite the Empros Theatre), Psyrri, 210/3214319, www.psirri.gr/central_hair
With its air of an English loft, this hair salon also doubles as an art gallery, displaying works by new Greek and foreign artists. No appointment necessary, and they're open on Sundays.

Daniel

20, Mavromichali St., Kolonaki, 210/3610278.
Eccentric and effective with

those who want a wild hair-do or a very stylish cut. If you want rasta or extensions, this is the place for you. The shop is fascinating - a cross between an operating theatre and a garage for Cadillacs.

Giorgos Doudesis
39, Voukourestiou St., 210/3629387.
Dynamic, quick, and a great favourite with models and celebrities. The staff are wonderful (ask for Ritsa) and the studio is modern and recently renovated.

Jacques Dessange
13, Spefsippou St., Kolonaki, 210/7214395.
The Parisian chain of hair salons has been warmly received in Athens. Elegant premises, expert staff (ask for Ms Syla Thomopoulou) and a magical palm oil mask (Creme de Palme) that make even the tiredest hair shine.

Ilias Zarmpalis
4, Spefsippou St., Kolonaki, 210/7232939.
Expensive cuts, but his clients wouldn't dream of going elsewhere. Tasteful and very modern, this salon is a model beauty parlour - but it's his skill with the scissors that has made Ilias Zarmpalis so famous.

Tommy
4, Eleftheroton Sq., Main Square Chalandri, 210/6856502, 210/6856286.
Bold new generation hair stylist (also a talented wedding dress designer), in an elegant, modern salon.

Vangelis Chatzis
196, Kifisias Ave., 210/6747011, 210/6774108.
Modern but classic, and a fabulous colourist (particularly famous for his highlights). Daring ideas and striking

results for those who aren't afraid to try something new and different. Very elegant premises, attentive service, and strictly punctual in their appointments.

Very Chic - Tryfon Samaras
28, Vas. Konstantinou St., Pagkrati, 210/7230890, 210/7235106.
A star in his own right, with a lavish book and innumerable fashion editorials. Very elegant salon (rococo), and although it will be difficult to book an appointment, it's well worth persevering - especially if, like Tryfon himself, you're partial to gorgeous warm chestnut shades.

HAIR CLUBS
Lazartigue
27, Lazaraki St., Glyfada, 210/8948108, 210/8942513. 16, Levidou St. & Argyropoulou, Kifisia, 210/6232014.
Hair health centre, with care based on the Lazartigue line of products. You can have a complete hair analysis, and treatment for any hair problem (hair loss, etc.).

Yianni Hair Spa
36, Plastira St., Nea Smyrni, 210/9340422, 210/9340444.
At Yianni Hair Spa, healthy hair is our prime and principal concern. A special spa room has been created for your shampoo and massage: abandon yourself to the hands of our expert masseurs and enjoy a truly rare experience, relaxing and revitalising. Essential oil-enriched natural oils, in conjunction with the special scalp massage, refresh and invigorate your weary head and leave your hair as soft and bright as a child's.

PERFUMER
Lino de Larossa
A unique parfumerie in a superb Kolonaki boutique. Perfumer Giorgos Karagiannis, a highly trained "nose" with years of experience in some of the biggest foreign firms, will create a perfume especially for you, based on your type and skin chemistry. He then files the code number and composition, so he can make it up again just for you.
5, Dexamenis Sq., Kolonaki, 210/3390871.

NAIL STUDIOS
Floral
14, Ag. Dimitriou St. & Ag. Theodoron, Kifisia, 210/8084800.
The most complete nail studio in Kifisia in an absolutely central location - and you won't even have trouble finding parking. Their best seller has to be the fancy painted nails with the Swarovski "insets", although their classic French manicures are fabulous. You can also enjoy a spa manicure, or an expert massage.

Glow Nail Studio
10, Irodotou St., Kolonaki, 210/7294936.
Hypermodern pop salon, offering every kind of nail care. Artificial nails, French manicure, accessories and rhinestone nails, toe rings and much more. Their fame, however, rests on their impeccable French manicures and their marvellous aromatic hydromassage.

LCN
451, Vouliagmenis Ave.,

Ilioupoli, 210/9920332, 210/9960247. LCN concept shop, 1, Solonos St. & Kanari, Kolonaki, 210/3630944.
The main salon in Ilioupoli has two foot booths and two hydromassage booths, a hamam, a large manicure salon cum waiting room and separate areas for facials and depilation treatments, all using nothing but the highly specialised German LCN line of products. The concept shop in Kolonaki has a nail treatment salon and you can also buy LCN products.

Mary's Nail Studio
43, Marasli St., Kolonaki, 210/7258785.
Elegant and very quiet, tucked away on the Marasli pedestrian precinct, this studio retains its demanding clientele by guaranteeing high quality and very careful work.

Nail & Hair Teta
294, Kifisias Ave. & Paritsi, Faros Shopping Centre, Neo Psychiko, 210/6722053, 210/6778727.
Kyria Teta is renowned not only for her perfect manicures and pedicures but also for her famous clientele: the pages of her appointment book are full of TV personalities, models and celebrities.

Nychi-Nychi
230, Kifisias Ave., Kifisia, 210/8080771. 111, Venizelou St., Nea Erythraia, 210/6200714, 210/6200717. 48, Pinelopis Delta St., Ag. Sofias Sq., Neo Psychiko, 210/6728268.
Nail care centre for men and women (the men have a salon of their own), where you can not only have your nails looked after but have a mehndi tattoo or a full make-up job - or even hold

a business meeting, over a light meal and a glass of wine, while your feet are relaxing in a mini hydromassage.

SWIMMING POOLS

Asteras Vouliagmenis
40, Apollonos St., Vouliagmeni, 210/8902000.
Swimming with style in three outdoor pools, one in each complex. The pool at the "Nafsicaa" complex is Olympic-size, the "Aphrodite" 28x16 metres. Both have adjacent bar and restaurant. The "Arionas" pool, next to the children's playground, is smaller (20x12 m).
Open: Mon.-Sun. 10.00-19.00. Admission: weekdays € 30. Sat., Sun. and holidays € 45. Annual membership: € 1400.

Asteria Seaside
58, Vas. Georgiou B', Glyfada, 210/8941062.
All day relaxation on the comfortable sunbeds beside the large pool in this elegant complex. A wonderful place for coffee, a meal and clubbing. Expert massage therapists on hand. Children's playground on the beach and in the water.
Open: daily 10.00-19.00. Admission: € 10.

Caprice Del Mar
Diadochou Pavlou, Glyfada waterfront, 210/8944048.
Chill out around the famous cafe's 25-metre pool, right by the sea. After your swim, relax over a cocktail on a sunbed or one of the lovely sofas and enjoy the music.
Open: Mon.-Sun. 10.00-19.00. Admission: € 7.

Divani Apollon Palace & Spa
10, Ag. Nikolaou St. & Iliou, Vouliagmeni, 210/8911100.
One indoor and two outdoor pools - one with fresh water and a Jacuzzi and one with seawater. After your swim, you can exercise on the apparatus around the indoor pool or relax at the poolside bar.
Open: Mon.-Sun. 8.00-21.00. Admission: weekdays € 20, children € 15. Sat., Sun. € 38, children € 20. One month pass: € 380.

Divani Caravel
2, Vas. Alexandrou St., Kaisariani, 210/7253725.
Roof garden pool, 12.5x8.5 metres. Sauna and gym adjacent.
Open: Mon.-Sun. 9.00-18.30. Admission: weekdays € 30, Sat., Sun. € 45.

Grand Resort Lagonissi
Km 40, Athens-Sounio Ave., 22910/76000.
26x12 metre pool in the luxurious gardens. Life guard and pool bar.
Open: Mon.-Sun. 11.00-19.00. Admission: weekdays € 30, Sat., Sun. and holidays € 44. Children 6 -12: half price.

Ledra Marriott
115, Syngrou Ave., 210/9300000.
Small roof garden pool with a fabulous view of the Acropolis and Lycabettus. Open to members of the Panorama Pool Club. € 35 assures you use of the pool, a room to relax in and entry to the Health Club, a free "welcome" cocktail and a 25% discount on the Panorama day menu.
Open: Mon.-Sun. 10.00-18.00.

Pentelikon
66, Diligianni St., Kefalari, 210/6230650.
20x10 metre pool, open only to members of the pool club. The water is renewed 4 times a day.
Open: Mon.-Sun. 10.00-18.00. Season membership (June-Sept.): € 590, children € 100.

St. George Lycabettus

2, Kleomenous St.,
Kolonaki, 210/7290711.
Roof garden pool (10x15 m)
with a view of the Acropolis.
Mini-gym, sauna and pool bar
adjacent.
Open: Mon.-Sun.: 10.00-19.00.
Open only to members:
€ 278.80 for the season.

The Margi

11, Litous St., Laimos Vouliagmenis, 210/8962061.
Small open pool in a tres
chic corner. After your
swim, relax on the comfortable sofas around the pool
or at the pool bar.
Open: until 19.00.
Admission: € 20.

TENNIS CLUBS

Asteras Vouliagmenis

40, Apollonos St., Vouliag-
meni, 210/8902000.
Four courts in the "woods"
on the Asteras grounds, near
the "Aphrodite" complex.
Fabulous view of the sea.
Open: Mon.-Sun. 8.00-22.00.
Rates: weekdays € 30, Sat.,
Sun. € 45.

Kavouri Tennis Club

1, Aktis St. & Litous, Megalo
Kavouri, 210/9670946.
Seven courts (4 with
Astroturf, 3 quick) in nicely
tended grounds with pines
and palms, 200 metres from
the sea. After your game
relax at the adjacent bar.
Coaching available.
Court fees depend on time of
day. Weekdays 8.00-15.00
€ 9. 15.00 to sunset: € 12,
with lights, till 23.00: € 18.
Sat., Sun. 8.00 to sunset € 12.
Evenings under lights € 18.

Politia Tennis Club

18, Aristotelous St., Politeia,
210/6200003.
Facilities with the unmistakeable air of the northern suburbs. Five tennis courts,
squash court, swimming
pool, gym, sauna, play

room, restaurant and bar
overlooking the courts. Call
the desk and they'll find you
a partner.
Open: Mon.-Sun. 8.00-22.00.
Annual subscription: € 1000
plus € 1500 initial membership
fee. Family package: € 1200.

Sunny Tennis Club

190, Kastritsas St.,
Nea Erythraia,
210/8136148, 210/8135101.
Classy facilities with 7 tennis
courts, open pool, brand
new aerobics and fitness
rooms.
Open: weekdays 9.00-23.00,
Sat., Sun. 9.00-22.00.
Members only. Annual fee
(covers tennis, pool and gym)
€ 1169.

RIDING

Athens Riding Club

3, Kazantzaki St., Gerakas,
210/6611088.

Attikos Riding Club

Tochi area, Koropi,
210/6626429.

Ekali Riding Club

6, Irakleiou St., Ekali,
210/6229773.

Greek Riding Club

18, Paradeisou St., Marousi,
210/6812506.

Marathonas Riding Club

3, Makedonias St.,
Marathonas, 22940/67002.

Northern Suburbs
Riding Club

137, Tatoiou Ave., Varym-
pompi, 210/8169564.

Panellinios Riding Club

Km 26, Paiania-Markopoulo
Ave., 210/6625690.

Tatoi Riding Club

Tatoiou Ave., Varympompi,
210/8169449.

Varympompi
Riding Club

107, Tatoiou Ave., Varym-
pompi, 210/8169383.

GO - KARTS

Agios Kosmas
Go Kart Center

Poseidonos Ave.,
opposite the old West
Air Terminal, 210/9851660,
210/9851546.
Next to the beach at Agios
Kosmas, this is one of the
biggest (1010 m) and most
popular tracks.
Coffee shop overlooking
the sea and karting till
dawn, since it's open every
day from 9.00 till 3.00 or
4.00 in the morning(!).
Workshop, parking for your
own kart, trainers. 25-30
karts, plus 2-3 two-seaters
for driving with company.
No mini-karts. Rate: € 10/10
minutes.

Kartodromlo

Afidnes, next to the toll
post, 22950/23265.
The biggest (1160 m long, 8
m wide) track in Greece and
the only one in Attica that is
used for National
Championship races. Coffee
shop, workshop, parking for
your own kart, shop for
equipment and 35 karts (200
and 300 cc, 2 two-seaters
and 5 for kids).
Open: Mon.-Sun. 10.00-
23.00. Rate: € 8-10/10 min-
utes.

Spata
Go Kart Track

Chorafi Zavou area,
Spata, 22940/88837.
Track 600 m long by 8 m
wide - ideal for beginners.
6 four-year-old 160 cc karts,
and 1 kiddy kart. Coffee
shop, workshop and parking
for your own kart, all for
€ 15 / month.
Open: Mon.-Sun. 10.00-
23.00. Rate: € 7/10 min.

Alpha Bank
business
solutions

ATHENS 2004

ALPHA BANK
OFFICIAL
BANK

Have you got something "cooking"? Alpha Bank is right beside you, with a wide range of financial solutions adapted to the particular requirements of your business.

Alpha Bank's financial solutions guarantee not only competitive interest rates and the best conditions of the market, but the additional advantage of the return of funds.

Because Alpha Bank is the first to return 10% of the interest on business loans* that are serviced punctually.

At Alpha Bank, punctuality is rewarded.

*Applies to Working Capital Loans of up to € 150,000 and Equipment or Business Vehicle Loans of up to € 300,000 to enterprises and professional clients with a gross annual turnover of up to € 1,000,000.

ALPHA BANK OFFICIAL BANK OF THE ATHENS 2004 OLYMPIC GAMES

Gastronomy

Athens Guide 2003

ATHENS 2004

ALPHA BANK

OFFICIAL BANK

Gastronomy

the
world of taste
at home

Where would you look for hand-made pasta, wines from the Lebanon, rare vintage Chablis, whole black truffles, tuna backs? Who makes the best sticky sweets and most delicious biscuits in Athens? Who has the best fish, meats, cured meats and cheeses? Which famous chef will teach you how to prepare and properly present a complete menu? If you've ever asked yourself questions like these and even more, then the pages that follow are bound to be of interest, for they constitute a mouth-watering tour of the most appetising and attractive sources of gastronomic pleasure in Athens.

Gastronomy in Athens is developing by leaps and bounds, keeping pace with the increasing numbers of flavour aficionados looking for sources of gustatory gratification. Treasure houses of fine foods are multiplying and at the same time becoming more attractive, more modern, more specialised. Which means that even the most demanding consumer can now readily find the rarest and most recherche products, the most curious ingredients, the most specialised items for the satisfaction of the palate and more. Wine cellars, delicatessens, patisseries, purveyors of local and organic products, cheesemongers and pork butchers, specialty fishmongers and meat markets, pasta fresca: it's all here, to bring luxury taste treats to your table or to be offered as unusual and sophisticated gifts. In this section of the Guide we have carefully selected for you the finest of these shops, chosen for their superior quality and unique features. The common denominator throughout is adherence to the basic principle that "luxury" is a value for life.

Al Dente

Bon Goût

Gastronomy

WINE CELLARS

Cava Anthidis
13-15, Ypsilantou St., Kolonaki, 210/7251050.
Huge variety of wines and spirits. You'll find rare whiskies, vintage champagnes, and a wide range of wines from Greece, Italy, Spain, France, Argentina, Chile, New Zealand, Australia, Africa, Lebanon and California.

Cellier
1, Kriezotou St., Kolonaki, 210/3610040. 10, Papadiamanti, Kifisia, 210/6233377.
One of the oldest cellars in Athens, with a large variety of Greek and imported wines and spirits. Exclusive representatives of Fortnum & Mason and other select deli products. Very elegant gift baskets with wine.

Methi
8, Veikou St., Galatsi, 210/2922879.
Well-selected cellar with a wide range of Greek wines, plus a few labels from France and Spain. Also fine foods from "Millelia" and Valrhona chocolates.

Oinou-Pnevmata
9a, Irakleitou St., Kolonaki, 210/3602932.
100 wines, spirits, fine French foods and related gift items. Interesting suggestions for composing lovely and unusual gifts, combining (for example) the wine of your choice with an art book or a book about wine.

Pavlidis Oinotrapeza
108, Achilleos St., Palaio Faliro, 210/9830000.
Representing Greek vintners, chiefly for the wholesale trade. They organise wine-tastings and will sell at retail prices to those who are interested.

Peri Karpou
324, Kifisias Ave., Nea Erythraia, 210/8081193.
Attractive, friendly and full of surprises. Fine dried fruits and nuts from Thessaloniki, chocolates from Valrhona as well as hand-made chocolates with almonds or pistachios, drinking chocolate, Queens label teas in many flavours and aromas, specialty jams and marmalades, preserves. Also everything you need to serve your tea, from fine china mugs to sugar sticks. Nor is that all: you'll also find grappas and liqueurs in special bottles, lovely bottles of liqueur fruits, tins of biscuits and original baskets with eco-organic touches. As for wines, there is a well-chosen selection of Greek and imported labels.

Vinifera
317, Kifisias Ave., Kifisia, 210/8077709.
A wine cellar that since 1983 has been specialising in rare and hard-to-find wines and spirits, both domestic and imported. Also a well-furnished deli, with fine foods from all over Greece.

Wine Garage
25, Xenokratous St., Kolonaki, 210/7213175.
Modern wine boutique with some 180 selected wines, ports and sherries from all over the world. By way of example, you will find labels like Chapoutier and Jadot (France), Lurton (Chile), Tommasi (Italy) and La Rioja Alta (Spain). On Saturdays they organise tastings for customers and friends.

DELICATESSEN

Alexis R. Delicatessen
29, Omirou St., Nea Smyrni, 210/9331435.
This delicatessen, a favourite local meeting-place, serves top quality, tasty fine foods - anything from a simple sandwich to a five-course dinner. Do try their authentic ratatouille with mozzarella, prosciutto, courgette, aubergine and tomato, or the shiitake mushrooms with red peppers in balsamic vinegar, and pick out a selection of goodies for your pantry: cured meat products from Frankfurt and Bohemia, salami abruzzese, Spanish Jabuco ham, chorizo sausage and, of course, Agilus Flensburg fine German chocolates.

Aria Gefseon
Vari-Koropi Ave. & Parou St., Vari, opposite "Scholi Evelpidon", 210/9656388-9. 19, 25th Martiou St., Nea Smyrni, 210/9329670.
Bright spacious shop, with separate product areas and a very impressive showroom. Exclusive imports of Italian pasta from the Adriatic and antipasti from Calabria, many different kinds of dried mushrooms, foie gras (goose and duck), Scottish salmon, Italian cured meat products and cheeses, hard roe from Mesolongi, French truffles. Small selection of Greek and foreign wines. They also have a take-away section, with a choice of at least ten different home-style dishes every day.

Arkefthos
12, Ag. Ioannou St., Glyfada, 210/9680968. 138, Grypari St., Kallithea, 210/9531042. 8, Ag. Foteinis St., Nea Ionia, 210/2710753.
Warm, friendly place, and

very functional with its endless rows of shelves, drawers and corners. Here you will find almost all the teas in the world, a wide range of essential oils for botanotherapy, all kinds of spices (grains, ground, powdered), traditional jams and honeys, pickles, and a whole section of flours.

Bon Goût
72, Strofiliou St. & Ch. Trikoupi, N. Erythraia, 210/6254628.
A good thousand product codes on fine foods from around the world in this delicatessen in Nea Erythraia. From wild Irish salmon to jumbo shrimp and from game (venison, pheasant, guinea fowl) to smoked Scottish lamb - even the most demanding will find what they want here. And then there are the fine grocery products: whole black truffles, solid meat tuna, Petrossian Beluga caviar, whole glace fruits from Hediart. And you can sample some of these gourmet products on the spot - either on the charmingly arranged mezzanine or in the lovely first floor restaurant, where they also serve a number of hot dishes.

Il Salumaio di Montenapoleone
3, Panagitsas St., Kifisia, 210/6233934.
Warm friendly place, with a few tables next to the deli counter. The proprietor is from Milan, and his trump card is the excellence of his products. Vast array of cured meat products (bresaola, prosciutto, cicciolo, capello da prete, etc.), salmon, antipasti (stuffed onions, Roman artichokes), truffles, vinegars, foie gras and caviar (black and red). The cellar boasts a wide range of grapas and wines from all over Italy. Delivery service.

Lutèce - Godiva
12, Botsari St. & Dousmani, Glyfada, 210/8945933-4.
5, Koumpari St., Kolonaki Sq., 210/3627744, 210/3629204.
The 65 m² of this shop conceal many fine food products and fine dining items. Here, apart from the famous Godiva chocolates in an endless variety of shapes and tastes, you will find Comtesse du Barry sweets and jams, Petrossian caviar, Bristol Spirits and Saint James Caribbean rum, Blue Mountain and Kona-Kai coffee from Suavor and pantry accessories from Gien-Artichaut-Jacquard and L' Esprit & Le Vin.

Maison du Fromage
10, Kapsali St., Kolonaki, 210/7248101.
Gourmet boutique with a broad range of items. The focus, of course, is on cheese: Dutch, Irish, Italian, Spanish, Swiss, with certain French and Greek cheeses that you'll find nowhere else. Also salmon, French sauces (Madeira, vegetable, fish, game), Italian pasta and delizie miste, etc.

Mandragoras
14, D. Gounari St., Central Market, Piraeus, 210/4172961.
Small in area, but not in variety. 2000 different herbs for cooking and seasoning, natural cosmetics and 1200 delicious traditional goodies from all over Greece in this microscopic shop located in the country's largest port.

Salamat
24, Korinthias St., Ampelokipoi, 210/7796766.
60 m² packed with more than 1200 different foodstuffs from the Philippines, China, Japan, Singapore, Malaysia, India, Vietnam, Mexico and a number of African countries. Do you want bottled fish or oyster sauces? Banana leaves? Plum wine? Milkfish? Twists of Japanese or Chinese rice or oat noodles? This is where to come.

Select Salmon House
33, Lasaraki St., Glyfada, 210/8945662.
3, K. Karamanli St., Melissia, 210/6133561.
Attractive small place, and a veritable cornucopia of gastronomic delicacies. Salmon, of course, black and red caviar, hard roe from Mesolongi, Italian cured meat products, sauces, pasta, dried mushrooms. The cellar includes a number of French whites to go with the salmon, Greek wines from boutique wineries and some good vintners' co-op Chablis. Special packaging available for dispatch all over Greece.

Simply Delicious
267, Kifisias Ave., 210/8089249.
Simple, uncluttered place, functionally arranged so products are easy to locate. Delicacies from five continents, imported mainly from the British islands: teas from India, Ceylon, Japan, Kenya, Nepal, Indonesia and China in a variety of flavours, home-style marmalades from England, Scotland, Wales and Australia, sweet and savoury sauces, innumerable spices, mustards, Asian seasonings and lots of books on foods, flavours and cuisines.

Sorpresa Italiana
6-8, Kyriazi St., Kifisia, 210/8017886.
Small shop filled with a wide range of Italian products.

Gastronomy

Cheeses (from dry, well-aged parmigiano reggiano to traditional soft cheeses from Alpine villages), cured meat products (Parma ham, prosciutto with truffles, salami cacciatorini), sauces, pasta, balsamic vinegars, mushrooms, fruits in syrup - the list is seemingly endless.

Spuntino
6, Omirou St., Neo Psychiko, 210/6745203.
13, Markou Botsari St., Glyfada, 210/8941649.
High ceiling, bare brick, strong colours, hidden corners, bar and deli counter, small tables. Cured meat products, interesting cheeses (real buffalo milk mozzarella), sun-dried tomatoes, truffles, risotto. The cellar contains wines from the Veneto, Piedmont, Tuscany and Friuli.

SWEET CORNERS

Alea
258, Kifisias Ave., Palaio Psychiko, 210/6748510.
9, Anagnostopoulou St., Kolonaki, 210/3625528.
One of the finest patisseries in the city, with a fabulous selection of feather-light sweets to suit modern tastes. Famous for their double mousse, wild cherry cheesecake, carre noir gateau and, of course, their cream puffs.

Asimakopoulos
82, Charilaou Trikoupi St., Exarcheia, 210/3610092.
French patisserie and traditional Greek sweets. Do try the chocolate mousse, the strawberry nougatina, the orange caramel gateau and - our favourite - the galaktompoureko.

Caravan
11, Voukourestiou St., 210/3641540. 26, Akadimias St., 210/3612864.
The most famous siropiasta in Athens. Our absolute

favourites are the mini baklava and the tavou kiokshou (a sweet made with chicken broth). You will also find delectably light savoury treats, including a first class brioche.

Eklektikon
4, Fokionos St., Syntagma, 210/3245040. 20, Eirinis Ave., Pefki, 210/8062557.
Microscopic in size, but vast in chocolaty prestige, since every year they handle some three tons of chocolate. Daskalides, Valor and Neuhaus are just some of the names on their shelves, alongside Kingsbridge, Toffies and Fats biscuits, preserves, jams, jellies and bottled fruits, petit fours from the French firm Rigeaut, and stuffed olives and aromatic olive oils.

Fresh
12, Kriezotou St., Kolonaki, 210/3642948. 20, Ydras St., Moschato, 210/4836900, e-mail: fresh@hol.gr
Fabulous chocolate desserts, hand made by Stelios Parliaros. And don't miss the rum prune cake, the tarts filled with giandujia chocolate or their best-seller champagne honey gateau.

Irène
57, Thiseos Ave., Ekali, 210/6229226.
Minimal decor setting for Irene Pappa's maxi-imaginative confections. A gateau with rose petals and tsikoudia, chocolate cake with four peppers, yoghurt mousse with honey, pistachios and black sesame - these are only a small selection of the delights on offer. Irene Pappa is famous for her chocolates and for her highly impressive profiterole. Everything is exceptionally well presented, right down to the ecological take-home packaging.

Layal
206, Kifisias Ave. & 2, Agamemnonos St., Chalandri, 210/6718888.
This Lebanese patisserie makes the best mini baklava in town, with a filling of pine nuts, cashews, pistachios and walnuts. Samir Nehime also makes Lebanese namora samali, Lebanese kinafa, kourabiedes stuffed with dates, pistachios or walnuts, as well as such Lebanese delicacies as hummus, tabbouleh and moutabal.
You will also find a whole collection of Lebanese craftwork, from backgammon boards inlaid with mother-of-pearl to lamps - interesting ideas (along with the sweets) for fine and unusual gifts.

To Biscotto
11, Spartis St., Chalandri, 210/6833598.
Their workshop prepares ten different sorts of homemade biscuits every day, using traditional and new recipes and the purest of ingredients. As they do for their chocolate and carrot cakes, their cheese pies and apple turnovers, and the Cretan skaltsounia they make every year during Lent.

LOCAL PRODUCTS

Gonia tou Agroti
94, Kallidromiou & 1, Plapouta St., Exarcheia, 210/8830410.
A shop that stocks a wide range of products: olives from Agrinio, cheeses, lasagne, rusks from Crete, vinegar and casks of Moschofilero wine from Ancient Olympia, feta from Aetos Xiromeri, rice, fat dried beans and coarse salt from Mesolongi, and a good selection of herbs.

Gastronomy

Kritiki Gonia
28, Sevastoupoleos St. & Fokidos, Ampelokipoi, 210/7485840.
Aka the "Psiloreitis Shepherd's Hut". This place has everything: Cretan cheeses (tyromalaka, xinomyzithra, fresh and hard anthotyro), apakia (smoked, pickled pork loin, a specialty of Rethymno), pure virgin olive oil, sweets and pasta from local co-ops and cottage industries, plus every wine produced in Crete and a wide selection of tsikoudias.

Mantineia
Dourou Sq., Chalandri, 210/6858366. 25, Trikalon St., Ampelokipoi, 210/6484272.
Good things from the countryside around Tripoli: fine cheeses (tin- or barrel-packed feta, graviera, kefalo-graviera, anthotyro, various myzithras), hand-made pasta (egg noodles, trachanas, lasagne), salt pork, country sausage, fresh butter, meadow and pine honey.

Mesogaia
52, Nikis St. & Kydathinaion, Plaka, 210/3229146.
Home-style goodies, cottage industry products and organic produce from ten sites in Greece, all in this little corner of Plaka. Anchovy fillets marinated in oil and garlic, yoghurt cheese in olive oil, eight kinds of lasagne, caper leaves, preservative-free jams, a variety of cheeses, sweets, rusks, biscuits, etc. Telephone orders accepted.

Naxos Cheese Factory
43, Kypselis St., Kypseli, 210/8222747.
The Koufopoulos family produce in Naxos and sell in Kypseli. You'll find the full range of Naxos cheeses (anthotyri, aged manouri, arseniko kefalotyri, goat's milk graviera, cream cheeses, etc.), plus strained yoghurt, raki, old mountain wine, sweets, jams and rare citrons (korgiolemono).

Rayan
Athinas & Andromachis, Kallithea, 210/9423230.
Aka "politiki gonia". For more than twenty years this shop has been supplying the city with delicacies from Pontus and Caucasia. From the depths of Kilkis they import solgun (a cow's milk cheese), baskitan (a slightly soured myzithra), smedana (cream), kvorak for cheese pies, sweet and sour trachanas, pickles, sweets and home-made jams. You can also get cartons of ariani here, the cultured dairy product to which the peoples of Caucasia attribute their longevity.

Tzekos - Naxos Foods
16, Ippokratous St., Galatsi, 210/2927803.
Galatsi is the city's Naxos quarter, and the natural home for this shop, which for the past twenty years has been a source of supply of the island's unique produce and products. Xinomyzithra and xinotyri (soured cheeses), gravieras, myzithras, potatoes, choice meats, Naxos bread, creamery butter, Probona wines and ouzo - they're all here. And every Wednesday they bring in fresh fish (red mullet, pandora, porgy, sea bream, sargo…).

ORGANIC PRODUCTS

Amaranto
6, Themistokleous St., Chalandri, 210/6832989.
Everybody in Chalandri knows Amaranto. Organically-grown fruit and vegetables, fresh Macrovita royal jelly, Perlier natural cosmetics made from honey and beeswax, health food products from Power Health, Ortis, Solgar, plus books on healthy eating.

Bionatura
2, Dimokratias Ave., Melissia.
Organic delicatessen with all the latest equipment, expert staff and windows full of familiar organic products. You can buy organic Scottish salmon, organic cured meat products (Parma ham, Milanese salami, organic Danish salami, etc.), organic cheeses (reggiano parmesan from Modena, feta from Grevena, etc.), olive paste and preserves (pistachio, plum, quince, fig and grape). You will also find a wide range of bottled wines produced from hand-grown grapes.

Green Farm
13, Dimokritou St., Kolonaki, 210/3614001. 8, D. Ralli St., Marousi, 210/6141914. 134, El. Venizelou Ave., Nea Erythraia, 210/6204044. 5, Dousmani St., Glyfada, 210/8985191-2.
A paradise for those who are devoted to healthy natural eating. Organic foods, fresh eggs, home-made sauces, all without preservatives and additives for a higher quality and healthier table. The wine cellar lists some 35 labels produced from organically-grown grapes. Delivery service available.

Nea Zoi
36, Protopapa St., Ilioupoli, 210/9912408.
Large shop with a wide product range and a steady clientele. Organic foodstuffs (pulses, pasta and flours), nuts, spaghetti, Cretan hondros from Varypetro (Chania county), dietary supplements and health foods.

A whole world of good things to discover:

why resist its sweet temptation?

αερι μαρθασ

MARTHA'S SWEETS & NUTS

ξηροί καρποί σοκολάτες γλυκά του

NUTS, CHOCOLATES, SWEETS, WINES, TEAS, GIFTS
324, Kifisias Ave. (next to the AB Vasilopoulos in Nea Erythraia),
tel.: 210 8081193

Gastronomy

PASTA FRESCA

Al Dente
230, Kifisias Ave., Kifisia, 210/8080140.
Pasta boutique, featuring a wide variety of home-made pastas, prepared according to traditional Italian recipes. Radiatori, conchiglie, mafaldine, fusilli, penne, linguini, spaghetti and spaghettini in unusual colours and shapes. Also home-made sauces to go with them (anchovy, vegetable, tomato, etc.), truffles, balsamic vinegar from Vecchia Emilia, Carearoli rice with truffles, tiramisu and pannacotta in individual portions. The wine cellar is small but representative, with a good selection of Greek wines and seven Italian labels.

MammaRò
238-240, Kifisias Ave., Mela Shopping Centre, Kifisia, 210/8083833.
Exceptionally well-made pasta in unusual shapes and flavours, and all so attractively packaged that you'll want some of each. Don't pass up the square "Germe di Grano" (wheat germ), green "Basilico", "Fungi Porcini" and "Peperoncino Rosso". Also cottage products (risotto, polenta, aromatic oils, cantuncini) prepared according to traditional Italian recipes. You will also find the famous glass and ceramics hand-crafted in Tuscany by Paolo and Mario Pierallini.

Santa Pasta in Cucina
114-118, Filolaou St., Pagkrati, 210/7013070.
The experience of the "Santa Pasta" restaurants transubstantiated into a tiny (45 m²) delicatessen for lovers of fresh pasta. Spaghetti, tagliatelle, linguini, pappardelle, stuffed pasta (ravioli with ricotta and spinach, tortelloni with mince), oven-ready pasta dishes (pasta mushroom roll, cannelloni with spinach) and more. You will also find 12 different sauces, salad dressings, aromatic oils, fresh sweets and a few kitchen gadgets and utensils.

CHARCUTERIE - CHEESES

A-B Mega
Km 20, Athens-Lamia Highway, 210/6229070.
All the AlphaVita stores have excellent charcuterie sections, but the twelve-metre counter at the Mega store out on the National Highway is truly awesome, both for the variety of products and the knowledgeability of the staff. You will find Greek sausages and salamis (Nikas, Myssor, Straka Volos), imported products from France, Italy and Spain, Negroni prosciutto, huge Negroni mortadellas, smoked French ham (Le Foue, from Paul Predault), chicken breast with orange.

Altro
57, Athinas St., 210/3211537.
Endless variety of cured meat products from all over Greece, at excellent prices. Smoked pork cortesinas, sausages (from Serres, Trikala, Volos, Artaki), soutzoukia, salamis and just about anything else you can think of.

Bavaria
113, Tatoiou Ave., Kifisia, 210/8073863.
This shop has no fewer than 300 sorts of cured meat products. A treasure house of German appellation d'origine sausages (Vienna, Frankfurt, Bohemia, Munich), Praggeschinken ham, Putenbrust roast turkey breast, Italian prosciutto, German sauces and mustards.

Mantri
41, Grammou St., Vrilissia, 210/8040484, 210/8041367.
Small purveyor of gastronomic cured meats and cheeses. Sausages from various parts of Greece, wine-cured ham, "turned" ham from Proussos, turkey breast from Israel, and an interesting quality of pastourmas made from the tenderloin. And probably the best collection of Greek cheeses.

Miran
45, Evripidou St., 210/3217187, 210/3250794.
In the same location since 1922, this shop has won medals at international food exhibitions. The selection is limited, but the quality is exceptional: pastourmas, soutzoukakia and sausages, all of their own production.

O Giorgos
21-23, D. Gounari St., Stoa Politi, Piraeus, 210/4112881, 210/4122604.
Known first and foremost for its pastourmas (the Balkan pastrami), and a fixture in Piraeus' central market since 1924. But apart from its feature specialty (which is available in two varieties: lean, from the ham, and tenderloin, with a bit of fat), this shop also carries another 50 kinds of cured meat products (Greek brands, plus an excellent Italian mortadella).

Select
26, Kanari St., Kolonaki, 210/3611671.
Excellent charcuterie, with a selection of 80 different products (Greek and imported), including Parma ham, Bresaola, authentic Hungarian salamis, German garlic sausage, Marox products from Germany and Israeli turkey (steamed and smoked).

Alpha Bank
is beside you,
wherever you may go

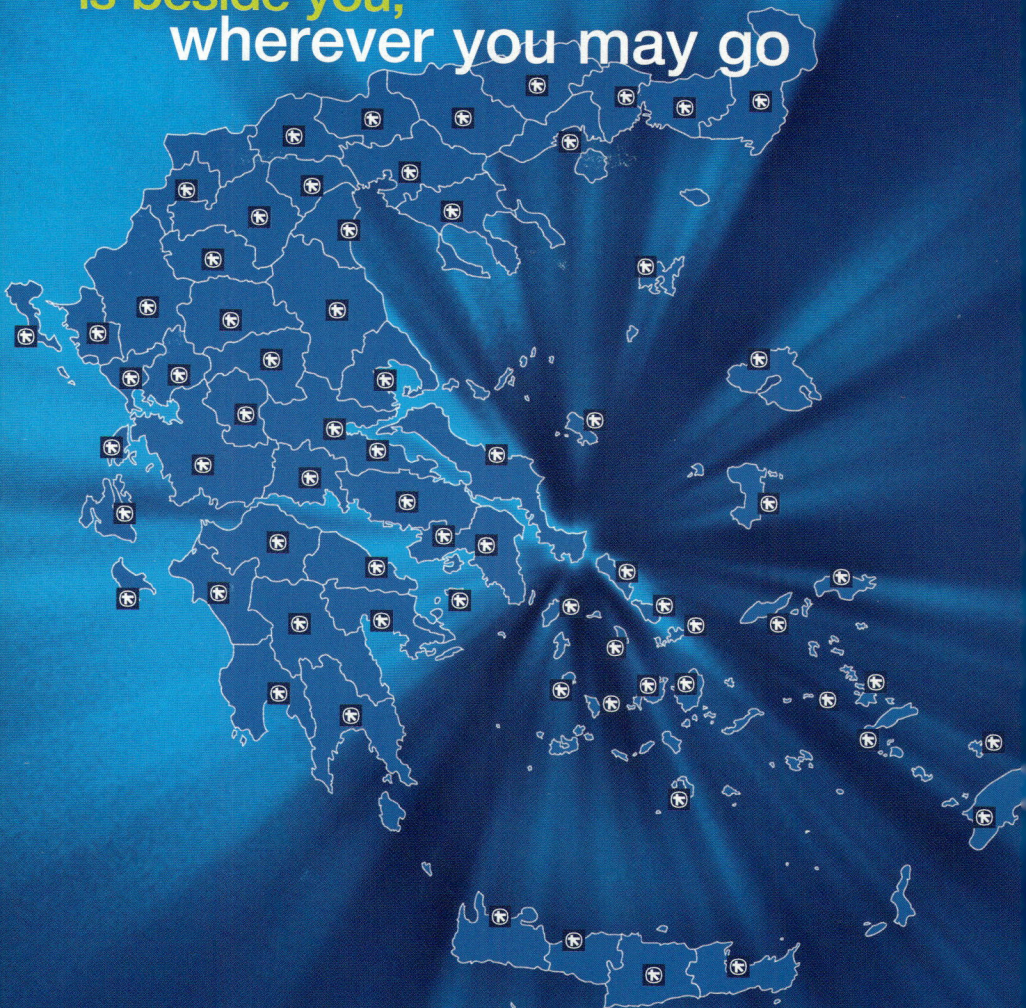

Wherever you travel, in every corner of Greece, you will find at least one Alpha Bank Branch. And thanks to the electronic services of the Bank's ATM Network, you can carry out your banking transactions directly at more than 730 points all over the country, 365 days a year, 24 hours a day. This means that you can enjoy freedom in full security, knowing that, wherever you are, Alpha Bank is there too. With pioneering programmes and services and above all with the spirit of collaboration that governs its employees' relationship with customers: "Mazi" *

"Mazi" in Greek means "together"

ATHENS 2004

ALPHA BANK
OFFICIAL
BANK

ALPHA BANK OFFICIAL BANK OF THE ATHENS 2004 OLYMPIC GAMES

Services

Athens Guide 2003

ATHENS 2004

ALPHA BANK
OFFICIAL BANK

make your life easier

This section contains a host of little secrets for the good life, tips to add a touch of luxury to your everyday existence and make life that little bit easier. From organising parties and other events, including the location and the people who will see to everything, to hiring a limousine, a yacht or an aircraft, finding home help or a courier or a special kind of florist to costume rentals, wigs and shops that specialise in repairing luxury goods: it's all in here, to help you when you're looking for the magic answer.

What is it that we call luxury, small or great? It is, in the end, all the things that save us time, quickly and easily. This may be an unusual definition, but I don't think many people would disagree with it. A carefully prepared meal delivered to your door when friends drop in unexpectedly, a repair shop that can fix a valuable item - these are everyday luxuries that are not expensive in themselves, but are invaluable to us in today's busy world.

This section of the Athens Guide may not appear particularly interesting at first glance, but it will provide solutions to any number of problems as if by magic. And for most of these services, you won't even need to leave home: with just a phone call or two you can organise a super party or dinner party, send gifts, find household help and much more - all you have to do is dial the right numbers. Everyday problems, large or small, solved in the way you want - this, too, is an invisible but substantial contribution to everyday quality of life.

Reception at Island

Reception by Party Mobile Services

RECEPTIONS
CATERING-
ORGANISERS
EVENTS

5 Aisthiseis

210/6646976, 0972956502.
Parties, openings, wedding receptions, baptisms, flower arrangements, balloon constructions, fireworks, decor, music, clowns, catering. They collaborate with several well-known reception venues (winter and summer places).

Aidinis

106, Iroon Polytechneiou St, Neo Psychiko, 210/6713883, 210/6713179.
A well-known name in the catering field. They will provide venues, food and drink (any sort of menu), staff and sound systems for your events.

Andriotis Catering

13, M. Lountemi St., Pefki (on the edge of Lykovrysi), 210/2841685.
Wonderful food, served in your home or in the company's special (winter and summer) facilities. Perfect solution for wedding receptions and other similar events.

Aria Getseon

Vari-Koropi Ave. & Parou, Vari (opposite Scholi Evelpidon), 210/9656388-90.
Original menu suggestions, well-prepared and beautifully presented, in three spacious halls (Limni Vouliagmenis, Ktima Flerianou, Asteria Seaside) to host your party or reception.

Berco

14, Ierou Lochou St, Marousi, 210/6105255, e-mail: berco@otenet.gr, www.berco.gr
The organisers of some of the most rarefied social events and parties in the country. They can provide

---

Bonsai

34, Laodikeias St., Nikaia, 210/4940660, www.asianfood-bonsai.gr
Specialising in Chinese buffets for parties in your home (up to 70 people). The menu might include anything from homemade lasagne and spring rolls to chicken in coconut cream. They will set up the buffet (red dragon-decked tableclocths), and can also provide sound systems/music for the event.

M. Panagiotidou

20, Tinou St, Alsoupoli, Kato Fliothel, 210/2772745, 210/6770291,
e-mail:pincom@otenet.gr
Receptions, business meetings and all kinds of events catered.

Friandises

6, Sp. Loui St. & Mitropoleos, Marousi, 210/8023949, 210/8088869.
Greek and French cuisine, in a home-cooked style. You must try their crepes (mushroom, spinach or chicken) and their quiches (herb and cheese, ardenoise, spinach). Another top seller is the pasticcio variant, made with green tagliatelle and prosciutto.

Ideal Catering

46, Panepistimiou St, 210/3303000-3.
The all time classic restaurant on Panepistimiou St, now in your own home. Greek and international cuisine prepared to order.

In Medias Res

16, Kifisias Ave., Marousi, 210/6850820.

DJs, any kind of band or orchestra, dance duos, fireworks, and even portable dance floors to save your precious hardwood floors.
Apart from its famous menus and cocktails, this caterer can also provide Chinese and Thai dishes and sushi.

Intercatering

3, Xanthou St., Glyfada, 210/8946625,
www.intercatering.gr
One of the biggest catering services in the country. Wide variety of menu suggestions and fine art de la table. They will undertake to organise your event in any of six venues of which they have exclusive use (Island at Limanakia Vouliagmenis, the Yacht Club at Microlimano, the Yacht Club at Agios Kosmas, Thexenia at Kefalari, the Pieridis Gallery in Glyfada and the Epistroff Gallery in Psyrri).

La Fourchette

22, Pigasou St., Polydroso Amarousiou, 210/6830165.
International and traditional cuisine specialties, impeccable presentation. Fine equipment, decoration by professional stylists, music. They will also arrange a venue for your reception.

Love & Marriage

19-21, Makrygianni St, 210/9241277,
e-mail: Love-mar@acci.gr
Imaginative ideas for the wedding of your dreams, with limousines, band, special decorations, etc. They will also organise bachelor parties, baptisms and other events.

Ma Cuisine

10, Panepistimiou St, 210/3636209, 210/3642154, 210/3619602, 210/3618073.
One of the best catering firms in the city. They will look after every detail (decoration, lighting, music, etc.) of

your party or reception, no matter how large (or small). Managers of the cafe in the Museum of Cycladic Art, which is available for children's parties, they also collaborate with reception gardens.

Pentelikon

66, Diligianni St., Kifisia, 210/6230650.
Greek, French, Polynesian, Chinese, and Mexican cuisine and whatever else you may want for a buffet or formal dinner. In fine weather you can hold a reception catering for up to 2000 people at Ktima Pentelikon!

Platis Gastronomie

29th St., Elliniko, 210/9636495.
Complete catering service for parties, receptions, dinners - from decoration and setting up to menu and music. Foreign and Greek cuisine.

Seven Stars

11, Efrosynis St., Kolonos, 210/5151155.
Receive your guests in fine style, with fireworks, balloons, confetti, candies shot out of cannons or champagne that creates a fountain of rose petals. Also very good for children's parties.

Waves Catering

3, Kantharou St., Piraeus, 210/4532391.
Full catering for any event, from food (international cuisine) and decoration to sound systems/music (orchestra, DJ). They also have a reception hall accommodating up to 400 (Peiraikos Syndesmos Hall).

PARTY PLANNERS

Anastazia Fotiadou

10, 28th October St., Palio
Making a wedding, a baptism, a reception something unique and very special is child's play for the imaginative talents of consultant Anastazia Fotiadou. She will fashion all the constructions - wreaths, bonbonnieres, etc. - herself and the results will surely bear her creative stamp. Psychiko, 210/6711420, 0932273323.

Klea Iliopoulou

210/9828498, 0932370469.
Klea Iliopoulou is both a personal shopper and a party planner. She will select the gifts for best man, godparents, etc., and help you in many other ways e.g. choosing furniture for your house.

Lia Kanari

210/8234382, 0932614572.
One of the first in Greece to use the term "wedding consultant" - and she really means it. If you want totally original hand-drawn invitations, a fabulous antique roadster, a string quartet and some swans or doves, then you can't do better than consult Ms Kanari.

Party Mobile Services (Elena Jeffrey)

42, G. Vlachou St., Neo Psychiko, 210/6744329, 210/6718531.
Elena studied photography, but very soon realised that what really interested her was to create her own atmospheric images. And so she specialised in interior styling and the art de la table. Consult her for your wedding arrangements, and of course any other reception or presentation.

Rania Stefanaki

210/6210746, 0977258233.
She organises wedding receptions, of course, but also all kinds of other events - baptisms, openings, conferences, even small dinner parties - arranging the food, the surprises, the atmosphere and the music. Consult her for your own bridal styling.

HOME CHEF

Aiman Elhambasi

210/8043117, 0977950797.
The Egyptian chef who can create exotic Egyptian dishes for you, or give cooking lessons in your home.

Rania Oraiopoulou

210/2770364, 210/2754779.
Will do all the cooking for you, with a different menu every day.

Rania Papadopoulou

210/6401431.
Delicious home style meals for any occasion.

SOUND SYSTEMS

Audio Coverage

3, Keas St., Chalandri, 210/6855789, 210/8386808.
Full sound coverage for any event, by experienced, professional DJs. Live music with orchestra.

Club Rackey's

27, Amarousiou Ave., Lykovrysi, 210/2823255, 210/2845799.
Wedding receptions, parties, openings. Seasonal engagements for clubs.

Jesto's Sound and Light Club

26, Dionysiou Solomou St., Nea Ionia, 210/2711124,
Sound and lighting for various events, weddings, conferences, parties. Famous DJs. Seasonal engagements, sales and installations.

Sonus Sound Systems

28, Myriofytou St., Nea Smyrni, 210/9340499, www.sonus.gr
Music and sound systems for

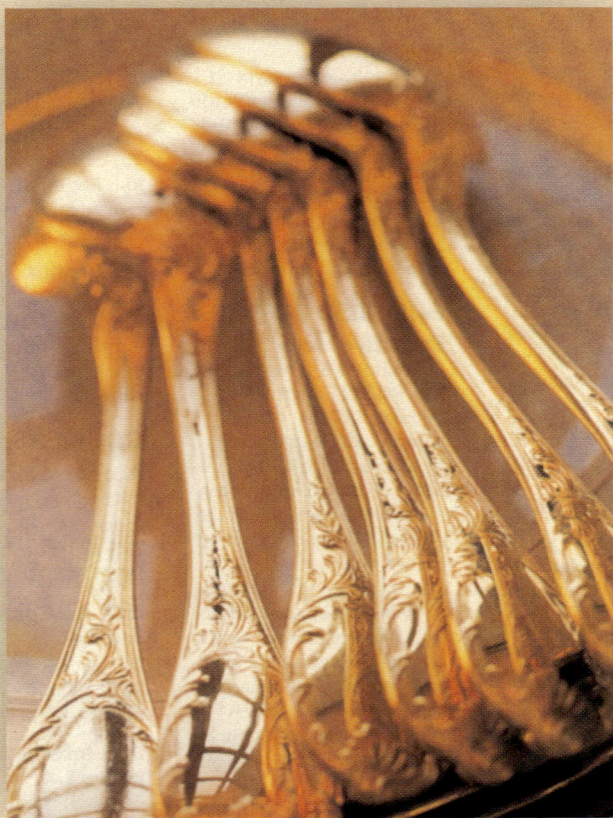

ma Cuisine

Reception services

10, Panepistimiou St., 106 71 Athens
Tel. 210/3636209, 210/3642154, 210/3619602, 210/3618073
Fax: 210/3636209

social and business/professional events, by experts.

Techno - Sound
30, Laodikeias St.,
"Notia" Shopping Centre,
Glyfada, 210/8946510,
0932956852.
Rental, sale and installation of professional sound and lighting systems.

PRIVATE MUSIC
Zontani Mousiki
210/8670120, 210/3231300,
e-mail: cosmicsound@
ath.forthnet.gr
One or more musicians,
even a full orchestra, to give a special note to your event.

DJs
Christos Giannikopoulos
210/9921664, 0932610106.
Plays all kinds of music, with the emphasis on the 25-50 year-old age group.

Giorgos Doxastakis
210/4113343, 0944360932.
Team of four DJs, for any kind of event, in Athens or elsewhere. Full repertory, sound and lighting systems.

Musico
37, K. Palaiologou,
210/6897247
Will supply experienced DJs with vast and flexible repertories for any kind of event.

Nikos Lymperopoulos
210/8230507, 0977677627.
Knowledgeable and experienced, with years in radio and major musical productions. For a high-flying musical evening.

Panagiotis Lyras
210/8962513, 0932236020.
Sound coverage by a team of six DJs.

KARAOKE
Karaoke Fun & Multi Media
4, Kallisperi St.,

Makrygianni, 210/9241568.
Karaoke events for your party or business reception.
They will lease and set up the equipment and, if you wish, provide DJs and MCs. Huge range of musical selections.

FACILITIES
HOME HELP
HEN (YWCA)
11, Amerikis St., Kolonaki,
210/3624291-4.
Will supply home help and baby-sitters, on a permanent or occasional basis.

Imigrante
116, Sapfous St., Kyprou
Sq., Kallithea, 210/9524510,
210/9565550, 0944501198.
Household staff (all kinds) supplied to the best Athenian houses. All arrangements are made through the bureau, and they bring the candidate(s) to your premises.

BUSINESS SERVICES
Executive Moto
5, Lachouri St., Athens,
210/9229800, e-mail:
info@executivemoto.gr,
www.executivemoto.gr
With their large fleet of heavy motorcycles they can take you to any point in the greater Athens region in record time.
The company has a travel division to look after ticketing, check-in, baggage services. They will also look after any kind of ex-office services: filing income tax and VAT returns, dealings with public services and banks, bill paying, etc.

Tilegrammateia
6, Lantza St., Athens,
210/2111666.
24-hour telephone service, notifying you of incoming calls if you are away, and notifying your clients of your absence and expected date of return.

BODYGUARD SERVICES
Falcon
Km 16, Lavriou Ave.,
Paiania, 210/6041270 (10 lines), 210/6041266,
e-mail: falcon@acn.gr,
www.falconsecurity.gr

Silver Guard Protection
6, Philippidi St., Nea
Filothei, 210/6912921-2,
e-mail: silvergroup@
b_online.gr

Special Security Office
3, Ch. Mouskou St., Ilisia,
210/7709708, 210/7751974.

Universal Security Service
16, Ellispontou St. & Bizaniou, Papagou, 210/6525211,
e-mail: info@uss.gr,
www.uss.gr

Wackenhut
7, Sorou St., Metamorfosi,
210/2896300, 210/2896362,
e-mail: hellaswack@
wackenhut.gr,
www.wackenhut.gr

COURIERS
Aces Couriers
8, Diocharous & 5-7,
Kleisouras St., Kaisariani,
210/7257783, fax
210/7249370, 210/7257780.

ACS Air Courier Services
25, Asklipiou St., Kryoneri,
210/8190000,
fax 210/8190261.

DHL International Hellas S.A.
44, Alimou Ave. & 17, Roma
St., Alimos, 210/9890800,
210/9890000,
fax 210/9841044.

Gold Mail
26, Thermopylon St.,
Agios Dimitrios,
210/9755555,
fax 210/9766623.

Exclusive

Services

Intermail Couriers S.A.
73, Machis Analatou St.,
Athens, 210/9019000,
fax 210/9029755.

Interpost Couriers
Kifisias Ave. &
4, Th. Oikonomou St.,
210/6743300,
fax 210/6743344.

Speedex Ltd
578A, Vouliagmenis Ave.,
Argyroupoli, 210/9943100,
fax 210/9943600.

TNT Express Worldwide
Z7 Elliniko, Elliniko,
210/8940062, 210/8983500,
fax 210/8949974.

Trust Mail
19, Koromila Ave., Athens,
210/9242080,
fax 210/9246637.

U.P.S. Hellas
98A, Alimou Ave.,
Argyroupoli, 210/9984000,
fax 210/9984099.

RENTALS
CARS
Auto Europe
2, Petmeza St., Koukaki,
210/9242206-7, e-mail:
aegreece@travelling.gr

Avis
46-48, Amalias Ave.,
Athens, 210/3224951-7,
www.avis.gr

Budget
94-96, Kifisou Ave., Agios
Ioannis Rentis,
210/3498800,
e-mail: reservations@
budget.gr, www.budget.gr

European
36-38, Syngrou Ave.,
210/9246778,
210/9246820-1,
e-mail: europea2@otenet.gr,
www.european-
rentacar.com

Hertz
12, Syngrou Ave.,
210/9982998-9,

210/9220102-4,
www.hertz.gr

Kosmos
4, Syngrou Ave.,
210/9234697-8, 210/9215430.

Luxury Cars for Rent
1, Syngrou Ave.,
210/9226666-9,
210/9222442-4, e-mail:
info@luxurycarsforrent.gr,
www.luxurycarsforrent.gr

Reliable International
3, Syngrou Ave.,
210/9249000,
www.reliable.gr

Sixt
138-140, Kifisou Ave.,
Peristeri, 210/5706895,
www.sixt.de

Thrifty
25, Syngrou Ave.,
210/9243310, e-mail:
dionisos@otenet.gr,
www.thriftygreece.gr

VIP's
Syngrou Ave. & 18,
Chatzichristou St.,
210/9246001, e-mail:
vipsrental@otenet.gr,
www.vipsrental.gr

CHAUFFEURED LIMOUSINES
Convecta
46, Amalias Ave.,
Syntagma, 210/3253286,
210/3221212,
e-mail: convecta@
travelling.gr
Mercedes models.

Royal Prestige
33, Perikleous St., Palio
Faliro, 210/9883221,
0944305000.
Luxury 7-seater Lincolns
with bar, Rolls Royce,
Mercedes.

PLANES - HELICOPTERS
Aegean Cronus
572, Vouliagmenis Ave.,

Argyroupoli, 210/9988350,
210/6694015, e-mail:
contact@aegeanair.com,
www.aegeanair.com
Two Lear Jet 55s, 6 and
7 passengers.

Air Miles
85, Vouliagmenis Ave., City
Plaza Shopping Centre,
Glyfada, 210/9603943-4,
e-mail: info@goairmiles.com,
www.goairmiles.com

Athens Aviation Services
18, Metsovou St., Glyfada,
210/3533717-8,
e-mail: aas@compulink.gr,
www.athensaviation.gr
Two 18-seater Jetstream 31
turbo props, one 7-seater
PA31, and one 5-seater heli-
copter.

Aviator
Athens International Air-
port, Spata, 210/3553713.
VIP aircraft: one 18-seater
Beach Craft 1900 and one
8-seater King Air 200.

Bellavia Ltd
95, El. Venizelou St., Nea
Ionia, 210/2759509,
e-mail: bellavia@hellasnet.gr
Two VIP helicopters: one
7-seater Bell 230 and one
4-seater Bell 206.

Chartair
21, Poseidonos Ave.,
Alimos, 210/9846165,
210/3617800, 0944394088
(24 hour line),
www.avinet.gr
Three aircraft: one 7-seater
executive Lear Jet 55 and two
18-seaters. Also 5- and 7-
seater executive helicopters.

Euroair
Athens International Air-
port, Spata, 210/3530123,
801-071070, 0945745200,
e-mail: info@euroair.gr,
www.euroair.gr
One 18-seater Embraer and
one 8-seater Piper Chieftain.

Ghiolman
7, Filellinon St., Syntagma, 210/3233696, 210/3230330, 0974500500 (24 hour line). Helicopters (2-5 seats) and aircraft, twin-engine 5-seaters, 8-11 passenger prop and jet planes.

Greek Air
81, Archimidous St., Mandra Tseva, Koropi, 210/6020609, 210/6020619, e-mail: greekair@otenet.gr, www.greekair.gr
Helicopters: single engine 5-seater and twin-engine 5 and 6-seaters, for domestic flights. 6-8 seat jet aircraft for domestic / international flights.

Interjet
32, El. Venizelou St., Glyfada, 210/9612050 (24 hour line), 210/3530132, e-mail: info@interjet.gr, www.interjet.gr

Three luxury jets: two 8-seaters (Falcon 2000 and Cessna Citation V Ultra) and one 9-seater (Cessna Citation Excel). Also one 4-seater and four 5-seater helicopters.

Karafil Ntoylis
602A, Vouliagmenis Ave., Argyroupoli, 210/9967870. Single- and twin-engine 7- and 5-seater helicopters.

Olympic Aviation
Athens International Airport, Spata, 210/9368600, 210/9368565, e-mail: charter@olav.gr
Four 4- and 5-seater helicopters, aircraft seating 18 and up.

YACHTS/SAILBOATS

Andros Yachting
245, Syngrou Ave., 210/9429006, 210/9429569, e-mail: androyacht@otenet.gr,

www.andros-yachting.gr
Sailboats, yachts and motor-sailers, with or without crew.

Atalanta Marine
9, Kassandras St., Kastella, Piraeus, 210/4174669, e-mail: gertsos@hol.gr
Sailboats (sleep 4-8), yachts (sleep 6-10), with or without crew.

Easy Sailing
4, N. Vrettakou St., Alimos, 210/9859363, www.easysailing.gr
Sailboats and motor yachts, with or without crew.

Ghiolman
7, Filellinon St., Syntagma, 210/3233696, 210/3230330, 0974500500 (24 hour line), e-mail: ghiolman@ghiolman.com, www.ghiolman.com
One of the best-known yacht brokers. Sailboats, lux-

Real Is Good...
...Interesting is Better
ST. KUBRICK

amuse
ARTIST MANAGEMENT | EVENTS PLANNING

ury mega yachts, catamarans, speedboats, motorsailers.

Kiriakoulis Mediterranean Cruises
7, Alimou Ave., Alimos, 210/9886187, e-mail: charter@kiriacoulis.com, www.kiriacoulis.com
Sailboats (sleep 6-10) and motor yachts (sleep 4-7), with or without skipper.

Nomicos Yachts
7, Eleftherias Ave., Alimos, 210/9851385-7, e-mail: nomicoya@otenet.gr
Sailboats, motor yachts and catamarans, with or without crew.

Vernicos Yachts
11, Poseidonos Ave., Alimos, 210/9896000, e-mail: info@vernicos.gr, www.vernicos.com
One of the biggest yacht brokers. Sailboats, motor yachts, catamarans (with or without skipper), mega yachts with full crew.

FOR SPECIAL CASES

REPAIRS
FURS - LEATHERS
Posto Pelle
28, Emm. Benaki St. & Akadimias, Athens, 210/3640488.
Will repair tears and any other damage to leather goods. Also dyeing and cleaning.

Spyros & Kostas Kogios
10, Kleitiou St. & Evangelistrias, 210/3218536, 210/3223964.
Will give old-fashioned furs a new look and repair any damage.

JEWELLERY
Lefteris Paradias
170, Filolaou St., Pagkrati, 210/7017801.

Lefteris will repair the jewellery you bring him while you wait. He will also engrave a name or date on the back of a wedding wreath case, icon or other object.

Lydia Lithos
51, Protopappa St., Ano Ilioupoli, 210/9938061.
Spyros Charalambidis will repair jewellery, string pearls, or set pearls and/or other precious or semi-precious stones into a handsome necklace.

GLASS - CRYSTAL
Alexandros Papadopoulos
16, Pallados St., Psyrri, 210/3247609, 210/3243009.
Etching, glass sculpture, repairs to crystal.

Stavros Stratou
5, M. Alexandrou St., Kalogiron Sq., Dafni, 210/9717015.
Experienced glass-cutter. Apart from repairs, he will also decorate glasses, carafes, mirrors, with modern motifs. If you wish, he can also give them an air of antiquity, using gilding and appropriate designs.

ANTIQUES
Ioannis Papanikitas
26, Metsovou St. & Zaimi, Exarcheia, 210/8226977.
Mr Papanikitas will polish the hand-finish, clean the upholstery and burnish the gold leaf on your antiques.

Nikolaos Roussos
3, Stadiou St., 210/3222815.
Antiquaire who will restore ivories, jewellery, ancient pottery.

Rodios
5 & 7, Pindarou St., Kolonaki, 210/3611239, 210/3616046.
Three generations of experi-

ence accumulated. They will repair broken porcelain, crystal, ivories and enamels so perfectly that they look like new.

ICONS - PAINTINGS
Dora Christopoulou
210/6721833.
Dora, who studied art restoration, knows how to expertly clean and protect your valuable treasures.

LAMPS
Stelios Mousadakos
10, Vas. Georgiou Ave., Chalandri, 210/6831368.
Workshop/atelier where, with patience and expertise, they will repair any damage to your lampshades or chandeliers.

FURNITURE
Giorgos Mavrakis
13, Gr. Lampraki St., Agios Dimitrios, 210/9707530, 210/9707996 (residence).
Sanding, restoring, turning, carving, re-upholstering.

Manos Nazos
14, Alamanas St., Dafni, 210/9731239, 0945740091.
Skilful upholstery repairs to furniture, buildings, ships, bars, at reasonable prices by Mr Manos.

Pavlos Poulis
40, Sp. Trikoupi St., Exarcheia, 210/8219646.
Restoration and repairs to classic or modern furniture.

RUGS & CARPETS
Edward Georgiou
31, Marasli St., Kolonaki, 210/7215923.
Restoration, valuation and sale of hand-knotted carpets from all over the world. They will also repair patterns, re-edge and fringe, and dye carpets.

Dareios Carpets
46, Kifisias Ave.,
Ampelokipoi, 210/7751187,
210/7771335.
Dareios came from Persia,
and he brought with him the
secrets of proper restoration
of hand-knotted carpets. The
one inflexible rule: nothing
but hand work.

Soutzoglou
2, Skoufa St. (1st floor),
Kolonaki, 210/3607779.
The Soutzoglou family has
been working with carpets
for over a century.
They will repair damage,
restore colour and re-
weave patterns in hand-
knotted carpets, tapestries
and kilimia.

MUSICAL INSTRUMENTS

Evangelos Kagmakis
36, Emmanouil Benaki St.,
Exarcheia, 210/3803727.
Will repair any damage to,
and improve the acoustics
of, your guitar.

Petros Michalitsianos
25, G. Vlachouli St., Neo
Psychiko, 210/6770737.
Anything to do with wind
instruments.

LUGGAGE

Adonini
22, Doukissis Plakentias,
Ampelokipoi, 210/6917191.
Have your favourite
bag repaired, or choose a
new one of their manufac-
ture, at very reasonable
prices.

Sofos
54, Agias Foteinis St.,
Nea Ionia, 210/2798993.
5, Agiou Vasiliou St.,
N. Ionia.
Take advantage of their experience - for 50 years they
have been repairing handbags,
luggage, vanity cases.

SPECIAL CLEANERS

Lymperopoulos Panagiotis
51, Plataion St. & Parnithos,
Vrilissia, 210/6131924.
Experts in cleaning haute
couture garments. Even the
most difficult cases.

Lazaridis Hat Cleaners
1, Peiraios St. (in the stoa),
Omonoia Sq., 210/3249082.
We brought in our hats and
they cleaned them, starched
them, pressed them,
refreshed them. Now, with
the brims smoothed, the
crowns steam-cleaned and
the bands changed, if necessary, they look like new.

FLORISTS

Antonello
11, Syngrou Ave.,
210/9234305, 210/9242455.
2, Skoufa St., Kolonaki,
210/3624586.
Progressive florist shop, that
"plays" with fruit and curious
objects. Abstract arrangements inspired by Ikebana,
also lavish fruity compositions. Ask them to encircle
a teddy bear with flowers
(for a friend who's just had
a baby), or let them indulge
in tender white creations for
your dinner party table. In
everything they are both
imaginative and flexible.

Bouquet
43, Anagnostopoulou St.,
Kolonaki, 210/3616454.
Unusual fastenings for bouquets, beautiful youthful
posies of tiny fresh rosebuds.
Special arrangements for
lovers. Beautifully fresh buds
without fancy trimmings, and
tender bouquets for romantic weddings and other
events. Personally supervised
by Mrs Eleni Oikonomou.

Fleria
35, Patriarchou Ioakeim St.,

Kolonaki, 210/7229697,
210/7229698. 363, Kifisias
Ave., Nea Erythraia,
210/6209382. 73, Pentelis
Ave., Chalandri,
210/6814425, 210/6842568.
74, Kyprou St., Glyfada,
210/9680296, 210/9680064.
It is nearly ten years since
Nina Ioannidi shook the status quo of flower arranging
to its foundations, with
lemons in her windows, artichokes in wedding bouquets
and Christmas cone arrangements of apples. Since then,
of course, she has become
an institution, and everybody
raves about all her ideas -
from a flying vase of freesias
to one of her famous pop
flower pots!

Petridis
314, Kifisias Ave., Psychiko,
210/6728370-5. 81, Posei-
donos Ave. & Dousmani,
Glyfada, 210/9681230.
Classic creative florist, with
quality and inspiration.
Seasonal arrangements, magnificent bouquets, tender
posies of rare flowers - all
elegantly wrapped and presented.

Ponirakis
45, Patriarchou Ioakeim St.,
Kolonaki, 210/7220662.
5, Ang. Metaxa St., Glyfada, 210/8945496,
210/8943635.
A family with a long tradition
in the flower business that
has created elegant shops all
over Athens. The Ponirakis
florists shops are supplied
from their nurseries in Marathonas - the family controls
the whole cycle, from production to sale, you see,
which explains their low
prices and rapid execution
of orders.

excursions
in the best
of company

Nafplion or Olympia? Hydra or Spetses? Whatever the choice, you know that what really counts is the mood - and of course the company. And in your case, you're always assured of the very best. With the ATHENS 2004 Silver VISA, the card created by Alpha Bank, the Official Bank of the ATHENS 2004 Olympic Games, travelling is totally carefree. For just € 3 per month, it will escort you to the best hotels, take you out to dinner and go shopping with you. With the ATHENS 2004 Silver VISA Card you can move around freely and enjoy your excursion, without any worries. All you have to do is make the right choice! Are we off?

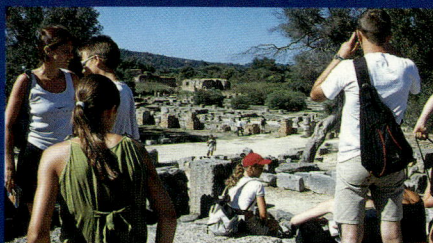

ALPHA BANK OFFICIAL BANK OF THE ATHENS 2004 OLYMPIC GAMES

Excursions

Athens Guide 2003

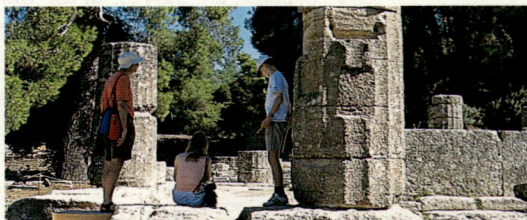

short
breaks

This section outlines six short tours
of archaeological and natural interest,
organised to the smallest detail.
All can be done as day trips,
if you wish. We take you by road
to Olympia, Delphi, Epidaurus,
Mycenae and Nafplio, places of
exceptional archaeological value
and epicentres of the cultural life of
Ancient Greece. As for our maritime
excursions, to Hydra, Poros,
Aegina and Spetses, they provide a
first taste of the beauties of the
Aegean and its islands.

OLYMPIA

**For the Greeks, it is a sacred
place; for the rest of the world,
the site of the Olympic Games.
This pilgrimage to Ancient
Olympia completes our journey
of discovery of Classical Greece.
The 2004 Games will simply
shed more light on this part of
Greece.**

The landscape is imposing, the
sense of history all-pervasive, the
serenity of the natural setting
soothing and relaxing. Occupying
a privileged situation of tranquil
Mediterranean beauty among the
foothills of the verdant Hill of
Cronius, at the confluence of the
Alpheios and Cladeos rivers, the
archaeological site of Olympia is
one of the most important and
most beautiful in Greece.
And in view of the 2004 Olympiad,
the sacred grove in which the
Olympic Games were born and
took place in ancient times acquires
additional interest and is expected
to be included in the itineraries of

Temple of Hera, Ancient Olympia

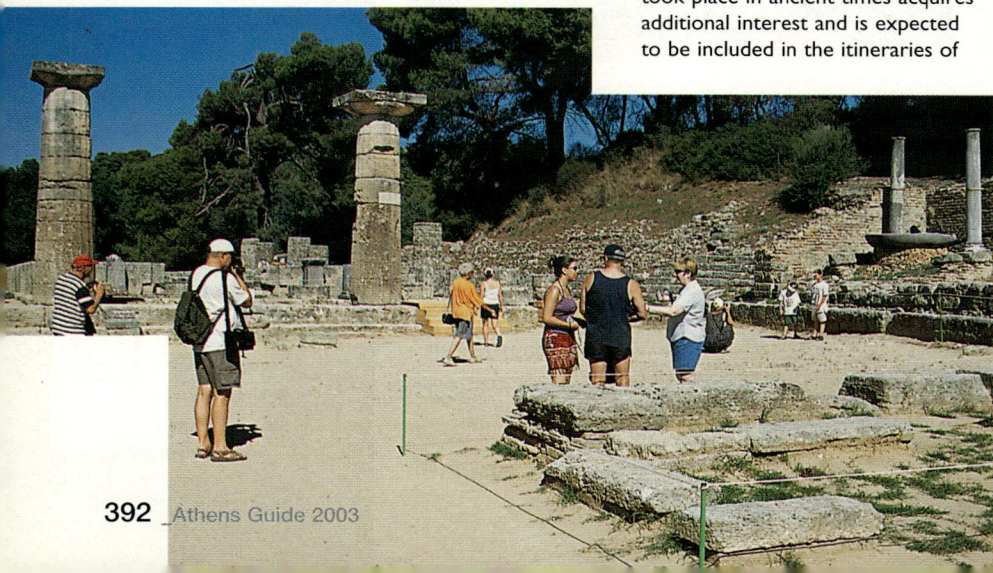

The beach at Skafidia

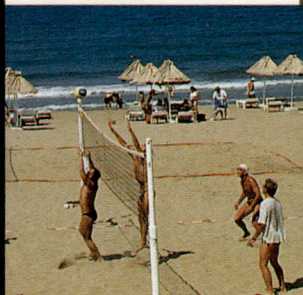

The Modern Olympic Games Museum

Agios Andreas

an ever-increasing number of visitors to this country. Particularly in the summer months, hundreds of tourists come here every day, many of them by coach from Athens on an organised day trip. And although the modern town of Olympia is of little interest, the surrounding area has much to attract the nature-lover, plus some of the finest sandy beaches in Greece and a selection of perfectly adequate accommodation, making Olympia a good base for a weekend jaunt.

The archaeological site

Olympia is one of the most important sanctuaries in the ancient world, it began to develop in the 10th - 9th century BC and was dedicated to Zeus, the father of the gods. The first monument that you come to as you enter the archaeological site is the Gymnasium (2nd century BC), a large rectangular building with a central courtyard surrounded by Doric colonnades. Here the athletes trained in the sports that required a lot of space: running, discus, javelin. The next building is the Palaestra (3rd century BC), where competitors in wrestling, boxing and jumping events trained. A little farther along is the workshop where the famous sculptor Pheidias created the gold and ivory (chryselephantine) statue of the god that adorned the Temple of Zeus, dominant on your left. This gigantic temple (470-456 BC), built by the Elean architect Libon and occupying the most prominent position on the site, is considered the most important building in the complex and the perfect expression of Doric temple architecture. From here you can survey the entire archaeological site, and decide which way to go next. The altar of Hera, next to the temple of the goddess, where every four years the Olympic Flame is kindled; the

tip
The best time of year to visit Ancient Olympia is in the spring, when the trees are in flower and the sun not too strong.

Ancient Olympia

Pheidias' Workshop

ATHENS 2004

ALPHA BANK
OFFICIAL BANK

Stadium (5th century BC), into which the sacred flame is carried in procession and where in ancient times as many as 45,000 spectators, seated on the ground, would watch the naked athletes compete; the Zanes (16 bases for bronze statues of Zeus erected with money from fines imposed on those who violated the rules of the Games); the (Roman) Western Thermes next to the baths, their mosaic floors still in fairly good condition: these are just some of the remaining monuments on the site that you should see.

The archaeological museum

The archaeological museum of Olympia, opposite the archaeological site, houses the finds from the excavations of the Sanctuary. The "Nike" of Paionios (5th c. BC), with her flowing garments, and Praxiteles' harmonious "Hermes carrying the young Dionysus" (4th c. BC), both

carved out of Parian marble, are two of the finest sculptures of classical antiquity and among the museum's most prized possessions. The central gallery is dominated by the two magnificent pediments from the Temple of Zeus: the scene on the east pediment - the chariot race between Pelops and Oinomaos - is arranged around the central figure of Zeus the judge, and that on the west pediment - the Battle of the Lapiths and Centaurs - around the figure of Apollo. In the pottery room, don't miss the group of Zeus and Ganymede (480-470 BC), a marvellous piece from a Corinthian workshop, or the oenochoe with the words "I am (the property) of Pheidias" inscribed on the base, which was found in the sculptor's workshop. Also remarkable is the collection of some 14,000 bronze items, thought to be the largest in the world, which includes weapons,

tip
Come early, before the parking lot fills up with coaches and campers and the ancient columns are swamped by tour groups and their guides.

ANCIENT OLYMPIA

The valley between the rivers Alpheios and Cladeos, where the sanctuary lies, was in ancient times lush with wild olives, poplars, oaks, pines and plane trees, and for that reason the sanctuary was known as the Altis, or Grove.
The cult of Zeus was probably introduced into this area about 1200 BC, when the Aetolians, a Doric tribe ruled by Oetylus, settled in the region. The Olympic Games were established in 776 BC in honour of Zeus. They were held every four years, a religious festival that followed a strict ritual. In the beginning they were held in the area in front of the altars and, as the years passed, in the various installations that were continually being added to. The victors were crowned with the cotinus, a wreath made from a

branch of the olive tree that grew near the Temple of Zeus.
The Temple of Zeus was destroyed in 393 AD, when the Byzantine Emperor Theodosius I condemned all the ancient temples. In 426 AD, Theodosius II ordered the destruction of all the buildings in the Sanctuary, a work of destruction that was completed by two severe earthquakes, in 522 and 551 AD. The archaeological excavation of the site began in May 1829 by a team of French archaeologists. Their finds were taken to the Louvre, where they still remain. The excavation work was interrupted, taken up again in 1875 by German archaeologists, and is now carried out by the German Archaeological Institute in Athens under the supervision of the Ephorate of Antiquities of Olympia.

statuettes, tripod cauldrons, helmets and other articles, most of which were votive offerings to Zeus.

If you are interested in the modern history of the Olympic Games, pay a visit to the Museum of the Modern Olympic Games which, although not very well tended, contains a large collection of related items (medals, torches, posters, copper-plates, etc.) from the first International Olympic Committee in Paris (1864) to the most recent Games.

If you're visiting Olympia in the summer, you might want to check out the programme of the Flokas Festival (there will be posters everywhere). The events (varied) are held in the 3500-place Flokas Amphitheatre, which was built for the Festival a few years ago of stone brought from nearby Andritsaina (the same as that used for the Temple of Apollo). The venue has a coffee shop and parking area.

DATA

How to get there

By car: via the Athens-Patra-Pyrgos-Olympia national highway.
By train: OSE, 210/3624402.
By bus: KTEL, 210/5124910. Many tour operators organise day trips.

Where to stay

At the *Amalia* (26240/22190), a standard establishment from the familiar Greek chain, at the refur-

bished *Antonios* (26240/22348-9), with a marvellous view of Ancient Olympia, at the handsome *Europa* (26240/22650), a Best Western hotel, at the luxurious *Olympia Palace* (26240/23101), at the new and very comfortable *Olympion Asty* (26240/23665-7), with a fabulous view of the valley of Alpheios.

Where to eat

Cooked dishes - specialties include rabbit in lemon sauce and lamb with oil and oregano - in the family taverna *Amvrosia* (26240/23414, 26240/23755), and simple short order dishes in the *Cladeos* (26240/23322), beside the little tributary of the Alpheios behind the railway station in Olympia. Fish at *Glyfada*, in Katakolo (26240/41204). If you're hungry on the road, the must place to stop is at *Aigli* (26210/22502), at km 4 on the Pyrgos-Patra national highway, for cooked dishes.

Archaeological site and museum

Opening hours: Winter (29/9-27/4): daily 8.00-17.00. Only for the museum: Mon. 10.30-17.00. Summer (28/4-28/9): daily 8.00-19.00.
Admission: Single ticket for the archaeological site and the museum € 9. Separate tickets for each € 6. Reduced rate: € 5 and € 3 respectively.
Information: 26240/22742, 26240/22517, 26240/22529.

INFORMATION ABOUT ARCHAEOLOGICAL SITES

Holiday hours: 6/1, "Clean Monday" (1st day of Lent), Saturday of Holy Week, Easter Monday, Whit Monday, 15/8, 28/10, 6/3 (Melina Merkouri Day), 18/4, 18/5, 5/6 and the last weekend in September: 8.30-15.00. Good Friday: 12.00-17.00.
Reduced rates: For EU citizens over 65 years of age and students from countries outside the EU.
Free admission: For students from EU countries, families with 4 or more children, teachers and archaeologists. Free general admission on holidays and on Sundays from 1/11 to 31/3.
Valid for all the archaeological sites recommended in the excursions to follow.

Bourtzi

Syntagma Square

NAFPLIO, MYCENAE, EPIDAURUS

The neo-romantic atmosphere of Nafplio encounters ancient tragedy at Epidaurus and the mythological history of the House of Atreus at Mycenae. Truly a place for all seasons.

tip
In Nafplio you'll do a lot of walking, so you'll need comfortable shoes, a hat, sunglasses... and plenty of film.

NAFPLIO

Nafplio, with its majestic twin look-outs of Palamidi and Akronafplia offering spectacular views of Bourtzi and the Argolic Gulf, is a favourite destination for a weekend break at any time of year. Narrow lanes in the old town a-buzz with tourists, the waterfront promenade constantly animated with strollers, museums for every taste, streets lit by lanterns hanging outside traditional tavernas, and secrets waiting to be winkled out of back streets lined with little bars: all make up the very special place that is Nafplio.

The first thing on any historic sight-seeing tour's agenda are the 999 (or possibly 857 - people's tallies differ) steps to the Palamidi, the famous castle built in the second Venetian period (1686-1715). It rises to a height of 216 metres, and surveys the city and the sea lying behind it like a backdrop. At the top you can visit the historic Church of Agios Andreas (dating from the time of the Venetians) with the "lion of St Mark" on its escutcheon, and the historic cell where Kolokotronis was imprisoned. Both the Palamidi and its twin fortress of Akronafplia offer interesting climbs with spectacular views. The fortifications of the Akronafplia (or Itz Kale) are the result of multiple stages of construction, from the 2nd century BC to the Venetian fortifications we see today. Beneath the south face of both castles stretches the municipal beach of Arvanitia, whose turquoise waters are perfect for idyllic summer swimming. The Indian figs clinging to the imposing rock on which Akronafplia is built add a note of wild beauty to this lovely little bay.

The neo-romantic atmosphere of the old town, however, is quite unlike anything else. You will feel it in cobbled Syntagmatos square, with its Italianate air and its all-day cafes, where the local people sit sipping their coffee and watching the tourists looking at the two great buildings facing each other across the square: the Archaeological Museum (with finds mainly from the Mycenaean period), housed in an old Venetian naval stores depot, and the Old Mosque (Palio Tzami), a Lancasterian school in the days of Kapodistrias and now the "Trianon" cinema. The best tavernas in the old town are strung

out in a row on Staikopoulou Street, the road that runs just above the piazza. In the summer it can be almost impossible to squeeze your way past the crowded tables; but if you do, you will come out in front of the Worry Bead Museum, with a collection of kompologia from all over the world as well as some rare photographic material; there is also a gift and souvenir shop on the ground floor.

And if in 1964, the Canadian thinker Marshall McLuhan ("the medium is the message") observed that, in their manner of playing with their beads, the Greek peasants click off the passage of time and repeat to themselves memories and histories, the modern visitor should let time look after itself and Nafplio tell its own story. Lose yourself in the side roads leading off Staikopoulou, and let your feet take you where they will. In this part of the old town a monument, a church, a Turkish fountain are so many mementoes of the city's turbulent history. You will pass by the historic church of Agios Spyridonas (Papanikolaou St.), where Ioannis Kapodistrias, Greece's first Governor, was assassinated.

A few more steps will bring you to the Catholic Church (or Fragoklisia: Frankish Church), where you will probably find a flock of tourists who have lost their way in the back streets and are looking for their hotel. The flower-decked Venetian balconies all look very much alike, and it's easy to lose your sense of direction; but the ladies watching the goings-on from their windows will be glad to point you in the right direction.

If sunset does not find you up on the castles of Nafplio, it will surely find you down on the waterfront. Just a stone's throw from the tavernas on Akti Miaouli and the cafe-bars of Akti Bouboulina, the microscopic but always impressive Bourtzi stands alone, the rocky islet with the Venetian fortress by the same name dating from the first Venetian period (1389-1540), guarding the harbour entrance just 450 metres from the mole of Nafplio. Cross by motorboat from the port, for a draught of mediaeval Venice and a different view of Nafplio.

In the evening everyone takes a stroll along Akti Bouboulina, for this is where the residents of the town meet for an early drink in summer. The thirtysomethings and their seniors tend to hold the front line of tables against the influx of tourists, while the students congregate in the old town, and particularly in Vasileos Konstantinou Street (which ends at Syntagmatos square). This is

tip
Akti Bouboulinas is where people meet before heading out for the evening.

The Lathos bar

Nafplio: the old town

where you'll find all the most interesting little bars.

The pebble beach at Arvanitia is frequented chiefly by those of a certain age, although you will always find a scattering of young couples there too. The main beach however at Nafplio is Karathonas, broad and sandy, with two large beach bars and an excellent place for wind surfing and other water sports.

MYCENAE

Your weekend in Nafplio will be incomplete if you do not take time to visit Mycenae, one of the most important archaeological sites in Greece, and just 24 km north of Nafplio. The ancient city of Mycenae, known from the works of Homer, was brought to light by Schliemann, whose excavations revealed the existence of a city with an extremely high level of civilisation in 3000 BC. The administrative centre of the Achaeans, ruled by Atreus, Thyestes and Agamemnon, Mycenae began to fail with the descent of the Dorians and the attacks of the Argives (468-463 BC); and while the city continued to be inhabited until at least the 10th century AD, it was with none of its former glory. Of the preserved archaeological monuments, the most famous and characteristic is the Lion Gate, which displays the oldest example of monumental sculpture in Europe on a strong wall dating from the end of the 13th century BC. On the north side of the palace complex, which occupies the highest elevation, the foundations of a temple dating from the archaic and Hellenistic period may be discerned, as well as buildings such as the workshops of artists and artisans. Outside the acropolis are the beehive tombs or tholoi, small burial structures preserved in relatively good condition, the most important being those of

tip

The information centre at the archaeological site of Mycenae (27510/76585) will give you the telephone numbers of guides you can call to arrange for a tour at your convenience.

the Lions and of Aigisthus and Clytemnaestra. The most magnificent of the Mycenaean beehive tombs, the Tomb of Agamemnon (50 metres from the acropolis) lies at the end of a ceremonial passageway 36 metres long, and has a facade richly ornamented with relief plaques. The most important finds from Mycenae are displayed in the Archaeological Museum in Athens, including the gold death mask that Schliemann attributed to Agamemnon.

The archaeological site is open to visitors every day from 8.00 to 18.00 (depending on the season, it may close a little earlier or later - you can check by telephone in 27510/76585).
Admission € 6.

EPIDAURUS

Anyone who has never visited the theatre of Polycleitus at the Asklepieion of Epidaurus (29 km east of Nafplio) has missed not only the jewel of Argolida but also the most important theatrical monument anywhere in the world. This most beautiful of theatres, built in the 4th century BC by the architect and sculptor Polycleitus, is still one of the finest architectural monuments in the world and a model of perfect symmetry and faultless acoustics. It has the standard Hellenistic theatre structure, with tiers of seats arranged in a hollow curve (koilos) facing a flat circular space (orchestra) backed by a low building (skene) in which the actors dressed and awaited their entry, and was built in two phases: the orchestra, the lower tier of seats and the pre-Hellenistic skene were built in the first phase (late 4th c. BC), while the upper tier of seats and the Late Hellenistic skene were constructed later (mid 2nd c. BC). Today, the theatre comes alive every summer (July, August, September) with performances of ancient

The ancient theatre of Epidaurus

drama in the Epidavria Festival, which is part of the annual Athens Festival and draws thousands of spectators to the archaeological site. (Information: 27530/22006).

The theatre is part of the archaeological site of the Asklepieion (outside the village of Lygourio), a splendid centre of healing in ancient times. The cult of Asklepios, the god of healing, began in the middle of the 6th century BC and flourished until the 2nd century AD. Important finds (inscriptions on votive offerings, Greek and Roman votive sculpture, architectural elements from monuments in the compound, etc.) are exhibited in the Archaeological Museum of Epidaurus (27530/22009).

DATA
How to get there
By car: via the Athens-Argos-Nafplio highway (the fastest route, and slight detour will take you to Mycenae) or via Athens-Epidaurus-Lygourio-Nafplio.
By train: OSE, 210/5297777.
By coach: KTEL, 210/5134588.

Where to stay
Nafplio: At the *Nafplia Palace* for its unbeatable location on Akronafplia (27520/28981-5), for

accommodation with style and character, at the *Ilion Hotel Suites* (27520/25114) or the *Nafsimedon* (27520/26913). Urban atmosphere at the *Kapodistrias* (27520/29366), the *King Othon* (27520/27585) and the *Lord Byron* (27520/22351).

Where to eat
Nafplio: Cooked dishes at *Vasilis* (27520/25114) and *Karamanlis* (27520/27668). For fish, at *Savvouras* (27520/27704) or *Taverna tou Stelara* (27520/28818). For Serbian cuisine, at the new *Vyzantio* (27520/21631).
Lygourio: Cooked dishes at *Leonidas* (27530/22115), where for decades the troupes from Epidaurus have been coming to eat after the show.

Night life
The most curious bar in Nafplio could double as an antique store, with its fantastic decor and dozens of mechanical contrivances patented by the proprietor: this is the *Lathos*, and they play everything from rock to classical music. The *Lyrikon* is a student hangout featuring mainstream music, while the *Allotino* is more elegant, more arty, more jazzy. All three are in Vasileos Konstantinou Street, in the old town of Nafplio.

Excursions

DELPHI

Centre of the world to the Ancient Greeks, its famous oracle making it a shrine of supranational significance, Delphi is still a supremely beautiful place with an intense aura of mystery. Just two hours from Athens, it is an ideal day trip of great archaeological interest - or why not make a weekend of it, and explore Mt Parnassos at the same time?

Dramatically situated high on the southern slopes of Mt Parnassos, and with an incomparable view of the olive plantations of Amfissa and the Gulf of Itea, Delphi is a place for all seasons. In wintertime it hosts sophisticated skiing parties from Parnassos; in spring and autumn it welcomes nature lovers, hikers and with-it weekenders, who roam the area from the mountain villages to the picturesque seaside village of Galaxidi down below; in the summer it attracts thousands of tourists, who come from every corner of the earth to visit the antiquities of the famous "navel of

EUROPEAN CULTURAL CENTRE OF DELPHI

Every summer, Delphi is the site of the International Congress of Ancient Greek Drama, which brings together outstanding companies and artists from all over the world to participate in performances, conferences and training programmes. This is the best known of the many activities of the European Cultural Centre of Delphi, which was founded in 1960 with the aim of restoring to Delphi its universal spiritual character. It is located to the west of the modern town, on a pine-clad site with an incomparable view of the Gulf of Corinth. Initially held in the ancient Stadium at Delphi, performances are now staged in the Centre's own prefabricated theatre, since the archaeological site only opens on the evening of the August full moon. The Centre is to some extent continuing the work of the poet Angelos and his wife Eva Sikelianos, who in 1927 organised the first Delphic Festival, a landmark in the cultural life of Greece and for contemporary perceptions of ancient drama. The Centre also sponsored the restoration of the poet's house, which now houses the Delphic Festival Museum, exhibiting photographs and costumes from theatrical performances as well as items from the poet's personal life.

the world", the place considered to be the centre of the world by the Ancient Greeks.

Sacred to Apollo and Dionysus, site of the famous oracle and seat of the Delphic Amphictyony, the first political alliance in the ancient world, Delphi was, with Olympia and Delos, one of Ancient Greece's most important sanctuaries. The excavation work begun in 1892 by the French Archaeological School discovered on the site of the mediaeval village of Kastri an extensive network of temples and treasuries (buildings that held the offerings of the city-states).

Your tour of the archaeological site begins on the left side of the road leading up from Arachova. Here are the sacred precincts of Athena Pronaia: treasuries, two temples dedicated to the goddess, and the much-photographed circular marble Tholos, which was probably dedicated to the cult of the underworld divinities. Passing the ruins of the adjacent Gymnasium, where the youths of Delphi practised their athletic exercises, we see on the right the Phaedriads, the two facing pillars of rock guarding the Castalian Spring, where the Pythia and her visitors purged themselves before consulting the oracle. The site is closed because of the danger of falling rock, but the springs (Archaic and Roman) are visible from the fence.

The stone-flagged path, still running parallel to the road, leads to the entrance of the Sanctuary of Apollo. This is the point where the Sacred Way begins, the broad ceremonial highway followed by the ancient pilgrims. Although it had been inhabited since the Mycenaean age, Delphi's age of glory was the period from the 6th to the 4th century BC, and the numerous buildings and offerings you see around you all date from this era. The most important treasuries are those of Sicyon, Sifnos, Megara and the well-preserved treasury of the Athenians with its ornate sculptural decoration (currently being restored).

Continuing on up the path, we pass the rock of the Sibyl and the Stoa of the Athenians before reaching the Temple of Apollo. Here, deep inside the temple, was the sanctuary of the Oracle, the place where, in a state of sacred intoxication, the Pythia uttered her incomprehensible prophecies. The existing site contains the ruins of the third temple, an imposing building erected in the 4th century BC. Above the Temple of Apollo, on a site that commands a magnificent view (perfect photo material), stands the Theatre, where in ancient times competitions in drama and poetry were held. The path ends at the Stadium, which every four years hosted the Pythian Games, a festival celebrated with a variety of athletic and artistic competitions and second only to the "Olympia" in their importance in the ancient world.

The archaeological tour ends at the museum, which houses some of the most famous archaeological finds in the world: the unique bronze statue of the Charioteer, the reliefs from the metopes of the Treasury of the Athenians, the Sphinx of Naxos from the Treasury of Sifnos, the silver bull, the statue of Antinoos, and the Omphalos (or navel) that marked the centre of the world. Because of the on-going renovations (the charming little refreshment area and washrooms are new), the rooms housing the gold and ivory statues of Apollo and Artemis, the Kouroi, the east pediment from the Temple of Apollo, the architectural sculptures of the Tholos, the votive offering of

tip
Memo to hikers: Euro trail E4 goes through Delphi. The ancient path (marked and maintained) from the Stadium towards the Parnassos National Forest takes you to the Korycian Cave (2½ hours), which, according to Pausanias, was dedicated to the cult of Pan and the Nymphs. The view of the sea is absolutely breathtaking.

Excursions

Daochus and the acanthus-flower column with the dancers will remain closed until April 2003. The modern-day town of Delphi, adjacent to the ancient site, has no particular traditional colour. Tourist activity focuses on the two (parallel) main streets (Pavlou & Freiderikis and Apollonos), full of tourist shops and tavernas. The local Tourist Information Centre opens onto both streets (at 12, Pavlou & Freiderikis St. and 11, Apollonos St., tel. 22650/82900).

On your way back to Athens, you can visit the little town of Arachova. This picturesque place, with its stone houses and narrow lanes, is always terribly busy in the winter, with people flocking up from Athens to dance in its night clubs and ski at Greece's biggest winter sports centre on Mt Parnassos. Also on the road back to Athens is Livadeia, with its all time classic souvlaki and the idyllic Krya springs, a delightful place to stop for coffee.

DATA

How to get there

By car: via the Athens-Lamia national highway: turn left at Thebes (Thiva) and follow the signs for Livadeia - Arachova - Delphi.

By coach: KTEL Fokidas, 210/8317096.

Where to stay

Attractive rooms, extensive gardens and magnificent views at the hotels *Xenia* (22650/82151-2) and *Amalia* (22650/82101). Balconies overlooking the olive groves at the very central *Apollo* (22650/82244) and the quieter *Acropole* (22650/82675).

Where to eat

Family atmosphere at the *Vakhos* taverna. Greek specialties at the *Epikouros*.

Opening hours - admission prices

Sanctuary of Apollo (open areas)
Summer (28/4-28/9): 7.30-19.00.
Winter (29/9-27/4): 8.30-15.00.

Delphi Museum
Summer (28/4-28/9): 7.30-19.00,
Mon. 12.00-18.30.
Winter (29/9-27/4): 8.30-15.00.

Athena Pronaia
Summer: 7.30-20.00.
Winter: from 7.30 till sunset.

Admission

Athena Pronaia: Admission free. Single ticket for the Museum and the Temple of Apollo: € 9. For each site separately: € 6. Reduced rate: € 5 and € 3 respectively. Information: 22650/82312.

The Charioteer

Delphi

resort hotel apollo

Occupying one of the most beautiful sites on the island, amid the pines and right by the sea, the Apollo is the perfect choice for those who want a quiet country holiday with all the amenities of a large hotel. The relaxing atmosphere of the verdant landscape, the fabulous view from the 107 comfortable rooms, the family-style public areas and the heightened beats of the beach bar will accommodate your every mood.

Agia Marina, Aegina, 22970/32271-4, 22970/32281, fax 22970/32688, e-mail: apolo@otenet.gr

HOTEL GALINI AEGINA

Built in a lovely quiet spot, amid 2 acres of pine trees just 350 metres from the harbour and sandy beach of Agia Marina, the Hotel Galini has 74 comfortable rooms, perfect for families (with refrigerator, TV and air-conditioning), pool, bar, restaurant, parking, billiards room and conference facility.

Agia Marina, Aegina
Tel. 22970/32203, 22970/32216, fax 22970/32216. Winter tel.: 22970/71395.
www.galinihotel.gr e-mail:galinihotel@hellasnet.gr

Aegina: views of the port

AEGINA

Classic solution for a last-minute weekend or low-budget excursion near home (even a day trip), Aegina is just 35 minutes by Flying Dolphin from Piraeus - but once there, you're in a different world.
However picturesque you may find Aegina's waterfront promenade, with its horse-drawn carriages, neoclassic buildings and floating fruit-and-vegetable stalls, there is far more to the island than that. Yes, the port is lively and colourful, but the interior of the island has a wealth of archaeological and religious sites that are well worth a visit. 15 km from the port, on a hill opposite the crowd-infested monastery of St Nektarios, lies Paliachora, the mediaeval capital of the island and a place just made for exploring on foot. Spring is the best time of year to stroll through Attica's largest Byzantine necropolis and gather wildflowers among the ruins of the stone houses and churches built in this rocky fastness to discourage pirates.
The next stop is - and rightfully so - the Temple of Aphaia, a local goddess later identified with Athena. No matter how often you return, the classic perfection of this site - serenely occupying the summit of a pine-clad hill above the seaside resort of Agia Marina - is always a revelation. The Doric temple we see today acquired its final form in about 500 BC; the small archaeological museum adjacent has models of the earlier temples, and replicas of its sculptured decoration (the originals are in the Pinakothek in Munich). Tradition has it that this temple, the Parthenon in Athens and the Temple of Poseidon on Cape Sounio form an imaginary equilateral triangle - when you go home, get out the map and a ruler and see if it's true!
Admirers of antiquities will also want to visit Aegina's archaeological museum. Located on the archaeological site of Kolona down by the harbour (the name comes from the single column - in Greek, kolona - that is all that remains of the Archaic Temple of Apollo), this was modern Greece's first museum, founded in 1829 by Governor Ioannis Kapodistrias. Another interesting place is the small private Kapralos Museum, with quite an extensive collection of the sculptor's works, and a mini open-air sculpture gallery in the garden that conveys something of the artistic aura that has been inspiring artists-devotees of the island for the best part of a century.

tip
If you're staying for more than a day, you'll need some form of transportation to explore the island. Cyclists, bring your wheels with you - the shore road is a great place for biking.

tip
And before you leave, don't forget to buy a supply of the island's most famous product - pistachios - from the Growers' Co-operative outlet in the port.

Taverna «o Tholos»

Beneath the century-old pine tree overlooking Agia Marina or in the warmly attractive dining room with its stone fireplace, either way the home-style Greek cooking is delicious.

Charcoal-broiled fresh fish or meat, grilled bread, wine from the barrel, delectable treats from the old stone oven, hospitable family service and friendly prices - what more could you want!

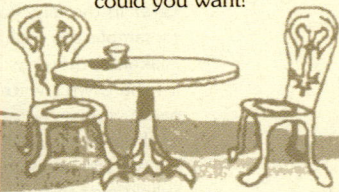

Agia Marina, Aegina, 22970/32129

HIPP◯CAMPUS HOTEL

Bed and Breakfast

Facilities: air-condition, TV, room service, breakfast, bar, fireplace

Perdika Aegina
Tel. 22970/61363-61459, 210/4512214

Excursions

Agios Nikolaos and the Marcellus Tower

Traditional coffee shop

Later in the day, you might want to sample the moka special at Aiakeion, the classic coffee shop on the town's waterfront promenade, savour the octopus at one of the ouzeries behind the fish market, go shopping at Fystiki or Syllektis or in Nikos Kontakis' pottery workshop, and then head to On the beach (which it is) for a sundowner.

The best swimming spots are the rocks to the left of the Agia Marina beach, below the Apollo hotel, the little bays of Kleidi and Keri near Perdika (sand, fine pebbles and total tranquillity), Tourlos (rocky outside, sandy inside) at Vagia and the organised area in front of the Baracuda beach bar on the sands of Agia Marina - especially popular with the young set.

tip

One of the... coolest spots for young and old is the Pipini Water Park, just outside the town. Open all day, with lots of attraction and live surprises every evening.

DATA

How to get there
By boat or Flying Dolphin: from Piraeus. Piraeus Port Authority, 210/4117341, Hellas Flying Dolphins 210/4199000.

Where to stay
The *Apollo* (22970/32271-4) and the *Galini* in Agia Marina and the *Moondy Bay* (22970/61215) in Perdika are standard hotels. In town, the *Pension Rena* (22970/24760, 22970/22086), *Petrino Spiti* (22970/23837-8) - ask

for the suite - and *Aiginitiko Archontiko* (22970/24968) are all friendly, companionable places. *Irides* is a new apartment complex (22970/52215) in Agioi, near Souvala.

Where to eat
Ouzo and fried whitebait in a place straight out of an old Greek film - that's *Agora* (22970/27308), behind the fish market. Home-style cooking and short order dishes at the simple family tavernas *Argyris* (22970/71313) in Mesagros and *Tholos* (22970/32129) in Agia Marina. Peace and quiet and fresh fish at *Akrogiali* (22970/31335) in Portes, a little harbour just past Agia Marina. Fish cheek by jowl with VIPs from Athens at *Antonis* (22970/61443), Perdika's most famous fish taverna.

Night life
The classic night spots - and for good reason - are *Elliniko* (mainstream and Greek) in town and *Baracuda* (beach bar) in Agia Marina. Live ethnic-jazz and a fabulous view at *Pelaginoi* (Perdika), live popular music at *En Aigini* and mainstream clubbing along the waterfront, where the young generation swarms in and out of the countless clubs that change their name (and management) every year.

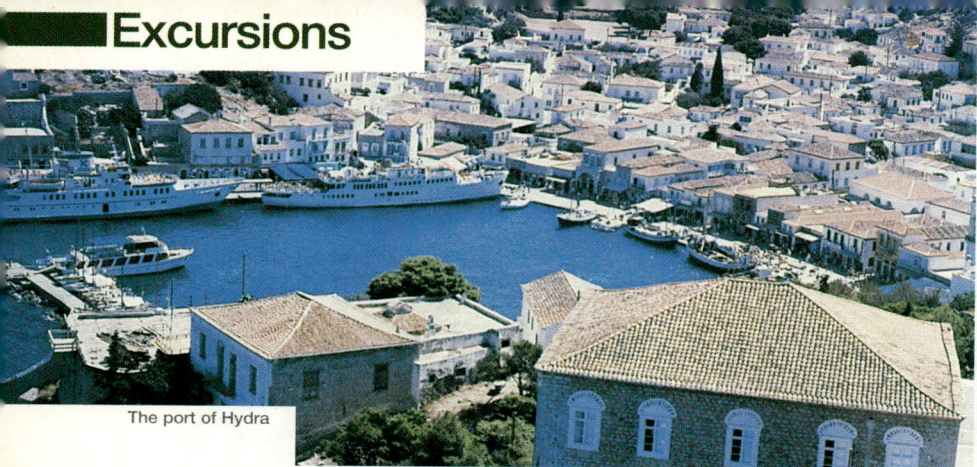

The port of Hydra

HYDRA

Picturesque, aristocratic, traditional, beloved of artists and art lovers, best preserved of the islands in the Saronikos Gulf, Hydra is the perfect place for trendy art weekends. Its stone mansions and cobbled lanes have inspired writers, painters and directors, and continue to attract artists and art lovers who have bought houses here or come regularly to stay in its tiny private hotels. In the 1960s, popularised by Sophia Loren and "The Boy and the Dolphin", it became the in place for the international jet set. Leonard Cohen (still a frequent visitor) wrote some of his superb ballads here, and artists like Chatzikyriakos-Ghikas, Tsoklis, Kounelis and Tetsis, who had or still have houses and studios on the island, recorded it endlessly on their canvases. More recently, a new generation of artists, like Dimitris Antonitsis, organise annual summer exhibitions at the local Primary school, with works by outstanding modern artists from all over the world. Which is only fitting, since this little stone town, spread amphitheatrically on the hill above the port, is itself an eternal work of art. Emblems of the great shipping wealth and cosmopolitan society of the late 18th and early 19th centuries, Hydra's mansions will again and again stop you in your tracks and look up, as you stroll along the waterfront or through the cobbled lanes winding up the hill (be prepared for loads of steps in Hydra: sometimes you even need to negotiate steps to get to your hotel). Some of the finest are the four-storey Tombazis House, which today houses a branch of the School of Fine Arts, the Tsamados House, home of the Merchant Marine Officers School after the 1821 Revolution, the Lazaros Kountouriotis House, today the Historical and Folk Museum and Public Art Gallery, the George Kountouriotis House, also a museum, and of course the Hydra Historical Archives and Museum, with its rich collection of artefacts from the First and Second World Wars, a gallery of paintings of the ships and historical figures of the 1821 Revolution by Greek and other painters, plus costumes, weapons belonging to local heroes, a 5500 volume library, etc.

While Hydra is not famous for its beaches, its waters are deep and clean and eminently suitable for swimming and diving. The nearest beaches are within easy walking distance; for the more distant you will need a boat (hire one, if you're not one of the yachting or sailing fraternity that tend to congregate at Hydra). You'll find an organised beach with water

tip
There are no wheeled vehicles in Hydra. Transportation is by mule or water taxi.

tip
In the summer Hydra is the place to go for art weekends, with exhibitions of famous artists who have been inspired by the island and of rising stars on the international plastic arts scene.

𝐵

Pension Bouayia
Barbara Laxou
HYDRA - GREECE

The atmosphere of the aristocratic
Hydra of a bygone age pervades the
experience of a stay at the Pension
Bouayia. This superb 1892 building
has been restored in accordance with
traditional Hydra style, and its five
spacious rooms combine modern
comfort and convenience with an
elegant period décor. The flagged terrace with its flowery pergola is the
perfect setting in which to enjoy
a home-style breakfast, with a view
of the picturesque little harbour and
its stone-built captain's houses.
The hospitality of the owners and the
central location of the Pension Bouayia,
just 200 metres from the port, make it
the ideal choice for maximum enjoyment
of your sojourn on one of Greece's most
atmospheric and popular islands.

Hydra, 22980/22890,
22980/52869, 22980/53883,
fax 22980/22890, 22980/54083.

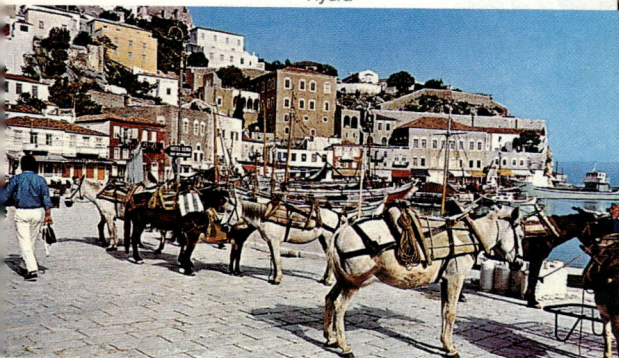
Hydra

Breakfast with a view at Bouayia

sports at Mandraki, rocks and a beach bar and lots of action at nearby Lagoudera, Spilia and Ydroneta, pebbles and fish tavernas at Kaminia. For greater solitude, sand or fine pebbles and pine trees, you will have to head for Palamida, Kaoumidi or Bisti. As for shopping, Elena Votsi's famous jewellery boutique and the classic ethnic Loulaki are the two most popular choices.

tip
Before you leave, be sure to buy a box of almond confectionery from Tsagaris.

DATA

How to get there
By ferry or Flying Dolphin from Piraeus: Piraeus Port Authority, 210/4117341, Hellas Flying Dolphins 210/4199000.

Where to stay
Hydra's hotel infrastructure has a few peculiarities of which the visitor should be aware. Since most of the island's hotels are in traditional stone houses, once the property of wealthy ships' captains and other notables, the rooms may differ in size and amenities in order to preserve the original style of the building. You should also be aware that for some hotels there may be a fair number of steps to negotiate. In most cases, however, any inconveniences are more than compensated by the atmosphere of these island mansions, which are decorated with antiques and works of art. Particularly recommended for lovers of the tradi-

tional, for couples and for the romantically-disposed, they are less suitable for families and those who demand the classic facilities and comforts of a standard hotel. Most of these places have just a few rooms, and provide friendly service and home-style care, paying particular attention to the breakfasts they serve, usually on a lovely courtyard or patio shaded by a pergola and dripping with bougainvillaea. Family atmosphere at the *Bouayia* (22980/52869). For atmospheric comfort in *Bratsera* (22980/53971), at the *Orlof* (22980/52564, 22980/52495) or the *Miranta* (22980/52230, 22980/53953). Elegance and understated luxury at the *Lito* (22980/53385). Warm hospitality at the *Nefeli* (22980/53297), the perfect place for large parties. Classic hotel style at the *Mistral* (22980/52509, 22980/53411).

Where to eat
Mediterranean cuisine at *Moita*, atmosphere and Italian flavours at the *Caprice* bar-restaurant, original dishes and youthful ambience at *Hydrargyros* and *Veranda*, international cuisine and great sunsets at *Sunset*, traditional flavours at *Porfyra* and *Geitoniko*, mezedes at *Paradosiako*, *Tzivaeri* and *Xeri Elia*, cooked dishes and '60s atmosphere at *Steki*. Fish on the waterfront at *Kondylenia*, in Kaminia.

Poros

POROS

Deep green pine forests that fringe the sands, neoclassical villas reflected in the calm waters, picturesque little tavernas and cafes and, of course, the famous Clock Tower standing above the port and welcoming you to Poros, the island that for years was the summer playground of the bourgeoisie of Athens.

A narrow strait separates Poros from Galatas on the Peloponnesian coast. And indeed for most people this island in the Argosaronikos Gulf is an extension of the Peloponnesian mainland, whose history it shared. Its beauty lies in the picturesque situation of the town of Poros, which sprawls, amphitheatre-fashion, over a pair of rocky hills. On one of these stands the Clock Tower (Roloi), the symbol of the island, which will draw your eye like a magnet from the moment your ship enters the harbour. Sooner or later you will climb up here, through the narrow lanes of Kasteli, the oldest part of town, past the handsome two-storey neoclassical buildings that bear witness to the prosperity of the island's middle classes in the 19th century.

From the Clock Tower let your gaze wander over the horizon. The channel between Poros and the opposite shore lies before you like a peaceful lagoon. (At sunset, the view is truly magical.)

A little outside the town, take the road heading west. Beyond the superb neoclassical Villa Dragoumi, you will come to the loveliest beaches on the island: Neorio, the little cove of Agapi and Apothikes. Here the pines come almost down to the water, creating a succession of marvellous landscapes with the green of the land embracing the blue of the sea. Continuing on your way, you will pass the lush green Askeli, the most touristy area on the island and turn north, towards the ruins of the Temple of Poseidon, heart of the ancient Amphictyony of Kalavria and refuge of the exiled orator Demosthenes.

DATA

How to get there

By ferry or Flying Dolphin from Piraeus: Piraeus Port Authority, 210/4117341, Hellas Flying Dolphins, 210/4199000.

Where to stay

In one of the charming apartments of the guesthouse *Sto Roloi*, housed in a restored neoclassical mansion (22980/25808), at the traditional *Dionysos* (22980/23511) or at the *Poros*, in Neorio (22980/22216).

Where to eat

For home style cooking and cooked dishes, at *Kathestos* down by the port, and for fresh fish at *Nikolas* in Monastiraki.

tip

Poros is a good base for exploring the Peloponnese. Cross over to the little town of Galatas, with its famous Lemon Grove, and visit the important archaeological sites of Troezen and Epidaurus.

ATHENS 2004

ALPHA BANK

OFFICIAL BANK

Spetses

SPETSES

Elegant, cosmopolitan and close by, Spetses is a favourite getaway spot for Athenians out for a weekend - or longer - break. Get there quickly by "Flying Dolphin" from Piraeus, or enjoy the beautiful drive through the Prefecture of Argolida.

Dapia: in 1821 the emplacement of the island's artillery and rallying point of the Revolution, and still the commercial centre and heart of the island. Dapia is cannons, neoclassical mansions and beautifully patterned pebble-paved streets. Dapia is where the most interesting museums (and most of the town's shops) are and where the "Dolphins" dock at the small harbour.

Of particular interest are the Museum of Spetses, with a collection of important historic treasures from the 1821 Revolution, which is housed in the mansion that once belonged to the first governor of the island, Chatzigiannis Mexis, and the lovely Laskarina Bouboulina House, where a direct descendant of the heroine of the Revolution, Filippos Demertzis Bouboulis, is pleased to conduct visitors on a touching tour of her life and her home.

The four rooms on the first floor display personal items that once belonged to the heroine of the

tip
The island's biggest festival is the Armata (usually the first weekend in September), when hundreds of visitors gather to watch the spectacular re-enactment of the 1822 naval battle of Spetses.

1821 Revolution, plus items relating to her activities. Her collection of weapons was quite astonishing, including a horse pistol picked out in gold and a Mongol sword that was a gift from Russia's Czar Alexander I. The furniture in the house comes from Florence, unique pieces that, particularly in the Great Hall with its beautifully carved wooden ceiling, create a striking ensemble. A portrait painted by famous Greek painter G. Prosalentis will make you pause for a few moments to admire the woman who came to symbolise the Greek Revolution. Apart from the classic stroll down to the old port and its boatyards, another delightful walk is up towards Kastelli - just a few minutes walk from the busy centre at Dapia, but with the feel of a country village.

The best beaches (Xylokeriza, Agioi Anargyroi with its water sports and tavernas, Agia Paraskevi, Zogeria and Vrellos) are on the north shore: take a fishing boat or water taxi from the port. A good alternative nearer the centre is Agia Marina, which offers an organised beach, beach bar and water sports. Directly opposite is the little island of Spetsopoula, the famous retreat of the Greek shipping magnate Niarchos. The little church of Panagia Daskalaki on the top of the mountain is well worth a visit (take the dirt road

VRACHOS

Welcome to VRACHOS, the restaurant with the panoramic view and the fabulous food. Our varied cuisine, featuring Greek and international specialties, our superb service and our idyllic situation right by the water are the three reasons why we stand out above the rest.
You will find us on the shore road, 200 metres past the town hall.

Tel.: 22980/73070.
Open daily, 12.30-00.30.

that starts from the pine-clad shore at Vrellos and runs through the Spetses pine forest), and also the village of Kounoupitsa on the northwest side of the island and the premises of the Anargyreio and Korgialeneio College of Spetses, once one of the country's finest schools. The beach just in front of it (Scholes), with its beach bars and water sports, is a favourite with the younger set. Spetses bids farewell to summer in style with the festival of the Armata early in September (usually the first weekend). This is an opportunity for hundreds of Athenians to gather on the island to watch a re-enactment of the victory of the Spetsiot fire ships over the Turkish fleet in 1822. The festivities last for several days, and include concerts, theatre performances, sporting events, etc. The most spectacular event takes place on the Saturday night, with the firing of a ship in front of the port, to the accompaniment of a grand display of fireworks. But whenever you come, you should certainly take time to go out to the little church of Panagia Armata, built to commemorate that victory, and follow the path that leads from the courtyard of the church up to the statue of the hero Kostas Barbatsis - and the best vantage point for enjoying a view of the old harbour.

tip
For the island's most beautiful beaches, catch a water taxi or caique.

Things to remember
No cars are allowed on Spetses. The best way to get around is by bicycle, scooter or motorcycle (although these are very noisy). But the most enjoyable way to get to know the island is by horse-drawn buggy. So take a romantic drive, but don't forget that it will cost you at least as much as an ordinary taxi. Water taxis are equally popular, ferrying visitors from the shore of Argolida opposite or to secluded lush green beaches.

DATA
How to get there
By boat or Flying Dolphin from Piraeus: Piraeus Port Authority, 210/4117341, Hellas Flying Dolphins 210/4199000.

Where to stay
Luxurious comfort at *Nisia* (22980/75000-11), atmosphere at

MUSEUM OF SPETSES

Finds spanning a period of 4000 years are housed in the Chatzigiannis Mexis House, one of the island's loveliest mansions. Chatzigiannis Mexis was a leader of the 1821 Revolution and one of the most powerful men on the island. Displayed on the ground floor of the museum are many of his personal belongings, while the wealth of exhibits on the upper floors cover every period in the island's life. The oldest artefacts come from the proto-Helladic settlement at Agia Marina, while the Roman period is represented by funerary steles, sculptures and coins. A collection of 6th century coins demonstrates the island's role in the early Byzantine period, with Byzantium represented by an array of rare icons, vestments and woodcarving. Rare ceramics and other objects from all over the world speak of thriving trade and commerce, and of the prosperity of the ships' captains who became the principal financiers of the war against the Turks. One whole room is dedicated to the contribution of the island to the 1821 Revolution, with historical documents, personal items, weapons, and wonderful painted figureheads from the prows of their ships.
22980/72994.

Spetses

Hotel Poseidonio

Zoes Club (22980/74447-8) and at the two studios at *Economou Mansion* (22980/73400-2). Care and comfort at Spetses (22980/72602). A feeling of home in the *Mimoza II* studio-apartments (22980/74087).

Where to eat

Fish and lobster spaghetti at *Patralis* (22980/72134) in Kounoupitsa. Fish and ouzomezedes at *Exedra* (22980/73497), *Liotrivi* (22980/72269), *Tarsanas* (22980/74490) and *Orloff* (22980/75255) in the old harbour. Choose from a selection of Greek and international dishes and enjoy the marvellous view at Vrachos (22980/73070), on the shore road.

Cooked dishes at *Lazaros* (22980/72600) in Kastelli, and cooked and short order dishes at *Stelios* (22980/73748) on the Dapia.

Night life

The two best clubs on the island are *Bracciera* (mainstream and Greek) and *Figaro* (mainly Greek, also mainstream), which also has a courtyard for chilling out by the sea. *Throumbi* (ethnic, jazz) and *Stavento* (mainstream and Greek), high spirits and live Greek music at *Remezzo*.

THE HOUSES OF SPETSES AND THEIR COURTYARDS

Anyone who is a fan of architecture will want to prolong his stay on the island, admiring the architecture of the houses, the beauty of the pebbled courtyards, the approach to interior decoration. And anyone who appreciates elegance and dignity will be struck by how simplicity can conceal such loveliness. The mansions are the outstanding features of the city's residential fabric, but the visitor will have to be rather "curious" if he is to see the hidden beauties of the island. For most of its houses stand behind high walls that conceal veritable architectural gems. The first surprise comes with the courtyard, which is the main feature of these houses. For here, among the trees and flowers, are ornate pebble-mosaic floors, representational rather than merely decorative, their subject matter drawn from daily life, folk tradition, Byzantium and antiquity. They are constructed of white pebbles, collected from the shores of the island or the Peloponnesian coast opposite. Fine examples of this type of work can also be seen in the courtyards of a number of public places, the most characteristic examples of which can be seen in the yard at Bouboulina's House, the Boukouri House in Kasteli, and the Church of Agios Nikolaos.

together
in the Athens
of 2004

A dream is becoming reality. The Olympic Games are returning to the country where they were born more than two thousand years ago and the city where they were revived a century or so ago. In 2004, the eyes of the world will be turned to Athens, where the high ideals of the Olympic spirit will meet their history, in this greatest of all athletic and cultural events. And Alpha Bank, the second largest Bank in Greece, will be there too. On February 8, 2001, Alpha Bank was proclaimed Grand National Sponsor of the ATHENS 2004 Olympic Games. The aim is to support the ATHENS 2004 Olympic Games Organising Committee and any private initiative that will do its utmost to help with the excellent preparation and hosting of the Games that will promote both our country and the Olympic Ideals on the world stage. Success is assured mainly through the support of all the people of Alpha Bank, who are working to turn this dream into reality.

ALPHA BANK OFFICIAL BANK OF THE ATHENS 2004 OLYMPIC GAMES

Olympic Games
the preliminary stages

Athens Guide 2003

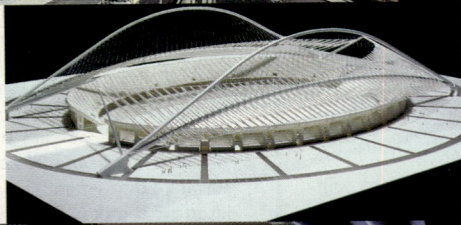

ATHENS 2004

ALPHA BANK

OFFICIAL BANK

Athens
is getting ready

The 2004 Olympic Games are only a pretext. In addition to a slew of sports facilities, Athens is acquiring a whole new face, as the great changes planned for the city's urban fabric are at last taking on solid form: new and more efficient public transport, extensive interventions to the major road arteries with lane widenings and a host of flyovers, large-scale regeneration and modernisation in key areas of the centre, the waterfront and many city districts. A solidinfrastructure that will remain with Athens long after the closing ceremonies...

"Greece's capital looks like the Athens of Pericles", wrote the editor of Time Europe in October 2002. For all their exaggeration, these words are fundamentally true: they capture the flavour of the times. The Athens of today, from Piraeus to Marathon, from Vouliagmeni to Thrakomakedones, is one vast construction site.

As it moves towards the great moment of the Olympics, the Athens of 2003 is changing day by day, constantly stimulating the imagination. Amid the dust and noise of the construction work we see the golden Athens of 2004 slowly emerging, the city whose image will be carried to the TV screens of some 5 billion viewers around the world. If last year - 2002 - was the turning point when "the projects lifted off the drawing board", as we head into 2003 we are nearing the final creative burst. After this year, Athens will be different. For the people of Athens the first

Work on the Attiki Odos

The Syntagma Metro station

The Roman Forum

and most visible change will be the disappearance of the billboards. All billboards. Not just for aesthetic reasons, but as a legal requirement - this is one of the terms of the contract under which the city will be hosting the Olympics. The sight of the Acropolis "brought to you by…" is a thing of the past.

Most projects are scheduled for completion in the early months of 2004. As the ribbons are cut, a different Athens will be delivered to its residents. And the consequences will be immediately sensible in people's everyday lives. In 2004, a Saturday lunchtime outing to Glyfada, for example, will no longer be a 1½-hour nightmare: the tram, from Syntagma via Venizelou and Nea Smyrni, will take you to the waterfront in twenty minutes. Or you could pay a visit to the Acropolis in the morning (by metro), and then take the tram

down to the sea. Get off at the end of Syngrou and walk across the "Esplanade", the suspension bridge that will carry pedestrian traffic between Syngrou and the waterfront. And what a waterfront! Totally different from the waste of reclaimed but unimproved ground that once lay between the Peace & Friendship Stadium and the Faliro Delta.

By spring 2004 this stretch of waterfront will have parks, canals (for flood control) and a new marina, plus elegant cafes and restaurants overlooking the yacht basin and the sea. This same area will also have the Olympic beach-volley pitches.

At the other end of the city, the flyovers at Faros Psychikou and Paradeisos Amarousiou will change the whole face of Kifisias Ave., providing two large breathing spaces in the flow of traffic. At the same time, the widening of the Vari-Koropi road will signifi-

In the first months of 2004, as inaugural ribbons are cut all over the city, a new and different Athens will be delivered to its residents for their use and enjoyment.

The new look of Omonoia Square

The Olympic Stadium, with the signature of Santiago Calatrava

The chaos and confusion that will mark 2003 are the price that has to be paid for the transformation of the city's traffic system.

cantly reduce traffic tie-ups in that area. Which means that, with the completion of the Attiki Odos, also scheduled for early 2004, you will be able to cross half the county, from Thrakomakedones to the Greek Ascot in no more than an hour. Ascot? The new Hippodrome, of course, to be built between Anavyssos and Markopoulo, to specifications that seem designed for glamorously dressed ladies with elegant escorts enjoying picnics of salmon and chilled white wine on the grass under the clear Attic sky. Yes, Athens is being transformed. And the transformation is taking place day by day. What is changing? The roads, the gateways into the city, the squares, the city centre, whole neighbourhoods and districts (with the creation of Olympic installations), communications between districts, building facades and street fronts. The changes are occurring on all levels - even underground: witness the extensions to the Metro! - and they are transforming the everyday life of the city's residents. What is changing? In a word, everything. So let's come back to the present and take a closer look at what is being done, focusing on the creative explosion that marked the city in the year 2002.

DISTRICTS

City centre

After Omonoia - where the results are already visible - three more major squares are in line for refurbishment: Syntagma, Koumoundourou (or Eleftherias, as it is now known) and Monastiraki, where the changes will be spectacular. Construction is underway on the new Metro station at the intersection of Ermou and Athinas, while the modern square that is taking shape in front of the old "electric train" station will include features that harmonise with the particular character and tradition of this district.

There will also be conspicuous changes to the main streets in the city centre. We are already enjoying the new street lights and the broad (and beautifully laid) pavements along Agiou Konstantinou, while, arriving at Karaiskaki Sq. and turning towards Omonoia, we catch a magnificent slice of the view of St George's church atop Lycabettus. Extensive tree planting is planned for all the central thoroughfares, as well as in squares and parklets, giving the city a substantial injection of chlorophyll. At the same time, the ambitious project for the unification of the archaeological sites includes the revamping of a num-

Interchange between Kifisias Ave. and the Attiki Odos

Roadworks at Faros·Psychikou

ber of main streets (redevelopment of Athinas and Aiolou, interventions to Mitropoleos and Kolokotroni, pedestrianization of Vasilissis Olgas), restoration of the facades of buildings around Plaka and the archaeological sites and the construction of a Cultural Park at Kerameikos.

But apart from the work being done in the framework of the unification of archaeological sites project, a whole series of interventions will enhance another forgotten face of the city, full of colour and memory. We note, by way of example, the extensive renewal work being done (on Panepistimiou, part of Patision, Alexandras Ave., Kountouriotika), the unification of the park systems from Lycabettus to Goudi, the refurbishing of building facades (Akadimias) and the redevelopment of the environs of the Archaeological Museum and the church of Agios Konstantinos (Omonoia).

Faliro

Forget your mental picture of the shoreline facing the Hippodrome - this is one of the districts that is going to be totally transformed. Today, this area (2.5 kilometres along the waterfront by a depth of about 400 metres) looks like a firing range - especially seen from above. By 2004, however, it will

not only have a number of Olympic facilities (beach-volley, handball and tae kwon do pitches) but also a host of other amenities that will radically revitalise the tourism infrastructure. The "Esplanade", a landscaped (with flowers and low bushes) pedestrian bridge 6 metres above the waterfront boulevard, will link Syngrou Ave. and the shore area. The two beach-volley pitches will be located between Ilisos and Kifisos, and canals will be built as part of the flood control programme. The marina that is planned for the area directly in front of Syngrou, between the beach-volley and tae kwon do pitches, will have restaurants and cafes and other recreational amenities/facilities.

Waterfront

Extensive redevelopment is planned for the entire length of the waterfront from Faliro to Vouliagmeni. One of the designs, in fact, is signed by Vittorio Gregotti, the Italian architect who designed the new wonderful Teatro degli Arcimboldi in Milan, which is serving the city's opera house while the famous Teatro alla Scala is being renovated. The main concept behind the Gregotti-Digenis design (named after its two architect-creators) is the development of a long

The city centre is acquiring more green space, and all the main streets are being refurbished.

There won't be much you can do to survive the trial by traffic on the city's main roads in 2003: just watch for notices about construction and alternate routes, and stock up on patience!

ALPHA BANK Panorama of Olympic Sports is the largest athletic, informative and recreational event ever carried out in Greece, an initiative of Alpha Bank, the Official Bank of the ATHENS 2004 Olympic Games. By June 2004, the Panorama will have visited every corner of Greece and Cyprus, promoting the Olympic Spirit. Its visit in each city lasts at least three days and is an exceptional event. It is the grand festival of sport, in each of the 64 cities of Greece and Cyprus it has been planned to visit. A festival that you'll have the opportunity to experience in person!

2003 TOUR PROGRAMME

1.	AMAROUSSION	13.	KOS
2.	LEIVADIA	14.	RHODES
3.	KARDITSA	15.	CHANIA
4.	GREVENA	16.	AGIOS NIKOLAOS
5.	GIANNITSA	17.	KORINTHOS
6.	MOUDANIA	18.	FLORINA
7.	IGOUMENITSA	19.	DRAMA
8.	MESSOLONGI	20.	SERRES
9.	LEFKADA	21.	THESSALONIKI
10.	ZAKYNTHOS	22.	PIRAEUS
11.	SPARTI	23.	AGHIA PARASKEVI
12.	NAFPLION	24.	AGHIOI ANARGYROI

OF THE ATHENS 2004 OLYMPIC GAMES

ALPHA BANK

Official Bank of the ATHENS 2004 Olympic Games

In 2004, the Olympic Games, the largest international sports event, return to Greece, where they were initially born. Greece has the unique opportunity to prove to the whole world that it is capable of not only organising the best Olympic Games, but also to infuse them with the spirit of a new era. In this national attempt, Alpha Bank, the leading Bank of the private sector will be present. During the next four years Alpha Bank will support the ATHENS 2004 Organising Committee as well as every business or individual to participate in the successful preparation of the Games. Having offered the largest sponsorship for the ATHENS 2004 Olympic Games, the Alpha Bank will develop new pioneering programmes and services guided above all by the basic spirit that governs its employees' relationship with its customers: mazi.*

* mazi in Greek means together.

ATHENS 2004 ™ ©

ALPHA BANK
OFFICIAL BANK

Piraeus Station

The new face of the shore road

waterfront promenade with paths and trails, recreation areas (floating squares), restaurants and cafes.

Elliniko

Formula 1 racetrack or city park? Whatever the final decision for this area, the site of the former airport is definitely going to be the city's next hot spot. Not least because the Olympic facilities scheduled for this site include the canoe/kayak slalom course. For those of you who are not familiar with it, this is one of the most spectacular Olympic events, with paddlers descending a giant artificial watercourse. Which - and this is just as exciting - will remain in place after the Games as the country's largest waterslide!

Piraeus

During the period of the Olympics a second city will come into being right next to Piraeus, in the form of ten luxury cruise ships (4 and 5 stars) that will provide accommodation for (mainly) guests of the sponsors of the Games and members of the Olympic family. Among these beautiful liners is the famous Queen Mary 2, a veritable miracle of technology, incredibly luxurious and taller than the Statue of Liberty. This floating city will have a total population of fifteen thousand people, who will lead a fabulous shipboard existence throughout the duration of the Games. To provide for them and their enter-

tainment, a whole series of projects are scheduled for the Piraeus area, with the emphasis on traffic arrangements and enhancement of the character of the port.

Gone will be the drunkards familiar from the rebetika: a well-lit promenade along the ancient walls, with benches and all the necessary civic amenities, will reflect the identity of persons enjoying a stroll with a view of the sea. At the same time, an Archaeological Park will be developed between Skylitsi, Kolokotroni, 34th Regiment, Kodrou and Zanni streets and down to the sea, with pedestrian precincts that will enhance the monuments at the gates of Piraeus. Nor is this all: other projects include the refurbishment of the hill at Kastella (pedestrian precincts, rest areas, lighting, improved pavements), the old commercial centre (between Loudovikou Sq., Ippodameias, Ethnikis Antistaseos and Akti Poseidonos) and Akti Protopsalti (repairs to building facades, lighting, creation of pedestrian precincts).

Work is also scheduled for Korai Sq. and Kanari Sq. (Pasalimani), to improve the front at Mikrolimano and in general to improve the aspect of all the major roads (Iroon Polytechneiou Ave., Vasileos Georgiou Ave., Grigoriou Lampraki Ave., Bouboulinas St.).

Schinias

Welcome to the Olympic rowing course! This long narrow strip of

Piraeus will be showing off its charms, with extensive landscaping and redevelopment.

The post-Olympic destiny of certain sites is going to be impressive: the artificial canoe slalom run is set to become a giant water slide, and Schinias will be turned into an ecological park.

water, which has already attracted a population of water birds and herons, will be a competition centre in the summer of 2004 and then a sports and recreation area.

The lake has natural sides (meaning that the lake bed has not been concrete-lined) and, with appropriate interventions and in conjunction with the canals and other smaller lakes in the region, will revitalise the beautiful pine forest on the Schoinias shore, where the trees had stopped growing on account of the brackish and increasingly salty water.

The new rowing lake will, among other things, be a wonderful destination for a day trip on the east side of the city. But don't head out that way yet. Better wait until after the Olympics, when the widening of Marathonos Ave. has been completed. And when you get there, remember that you will probably have to park about 500 metres away from the park entrance and walk down to the three tavernas and two or three cafes that will be allowed on the waterfront there. Cars and natural landscapes don't always mix, right?

The Athenian waterfront is turning into a real hot spot. Marinas, flyovers and other impressive projects are totally transforming it.

MAP OF OLYMPIC EVENTS

Elliniko
Basketball (quarter finals)
Handball (finals)
Hockey
Fencing
Canoe/kayak slalom
Softball
Baseball

Panathenian Stadium
Archery
Marathon (finish)

City centre
Cycling (road race)

Goudi
Modern pentathlon
Badminton

Galatsi
Table tennis
Rhythmic gymnastics

Marathonas
Rowing
Canoe/kayak sprint events

Markopoulo
Equestrian three-day event
Equestrian jumping grand prix
Equestrian dressage grand prix
Shooting

Vouliagmeni
Cycling: individual time trials,
Triathlon

Agios Kosmas
Sailing

Nikaia
Weight-lifting

Ano Liosia
Judo,
Greco-Roman wrestling,
Freestyle wrestling

Peristeri
Boxing

Peace & Friendship Stadium
Basketball

Faliro
Beach-volley
Handball (quarter finals)
Tae kwon do

Olympic Sports Complex (Marousi)
Opening and closing ceremonies
Swimming, Water polo
(quarter finals - finals),
Synchronised swimming,
Diving, Track and field events,
Tennis, Artistic gymnastics,
Trampoline, Cycling (track races)

Parnitha
Mountain biking

Marathon race
Starts at the Tumulus in
Marathon, follows the route
Mesogeion-Vas. Konstantinou-
Hilton-Zappeio and finishes
at the Panathenian Stadium

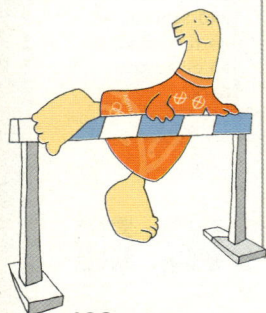

Practical informations

Athens Guide 2003

ATHENS 2004

ALPHA BANK
OFFICIAL BANK

USEFUL TELEPHONE NUMBERS

TRANSPORTATION

Airlines

Aegean Cronus:
Reservations: 8011120000 (from wire line), 210/9988300 (from wire line or cell phone).
www.aegeanair.com

Olympic Airways:
Reservations: 8011144444 (from wire line), 210/9666666 (from wire line or cell phone).

Eleftherios Venizelos International Airport:
210/3530000.

Boats

G.A. Ferries-Agoudimos:
210/4582640.
Boats for: Mykonos, Naxos, Paros, Syros, Tinos, the Dodecanese, the Sporades and the islands of the Eastern Aegean.

ANEK:
210/4197420, 210/3233481.
Boats for Crete.

Blue Star Ferries/Strintzis:
210/4141140, 210/8919940, 210/8236011-13.
Boats for: Amorgos, Cephalonia, Ios, Ithaki, Koufonisia, Mykonos, Naxos, Paros, Santorini, Syros, Tinos.

DANE: 210/4529360-1.
Boats for: Kalymnos, Kos, Leros, Patmos, Rhodes, Symi, Tilos.

Hellas Flying Dolphins:
210/4199000.
Boats for: the Argosaronikos, the Cyclades, Ikaria, Kithira, Leonidio, Monemvasia, Samos, the Sporades.

L.A.N.E.: 210/4274009, 210/4113855, 210/4110716.
Boats for: Agios Nikolaos (Crete), Chalki, Karpathos, Milos, Rhodes, Sitia.

Minoan: 210/4145700.
Boats for: Heraklion (Crete).

NEL: 210/4115015-18, 210/4223185.
Boats for: Ikaria, Kavala, Kos, Mykonos, Naxos, Paros, Rhodes, Samos, Syros, Tinos, Thessaloniki and the islands of the Eastern Aegean.

Harbourmasters

Agios Konstantinos:
22350/31759 (for Alonnisos, Skiathos, Skopelos).

Lavrio: 22920/25249, 22920/26859 (for Kea, Kythnos, Limnos).

Piraeus: 210/4226000-4,

TAXIS

A lot of stories are told about Athens' taxi drivers, especially concerning the way they treat tourists. One of their special characteristics (apart from their yellow colour) is that, even if there are already passengers inside, the driver may stop and take new passengers that are going in the same direction. To hail a taxi, people stand on the pavement, wave their hand and yell their destination to the driver. To make sure you pay the right amount of money if there are already passengers inside, don't forget to look at the meter as you enter. The flag fall is € 0,75 and the minimum fare is € 1,5. There are surcharges from ports, airport and stations that are usually indicated on a card hanging next to the meter. The rate doubles between midnight and early in the morning - make sure "tariff 2" doesn't appear on the meter during the rest of the day, a common trick taxi drivers are said to be using to cheat on tourists. It's better to avoid places such as the port of Piraeus, the main bus terminals and train stations after midnight, because taxi drivers impose their own rules, refusing to use the meter and negotiating a price with the passenger in advance. In order to avoid trouble and get to your destination in time, especially when you are trying to catch a plane for example, it is advisable to call for a radio taxi, which is charged extra. Otherwise, if you feel you have been ripped off, ask for a receipt or write down the taxi number and report it to the tourist police.

210/4593000, 210/4593140 (for the islands of the Argosaronikos, Cyclades, Dodecanese, Eastern Aegean and Northern Aegean, Crete and Kavala).
Rafina: 22940/22300, 22940/28888, (for Amorgos, Andros, Ios, Lesbos, Limnos, Mykonos, Paros, Syros, Tinos).
Flying Dolphins for the Argosaronikos: 210/4124585.

KTEL (intercity coaches)
KTEL Kifisou, 100, Kifisou St., 210/5124910.
Coaches for: the Peloponnese, Aitoloakarnania, Epirus, Macedonia, Ionian Islands (Cephalonia, Corfu, Lefkada, Zakynthos).
KTEL Liossion, 260, Liossion St., "Treis Gefyres", 210/8317153.
Coaches for: Central Greece, Evoia, Thessaly.
KTEL Attikis 210/8230179 (for Kalamos, Kalyvia, Keratea, Lavrio, Markopoulo, Oropos, Porto Rafti, Rafina, Sounio). Departures from the Pedion tou Areos.
KTEL Attikis 210/8210872 for Marathon, Nea Makri. Departures from the Pedion tou Areos.
KTEL Attikis 210/3464731

for Megara, Megalo Pefko. Departures from in front of the "Theseion" train station.

OSE
Reservations / ticket information 6, Sina St., 210/5297313 (Telephone bookings 08:00-14:30, at least two days before departure)
Railway Station (Peloponnese line) 3, Sidirodromon St., Athens, 210/5131601.
Railway Station (Larissa line) 31, Deligianni St., Athens, 210/5297777.

ROAD ASSISTANCE
ELPA (road assistance) 104
ELPA (information) 210/6068800
Express Service 154
Hellas Service 157
Interamerican 168

RADIO TAXI
Athens I 210/9217942
Dimitra 210/5560800, 210/5543065, 210/5546993
Ellas 210/6457000, 210/6451910, **Northern Suburbs** 210/8014000, **Southern Suburbs** 210/9961420-4
Enotita 210/6459000-5
Ermis 210/4115200, 210/4115277
Evropi 210/5023583,

210/5023783, 210/5020357
Express 210/9943000
Glyfada 210/9605600-7
Ikaros 210/5130640, 210/5132316, 210/5132319, 210/5132465
Kifisia 210/8014867, 210/8084000, 210/8084408, 210/8084101, 210/8012270, 210/8018820
Kosmos 210/8019000, 210/8088000
Parthenon 210/5814711, 210/5821292, 210/5811809
Piraeus I 210/4182333-5
Protoporia 210/2928150, 210/2221623, 210/2919016
Mototaxi 210/9029333

HOSPITALS
"Agia Sophia" Children's Hospital
Thivon & Livadias, Goudi, 210/7467000.
"Agios Savvas" Cancer Hospital Athens
171, Alexandras Ave., Athens, 210/6409000.
"Aglaia Kyriakou" Children's Hospital
Thivon & Livadias, Goudi, 210/7775610.
Alexandra Regional General Hospital Athens
80, Vasilissis Sofias St. & Lourou, Ilisia, 210/7770501.
Andreas Syngros
5, Ionos Dragoumi St., Athens, 210/7265100.
"Apostolos Pavlos" (KAT) Emergency Hospital
2, Nikis St., Kifisia, 210/6280000.
Asklipieio Voulas
1, Vasileos Pavlou St., Voula, 210/8958301.
"Elpis" General Prefectural Hospital
7, Dimitsanis St., Ampelokipoi, 210/6434001.
"Georgios Gennimatas" General Hospital Athens
154, Mesogeion Ave., Athens, 210/7701211.

BUSES AND TROLLEYS

Both buses and trolleys cover Athens and the suburbs and run every 10 to 15 minutes from 5 a.m. until midnight. There are no night buses. Blue signs indicate the stops for buses and yellow for trolleys. The fare is € 0,45 for both. Tickets must be purchased before boarding at a transport kiosk or a regular kiosk (periptero). Buses serve mainly those who want to travel to the suburbs, while trolleys are more helpful for

moving around in the city center, from the museums of Vasilissis Sofias Ave., for example, to Syntagma and Omonoia Square. There are two special express buses running between the airport and the city centre (either to Ethnikis Amynis, every 15 to 30 minutes, from 6 a.m. to midnight, or to Syntagma, every 25 to 35 min, 24hrs a day) and one between the airport and the port of Piraeus (every 20 to 40 min, 24hrs a day).

Data

Errikos Dinan (Henri Dunant) Hospital
107, Mesogeion Ave., Athens, 210/6972000.
Evangelismos 45-47, Ypsilantou St., Athens, 210/7201001.
Hippokrateio Regional General Hospital Athens
114, Vasilissis Sofias St., Athens, 210/7483770.
Laiko General Hospital Athens
17, Agiou Thoma St., Goudi, 210/7456000.
Metaxas Regional General Cancer Hospital Piraeus
51, Botasi St., Piraeus, 210/4284444.
Tzanneio General Hospital Piraeus
1, Afentouli St. & Zanni, Freatida, 210/4592911.

EMBASSIES - CONSULATES
Albania
1, Karachristou St., Athens, 210/7234412, 210/7232457.
Algeria
14, Vasileos Konstantinou St., Pagrati 210/7564191-2.
Argentina
59, Vasilissis Sofias St., Athens, 210/7224753, 210/7224710.

Armenia
159, Syngrou St., Nea Smyrni, 210/9345727.
Australia
37, Soutsou St. & 24, An. Tsocha, Athens, 210/6450404, 210/6450079.
Austria
26, Alexandras Ave., Athens, 210/8257240, 210/8257230.
Belgium
3, Sekeri St., Athens, 210/3617886-7.
Brazil
14, Filikis Etaireias St., Kolonaki Sq., 210/7213039.
Bulgaria
33 A, Stratigou Kalari St., Palio Psychiko, 210/6748106-8.
Canada
4, Ioanni Gennadiou St., Athens, 210/7273400.
Chile
25, Vasilissis Sofias St., Athens, 210/7252574.
China
2 A, Krinon St., Palio Psychiko, 210/6723282.
Columbia
3, Vrasida St., Athens, 210/7236848.
Costa Rica
4, Grigoriou Lambraki St., Glyfada, 210/9680620.

Croatia
4, Tzavella St., Neo Psychiko, 210/6777033.
Cuba
5, Sofokleous St., Filothei, 210/6842807.
Cyprus
16, Irodotou St., Kolonaki, 210/7237883.
Czech Republic
6, Georgiou Seferi St., Palio Psychiko, 210/6713755.
Denmark
11, Vasilissis Sofias St., Athens, 210/3608315.
Egypt
3, Vasilissis Sofias St., Athens, 210/3618612-3.
Eire
7, Vasileos Konstantinou St., Athens, 210/7232771-2.
Estonia
48-50, Patriarchou Ioakeim St., Kolonaki, 210/7229803.
Finland
1, Eratosthenous St. & Vasileos Konstantinou, Athens, 210/7011775.
France
7, Vasilissis Sofias St., Athens, 210/3391000.
Georgia
24, Agiou Dimitriou St., Psychiko, 210/6716737.
Germany
3, Karaoli Dimitriou St., Athens, 210/7285111.

METRO

There are 3 metro lines. Trains run from 5 a.m. to midnight. Tickets can be bought at the stations and must be validated at the machines at the entrance. The fare is € 0,70 for line 2 and 3. Line I is divided into 3 sections and there is an extra cost if the ticket covers two or more sections. Line I is the old Kifisia - Piraeus line, and popular destinations include Omonoia, Thiseio, Monastiraki, Piraeus. Line 2 runs from Dafni, in the southeast, to Sepolia, in the north-west, and popular stops include Akropoli, Panepistimio, Omonoia, Syntagma and Larissis for the railway station. Line 3 runs from Syntagma to Ethnikis Amynis in the north-east and a popular stop is Evangelismos for the museums on Vasilissis Sofias Avenue. You can ask for a map at the ticket kiosks.

Honduras
5, Karagiorgi Servias St., Piraeus, 210/4116105.
Hungary
16, Kalvou St., Palio Psychiko, 210/6725337.
India
3, Kleanthous St., Athens, 210/7216227.
Indonesia
55, Papanastasiou St., Palio Psychiko, 210/6712737.
Iran
16, Stratigou Kalari St., Palio Psychiko, 210/6741436.
Iraq
4, Mazaraki St., Palio Psychiko, 210/6722330.
Israel
1, Marathonodromon St., Palio Psychiko, 210/6719530-1.
Italy
2, Sekeri St., Athens, 210/3617260.
Japan
2-4, Mesogeion Ave., Athens Tower, 210/7758101-3.
Jordan
30, Zervou St., Palio Psychiko, 210/6744161.
Korea
124, Kifisias Ave., Athens, 210/6984080.
Kuwait
27, Marathonodromon St., Palio Psychiko, 210/6743593.

Lebanon
6, 25th March St., Palio Psychiko, 210/6755873.
Libya
13, Vryonos St., Palio Psychiko, 210/6742120-2.
Lithuania
40, Dimosthenous St., Chalandri, 210/6848204.
Luxembourg
11-13, Skoufa St., Kolonaki, 210/3640040.
Mexico
14, Filikis Etaireias St., Kolonaki, 210/7294780.
Morocco
14, Mouson St., Palio Psychiko, 210/6744209-10.
Netherlands
5-7, Vasileos Konstantinou St., Athens, 210/7239701-4.
Norway
23, Vasilissis Sofias St., Athens, 210/7246173-4.
Pakistan
6, Loukianou St., Kolonaki, 210/7290214.
Panama
42, Panepistimiou St., Athens, 210/3636121.
Peru
105-107, Vasilissis Sofias St., Athens, 210/6411221.
Philippines
26, Antheon St., Palio Psychiko, 210/6721837.
Poland
22, Chrysanthemon St., Palio Psychiko, 210/6775742.
Portugal
44, Karneadou St., Kolona-

ki, 210/7290096.
Romania
7, Emmanouil Benaki St., Palio Psychiko, 210/6728875-6.
Russian Confederation
28, Nikiforou Lytra St., Palio Psychiko, 210/6725235.
Saudi Arabia
71, Marathonodromon St., Palio Psychiko, 210/6716911-3.
Slovakia
4, Georgiou Seferi St., Psychiko, 210/6776757-8.
Slovenia
10, Mavili St., Athens, Palio Psychiko, 210/6775683-5.
South Africa
60, Kifisias Ave., Marousi, 210/6106645.
Spain
21, Dionysiou Areopagitou St., Makrygianni, 210/9213237.
Sudan
44, Amalias St., Athens, 210/3313261-2.
Sweden
7, Vasileos Konstantinou St., Athens, 210/7290421-4.
Switzerland
2, Iasiou St., Athens, 210/7230364-6.
Syria
61, Diamantidou St., Palio Psychiko, 210/6725577.
Thailand
23, Taygetou St., Palio Psychiko, 210/6717969.
Tunisia
2, Antheon St. & Marathonodromon, Palio Psychiko, 210/6717590.
Turkey
8, Vasileos Georgiou St., Athens, 210/7245915-7.
Ukraine
4, Stefanou Delta St., Filothei, 210/6800230.
United Kingdom
1, Ploutarchou St., Kolonaki, 210/7212951-9.

PERIPTERO (KIOSK)

You will find them everywhere in Athens, especially in the city centre, selling just about everything you might need (from cigarettes, newspapers and candies to refreshments and bus tickets). Some of them, mainly those around Syntagma and Omonoia, stay open all night and offer a wide range of foreign newspapers and magazines.

ATHENS 2004 | ALPHA BANK OFFICIAL BANK

Data

Uruguay
1c, Lykavittou St., Athens,
210/3602635.
Venezuela
112, Vasilissis Sofias St.,
210/7709962.
Yugoslavia
106, Vasilissis Sofias St.,
Athens, 210/7774355.

EMERGENCY & OTHER SERVICES
City of Athens
(Interventions) 195
Coast Guard 108
Consumer Protection
(INKA) 1721, 210/3632443
Doctors (for house calls)
210/6801555.
Duty Hospitals, Doctors, Pharmacies 1434
Fire Department 199
Fire Department
(Forest Fires) 191

First Aid Centre 166
First Aid Service
(Telemedics) 210/6801555
Market Police 210/3217056
Mental Health
Help Line 175
Narcotics Police 109
OTE directory information
131
OTE directory information
outside Greece 161
Poison Centre
210/7793777
Police 100
Public Services Centre
1464
Red Cross Blood Donor
Clinic 210/8219391
SOS Doctors 1016
Stock Exchange 1424
Theatres 1422
Time 141
Timetable information
(city transit) 185

Timetable information
(flights, intercity coaches,
boats) 1440
Tourist Board (EOT)
210/3271300-1
Tourist Police 171
Traffic Police: Athens
210/5230111
Traffic Police: Piraeus
210/4113832
Wake-up / Reminder service 182
Weather & Pollution
Bulletin (Attica) 1448

MONEY
The Greek currency is the
Euro. ATMs can be found at
banks, metro stations, the
airport and other public
areas. Bureaux de change are
located in the city centre,
especially around Syntagma
and Omonoia square.

VOCABULARY

The majority of people in
Athens speak English, and
you will certainly be able to
get by without a word of
Greek during your stay.
Moreover, signs in public
areas and places of interest
are usually also written in
English. However, here are
some basic words and
phrases that might help you
during your stay.

BASICS
Good morning Kalimera
Good evening Kalispera
Good night Kalinihta
Hello Yassu (informal),
yassas (formal)
Goodbye Ya or Antio
Please/you are welcome
Parakalo
Thank you Efharisto
Yes Ne
No Ohi
Excuse me (Sorry)
Sighnomi
Help! Voithia!
Police! Astinomia!
What's the time? Ti ora ine?

GETTING AROUND
Taxi Taxi
Bus Leoforio
Car Aftokinito
Tube/Metro Metro
Boat plio/ karavi
Plane aeroplano
Where is ..? Pou ine…?
Ticket Isitirio

TOURIST INFORMATION
Hotel xenodohio
Restaurant estiatorio
Bar bar
Club club
Museum mussio
Bank trapeza
Post office tahydhromio
Pharmacy pharmakio
Hospital Nosokomio

SHOPPING
How much? Poso kani?
Do you accept credit cards?
Dheheste pistotikes kartes?
Could I have a receipt?
Boro na eho apodiksi?

DAYS
Monday Dheftera

Tuesday Triti
Wednesday Tetarti
Thursday Pempti
Friday Paraskevi
Saturday Savato
Sunday Kiriaki

NUMBERS
0 midhen
1 ena
2 dhio
3 tria
4 tessera
5 pende
6 exi
7 epta
8 okto
9 enia
10 dheka
20 ikosi
30 trianda
40 saranda
50 peninda
60 exinda
70 evdhominda
80 oghdonda
90 eneninta
100 ekato
1000 hilia

ATTIKO METRO
METRO LINES DEVELOPMENT PLAN

ANO LIOSIA

KIFISIA

KIFISSIA

KAT

METAMORFOSI

MAROUSSI

KAMATERO

MELISSIA

IRAKLIO

IRAKLIO

NEA PENTELI

NERATZIOTISSA

PAHADISOS

NEA IONIA

RIMI

ILION

PEFKAKIA

MAROUSI

DOUK. PLAKENTIAS

PERISSOS

NEA IONIA

GAKA

ANO PATISSIA

TRALLEON

SIDERA

HALANDRI

HALANDRI

AG. ELEFTHERIOS

GALATSI

FILOTHEI

AG.PARASKEVI

THIVON

KATO PATISSIA

AGIA PARASKEVI

PERISTERI

GALATSI

NOMISMATOKOPIO

PERISTERI

AG.NIKOLAOS

PEIRISTERI

AG.ANTONIOS

KYPSELI

FAROS

HOLARGOS

SEPOLIA

ATTIKI

DIKASTIRIA

ETHNIKI AMYNA

HAIDARI

HAIDARI

VICTORIA

PANORMOU

KATEHAKI

ARISA

ATHENS

ALEXANDRAS

AMBELOKIPI

AG. SAVAS

EGALEO

METAXOURGHIO

OMONIA

EXARHIA

MEGARO MOUSSIKIS

EGALEO

PANEPISTIMIO

EVANGELISMOS

GLIKA N

AG. VARVARA

VOTANIKOS

THISSIO

MONASTIRAKI

SYNTAGMA

KORYDALLOS

ZOGRAFOU

KEA

PETRALONA

AKROPOLI

TAVROS

NIKEA

SYGROU-FIX

KALLITHEA

AG.IOANNIS

TAMBOURIA

PIRAEUS

MOSHATO

NEOS KOSMOS

DAFNI

VIRONAS

PIREAS

FALIRO

KALLITHEA

AL.PANAGOULIS

PALEO FALIRO

AGIOS DIMITRIOS

ILIOUPOLI

MOUNT IMITTOS

ILIOUPOLI

ALIMOS

ARGYROUPOLI

ELLINIKO

HELLINIKO

AIRPORT HELLINIKO

GLIFAD

ATTIKO METPO A.E.

PLANNING, GENERAL STUDIES AND
FACILITIES ENGINEERING DIVISION

OPERATING LINES

- LINE 1, ISAP
- LINE 2, ATTIKO METRO
- LINE 3, ATTIKO METRO

EXTENSIONS

- Under Construction
- Planned
- Possible - Under Consideration
- Suburban Railway Section
  Also Used By Attiko Metro

P — PARKING FACILITY - ATTIKO METRO

0m   5000m   10000m

KERAMEON
KORDATOU
PINELOPIS
ODYSSEOS
V. HUGO
CHALKOKONDYLI
GEORGE
LENORMAN
ACHILLEOS
KARAISKAKI SQ.
IEROTHEOU
AG. KONSTANTINOU
NIKIFOROU
KOUMOUNDOUROU
VERANZEROU
XOUNTHOU
SATOVRIANDOU
TOPOU
DOROU
28th OKTOVRIOU
KANINGOS SQ.
AKADIMIAS
OMONIAS SQ.
GLADSTONOS
GAMVETTA
FEIDIOU
NIKITARA
MEG. ALEXANDROU
KOLONOU
KALLERGI
VILARA
MENANDROU
SOKRATOUS
EM. BENAKI
SANTAROZA
ARSAKI
PANEPISTIMIOU (EL. VENIZ.)
METAXOURGEIO
GERMANIKOU
GIATRAKOU
LEONIDOU
KOLOKYNTHOUS
KERAMEIKOU
DELIGIORGI
VOULGARI
ZINONOS
IASONOS
STADIOU
PESMAZOGLOU
MARATHONOS
AKADIMOU
TSALDARI (PEIRAIOS)
ANAXAGORA
GERANIOU
LYKOURGOU
EFPOLIDOS
KOTZIA SQ.
KRATINOU
STAVROU
AGISILAOU
THERMOPYLON
MYLLEROU
EPIKOUROU
SAPFOUS
SOFOKLEOUS
MENANDROU
IKTINOU
KLEISTHENOUS
ARMODIOU
ARISTOGEITONOS
ATHINAS
AIOLOU
ARISTEIDOU
DRAGATSANIOU
GERMANOU
KLAFTHMONOS SQ.
PAPARRIGOPOULOU
ELEFTHERIAS SQ.
(KOUMOUNDOUROU)
SACHTOURI
DIPYLOU
SARRI
KRIEZI
TOMPAZI
LOUKA NIKA
AG. ANARGYRON
DIPLARI
AG. DIMITRIOU
EVRIPIDOU
ARISTOFAOUS
AISCHYLOU
POLYKLEITOU
PRAXITELOUS
LADA
KEMEIKOS
PSAROMILIGOU
AG. ASOMATON
KALOG. SAMOUIL
LEOKORIOU
IVIS
TAKI
CHRISTOKOPIDOU
AISOPOU
KARAISKAKI
PALLADOS
PSYRRI
PROTOGENOUS
AGATHONOS
MILTIADOU
KOLOKOTRONI
THISEOS
LEKKA
MELIDONI
ERMOU
ASOMATON SQ.
ERMOU
POSEIDONOS
ASTINGOS
KYNETOU
AG. THEKLAS
VOREOU
KARORI
AVRAMIOTOU
SKOUZE
VASILIS LIMONA
KALAMIOTOU
ATHINAIDOS
EVANGELISTRIAS
ROMVIS
PERIKLEOUS
KORNAROU
THISIOU STATION
ADRIANOU
IFAISTOU
MONASTIRAKI
PANDROSOU
KYRRIKOU
MITROPOLEOS
ERMOU
FOKIONOS
THISEIO
AREIOU PAGOU
AREOS
MUSEUM OF POPULAR ART
DEXIPPOU
AGORAS SQ.
ADRIANOU
KALOGRIONI
BENIZELOU
MITROPOLEOS SQ.
MITROPOLI
PENTELIS
PETR.
PATROOU
YPATIAS
FAIDRAS
IRAKLEIDON
NILEOS
AKAMANTOS
ANCIENT AGORA
AG. APOSTOLON
VRYSAKIOU
KREVATA
KLADOU
EPAMEINONDA
POIKILIS
PELOPIDA
ROLOI
ROMAN FORUM
KYRRISTOU
POLY GNOTOU
DIOGENOUS
FILOTHEIS
APOLLONOS
THOUKYDIDOU
NIK.
AG. MARINIS
OTRYNEON
ALSOS THISEIOU
ASTERO SKOPEIOU
VOULEFTIRIOU
MOUSAIOU
LYSIOU
ERECHTHEOS
FLESSA
SCHOLIOU
KEKROPOS
YPEREIDOU
AIGINITOU
DIMITRIOU
PNYKOS
AP. PAVLOU
AREIOS PAGOS
THEORIAS
DIOSKOURON
MITROOU
ARETOUSAS
KLEPSYDRAS
PANOS
ANDOKIDOU
THRASYVOULOU
PRYTANIOU
TRIPODON
EPICHARMOU
RAGKAVA
PLAKA
GERONTA
PNYKA
HILL OF THE NYMPHS
AKROPOLIS HILL
PARTHENONAS
MUSEUM OF ACROPOLIS
STRATONOS
THESPIDOS
EPIMENIDOU
VAKCHOU
KYDATHINEON
CHAIREFONTOS
LYSIKRATOUS
GKOLI
IRODOU ATTIKOU THEATRE
DIONYSOS THEATRE
VYRONOS
FRYNICHOU
AISCHYLOU
FILOPAPPOU HILL
GAVRIALDI
KALLISPERI
ROV. GALI
FRATTI
PROPYLAION
PROMACHOU
KAVALLOTI
MITSAION
KRYATIDON
ANGELIKARA
RATZIERI
DIONYSIOU AREOPAGITOU
STRATIGOU MAKRYGIANNI
MAKRYGIANNI
MAKRI
TZIRAION
CHAT.
DIAKOU

SYNTAGMA SQ.

VAS. AMALIAS AVE.

VAS. OLGAS AVE.

NATIONAL GARDEN

ERMOU

ERMOU

ERMOU

NIKODIMOU

ADRIANOU

ADRIANOU

MITROPOLEOS SQ.

MITROPOLEOS

MITROPOLI

MONASTIRAKI

PLAKA

PYLI ADRIANOU

STYLOI OLYMPIOU DIOS

ACROPOLIS HILL

ACROPOLIS MUSEUM

DIONYSOS THEATRE

DIONYSIOU AREOPAGITOU AVE.

THEORIAS

IRODOU ATTIKOU THEATRE

THISEIO

ANCIENT AGORA

AREIOS PAGOS

AP. PAVLOU

ROVERTOU GALLI

PNYKA

HILL OF THE NYMPHS

ERMOU

ADRIANOU

Herodion

Temple of Hephaestus, Ancient Agora

Ancient Theatre of Dionysus

Acropolis - Erechtheum

MAIN ARCHAEOLOGICAL WALK